THE *Art* OF SHORT *Fiction*

BRIEF EDITION

THE *Art* OF SHORT *Fiction*

BRIEF EDITION

Edited by **Gary Geddes**

Addison-Wesley

An imprint of Addison Wesley Longman Ltd.

Don Mills, Ontario • Reading, Massachusetts • Harlow, England
Melbourne, Australia • Amsterdam, The Netherlands • Bonn, Germany

Publisher: Brian Henderson
Managing Editor: Linda Scott
Copy Editor: Pamela Erlichman
Cover Design: Anthony Leung
Page Design and Layout: Heidy Lawrance Associates
Production Coordinator: Alexandra Odulak
Manufacturing Coordinator: Sharon Latta Paterson
Printing and Binding: Webcom

The acknowledgments on pages xiii–xv are an extension of this copyright page. The publishers will gladly receive information enabling them to rectify any errors in references or credits.

Canadian Cataloguing in Publication Data

Main entry under title:
The art of short fiction

Brief ed.
ISBN 0-201-39617-3

1. Short stories. 2. Fiction—20th century. 3. Fiction—19th century. I. Geddes, Gary, 1940– .

PN6120.2.A745 1999 808.83'1 C99-930441-0

ISBN 0-201-39617-3

Printed and bound in Canada.

A B C D E—WC—03 02 01 00 99

Table of Contents

Publisher's Preface

Thank you for selecting *The Art of Short Fiction: Brief Edition*, edited by Gary Geddes. We appreciate your recognition of the considerable time and care the editor and publisher have devoted to the development of this book.

The new, brief edition of *The Art of Short Fiction* is more than just a reduction of the bigger edition; it is in many ways a significant departure in approach and coverage. Professor Geddes has indeed pared down the number of stories—no easy task in the face of such wonderful work in the genre—but he has also honed the international focus and centred the book more firmly on reading the short story rather than on writing. He has included a novella, Joseph Conrad's *Heart of Darkness*, in order to better represent the range of short fiction, from the miniatures of "postcard fiction" to the edge of the novel.

There is still a broad selection of critical writing—"Writers on Writing"—and each piece of fiction is still prefaced by the very informative notes on the author, all of which have been updated for this edition. The Instructor's Manual, available to adopters, contains more discussion notes that can enrich each class.

We would like to thank the editorial board for their invaluable suggestions throughout the compilation of this text: Martin Hallett (Vanier College), Anne McWhir (University of Calgary), and Antanas Sileika (Humber College).

We want to hear what you think about *The Art of Short Fiction: Brief Edition*. Your comments and suggestions will be valuable to us as we prepare new editions and other books.

Introduction

One of my aims in putting together the materials in this anthology has been to provide, within a single volume, a critical milieu for the enjoyment and gradual understanding of short fiction. The stories gathered together here represent a cross-section of the best of what has been written in the past century and a half in the arena of short fiction. For a variety of reasons, short fiction, more specifically the short story, came into prominence only as recently as the nineteenth century, though its roots are deep in the folk tradition and in such well-known literary models as *A Thousand and One Nights*, *The Decameron*, and *Canterbury Tales*. Industrialization, which regimented the workplace and stimulated the demand for education, also spawned both a professional and entrepreneurial middle class and the phenomenon of leisure time. The worker, previously sustained by his or her feelings of solidarity within the community and by participation in a largely oral culture, became more or less isolated—some would say alienated—and had to depend on written stories, or narratives, for information, instruction, and entertainment. Newspaper and magazine publications, catering to the reading demands of a new urban public, began to serialize novels and provide a venue for self-contained shorter fictions, which could be more readily consumed in the brief periods punctuating the work schedule.

The growth and development of short fiction did not occur without a battle. Its arrival threatened certain vested interests in longer fiction. In the pages of *Dial* in 1917, Herbert Ellsworth Cory launched an attack on the fledgling form, equating its success with the shallowness of contemporary life. "The short story," he said, "is the blood kinsman of the quick-lunch, the vaudeville, and the joy-ride. It is the supreme art-form of those who believe in the philosophy of quick results." Cory considered the short story not only trivial and egocentric, but also lacking in spiritual nourishment; he described it as "a morbidly perfected miniature," and dismissed it as "a more delicate manifestation of that universal fever that has bankrupted mankind, and from which our deepest instincts of self-preservation urge us with tremendous pressure to arouse ourselves."

I'm reluctant to link my own interest in this exciting literary form with membership in the quick-fix and junk-food crowd, that ocean of lost souls addicted to shortcuts, shorthand, and short-order lunches. However, even V. S. Pritchett, himself no casual scribbler, had to confess that no longer "the poor relation of the novel," the short story is nonetheless a product of our keyed-up modern nervous system: "It is a hybrid. It owes much to the quickness, the objectivity and cutting of the cinema; it owes much to the poet on the one hand and the newspaper reporter on the other; something also to the dramatic compression of the theatre, and everything to the restlessness, the alert nerve, the scientific eye and the short breath of contemporary life ... it answers the primitive craving for art, the wit, paradox and beauty of shape, the longing to see a dramatic pattern and significance in our experience, the desire for the electric shock."

Short fiction is not only compared by many of its finest practitioners with the rigours of poetry, particularly the lyric, but also described as a "fierce pleasure" (Raymond Carver), a "healing riddle" (Tillie Olsen), an art of "snapshots" (Alice Munro), a "redemptive act" (Flannery O'Connor), a "joke" (Robert Stone and Leandro Urbina), a "wonderfully evolved mandible" (Terence Byrnes), "a form of prayer" (John Berger), "an act of rebellion" (John Hawkes), and a "musical composition" (Katherine Mansfield). Nadine Gordimer, recipient of the Nobel Prize for Literature in 1991, is famous for her description of the short story in her *Selected Stories* (1975) as "the life-giving drop—sweat, tear, semen, saliva—that will spread an intensity on the page; burn a hole in it"; however, an even more useful statement is to be found in her essay "The Flash of Fireflies":

"Certainly the short story has always been more flexible and open to experiment than the novel. Short-story writers always have been subject at the same time to both a stricter technical discipline and a wider freedom than the novelist. Short-story writers have known—and solved by the nature of their choice of form—what novelists seem to have discovered in despair only now: the strongest convention of the novel, prolonged coherence of time, to which even the most experimental of novels must conform unless it is to fall apart, is false to the nature of whatever can be grasped of human reality. How shall I put it? Each of us has a thousand lives and a novel gives a character only one. *For the sake of the form.* The novelist may juggle about with chronology and throw narrative overboard; all the time his characters have the reader by the hand, there is a consistency of relationship throughout the experience that cannot and does not convey the quality of human life, where contact is more like the flash of fireflies, in and out, now here, now there, in darkness. Short-story writers see by the light of the flash; theirs is the art of the only thing one can be sure of—the present moment. Ideally, they have learned to do without explanation of what went before, and what happens beyond this point. How the characters will appear, think, behave, comprehend, tomorrow or at any other time in their lives, is irrelevant. A discrete moment of truth is aimed at—not *the* moment of truth, because the short story doesn't deal in cumulatives. ... The short story recognizes that full comprehension of a particular kind in the reader, like full apprehension of a particular kind in the writer, is something of limited duration. The short story is a fragmented and restless form, a matter of hit or miss, and it is perhaps for this reason that it suits modern consciousness—which seems best expressed as flashes of fearful insight alternating with near-hypnotic states of indifference."

Seeing by the light of the flash. That requires an art of extreme delicacy and precision, of understatement. Valerie Shaw, in *The Short Story: A Critical Introduction*, insists that "It seems reasonable to say that a firm definition of the short story is impossible." And yet, in those same pages, she identifies *reticence* as one of the most striking features of the short story: "It is the degree and nature of the reticence conveyed by the short story at its best that give the genre its own decorum, a tactfulness consisting of respect for silences or unstated feelings, and displaying itself formally in the 'artful compromise' by which, Henry James proposed, the 'space-hunger and space-cunning' of a writer's material can be 'kept down.' The surface of a story, James explained, was made 'iridescent, even in the short piece, or what is beneath it and what probes and gleams through,' and it is this that produces 'the only compactness that has a charm ... the only sparseness that has a force ... the only simplicity that has a grace—those, in each order, that produce the rich effect.' In many of the stories presented in this study as attaining a 'rich effect,' silence is of paramount significance."

Truman Capote calls the short story "the most difficult and disciplining form of prose writing extant. Whatever control and technique I may have I owe entirely to my training in this medium." When asked in *The Paris Review* interview to explain what he meant by control, Capote said: "I mean maintaining a stylistic and emotional upper hand over your material. Call it precious and go to hell, but I believe a story can be wrecked by a faulty rhythm in a sentence—especially if it occurs toward the end—or a mistake in paragraphing, even punctuation. Henry James is the maestro of the semicolon. Hemingway is a first-rate paragrapher. From the point of view of ear, Virginia Woolf never wrote a bad sentence." In the same interview, he concludes: "Even Joyce, our most extreme disregarder [of rules], was a superb craftsman; he could write *Ulysses* because he could write *Dubliners*. Too many writers seem to consider the writing of short stories as a kind of finger exercise. Well, in such cases, it is certainly only their fingers they are exercising. ..."

The range of stories included in *The Art of Short Fiction* should encompass most of the forms and "-isms" that have been associated with short fiction: naturalism, all the brands of realism (including Virginia Woolf's psychological realism and that brand of the fantastical in Latin American writing now described as magic realism), surrealism, modernism, postmodernism, and metafiction. Readers interested in form will find here, in various disguises, confession, fable, parable, myth, allegory, pastoral, the tall tale, science fiction, the detective story, and the dramatic monologue. I prefer not to label or categorize, since that is often reductive and distracting to first-time readers of a text; besides, most good short fiction defies simple pigeon-holing and demands the freedom of the field or city. A reader with a sociological bent will find stories that deal with race, politics, love, loneliness, despair, tribal breakdown, war, the battle of the sexes, and a host of contemporary maladies. The formalist will be able to chart the decline, fall, and restoration of such concerns as unity of effect, plot, character, setting, texture, patterning, *progression d'effets*, and closure. The notes and statements on the art of fiction should be useful in both cases, providing the often conflicting views of writers.

In keeping with Chaucer's habit (as Dryden saw it) of loading every rift with ore, I have tried to stuff as much useful information as possible into the notes. My assumption has been that these snippets and quotations will stimulate debate and not interfere with either the student's first reading of the text or the teacher's Socratic probings. As a student, a teacher, and, then, as a beginning writer, I found nothing, outside the texts themselves, quite as inspiring and provocative as authors' attempts to talk about—and, at times, *around*—the creative process.

Granted, much of what authors have to say is impressionistic and usually written after the fact, so that it sometimes has the cast of yet another personal fiction. Plato gave a clear warning in the *Apology*: "Will you believe me? I am almost ashamed to confess the truth, but I must say that there is hardly a person present who would not have talked better about their poetry than did the poets." I'm sure Plato would have been equally sceptical of writers of short fiction. So, with fair warning from the ancients, from modernists who counsel against committing the "intentional fallacy"—mistaking an artist's expressed aims for what is actually achieved in the completed text—and from postmodernists such as Roland Barthes who announce the "death of the Author," I still find myself on the side of Albert Guerard, who declared himself "sufficiently 'intentionalist' to remain incorrigibly interested in the psychology of composition." I would, most often, rather read what an author has to say about his craft than a dozen so-called "interpretations" of his work.

In order to make this anthology even more useful, I have decided to include a number of excerpts and essays, some of which discuss problems unique to short fiction and to the history and definition of the short story, and others that are more general. Rather than offer a potted history of the short story, in which I would have to paraphrase or quote extensively, I have decided to include Ian Reid's pithy and epigrammatic opening chapter in *The Short Story*, called "Problems of Definition." Students who want to go deeper into genre study or see how contemporary critical modes are being applied to short fiction might well dip into back issues of the periodical *Studies in Short Fiction* and such works as *Short Story Theory at the Crossroads*, edited by Susan Lohafer and Jo Ellyn Clarey.

In order to balance the losses and increase the usefulness of a shorter edition, I have made a number of important additions—an essay on how to read and write about short fiction and stories by Kate Chopin and Vladimir Nabokov—and have altered my selections from Audrey Thomas, Mavis Gallant, Alice Munro, Joseph Conrad, William Faulkner, and Edgar Allan Poe. The longer work—*Heart of Darkness*—should now make it possible for students and teachers to cover a fuller range of fiction, from the short "postcard fictions" of Urbina and Phillips, where minimalist techniques reveal a barely submerged narrative machinery that has something in common with the structure of the joke, to the strangely intense and evocative form of the short story, or novella, which Henry James considered so *shapely*. I attempt to identify some characteristics of the novella in the Glossary, but have also provided a section called "Some Notes on the Novella," in which I offer a miscellany of quotations from a number of critics whose ideas you may find worth seeking out in their entirety.

In his fascinating essay "The Writing Lesson," the cultural anthropologist Claude Lévi-Strauss suggests that "the primary function of writing, as a means of communication, is to facilitate the enslavement of other human beings." We know something about the power and authority invested in written language from current challenges to the so-called "contracts" by which imperial nations and vested interests justified their theft of aboriginal lands; and we know even more about the power of written language by observing—with or without the records provided by

Amnesty International—how writings are censored or condemned and how writers are harassed, jailed, or murdered by the State for the exercise of their peculiar magic. Story is the text, and sub-text, by which we analyze and record our passage through time and our occupation of space. We cannot survive, individually or tribally, without story any more than we can survive without hope; it is our link with the past and our gift to, and promise in, the future. To know our stories—what they say and how they are constructed—is to begin to understand the nature of that passage. In fact, it is the beginning of freedom.

This paradox—that written communication may have originated to enslave, but now has the potential to free mankind—is nowhere better expressed than in Paulo Freire's *The Pedagogy of the Oppressed* and Jean-Paul Sartre's essay "Why Write?" Freire shows how peasants in the Third World are politicized by the acquisition of literacy, especially when the vocabulary learned speaks directly to the terms of their oppression. And Sartre, a keen observer of the moral failings of capitalistic and socialistic political structures, makes a powerful case for writing as a means to individual and collective liberation: "The art of prose is bound up with the only régime in which prose has meaning, democracy. When one is threatened, the other is too. And it is not enough to defend them with the pen. A day comes when the pen is forced to stop, and the writer must take up arms. Thus, however you might have come to it, whatever opinions you might have professed, literature throws you into battle. Writing is a certain way of wanting freedom; once you have begun, you are committed, willy-nilly."

• • •

I would like to reiterate here my gratitude for those who contributed to the larger edition of *The Art of Short Fiction*, including the original advisory editors. In addition to Anne McWhir, Antanas Sileika, and Martin Hallett, I would like to thank P. Scott Lawrence, Jean Clifford, John Ball, Wendy Robbins, Joan Langevin, and Brian Henderson for their invaluable advice.

Gary Geddes

Acknowledgments

Chinua Achebe: "The Sacrificial Egg" from *Girls at War and Other Stories*. Copyright © 1972, 1973 by Chinua Achebe. Reprinted by permission of Harold Ober Associates Incorporated.

Ryūnosuke Akutagawa: "In a Grove," reprinted from *Rashomon and Other Stories* by Ryūnosuke Akutagawa, translated by Takashi Kojima. Copyright © 1952, 1970 by Liveright Publishing Corporation. Reprinted by permission of Liveright Publishing Corporation.

Margaret Atwood: "Hairball" from *Wilderness Tips* by Margaret Atwood. Used by permission, McClelland & Stewart, Inc. *The Canadian Publishers*. "An End to Audience?" from *Second Words*, published by The House of Anansi. Copyright © 1982 by Margaret Atwood.

Clark Blaise: "A Class of New Canadians" from *A North American Education* (Doubleday & Co., Toronto) by Clark Blaise. Copyright © 1973 by Clark Blaise. Reprinted by permission of the author.

Jorge Luis Borges: "The Book of Sand" from *The Book of Sand* by Jorge Luis Borges, translated by Norman Thomas di Giovanni. Translation copyright © 1971, 1975, 1976, 1977 by Emece Editores, S.A., and Norman Thomas di Giovanni. Used by permission of Dutton, a division of Putnam Penguin Inc.

Tadeusz Borowski: "This Way for the Gas, Ladies and Gentlemen" from *This Way for the Gas, Ladies and Gentlemen* by Tadeusz Borowski, selected and translated by Barbara Vedder (Penguin Books, 1976), copyright © by Maria Borowski, 1959; this translation copyright © Penguin Books Ltd., 1967.

Anton Chekhov: "The Lady with the Pet Dog" by Anton Chekhov, from *The Portable Chekhov* by Anton Chekhov, edited by Avrahm Yarmolinsky. Copyright 1947, © 1968 by Viking Penguin, Inc. Renewed © 1975 by Avrahm Yarmolinsky. Used by permission of Viking Penguin, a division of Penguin Putnam Inc. "The Matter of Technique in Short-Story Writing," excerpts from *Letters on the Short Story, the Drama, and Other Literary Topics*, by Anton Chekhov, ed. L. Friedland.

William Faulkner: "A Rose for Emily" from *Collected Stories of William Faulkner* by William Faulkner. Copyright © 1930 and renewed 1958 by William Faulkner. Reprinted by permission of Random House, Inc.

Mavis Gallant: "Rue de Lille" from *Overhead in a Balloon* by Mavis Gallant. Copyright © 1979, 1981, 1982, 1983, 1984, 1985 by Mavis Gallant. Reprinted by permission of Macmillan Canada. "What Is Style?" from *Paris Notebooks* by Mavis Gallant. Copyright © 1982 by Mavis Gallant. Reprinted by permission of Macmillan Canada.

Gabriel Garcia Marquez: "One of These Days" from *No One Writes to the Colonel and Other Stories* by Gabriel Garcia Marquez. Copyright © 1968 in the English translation by Harper & Row, Publishers, Inc. Reprinted by permission of HarperCollins Publishers, Inc.

Nadine Gordimer: "The Ultimate Safari" from *Jump and Other Stories* by Nadine Gordimer. Copyright © 1991 by Felix Licensing, B.V. Reprinted by permission of Penguin Books Canada Limited. "The Flash of Fireflies," first published in *The Kenyon Review*, 1968, OS, Vol. XXX, No. 4. Copyright The Kenyon Review.

Ernest Hemingway: "Hills Like White Elephants," reprinted with permission of Scribner, a Division of Simon & Schuster, from *Men Without Women* by Ernest Hemingway. Copyright 1927 Charles Scribner's Sons. Copyright renewed 1955 by Ernest Hemingway.

Amy Hempel: "The Harvest" from *At the Gates of the Animal Kingdom* by Amy Hempel. Copyright © 1990 by Amy Hempel. Published by Alfred A. Knopf, Inc.

Thomas King: "Borders" by Thomas King. Copyright © 1991 by Thomas King. First appeared in *Saturday Night*. Reprinted by permission of The Bukowski Agency.

Margaret Laurence: "The Loons" from *A Bird in the House* by Margaret Laurence. Used by permission, McClelland & Stewart, Inc. *The Canadian Publishers.*

Alistair MacLeod: "As Birds Bring Forth the Sun" from *As Birds Bring Forth the Sun* by Alistair MacLeod. Used by permission, McClelland & Steward, Inc. *The Canadian Publishers.* "At the Moment: Notes on the Craft of Fiction" by Alistair MacLeod first appeared in *Event* and is reprinted by permission of the author.

Alice Munro: "The Shining Houses" from *Dance of the Happy Shades* by Alice Munro. Reprinted by permission of McGraw-Hill Ryerson. "What Is Real?" from *Making It New*, edited by John Metcalf.

Vladimir Nabokov: "Signs and Symbols" from *The Stories of Vladimir Nabokov* by Vladimir Nabokov. Copyright © 1995 by Dmitri Nabokov. Reprinted by permission of Alfred A. Knopf, Inc.

Flannery O'Connor: "Good Country People" from *A Good Man Is Hard to Find and Other Stories*, copyright © 1955 by Flannery O'Connor and renewed 1983 by Regina O'Connor, reprinted by permission of Harcourt Brace & Company. "Writing Short Stories" from *Mystery and Manners: Occasional Prose* by Flannery O'Connor, selected and edited by Sally and Robert Fitzgerald. Copyright © 1969 by The Estate of Mary Flannery O'Connor. Reprinted by permission of Farrar, Straus & Giroux, Inc.

Tillie Olsen: "I Stand Here Ironing" from *Tell Me a Riddle* by Tillie Olsen. Copyright © 1956, 1957, 1960, 1961 by Tillie Olsen. Introduction by John Leonard. Used by permission of Delacorte Press/Seymour Lawrence, a division of Random House, Inc. "Silences," from *Silences* by Tillie Olsen. Copyright © 1965, 1972, 1978 by Tillie Olsen. Used by permission of Delacorte Press/Seymour Lawrence, a division of Random House, Inc.

Jayne Anne Phillips: "The Stripper" from *Black Tickets* by Jayne Anne Phillips. Copyright © 1979 by Jayne Anne Phillips. Used by permission of Delacorte Press/Seymour Lawrence, a division of Random House, Inc.

Katherine Anne Porter: "Flowering Judas" from *Flowering Judas and Other Stories*, copyright 1930 and renewed 1958 by Katherine Anne Porter. Reprinted by permission of Harcourt Brace & Company.

Ian Reid: "Problems of Definitions" from *The Short Story* (Methuen) by Ian Reid. Copyright © 1977 by Ian Reid. Reprinted by permission of Routledge.

Audrey Thomas: "Mothering Sunday" from *Goodbye Harold, Good Luck* by Audrey Thomas. Copyright © 1986 by Audrey Thomas. Reprinted by permission of Penguin Books Canada Limited.

José Leandro Urbina: "Our Father Who Art in Heaven" and "Portrait of a Lady" from *Lost Causes* (Cormorant Books, 1987) by José Leandro Urbina. First appeared in Spanish in part in Ediciones Cordillera in Ottawa in 1978, then in full as *Las malas juntas* by Ediciones Obsidiana in Santiago, Chile, in 1986. Translation copyright © by Christina Shantz. Reprinted by permission of the author, the translator, and Cormorant Books.

W.D. Valgardson: "Celebration" from *Red Dust* by W.D. Valgardson. Reprinted by permission of Oberon Press.

Alice Walker: "The Child Who Favored Daughter" from *In Love and Trouble: Stories of Black Women*, copyright © 1967 and renewed 1995 by Alice Walker. Reprinted by permission of Harcourt Brace & Company.

Eudora Welty: "A Worn Path" from *A Curtain of Green and Other Stories*, copyright 1941 and renewed 1969 by Eudora Welty. Reprinted by permission of Harcourt Brace & Company.

Chinua Achebe

Chinua Achebe, one of the foremost African writers, was born in Ogidi, Nigeria, in 1930. After graduating from University College, Ibadan, he worked for a number of years as director of the Nigerian Broadcasting Corporation before pursuing his writing career full time. His publications include several volumes of poetry, one of which won the Commonwealth Poetry Prize in 1974, five novels, *Things Fall Apart* (1958), *No Longer at Ease* (1960), *Arrow of God* (1964), *A Man of the People* (1966), and *Anthills of the Savannah* (1988), two books of short stories, *The Sacrificial Egg* (1962) and *Girls at War* (1972), and several books of essays, including *Morning Yet on Creation Day* (1975), *Hopes and Impediments: Selected Essays* (1988), and *Beyond Hunger in Africa: Conventional Wisdom and A Vision of Africa in 2057*, which he co-edited.

As the titles of his first two novels suggest, Achebe has been particularly conscious of the dislocation, the dis-ease, that is the legacy of colonialism in Africa. Having been raised a Christian and educated in English, he is particularly well placed to explore the cultural rift—what Roland Barthes calls the "site of a loss"—in Nigerian society, where the cost of acquiring imperial culture has too often been a loss of dignity and power for indigenous peoples. "I would be quite satisfied," Achebe writes in "The Novelist As Teacher," "if my novels (especially the ones I set in the past) did no more than teach my readers that their past—with all its imperfections—was not one long night of savagery from which the first Europeans acting on God's behalf delivered them."

In addition to reclaiming African subjects and settings, Achebe has been concerned with the issue of language. Margaret Laurence has written of Achebe that "there is one theme which runs through everything he has written—human communication and the lack of it." He found, in a country of so many languages, that writing in English made it easier for him to address national issues. In response to the question of whether the African writer can master English, Achebe gives a resounding yes: "If on the other hand you ask: Can he ever learn to use it like a native speaker? I should say: I hope not. It is neither necessary nor desirable for him to be able to do so. ... The African writer should aim to use English in a way that brings out his message best without altering the language to the extent that its value as a medium of international exchange is lost. He should aim at fashioning out an English which is at once universal and able to carry his experience."

In order to do this, Achebe has had to work out his own unique linguistic strategies. "Among the Ibo," he writes in *Things Fall Apart*, "the art of conversation is regarded very highly and proverbs are the palm-oil with which words are eaten." His own narratives embody the spirit and many techniques of the oral tradition—the use of proverbs, parables, and a very conversational language—while maintaining the subtlety and allusiveness of the written language, an achievement that reflects the high regard in which he holds the profession of story-teller. "Story-tellers are a threat," he writes in *Anthills of the Savannah*. "They threaten all the champions of control, they frighten usurpers of the right-to-freedom of the human spirit—in state, in church or mosque, in party congresses, in the university or wherever."

"I think writing is such a serious thing that one ought to take it fairly easily and slowly, you know, at its own pace," he said in an interview with Lewis Nkosi in 1962. "I don't like forcing a story. Some days, weeks even, I can't write anything, and I don't want to go to the table and start scribbling, you see, I feel it's—it is an important thing and ought to be taken seriously." Achebe rejects the notion of a pure, disinterested art, arguing instead for writing that is both morally and aesthetically engaged: "Perhaps what I write is applied art as distinct from pure. But who cares? Art is important but so is education of the kind I have in mind. And I don't see that the two need be mutually exclusive."

Achebe accepts the traditional role of artist as myth-maker. He quotes Claude Lévi-Strauss on the subject of ancestors as the *senders* of messages (myths) and us as *receivers* of messages about the meaning of life and the values that are worth preserving. "This, to my mind, is the great myth about language and the destiny of man. Its lesson should be clear to all. It is as though the ancestors who made language and knew from what bestiality its use rescued them are saying to us: Beware of interfering with its purpose! For when language is seriously interfered with, when it is disjoined from truth, be it from mere incompetence or worse, from malice, horrors can descend again on mankind."

The Sacrificial Egg

Julius Obi sat gazing at his typewriter. The fat Chief Clerk, his boss, was snoring at his table. Outside, the gatekeeper in his green uniform was sleeping at his post. You couldn't blame him; no customer had passed through the gate for nearly a week. There was an empty basket on the giant weighing machine. A few palm-kernels lay desolately in the dust around the machine. Only the flies remained in strength.

Julius went to the window that overlooked the great market on the bank of the River Niger. This market, though still called Nkwo, had long spilled over into Eke, Oye, and Afo with the coming of civilization and the growth of the town into a big palm-oil port. In spite of this encroachment, however, it was still busiest on its original Nkwo day, because the deity who had presided over it from antiquity still cast her spell only on her own day—let men in their greed spill over themselves. It was said that she appeared in the form of an old woman in the centre of the market just before cock-crow and waved her magic fan in the four directions of the earth—in front of her, behind her, to the right and to the left—to draw to the market men and women from distant places. And they came bringing the produce of their lands—palm-oil and kernels, kola nuts, cassava, mats, baskets and earthenware pots; and took home many-coloured cloths, smoked fish, iron pots and plates. These were the forest peoples. The other half of the world who lived by the great rivers came down also—by canoe, bringing yams and fish. Sometimes it was a big canoe with a dozen or more people in it; sometimes it was a lone fisherman and his wife in a small vessel from the swift flowing Anambara. They moored their canoe on the bank and sold their fish, after much haggling. The woman then walked up the steep banks of the river to the heart of the market to buy salt and oil and, if the sales had been very good, even a length of cloth. And for her children at home she bought bean cakes and mai-mai which the Igara women cooked. As evening approached, they took up their paddles again and paddled away, the water shimmering in the sunset and their canoe becoming smaller and smaller in the distance until it was just a dark crescent on the water's face and two dark bodies swaying forwards and backwards in it. Umuru then was the meeting place of the forest people who were called Igbo and the alien riverain folk whom the Igbo called Olu and beyond whom the world stretched in indefiniteness.

Julius Obi was not a native of Umuru. He had come like countless others from some bush village inland. Having passed his Standard Six in a mission school he had come to Umuru to work as a clerk in the offices of the all-powerful European trading company which bought palm-kernels at its own price and sold cloth and metalware, also at its own price. The offices were situated beside the famous market so that in his first two or three weeks Julius had to learn to work within its huge enveloping hum. Sometimes when the Chief Clerk was away he walked to the window and looked down on the vast anthill activity. Most of these people were not there yesterday, he thought, and yet the market had been just as full. There must be many, many people in the world to be able to fill the market day after day like this. Of course they say not all who came to the great market were real people. Janet's mother, Ma, had said so.

"Some of the beautiful young women you see squeezing through the crowds are not people like you or me but mammy-wota who have their town in the depths of the river," she said. "You can always tell them, because they are beautiful with a beauty that is too perfect and too cold. You catch a glimpse of her with the tail of your eye, then you blink and look properly, but she has already vanished in the crowd."

Julius thought about these things as he now stood at the window looking down on the silent, empty market. Who would have believed that the great boisterous market could ever be quenched like this? But such was the strength of Kitikpa, the incarnate power of smallpox. Only he could drive away all those people and leave the market to the flies.

When Umuru was a little village, there was an age-grade who swept its market-square every Nkwo day. But progress had turned it into a busy, sprawling, crowded and dirty river port, a no-man's-land where strangers outnumbered by far the sons of the soil, who could do nothing about it except shake their heads at this gross perversion of their prayer. For indeed they had prayed—who will blame them—for their town to grow and prosper. And it had grown. But there is good growth and there is bad growth. The belly does not bulge out only with food and drink; it might be the abominable disease which would end by sending its sufferer out of the house even before he was fully dead.

The strangers who came to Umuru came for trade and money, not in search of duties to perform, for they had those in plenty back home in their village which was real home.

And as if this did not suffice, the young sons and daughters of Umuru soil, encouraged by schools and churches were behaving no better than the strangers. They neglected all their old tasks and kept only the revelries.

Such was the state of the town when Kitikpa came to see it and to demand the sacrifice the inhabitants owed the gods of the soil. He came in confident knowledge of the terror he held over the people. He was an evil deity, and boasted it. Lest he be offended those he killed were not killed but decorated, and no one dared weep for them. He put an end to the coming and going between neighbours and between villages. They said, "Kitikpa is in that village," and immediately it was cut off by its neighbours.

Julius was sad and worried because it was almost a week since he had seen Janet, the girl he was going to marry. Ma had explained to him very gently that he should no longer go to see them "until this thing is over, by the power of Jehovah." (Ma was a very devout Christian convert and one reason why she approved of Julius for her only daughter was that he sang in the choir of the CMS church.)

"You must keep to your rooms," she had said in hushed tones, for Kitikpa strictly forbade any noise or boisterousness. "You never know whom you might meet on the streets. That family has got it." She lowered her voice even more and pointed surreptitiously at the house across the road whose doorway was barred with a yellow palm-frond. "He has decorated one of them already and the rest were moved away today in a big government lorry."

Janet walked a short way with Julius and stopped; so he stopped too. They seemed to have nothing to say to each other yet they lingered on. Then she said goodnight and he said goodnight. And they shook hands, which was very odd, as though parting for the night were something new and grave.

He did not go straight home, because he wanted desperately to cling, even alone, to this strange parting. Being educated he was not afraid of whom he might meet, so he went to the bank of the river and just walked up and down it. He must have been there a long time because he was still there when the wooden gong of the night-mask sounded. He immediately set out for home, half-walking and half-running, for night-masks were not a matter of superstition; they were real. They chose the night for their revelry because like the bat's their ugliness was great.

In his hurry he stepped on something that broke with a slight liquid explosion. He stopped and peeped down at the footpath. The moon was not up yet but there was a faint light in the sky which showed that it would not be long delayed. In this half-light he saw that he had stepped on an egg offered in sacrifice. Someone oppressed by misfortune had brought the offering to the crossroad in the dusk. And he had stepped on it. There were the usual young palm-fronds around it. But Julius saw it differently as a house where the terrible artist was at work. He wiped the sole of his foot on the sandy path and hurried away, carrying another vague worry in his mind. But hurrying was no use now; the fleet-footed mask was already abroad. Perhaps it was impelled to hurry by the threatening imminence of the moon. Its voice rose high and clear in the still night air like a flaming sword. It was yet a long way away, but Julius knew that distances vanished before it. So he made straight for the cocoyam farm beside the road and threw himself on his belly, in the shelter of the broad leaves. He had hardly done this when he heard the rattling staff of the spirit and a thundering stream of esoteric speech. He shook all over. The sounds came bearing down on him almost pressing his face into the moist earth. And now he could hear the footsteps as if twenty evil men were running together. Panic sweat broke out all over him and he was nearly impelled to get up and run. Fortunately he kept a firm hold on himself ... In no time at all the commotion in the air and on the earth—the thunder and torrential rain, the earthquake and flood—passed and disappeared in the distance on the other side of the road.

The next morning, at the office the Chief Clerk, a son of the soil spoke bitterly about last night's provocation of Kitikpa by the headstrong youngsters who had launched the noisy fleet-footed mask in defiance of their elders, who knew that Kitikpa would be enraged, and then ...

The trouble was that the disobedient youths had never yet experienced the power of Kitikpa themselves; they had only heard of it. But soon they would learn.

As Julius stood at the window looking out on the emptied market he lived through the terror of that night again. It was barely a week ago but already it seemed like another life, separated from the present by a vast emptiness. This emptiness deepened with every passing day. On this side of it stood Julius, and on the other Ma and Janet whom the dread artist decorated.

Ryūnosuke Akutagawa

Born in Tokyo in 1892, Ryūnosuke Akutagawa became well known as an art collector, teacher, traveller, and writer and is the first Japanese writer to achieve distinction in a Western genre. He was a precocious child, writing stories at age ten and reading foreign authors in his early teens. His most famous collection, *Rashomon and Other Stories*, was published in Japan in 1916 when he was only twenty-three, but did not appear in English until 1948. He graduated from Tokyo Imperial University in 1916 with distinction in English Studies, having already translated numerous Western works, published widely in periodicals, and been active in editing and publishing a student literary magazine. Like many of his contemporaries, he was interested in socialism and this is reflected in his graduating thesis, "A Study of William Morris." Sent to China as an observer in 1921 by the Japanese newspaper that regularly published his fiction, Akutagawa suffered a severe physical and emotional debilitation that left him depressed and fearful of the mental collapse that had claimed his mother as a young woman. This condition was exacerbated by the death of his father and uncle, when he had to take financial responsibility for a sister whose house had burned down and whose husband had committed suicide, and by the loss of all his belongings, art objects, and early editions in the major Tokyo earthquake and fire of 1923. He became excessively inward-looking and dependent on drugs before taking his own life in 1927 by an overdose of barbiturates.

Although he was certainly a moralist in fiction, Akutagawa was nonetheless an exacting craftsman and an adherent to the notion that the artist must be free to find and explore his own materials. His aim seems to have been to create a fiction that was spare and starkly poetic, but capable of objectivity in rendering what Virginia Woolf calls "the dark places of psychology," and committed to a rigorous analysis of human behaviour. His belief in art as a form of religion, in which perfection is the aim and self-reliance the method, is reflected throughout his writings, particularly in "Art, etc." and the preface to his second volume of stories, *Tobacco and the Devil* (1917): "To speak of my feelings while I am at work, it seems like growing rather than making something. Every phenomenon, human and otherwise, follows its own unique course of development in that it happens in the way it must. So as I write I proceed from point to point, from moment to moment. If I miss one step, then I am stuck. I can not go even one step further. If I force myself, something is bound to go wrong. I must always be alert. No matter how alert, it often happens that I miss it. That is my trouble."

Although his pronouncements on art show Akutagawa to be a believer in organic form, he was enough of a formalist to suffer from divided loyalties, his urge for order and perfection driving him towards art, but the body and its needs always reclaiming him for the instinctual life. Had he been able to view his writing as an act of profound solidarity with, rather than a continually revised performance for, mankind, he might have triumphed over both the writer's blocks and the emotional depressions that continued to plague him until his death. However, his poetic temperament and the techniques of Western realism did enable him to create a vivid and gripping portrayal of the social and moral quagmires of ancient and contemporary life in Japan. The famous Japanese film-maker Akira Kurosawa adapted Akutagawa's work in 1950, using both "Rashomon" and "In a Grove" as the basis for his film classic *Rashomon*.

Like Shakespeare with his Holinshed *Chronicles*, Akutagawa found some of his most congenial material in history, particularly in the Japanese classic "Tales Old and New." His short story "In a Grove," with its multiple perspectives of a single event, is said to owe something to Robert Browning's "The Ring and the Book."

In a Grove

Translated by Takashi Kojima

THE TESTIMONY OF A WOODCUTTER QUESTIONED BY A HIGH POLICE COMMISSIONER

Yes, sir. Certainly, it was I who found the body. This morning, as usual, I went to cut my daily quota of cedars, when I found the body in a grove in a hollow in the mountains. The exact location? About 150 meters off the Yamashina stage road. It's an out-of-the-way grove of bamboo and cedars.

The body was lying flat on its back dressed in a bluish silk kimono and a wrinkled head-dress of the Kyoto style. A single sword-stroke had pierced the breast. The fallen bamboo-blades around it were stained with bloody blossoms. No, the blood was no longer running. The wound had dried up, I believe. And also, a gadfly was stuck fast there, hardly noticing my footsteps.

You ask me if I saw a sword or any such thing?

No, nothing, sir. I found only a rope at the root of a cedar near by. And ... well, in addition to a rope, I found a comb. That was all. Apparently he must have made a battle of it before he was murdered, because the grass and fallen bamboo-blades had been trampled down all around.

"A horse was near by?"

No, sir. It's hard enough for a man to enter, let alone a horse.

THE TESTIMONY OF A TRAVELING BUDDHIST PRIEST QUESTIONED BY A HIGH POLICE COMMISSIONER

The time? Certainly, it was about noon yesterday, sir. The unfortunate man was on the road from Sekiyama to Yamashina. He was walking toward Sekiyama with a woman accompanying him on horseback, who I have since learned was his wife. A scarf hanging from her head hid her face from view. All I saw was the color of her clothes, a lilac-colored suit. Her horse was a sorrel with a fine mane. The lady's height? Oh, about four feet five inches. Since I am a Buddhist priest, I took little notice about her details. Well, the man was armed with a sword as well as a bow and arrows. And I remember that he carried some twenty odd arrows in his quiver.

Little did I expect that he would meet such a fate. Truly human life is as evanescent as the morning dew or a flash of lightning. My words are inadequate to express my sympathy for him.

The testimony of a policeman questioned by a high police commissioner

The man that I arrested? He is a notorious brigand called Tajomaru. When I arrested him, he had fallen off his horse. He was groaning on the bridge at Awataguchi. The time? It was in the early hours of last night. For the record, I might say that the other day I tried to arrest him, but unfortunately he escaped. He was wearing a dark blue silk kimono and a large plain sword. And, as you see, he got a bow and arrows somewhere. You say that this bow and these arrows look like the ones owned by the dead man? Then Tajomaru must be the murderer. The bow wound with leather strips, the black lacquered quiver, the seventeen arrows with hawk feathers—these were all in his possession I believe. Yes, sir, the horse was, as you say, a sorrel with a fine mane. A little beyond the stone bridge I found the horse grazing by the roadside, with his long rein dangling. Surely there is some providence in his having been thrown by the horse.

Of all the robbers prowling around Kyoto, this Tajomaru has given the most grief to the women in town. Last autumn a wife who came to the mountain back of the Pindora of the Toribe Temple, presumably to pay a visit, was murdered, along with a girl. It has been suspected that it was his doing. If this criminal murdered the man, you cannot tell what he may have done with the man's wife. May it please your honor to look into this problem as well.

The testimony of an old woman questioned by a high police commissioner

Yes, sir, that corpse is the man who married my daughter. He does not come from Kyoto. He was a samurai in the town of Kokufu, in the province of Wakasa. His name was Kanazawa no Takehiko, and his age was twenty-six. He was of a gentle disposition, so I am sure he did nothing to provoke the anger of others.

My daughter? Her name is Masago, and her age is nineteen. She is a spirited, fun-loving girl, but I am sure she has never known any man except Takehiko. She has a small, oval, dark-complected face with a mole at the corner of her left eye.

Yesterday Takehiko left for Wakasa with my daughter. What bad luck it is that things should have come to such a sad end! What has become of my daughter? I am resigned to giving up my son-in-law as lost, but the fate of my daughter worries me sick. For heaven's sake leave no stone unturned to find her. I hate that robber Tajomaru, or whatever his name is. Not only my son-in-law, but my daughter ... (Her later words were drowned in tears.)

Tajomaru's confession

I killed him, but not her. Where's she gone? I can't tell. Oh, wait a minute. No torture can make me confess what I don't know. Now things have come to such a head, I won't keep anything from you.

Yesterday a little past noon I met that couple. Just then a puff of wind blew, and raised her hanging scarf, so that I caught a glimpse of her face. Instantly it was again covered from my view. That may have been one reason; she looked like a Bodhisattva. At that moment I made up my mind to capture her even if I had to kill her man.

Why? To me killing isn't a matter of such great consequence as you might think. When a woman is captured, her man has to be killed anyway. In killing, I use the sword I wear at my side. Am I the only one who kills people? You, you don't use your swords. You kill people with your power, with your money. Sometimes you kill them on the pretext of working for their good. It's true they don't bleed. They are in the best of health, but all the same you've killed them. It's hard to say who is a greater sinner, you or me. (An ironical smile.)

But it would be good if I could capture a woman without killing her man. So, I made up my mind to capture her, and do my best not to kill him. But it's out of the question on the Yamashina stage road. So I managed to lure the couple into the mountains.

It was quite easy. I became their traveling companion, and I told them there was an old mound in the mountain over there, and that I had dug it open and found many mirrors and swords. I went on to tell them I'd buried the things in a grove behind the mountain, and that I'd like to sell them at a low price to anyone who would care to have them. Then ... you see, isn't greed terrible? He was beginning to be moved by my talk before he knew it. In less than half an hour they were driving their horse toward the mountain with me.

When he came in front of the grove, I told them that the treasures were buried in it, and I asked them to come and see. The man had no objection—he was blinded by greed. The woman said she would wait on horseback. It was natural for her to say so, at the sight of a thick grove. To tell you the truth, my plan worked just as I wished, so I went into the grove with him, leaving her behind alone.

The grove is only bamboo for some distance. About fifty yards ahead there's a rather open clump of cedars. It was a convenient spot for my purpose. Pushing my way through the grove, I told him a plausible lie that the treasures were buried under the cedars. When I told him this, he pushed his laborious way toward the slender cedar visible through the grove. After a while the bamboo thinned out, and we came to where a number of cedars grew in a row. As soon as we got there, I seized him from behind. Because he was a trained, sword-bearing warrior, he was quite strong, but he was taken by surprise, so there was no help for him. I soon tied him up to the root of a cedar. Where did I get the rope? Thank heaven, being a robber, I had a rope with me, since I might have to scale a wall at any moment. Of course it was easy to stop him from calling out by gagging his mouth with fallen bamboo leaves.

When I disposed of him, I went to his woman and asked her to come and see him, because he seemed to have been suddenly taken sick. It's needless to say that this plan also worked well. The woman, her sedge hat off, came into the depths of the grove, where I led her by the hand. The instant she caught sight of her husband, she drew a small sword. I've never seen a woman of such violent temper. If I'd been off guard, I'd have got a thrust in my side. I dodged, but she kept on slashing at me. She might have wounded me deeply or killed me. But I'm Tajomaru. I managed to strike down her small sword without drawing my own.

The most spirited woman is defenseless without a weapon. At least I could satisfy my desire for her without taking her husband's life.

Yes, ... without taking his life. I had no wish to kill him. I was about to run away from the grove, leaving the woman behind in tears, when she frantically clung to my arm. In broken fragments of words, she asked that either her husband or I die. She said it was more trying than death to have her shame known to two men. She gasped out that she wanted to be the wife of whichever survived. Then a furious desire to kill him seized me. (Gloomy excitement.)

Telling you in this way, no doubt I seem a crueler man than you. But that's because you didn't see her face. Especially her burning eyes at that moment. As I saw her eye to eye, I wanted to make her my wife even if I were to be struck by lightning; I wanted to make her my wife ... this single desire filled my mind. This was not only lust, as you might think. At that time if I'd had no other desire than lust, I'd surely not have minded knocking her down and running away. Then I wouldn't have stained my sword with his blood. But the moment I gazed at her face in the dark grove, I decided not to leave there without killing him.

But I didn't like to resort to unfair means to kill him. I untied him and told him to cross swords with me. (The rope that was found at the root of the cedar is the rope I dropped at the time.) Furious with anger, he drew his thick sword. And quick as thought, he sprang at me ferociously, without speaking a word. I needn't tell you how our fight turned out. The twenty-third stroke ... please remember this. I'm impressed with this fact still. Nobody under the sun has ever clashed swords with me twenty strokes. (A cheerful smile.)

When he fell, I turned toward her, lowering my bloodstained sword. But to my great astonishment she was gone. I wondered to where she had run away. I looked for her in the clump of cedars. I listened, but heard only a groaning sound from the throat of the dying man.

As soon as we started to cross swords, she may have run away through the grove to call for help. When I thought of that, I decided it was a matter of life and death to me. So, robbing him of his sword, and bow and arrows, I ran out to the mountain road. There I found her horse still grazing quietly. It would be a mere waste of words to tell you the later details, but before I entered town I had already parted with the sword. That's all my confession. I know that my head will be hung in chains anyway, so put me down for the maximum penalty. (A defiant attitude.)

THE CONFESSION OF A WOMAN WHO HAS COME TO THE SHIMIZU TEMPLE

That man in the blue silk kimono, after forcing me to yield to him, laughed mockingly as he looked at my bound husband. How horrified my husband must have been! But no matter how hard he struggled in agony, the rope cut into him all the more tightly. In spite of myself I ran stumblingly toward his side. Or rather I tried to run toward him, but the man instantly knocked me down. Just at that moment I saw an indescribable light in my husband's eyes. Something beyond expression ... his eyes make me shudder even now. That instantaneous look of my husband, who couldn't speak a word, told me all his heart. The flash in his eyes was neither anger nor sorrow ... only a cold light, a look of loathing. More struck by the look in his eyes than by the blow of the thief, I called out in spite of myself and fell unconscious.

In the course of time I came to, and found that the man in blue silk was gone. I saw only my husband still bound to the root of the cedar. I raised myself from the bamboo-blades with difficulty, and looked into his face; but the expression in his eyes was just the same as before.

Beneath the cold contempt in his eyes, there was hatred. Shame, grief, and anger ... I don't know how to express my heart at that time. Reeling to my feet, I went up to my husband.

"Takejiro," I said to him, "since things have come to this pass I cannot live with you. I'm determined to die, ... but you must die, too. You saw my shame. I can't leave you alive as you are."

This was all I could say. Still he went on gazing at me with loathing and contempt. My heart breaking, I looked for his sword. It must have been taken by the robber. Neither his sword nor his bow and arrows were to be seen in the grove. But fortunately my small sword was lying at my feet. Raising it over head, once more I said, "Now give me your life. I'll follow you right away."

When he heard these words, he moved his lips with difficulty. Since his mouth was stuffed with leaves, of course his voice could not be heard at all. But at a glance I understood his words. Despising me, his look said only, "Kill me." Neither conscious nor unconscious, I stabbed the small sword through the lilac-colored kimono into his breast.

Again at this time I must have fainted. By the time I managed to look up, he had already breathed his last—still in bonds. A streak of sinking sunlight streamed through the clump of cedars and bamboos, and shone on his pale face. Gulping down my sobs, I untied the rope from his dead body. And ... and what has become of me since I have no more strength to tell you. Anyway I hadn't the strength to die. I stabbed my own throat with the small sword, I threw myself into a pond at the foot of the mountain, and I tried to kill myself in many ways. Unable to end my life, I am still living in dishonor. (A lonely smile.) Worthless as I am, I must have been forsaken even by the most merciful Kwannon. I killed my own husband. I was violated by the robber. Whatever can I do? Whatever can I ... I ... (Gradually, violent sobbing.)

THE STORY OF THE MURDERED MAN, AS TOLD THROUGH A MEDIUM

After violating my wife, the robber, sitting there, began to speak comforting words to her. Of course I couldn't speak. My whole body was tied fast to the root of a cedar. But meanwhile I winked at her many times, as much as to say "Don't believe the robber." I wanted to convey some such meaning to her. But my wife, sitting dejectedly on the bamboo leaves, was looking hard at her lap. To all appearances, she was listening to his words. I was agonized by jealousy. In the meantime the robber went on with his clever talk, from one subject to another.

The robber finally made his bold, brazen proposal. "Once your virtue is stained, you won't get along well with your husband, so won't you be my wife instead? It's my love for you that made me be violent toward you."

While the criminal talked, my wife raised her face as if in a trance. She had never looked so beautiful as at that moment. What did my beautiful wife say in answer to him while I was sitting bound there? I am lost in space, but I never thought of her answer without burning with anger and jealousy. Truly she said, ... "Then take me away wherever you go."

This is not the whole of her sin. If that were all, I would not be tormented so much in the dark. When she was going out of the grove as if in a dream, her hand in the robber's, she suddenly turned pale, and pointed at me tied to the root of the cedar, and said, "Kill him! I cannot marry you as long as he lives." "Kill him!" she cried many times, as if she had gone crazy. Even now these words threaten to blow me headlong into the bottomless abyss of darkness. Has such a hateful thing come out of a human mouth ever before? Have such cursed words ever struck a human ear, even once! Even once such a ... (A sudden cry of scorn.) At these words the robber himself turned pale. "Kill him," she cried, clinging to his arms. Looking hard at her, he answered neither yes nor no ... but hardly had I thought about his answer before she had been knocked down into the bamboo leaves. (Again a cry of scorn.) Quietly folding his arms, he looked at me and said, "What will you do with her? Kill her or save her? You have only to nod. Kill her?" For these words alone I would like to pardon his crime.

While I hesitated, she shrieked and ran into the depths of the grove. The robber instantly snatched at her, but he failed even to grasp her sleeve.

After she ran away, he took up my sword, and my bow and arrows. With a single stroke he cut one of my bonds. I remember his mumbling, "My fate is next." Then he disappeared from the grove. All was silent after that. No, I heard someone crying. Untying the rest of my bonds, I listened carefully, and I noticed that it was my own crying. (Long silence.)

I raised my exhausted body from the root of the cedar. In front of me there was shining the small sword which my wife had dropped. I took it up and stabbed it into my breast. A bloody lump rose to my mouth, but I didn't feel any pain. When my breast grew cold, everything was as silent as the dead in their graves. What profound silence! Not a single bird-note was heard in the sky over this grave in the hollow of the mountains. Only a lonely light lingered on the cedars and mountains. By and by the light gradually grew fainter, till the cedars and bamboo were lost to view. Lying there, I was enveloped in deep silence.

Then someone crept up to me. I tried to see who it was. But darkness had already been gathering around me. Someone ... that someone drew the small sword softly out of my breast in its invisible hand. At the same time once more blood flowed into my mouth. And once and for all I sank down into the darkness of space.

Margaret Atwood

Margaret Atwood was born in Ottawa in 1939, but spent most of her early years in the bush country of northern Ontario and Quebec, where her father was engaged in research as an entomologist. She did not spend a full year in school until Grade 8, but had already begun to write poems and stories and plays at age five. She completed her B.A. at Victoria College, University of Toronto, and her M.A. at Radcliffe College, then won a Woodrow Wilson Fellowship to Harvard, where she studied Victorian Literature. She spent the next ten years alternating between teaching and writing until she could afford to write full time. She lives with her companion, the writer Graeme Gibson, and their daughter in Toronto. Her first book of poems, *The Circle Game* (1964), won the Governor General's Award and was followed by a prodigious output of more than a dozen books of poetry; three collections of short stories, *Dancing Girls* (1977), *Bluebeard's Egg* (1983), and *Wilderness Tips* (1991); and the following novels, *The Edible Woman* (1969), *Surfacing* (1972), *Lady Oracle* (1976), *Life before Man* (1979), *Bodily Harm* (1980), *The Handmaid's Tale* (1985), which won the Governor General's Award and was made into a film, *Cat's Eye* (1988), *The Robber Bride* (1993), and *Alias Grace* (1996), which was nominated for the Booker prize. Atwood is also the author of a collection of essays, *Second Words* (1982), and a controversial study of Canadian literature, *Survival* (1972).

Although she considers interviews with authors as suspect fictions, many of Atwood's most engaging comments on the nature and aims of fiction are to be found in her playful, often acerbic, replies to questions posed by interviewers. She argues, in an interview with Geoff Hancock (*Canadian Writers at Work*), that fiction should surprise, satisfy the reader's nosiness or curiosity; should evoke emotion from the reader rather than settle for self-expression; and should also "expand the possibilities of the language." In a sympathetic review (in *Second Words*) of Audrey Thomas's short fiction, Atwood praises qualities that might well be singled out in her own work: "enormous verbal skills: a passion for words—words as games, words as magic or refrain, words as puzzle or multi-levelled pun—a wonderful ear for dialogue and dialect, a flexible style."

Her comments about the genesis of stories—"As I do in the novels, I start with a scene of some kind. Or an image. Or a voice. I don't work much from an idea"—stress the importance of observation; so, too, does her discussion of character underline the centrality of plot, or action, in her stories. "People ask me, why do your characters have these problems? If the characters have no problems, what's the book going to be about? The problem has to be an internal one, or a problem with another character, or an external problem like the Great White Shark, or the end of the world, or the people from Mars, or vampires. Something has to be there to disturb the stasis. Think of a play in which the characters do nothing at all, ever, throughout the play."

When asked about rules, or prescriptive criteria for story-writing, Atwood recalled writing *The Edible Woman* in four months in University of B.C. exam booklets, thinking that each book would contain a chapter; but the process proved unrepeatable: "Nothing works, necessarily, dependably, infallibly. No regime, no scheme, no incantation. If we knew what worked, we could sell it as an unbeatable program for writing masterpieces. Writing is very improvisational. It's like trying to fix a broken sewing machine with safety pins and rubber bands. A lot of tinkering."

When asked about hope, and the idea of art as capable of affirmation, Atwood replied: "When I finish a book I really like, no matter what the subject matter, or see a play or film, like Kurosawa's *Ran*, which is swimming in blood and totally pessimistic, but so well done, I feel very good. I *do* feel hope. It's the *well-doneness* that has that effect on me. Not the conclusion—not what is said, *per se*. ...

"If you are tone deaf, you are not going to get much out of Beethoven. If you are colour blind, you won't get much out of Monet. But if you have those capabilities, and you see something done very, very well, something that is true to itself, you can feel for two or three minutes that the clouds have parted and you've had a vision, of something of what music or art or writing can do, at its best. A revelation of the full range of our human response to the world—this is what it means to be human, on earth. That seems to be what 'hope' is about in relation to art. Nothing so simple as 'happy endings.'"

In an article entitled "On Being a Woman Writer," Atwood declares that "the proper path for a woman writer is not an all-out manning (or womaning) of the barricades, however much she may agree with the aims of the Movement. The proper path is to become better as a writer." Much of her creative life has been devoted to working with Amnesty International, PEN, and various writers' organizations, speaking out and writing against totalitarianism at the domestic or institutional level. Atwood is a radical, a feminist, and a nationalist, in the best sense of all three strategies; the operative phrase for her is *power politics*, which encompasses the domination of women, races, and other targets of tyranny, such as writers, the poor, progressives, and, of course, the environment. While she claims that, in fiction, "engagement is unavoidable," Atwood advises putting writing first. "Writers, as writers, are not propagandists or examples of social trends or preachers or politicians. They are makers of books, and unless they can make books well they will be bad writers, no matter what the social validity of their views."

Hairball

On the thirteenth of November, day of unluck, month of the dead, Kat went into the Toronto General Hospital for an operation. It was for an ovarian cyst, a large one.

Many women had them, the doctor told her. Nobody knew why. There wasn't any way of finding out whether the thing was malignant, whether it contained, already, the spores of death. Not before they went in. He spoke of "going in" the way she'd heard old veterans in TV documentaries speak of assaults on enemy territory. There was the same tensing of the jaw, the same fierce gritting of the teeth, the same grim enjoyment. Except that what he would be going into was her body. Counting down, waiting for the anaesthetic, Kat too gritted her teeth fiercely. She was terrified, but also she was curious. Curiosity has got her through a lot.

She'd made the doctor promise to save the thing for her, whatever it was, so she could have a look. She was intensely interested in her own body, in anything it might choose to do or produce; although when flaky Dania, who did layout at the magazine, told her this growth was a message to her from her body and she ought to sleep with an amethyst under her pillow to calm her vibrations, Kat told her to stuff it.

The cyst turned out to be a benign tumour. Kat liked that use of *benign*, as if the thing had a soul and wished her well. It was big as a grapefruit, the doctor said. "Big as a coconut," said Kat. Other people had grapefruits. "Coconut" was better. It conveyed the hardness of it, and the hairiness, too.

The hair in it was red—long strands of it wound round and round inside, like a ball of wet wool gone berserk or like the guck you pulled out of a clogged bathroom-sink drain. There were little bones in it too, or fragments of bone; bird bones, the bones of a sparrow crushed by a car. There was a scattering of nails, toe or finger. There were five perfectly formed teeth.

"Is this abnormal?" Kat asked the doctor, who smiled. Now that he had gone in and come out again, unscathed, he was less clenched.

"Abnormal? No," he said carefully, as if breaking the news to a mother about a freakish accident to her newborn. "Let's just say it's fairly common." Kat was a little disappointed. She would have preferred uniqueness.

She asked for a bottle of formaldehyde, and put the cut-open tumour into it. It was hers, it was benign, it did not deserve to be thrown away. She took it back to her apartment and stuck it on the mantelpiece. She named it Hairball. It isn't that different from having a stuffed bear's head or a preserved ex-pet or anything else with fur and teeth looming over your fireplace; or she pretends it isn't. Anyway, it certainly makes an impression.

Ger doesn't like it. Despite his supposed yen for the new and outré, he is a squeamish man. The first time he comes around (sneaks around, creeps around) after the operation, he tells Kat to throw Hairball out. He calls it "disgusting." Kat refuses point-blank, and says she'd rather have Hairball in a bottle on her mantelpiece than the soppy dead flowers he's brought her, which will anyway rot a lot sooner than Hairball will. As a mantelpiece ornament, Hairball is far superior. Ger says Kat has a tendency to push things to extremes, to go over the edge, merely from a juvenile desire to shock, which is hardly a substitute for wit. One of these days, he says, she will go way too far. Too far for him, is what he means.

"That's why you hired me, isn't it?" she says. "Because I go way too far." But he's in one of his analyzing moods. He can see these tendencies of hers reflected in her work on the magazine, he says. All that leather and those grotesque and tortured-looking poses are heading down a track he and others are not at all sure they should continue to follow. Does she see what he means, does she take his point? It's a point that's been made before. She shakes her head slightly, says nothing. She knows how that translates: there have been complaints from the advertisers. *Too bizarre, too kinky.* Tough.

"Want to see my scar?" she says. "Don't make me laugh, though, you'll crack it open." Stuff like that makes him dizzy: anything with a hint of blood, anything gynecological. He almost threw up in the delivery room when his wife had a baby two years ago. He'd told her that with pride. Kat thinks about sticking a cigarette into the side of her mouth, as in a black-and-white movie of the forties. She thinks about blowing the smoke into his face.

Her insolence used to excite him, during their arguments. Then there would be a grab of her upper arms, a smouldering, violent kiss. He kisses her as if he thinks someone else is watching him, judging the image they make together. Kissing the latest thing, hard and shiny, purple-mouthed, crop-headed; kissing a girl, a woman, a girl, in a little crotch-hugger skirt and skin-tight leggings. He likes mirrors.

But he isn't excited now. And she can't decoy him into bed; she isn't ready for that yet, she isn't healed. He has a drink, which he doesn't finish, holds her hand as an afterthought, gives her a couple of avuncular pats on the off-white outsized alpaca shoulder, leaves too quickly.

"Goodbye, Gerald," she says. She pronounces the name with mockery. It's a negation of him, an abolishment of him, like ripping a medal off his chest. It's a warning.

He'd been Gerald when they first met. It was she who transformed him, first to Gerry, then to Ger. (Rhymed with *flair*, rhymed with *dare*.) She made him get rid of those sucky pursed-mouth ties, told him what shoes to wear, got him to buy a loose-cut Italian suit, redid his hair. A lot of his current tastes—in food, in drink, in recreational drugs, in women's entertainment underwear—were once hers. In his new phase, with his new, hard, stripped-down name ending on the sharpened note of *r*, he is her creation.

As she is her own. During her childhood she was a romanticized Katherine, dressed by her misty-eyed, fussy mother in dresses that looked like ruffled pillow-cases. By high school she'd shed the frills and emerged as a bouncy, round-faced Kathy, with gleaming freshly washed hair and enviable teeth, eager to please and no more interesting than a health-food ad. At university she was Kath, blunt and no-bullshit in her Take-Back-the-Night jeans and checked shirt and her bricklayer-style striped-denim peaked hat. When she ran away to England, she sliced herself down to Kat. It was economical, street-feline, and pointed as a nail. It was also unusual. In England you had to do something to get their attention, especially if you weren't English. Safe in this incarnation, she Ramboed through the eighties.

It was the name, she still thinks, that got her the interview and then the job. The job with an avant-garde magazine, the kind that was printed on matte stock in black and white, with overexposed close-ups of women with hair blowing over their eyes, one nostril prominent: *the razor's edge*, it was called. Haircuts as art, some real art, film reviews, a little stardust, wardrobes of ideas that were clothes and of clothes that were ideas—the metaphysical shoulder pad. She learned her trade well, hands-on. She learned what worked.

She made her way up the ladder, from layout to design, then to the supervision of whole spreads, and then whole issues. It wasn't easy, but it was worth it. She had become a creator; she created total looks. After a while she could walk down the street in Soho or stand in the lobby at openings and witness her handiwork incarnate, strolling around in outfits she'd put together, spouting her warmed-over pronouncements. It was like being God, only God had never got around to off-the-rack lines.

By that time her face had lost its roundness, though the teeth of course remained: there was something to be said for North American dentistry. She'd shaved off most of her hair, worked on the drop-dead stare, perfected a certain turn of the neck that conveyed an aloof inner authority. What you had to make them believe was that you knew something they didn't know yet. What you also had to make them believe was that they too could know this thing, this thing that would give them eminence and power and sexual allure, that would attract envy to them but for a price. The price of the magazine. What they could never get through their heads was that it was done entirely with cameras. Frozen light, frozen time. Given the angle, she could make any woman look ugly. Any man as well. She could make anyone look beautiful, or at least interesting. It was all photography, it was all iconography. It was all in the choosing eye. This was the thing that could never be bought, no matter how much of your pitiful monthly wage you blew on snakeskin.

Despite the status, *the razor's edge* was fairly low-paying. Kat herself could not afford many of the things she contextualized so well. The grottiness and expense of London began to get to her; she got tired of gorging on the canapés at literary launches in order to scrimp on groceries, tired of the fuggy smell of cigarettes ground into the red-and-maroon carpeting of pubs, tired of the pipes bursting every time it froze in winter, and of the Clarissas and Melissas and Penelopes at the magazine rabbiting on about how they had been literally, absolutely, totally freezing all night, and how it literally, absolutely, totally, usually never got that cold. It always got that cold. The pipes always burst. Nobody thought of putting in real pipes, ones that would not burst next time. Burst pipes were an English tradition, like so many others.

Like, for instance, English men. Charm the knickers off you with their mellow vowels and frivolous verbiage, and then, once they'd got them off, panic and run. Or else stay and whinge. The English called it *whinging* instead of whining. It was better, really. Like a creaking hinge. It was a traditional compliment to be whinged at by an Englishman. It was his way of saying he trusted you, he was conferring upon you the privilege of getting to know the real him. The inner, whinging him. That was how they thought of women, secretly: whinge receptacles. Kat could play it, but that didn't mean she liked it.

She had an advantage over the English women, though: she was of no class. She had no class. She was in a class of her own. She could roll around among the English men, all different kinds of them, secure in the knowledge that she was not being measured against the class yardsticks and accent-detectors they carried around in their back pockets, was not subject to the petty snobberies and resentments that lent such richness to their inner lives. The flip side of this freedom was that she was beyond the pale. She was a colonial—how fresh, how vital, how anonymous, how finally of no consequence. Like a hole in the wall, she could be told all secrets and then be abandoned with no guilt.

She was too smart, of course. The English men were very competitive; they liked to win. Several times it hurt. Twice she had abortions, because the men in question were not up for the alternative. She learned to say that she didn't want children anyway, that if she longed for a rug-rat she would buy a gerbil. Her life began to seem long. Her adrenalin was running out. Soon she would be thirty, and all she could see ahead was more of the same.

This was how things were when Gerald turned up. "You're terrific," he said, and she was ready to hear it, even from him, even though *terrific* was a word that had probably gone out with fifties crew-cuts. She was ready for his voice by that time too: the flat, metallic nasal tone of the Great Lakes, with its clear hard *r*'s and its absence of theatricality. Dull normal. The speech of her people. It came to her suddenly that she was an exile.

Gerald was scouting, Gerald was recruiting. He'd heard about her, looked at her work, sought her out. One of the big companies back in Toronto was launching a new fashion-oriented magazine, he said: upmarket, international in its coverage, of course, but with some Canadian fashion in it too, and with lists of stores where the items portrayed could actually be bought. In that respect they felt they'd have it all over the competition, those American magazines that assumed you could only get Gucci in New York or Los Angeles. Heck, times had changed, you could get it in Edmonton! You could get it in Winnipeg!

Kat had been away too long. There was Canadian fashion now? The English quip would be to say that "Canadian fashion" was an oxymoron. She refrained from making it, lit a cigarette with her cyanide-green Covent Garden–boutique leather-covered lighter (as featured in the May issue of *the razor's edge*), looked Gerald in the eye. "London is a lot to give up," she said levelly. She glanced around the see-me-here Mayfair restaurant where they were finishing lunch, a restaurant she'd chosen because she'd known he was paying. She'd never spend that kind of money on food otherwise. "Where would I eat?"

Gerald assured her that Toronto was now the restaurant capital of Canada. He himself would be happy to be her guide. There was a great Chinatown, there was world-class Italian. Then he paused, took a breath. "I've been meaning to ask you," he said. "About the name. Is that Kat as in Krazy?" He thought this was suggestive. She'd heard it before.

"No," she said. "It's Kat as in KitKat. That's a chocolate bar. Melts in your mouth." She gave him her stare, quirked her mouth, just a twitch.

Gerald became flustered, but he pushed on. They wanted her, they needed her, they loved her, he said in essence. Someone with her fresh, innovative approach and her experience would be worth a lot of money to them, relatively speaking. But there were rewards other than the money. She would be in on the initial concept, she would have a formative influence, she would have a free hand. He named a sum that made her gasp, inaudibly of course. By now she knew better than to betray desire.

So she made the journey back, did her three months of culture shock, tried the world-class Italian and the great Chinese, and seduced Gerald at the first opportunity, right in his junior vice-presidential office. It was the first time Gerald had been seduced in such a location, or perhaps ever. Even though it was after hours, the danger frenzied him. It was the idea of it. The daring. The image of Kat kneeling on the broadloom, in a legendary bra that until now he'd seen only in the lingerie ads of the Sunday *New York Times*, unzipping him in full view of the silver-framed engagement portrait of his wife that complemented the impossible ball-point pen set on his desk. At that time he was so straight he felt compelled to take off his wedding ring and place it carefully in the ashtray first. The next day he brought her a box of David Wood Food Shop chocolate truffles. They were the best, he told her, anxious that she should recognize their quality. She found the gesture banal, but also sweet. The banality, the sweetness, the hunger to impress: that was Gerald.

Gerald was the kind of man she wouldn't have bothered with in London. He was not funny, he was not knowledgeable, he had little verbal charm. But he was eager, he was tractable, he was blank paper. Although he was eight years older than she was, he seemed much younger. She took pleasure from his furtive, boyish delight in his own wickedness. And he was so grateful. "I can hardly believe this is happening," he said, more frequently than was necessary and usually in bed.

His wife, whom Kat encountered (and still encounters) at many tedious company events, helped to explain his gratitude. The wife was a priss. Her name was Cheryl. Her hair looked as if she still used big rollers and embalm-your-hairdo spray; her mind was room-by-room Laura Ashley wallpaper: tiny, unopened pastel buds arranged in straight rows. She probably put on rubber gloves to make love, and checked it off on a list afterwards. One more messy household chore. She looked at Kat as if she'd like to spritz her with air deodorizer. Kat revenged herself by picturing Cheryl's bathrooms: hand towels embroidered with lilies, fuzzy covers on the toilet seats.

The magazine itself got off to a rocky start. Although Kat had lots of lovely money to play with, and although it was a challenge to be working in colour, she did not have the free hand Gerald had promised her. She had to contend with the company board of directors, who were all men, who were all accountants or indistinguishable from them, who were cautious and slow as moles.

"It's simple," Kat told them. "You bombard them with images of what they ought to be, and you make them feel grotty for being the way they are. You're working with the gap between reality and perception. That's why you have to hit them with something new, something they've never seen before, something they aren't. Nothing sells like anxiety."

The board, on the other hand, felt that the readership should simply be offered more of what they already had. More fur, more sumptuous leather, more cashmere. More established names. The board had no sense of improvisation, no wish to take risks; no sporting instincts, no desire to put one over on the readers just for the hell of it. "Fashion is like hunting," Kat told them, hoping to appeal to their male hormones, if any. "It's playful, it's intense, it's predatory. It's blood and guts. It's erotic." But to them it was about good taste. They wanted Dress-for-Success. Kat wanted scattergun ambush.

Everything became a compromise. Kat had wanted to call the magazine *All the Rage*, but the board was put off by the vibrations of anger in the word "rage." They thought it was too feminist, of all things. "It's a *forties* sound," Kat said.

"Forties is *back*. Don't you get it?" But they didn't. They wanted to call it *Or*. French for *gold*, and blatant enough in its values, but without any base note, as Kat told them. They sawed off at *Felice*, which had qualities each side wanted. It was vaguely French-sounding, it meant "happy" (so much less threatening than rage), and, although you couldn't expect the others to notice, for Kat it had a feline bouquet which counteracted the laciness. She had it done in hot-pink lipstick-scrawl, which helped some. She could live with it, but it had not been her first love.

This battle has been fought and refought over every innovation in design, every new angle Kat has tried to bring in, every innocuous bit of semi-kink. There was a big row over a spread that did lingerie, half pulled off and with broken glass perfume bottles strewn on the floor. There was an uproar over the two nouveau-stockinged legs, one tied to a chair with a third, different-coloured stocking. They had not understood the man's three-hundred-dollar leather gloves positioned ambiguously around a neck.

And so it has gone on, for five years.

After Gerald has left, Kat paces her living room. Pace, pace. Her stitches pull. She's not looking forward to her solitary dinner of microwaved leftovers. She's not sure now why she came back here, to this flat burg beside the polluted inland sea. Was it Ger? Ludicrous thought but no longer out of the question. Is he the reason she stays, despite her growing impatience with him?

He's no longer fully rewarding. They've learned each other too well, they take short-cuts now; their time together has shrunk from whole stolen rolling and sensuous afternoons to a few hours snatched between work and dinner-time. She no longer knows what she wants from him. She tells herself she's worth more, she should branch out; but she doesn't see other men, she can't, somehow. She's tried once or twice but it didn't work. Sometimes she goes out to dinner or a flick with one of the gay designers. She likes the gossip.

Maybe she misses London. She feels caged, in this country, in this city, in this room. She could start with the room, she could open a window. It's too stuffy in here. There's an undertone of formaldehyde, from Hairball's bottle. The flowers she got for the operation are mostly wilted, all except Gerald's from today. Come to think of it, why didn't he send her any at the hospital? Did he forget, or was it a message?

"Hairball," she says, "I wish you could talk. I could have a more intelligent conversation with you than with most of the losers in this turkey farm." Hairball's baby teeth glint in the light; it looks as if it's about to speak.

Kat feels her own forehead. She wonders if she's running a temperature. Something ominous is going on, behind her back. There haven't been enough phone calls from the magazine; they've been able to muddle on without her, which is bad news. Reigning queens should never go on vacation, or have operations either. Uneasy lies the head. She has a sixth sense about these things, she's been involved in enough palace coups to know the signs, she has sensitive antennae for the footfalls of impending treachery.

The next morning she pulls herself together, downs an espresso from her minimachine, picks out an aggressive touch-me-if-you-dare suede outfit in armour grey, and drags herself to the office, though she isn't due in till next week. Surprise, surprise. Whispering knots break up in the corridors, greet her with false welcome as she limps past. She settles herself at her minimalist desk, checks her mail. Her head is pounding, her stitches hurt. Ger gets wind of her arrival; he wants to see her a.s.a.p., and not for lunch.

He awaits her in his newly done wheat-on-white office, with the eighteenth-century desk they chose together, the Victorian inkstand, the framed blow-ups from the magazine, the hands in maroon leather, wrists manacled with pearls, the Hermès scarf twisted into a blindfold, the model's mouth blossoming lusciously beneath it. Some of her best stuff. He's beautifully done up, in a lick-my-neck silk shirt open at the throat, an eat-your-heart-out Italian silk-and-wool loose-knit sweater. Oh, cool insouciance. Oh, eyebrow language. He's a money man who lusted after art, and now he's got some, now he is some. Body art. Her art. She's done her job well; he's finally sexy.

He's smooth as lacquer. "I didn't want to break this to you until next week," he says. He breaks it to her. It's the board of directors. They think she's too bizarre, they think she goes way too far. Nothing he could do about it, although naturally he tried.

Naturally. Betrayal. The monster has turned on its own mad scientist. "I gave you life!" she wants to scream at him.

She isn't in good shape. She can hardly stand. She stands, despite his offer of a chair. She sees now what she's wanted, what she's been missing. Gerald is what she's been missing—the stable, unfashionable, previous, tight-assed Gerald. Not Ger, not the one she's made in her own image. The other one, before he got ruined. The Gerald with a house and a small child and a picture of his wife in a silver frame on his desk. She wants to be in that silver frame. She wants the child. She's been robbed.

"And who is my lucky replacement?" she says. She needs a cigarette, but does not want to reveal her shaking hands.

"Actually, it's me," he says, trying for modesty.

This is too absurd. Gerald couldn't edit a phone book. "You?" she says faintly. She has the good sense not to laugh.

"I've always wanted to get out of the money end of things here," he says, "into the creative area. I knew you'd understand, since it can't be you at any rate. I knew you'd prefer someone who could, well, sort of build on your foundations." Pompous asshole. She looks at his neck. She longs for him, hates herself for it, and is powerless.

The room wavers. He slides towards her across the wheat-coloured broadloom, takes her by the grey suede upper arms. "I'll write you a good reference," he says. "Don't worry about that. Of course, we can still see one another. I'd miss our afternoons."

"Of course," she says. He kisses her, a voluptuous kiss, or it would look like one to a third party, and she lets him. *In a pig's ear.*

She makes it home in a taxi. The driver is rude to her and gets away with it;

she doesn't have the energy. In her mailbox is an engraved invitation: Ger and Cheryl are having a drinks party, tomorrow evening. Postmarked five days ago. Cheryl is behind the times.

Kat undresses, runs a shallow bath. There's not much to drink around here, there's nothing to sniff or smoke. What an oversight; she's stuck with herself. There are other jobs. There are other men, or that's the theory. Still, something's been ripped out of her. How could this have happened, to her? When knives were slated for backs, she'd always done the stabbing. Any headed her way she's seen coming in time, and thwarted. Maybe she's losing her edge.

She stares into the bathroom mirror, assesses her face in the misted glass. A face of the eighties, a mask face, a bottom-line face; push the weak to the wall and grab what you can. But now it's the nineties. Is she out of style, so soon? She's only thirty-five, and she's already losing track of what people ten years younger are thinking. That could be fatal. As time goes by she'll have to race faster and faster to keep up, and for what? Part of the life she should have had is just a gap, it isn't there, it's nothing. What can be salvaged from it, what can be redone, what can be done at all?

When she climbs out of the tub after her sponge bath, she almost falls. She has a fever, no doubt about it. Inside her something is leaking, or else festering; she can hear it, like a dripping tap. A running sore, a sore from running so hard. She should go to the Emergency ward at some hospital, get herself shot up with antibiotics. Instead she lurches into the living room, takes Hairball down from the mantelpiece in its bottle, places it on the coffee table. She sits cross-legged, listens. Filaments wave. She can hear a kind of buzz, like bees at work.

She'd asked the doctor if it could have started as a child, a fertilized egg that escaped somehow and got into the wrong place. No, said the doctor. Some people thought this kind of tumour was present in seedling form from birth, or before it. It might be the woman's undeveloped twin. What they really were was unknown. They had many kinds of tissue, though. Even brain tissue. Though of course all of these tissues lack structure.

Still, sitting here on the rug looking in at it, she pictures it as a child. It has come out of her, after all. It is flesh of her flesh. Her child with Gerald, her thwarted child, not allowed to grow normally. Her warped child, taking its revenge.

"Hairball," she says. "You're so ugly. Only a mother could love you." She feels sorry for it. She feels loss. Tears run down her face. Crying is not something she does, not normally, not lately.

Hairball speaks to her, without words. It is irreducible, it has the texture of reality, it is not an image. What it tells her is everything she's never wanted to hear about herself. This is new knowledge, dark and precious and necessary. It cuts.

She shakes her head. What are you doing, sitting on the floor and talking to a hairball? You are sick, she tells herself. Take a Tylenol and go to bed.

The next day she feels a little better. Dania from layout calls her and makes dove-like, sympathetic coos at her, and wants to drop by during lunch hour to take a look at her aura. Kat tells her to come off it. Dania gets huffy, and says that Kat's losing her job is a price for immoral behaviour in a previous life. Kat tells her to stuff it; anyway, she's done enough immoral behaviour in this life to account for the whole thing. "Why are you so full of hate?" asks Dania. She doesn't say it like a point she's making, she sounds truly baffled.

"I don't know," says Kat. It's a straight answer.

After she hangs up she paces the floor. She's crackling inside, like hot fat under the broiler. What she's thinking about is Cheryl, bustling about her cosy house, preparing for the party. Cheryl fiddles with her freeze-framed hair, positions an overloaded vase of flowers, fusses about the caterers. Gerald comes in, kisses her lightly on the cheek. A connubial scene. His conscience is nicely washed. The witch is dead, his foot is on the body, the trophy; he's had his dirty fling, he's ready now for the rest of his life.

Kat takes a taxi to the David Wood Food Shop and buys two dozen chocolate truffles. She has them put into an oversized box, then into an oversized bag with the store logo on it. Then she goes home and takes Hairball out of its bottle. She drains it in the kitchen strainer and pats it damp-dry, tenderly, with paper towels. She sprinkles it with powdered cocoa, which forms a brown pasty crust. It still smells like formaldehyde, so she wraps it in Saran Wrap and then in tinfoil, and then in pink tissue paper, which she ties with a mauve bow. She places it in the David Wood box in a bed of shredded tissue, with the truffles nestled around. She closes the box, tapes it, puts it into the bag, stuffs several sheets of pink paper on top. It's her gift, valuable and dangerous. It's her messenger, but the message it will deliver is its own. It will tell the truth, to whoever asks. It's right that Gerald should have it; after all, it's his child too.

She prints on the card, "Gerald, Sorry I couldn't be with you. This is all the rage. Love, K."

When evening has fallen and the party must be in full swing, she calls a delivery taxi. Cheryl will not distrust anything that arrives in such an expensive bag. She will open it in public, in front of everyone. There will be distress, there will be questions. Secrets will be unearthed. There will be pain. After that, everything will go way too far.

She is not well; her heart is pounding, space is wavering once more. But outside the window it's snowing, the soft, damp, windless flakes of her childhood. She puts on her coat and goes out, foolishly. She intends to walk just to the corner, but when she reaches the corner she goes on. The snow melts against her face like small fingers touching. She has done an outrageous thing, but she doesn't feel guilty. She feels light and peaceful and filled with charity, and temporarily without a name.

Ambrose Bierce

Known as the author of *The Devil's Dictionary* (1906), which abounds in witty epigrams and scathing denunciations of all kinds of pretention, Ambrose Bierce is also the author of two collections of short stories, *In the Midst of Life*, which was privately published as *Tales of Soldiers and Civilians* in 1891, and *Can Such Things Be?* (1893). He loved the short-story form for its precision and economy, contrasting it with the novel, which he describes as "a diluted story—a story cumbered with trivialities and nonessentials." He adhered to Poe's notion that the best work might be "read at a single sitting" and have "unity, totality of effect." "The first three essentials of the literary art," he wrote, "are imagination, imagination, imagination."

In denigrating the novel—"a species of composition bearing the same relation to literature that panorama bears to art"—Bierce holds up for approval the model of the romance, which he claims "knows no law but that of its own artistic development"; it is vital, essential, and free to invent. Rejecting local colour and the excesses of realistic writing, Bierce seems a precursor of such European writers as Conrad, Joyce, and Virginia Woolf. He eschews not only novels, but also short stories written for the magazine market, a talent that, he says, "can not be acquired," but must be born into: "The torch must be passed down the line by the thumbless hands of an illustrious line of prognathous ancestors unacquainted with fire." Against such third-rate journalism, what he calls the Reporter School, stories laden down with sentiment and excessive documentation, in the interests of *vraisemblance* ("Are we given dialogue? It is not enough to report what was said, but the record must be authenticated by enumeration of the inanimate objects—commonly articles of furniture—which were privileged to be present at the conversation"), Bierce reasserts the cliché that "nothing is so probable as what is true": "Fiction has nothing to do with probability; the capable writer gives it not a moment's attention, except to make what is related *seem* probable in the reading—*seem* true."

Bierce's comments on William Dean Howells, in an essay called "The Short Story," constitute one of the finest satirical attacks ever written and reveal yet another example of his abilities as a stylist: "I want to be fair: Mr. Howells has considerable abilities. He is insufferable only in fiction and when, in criticism, he is making fiction's laws with one eye upon his paper and the other upon a catalogue of his own novels. When not carrying that heavy load, himself, he has a manly enough stride. He is not upon very intimate terms with the English language, but on many subjects, and when you least expect it of him, he thinks with such precision as momentarily to subdue a disobedient vocabulary and keep out the wrong word. Now and then he catches an accidental glimpse of his subject in a sidelight and tells with capital vivacity what it is not. The one thing that he never sees is the question that he has raised by inadvertence, deciding it by implication against his convictions. If Mr. Howells had never written fiction his criticism of novels would entertain, but the imagination which can conceive him as writing a good story under any circumstances would be a precious literary possession, enabling its owner to write a better one."

The humour and wonderfully biting satire of his critical writings might not prepare a reader for the dark intensity of Bierce's fictional vision. He was born in poverty in a log cabin in Horse Cave

Creek, Ohio (his date of birth, though uncertain, may have been 1842), the youngest of nine children. He had almost no formal education, except for a year at the Kentucky Military Institute. He joined the 9th Indiana Infantry as a drummer, fought throughout the Civil War, was wounded, and had the rank of major when he was discharged. Bierce found nothing glorious in war and described his career as that of a "hired assassin." He began his newspaper career in San Francisco, lived briefly in London, then settled down to write stories and columns in California until his wife left him and his two sons died tragically. Personal grief and professional neglect led him to an uncertain fate in Mexico in 1914, but not before he had supervised the publication of his twelve-volume *Collected Works*.

An Occurrence at Owl Creek Bridge

I

A man stood upon a railroad bridge in Northern Alabama, looking down into the swift waters twenty feet below. The man's hands were behind his back, the wrists bound with a cord. A rope loosely encircled his neck. It was attached to a stout cross-timber above his head, and the slack fell to the level of his knees. Some loose boards laid upon the sleepers supporting the metals of the railway supplied a footing for him and his executioners—two private soldiers of the Federal army, directed by a sergeant, who in civil life may have been a deputy sheriff. At a short remove upon the same temporary platform was an officer in the uniform of his rank, armed. He was captain. A sentinel at each end of the bridge stood with his rifle in the position known as "support," that is to say, vertical in front of the left shoulder, the hammer resting on the forearm thrown straight across the chest—a formal and unnatural position, enforcing an erect carriage of the body. It did not appear to be the duty of these two men to know what was occurring at the center of the bridge; they merely blockaded the two ends of the foot plank which traversed it.

Beyond one of the sentinels nobody was in sight; the railroad was lost to view. Doubtless there was an outpost further along. The other bank of the stream was open ground—a gentle acclivity crowned with a stockade of vertical tree trunks, loop-holed for rifles, with a single embrasure through which protruded the muzzle of a brass cannon commanding the bridge. Midway of the slope between bridge and fort were the spectators—a single company of infantry in line, at "parade rest," the butts of the rifles on the ground, the barrels inclining slightly backward against the right shoulder, the hands crossed upon the stock. A lieutenant stood at the right of the line, the point of his sword upon the ground, his left hand resting upon his right. Excepting the group of four at the center of the bridge not a man moved. The company faced the bridge staring stonily, motionless. The sentinels, facing the banks of the stream, might have been statues to adorn the bridge. The captain stood with folded arms, silent, observing the work of his subordinates but making no sign. Death is a dignitary who, when he comes announced, is to be received with formal manifestations of respect, even by those most familiar with him. In the code of military etiquette silence and fixity are forms of deference.

The man who was engaged in being hanged was apparently about thirty-five years of age. He was a civilian, if one might judge from his dress, which was that of a planter. His features were good—a straight nose, firm mouth, broad forehead, from which his long, dark hair was combed straight back, falling behind his ears to the collar of his well-fitting frock coat. He wore a mustache and pointed beard, but no whiskers; his eyes were large and dark grey and had a kindly expression which one would hardly have expected in one whose neck was in the hemp. Evidently this was no vulgar assassin. The liberal military code makes provision for hanging many kinds of people, and gentlemen are not excluded.

The preparations being complete, the two private soldiers stepped aside and each drew away the plank upon which he had been standing. The sergeant turned to the captain, saluted and placed himself immediately behind that officer who in turn moved apart one pace. These movements left the condemned man and the sergeant standing on the two ends of the same plank, which spanned three of the cross-ties of the bridge. The end upon which the civilian stood almost, but not quite, reached a fourth. This plank had been held in place by the weight of the captain; it was now held by that of the sergeant. At a signal from the former, the latter would step aside, the plank would tilt and the condemned man go down between two ties. The arrangement commended itself to his judgment as simple and effective. His face had not been covered nor his eyes bandaged. He looked a moment at his "unsteadfast footing," then let his gaze wander to the swirling water of the stream racing madly beneath his feet. A piece of dancing driftwood caught his attention and his eyes followed it down the current. How slowly it appeared to move! What a sluggish stream!

He closed his eyes in order to fix his last thoughts upon his wife and children. The water, touched to gold by the early sun, the brooding mists under the banks at some distance down the stream, the fort, the soldiers, the piece of drift—all had distracted him. And now he became conscious of a new disturbance. Striking through the thought of his dear ones was a sound which he could neither ignore nor understand, a sharp distinct metallic percussion like the stroke of blacksmith's hammer upon the anvil; it had the same ringing quality. He wondered what it was, and whether immeasurably distant or near by—it seemed both. Its recurrence was regular, but as slow as the tolling of a death knell. He awaited each stroke with impatience and—he knew not why—apprehension. The intervals of silence grew progressively longer; the delays became maddening. With their greater infrequency the sounds increased in strength and sharpness. They hurt his ear like the thrust of a knife; he feared he would shriek. What he heard was the ticking of his watch.

He unclosed his eyes and saw again the water below him. "If I could free my hands," he thought, "I might throw off the noose and spring into the stream. By diving I could evade the bullets, and, swimming vigorously, reach the bank, take to the woods, and get away home. My home, thank God, is as yet outside their lines; my wife and little ones are still beyond the invader's farthest advance."

As these thoughts, which have here to be set down in words, were flashed into the doomed man's brain rather than evolved from it, the captain nodded to the sergeant. The sergeant stepped aside.

II

Peyton Farquhar was a well-to-do planter, of an old and highly respected Alabama family. Being a slave owner, and, like other slave owners, a politician, he was naturally an original secessionist and ardently devoted to the Southern cause. Circumstances of an imperious nature which it is unnecessary to relate here, had prevented him from taking service with the gallant army which had fought the disastrous campaigns ending with the fall of Corinth, and he chafed under the inglorious restraint, longing for the release of his energies, the larger life of the soldier, the opportunity for distinction. That opportunity, he felt, would come, as it comes to all in war time. Meanwhile he did what he could. No service was too humble for him to perform in aid of the South, no adventure too perilous for him to undertake if consistent with the character of a civilian who was at heart a soldier, and who in good faith and without too much qualification assented to at least a part of the frankly villainous dictum that all is fair in love and war.

One evening while Farquhar and his wife were sitting on a rustic bench near the entrance to his grounds, a grey-clad soldier rode up to the gate and asked for a drink of water. Mrs. Farquhar was only too happy to serve him with her own white hands. While she was gone to fetch the water, her husband approached the dusty horseman and inquired eagerly for news from the front.

"The Yanks are repairing the railroads," said the man, "and are getting ready for another advance. They have reached the Owl Creek bridge, put it in order, and built a stockade on the other bank. The commandant has issued an order, which is posted everywhere, declaring that any civilian caught interfering with the railroad, its bridges, tunnels, or trains, will be summarily hanged. I saw the order."

"How far is it to the Owl Creek bridge?" Farquhar asked.

"About thirty miles."

"Is there no force on this side the creek?"

"Only a picket post half a mile out, on the railroad, and a single sentinel at this end of the bridge."

"Suppose a man—a civilian and student of hanging—should elude the picket post and perhaps get the better of the sentinel," said Farquhar, smiling, "what could he accomplish?"

The soldier reflected. "I was there a month ago," he replied. "I observed that the flood of last winter had lodged a great quantity of driftwood against the wooden pier at this end of the bridge. It is now dry and would burn like tow."

The lady had now brought the water, which the soldier drank. He thanked her ceremoniously, bowed to her husband, and rode away. An hour later, after nightfall, he repassed the plantation, going northward in the direction from which he had come. He was a Federal scout.

III

As Peyton Farquhar fell straight downward through the bridge, he lost consciousness and was as one already dead. From this state he was awakened—ages later, it seemed to him—by the pain of a sharp pressure upon his throat, followed by a sense of suffocation. Keen, poignant agonies seemed to shoot from his neck downward through every fiber of his body and limbs. These pains appeared to flash along well defined lines of ramification, and to beat with an inconceivably rapid periodicity. They seemed like streams of pulsating fire heating him to an intolerable temperature. As to his head, he was conscious of nothing but a feeling of fullness—of congestion. These sensations were unaccompanied by thought. The intellectual part of his nature was already effaced; he had power only to feel, and feeling was torment. He was conscious of motion. Encompassed in a luminous cloud, of which he was now merely the fiery heart, without material substance, he swung through unthinkable arcs of oscillation, like a vast pendulum. Then all at once, with terrible suddenness, the light about him shot upward with the noise of a loud splash; a frightful roaring was in his ears, and all was cold and dark. The power of thought was restored; he knew that the rope had broken and he had fallen into the stream. There was no additional strangulation; the noose about his neck was already suffocating him, and kept the water from his lungs. To die of hanging at the bottom of a river!—the idea seemed to him ludicrous. He opened his eyes in the blackness and saw above him a gleam of light, but how distant, how inaccessible! He was still sinking, for the light became fainter and fainter until it was a mere glimmer. Then it began to grow and brighten, and he knew that he was rising toward the surface—knew it with reluctance, for he was now very comfortable. "To be hanged and drowned," he thought, "that is not so bad; but I do not wish to be shot. No; I will not be shot; that is not fair."

He was not conscious of an effort, but a sharp pain in his wrist apprised him that he was trying to free his hands. He gave the struggle his attention, as an idler might observe the feat of a juggler, without interest in the outcome. What splendid effort!—what magnificent, what superhuman strength! Ah, that was a fine endeavor! Bravo! The cord fell away; his arms parted and floated upward, the hands dimly seen on each side in the growing light. He watched them with a new interest as first one and then the other pounced upon the noose at his neck. They tore it away and thrust it fiercely aside, its undulations resembling those of a water-snake. "Put it back, put it back!" He thought he shouted these words to his hands, for the undoing of the noose had been succeeded by the direst pang which he had yet experienced. His neck ached horribly; his brain was on fire; his heart, which had been fluttering faintly, gave a great leap, trying to force itself out at his mouth. His whole body was racked and wrenched with an insupportable anguish! But his disobedient hands gave no heed to the command. They beat the water vigorously with quick, downward strokes, forcing him to the surface. He felt his head emerge; his eyes were blinded by the sunlight; his chest expanded convulsively, and with supreme and crowning agony his lungs engulfed a great draught of air, which instantly he expelled in a shriek!

He was now in full possession of his physical senses. They were, indeed, preternaturally keen and alert. Something in the awful disturbance of his organic system had so exalted and refined them that they made record of things never before perceived. He felt the ripples upon his face and heard their separate sounds as they struck. He looked at the forest on the bank of the stream, saw the individual trees, the leaves and the veining of each leaf—saw the very insects upon them, the locusts, the brilliant-bodied flies, the grey spiders stretching their webs from twig to twig. He noted the prismatic colors in all the dewdrops upon a million blades of grass. The humming of the gnats that danced above the eddies of the stream, the beating of the dragon flies' wings, the strokes of the water spiders' legs, like oars which had lifted their boat—all these made audible music. A fish slid along beneath his eyes and he heard the rush of its body parting the water.

He had come to the surface facing down the stream; in a moment the visible world seemed to wheel slowly round, himself the pivotal point, and he saw the bridge, the fort, the soldiers upon the bridge, the captain, the sergeant, the two privates, his executioners. They were a silhouette against the blue sky. They shouted and gesticulated, pointing at him; the captain had drawn his pistol, but did not fire; the others were unarmed. Their movements were grotesque and horrible, their forms gigantic.

Suddenly he heard a sharp report and something struck the water smartly within a few inches of his head, spattering his face with spray. He heard a second report, and saw one of the sentinels with his rifle at his shoulder, a light cloud of blue smoke rising from the muzzle. The man in the water saw the eye of the man on the bridge gazing into his own through the sights of the rifle. He observed that it was a grey eye, and remembered having read that grey eyes were keenest and that all famous marksmen had them. Nevertheless, this one had missed.

A counter swirl had caught Farquhar and turned him half round; he was again looking into the forest on the bank opposite the fort. The sound of a clear, high voice in a monotonous singsong now rang out behind him and came across the water with a distinctness that pierced and subdued all other sounds, even the beating of the ripples in his ears. Although no soldier, he had frequented camps enough to know the dread significance of that deliberate, drawling, aspirated chant; the lieutenant on shore was taking a part in the morning's work. How coldly and pitilessly—with what an even, calm intonation, presaging and enforcing tranquillity in the men—with what accurately-measured intervals fell those cruel words:

"Attention, company. ... Shoulder arms. ... Ready. ... Aim. ... Fire."

Farquhar dived—dived as deeply as he could. The water roared in his ears like the voice of Niagara, yet he heard the dulled thunder of the volley, and rising again toward the surface, met shining bits of metal, singularly flattened, oscillating slowly downward. Some of them touched him on the face and hands, then fell away, continuing their descent. One lodged between his collar and neck; it was uncomfortably warm, and he snatched it out.

As he rose to the surface, gasping for breath, he saw that he had been a long time under water; he was perceptibly farther down stream—nearer to safety. The soldiers had almost finished reloading; the metal ramrods flashed all at once in the sunshine as they were drawn from the barrels, turned in the air; and thrust into their sockets. The two sentinels fired again, independently and ineffectually.

The hunted man saw all this over his shoulder; he was now swimming vigorously with the current. His brain was as energetic as his arms and legs; he thought with the rapidity of lightning.

"The officer," he reasoned, "will not make that martinet's error a second time. It is as easy to dodge a volley as a single shot. He has probably already given the command to fire at will. God help me, I cannot dodge them all!"

An appalling splash within two yards of him, followed by a loud rushing sound, diminuendo, which seemed to travel back through the air to the fort and died in an explosion which stirred the very river to its deeps! A rising sheet of water, which curved over him, fell down upon him, blinded him, strangled him! The cannon had taken a hand in the game. As he shook his head free from the commotion of the smitten water, he heard the deflected shot humming through the air ahead, and in an instant it was cracking and smashing the branches in the forest beyond.

"They will not do that again; the next time they will use a charge of grape. I must keep my eye upon the gun; the smoke will apprise me—the report arrives too late; it lags behind the missile. It is a good gun."

Suddenly he felt himself whirled round and round—spinning like a top. The water, the banks, the forest, the now distant bridge, fort and men—all were commingled and blurred. Objects were represented by their colors only; circular horizontal streaks of color—that was all he saw. He had been caught in a vortex and was being whirled on with a velocity of advance and gyration which made him giddy and sick. In a few moments he was flung upon the gravel at the foot of the left bank of the stream—the southern bank—and behind a projecting point which concealed him from his enemies. The sudden arrest of his motion, the abrasion of one of his hands on the gravel, restored him and he wept with delight. He dug his fingers into the sand, threw it over himself in handfuls and audibly blessed it. It looked like gold, like diamonds, rubies, emeralds; he could think of nothing beautiful which it did not resemble. The trees upon the bank were giant garden plants; he noted a definite order in their arrangement, inhaled the fragrance of their blooms. A strange, roseate light shone through the spaces among their trunks, and the wind made in their branches the music of aeolian harps. He had no wish to perfect his escape, was content to remain in that enchanting spot until retaken.

A whizz and rattle of grapeshot among the branches high above his head roused him from his dream. The baffled cannoneer had fired him a random farewell. He sprang to his feet, rushed up the sloping bank, and plunged into the forest.

All that day he travelled, laying his course by the rounding sun. The forest seemed interminable; nowhere did he discover a break in it, not even a woodman's road. He had not known that he lived in so wild a region. There was something uncanny in the revelation.

By nightfall he was fatigued, footsore, famishing. The thought of his wife and children urged him on. At last he found a road which led him in what he knew to be the right direction. It was as wide and straight as a city street, yet it seemed untravelled. No fields bordered it, no dwelling anywhere. Not so much as the barking of a dog suggested human habitation. The black bodies of the great trees formed a straight wall on both sides, terminating on the horizon in a point, like a diagram in a lesson in perspective. Overhead, as he looked up through this rift in the wood, shone great golden stars looking unfamiliar and grouped in strange constellations. He was sure they were arranged in some order which had a secret and malign significance. The wood on either side was full of singular noises, among which—once, twice, and again—he distinctly heard whispers in an unknown tongue.

His neck was in pain, and, lifting his hand to it, he found it horribly swollen. He knew that it had a circle of black where the rope had bruised it. His eyes felt congested; he could no longer close them. His tongue was swollen with thirst; he relieved its fever by thrusting it forward from between his teeth into the cool air. How softly the turf had carpeted the untravelled avenue! He could no longer feel the roadway beneath his feet!

Doubtless, despite his suffering, he fell asleep while walking, for now he sees another scene—perhaps he has merely recovered from a delirium. He stands at the gate of his own home. All is as he left it, and all bright and beautiful in the morning sunshine. He must have travelled the entire night. As he pushes open the gate and passes up the wide white walk, he sees a flutter of female garments; his wife, looking fresh and cool and sweet, steps down from the verandah to meet him. At the bottom of the steps she stands waiting, with a smile of ineffable joy, an attitude of matchless grace and dignity. Ah, how beautiful she is! He springs forward with extended arms. As he is about to clasp her, he feels a stunning blow upon the back of the neck; a blinding white light blazes all about him, with a sound like the shock of a cannon—then all is darkness and silence!

Peyton Farquhar was dead; his body, with a broken neck, swung gently from side to side beneath the timbers of the Owl Creek bridge.

Clark Blaise

Clark Blaise was born in 1940 in Fargo, North Dakota, to an English-Canadian mother and a French-Canadian father. Growing up in both Canada and the U.S., particularly in Florida and Pittsburgh, and the Canadian prairies, Blaise describes himself as sociologically an American, having as a child processed so much data about the U.S.; psychologically a Canadian, in the way he uses and interprets that data—the irony, the self-doubt, the sense of human limits; and emotionally, a Québécois. He has been a peripatetic teacher of Creative Writing, at Concordia University in Montreal, Saratoga Springs, Columbia, and the University of Iowa, where he received his M.F.A. and where he now directs the International Writers' Program. His publications include *A North American Education* (1973), *Tribal Justice* (1974), *Lunar Attractions* (1979), *Lusts* (1983), *Resident Alien* (1986), *If I Had a Father: A Post-Modern Autobiography* (1994), and *If I Were Me* (1997). He has collaborated on two non-fiction works with his wife, the fiction writer Bharati Mukherjee: *Days and Nights in Calcutta* (1977) and a book about the Air India disaster called *The Sorrow and the Terror* (1989), and another, *The Border as Fiction* (1990).

Clark Blaise's thoughts on the craft of fiction can be found in several essays written for anthologies edited by John Metcalf and in an interview conducted with Geoff Hancock published in *Canadian Fiction Magazine* (No. 34/35, 1980). He is perpetually interested in matters of form. He describes the writing of stories as "line-by-line creation"; and revision, as an exhausting process: "I don't have the construction engineer's sense of 'knock this out, knock that out' and it'll work. I am a bricklayer in that sense, I have to go from brick to brick." The short story, he says "is a delicate, fluted casting; what the writer is out to capture is the rough, shaggy and broken-open mold that surrounded it, at least in his imagination." His stories, which are often low-key, originate in memories and visual impressions: "Most of the deep emotional situations that hit me or that hit people I know are too hot for me to handle. I'm in possession of a great number of stories of vast interest. But they're thoroughly useless to me; I'd make pulp of them. If they'd give me a detail instead, then I could invent the situation."

Blaise claims that the centre of his stories is not in character, but elsewhere: "... I do not set out to create characters. I do not set out to write a psychological case study. I am really trying to talk about, as I understand it, the world, the nature of the world, the nature of event, happenstance, accident, beauty, permanence, change, violence. I'm trying to talk about things like that. You have to have in our humanist culture, in our humanist Western tradition, you have to have a human focus for those things or else you are writing allegory, or fable. And psychology has told us so much about probability that the character is bound to be fairly recognizable. I'm committed to representational fiction; otherwise you're doing stained-glass windows. ...

"Yes, or sociology. So that the agreed-upon way of registering shock waves is through a perceiving consciousness and so I do that. ... Things that really interest me are more aesthetic than psychological, so I'm willing to accept a fairly stable psychological receiver. I don't explore a great range of characterization, and I'm willing to accept that so long as I do have intensity and texture. To me that's where the interest lies, not in the characters."

The preoccupation with detail and with aesthetic questions is nowhere more evident than in Blaise's attitude to style. "Oh, I'm always very much aware of style. The style is the situation. If I want to be true to how something strikes me, I have to be as stylish or as style-conscious as that very thing that I found so gripping. I'm talking about very small things: a hedgerow, say. To do real justice to a hedgerow would require the work of a great lyric poet or Monet or (in prose) Proust—the only author I know who gives every element of nature and of character its proper space. To do real justice to anything is a matter of generosity, and character and style and you can't use the language of the butcher shop or the language of the newspaper or the textbook to do that hedgerow justice. That's the great challenge: to find language that fits the things that do not yield to language. We have no agreed-upon formula for that. We do have visual formulas in the arts, in painting and film and in music, but not in prose."

In terms of structure or design in fiction, Blaise places considerable emphasis on plot, but defines the word idiosyncratically. "For me and for me alone, plot is not planned but plot is the revelation of inevitability, the slow disclosure of something beautifully obvious, though hidden. ... I feel sometimes that you hurtle through the vastness of time—those two billion seconds that we all have allotted to us—towards some point that was always there, something that you feared and hoped to avoid, but it was always there. And you embrace it finally and that's a plot, but until that moment, you've had (seemingly) an infinite number of choices, and ways to avoid it." He believes form is organic, not inherited, that it emerges from the material and does not necessarily follow the conventional lines of conflict, crisis, and resolution.

Blaise's response to Hancock's question about shaping strategies suggests a fascinating link between art and life in his own work. "Who knows? It's deeply related to one's own psychology obviously; introspective people write inward-looking stories. The stories, in my own mind, tend towards a kind of confirmation and towards the discovery of that which you wanted to keep hidden, and to a kind of confirmation of what you hoped was not there. ... I hope to imply that the world was not created when the story started and it does not end when the story's over, but rather there is a continuum and the story is a plucked thread, one of possible thousands, from a sweater that remains indifferent to the process. We tease the story into a visible loop and we stare at this loop and it bothers us and it disrupts the harmony of the weave but it also goes back into the weave and disappears. End of story. For a while, it snagged at our eye. We even felt sorry for the owner of the sweater. But we also noticed that, snagged thread and all, it remains a handsome sweater. It doesn't destroy the sweater, it doesn't destroy the overall design, and there are millions more threads running in every which way which will eventually get snagged and which will become exposed and embarrassing. And that's my sense of the story. We are not talking about a whole sweater. We're talking about one out of several thousand intricately patterned, interwoven, anonymous threads and if we had the time and patience in our life we could look at every single strand, at every single moment of human life, and make of it a densely observed story. But no one has that. The sweater, however, is the shaggy old mold I was talking of earlier."

A Class of New Canadians

Norman Dyer hurried down Sherbrooke Street, collar turned against the snow. 'Superb!' he muttered, passing a basement gallery next to a French bookstore.

Bleached and tanned women in furs dashed from hotel lobbies into waiting cabs. Even the neon clutter of the side streets and the honks of slithering taxis seemed remote tonight through the peaceful snow. *Superb*, he thought again, waiting for a light and backing from a slushy curb: a word reserved for wines, cigars, and delicate sauces; he was feeling superb this evening. After eighteen months in Montreal, he still found himself freshly impressed by everything he saw. He was proud of himself for having steered his life north, even for jobs that were menial by standards he could have demanded. Great just being here no matter what they paid, looking at these buildings, these faces, and hearing all the languages. He was learning to be insulted by simple bad taste, wherever he encountered it.

Since leaving graduate school and coming to Montreal, he had sampled every ethnic restaurant downtown and in the old city, plus a few Levantine places out in Outremont. He had worked on conversational French and mastered much of the local dialect, done reviews for local papers, translated French-Canadian poets for Toronto quarterlies, and tweaked his colleagues for not sympathizing enough with Quebec separatism. He attended French performances of plays he had ignored in English, and kept a small but elegant apartment near a colony of *émigré* Russians just off Park Avenue. Since coming to Montreal he'd witnessed a hold-up, watched a murder, and seen several riots. When stopped on the street for directions, he would answer in French or accented English. To live this well and travel each long academic summer, he held two jobs. He had no intention of returning to the States. In fact, he had begun to think of himself as a semi-permanent, semi-political exile.

Now, stopped again a few blocks farther, he studied the window of Holt-Renfrew's exclusive men's shop. Incredible, he thought, the authority of simple good taste. Double-breasted chalk-striped suits he would never dare to buy. Knitted sweaters, and fifty-dollar shoes. One tanned mannequin was decked out in a brash checkered sportscoat with a burgundy vest and dashing ascot. Not a price tag under three hundred dollars. Unlike food, drink, cinema, and literature, clothing had never really involved him. Someday, he now realized, it would. Dyer's clothes, thus far, had all been bought in a chain department store. He was a walking violation of American law, clad shoes to scarf in Egyptian cottons, Polish leathers, and woolens from the People's Republic of China.

He had no time for dinner tonight; this was Wednesday, a day of lectures at one university, and then an evening course in English as a Foreign Language at McGill, beginning at six. He would eat afterwards.

Besides the money, he had kept this second job because it flattered him. There was to Dyer something fiercely elemental, almost existential, about teaching both his language and his literature in a foreign country—like Joyce in Trieste, Isherwood and Nabokov in Berlin, Beckett in Paris. Also it was necessary for his students. It was the first time in his life that he had done something socially useful. What difference did it make that the job was beneath him, a recent Ph.D., while most of his colleagues in the evening school at McGill were idle housewives and bachelor civil servants? It didn't matter, even, that this job was a perversion of all the sentiments he held as a progressive young teacher. He was a god two evenings a week, sometimes suffering and fatigued, but nevertheless an omniscient, benevolent god. His students were silent, ignorant, and dedicated to learning English. No discussions, no demonstrations, no dialogue.

I love them, he thought. They need me.

He entered the room, pocketed his cap and ear muffs, and dropped his brief-case on the podium. Two girls smiled good evening.

They love me, he thought, taking off his boots and hanging up his coat; I'm not like their English-speaking bosses.

I love myself, he thought with amazement even while conducting a drill on word order. I love myself for tramping down Sherbrooke Street in zero weather just to help them with noun clauses. I love myself standing behind this podium and showing Gilles Carrier and Claude Veilleux the difference between the past continuous and the simple past; or the sultry Armenian girl with the bewitching half-glasses that 'put on' is not the same as 'take on'; or telling the dashing Mr Miguel Mayor, late of Madrid, that simple futurity can be expressed in four different ways, at least.

This is what mastery is like, he thought. Being superb in one's chosen field, not merely in one's mother tongue. A respected performer in the lecture halls of the major universities, equipped by twenty years' research in the remotest libraries, and slowly giving it back to those who must have it. Dishing it out suavely, even wittily. Being a legend. Being loved and a little feared.

'Yes, Mrs David?'

A *sabra*: freckled, reddish hair, looking like a British model, speaks with a nifty British accent, and loves me.

'No,' he smiled, 'I *were* is not correct except in the present subjunctive, which you haven't studied yet.'

The first hour's bell rang. The students closed their books for the intermission. Dyer put his away, then noticed a page of his Faulkner lecture from the afternoon class. *Absalom, Absalom!* his favourite.

'Can anyone here tell me what the *impregnable citadel of his passive rectitude* means?'

'What, sir?' asked Mr Vassilopoulos, ready to copy.

'What about the *presbyterian and lugubrious effluvium of his passive vindictiveness*?' A few girls giggled. 'O.K.,' said Dyer, 'take your break.'

In the halls of McGill they broke into the usual groups. French Canadians and South Americans into two large circles, then the Greeks, Germans, Spanish, and French into smaller groups. The patterns interested Dyer. Madrid Spaniards and Parisian French always spoke English with their New World co-linguals. The Middle Europeans spoke German together, not Russian, preferring one occupier to the other. Two Israeli men went off alone. Dyer decided to join them for the break.

Not *sabras*, Dyer concluded, not like Mrs David. The shorter one, dark and wavy-haired, held his cigarette like a violin bow. The other, Mr Weinrot, was tall and pot-bellied, with a ruddy face and thick stubby fingers. Something about him suggested truck-driving, perhaps of beer, maybe in Germany. Neither one, he decided, could supply the name of a good Israeli restaurant.

'This is really hard, you know?' said Weinrot.

'Why?'

'I think it's because I'm not speaking much of English at my job.'

'French?' asked Dyer.

'French? Pah! All the time Hebrew, sometimes German, sometimes little Polish. Crazy thing, eh? How long you think they let me speak Hebrew if I'm working in America?'

'Depends on where you're working,' he said.

'Hell, I'm working for the Canadian government, what you think? Plant I work in—I'm engineer, see—makes boilers for the turbines going up North. Look. When I'm leaving Israel I go first to Italy. Right away-bamm I'm working in Italy I'm speaking Italian like a native. Passing for a native.'

'A native Jew,' said his dark-haired friend.

'Listen to him. So in Rome they think I'm from Tyrol—that's still native, eh? So I speak Russian and German and Italian like a Jew. My Hebrew is bad, I admit it, but it's a lousy language anyway. Nobody likes it. French I understand but English I'm talking like a bum. Arabic I know five dialects. Danish fluent. So what's the matter I can't learn English?'

'It'll come, don't worry,' Dyer smiled. *Don't worry, my son*; he wanted to pat him on the arm. 'Anyway, that's what makes Canada so appealing. Here they don't force you.'

'What's this *appealing*? Means nice? Look, my friend, keep it, eh? Two years in a country I don't learn the language means it isn't a country.'

'Come on,' said Dyer. 'Neither does forcing you.'

'Let me tell you a story why I come to Canada. Then you tell me if I was wrong, O.K.?'

'Certainly,' said Dyer, flattered.

In Italy, Weinrot told him, he had lost his job to a Communist union. He left Italy for Denmark and opened up an Israeli restaurant with five other friends. Then the six Israelis decided to rent a bigger apartment downtown near the restaurant. They found a perfect nine-room place for two thousand kroner a month, not bad shared six ways. Next day the landlord told them the deal was off. 'You tell me why,' Weinrot demanded.

No Jews? Dyer wondered. 'He wanted more rent,' he finally said.

'More—you kidding? More we expected. *Less* we didn't expect. A couple with eight kids is showing up after we're gone and the law in Denmark says a man has a right to a room for each kid plus a hundred kroner knocked off the rent for each kid. What you think of that? So a guy who comes in *after* us gets a nine-room place for a thousand kroner *less*. Law says no way a bachelor can get a place ahead of a family, and bachelors pay twice as much.'

Dyer waited, then asked, 'So?'

'So, I make up my mind the world is full of communismus, just like Israel. So I take out applications next day for Australia, South Africa, U.S.A., and Canada. Canada says come right away, so I go. Should have waited for South Africa.'

'How could you?' Dyer cried. 'What's wrong with you anyway? South Africa is fascist. Australia is racist.'

The bell rang, and the Israelis, with Dyer, began walking to the room.

'What I was wondering, then,' said Mr Weinrot, ignoring Dyer's outburst, 'was if my English is good enough to be working in the United States. You're American, aren't you?'

It was a question Dyer had often avoided in Europe, but had rarely been asked in Montreal. 'Yes,' he admitted, 'your English is probably good enough for the States or South Africa, whichever one wants you first.'

He hurried ahead to the room, feeling that he had let Montreal down. He wanted to turn and shout to Weinrot and to all the others that Montreal was the greatest city on the continent, if only they knew it as well as he did. If they'd just break out of their little ghettos.

At the door, the Armenian girl with the half-glasses caught his arm. She was standing with Mrs David and Miss Parizeau, a jolly French-Canadian girl that Dyer had been thinking of asking out.

'Please, sir,' she said, looking at him over the tops of her tiny glasses, 'what I was asking earlier—*put on*—I heard on the television. A man said *You are putting me on* and everybody laughed. I think it was supposed to be funny but *put on* we learned means get dressed, no?'

'Ah—don't put me on,' Dyer laughed.

'I yaven't erd it neither,' said Miss Parizeau.

'To put some*body* on means to make a fool of him. To put some*thing* on is to wear it. O.K.?' He gave examples.

'Ah, now I know,' said Miss Parizeau. 'Like bullshitting somebody. Is it the same?'

'Ah, yes,' he said, smiling. French-Canadians were like children learning the language. 'Your example isn't considered polite. "Put on" is very common now in the States.'

'Then maybe,' said Miss Parizeau, 'we'll ave it ere in twenty years.' The Armenian giggled.

'No—I've heard it here just as often,' Dyer protested, but the girls had already entered the room.

He began the second hour with a smile which slowly soured as he thought of the Israelis. America's anti-communism was bad enough, but it was worse hearing it echoed by immigrants, by Jews, here in Montreal. Wasn't there a psychological type who chose Canada over South Africa? Or was it just a matter of visas and slow adjustment? Did Johannesburg lose its Greeks, and Melbourne its Italians, the way Dyer's students were always leaving Montreal?

And after class when Dyer was again feeling content and thinking of approaching one of the Israelis for a restaurant tip, there came the flood of small requests: should Mrs Papadopoulos go into a more advanced course; could Mr Perez miss a week for an interview in Toronto; could Mr Giguère, who spoke English perfectly, have a harder book; Mr Coté an easier one?

Then as he packed his briefcase in the empty room, Miguel Mayor, the vain and impeccable Spaniard, came forward from the hallway.

'Sir,' he began, walking stiffly, ready to bow or salute. He wore a loud grey checkered sportscoat this evening, blue shirt, and matching ascot-handkerchief, slightly mauve. He must have shaved just before class, Dyer noticed, for two fresh daubs of antiseptic cream stood out on his jaw, just under his earlobe.

'I have been wanting to ask you something, as a matter of fact,' said Dyer. 'Do you know any good Spanish restaurants I might try tonight?'

'There are not any good Spanish restaurants in Montreal,' he said. He stepped closer. 'Sir?'

'What's on your mind, then?'

'Please—have you the time to look on a letter for me?'

He laid the letter on the podium.

'Look *over* a letter,' said Dyer. 'What is it for?'

'I have applied,' he began, stopping to emphasize the present perfect construction, 'for a job in Cleveland, Ohio, and I want to know if my letter will be good. Will an American, I mean—'

'Why are you going there?'

'It is a good job.'

'But Cleveland—'

'They have a blackman mayor, I have read. But the job is not in Cleveland.'

'Let me see it.'

Most honourable Sir: I humbly beg consideration for a position in your grand company ...

'Who are you writing this to?'

'The president,' said Miguel Mayor.

I am once a student of Dr Ramiro Gutierrez of the Hydraulic Institute of Sevilla Spain ...

'Does the president know this Ramiro Gutierrez?'

'Oh, everybody is knowing him,' Miguel Mayor assured, 'he is the most famous expert in all Spain.'

'Did he recommend this company to you?'

'No—I have said in my letter, if you look—'

An ancient student of Dr Gutierrez, Salvador del Este is actually a boiler expert who is being employed like supervisor is formerly a friend of mine ...

'Is he still your friend?'

Whenever you say come to my city Miguel Mayor for talking I will be coming. I am working in Montreal since two years and am now wanting more money than I am getting here now ...

'Well ...' Dyer sighed.

'Sir—what I want from you is knowing in good English how to interview me by this man. The letters in Spanish are not the same to English ones, you know?'

I remain humbly at your orders ...

'Why do you want to leave Montreal?'

'It's time for a change.'

'Have you ever been to Cleveland?'

'I am one summer in California. Very beautiful there and hot like my country.

Montreal is big port like Barcelona. Everybody mixed together and having no money. It is just a place to land, no?'

'Montreal? Don't be silly.'

'I thought I come here and learn good English but where I work I get by in Spanish and French. It's hard, you know?' he smiled. Then he took a few steps back and gave his cuffs a gentle tug, exposing a set of jade cufflinks.

Dyer looked at the letter again and calculated how long he would be correcting it, then up at his student. How old is he? My age? Thirty? Is he married? Where do the Spanish live in Montreal? He looks so prosperous, so confident, like a male model off a page of *Playboy*. For an instant Dyer felt that his student was mocking him, somehow pitting his astounding confidence and wardrobe, sharp chin and matador's bearing against Dyer's command of English and mastery of the side streets, bistros, and ethnic restaurants. Mayor's letter was painful, yet he remained somehow competent. He would pass his interview, if he got one. What would he care about America, and the odiousness he'd soon be supporting? It was as though a superstructure of exploitation had been revealed, and Dyer felt himself abused by the very people he wanted so much to help. It had to end someplace.

He scratched out the second 'humbly' from the letter, then folded the sheet of foolscap. 'Get it typed right away,' he said. 'Good luck.'

'Thank you, sir,' said his student, with a bow. Dyer watched the letter disappear in the inner pocket of the checkered sportscoat. Then the folding of the cashmere scarf, the draping of the camel's hair coat about the shoulders, the easing of the fur hat down to the rims of his ears. The meticulous filling of the pigskin gloves. Mayor's patent leather galoshes glistened.

'Good evening, sir,' he said.

'*Buenas noches*,' Dyer replied.

He hurried now, back down Sherbrooke Street to his daytime office where he could deposit his books. Montreal on a winter night was still mysterious, still magical. Snow blurred the arc lights. The wind was dying. Every second car was now a taxi, crowned with an orange crescent. Slushy curbs had hardened. The window of Holt-Renfrew's was still attractive. The legless dummies invited a final stare. He stood longer than he had earlier, in front of the sporty mannequin with a burgundy waistcoat, the mauve and blue ensemble, the jade cufflinks.

Good evening, sir, he could almost hear. The ascot, the shirt, the complete outfit, had leaped off the back of Miguel Mayor. He pictured how he must have entered the store with three hundred dollars and a prepared speech, and walked out again with everything off the torso's back.

I want that.

What, sir?

That.

The coat, sir?

Yes.

Very well, sir.

And *that*.

Which, sir?

All that.

'Absurd man!' Dyer whispered. There had been a moment of fear, as though the naked body would leap from the window, and legless, chase him down Sherbrooke Street. But the moment was passing. Dyer realized now that it was comic, even touching. Miguel Mayor had simply tried too hard, too fast, and it would be good for him to stay in Montreal until he deserved those clothes, that touching vanity and confidence. With one last look at the window, he turned sharply, before the clothes could speak again.

Jorge Luis Borges

Born in 1899 in Buenos Aires, where his father was a lawyer and teacher of psychology, Borges was a precocious child, who was writing in Spanish and English at age six and had published a translation before he was ten. He spent the war years at school in Geneva, studying in French, but also learning Latin, German, and Italian. On his return to Argentina from Spain in 1921, he founded the literary magazine *Sur* and embarked on his long career as a writer, writing mainly poetry and flirting with literary movements such as "Ultraism," a form of Spanish Expressionism. He was best known as an editor and essayist until the publication of *Ficciones* in 1945, a playful book of anti-realist fictions. This was followed by *Labyrinths* (1962), *The Aleph and Other Stories* (1970), and *Doctor Brodie's Report* (1973). Although he was not a politically engaged writer, Borges nonetheless ran afoul of dictator Juan Perón, who demoted him from librarian to chicken inspector. He was Charles Eliot Norton Professor of Poetry at Harvard in 1967–1968 and received various honours, including the Prix Internationale des Editeurs (Prix Formentor), which he shared with Samuel Beckett. Borges taught English and American Literature for many years at the University of Buenos Aires, until blindness forced him to retire. In his essay "Blindness," he speaks ironically, but not bitterly, of being reinstated as director of the Argentine National Library the year he became too blind to read books and of how he celebrated both events by taking up the study of Old English. Because of his remarkable memory and determination, Borges's range of literary reference was remarkable and he could recall enormous amounts of material for his lectures, conversations, and literary purposes. His ideas on the craft are gathered together in *Borges on Writing* (1973) and some of his lectures are available in *Seven Nights* (1984). He died in 1986.

Although he is a great stylist, Borges felt that style was not something to be consciously cultivated, but, rather, must grow out of a writer's convictions and long devotion to the craft. "If a writer disbelieves what he is writing, then he can hardly expect his readers to believe it. In this country, though, there is a tendency to regard any kind of writing—especially the writing of poetry—as a game of style. I have known many poets here who have written well—very fine stuff—with delicate moods and so on—but if you talk with them, the only thing they tell you is smutty stories or speak of politics in the way that everybody does, so that really their writing turns out to be a kind of sideshow. They had learned writing in the way that a man might learn to play chess or to play bridge. They were not really poets or writers at all. It was a trick they had learned, and they had learned it thoroughly. They had the whole thing at their finger ends."

His work is dominated by ideas, yet Borges insisted that a writer not be judged by the importance of his ideas, but rather by "the enjoyment he gives and by the emotion one gets" from his work. When asked in *The Paris Review* interview, conducted by Ronald Christ, about his interest in the fantastic, Borges quoted two of his favourite writers: "Conrad thought that when one wrote, even in a realistic way, about the world, one was writing a fantastic story because the world itself is fantastic and unfathomable and mysterious. ... I found that he was right. I talked to Bioy Cesares, who also writes fantastic stories—very, very fine stories—and he said, 'I think Conrad is right. Really, nobody knows whether the world is realistic or fantastic, that is to say, whether the world is a natural process or whether it is a kind of dream, a dream that we may or may not share with others.'"

His writing is highly allusive, but Borges argues for a plain style, unadorned, with no big dictionary words and nothing from the streets that will quickly go out of fashion. In terms of organizing principles in fiction, he says: "... generally speaking, what I think is most important in a short story is the plot or situation, while in a novel what's important are the characters." When asked if social or political issues should be dealt with in fiction, Borges, who has elsewhere declared himself an antagonist of *engaged writing*, plays down any links in his fiction with contemporary politics and tries to suggest that "perhaps it's about the politics of any time or any place." "Oscar Wilde said that modernity of treatment and subject should he carefully avoided by the modern artist. Of course, he was being witty, but what he was saying was based on an obvious truth. Homer, for example, wrote several centuries after the Trojan War. The idea that a writer should be contemporaneous is itself modern, but I should say it belongs more to journalism than to literature. No real writer ever tried to be contemporary."

In an essay called "The Writer's Apprenticeship," Borges quotes Chesterton's famous remark about writing: "Only one thing is needful—everything." Addressing himself to the question of what a great university, or education, should give the young writer, he includes "conversation, discussion, the art of agreeing, and, what is perhaps most important, the art of disagreeing." He echoes Camus's dictum that creating is living doubly and urges the beginning writer to remember that "Literature is not a mere juggling of words; what matters is what is left unsaid, or what may be read between the lines. Were it not for this deep inner feeling, literature would be no more than a game, and we all know that it can be much more than that."

The Book of Sand

Translated by Norman Thomas di Giovanni

Thy rope of sands...

—George Herbert

The line is made up of an infinite number of points; the plane of an infinite number of lines; the volume of an infinite number of planes; the hypervolume of an infinite number of volumes. ... No, unquestionably this is not—*more geometrico*—the best way of beginning my story. To claim that it is true is nowadays the convention of every made-up story. Mine, however, is true.

I live alone in a fourth-floor apartment on Belgrano Street, in Buenos Aires. Late one evening, a few months back, I heard a knock at my door. I opened it and a stranger stood there. He was a tall man, with nondescript features—or perhaps it was my myopia that made them seem that way. Dressed in gray and carrying a gray suitcase in his hand, he had an unassuming look about him. I saw at once that he was a foreigner. At first, he struck me as old; only later did I realize that I had been misled by his thin blond hair, which was, in a Scandinavian sort of way, almost white. During the course of our conversation, which was not to last an hour, I found out that he came from the Orkneys.

I invited him in, pointing to a chair. He paused awhile before speaking. A kind of gloom emanated from him—as it does now from me.

"I sell Bibles," he said.

Somewhat pedantically, I replied, "In this house are several English Bibles, including the first—John Wiclif's. I also have Cipriano de Valera's, Luther's—which, from a literary viewpoint, is the worst—and a Latin copy of the Vulgate. As you see, it's not exactly Bibles I stand in need of."

After a few moments of silence, he said, "I don't only sell Bibles. I can show you a holy book I came across on the outskirts of Bikaner. It may interest you."

He opened the suitcase and laid the book on a table. It was an octavo volume, bound in cloth. There was no doubt that it had passed through many hands. Examining it, I was surprised by its unusual weight. On the spine were the words "Holy Writ" and, below them, "Bombay."

"Nineteenth century, probably," I remarked.

"I don't know," he said. "I've never found out."

I opened the book at random. The script was strange to me. The pages, which were worn and typographically poor, were laid out in double columns, as in a Bible. The text was closely printed, and it was ordered in versicles. In the upper corners of the pages were Arabic numbers. I noticed that one left-hand page bore the number (let us say) 40,514 and the facing right-hand page 999. I turned the leaf; it was numbered with eight digits. It also bore a small illustration, like the kind used in dictionaries—an anchor drawn with pen and ink, as if by a schoolboy's clumsy hand.

It was at this point that the stranger said, "Look at the illustration closely. You'll never see it again."

I noted my place and closed the book. At once, I reopened it. Page by page, in vain, I looked for the illustration of the anchor. "It seems to be a version of Scriptures in some Indian language, is it not?" I said to hide my dismay.

"No," he replied. Then, as if confiding a secret, he lowered his voice. "I acquired the book in a town out on the plain in exchange for a handful of rupees and a Bible. Its owner did not know how to read. I suspect that he saw the Book of Books as a talisman. He was of the lowest caste; nobody but other untouchables could tread his shadow without contamination. He told me his book was called the Book of Sand, because neither the book nor the sand has any beginning or end."

The stranger asked me to find the first page.

I laid my left hand on the cover and, trying to put my thumb on the flyleaf, I opened the book. It was useless. Every time I tried, a number of pages came between the cover and my thumb. It was as if they kept growing from the book.

"Now find the last page."

Again I failed. In a voice that was not mine, I barely managed to stammer, "This can't be."

Still speaking in a low voice, the stranger said, "It can't be, but it is. The number of pages in this book is no more or less than infinite. None is the first page, none the last. I don't know why they're numbered in this arbitrary way. Perhaps to suggest that the terms of an infinite series admit any number."

Then, as if he were thinking aloud, he said, "If space is infinite, we may be at any point in space. If time is infinite, we may be at any point in time."

His speculations irritated me. "You are religious, no doubt?" I asked him.

"Yes, I'm a Presbyterian. My conscience is clear. I am reasonably sure of not having cheated the native when I gave him the Word of God in exchange for his devilish book."

I assured him that he had nothing to reproach himself for, and I asked if he were just passing through this part of the world. He replied that he planned to return to his country in a few days. It was then that I learned that he was a Scot from the Orkney Islands. I told him I had a great personal affection for Scotland, through my love of Stevenson and Hume.

"You mean Stevenson and Robbie Burns," he corrected.

While we spoke, I kept exploring the infinite book. With feigned indifference, I asked, "Do you intend to offer this curiosity to the British Museum?"

"No. I'm offering it to you," he said, and he stipulated a rather high sum for the book.

I answered, in all truthfulness, that such a sum was out of my reach, and I began thinking. After a minute or two, I came up with a scheme.

"I propose a swap," I said. "You got this book for a handful of rupees and a copy of the Bible. I'll offer you the amount of my pension check, which I've just collected, and my black-letter Wiclif Bible. I inherited it from my ancestors."

"A black-letter Wiclif!" he murmured.

I went to my bedroom and brought him the money and the book. He turned the leaves and studied the title page with all the fervor of a true bibliophile.

"It's a deal," he said.

It amazed me that he did not haggle. Only later was I to realize that he had entered my house with his mind made up to sell the book. Without counting the money, he put it away.

We talked about India, about Orkney, and about the Norwegian jarls who once ruled it. It was night when the man left. I have not seen him again, nor do I know his name.

I thought of keeping the Book of Sand in the space left on the shelf by the Wiclif, but in the end I decided to hide it behind the volumes of a broken set of The Thousand and One Nights. I went to bed and did not sleep. At three or four in the morning, I turned on the light. I got down the impossible book and leafed through its pages. On one of them I saw engraved a mask. The upper corner of the page carried a number, which I no longer recall, elevated to the ninth power.

I showed no one my treasure. To the luck of owning it was added the fear of having it stolen, and then the misgiving that it might not truly be infinite. These twin preoccupations intensified my old misanthropy. I had only a few friends left; I now stopped seeing even them. A prisoner of the book, I almost never went out anymore. After studying its frayed spine and covers with a magnifying glass, I rejected the possibility of contrivance of any sort. The small illustrations, I verified, came two thousand pages apart. I set about listing them alphabetically in a notebook, which I was not long in filling up. Never once was an illustration repeated. At night, in the meager intervals my insomnia granted, I dreamed of the book.

Summer came and went, and I realized that the book was monstrous. What good did it do me to think that I, who looked upon the volume with my eyes, who held it in my hands, was any less monstrous? I felt that the book was a nightmarish object, an obscene thing that affronted and tainted reality itself.

I thought of fire, but I feared that the burning of an infinite book might likewise prove infinite and suffocate the planet with smoke. Somewhere I recalled reading that the best place to hide a leaf is in a forest. Before retirement, I worked on Mexico Street, at the Argentine National Library, which contains nine hundred thousand volumes. I knew that to the right of the entrance a curved staircase leads down into the basement, where books and maps and periodicals are kept. One day I went there and, slipping past a member of the staff and trying not to notice at what height or distance from the door, I lost the Book of Sand on one of the basement's musty shelves.

Tadeusz Borowski

Born in 1922 in Zytomierz, Poland, to a dissident father who was subsequently interned in a labour camp in the Arctic and a mother who was sent to Siberia, Tadeusz Borowski not surprisingly later ran afoul of the authorities during the German occupation. His literary career and studies at underground universities were interrupted when he was arrested for his activist associations. He was incarcerated in Auschwitz, then in Dachau, where he witnessed and participated in the Nazi torture and killing of countless thousands. After the war, he published two volumes of poems, *Imiona nurtu* (1945) and *Poszukiwania* (1945), and three collections of stories, including *This Way for the Gas, Ladies and Gentlemen* (1976), which Jan Kott describes as "one of the cruellest testimonies to what men did to men, and a pitiless verdict that anything can be done to a human being." He worked, for a time, as a propagandist for a new socialist order in Poland, but his searing memories proved too great a burden. He committed suicide by asphyxiation in 1951.

Instead of cherishing an undying hope, which was the credo of that other great Polish writer Joseph Conrad, Borowski's narrator in "Auschwitz, Our Home," attacks the "hope that makes people go without a murmur to the gas chambers, keeps them from risking revolt ... compels man to hold on to one more day of life." As an intimate participant in these horrific events, Borowski refused to sentimentalize the victims or demonize the criminals. Critic Andrzej Wirth suggests that Borowski's narrative focus on the Kapos, the go-betweens, provides a morally ambivalent point of view that forces the reader to internalize the evil and allows both reader and author to direct their rage against the system that is responsible for creating these conditions. And, of course, the buck does not stop with the Nazis, but with the whole of Western civilization, which laid the groundwork for so colossal a slaughter.

Borowski's work raises important questions about both the nature and function of art. After the war, many German writers chose silence, rather than use a language that was in complicity with the Nazi regime; others felt that language itself was inadequate to convey the true horror of events. Some few Europeans, among them Borowski, had no option but to try to give imaginative expression to what they had experienced, creating what has been called a "literature of atrocity." While the landscape of his fiction seems devoid of values—one of his characters says that "in this war morality, justice, and human dignity had all slid off man like a rotten rag. ... There is no crime a man will not commit to save himself"—Borowski's task is a painfully moral one, to draw us inescapably into a world where there seem to be no heroes and no simple moral choices.

More searing even than Hubert Selby's *Last Exit to Brooklyn*, Borowski's work is, nonetheless, an affirmation of the need to bear witness and calls to mind Albert Camus's remarks in *The Rebel* that even if literature "describes nostalgia, despair, frustration, it still creates a form of salvation. To talk of despair is to conquer it. Despairing literature is a contradiction in terms."

This Way for the Gas, Ladies and Gentlemen

Translated by Barbara Vedder

All of us walk around naked. The delousing is finally over, and our striped suits are back from the tanks of Cyclone B solution, an efficient killer of lice in clothing and of men in gas chambers. Only the inmates in the blocks cut off from ours by the 'Spanish goats'[1] still have nothing to wear. But all the same, all of us walk around naked: the heat is unbearable. The camp has been sealed off tight. Not a single prisoner, not one solitary louse, can sneak through the gate. The labour Kommandos have stopped working. All day, thousands of naked men shuffle up and down the roads, cluster around the squares, or lie against the walls and on top of the roofs. We have been sleeping on plain boards, since our mattresses and blankets are still being disinfected. From the rear blockhouses we have a view of the F.K.L.—*Frauen Konzentration Lager*; there too the delousing is in full swing. Twenty-eight thousand women have been stripped naked and driven out of the barracks. Now they swarm around the large yard between the blockhouses.

The heat rises, the hours are endless. We are without even our usual diversion: the wide roads leading to the crematoria are empty. For several days now, no new transports have come in. Part of 'Canada'[2] has been liquidated and detailed to a labour Kommando—one of the very toughest—at Harmenz. For there exists in the camp a special brand of justice based on envy: when the rich and mighty fall, their friends see to it that they fall to the very bottom. And Canada, our Canada, which smells not of maple forests but of French perfume, has amassed great fortunes in diamonds and currency from all over Europe.

Several of us sit on the top bunk, our legs dangling over the edge. We slice the neat loaves of crisp, crunchy bread. It is a bit coarse to the taste, the kind that stays fresh for days. Sent all the way from Warsaw—only a week ago my mother held this white loaf in her hands ... dear Lord, dear Lord ...

We unwrap the bacon, the onion, we open a can of evaporated milk. Henri, the fat Frenchman, dreams aloud of the French wine brought by the transports from Strasbourg, Paris, Marseille ... Sweat streams down his body.

'Listen, *mon ami*, next time we go up on the loading ramp, I'll bring you real champagne. You haven't tried it before, eh?'

'No. But you'll never be able to smuggle it through the gate, so stop teasing. Why not try and "organize" some shoes for me instead—you know, the perforated kind, with a double sole, and what about that shirt you promised me long ago?'

'*Patience, patience*. When the new transports come, I'll bring all you want. We'll be going on the ramp again!'

'And what if there aren't any more "cremo" transports?' I say spitefully. 'Can't you see how much easier life is becoming around here: no limit on packages, no more beatings? You even write letters home ... One hears all kind of talk, and, dammit, they'll run out of people!'

'Stop talking nonsense.' Henri's serious fat face moves rhythmically, his mouth is full of sardines. We have been friends for a long time, but I do not even know his last name. 'Stop talking nonsense,' he repeats, swallowing with effort. 'They can't run out of people, or we'll starve to death in this blasted camp. All of us live on what they bring.'

'All? We have our packages ...'

'Sure, you and your friend, and ten other friends of yours. Some of you Poles get packages. But what about us, and the Jews, and the Russkis? And what if we had no food, no "organization" from the transports, do you think you'd be eating those packages of yours in peace? We wouldn't let you!'

'You would, you'd starve to death like the Greeks. Around here, whoever has grub, has power.'

'Anyway, you have enough, we have enough, so why argue?'

Right, why argue? They have enough, I have enough, we eat together and we sleep on the same bunks. Henri slices the bread, he makes a tomato salad. It tastes good with the commissary mustard.

Below us, naked, sweat-drenched men crowd the narrow barracks aisles or lie packed in eights and tens in the lower bunks. Their nude, withered bodies stink of sweat and excrement; their cheeks are hollow. Directly beneath me, in the bottom bunk, lies a rabbi. He has covered his head with a piece of rag torn off a blanket and reads from a Hebrew prayer book (there is no shortage of this type of literature at the camp), wailing loudly, monotonously.

'Can't somebody shut him up? He's been raving as if he'd caught God himself by the feet.'

'I don't feel like moving. Let him rave. They'll take him to the oven that much sooner.'

'Religion is the opium of the people,' Henri, who is a Communist and a *rentier*, says sententiously. 'If they didn't believe in God and eternal life, they'd have smashed the crematoria long ago.'

'Why haven't you done it then?'

The question is rhetorical; the Frenchman ignores it.

'Idiot,' he says simply, and stuffs a tomato in his mouth.

Just as we finish our snack, there is a sudden commotion at the door. The Muslims[3] scurry in fright to the safety of their bunks, a messenger runs into the Block Elder's shack. The Elder, his face solemn, steps out at once.

'Canada! *Antreten*! But fast! There's a transport coming!'

'Great God!' yells Henri, jumping off the bunk. He swallows the rest of his tomato, snatches his coat, screams '*Raus*' at the men below, and in a flash is at the door. We can hear a scramble in the other bunks. Canada is leaving for the ramp.

'Henri, the shoes!' I call after him.

'*Keine Angst!*' he shouts back, already outside.

I proceed to put away the food. I tie a piece of rope around the suitcase where the onions and the tomatoes from my father's garden in Warsaw mingle with Portuguese sardines, bacon from Lublin (that's from my brother), and authentic sweetmeats from Salonica. I tie it all up, pull on my trousers, and slide off the bunk.

'*Platz!*' I yell, pushing my way through the Greeks. They step aside. At the door I bump into Henri.

'*Was ist los?*'

'Want to come with us on the ramp?'

'Sure, why not?'

'Come along then, grab your coat! We're short of a few men. I've already told the Kapo,' and he shoves me out of the barracks door.

We line up. Someone has marked down our numbers, someone up ahead yells, 'March, march,' and now we are running towards the gate, accompanied by the shouts of a multilingual throng that is already being pushed back to the barracks. Not everybody is lucky enough to be going on the ramp ... We have almost reached the gate. *Links, zwei, drei, vier! Mützen ab!* Erect, arms stretched stiffly along our hips, we march past the gate briskly, smartly, almost gracefully. A sleepy S.S. man with a large pad in his hand checks us off, waving us ahead in groups of five.

'*Hundert!*' he calls after we have all passed.

'*Stimmt!*' comes a hoarse answer from out front.

We march fast, almost at a run. There are guards all around, young men with automatics. We pass camp II B, then some deserted barracks and a clump of unfamiliar green—apple and pear trees. We cross the circle of watchtowers and, running, burst on to the highway. We have arrived. Just a few more yards. There, surrounded by trees, is the ramp.

A cheerful little station, very much like any other provincial railway stop: a small square framed by tall chestnuts and paved with yellow gravel. Not far off, beside the road, squats a tiny wooden shed, uglier and more flimsy than the ugliest and flimsiest railway shack; farther along lie stacks of old rails, heaps of wooden beams, barracks parts, bricks, paving stones. This is where they load freight for Birkenau: supplies for the construction of the camp, and people for the gas chambers. Trucks drive around, load up lumber, cement, people—a regular daily routine.

And now the guards are being posted along the rails, across the beams, in the green shade of the Silesian chestnuts, to form a tight circle around the ramp. They wipe the sweat from their faces and sip out of their canteens. It is unbearably hot; the sun stands motionless at its zenith.

'Fall out!'

We sit down in the narrow streaks of shade along the stacked rails. The hungry Greeks (several of them managed to come along, God only knows how) rummage underneath the rails. One of them finds some pieces of mildewed bread, another a few half-rotten sardines. They eat.

'*Schweinedreck*,' spits a young, tall guard with corn-coloured hair and dreamy blue eyes. 'For God's sake, any minute you'll have so much food to stuff down your guts, you'll bust!' He adjusts his gun, wipes his face with a handkerchief.

'Hey you, fatso!' His boot lightly touches Henri's shoulder. '*Pass mal auf*, want a drink?'

'Sure, but I haven't got any marks,' replies the Frenchman with a professional air.

'*Schade*, too bad.'

'Come, come, Herr Posten, isn't my word good enough any more? Haven't we done business before? How much?'

'One hundred. *Gemacht?*'

'*Gemacht.*'

We drink the water, lukewarm and tasteless. It will be paid for by the people who have not yet arrived.

'Now you be careful,' says Henri, turning to me. He tosses away the empty bottle. It strikes the rails and bursts into tiny fragments. 'Don't take any money, they might be checking. Anyway, who the hell needs money? You've got enough to eat. Don't take suits, either, or they'll think you're planning to escape. Just get a shirt, silk only, with a collar. And a vest. And if you find something to drink, don't bother calling me. I know how to shift for myself, but you watch your step or they'll let you have it.'

'Do they beat you up here?'

'Naturally. You've got to have eyes in your ass. *Arschaugen.*'

Around us sit the Greeks, their jaws working greedily, like huge human insects. They munch on stale lumps of bread. They are restless, wondering what will happen next. The sight of the large beams and the stacks of rails has them worried. They dislike carrying heavy loads.

'*Was wir arbeiten?*' they ask.

'*Niks. Transport kommen, alles Krematorium, compris?*'

'*Alles verstehen*,' they answer in crematorium Esperanto. All is well—they will not have to move the heavy rails or carry the beams.

In the meantime, the ramp has become increasingly alive with activity, increasingly noisy. The crews are being divided into those who will open and unload the arriving cattle cars and those who will be posted by the wooden steps. They receive instructions on how to proceed most efficiently. Motor cycles drive up, delivering S.S. officers, bemedalled, glittering with brass, beefy men with highly polished boots and shiny, brutal faces. Some have brought their briefcases, others hold thin, flexible whips. This gives them an air of military readiness and agility. They walk in and out of the commissary—for the miserable little shack by the road serves as their commissary, where in the summertime they drink mineral water, *Studentenquelle*, and where in winter they can warm up with a glass of hot wine. They greet each other in the state-approved way, raising an arm Roman fashion, then shake hands cordially, exchange warm smiles, discuss mail from home, their children, their families. Some stroll majestically on the ramp. The silver squares on their collars glitter, the gravel crunches under their boots, their bamboo whips snap impatiently.

We lie against the rails in the narrow streaks of shade, breathe unevenly, occasionally exchange a few words in our various tongues, and gaze listlessly at the majestic men in green uniforms, at the green trees, and at the church steeple of a distant village.

'The transport is coming,' somebody says. We spring to our feet, all eyes turn in one direction. Around the bend, one after another, the cattle cars begin rolling in. The train backs into the station, a conductor leans out, waves his hand, blows a whistle. The locomotive whistles back with a shrieking noise, puffs, the train rolls slowly alongside the ramp. In the tiny barred windows appear pale, wilted, exhausted human faces, terror-stricken women with tangled hair, unshaven men. They gaze at the station in silence. And then, suddenly, there is a stir inside the cars and a pounding against the wooden boards.

'Water! Air!'—weary, desperate cries.

Heads push through the windows, mouths gasp frantically for air. They draw a few breaths, then disappear; others come in their place, then also disappear. The cries and moans grow louder.

A man in a green uniform covered with more glitter than any of the others jerks his head impatiently, his lips twist in annoyance. He inhales deeply, then with a rapid gesture throws his cigarette away and signals to the guard. The guard removes the automatic from his shoulder, aims, sends a series of shots along the train. All is quiet now. Meanwhile, the trucks have arrived, steps are being drawn up, and the Canada men stand ready at their posts by the train doors. The S.S. officer with the briefcase raises his hand.

'Whoever takes gold, or anything at all besides food, will be shot for stealing Reich property. Understand? *Verstanden?*'

'*Jawohl!*' we answer eagerly.

'*Also los!* Begin!'

The bolts crack, the doors fall open. A wave of fresh air rushes inside the train. People ... inhumanly crammed, buried under incredible heaps of luggage, suitcases, trunks, packages, crates, bundles of every description (everything that had been their past and was to start their future). Monstrously squeezed together, they have fainted from heat, suffocated, crushed one another. Now they push towards the opened doors, breathing like fish cast out on the sand.

'Attention! Out, and take your luggage with you! Take out everything. Pile all your stuff near the exits. Yes, your coats too. It is summer. March to the left. Understand?'

'Sir, what's going to happen to us?' They jump from the train on to the gravel, anxious, worn-out.

'Where are you people from?'

'Sosnowiec-Będzin. Sir, what's going to happen to us?' They repeat the question stubbornly, gazing into our tired eyes.

'I don't know, I don't understand Polish.'

It is the camp law: people going to their death must be deceived to the very end. This is the only permissible form of charity. The heat is tremendous. The sun hangs directly over our heads, the white, hot sky quivers, the air vibrates, an occasional breeze feels like a sizzling blast from a furnace. Our lips are parched, the mouth fills with the salty taste of blood, the body is weak and heavy from lying in the sun. Water!

A huge, multicoloured wave of people loaded down with luggage pours from the train like a blind, mad river trying to find a new bed. But before they have a chance to recover, before they can draw a breath of fresh air and look at the sky, bundles are snatched from their hands, coats ripped off their backs, their purses and umbrellas taken away.

'But please, sir, it's for the sun, I cannot ...'

'*Verboten!*' one of us barks through clenched teeth. There is an S.S. man standing behind your back, calm, efficient, watchful.

'*Meine Herrschaften*, this way, ladies and gentlemen, try not to throw your things around, please. Show some goodwill,' he says courteously, his restless hands playing with the slender whip.

'Of course, of course,' they answer as they pass, and now they walk alongside the train somewhat more cheerfully. A woman reaches down quickly to pick up her handbag. The whip flies, the woman screams, stumbles, and falls under the feet of the surging crowd. Behind her, a child cries in a thin little voice 'Mamele!'—a very small girl with tangled black curls.

The heaps grow. Suitcases, bundles, blankets, coats, handbags that open as they fall, spilling coins, gold, watches; mountains of bread pile up at the exits, heaps of marmalade, jams, masses of meat, sausages; sugar spills on the gravel. Trucks, loaded with people, start up with a deafening roar and drive off amidst the wailing and screaming of the women separated from their children, and the stupefied silence of the men left behind. They are the ones who had been ordered to step to the right—the healthy and the young who will go to the camp. In the end, they too will not escape death, but first they must work.

Trucks leave and return, without interruption, as on a monstrous conveyor belt. A Red Cross van drives back and forth, back and forth, incessantly: it transports the gas that will kill these people. The enormous cross on the hood, red as blood, seems to dissolve in the sun.

The Canada men at the trucks cannot stop for a single moment, even to catch their breath. They shove the people up the steps, pack them in tightly, sixty per truck, more or less. Near by stands a young, clean-shaven 'gentleman', an S.S. officer with a notebook in his hand. For each departing truck he enters a mark; sixteen gone means one thousand people, more or less. The gentleman is calm, precise. No truck can leave without a signal from him, or a mark in his notebook: *Ordnung muss sein*. The marks swell into thousands, the thousands into whole transports, which afterwards we shall simply call 'from Salonica', 'from Strasbourg', 'from Rotterdam'. This one will be called 'Sosnowiec-Będzin'. The new prisoners from Sosnowiec-Będzin will receive serial numbers 131-2-thousand, of course, though afterwards we shall simply say 131-2, for short.

The transports swell into weeks, months, years. When the war is over, they will count up the marks in their notebooks—all four and a half million of them. The bloodiest battle of the war, the greatest victory of the strong, united Germany. *Ein Reich, ein Volk, ein Führer*—and four crematoria.

The train has been emptied. A thin, pock-marked S.S. man peers inside, shakes his head in disgust and motions to our group, pointing his finger at the door.

'*Rein*. Clean it up!'

We climb inside. In the corners amid human excrement and abandoned wristwatches lie squashed, trampled infants, naked little monsters with enormous heads and bloated bellies. We carry them out like chickens, holding several in each hand.

'Don't take them to the trucks, pass them on to the women,' says the S.S. man, lighting a cigarette. His cigarette lighter is not working properly; he examines it carefully.

'Take them, for God's sake!' I explode as the women run from me in horror, covering their eyes.

The name of God sounds strangely pointless, since the women and the infants will go on the trucks, every one of them, without exception. We all know what this means, and we look at each other with hate and horror.

'What, you don't want to take them?' asks the pock-marked S.S. man with a note of surprise and reproach in his voice, and reaches for his revolver.

'You mustn't shoot, I'll carry them.' A tall, grey-haired woman takes the little corpses out of my hands and for an instant gazes straight into my eyes.

'My poor boy,' she whispers and smiles at me. Then she walks away, staggering along the path. I lean against the side of the train. I am terribly tired. Someone pulls at my sleeve.

'*En avant*, to the rails, come on!'

I look up, but the face swims before my eyes, dissolves, huge and transparent, melts into the motionless trees and the sea of people ... I blink rapidly: Henri.

'Listen, Henri, are we good people?'

'That's stupid. Why do you ask?'

'You see, my friend, you see, I don't know why, but I am furious, simply furious with these people—furious because I must be here because of them. I feel no pity. I am not sorry they're going to the gas chamber. Damn them all! I could throw myself at them, beat them with my fists. It must be pathological, I just can't understand ...'

'Ah, on the contrary, it is natural, predictable, calculated. The ramp exhausts you, you rebel—and the easiest way to relieve your hate is to turn against someone weaker. Why, I'd even call it healthy. It's simple logic, *compris*?' He props himself up comfortably against the heap of rails. 'Look at the Greeks, they know how to make the best of it! They stuff their bellies with anything they find. One of them has just devoured a full jar of marmalade.'

'Pigs! Tomorrow half of them will die of the shits.'

'Pigs? You've been hungry.'

'Pigs!' I repeat furiously. I close my eyes. The air is fitted with ghastly cries, the earth trembles beneath me, I can feel sticky moisture on my eyelids. My throat is completely dry.

The morbid procession streams on and on—trucks growl like mad dogs. I shut my eyes tight, but I can still see corpses dragged from the train, trampled infants, cripples piled on top of the dead, wave after wave ... freight cars roll in, the heaps of clothing, suitcases and bundles grow, people climb out, look at the sun, take a few breaths, beg for water, get into the trucks, drive away. And again freight cars roll in, again people ... The scenes become confused in my mind—I am not sure if all of this is actually happening, or if I am dreaming. There is a humming inside my head; I feel that I must vomit.

Henri tugs at my arm.

'Don't sleep, we're off to load up the loot.'

All the people are gone. In the distance, the last few trucks roll along the road in clouds of dust, the train has left, several S.S. officers promenade up and down the ramp. The silver glitters on their collars. Their boots shine, their red, beefy faces shine. Among them there is a woman—only now I realize she has been here all along—withered, flat-chested, bony, her thin, colourless hair pulled back and tied in a 'Nordic' knot; her hands are in the pockets of her wide skirt. With a rat-like, resolute smile glued on her thin lips she sniffs around the corners of the ramp. She detests feminine beauty with the hatred of a woman who is herself repulsive, and knows it. Yes, I have seen her many times before and I know her well: she is the commandant of the F.K.L. She has come to look over the new crop of women, for some of them, instead of going on the trucks, will go on foot—to the concentration camp. There our boys, the barbers from the Zauna, will shave their heads and will have a good laugh at their 'outside world' modesty.

We proceed to load the loot. We lift huge trunks, heave them on to the trucks. There they are arranged in stacks, packed tightly. Occasionally somebody slashes one open with a knife, for pleasure or in search of vodka and perfume. One of the crates falls open; suits, shirts, books drop out on the ground ... I pick up a small, heavy package. I unwrap it—gold, about two handfuls, bracelets, rings, brooches, diamonds ...

'*Gib hier*,' an S.S. man says calmly, holding up his briefcase already full of gold and colourful foreign currency. He locks the case, hands it to an Officer, takes another, an empty one, and stands by the next truck, waiting. The gold will go to the Reich.

It is hot, terribly hot. Our throats are dry, each word hurts. Anything for a sip of water! Faster, faster, so that it is over, so that we may rest. At last we are done, all the trucks have gone. Now we swiftly clean up the remaining dirt: there must be 'no trace left of the *Schweinerei*'. But just as the last truck disappears behind the trees and we walk, finally, to rest in the shade, a shrill whistle sounds around the bend. Slowly, terribly slowly, a train rolls in, the engine whistles back with a deafening shriek. Again weary, pale faces at the windows, flat as though cut out of paper, with huge, feverishly burning eyes. Already trucks are pulling up, already the composed gentleman with the notebook is at his post, and the S.S. men emerge from the commissary carrying briefcases for the gold and money. We unseal the train doors.

It is impossible to control oneself any longer. Brutally we tear suitcases from their hands, impatiently pull off their coats. Go on, go on, vanish! They go, they vanish. Men, women, children. Some of them know.

Here is a woman—she walks quickly, but tries to appear calm. A small child with a pink cherub's face runs after her and, unable to keep up, stretches out his little arms and cries: 'Mama! Mama!'

'Pick up your child, woman!'

'It's not mine, sir, not mine!' she shouts hysterically and runs on, covering her face with her hands. She wants to hide, she wants to reach those who will not ride the trucks, those who will go on foot, those who will stay alive. She is young, healthy, good-looking, she wants to live.

But the child runs after her, wailing loudly: 'Mama, mama, don't leave me!'

'It's not mine, not mine, no!'

Andrei, a sailor from Sevastopol, grabs hold of her. His eyes are glassy from vodka and the heat. With one powerful blow he knocks her off her feet, then, as she falls, takes her by the hair and pulls her up again. His face twitches with rage.

'Ah, you bloody Jewess! So you're running from your own child! I'll show you, you whore!' His huge hand chokes her, he lifts her in the air and heaves her on to the truck like a heavy sack of grain.

'Here! And take this with you, bitch!' and he throws the child at her feet.

'*Gut gemacht*, good work. That's the way to deal with degenerate mothers,' says the S.S. man standing at the foot of the truck. '*Gut, gut, Russki.*'

'Shut your mouth,' growls Andrei through clenched teeth, and walks away. From under a pile of rags he pulls out a canteen, unscrews the cork, takes a few deep swallows, passes it to me. The strong vodka burns the throat. My head swims, my legs are shaky, again I feel like throwing up.

And suddenly, above the teeming crowd pushing forward like a river driven by an unseen power, a girl appears. She descends lightly from the train, hops on to the gravel, looks around inquiringly, as if somewhat surprised. Her soft, blonde hair has fallen on her shoulders in a torrent, she throws it back impatiently. With a natural gesture she runs her hands down her blouse, casually straightens her skirt. She stands like this for an instant, gazing at the crowd, then turns and with a gliding look examines our faces, as though searching for someone. Unknowingly, I continue to stare at her, until our eyes meet.

'Listen, tell me, where are they taking us?'

I look at her without saying a word. Here, standing before me, is a girl, a girl with enchanting blonde hair, with beautiful breasts, wearing a little cotton blouse, a girl with a wise, mature look in her eyes. Here she stands, gazing straight into my face, waiting. And over there is the gas chamber: communal death, disgusting and ugly. And over in the other direction is the concentration camp: the shaved head, the heavy Soviet trousers in sweltering heat, the sickening, stale odour of dirty, damp female bodies, the animal hunger, the inhuman labour, and later the same gas chamber, only an even more hideous, more terrible death ...

Why did she bring it? I think to myself, noticing a lovely gold watch on her delicate wrist. They'll take it away from her anyway.

'Listen, tell me,' she repeats.

I remain silent. Her lips tighten.

'I know,' she says with a shade of proud contempt in her voice, tossing her head. She walks off resolutely in the direction of the trucks. Someone tries to stop her; she boldly pushes him aside and runs up the steps. In the distance I can only catch a glimpse of her blonde hair flying in the breeze.

I go back inside the train; I carry out dead infants; I unload luggage. I touch corpses, but I cannot overcome the mounting, uncontrollable terror. I try to escape from the corpses, but they are everywhere: lined up on the gravel, on the cement edge of the ramp, inside the cattle cars. Babies, hideous naked women, men twisted by convulsions. I run off as far as I can go, but immediately a whip slashes across my back. Out of the corner of my eye I see an S.S. man, swearing profusely. I stagger forward and run, lose myself in the Canada group. Now, at last, I can once more rest against the stack of rails. The sun has leaned low over the horizon and illuminates the ramp with a reddish glow; the shadows of the trees have become elongated, ghostlike. In the silence that settles over nature at this time of day, the human cries seem to rise all the way to the sky.

Only from this distance does one have a full view of the inferno on the teeming ramp. I see a pair of human beings who have fallen to the ground locked in a last desperate embrace. The man has dug his fingers into the woman's flesh and has caught her clothing with his teeth. She screams hysterically, swears, cries, until at last a large boot comes down over her throat and she is silent. They are pulled apart and dragged like cattle to the truck. I see four Canada men lugging a corpse: a huge, swollen female corpse. Cursing, dripping wet from the strain, they kick out of their way some stray children who have been running all over the ramp, howling like dogs. The men pick them up by the collars, heads, arms, and toss them inside the trucks, on top of the heaps. The four men have trouble lifting the fat corpse on to the car, they call others for help, and all together they hoist up the mound of meat. Big, swollen, puffed-up corpses are being collected from all over the ramp; on top of them are piled the invalids, the smothered, the sick, the unconscious. The heap seethes, howls, groans. The driver starts the motor, the truck begins rolling.

'Halt! Halt!' an S.S. man yells after them. 'Stop, damn you!'

They are dragging to the truck an old man wearing tails and a band around his arm. His head knocks against the gravel and pavement; he moans and wails in an uninterrupted monotone: '*Ich will mit dem Herrn Kommandanten sprechen*—I wish to speak with the commandant ...' With senile stubbornness he keeps repeating these words all the way. Thrown on the truck, trampled by others, choked, he still wails: '*Ich will mit dem ...*'

'Look here, old man!' a young S.S. man calls, laughing jovially. 'In half an hour you'll be talking with the top commandant! Only don't forget to greet him with a *Heil Hitler!*'

Several other men are carrying a small girl with only one leg. They hold her by the arms and the one leg. Tears are running down her face and she whispers faintly: 'Sir, it hurts, it hurts ...' They throw her on the truck on top of the corpses. She will burn alive along with them.

The evening has come, cool and clear. The stars are out. We lie against the rails. It is incredibly quiet. Anaemic bulbs hang from the top of the high lampposts; beyond the circle of light stretches an impenetrable darkness. Just one step, and a man could vanish for ever. But the guards are watching, their automatics ready.

'Did you get the shoes?' asks Henri.

'No.'

'Why?'

'My God, man, I am finished, absolutely finished!'

'So soon? After only two transports? Just look at me, I ... since Christmas, at least a million people have passed through my hands. The worst of all are the transports from around Paris—one is always bumping into friends.'

'And what do you say to them?'

'That first they will have a bath, and later we'll meet at the camp. What would you say?'

I do not answer. We drink coffee with vodka; somebody opens a tin of cocoa and mixes it with sugar. We scoop it up by the handful, the cocoa sticks to the lips. Again coffee, again vodka.

'Henri, what are we waiting for?'

'There'll be another transport.'

'I'm not going to unload it! I can't take any more.'

'So, it's got you down? Canada is nice, eh?' Henri grins indulgently and disappears into the darkness. In a moment he is back again.

'All right. Just sit here quietly and don't let an S.S. man see you. I'll try to find you your shoes.'

'Just leave me alone. Never mind the shoes.' I want to sleep. It is very late.

Another whistle, another transport. Freight cars emerge out of the darkness, pass under the lamp-posts, and again vanish in the night. The ramp is small, but the circle of lights is smaller. The unloading will have to be done gradually. Somewhere the trucks are growling. They back up against the steps, black, ghost-like, their searchlights flash across the trees. *Wasser! Luft!* The same all over again, like a late showing of the same film: a volley of shots, the train falls silent. Only this time a little girl pushes herself halfway through the small window and, losing her balance, falls out on to the gravel. Stunned, she lies still for a moment, then stands up and begins walking around in a circle, faster and faster, waving her rigid arms in the air, breathing loudly and spasmodically, whining in a faint voice. Her mind has given way in the inferno inside the train. The whining is hard on the nerves: an S.S. man approaches calmly, his heavy boot strikes between her shoulders. She falls. Holding her down with his foot, he draws his revolver, fires once, then again. She remains face down, kicking the gravel with her feet, until she stiffens. They proceed to unseal the train.

I am back on the ramp, standing by the doors. A warm, sickening smell gushes from inside. The mountain of people filling the car almost halfway up to the ceiling is motionless, horribly tangled, but still steaming.

'*Ausladen!*' comes the command. An S.S. man steps out from the darkness. Across his chest hangs a portable searchlight. He throws a stream of light inside.

'Why are you standing about like sheep? Start unloading!' His whip flies and falls across our backs. I seize a corpse by the hand; the fingers close tightly around mine. I pull back with a shriek and stagger away. My heart pounds, jumps up to my throat. I can no longer control the nausea. Hunched under the train I begin to vomit. Then, like a drunk, I weave over to the stack of rails.

I lie against the cool, kind metal and dream about returning to the camp, about my bunk, on which there is no mattress, about sleep among comrades who are not going to the gas tonight. Suddenly I see the camp as a haven of peace. It is true, others may be dying, but one is somehow still alive, one has enough food, enough strength to work ...

The lights on the ramp flicker with a spectral glow, the wave of people—feverish, agitated, stupefied people—flows on and on, endlessly. They think that now they will have to face a new life in the camp, and they prepare themselves emotionally for the hard struggle ahead. They do not know that in just a few moments they will die, that the gold, money, and diamonds which they have so prudently hidden in their clothing and on their bodies are now useless to them. Experienced professionals will probe into every recess of their flesh, will pull the gold from under the tongue and the diamonds from the uterus and the colon. They will rip out gold teeth. In tightly sealed crates they will ship them to Berlin.

The S.S. men's black figures move about, dignified, businesslike. The gentleman with the notebook puts down his final marks, rounds out the figures: fifteen thousand.

Many, very many, trucks have been driven to the crematoria today.

It is almost over. The dead are being cleared off the ramp and piled into the last truck. The Canada men, weighed down under a load of bread, marmalade and sugar, and smelling of perfume and fresh linen, line up to go. For several days the entire camp will live off this transport. For several days the entire camp will talk about 'Sosnowiec-Będzin'. 'Sosnowiec-Będzin' was a good, rich transport.

The stars are already beginning to pale as we walk back to the camp. The sky grows translucent and opens high above our heads—it is getting light.

Great columns of smoke rise from the crematoria and merge up above into a huge black river which very slowly floats across the sky over Birkenau and disappears beyond the forests in the direction of Trzebinia. The 'Sosnowiec-Będzin' transport is already burning.

We pass a heavily armed S.S. detachment on its way to change guard. The men march briskly, in step, shoulder to shoulder, one mass, one will.

'*Und morgen die ganze Welt* ...' they sing at the top of their lungs.

'*Rechts ran!* To the right march!' snaps a command from up front. We move out of their way.

---

1. Crossed wooden beams wrapped in barbed wire.
2. 'Canada' refers to the labour gang who helped to unload the incoming transports of people destined for gas chambers. The term also designated a state of well-being and plenty.
3. 'Muslim' was the name used in camp to describe prisoners who had lost all will to survive, physical and emotional zombies whose days were numbered.

Anton Chekhov

Anton Chekhov was born in 1860 in Taganrog, southwestern Russia, where his grandfather had been an indentured peasant and his father was a grocer. He studied medicine at the University of Moscow, publishing sketches in newspapers and magazines to support himself and help the family. "I have two professions and not one," he wrote. "Medicine is my lawful wife and literature is my mistress. When I get tired of one, I spend the night with the other." After practising in a provincial setting, he eventually, with the success of *Particoloured Stories* (1886) and a second volume in 1887, was able to write full time, purchasing a small estate outside Moscow, where, in addition to his abundant writing and correspondence, he gave free medical advice to peasants. The Pushkin Prize and the success he achieved in his own lifetime were the result not only of a prodigious talent, but also of amazing productivity: "I am leading the life of a privileged vegetable which is constantly poisoned by the thought that it must write, eternally write." To a young writer, he said: "But can you have written only fifteen stories?—at this rate you won't learn to write till you are fifty. Write another twenty stories and send them. ... Practice is essential for you." During the last decade of his life, Chekhov became involved with the Moscow Art Theatre, under the direction of Konstantin Stanislavsky, and wrote *The Seagull* (1896), *Uncle Vanya* (1898), *The Three Sisters* (1901), and *The Cherry Orchard* (1904). He married the actress Olga Knipper in 1901, but died of tuberculosis three years later.

Chekhov's abundant letters reveal him to be a dedicated craftsman and a painstakingly generous critic of the work of other writers. He praised Maxim Gorky highly, but criticized his floridity and lack of restraint; to others, he argued for more "art," "polish," compression, and objectivity; concern for the story's "architecture," which often meant trimming the beginning and end and beefing up the middle; and developing an eye for the total picture rather than "a mere summary, a dry inventory of impressions." He advised the young writer to "seize upon the little particulars" that will create a picture, that "it is better to say not enough than to say too much": "To make a face from marble means to remove everything that is not the face."

Although he has been described as a minimalist in fiction (William Trevor calls it "the art of the glimpse"), who needs the slightest detail to create a sense of character and only a hint of conflict to give momentum to his own stories, Chekhov did not underplay the importance of action in the works of others: "Your story is a good, charming, clever thing. But the action is, as always, slow, and therefore the story seems in some places to drag. Imagine a great pond out of which flows a slender current of water; imagine on the surface of the pond a number of things:—chips of wood, boards, empty barrels, leaves,—all of them, because of the slow flowing of the water, seeming to be stationary and heaped up at the mouth of the stream. This is what occurs in your story,—no movement, and a multitude of details that pile up into a great heap."

A constant concern expressed in his letters was the freedom of the writer to say what must be said. He took a number of humorous swipes at the academy of "lop-eared critics," insisting that "one cannot escape this abuse, because in our age of telegraphy, and hypercritical journalism, and telephones, abuse is the sister of advertising." However, he was a vigorous opponent of censorship of any kind, as is evident in a letter to M. V. Kiselev (1887): "But to think that the task of literature is to gather the pure grain from the muck heap, is to reject literature itself. Artistic literature is called so just because it depicts life as it really is. Its aim is truth,—unconditional and honest." The writer, he insists, is not a cosmetician, but a reporter, an analyst, for whom nothing, not even the dung heap, is unclean or unfit for attention.

Two years later, he wrote to A. N. Pleshcheyev: "I am not a liberal, not a conservative, not a believer in gradual progress, not a monk, not an indifferentist. I should like to be a free artist and nothing more, and I regret that God has not given me the power to be one. I hate lying and violence in all their forms, and am equally repelled by the secretaries of consistories and by Notovich and Gradovksy. Pharisaism, stupidity, and despotism reign not in merchants' houses and prisons alone. I see them in science, in literature, in the younger generation. ... That is why I have no preference either for gendarmes, or for butchers, or for scientists, or for writers, or for the younger generation. I regard trademarks and labels as a superstition. My holy of holies is the human body, health, intelligence, talent, inspiration, love, and the most absolute freedom—freedom from violence and lying, whatever forms they take. This is the program I would follow if I were a great artist."

If he demanded absolute freedom from rules in content and form, Chekhov was nonetheless increasingly concerned with economy and precision in his writing. Of "The Lady with the Pet Dog," Vladimir Nabokov has written: "All the traditional rules of story telling have been broken in his wonderful story of twenty pages or so. There is no problem, no regular climax, no point at the end. And it is one of the greatest stories ever written."

The Lady with the Pet Dog

Translated by Avrahm Yarmolinsky

I

A new person, it was said, had appeared on the esplanade: a lady with a pet dog. Dmitry Dmitrich Gurov, who had spent a fortnight at Yalta and had got used to the place, had also begun to take an interest in new arrivals. As he sat in Vernet's confectionery shop, he saw, walking on the esplanade, a fair-haired young woman of medium height, wearing a beret; a white Pomeranian was trotting behind her.

And afterwards he met her in the public garden and in the square several times a day. She walked alone, always wearing the same beret and always with the white dog; no one knew who she was and everyone called her simply "the lady with the pet dog."

"If she is here alone without husband or friends," Gurov reflected, "it wouldn't be a bad thing to make her acquaintance."

He was under forty, but he already had a daughter twelve years old, and two sons at school. They had found a wife for him when he was very young, a student in his second year, and by now she seemed half as old again as he. She was a tall, erect woman with dark eyebrows, stately and dignified and, as she said of herself, intellectual. She read a great deal, used simplified spelling in her letters, called her husband, not Dmitry, but Dimitry, while he privately considered her of limited intelligence, narrow-minded, dowdy, was afraid of her, and did not like to be at home. He had begun being unfaithful to her long ago—had been unfaithful to her often and, probably for that reason, almost always spoke ill of women, and when they were talked of in his presence used to call them "the inferior race."

It seemed to him that he had been sufficiently tutored by bitter experience to call them what he pleased, and yet he could not have lived without "the inferior race" for two days together. In the company of men he was bored and ill at ease, he was chilly and uncommunicative with them; but when he was among women he felt free, and knew what to speak to them about and how to comport himself; and even to be silent with them was no strain on him. In his appearance, in his character, in his whole make-up there was something attractive and elusive that disposed women in his favor and allured them. He knew that, and some force seemed to draw him to them, too.

Oft-repeated and really bitter experience had taught him long ago that with decent people—particularly Moscow people—who are irresolute and slow to move, every affair which at first seems a light and charming adventure inevitably grows into a whole problem of extreme complexity, and in the end a painful situation is created. But at every new meeting with an interesting woman this lesson of experience seemed to slip from his memory, and he was eager for life, and everything seemed so simple and diverting.

One evening while he was dining in the public garden the lady in the beret walked up without haste to take the next table. Her expression, her gait, her dress, and the way she did her hair told him that she belonged to the upper class, that she was married, that she was in Yalta for the first time and alone, and that she was bored there. The stories told of the immorality in Yalta are to a great extent untrue; he despised them, and knew that such stories were made up for the most part by persons who would have been glad to sin themselves if they had had the chance; but when the lady sat down at the next table three paces from him, he recalled these stories of easy conquests, of trips to the mountains, and the tempting thought of a swift, fleeting liaison, a romance with an unknown woman of whose very name he was ignorant suddenly took hold of him.

He beckoned invitingly to the Pomeranian, and when the dog approached him, shook his finger at it. The Pomeranian growled; Gurov threatened it again.

The lady glanced at him and at once dropped her eyes.

"He doesn't bite," she said and blushed.

"May I give him a bone?" he asked; and when she nodded he inquired affably, "Have you been in Yalta long?"

"About five days."

"And I am dragging out the second week here."

There was a short silence.

"Time passes quickly, and yet it is so dull here!" she said, not looking at him.

"It's only the fashion to say it's dull here. A provincial will live in Belyov or

Zhizdra and not be bored, but when he comes here it's 'Oh, the dullness! Oh, the dust!' One would think he came from Granada."

She laughed. Then both continued eating in silence, like strangers, but after dinner they walked together and there sprang up between them the light banter of people who are free and contented, to whom it does not matter where they go or what they talk about. They walked and talked of the strange light on the sea: the water was a soft, warm, lilac color, and there was a golden band of moonlight upon it. They talked of how sultry it was after a hot day. Gurov told her that he was a native of Moscow, that he had studied languages and literature at the university, but had a post in a bank; that at one time he had trained to become an opera singer but had given it up, that he owned two houses in Moscow. And he learned from her that she had grown up in Petersburg, but had lived in S—— since her marriage two years previously, that she was going to stay in Yalta for about another month, and that her husband, who needed a rest, too, might perhaps come to fetch her. She was not certain whether her husband was a member of a Government Board or served on a Zemstvo Council, and this amused her. And Gurov learned too that her name was Anna Sergeyevna.

Afterwards in his room at the hotel he thought about her—and was certain that he would meet her the next day. It was bound to happen. Getting into bed he recalled that she had been a schoolgirl only recently, doing lessons like his own daughter; he thought how much timidity and angularity there was still in her laugh and her manner of talking with a stranger. It must have been the first time in her life that she was alone in a setting in which she was followed, looked at, and spoken to for one secret purpose alone, which she could hardly fail to guess. He thought of her slim, delicate throat, her lovely gray eyes.

"There's something pathetic about her, though," he thought, and dropped off.

II

A week had passed since they had struck up an acquaintance. It was a holiday. It was close indoors, while in the street the wind whirled the dust about and blew people's hats off. One was thirsty all day, and Gurov often went into the restaurant and offered Anna Sergeyevna a soft drink or ice cream. One did not know what to do with oneself.

In the evening when the wind had abated they went out on the pier to watch the steamer come in. There were a great many people walking about the dock; they had come to welcome someone and they were carrying bunches of flowers. And two peculiarities of a festive Yalta crowd stood out: the elderly ladies were dressed like young ones and there were many generals.

Owing to the choppy sea, the steamer arrived late, after sunset, and it was a long time tacking about before it put in at the pier. Anna Sergeyevna peered at the steamer and the passengers through her lorgnette as though looking for acquaintances, and whenever she turned to Gurov her eyes were shining. She talked a great deal and asked questions jerkily, forgetting the next moment what she had asked; then she lost her lorgnette in the crush.

The festive crowd began to disperse; it was now too dark to see people's faces; there was no wind any more, but Gurov and Anna Sergeyevna still stood as though waiting to see someone else come off the steamer. Anna Sergeyevna was silent now, and sniffed her flowers without looking at Gurov.

"The weather has improved this evening," he said. "Where shall we go now? Shall we drive somewhere?"

She did not reply.

Then he looked at her intently, and suddenly embraced her and kissed her on the lips, and the moist fragrance of her flowers enveloped him; and at once he looked round him anxiously, wondering if anyone had seen them.

"Let us go to your place," he said softly. And they walked off together rapidly.

The air in her room was close and there was the smell of the perfume she had bought at the Japanese shop. Looking at her, Gurov thought: "What encounters life offers!" From the past he preserved the memory of carefree, good-natured women whom love made gay and who were grateful to him for the happiness he gave them, however brief it might be; and of women like his wife who loved without sincerity, with too many words, affectedly, hysterically, with an expression that it was not love or passion that engaged them but something more significant; and of two or three others, very beautiful, frigid women, across whose faces would suddenly flit a rapacious expression—an obstinate desire to take from life more than it could give, and these were women no longer young, capricious, unreflecting, domineering, unintelligent, and when Gurov grew cold to them their beauty aroused his hatred, and the lace on their lingerie seemed to him to resemble scales.

But here there was the timidity, the angularity of inexperienced youth, a feeling of awkwardness; and there was a sense of embarrassment, as though someone had suddenly knocked at the door. Anna Sergeyevna, "the lady with the pet dog," treated what had happened in a peculiar way, very seriously, as though it were her fall—so it seemed, and this was odd and inappropriate. Her features drooped and faded, and her long hair hung down sadly on either side of her face; she grew pensive and her dejected pose was that of a Magdalene in a picture by an old master.

"It's not right," she said. "You don't respect me now, you first of all."

There was a watermelon on the table. Gurov cut himself a slice and began eating it without haste. They were silent for at least half an hour.

There was something touching about Anna Sergeyevna; she had the purity of a well-bred, naive woman who has seen little of life. The single candle burning on the table barely illumined her face, yet it was clear that she was unhappy.

"Why should I stop respecting you, darling?" asked Gurov. "You don't know what you're saying."

"God forgive me," she said, and her eyes filled with tears. "It's terrible."

"It's as though you were trying to exonerate yourself."

"How can I exonerate myself? No. I am a bad, low woman; I despise myself and I have no thought of exonerating myself. It's not my husband but myself I have deceived. And not only just now; I have been deceiving myself for a long time. My husband may be a good, honest man, but he is a flunkey! I don't know what he does, what his work is, but I know he is a flunkey! I was twenty when I married him. I was tormented by curiosity; I wanted something better. 'There must be a different sort of life,' I said to myself. I wanted to live! To live, to live! Curiosity kept eating at me—you don't understand it, but I swear to God I could no longer control myself; something was going on in me; I could not be held back. I told my husband I was ill, and came here. And here I have been walking about as though in a daze, as though I were mad; and now I have become a vulgar, vile woman whom anyone may despise."

Gurov was already bored with her; he was irritated by her naive tone, by her repentance, so unexpected and so out of place, but for the tears in her eyes he might have thought she was joking or play-acting.

"I don't understand, my dear," he said softly. "What do you want?"

She hid her face on his breast and pressed close to him.

"Believe me, believe me, I beg you," she said, "I love honesty and purity, and sin is loathsome to me; I don't know what I'm doing. Simple people say, 'The Evil One has led me astray.' And I may say of myself now that the Evil One has led me astray."

"Quiet, quiet," he murmured.

He looked into her fixed, frightened eyes, kissed her, spoke to her softly and affectionately, and by degrees she calmed down, and her gaiety returned; both began laughing.

Afterwards when they went out there was not a soul on the esplanade. The town with its cypresses looked quite dead, but the sea was still sounding as it broke upon the beach; a single launch was rocking on the waves and on it a lantern was blinking sleepily.

They found a cab and drove to Oreanda.

"I found out your surname in the hall just now: it was written on the board—von Dideritz," said Gurov. "Is your husband German?"

"No; I believe his grandfather was German, but he is Greek Orthodox himself."

At Oreanda they sat on a bench not far from the church, looked down at the sea, and were silent. Yalta was barely visible through the morning mist; white clouds rested motionlessly on the mountaintops. The leaves did not stir on the trees, cicadas twanged, and the monotonous muffled sound of the sea that rose from below spoke of the peace, the eternal sleep awaiting us. So it rumbled below when there was no Yalta, no Oreanda here; so it rumbles now, and it will rumble as indifferently and as hollowly when we are no more. And in this constancy, in this complete indifference to the life and death of each of us, there lies, perhaps, a pledge of our eternal salvation, of the unceasing advance of life upon earth, of unceasing movement towards perfection. Sitting beside a young woman who in the dawn seemed so lovely, Gurov, soothed and spellbound by these magical surroundings—the sea, the mountains, the clouds, the wide sky—thought how everything is really beautiful in this world when one reflects: everything except what we think or do ourselves when we forget the higher aims of life and our own human dignity.

A man strolled up to them—probably a guard—looked at them and walked away. And this detail, too, seemed so mysterious and beautiful. They saw a steamer arrive from Feodosia, its lights extinguished in the glow of dawn.

"There is dew on the grass," said Anna Sergeyevna, after a silence.

"Yes, it's time to go home."

They returned to the city.

Then they met every day at twelve o'clock on the esplanade, lunched and dined together, took walks, admired the sea. She complained that she slept badly, that she had palpitations, asked the same questions, troubled now by jealousy and now by the fear that he did not respect her sufficiently. And often in the square or the public garden, when there was no one near them, he suddenly drew her to him and kissed her passionately. Complete idleness, these kisses in broad daylight exchanged furtively in dread of someone's seeing them, the heat, the smell of the sea, and the continual flitting before his eyes of idle, well-dressed, well-fed people, worked a complete change in him; he kept telling Anna Sergeyevna how beautiful she was, how seductive, was urgently passionate; he would not move a step away from her, while she was often pensive and continually pressed him to confess that he did not respect her, did not love her in the least, and saw in her nothing but a common woman. Almost every evening rather late they drove somewhere out of town, to Oreanda or to the waterfall; and the excursion was always a success, the scenery invariably impressed them as beautiful and magnificent.

They were expecting her husband, but a letter came from him saying that he had eye-trouble, and begging his wife to return home as soon as possible. Anna Sergeyevna made haste to go.

"It's a good thing I am leaving," she said to Gurov. "It's the hand of Fate!"

She took a carriage to the railway station, and he went with her. They were driving the whole day. When she had taken her place in the express, and when the second bell had rung, she said, "Let me look at you once more—let me look at you again. Like this."

She was not crying but was so sad that she seemed ill and her face was quivering.

"I shall be thinking of you—remembering you," she said. "God bless you; be happy. Don't remember evil against me. We are parting forever—it has to be, for we ought never to have met. Well, God bless you."

The train moved off rapidly, its lights soon vanished, and a minute later there was no sound of it, as though everything had conspired to end as quickly as possible that sweet trance, that madness. Left alone on the platform, and gazing into the dark distance, Gurov listened to the twang of the grasshoppers and the hum of the telegraph wires, feeling as though he had just waked up. And he reflected, musing, that there had now been another episode or adventure in his life, and it, too, was at an end, and nothing was left of it but a memory. He was moved, sad, and slightly remorseful: this young woman whom he would never meet again had not been happy with him; he had been warm and affectionate with her, but yet in his manner, his tone, and his caresses there had been a shade of light irony, the slightly coarse arrogance of a happy male who was, besides, almost twice her age. She had constantly called him kind, exceptional, high-minded; obviously he had seemed to her different from what he really was, so he had involuntarily deceived her.

Here at the station there was already a scent of autumn in the air; it was a chilly evening.

"It is time for me to go north, too," thought Gurov as he left the platform. "High time!"

III

At home in Moscow the winter routine was already established; the stoves were heated, and in the morning it was still dark when the children were having breakfast and getting ready for school, and the nurse would light the lamp for a short time. There were frosts already. When the first snow falls, on the first day the sleighs are out, it is pleasant to see the white earth, the white roofs; one draws easy, delicious breaths, and the season brings back the days of one's youth. The old limes and birches, white with hoar-frost, have a good-natured look; they are closer to one's heart than cypresses and palms, and near them one no longer wants to think of mountains and the sea.

Gurov, a native of Moscow, arrived there on a fine frosty day, and when he put on his fur coat and warm gloves and took a walk along Petrovka, and when on Saturday night he heard the bells ringing, his recent trip and the places he had visited lost all charm for him. Little by little he became immersed in Moscow life, greedily read three newspapers a day, and declared that he did not read the Moscow papers on principle. He already felt a longing for restaurants, clubs, formal dinners, anniversary celebrations, and it flattered him to entertain distinguished lawyers and actors, and to play cards with a professor at the physicians' club. He could eat a whole portion of meat stewed with pickled cabbage and served in a pan, Moscow style.

A month or so would pass and the image of Anna Sergeyevna, it seemed to him, would become misty in his memory, and only from time to time he would dream of her with her touching smile as he dreamed of others. But more than a month went by, winter came into its own, and everything was still clear in his memory as though he had parted from Anna Sergeyevna only yesterday. And his memories glowed more and more vividly. When in the evening stillness the voices of his children preparing their lessons reached his study, or when he listened to a song or to an organ playing in a restaurant, or when the storm howled in the chimney, suddenly everything would rise up in his memory; what had happened on the pier and the early morning with the mist on the mountains, and the steamer coming from Feodosia, and the kisses. He would pace about his room a long time, remembering and smiling; then his memories passed into reveries, and in his imagination the past would mingle with what was to come. He did not dream of Anna Sergeyevna, but she followed him about everywhere and watched him. When he shut his eyes he saw her before him as though she were there in the flesh, and she seemed to him lovelier, younger, tenderer than she had been, and he imagined himself a finer man than he had been in Yalta. Of evenings she peered out at him from the bookcase, from the fireplace, from the corner—he heard her breathing, the caressing rustle of her clothes. In the street he followed the women with his eyes, looking for someone who resembled her.

Already he was tormented by a strong desire to share his memories with someone. But in his home it was impossible to talk of his love, and he had no one to talk to outside; certainly he could not confide in his tenants or in anyone at the bank. And what was there to talk about? He hadn't loved her then, had he? Had there been anything beautiful, poetical, edifying, or simply interesting in his relations with Anna Sergeyevna? And he was forced to talk vaguely of love, of women, and no one guessed what he meant; only his wife would twitch her black eyebrows and say, "The part of a philanderer does not suit you at all, Dimitry."

One evening, coming out of the physicians' club with an official with whom he had been playing cards, he could not resist saying:

"If you only knew what a fascinating woman I became acquainted with at Yalta!"

The official got into his sledge and was driving away, but turned suddenly and shouted:

"Dmitry Dmitrich!"

"What is it?"

"You were right this evening: the sturgeon was a bit high."

These words, so commonplace, for some reason moved Gurov to indignation, and struck him as degrading and unclean. What savage manners, what mugs! What stupid nights, what dull, humdrum days! Frenzied gambling, gluttony, drunkenness, continual talk always about the same thing! Futile pursuits and conversations always about the same topics take up the better part of one's time, the better part of one's strength, and in the end there is left a life clipped and wingless, an absurd mess, and there is no escaping or getting away from it—just as though one were in a madhouse or a prison.

Gurov, boiling with indignation, did not sleep all night. And he had a headache all the next day. And the following nights too he slept badly; he sat up in bed, thinking, or paced up and down his room. He was fed up with his children, fed up with the bank; he had no desire to go anywhere or to think of anything.

In December during the holidays he prepared to take a trip and told his wife he was going to Petersburg to do what he could for a young friend—and he set off for S——. What for? He did not know, himself. He wanted to see Anna Sergeyevna and talk with her, to arrange a rendezvous if possible.

He arrived at S—— in the morning, and at the hotel took the best room, in which the floor was covered with gray army cloth, and on the table there was an inkstand, gray with dust and topped by a figure on horseback, its hat in its raised hand and its head broken off. The porter gave him the necessary information: von Dideritz lived in a house of his own on Staro-Goncharnaya Street, not far from the hotel: he was rich and lived well and kept his own horses; everyone in the town knew him. The porter pronounced the name: "Dridiritz."

Without haste Gurov made his way to Staro-Goncharnaya Street and found the house. Directly opposite the house stretched a long gray fence studded with nails.

"A fence like that would make one run away," thought Gurov, looking now at the fence, now at the windows of the house.

He reflected: this was a holiday, and the husband was apt to be at home. And in any case, it would be tactless to go into the house and disturb her. If he were to send her a note, it might fall into her husband's hands, and that might spoil everything. The best thing was to rely on chance. And he kept walking up and down the street and along the fence, waiting for the chance. He saw a beggar go in at the gate and heard the dogs attack him; then an hour later he heard a piano, and the sound came to him faintly and indistinctly. Probably it was Anna Sergeyevna playing. The front door opened suddenly, and an old woman came out, followed by the familiar white Pomeranian. Gurov was on the point of calling to the dog, but his heart began beating violently, and in his excitement he could not remember the Pomeranian's name.

He kept walking up and down, and hated the gray fence more and more, and by now he thought irritably that Anna Sergeyevna had forgotten him, and was perhaps already diverting herself with another man, and that that was very natural in a young woman who from morning till night had to look at that damn fence. He went back to his hotel room and sat on the couch for a long while, not knowing what to do, then he had dinner and a long nap.

"How stupid and annoying all this is!" he thought when he woke and looked at the dark windows: it was already evening. "Here I've had a good sleep for some reason. What am I going to do at night?"

He sat on the bed, which was covered with a cheap gray blanket of the kind seen in hospitals, and he twitted himself in his vexation:

"So there's your lady with the pet dog. There's your adventure. A nice place to cool your heels in."

That morning at the station a playbill in large letters had caught his eye. *The Geisha* was to be given for the first time. He thought of this and drove to the theater.

"It's quite possible that she goes to first nights," he thought.

The theater was full. As in all provincial theaters, there was a haze above the chandelier, the gallery was noisy and restless; in the front row, before the beginning of the performance the local dandies were standing with their hands clasped behind their backs; in the Governor's box the Governor's daughter, wearing a boa, occupied the front seat, while the Governor himself hid modestly behind the portiere and only his hands were visible; the curtain swayed; the orchestra was a long time tuning up. While the audience was coming in and taking their seats, Gurov scanned the faces eagerly.

Anna Sergeyevna, too, came in. She sat down in the third row, and when Gurov looked at her his heart contracted, and he understood clearly that in the whole world there was no human being so near, so precious, and so important to him; she, this little, undistinguished woman, lost in a provincial crowd, with a vulgar lorgnette in her hand, filled his whole life now, was his sorrow and his joy, the only happiness that he now desired for himself, and to the sounds of the bad orchestra, of the miserable local violins, he thought how lovely she was. He thought and dreamed.

A young man with small side-whiskers, very tall and stooped, came in with Anna Sergeyevna and sat down beside her; he nodded his head at every step and seemed to be bowing continually. Probably this was the husband whom at Yalta, in an excess of bitter feeling, she had called a flunkey. And there really was in his lanky figure, his side-whiskers, his small bald patch, something of a flunkey's retiring manner; his smile was mawkish, and in his buttonhole there was an academic badge like a waiter's number.

During the first intermission the husband went out to have a smoke; she remained in her seat. Gurov, who was also sitting in the orchestra, went up to her and said in a shaky voice, with a forced smile:

"Good evening!"

She glanced at him and turned pale, then looked at him again in horror, unable to believe her eyes, and gripped the fan and the lorgnette tightly together in her hands, evidently trying to keep herself from fainting. Both were silent. She was sitting, he was standing, frightened by her distress and not daring to take a seat beside her. The violins and the flute that were being tuned up sang out. He suddenly felt frightened: it seemed as if all the people in the boxes were looking at them. She got up and went hurriedly to the exit; he followed her, and both of them walked blindly along the corridors and up and down stairs, and figures in the uniforms prescribed for magistrates, teachers, and officials of the Department of Crown Lands, all wearing badges, flitted before their eyes, as did also ladies, and fur coats on hangers; they were conscious of drafts and the smell of stale tobacco. And Gurov, whose heart was beating violently, thought:

"Oh, Lord! Why are these people here and this orchestra!"

And at that instant he suddenly recalled how when he had seen Anna Sergeyevna off at the station he had said to himself that all was over between them and that they would never meet again. But how distant the end still was!

On the narrow, gloomy staircase over which it said "To the Amphitheater," she stopped.

"How you frightened me!" she said, breathing hard, still pale and stunned. "Oh, how you frightened me! I am barely alive. Why did you come? Why?"

"But do understand, Anna, do understand—" he said hurriedly, under his breath. "I implore you, do understand—"

She looked at him with fear, with entreaty, with love; she looked at him intently, to keep his features more distinctly in her memory.

"I suffer so," she went on, not listening to him. "All this time I have been thinking of nothing but you; I live only by the thought of you. And I wanted to forget, to forget; but why, oh, why have you come?"

On the landing above them two high school boys were looking down and smoking, but it was all the same to Gurov; he drew Anna Sergeyevna to him and began kissing her face and hands.

"What are you doing, what are you doing!" she was saying in horror, pushing him away. "We have lost our senses. Go away today; go away at once—I conjure you by all that is sacred, I implore you—People are coming this way!"

Someone was walking up the stairs.

"You must leave," Anna Sergeyevna went on in a whisper. "Do you hear, Dmitry Dmitrich? I will come and see you in Moscow. I have never been happy; I am unhappy now, and I never, never shall be happy, never! So don't make me suffer still more! I swear I'll come to Moscow. But now let us part. My dear, good, precious one, let us part!"

She pressed his hand and walked rapidly downstairs, turning to look round at him, and from her eyes he could see that she really was unhappy. Gurov stood for a while, listening, then when all grew quiet, he found his coat and left the theater.

IV

And Anna Sergeyevna began coming to see him in Moscow. Once every two or three months she left S—— telling her husband that she was going to consult a doctor about a woman's ailment from which she was suffering—and her husband did and did not believe her. When she arrived in Moscow she would stop at the Slavyansky Bazar Hotel, and at once send a man in a red cap to Gurov. Gurov came to see her, and no one in Moscow knew of it.

Once he was going to see her in this way on a winter morning (the messenger had come the evening before and not found him in). With him walked his daughter, whom he wanted to take to school; it was on the way. Snow was coming down in big wet flakes.

"It's three degrees above zero, and yet it's snowing," Gurov was saying to his daughter. "But this temperature prevails only on the surface of the earth; in the upper layers of the atmosphere there is quite a different temperature."

"And why doesn't it thunder in winter, papa?"

He explained that, too. He talked, thinking all the while that he was on his way to a rendezvous, and no living soul knew of it, and probably no one would ever know. He had two lives, an open one, seen and known by all who needed to know it, full of conventional truth and conventional falsehood, exactly like the lives of his friends and acquaintances; and another life that went on in secret. And through some strange, perhaps accidental, combination of circumstances, everything that was of interest and importance to him, everything that was essential to him, everything about which he felt sincerely and did not deceive himself, everything that constituted the core of his life, was going on concealed from others; while all that was false, the shell in which he hid to cover the truth—his work at the bank, for instance, his discussions at the club, his references to the "inferior race," his appearances at anniversary celebrations with his wife—all that went on in the open. Judging others by himself, he did not believe what he saw, and always fancied that every man led his real, most interesting life under cover of secrecy as under cover of night. The personal life of every individual is based on secrecy, and perhaps it is partly for that reason that civilized man is so nervously anxious that personal privacy should be respected.

Having taken his daughter to school, Gurov went on to the Slavyansky Bazar Hotel. He took off his fur coat in the lobby, went upstairs, and knocked gently at the door. Anna Sergeyevna, wearing his favorite gray dress, exhausted by the journey and by waiting, had been expecting him since the previous evening. She was pale, and looked at him without a smile, and he had hardly entered when she flung herself on his breast. That kiss was a long, lingering one, as though they had not seen one another for two years.

"Well, darling, how are you getting on there?" he asked. "What news?"

"Wait; I'll tell you in a moment—I can't speak."

She could not speak; she was crying. She turned away from him, and pressed her handkerchief to her eyes.

"Let her have her cry; meanwhile I'll sit down," he thought, and he seated himself in an armchair.

Then he rang and ordered tea, and while he was having his tea she remained standing at the window with her back to him. She was crying out of sheer agitation, in the sorrowful consciousness that their life was so sad; that they could only see each other in secret and had to hide from people like thieves! Was it not a broken life?

"Come, stop now, dear!" he said.

It was plain to him that this love of theirs would not be over soon, that the end of it was not in sight. Anna Sergeyevna was growing more and more attached to him. She adored him, and it was unthinkable to tell her that their love was bound to come to an end some day; besides, she would not have believed it!

He went up to her and took her by the shoulders, to fondle her and say something diverting, and at that moment he caught sight of himself in the mirror.

His hair was already beginning to turn gray. And it seemed odd to him that he had grown so much older in the last few years, and lost his looks. The shoulders on which his hands rested were warm and heaving. He felt compassion for this life, still so warm and lovely, but probably already about to begin to fade and wither like his own. Why did she love him so much? He always seemed to women different from what he was, and they loved in him not himself, but the man whom their imagination created and whom they had been eagerly seeking all their lives; and afterwards, when they saw their mistake, they loved him nevertheless. And not one of them had been happy with him. In the past he had met women, come together with them, parted from them, but he had never once loved; it was anything you please, but not love. And only now when his head was gray he had fallen in love, really, truly—for the first time in his life.

Anna Sergeyevna and he loved each other as people do who are very close and intimate, like man and wife, like tender friends; it seemed to them that Fate itself had meant them for one another, and they could not understand why he had a wife and she a husband; and it was as though they were a pair of migratory birds, male and female, caught and forced to live in different cages. They forgave each other what they were ashamed of in their past, they forgave everything in the present, and felt that this love of theirs had altered them both.

Formerly in moments of sadness he had soothed himself with whatever logical arguments came into his head, but now he no longer cared for logic, he felt profound compassion, he wanted to be sincere and tender.

"Give it up now, my darling," he said. "You've had your cry; that's enough. Let us have a talk now, we'll think up something."

Then they spent a long time taking counsel together, they talked of how to avoid the necessity for secrecy, for deception, for living in different cities, and not seeing one another for long stretches of time. How could they free themselves from these intolerable fetters?

"How? How?" he asked, clutching his head. "How?"

And it seemed as though in a little while the solution would he found, and then a new and glorious life would begin; and it was clear to both of them that the end was still far off, and that what was to be most complicated and difficult for them was only just beginning.

Kate Chopin

Kate O'Flaherty was born in 1851 in St. Louis, Missouri to an Irish father and a Creole mother. At age four she lost her father when he was killed in the wreck of a train belonging to his own company; then she lost in quick succession a half-brother in the Civil War, another brother who fell from a runaway horse, her mother, and grandmother. After being educated in the Academy of the Sacred Heart convent, she married cotton broker Oscar Chopin in 1870, living first in Louisiana and New Orleans and then on a large plantation among French-speaking Acadians, a milieu that richly supplied her later fiction. After her husband's death in 1882, Chopin returned with her six children to St. Louis, where she was encouraged to write professionally, publishing two novels, *At Fault* (1890) and *The Awakening* (1899) and two collections of short stories, *Bayou Folk* (1894) and *A Night in Arcadie* (1897), several of which appeared in *Century* and *Harper's*. Her frank and candid treatment of issues such as sexuality and slavery, and her espousal of Darwinism, brought public scorn and rejection from publishers, so that she spent her final years in relative silence. Her works were removed from libraries and she was barred from joining literary societies in St. Louis. Chopin died in 1904 and remained unknown until her work was rediscovered by feminist critics in the 1960s.

Chopin was so fascinated with and empowered by the stories of Guy de Maupassant that she translated many of them into English. As she explains in an essay reprinted in *The Complete Works of Kate Chopin* (1969, Volume 2): "About eight years ago there fell accidentally into my hands a volume of Maupassant's tales. These were new to me. I had been in the woods, in the fields, groping around; looking for something big, satisfying, convincing, and finding nothing but—myself; a something neither big nor satisfying but wholly convincing. It was at this period of my emerging from the vast solitude in which I had been making my own acquaintance, that I stumbled upon Maupassant. I read his stories and marvelled at them. Here was life, not fiction; for where were the plots, the old fashioned mechanism and stage trapping that in a vague unthinking way I had fancied were essential to the art of story making? Here was a man who had escaped from tradition and authority, who had entered into himself and looked out upon life through his own eyes; and who, in a direct and simple way, told us what he saw. When a man does this, he gives us the best that he can; something valuable for it is genuine and spontaneous. He gives us his impressions. Someone told me the other day that Maupassant had gone out of fashion. I was not grieved to hear it. He has never seemed to me to belong to the multitude, but rather to the individual."

Like her mentor, Chopin was deeply interested in the inner life of her characters, particularly the conflict between appearance and reality. In many of her stories, she explores those intersections of character and experience that cut to the quick of human feeling, revealing heretofore unacknowledged griefs and yearnings. In her story "Regret," for example, she presents a character called Mamzelle Aurélie who has never married and who lives alone with her dog Ponto, apparently content with her life. The unexpected task of caring for a neighbour's four children for two weeks unsettles both her domestic routines and her emotional balance, bringing to the surface her own maternal feelings and her acute awareness of loss: "She turned into the house. There was much work awaiting her, for the children had left a sad disorder behind them; but she did not at once set about the task of righting it. Mamzelle Aurélie seated herself beside the table. She gave one slow glance through the room, into which the evening shadows were creeping and deepening around her solitary figure. She let her head fall down upon her bended arm, and began to cry. Oh, but she cried! Not softly, as women often do. She cried like a man, with sobs that seemed to tear her very soul. She did not notice Ponto licking her hand."

As in "The Story of an Hour," Chopin employs a rather severe shorthand, providing very little information about character and situation but expecting readers to grasp in an instant the underlying psychology. You can imagine how Mavis Gallant or Alice Munro would handle the material of "Regret," weaving in and out of past and present, providing many more scenes between Mamzelle Aurélie and the children, so that we are not so much startled by the final revelation as deeply moved from having invested so much in getting to know the central character. However, it's not surprising, given the risks and pressures and blows to her confidence that Chopin experienced, that she could not fully escape the very mechanisms and stage trappings of the genre (particularly the abrupt, surprise ending) that she had inherited from Poe and others.

The Story of an Hour

Knowing that Mrs. Mallard was afflicted with a heart trouble, great care was taken to break to her as gently as possible the news of her husband's death.

It was her sister Josephine who told her, in broken sentences; veiled hints that revealed in half concealing. Her husband's friend Richards was there, too, near her. It was he who had been in the newspaper office when intelligence of the railroad disaster was received, with Brently Mallard's name leading the list of "killed." He had only taken the time to assure himself of its truth by a second telegram, and had hastened to forestall any less careful, less tender friend in bearing the sad message.

She did not hear the story as many women have heard the same, with a paralyzed inability to accept its significance. She wept at once, with sudden, wild abandonment, in her sister's arms. When the storm of grief had spent itself she went away to her room alone. She would have no one follow her.

There stood, facing the open window, a comfortable, roomy armchair. Into this she sank, pressed down by a physical exhaustion that haunted her body and seemed to reach into her soul.

She could see in the open square before her house the tops of trees that were all aquiver with the new spring life. The delicious breath of rain was in the air. In the street below a peddler was crying his wares. The notes of a distant song which some one was singing reached her faintly, and countless sparrows were twittering in the eaves.

There were patches of blue sky showing here and there through the clouds that had met and piled one above the other in the west facing her window.

She sat with her head thrown back upon the cushion of the chair, quite motionless, except when a sob came up into her throat and shook her, as a child who had cried itself to sleep continues to sob in its dreams.

She was young, with a fair, calm face, whose lines bespoke repression and even a certain strength. But now there was a dull stare in her eyes, whose gaze was fixed away off yonder on one of those patches of blue sky. It was not a glance of reflection, but rather indicated a suspension of intelligent thought.

There was something coming to her and she was waiting for it, fearfully. What was it? She did not know; it was too subtle and elusive to name. But she felt it, creeping out of the sky, reaching toward her through the sounds, the scents, the color that filled the air.

Now her bosom rose and fell tumultuously. She was beginning to recognize this thing that was approaching to possess her, and she was striving to beat it back with her will—as powerless as her two white slender hands would have been.

When she abandoned herself a little whispered word escaped her slightly parted lips. She said it over and over under her breath: "free, free, free!" The vacant stare and the look of terror that had followed it went from her eyes. They stayed keen and bright. Her pulses beat fast, and the coursing blood warmed and relaxed every inch of her body.

She did not stop to ask if it were or were not a monstrous joy that held her. A clear and exalted perception enabled her to dismiss the suggestion as trivial.

She knew that she would weep again when she saw the kind, tender hands folded in death; the face that had never looked save with love upon her, fixed and gray and dead. But she saw beyond that bitter moment a long procession of years to come that would belong to her absolutely. And she opened and spread her arms out to them in welcome.

There would be no one to live for her during those coming years: she would live for herself. There would be no powerful will bending hers in that blind persistence with which men and women believe they have a right to impose a private will upon a fellow-creature. A kind intention or a cruel intention made the act seem no less a crime as she looked upon it in that brief moment of illumination.

And yet she had loved him—sometimes. Often she had not. What did it matter! What could love, the unsolved mystery, count for in face of this possession of self-assertion which she suddenly recognized as the strongest impulse of her being!

"Free! Body and soul free!" she kept whispering.

Josephine was kneeling before the closed door with her lips to the keyhole, imploring for admission. "Louise, open the door! I beg; open the door—you will make yourself ill. What are you doing, Louise? For heaven's sake open the door."

"Go away. I am not making myself ill." No; she was drinking in a very elixir of life through that open window.

Her fancy was running riot along those days ahead of her. Spring days, and summer days, and all sorts of days that would be her own. She breathed a quick prayer that life might be long. It was only yesterday she had thought with a shudder that life might be long.

She arose at length and opened the door to her sister's importunities. There was a feverish triumph in her eyes, and she carried herself unwittingly like a goddess of Victory. She clasped her sister's waist, and together they descended the stairs. Richards stood waiting for them at the bottom.

Some one was opening the front door with a latchkey. It was Brently Mallard who entered, a little travel-stained, composedly carrying his grip-sack and umbrella. He had been far from the scene of accident, and did not even know there had been one. He stood amazed at Josephine's piercing cry; at Richards' quick motion to screen him from the view of his wife.

But Richards was too late.

When the doctors came they said she had died of heart disease—of joy that kills.

Joseph Conrad

Jozef Teodor Konrad Nalecz Korzeniowski was born near Kiev in 1857, at a time when much of Poland was under the heel of Czarist Russia. His father, a poet, translator of Shakespeare, and a strong advocate of Polish independence, was exiled to Russia; his mother died three years later in exile, leaving Conrad in the care of his wealthy uncle, Tadeusz Bobrowski. At the age of seventeen, Conrad left for Marseilles, where he lived beyond his means and became enamoured of personalities associated with the cause of restoring the Carlist monarchy to Spain. He described himself at that stage as "an incorrigible Don Quixote." His extravagant affairs and dangerous skirmishes as a gun-runner for the Carlists brought on what appears to have been a nervous breakdown and attempted suicide. The long apprenticeship with the sea in the French and British merchant service that followed gave Conrad the stability, not to mention the varied experiences, that would serve him so well in his career as a writer. He published his first novel, *Almayer's Folly*, in 1895 and shortly after settled to write in England, whose language he had adopted. He is best known for *The Nigger of the "Narcissus"* (1897), *Lord Jim* (1900), *Heart of Darkness* (1902), *Nostromo* (1904), *The Secret Agent* (1907), and *Victory* (1915).

Conrad's romantic temperament and his sceptical cast of mind produced in him an existential awareness that, in his early years, often found extreme expression, as in this letter to R. B. Cunninghame Graham: "'Put out the tongue,' why not? One ought to really and the machine will run all the same. The question is whether the fatigue of the muscular exertion is worth the transient pleasure of indulgent scorn. On the other hand one may ask whether scorn, love or hate are justified in the face of such shadowy illusions. The machine is thinner than air and as evanescent as a flash of lightning. The attitude of cold unconcern is the only reasonable one. Of course reason is hateful,—but why? Because it demonstrates (to those who have the courage) that we, living, are out of life,—utterly out of it. The mysteries of a universe made up of drops of fire and clods of mud do not concern us in the least. The fire of a humanity condemned ultimately to perish from cold is not worth troubling about. If you take it to heart it becomes an unendurable tragedy. ... Life knows us not and we do not know life,—we don't even know our own thoughts. Half the words we use have no meaning whatever and of the other half each man understands each word after the fashion of his own folly and conceit. Faith is a myth and beliefs shift like mists on the shore: thoughts vanish: words, once pronounced, die: and the memory of yesterday is as shadowy as the hope of tomorrow—only the string of my platitudes seems to have no end. As our peasants say: 'Pray, brother, forgive me for the love of God.' And we don't know what forgiveness is, nor what love is, nor where God is. *Assez!*"

The bleakness of this vision is modified somewhat in the later writings. As he says in his essay "Books," "To be hopeful in an artistic sense it is not necessary to think that the world is good. It is enough to believe that there is no impossibility of its being made so." Work, particularly the work of writing, was for Conrad a great moral comfort, though he had few illusions about its potential for finding political cures. As he says in "Autocracy and War," "The true peace of the world will be a place of refuge much less like a beleaguered fortress and more, let us hope, in the nature of an Inviolable Temple. It will be built on less perishable foundations than those of material interests. But it must be confessed that the architectural aspect of the universal city remains as yet inconceivable—that the very ground for its erection has not been cleared of the jungle."

Conrad's aesthetic may be gleaned from the fiction, of course, but also by a careful reading of his letters, essays, prefaces, and *A Personal Record.* Writing to Arnold Bennett, he said: "Now realism in art will never approach reality. And your art, your gift, should be put to the service of a larger and freer faith." Instead, he advised the writer to "cultivate his poetic faculty," to aim for plasticity, suggestiveness, and "an unremitting never-discouraged care for the shape and ring of sentences." Conrad's imagery here—*faith, temple, hope, forgiveness*—is significant, for it reflects his view of art as a sacred trust, a religious commitment. In a letter to Arthur Symons, he says: "One thing I am certain of is that I have approached the object of my task, things human, in a spirit of piety. The earth is a temple where there is going on a mystery play, childish and poignant, ridiculous and awful enough, in all conscience. Once in I've tried to behave decently. I have not degraded any quasi-religious sentiment by tears and groans; and if I have been amused or indignant, I've neither grinned nor gnashed my teeth. In other words, I've tried to write with dignity, not out of a regard for myself, but for the sake of the spectacle, the play with an obscure beginning and an unfathomable dénouement. I don't think this has been noticed. It is your penitent beating the floor with his forehead and the ecstatic worshipper at the rails that are obvious to the public's eye. The man standing quietly in the shadow of the pillar, if noticed at all, runs the risk of being suspected of sinister designs. Thus I've been called a heartless wretch, a man without ideals and a poseur of brutality. But I will confess to you under seal of secrecy that I *don't believe* I am such as I appear to mediocre minds."

Heart of Darkness

I

The *Nellie*, a cruising yawl, swung to her anchor without a flutter of the sails, and was at rest. The flood had made, the wind was nearly calm, and being bound down the river, the only thing for it was to come to and wait for the turn of the tide.

The sea-reach of the Thames stretched before us like the beginning of an interminable waterway. In the offing the sea and the sky were welded together without a joint, and in the luminous space the tanned sails of the barges drifting up with the tide seemed to stand still in red clusters of canvas sharply peaked, with gleams of varnished sprits. A haze rested on the low shores that ran out to sea in vanishing flatness. The air was dark above Gravesend, and farther back still seemed condensed into a mournful gloom, brooding motionless over the biggest, and the greatest, town on earth.

The Director of Companies was our captain and our host. We four affectionately watched his back as he stood in the bows looking to seaward. On the whole river there was nothing that looked half so nautical. He resembled a pilot, which to a seaman is trustworthiness personified. It was difficult to realise his work was not out there in the luminous estuary, but behind him, within the brooding gloom.

Between us there was, as I have already said somewhere, the bond of the sea. Besides holding our hearts together through long periods of separation, it had the effect of making us tolerant of each other's yarns—and even convictions. The Lawyer—the best of old fellows—had, because of his many years and many virtues, the only cushion on deck, and was lying on the only rug. The Accountant had brought out already a box of dominoes, and was toying architecturally with the bones. Marlow sat cross-legged right aft, leaning against the mizzen-mast. He had sunken cheeks, a yellow complexion, a straight back, an ascetic aspect, and, with his arms dropped, the palms of hands outwards, resembled an idol. The Director, satisfied the anchor had good hold, made his way aft and sat down amongst us. We exchanged a few words lazily. Afterwards there was silence on board the yacht. For some reason or other we did not begin that game of dominoes. We felt meditative, and fit for nothing but placid staring. The day was ending in a serenity of still and exquisite brilliance. The water shone pacifically; the sky, without a speck, was a benign immensity of unstained light; the very mist on the Essex marshes was like a gauzy and radiant fabric, hung from the wooded rises inland, and draping the low shores in diaphanous folds. Only the gloom to the west, brooding over the upper reaches, became more sombre every minute, as if angered by the approach of the sun.

And at last, in its curved and imperceptible fall, the sun sank low, and from glowing white changed to a dull red without rays and without heat, as if about to go out suddenly, stricken to death by the touch of that gloom brooding over a crowd of men.

Forthwith a change came over the waters, and the serenity became less brilliant but more profound. The old river in its broad reach rested unruffled at the decline of day, after ages of good service done to the race that peopled its banks, spread out in the tranquil dignity of a waterway leading to the uttermost ends of the earth. We looked at the venerable stream not in the vivid flush of a short day that comes and departs for ever, but in the august light of abiding memories. And indeed nothing is easier for a man who has, as the phrase goes, "followed the sea" with reverence and affection, than to evoke the great spirit of the past upon the lower reaches of the Thames. The tidal current runs to and fro in its unceasing service, crowded with memories of men and ships it has borne to the rest of home or to the battles of the sea. It had known and served all the men of whom the nation is proud, from Sir Francis Drake to Sir John Franklin, knights all, titled and untitled—the great knights-errant of the sea. It had borne all the ships whose names are like jewels flashing in the night of time, from the *Golden Hind* returning with her round flanks full of treasure, to be visited by the Queen's Highness and thus pass out of the gigantic tale, to the *Erebus* and *Terror*, bound on other conquests—and that never returned. It had known the ships and the men. They had sailed from Deptford, from Greenwich, from Erith—the adventurers and the settlers; kings' ships and the ships of men on 'Change; captains, admirals, the dark "interlopers" of the Eastern trade, and the commissioned "generals" of East India fleets. Hunters for gold or pursuers of fame, they all had gone out on that stream, bearing the sword, and often the torch, messengers of the might within the land, bearers of a spark from the sacred fire. What greatness had not floated on the ebb of that river into the mystery of an unknown earth! ... The dreams of men, the seed of commonwealths, the germs of empires.

The sun set; the dusk fell on the stream, and lights began to appear along the shore. The Chapman lighthouse, a three-legged thing erect on a mud-flat, shone strongly. Lights of ships moved in the fairway—a great stir of lights going up and going down. And farther west on the upper reaches the place of the monstrous town was still marked ominously on the sky, a brooding gloom in sunshine, a lurid glare under the stars.

"And this also," said Marlow suddenly, "has been one of the dark places of the earth."

He was the only man of us who still "followed the sea." The worst that could be said of him was that he did not represent his class. He was a seaman, but he was a wanderer too, while most seamen lead, if one may so express it, a sedentary life. Their minds are of the stay-at-home order, and their home is always with them—the ship; and so is their country—the sea. One ship is very much like another, and the sea is always the same. In the immutability of their surroundings the foreign shores, the foreign faces, the changing immensity of life, glide past, veiled not by a sense of mystery but by a slightly disdainful ignorance; for there is nothing mysterious to a seaman unless it be the sea itself, which is the mistress of his existence and as inscrutable as Destiny. For the rest, after his hours of work, a casual stroll or a casual spree on shore suffices to unfold for him the secret of a whole continent, and generally he finds the secret not worth knowing. The yarns of seamen have a direct simplicity, the whole meaning of which lies within the shell of a cracked nut. But Marlow was not typical (if his propensity to spin yarns be excepted), and to him the meaning of an episode was not inside like a kernel but outside, enveloping the tale which brought it out only as a glow brings out a haze, in the likeness of one of these misty halos that sometimes are made visible by the spectral illumination of moonshine.

His remark did not seem at all surprising. It was just like Marlow. It was accepted in silence. No one took the trouble to grunt even; and presently he said, very slow:

"I was thinking of very old times, when the Romans first came here, nineteen hundred years ago—the other day. ... Light came out of this river since—you say Knights? Yes; but it is like a running blaze on a plain, like a flash of lightning in the clouds. We live in the flicker—may it last as long as the old earth keeps rolling! But darkness was here yesterday. Imagine the feelings of a commander of a fine—what d'ye call 'em?—trireme in the Mediterranean, ordered suddenly to the north; run overland across the Gauls in a hurry; put in charge of one of these craft the legionaries—a wonderful lot of handy men they must have been too—used to build, apparently by the hundred, in a month or two, if we may believe what we read. Imagine him here—the very end of the world, a sea the colour of lead, a sky the colour of smoke, a kind of ship about as rigid as a concertina—and going up this river with stores, or orders, or what you like. Sandbanks, marshes, forests, savages—precious little to eat fit for a civilised man, nothing but Thames water to drink. No Falernian wine here, no going ashore. Here and there a military camp lost in a wilderness, like a needle in a bundle of hay—cold, fog, tempests, disease, exile, and death—death skulking in the air, in the water, in the bush. They must have been dying like flies here. Oh yes—he did it. Did it very well, too, no doubt, and without thinking much about it either, except afterwards to brag of what he had gone through in his time, perhaps. They were men enough to face the darkness. And perhaps he was cheered by keeping his eye on a chance of promotion to the fleet at Ravenna by and by, if he had good friends in Rome and survived the awful climate. Or think of a decent young citizen in a toga—perhaps too much dice, you know—coming out here in the train of some prefect, or tax-gatherer, or trader, even, to mend his fortunes. Land in a swamp, march through the woods, and in some inland post feel the savagery, the utter savagery, had closed round him—all that mysterious life of the wilderness that stirs in the forest, in the jungles, in the hearts of wild men. There's no initiation either into such mysteries. He has to live in the midst of the incomprehensible, which is also detestable. And it has a fascination, too, that goes to work upon him. The fascination of the abomination—you know. Imagine the growing regrets, the longing to escape, the powerless disgust, the surrender, the hate."

He paused.

"Mind," be began again, lifting one arm from the elbow, the palm of the hand outwards, so that, with his legs folded before him, he had the pose of a Buddha preaching in European clothes and without a lotus-flower—"Mind, none of us would feel exactly like this. What saves us is efficiency—the devotion to efficiency. But these chaps were not much account, really. They were no colonists; their administration was merely a squeeze, and nothing more, I suspect. They were conquerors, and for that you want only brute force—nothing to boast of, when you have it, since your strength is just an accident arising from the weakness of others. They grabbed what they could get for the sake of what was to be got. It was just robbery with violence, aggravated murder on a great scale, and men going at it blind—as is very proper for those who tackle a darkness. The conquest of the earth, which mostly means the taking it away from those who have a different complexion or slightly flatter noses than ourselves, is not a pretty thing when you look into it too much. What redeems it is the idea only. An idea at the back of it; not a sentimental pretence but an idea; and an unselfish belief in the idea—something you can set up, and bow down before, and offer a sacrifice to. ..."

He broke off. Flames glided in the river, small green flames, red flames, white flames, pursuing, overtaking, joining, crossing each other—then separating slowly or hastily. The traffic of the great city went on in the deepening night upon the sleepless river. We looked on, waiting patiently—there was nothing else to do till the end of the flood; but it was only after a long silence, when he said, in a hesitating voice, "I suppose you fellows remember I did once turn fresh-water sailor for a bit," that we knew we were fated, before the ebb began to run, to hear about one of Marlow's inconclusive experiences.

"I don't want to bother you much with what happened to me personally," he began, showing in this remark the weakness of many tellers of tales who seem so often unaware of what their audience would best like to hear; "yet to understand the effect of it on me you ought to know how I got out there, what I saw, how I went up that river to the place where I first met the poor chap. It was the farthest point of navigation and the culminating point of my experience. It seemed somehow to throw a kind of light on everything about me—and into my thoughts. It was sombre enough too—and pitiful—not extraordinary in any way—not very clear either. No, not very clear. And yet it seemed to throw a kind of light.

"I had then, as you remember, just returned to London after a lot of Indian Ocean, Pacific, China Seas—a regular dose of the East—six years or so, and I was loafing about, hindering you fellows in your work and invading your homes, just as though I had got a heavenly mission to civilise you. It was very fine for a time, but after a bit I did get tired of resting. Then I began to look for a ship—I should think the hardest work on earth. But the ships wouldn't even look at me. And I got tired of that game too.

"Now when I was a little chap I had a passion for maps. I would look for hours at South America, or Africa, or Australia, and lose myself in all the glories of exploration. At that time there were many blank spaces on the earth, and when I saw one that looked particularly inviting on a map (but they all look that) I would put my finger on it and say, When I grow up I will go there. The North Pole was one of these places, I remember. Well, I haven't been there yet, and shall not try now. The glamour's off. Other places were scattered about the Equator, and in every sort of latitude all over the two hemispheres. I have been in some of them, and ... well, we won't talk about that. But there was one yet—the biggest, the most blank, so to speak—that I had a hankering after.

"True, by this time it was not a blank space any more. It had got filled since my boyhood with rivers and lakes and names. It had ceased to be a blank space of delightful mystery—a white patch for a boy to dream gloriously over. It had become a place of darkness. But there was in it one river especially, a mighty big river, that you could see on the map, resembling an immense snake uncoiled, with its head in the sea, its body at rest curving afar over a vast country, and its tail lost in the depths of the land. And as I looked at the map of it in a shop-window, it fascinated me as a snake would a bird—a silly little bird. Then I remembered there was a big concern, a Company for trade on that river. Dash it all! I thought to myself, they can't trade without using some kind of craft on that lot of fresh water—steamboats! Why shouldn't I try to get charge of one? I went on along Fleet Street, but could not shake off the idea. The snake had charmed me.

"You understand it was a Continental concern, that Trading Society; but I have a lot of relations living on the Continent, because it's cheap and not so nasty as it looks, they say.

"I am sorry to own I began to worry them. This was already a fresh departure for me. I was not used to get things that way, you know. I always went my own road and on my own legs where I had a mind to go. I wouldn't have believed it of myself; but, then—you see—I felt somehow I must get there by hook or by crook. So I worried them. The men said, 'My dear fellow,' and did nothing. Then—would you believe it?—I tried the women. I, Charlie Marlow, set the women to work—to get a job. Heavens! Well, you see, the notion drove me. I had an aunt, a dear enthusiastic soul. She wrote: 'It will be delightful. I am ready to do anything, anything for you. It is a glorious idea. I know the wife of a very high personage in the Administration, and also a man who has lots of influence with,' etc. etc. She was determined to make no end of fuss to get me appointed skipper of a river steamboat, if such was my fancy.

"I got my appointment—of course; and I got it very quick. It appears the Company had received news that one of their captains had been killed in a scuffle with the natives. This was my chance, and it made me the more anxious to go. It was only months and months afterwards, when I made the attempt to recover what was left of the body, that I heard the original quarrel arose from a misunderstanding about some hens. Yes, two black hens. Fresleven—that was the fellow's name, a Dane—thought himself wronged somehow in the bargain, so he went ashore and started to hammer the chief of the village with a stick. Oh, it didn't surprise me in the least to hear this, and at the same time to be told that Fresleven was the gentlest, quietest creature that ever walked on two legs. No doubt he was; but he had been a couple of years already out there engaged in the noble cause, you know, and he probably felt the need at last of asserting his self-respect in some way. Therefore he whacked the old nigger mercilessly, while a big crowd of his people watched him, thunderstruck, till some man—I was told the chief's son—in desperation at hearing the old chap yell, made a tentative jab with a spear at the white man—and of course it went quite easy between the shoulder-blades. Then the whole population cleared into the forest, expecting all kinds of calamities to happen, while, on the other hand, the steamer Fresleven commanded left also in a bad panic, in charge of the engineer, I believe. Afterwards nobody seemed to trouble much about Fresleven's remains, till I got out and stepped into his shoes. I couldn't let it rest, though; but when an opportunity offered at last to meet my predecessor, the grass growing through his ribs was tall enough to hide his bones. They were all there. The supernatural being had not been touched after he fell. And the village was deserted, the huts gaped black, rotting, all askew within the fallen enclosures. A calamity had come to it, sure enough. The people had vanished. Mad terror had scattered them, men, women, and children, through the bush, and they had never returned. What became of the hens I don't know either. I should think the cause of progress got them, anyhow. However, through this glorious affair I got my appointment, before I had fairly begun to hope for it.

"I flew around like mad to get ready, and before forty-eight hours I was crossing the Channel to show myself to my employers, and sign the contract. In a very few hours I arrived in a city that always makes me think of a whited sepulchre. Prejudice no doubt. I had no difficulty in finding the Company's offices. It was the biggest thing in the town, and everybody I met was full of it. They were going to run an oversea empire, and make no end of coin by trade.

"A narrow and deserted street in deep shadow, high houses, innumerable windows with venetian blinds, a dead silence, grass sprouting between the stones, imposing carriage archways right and left, immense double doors standing ponderously ajar. I slipped through one of these cracks, went up a swept and ungarnished staircase, as arid as a desert, and opened the first door I came to. Two women, one fat and the other slim, sat on straw-bottomed chairs, knitting black wool. The slim one got up and walked straight at me—still knitting with downcast eyes—and only just as I began to think of getting out of her way, as you would for a somnambulist, stood still, and looked up. Her dress was as plain as an umbrella-cover, and she turned round without a word and preceded me into a waiting-room. I gave my name, and looked about. Deal table in the middle, plain chairs all round the walls, on one end a large shining map, marked with all the colours of a rainbow. There was a vast amount of red—good to see at any time, because one knows that some real work is done in there, a deuce of a lot of blue, a little green, smears of orange, and, on the East Coast, a purple patch, to show where the jolly pioneers of progress drink the jolly lager-beer. However, I wasn't going into any of these. I was going into the yellow. Dead in the centre. And the river was there—fascinating—deadly—like a snake. Ough! A door opened, a white-haired secretarial head, but wearing a compassionate expression, appeared, and a skinny forefinger beckoned me into the sanctuary. Its light was dim, and a heavy writing-desk squatted in the middle. From behind that structure came out an impression of pale plumpness in a frock-coat. The great man himself. He was five feet six, I should judge, and had his grip on the handle-end of ever so many millions. He shook hands, I fancy, murmured vaguely, was satisfied with my French. *Bon voyage.*

"In about forty-five seconds I found myself again in the waiting-room with the compassionate secretary, who, full of desolation and sympathy, made me sign some document. I believe I undertook amongst other things not to disclose any trade secrets. Well, I am not going to.

"I began to feel slightly uneasy. You know I am not used to such ceremonies, and there was something ominous in the atmosphere. It was just as though I had been let into some conspiracy—I don't know—something not quite right; and I was glad to get out. In the outer room the two women knitted black wool feverishly. People were arriving, and the younger one was walking back and forth introducing them. The old one sat on her chair. Her flat cloth slippers were propped up on a foot-warmer, and a cat reposed on her lap. She wore a starched white affair on her head, had a wart on one cheek, and silver-rimmed spectacles hung on the tip of her nose. She glanced at me above the glasses. The swift and indifferent placidity of that look troubled me. Two youths with foolish and cheery countenances were being piloted over, and she threw at them the same quick glance of unconcerned wisdom. She seemed to know all about them and about me too. An eerie feeling came over me. She seemed uncanny and fateful. Often far away there I thought of these two, guarding the door of Darkness, knitting black wool as for a warm pall, one introducing, introducing continuously to the unknown, the other scrutinising the cheery and foolish faces with unconcerned old eyes. *Ave!* Old knitter of black wool. *Morituri te salutant.* Not many of those she looked at ever saw her again—not half, by a long way.

"There was yet a visit to the doctor. 'A simple formality,' assured me the secretary, with an air of taking an immense part in all my sorrows. Accordingly a young chap wearing his hat over the left eyebrow, some clerk I suppose—there must have been clerks in the business, though the house was as still as a house in a city of the dead—came from somewhere upstairs, and led me forth. He was shabby and careless, with ink-stains on the sleeves of his jacket, and his cravat was large and billowy, under a chin shaped like the toe of an old boot. It was a little too early for the doctor, so I proposed a drink, and thereupon he developed a vein of joviality. As we sat over our vermouths he glorified the Company's business, and by and by I expressed casually my surprise at him not going out there. He became very cool and collected all at once. 'I am not such a fool as I look, quoth Plato to his disciples,' he said sententiously, emptied his glass with great resolution, and we rose.

"The old doctor felt my pulse, evidently thinking of something else the while. 'Good, good for there,' he mumbled, and then with a certain eagerness asked me whether I would let him measure my head. Rather surprised, I said Yes, when he produced a thing like callipers and got the dimensions back and front and every way, taking notes carefully. He was an unshaven little man in a thread-bare coat like a gaberdine, with his feet in slippers, and I thought him a harmless fool. 'I always ask leave, in the interests of science, to measure the crania of those going out there,' he said. 'And when they come back too?' I asked. 'Oh, I never see them,' he remarked; 'and, moreover, the changes take place inside, you know.' He smiled, as if at some quiet joke. 'So you are going out there. Famous. Interesting too.' He gave me a searching glance, and made another note. 'Ever any madness in your family?' he asked, in a matter-of-fact tone. I felt very annoyed. 'Is that question in the interests of science too?' 'It would be,' he said, without taking notice of my irritation, 'interesting for science to watch the mental changes of individuals, on the spot, but ...' 'Are you an alienist?' I interrupted. 'Every doctor should be—a little,' answered that original imperturbably. 'I have a little theory which you Messieurs who go out there must help me to prove. This is my share in the advantages my country shall reap from the possession of such a magnificent dependency. The mere wealth I leave to others. Pardon my questions, but you are the first Englishman coming under my observation ...' I hastened to assure him I was not in the least typical. 'If I were,' said I, 'I wouldn't be talking like this with you.' 'What you say is rather profound, and probably erroneous,' he said, with a laugh. 'Avoid irritation more than exposure to the sun. Adieu. How do you English say, eh? Good-bye. Ah! Good-bye. Adieu. In the tropics one must before everything keep calm.' ... He lifted a warning forefinger. ... '*Du calme, du calme. Adieu.*'

"One thing more remained to do—say good-bye to my excellent aunt. I found her triumphant. I had a cup of tea—the last decent cup of tea for many days—and in a room that most soothingly looked just as you would expect a lady's drawing-room to look, we had a long quiet chat by the fireside. In the course of these confidences it became quite plain to me I had been represented to the wife of the high dignitary, and goodness knows to how many more people besides, as an exceptional and gifted creature—a piece of good fortune for the Company—a man you don't get hold of every day. Good Heavens! and I was going to take charge of a two-penny-half-penny river-steamboat with a penny whistle attached! It appeared, however, I was also one of the Workers, with a capital—you know. Something like an emissary of light, something like a lower sort of apostle. There had been a lot of such rot let loose in print and talk just about that time, and the excellent woman, living right in the rush of all that humbug, got carried off her feet. She talked about 'weaning those ignorant millions from their horrid ways,' till, upon my word, she made me quite uncomfortable. I ventured to hint that the Company was run for profit.

"'You forget, dear Charlie, that the labourer is worthy of his hire,' she said brightly. It's queer how out of touch with truth women are. They live in a world of their own, and there had never been anything like it, and never can be. It is too beautiful altogether, and if they were to set it up it would go to pieces before the first sunset. Some confounded fact we men have been living contentedly with ever since the day of creation would start up and knock the whole thing over.

"After this I got embraced, told to wear flannel, be sure to write often, and so on—and I left. In the street—I don't know why—a queer feeling came to me that I was an impostor. Odd thing that I, who used to clear out for any part of the world at twenty-four hours' notice, with less thought than most men give to the crossing of a street, had a moment—I won't say of hesitation, but of startled pause, before this commonplace affair. The best way I can explain it to you is by saying that, for a second or two, I felt as though, instead of going to the centre of a continent, I were about to set off for the centre of the earth.

"I left in a French steamer, and she called in every blamed port they have out there, for, as far as I could see, the sole purpose of landing soldiers and custom-house officers. I watched the coast. Watching a coast as it slips by the ship is like thinking about an enigma. There it is before you—smiling, frowning, inviting, grand, mean, insipid, or savage, and always mute with an air of whispering, Come and find out. This one was almost featureless, as if still in the making, with an aspect of monotonous grimness. The edge of a colossal jungle, so dark green as to be almost black, fringed with white surf, ran straight, like a ruled line, far, far away along a blue sea whose glitter was blurred by a creeping mist. The sun was fierce, the land seemed to glisten and drip with steam. Here and there greyish-whitish specks showed up clustered inside the white surf, with a flag flying above them perhaps—settlements some centuries old, and still no bigger than pin-heads on the untouched expanse of their background. We pounded along, stopped, landed soldiers; went on, landed custom-house clerks to levy toll in what looked like a God-forsaken wilderness, with a tin shed and a flag-pole lost in it; landed more soldiers—to take care of the custom-house clerks presumably. Some, I heard, got drowned in the surf; but whether they did or not, nobody seemed particularly to care. They were just flung out there, and on we went. Every day the coast looked the same, as though we had not moved; but we passed various places—trading places—with names like Gran' Bassam, Little Popo; names that seemed to belong to some sordid farce acted in front of a sinister back-cloth. The idleness of a passenger, my isolation amongst all these men with whom I had no point of contact, the oily and languid sea, the uniform sombreness of the coast, seemed to keep me away from the truth of things, within the toil of a mournful and senseless delusion. The voice of the surf heard now and then was a positive pleasure, like the speech of a brother. It was something natural, that had its reason, that had a meaning. Now and then a boat from the shore gave one a momentary contact with reality. It was paddled by black fellows. You could see from afar the white of their eyeballs glistening. They shouted, sang; their bodies streamed with perspiration; they had faces like grotesque masks—these chaps; but they had bone, muscle, a wild vitality, an intense energy of movement, that was as natural and true as the surf along their coast. They wanted no excuse for being there. They were a great comfort to look at. For a time I would feel I belonged still to a world of straightforward facts; but the feeling would not last long. Something would turn up to scare it away. Once, I remember, we came upon a man-of-war anchored off the coast. There wasn't even a shed there, and she was shelling the bush. It appears the French had one of their wars going on thereabouts. Her ensign dropped limp like a rag; the muzzles of the long six-inch guns stuck out all over the low hull; the greasy, slimy swell swung her up lazily and let her down, swaying her thin masts. In the empty immensity of earth, sky, and water, there she was, incomprehensible, firing into a continent. Pop, would go one of the six-inch guns; a small flame would dart and vanish, a little white smoke would disappear, a tiny projectile would give a feeble screech—and nothing happened. Nothing could happen. There was a touch of insanity in the proceeding, a sense of lugubrious drollery in the sight; and it was not dissipated by somebody on board assuring me earnestly there was a camp of natives—he called them enemies!—hidden out of sight somewhere.

"We gave her her letters (I heard the men in that lonely ship were dying of fever at the rate of three a day) and went on. We called at some more places with farcical names, where the merry dance of death and trade goes on in a still and earthy atmosphere as of an overheated catacomb; all along the formless coast bordered by dangerous surf, as if Nature herself had tried to ward off intruders; in and out of rivers, streams of death in life, whose banks were rotting into mud, whose waters, thickened into slime, invaded the contorted mangroves, that seemed to writhe at us in the extremity of an impotent despair. Nowhere did we stop long enough to get a particularised impression, but the general sense of vague and oppressive wonder grew upon me. It was like a weary pilgrimage amongst hints for nightmares.

"It was upward of thirty days before I saw the mouth of the big river. We anchored off the seat of the government. But my work would not begin till some two hundred miles farther on. So as soon as I could I made a start for a place thirty miles higher up.

"I had my passage on a little sea-going steamer. Her captain was a Swede, and knowing me for a seaman, invited me on the bridge. He was a young man, lean, fair, and morose, with lanky hair and a shuffling gait. As we left the miserable little wharf, he tossed his head contemptuously at the shore. 'Been living there?' he asked. I said, 'Yes.' 'Fine lot these government chaps—are they not?' he went on, speaking English with great precision and considerable bitterness. 'It is funny what some people will do for a few francs a month. I wonder what becomes of that kind when it goes up country?' I said to him I expected to see that soon. 'So-o-o!' he exclaimed. He shuffled athwart, keeping one eye ahead vigilantly. 'Don't be too sure,' he continued. 'The other day I took up a man who hanged himself on the road. He was a Swede, too.' 'Hanged himself! Why, in God's name?' I cried. He kept on looking out watchfully. 'Who knows? The sun too much for him, or the country perhaps.'

"At last we opened a reach. A rocky cliff appeared, mounds of turned-up earth by the shore, houses on a hill, others with iron roofs, amongst a waste of excavations, or hanging to the declivity. A continuous noise of the rapids above hovered over this scene of inhabited devastation. A lot of people, mostly black and naked, moved about like ants. A jetty projected into the river. A blinding sunlight drowned all this at times in a sudden recrudescence of glare. 'There's your Company's station,' said the Swede, pointing to three wooden barrack-like structures on the rocky slope. 'I will send your things up. Four boxes did you say? So. Farewell.'

"I came upon a boiler wallowing in the grass, then found a path leading up the hill. It turned aside for the boulders, and also for an undersized railway truck lying there on its back with its wheels in the air. One was off. The thing looked as dead as the carcass of some animal. I came upon more pieces of decaying machinery, a stack of rusty rails. To the left a clump of trees made a shady spot, where dark things seemed to stir feebly. I blinked, the path was steep. A horn tooted to the right, and I saw the black people run. A heavy and dull detonation shook the ground, a puff of smoke came out of the cliff, and that was all. No change appeared on the face of the rock. They were building a railway. The cliff was not in the way or anything; but this objectless blasting was all the work going on.

"A slight clinking behind me made me turn my head. Six black men advanced in a file, toiling up the path. They walked erect and slow, balancing small baskets full of earth on their heads, and the clink kept time with their footsteps. Black rags were wound round their loins, and the short ends behind waggled to and fro like tails. I could see every rib, the joints of their limbs were like knots in a rope; each had an iron collar on his neck, and all were connected together with a chain whose bights swung between them, rhythmically clinking. Another report from the cliff made me think suddenly of that ship of war I had seen firing into a continent. It was the same kind of ominous voice; but these men could by no stretch of imagination be called enemies. They were called criminals, and the outraged law, like the bursting shells, had come to them, an insoluble mystery from the sea. All their meagre breasts panted together, the violently dilated nostrils quivered, the eyes stared stonily uphill. They passed me within six inches, without a glance, with that complete, deathlike indifference of unhappy savages. Behind this raw matter one of the reclaimed, the product of the new forces at work, strolled despondently, carrying a rifle by its middle. He had a uniform jacket with one button off, and seeing a white man on the path, hoisted his weapon to his shoulder with alacrity. This was simple prudence, white men being so much alike at a distance that he could not tell who I might be. He was speedily reassured, and with a large, white, rascally grin, and a glance at his charge, seemed to take me into partnership in his exalted trust. After all, I also was a part of the great cause of these high and just proceedings.

"Instead of going up, I turned and descended to the left. My idea was to let that chain-gang get out of sight before I climbed the hill. You know I am not particularly tender; I've had to strike and to fend off. I've had to resist and to attack sometimes—that's only one way of resisting—without counting the exact cost, according to the demands of such sort of life as I had blundered into—I've seen the devil of violence, and the devil of greed, and the devil of hot desire; but, by all the stars! these were strong, lusty, red-eyed devils, that swayed and drove men—men, I tell you. But as I stood on this hillside, I foresaw that in the blinding sunshine of that land I would become acquainted with a flabby, pretending, weak-eyed devil of a rapacious and pitiless folly. How insidious he could be, too, I was only to find out several months later and a thousand miles farther. For a moment I stood appalled, as though by a warning. Finally I descended the hill, obliquely, towards the trees I had seen.

"I avoided a vast artificial hole somebody had been digging on the slope, the purpose of which I found it impossible to divine. It wasn't a quarry or a sandpit, anyhow. It was just a hole. It might have been connected with the philanthropic desire of giving the criminals something to do. I don't know. Then I nearly fell into a very narrow ravine, almost no more than a scar in the hillside. I discovered that a lot of imported drainage-pipes for the settlement had been tumbled in there. There wasn't one that was not broken. It was a wanton smash-up. At last I got under the trees. My purpose was to stroll into the shade for a moment; but no sooner within than it seemed to me I had stepped into the gloomy circle of some Inferno. The rapids were near, and an uninterrupted, uniform, headlong, rushing noise filled the mournful stillness of the grove, where not a breath stirred, not a leaf moved, with a mysterious sound—as though the tearing pace of the launched earth had suddenly become audible.

"Black shapes crouched, lay, sat between the trees, leaning against the trunks, clinging to the earth, half coming out, half effaced within the dim light, in all the attitudes of pain, abandonment, and despair. Another mine on the cliff went off, followed by a slight shudder of the soil under my feet. The work was going on. The work! And this was the place where some of the helpers had withdrawn to die.

"They were dying slowly—it was very clear. They were not enemies, they were not criminals, they were nothing earthly now—nothing but black shadows of disease and starvation, lying confusedly in the greenish gloom. Brought from all the recesses of the coast in all the legality of time contracts, lost in uncongenial surroundings, fed on unfamiliar food, they sickened, became inefficient, and were then allowed to crawl away and rest. These moribund shapes were free as air—and nearly as thin. I began to distinguish the gleam of the eyes under the trees. Then, glancing down, I saw a face near my hand. The black bones reclined at full length with one shoulder against the tree, and slowly the eyelids rose and the sunken eyes looked up at me, enormous and vacant, a kind of blind, white flicker in the depths of the orbs, which died out slowly. The man seemed young—almost a boy—but you know with them it's hard to tell. I found nothing else to do but to offer him one of my good Swede's ship's biscuits I had in my pocket. The fingers closed slowly on it and held—there was no other movement and no other glance. He had tied a bit of white worsted round his neck—Why? Where did he get it? Was it a badge—an ornament—a charm—a propitiatory act? Was there any idea at all connected with it? It looked startling round his black neck, this bit of white thread from beyond the seas.

"Near the same tree two more bundles of acute angles sat with their legs drawn up. One, with his chin propped on his knees, stared at nothing, in an intolerable and appalling manner: his brother phantom rested its forehead, as if overcome with a great weariness; and all about others were scattered in every pose of contorted collapse, as in some picture of a massacre or a pestilence. While I stood horror-struck, one of these creatures rose to his hands and knees, and went off on all-fours towards the river to drink. He lapped out of his hand, then sat up in the sunlight, crossing his shins in front of him, and after a time let his woolly head fall on his breastbone.

"I didn't want any more loitering in the shade, and I made haste towards the station. When near the buildings I met a white man, in such an unexpected elegance of get-up that in the first moment I took him for a sort of vision. I saw a high starched collar, white cuffs, a light alpaca jacket, snowy trousers, a clean necktie, and varnished boots. No hat. Hair parted, brushed, oiled, under a green-lined parasol held in a big white hand. He was amazing, and had a pen-holder behind his ear.

"I shook hands with this miracle, and I learned he was the Company's chief accountant, and that all the book-keeping was done at this station. He had come out for a moment, he said, 'to get a breath of fresh air.' The expression sounded wonderfully odd, with its suggestion of sedentary desk-life. I wouldn't have mentioned the fellow to you at all, only it was from his lips that I first heard the name of the man who is so indissolubly connected with the memories of that time. Moreover, I respected the fellow. Yes; I respected his collars, his vast cuffs, his brushed hair. His appearance was certainly that of a hairdresser's dummy; but in the great demoralisation of the land he kept up his appearance. That's backbone. His starched collars and got-up shirt-fronts were achievements of character. He had been out nearly three years; and, later, I could not help asking him how he managed to sport such linen. He had just the faintest blush, and said modestly, 'I've been teaching one of the native women about the station. It was difficult. She had a distaste for the work.' Thus this man had verily accomplished something. And he was devoted to his books, which were in apple-pie order.

"Everything else in the station was in a muddle,—heads, things, buildings. Strings of dusty niggers with splay feet arrived and departed; a stream of manufactured goods, rubbishy cottons, beads, and brass-wire set into the depths of darkness, and in return came a precious trickle of ivory.

"I had to wait in the station for ten days—an eternity. I lived in a hut in the yard, but to be out of the chaos I would sometimes get into the accountant's office. It was built of horizontal planks, and so badly put together that, as he bent over his high desk, he was barred from neck to heels with narrow strips of sunlight. There was no need to open the big shutter to see. It was hot there too; big flies buzzed fiendishly, and did not sting, but stabbed. I sat generally on the floor, while, of faultless appearance (and even slightly scented), perching on a high stool, he wrote, he wrote. Sometimes he stood up for exercise. When a truckle-bed with a sick man (some invalided agent from up-country) was put in there, he exhibited a gentle annoyance. 'The groans of this sick person,' he said, 'distract my attention. And without that it is extremely difficult to guard against clerical errors in this climate.'

"One day he remarked, without lifting his head, 'In the interior you will no doubt meet Mr. Kurtz.' On my asking who Mr. Kurtz was, he said he was a first-class agent; and seeing my disappointment at this information, he added slowly, laying down his pen, 'He is a very remarkable person.' Further questions elicited from him that Mr. Kurtz was at present in charge of a trading-post, a very important one, in the true ivory-country, at 'the very bottom of there. Sends in as much ivory as all the others put together ...' He began to write again. The sick man was too ill to groan. The flies buzzed in a great peace.

"Suddenly there was a growing murmur of voices and a great tramping of feet. A caravan had come in. A violent babble of uncouth sounds burst out on the other side of the planks. All the carriers were speaking together, and in the midst of the uproar the lamentable voice of the chief agent was heard 'giving it up' tearfully for the twentieth time that day. ... He rose slowly. 'What a frightful row,' he said. He crossed the room gently to look at the sick man, and returning, said to me, 'He does not hear.' 'What! Dead?' I asked, startled. 'No, not yet,' he answered, with great composure. Then, alluding with a toss of the head to the tumult in the station-yard, 'When one has got to make correct entries, one comes to hate those savages—hate them to the death.' He remained thoughtful for a moment. 'When you see Mr. Kurtz,' he went on, 'tell him from me that everything here'—he glanced at the desk—'is very satisfactory. I don't like to write to him—with those messengers of ours you never know who may get hold of your letter—at that Central Station.' He stared at me for a moment with his mild, bulging eyes. 'Oh, he will go far, very far,' he began again. 'He will be a somebody in the Administration before long. They, above—the Council in Europe, you know—mean him to be.'

"He turned to his work. The noise outside had ceased, and presently in going out I stopped at the door. In the steady buzz of flies the homeward-bound agent was lying flushed and insensible; the other, bent over his books, was making correct entries of perfectly correct transactions; and fifty feet below the doorstep I could see the still tree-tops of the grove of death.

"Next day I left that station at last, with a caravan of sixty men, for a two-hundred-mile tramp.

"No use telling you much about that. Paths, paths, everywhere; a stamped-in network of paths spreading over the empty land, through long grass, through burnt grass, through thickets, down and up chilly ravines, up and down stony hills ablaze with heat; and a solitude, a solitude, nobody, not a hut. The population had cleared out a long time ago. Well, if a lot of mysterious niggers armed with all kinds of fearful weapons suddenly took to travelling on the road between Deal and Gravesend, catching the yokels right and left to carry heavy loads for them, I fancy every farm and cottage thereabouts would get empty very soon. Only here the dwellings were gone too. Still, I passed through several abandoned villages. There's something pathetically childish in the ruins of grass walls. Day after day, with the stamp and shuffle of sixty pair of bare feet behind me, each pair under a 60-lb. load. Camp, cook, sleep; strike camp, march. Now and then a carrier dead in harness, at rest in the long grass near the path, with an empty water-gourd and his long staff lying by his side. A great silence around and above. Perhaps on some quiet night the tremor of far-off drums, sinking, swelling, a tremor vast, faint; a sound weird, appealing, suggestive, and wild—and perhaps with as profound a meaning as the sound of bells in a Christian country. Once a white man in an unbuttoned uniform, camping on the path with an armed escort of lank Zanzibaris, very hospitable and festive—not to say drunk. Was looking after the upkeep of the road, he declared. Can't say I saw any road or any upkeep, unless the body of a middle-aged negro, with a bullet-hole in the forehead, upon which I absolutely stumbled three miles farther on, may be considered as a permanent improvement. I had a white companion too, not a bad chap, but rather too fleshy and with the exasperating habit of fainting on the hot hillsides, miles away from the least bit of shade and water. Annoying, you know, to hold your own coat like a parasol over a man's head while he is coming to. I couldn't help asking him once what he meant by coming there at all. 'To make money, of course. What do you think?' he said scornfully. Then he got fever, and had to be carried in a hammock slung under a pole. As he weighed sixteen stone I had no end of rows with the carriers. They jibbed, ran away, sneaked off with their loads in the night—quite a mutiny. So, one evening, I made a speech in English with gestures, not one of which was lost to the sixty pairs of eyes before me, and the next morning I started the hammock off in front all right. An hour afterwards I came upon the whole concern wrecked in a bush—man, hammock, groans, blankets, horrors. The heavy pole had skinned his poor nose. He was very anxious for me to kill somebody, but there wasn't the shadow of a carrier near. I remembered the old doctor—'It would be interesting for science to watch the mental changes of individuals, on the spot.' I felt I was becoming scientifically interesting. However, all that is to no purpose. On the fifteenth day I came in sight of the big river again, and hobbled into the Central Station. It was on a back water surrounded by scrub and forest, with a pretty border of smelly mud on one side, and on the three others enclosed by a crazy fence of rushes. A neglected gap was all the gate it had, and the first glance at the place was enough to let you see the flabby devil was running that show. White men with long staves in their hands appeared languidly from amongst the buildings, strolling up to take a look at me, and then retired out of sight somewhere. One of them, a stout, excitable chap with black moustaches, informed me with great volubility and many digressions, as soon as I told him who I was, that my steamer was at the bottom of the river. I was thunderstruck. What, how, why? Oh, it was 'all right.' The 'manager himself' was there. All quite correct. 'Everybody had behaved splendidly! splendidly!'—'You must,' he said in agitation, 'go and see the general manager at once. He is waiting.'

"I did not see the real significance of that wreck at once. I fancy I see it now, but I am not sure—not at all. Certainly the affair was too stupid—when I think of it—to be altogether natural. Still ... But at the moment it presented itself simply as a confounded nuisance. The steamer was sunk. They had started two days before in a sudden hurry up the river with the manager on board, in charge of some volunteer skipper, and before they had been out three hours they tore the bottom out of her on stones, and she sank near the south bank. I asked myself what I was to do there, now my boat was lost. As a matter of fact, I had plenty to do in fishing my command out of the river. I had to set about it the very next day. That, and the repairs when I brought the pieces to the station, took some months.

"My first interview with the manager was curious. He did not ask me to sit down after my twenty-mile walk that morning. He was commonplace in complexion, in feature, in manners, and in voice. He was of middle size and of ordinary build. His eyes, of the usual blue, were perhaps remarkably cold, and he certainly could make his glance fall on one as trenchant and heavy as an axe. But even at these times the rest of his person seemed to disclaim the intention. Otherwise there was only an indefinable, faint expression of his lips, something stealthy—a smile—not a smile—I remember it, but I can't explain. It was unconscious, this smile was, though just after he had said something it got intensified for an instant. It came at the end of his speeches like a seal applied on the words to make the meaning of the commonest phrase appear absolutely inscrutable. He was a common trader, from his youth up employed in these parts—nothing more. He was obeyed, yet he inspired neither love nor fear, nor even respect. He inspired uneasiness. That was it! Uneasiness. Not a definite mistrust—just uneasiness—nothing more. You have no idea how effective such a ... a ... faculty can be. He had no genius for organising, for initiative, or for order even. That was evident in such things as the deplorable state of the station. He had no learning, and no intelligence. His position had come to him—why? Perhaps because he was never ill ... He had served three terms of three years out there ... Because triumphant health in the general rout of constitutions is a kind of power in itself. When he went home on leave he rioted on a large scale—pompously. Jack ashore—with a difference—in externals only. This one could gather from his casual talk. He originated nothing, he could keep the routine going—that's all. But he was great. He was great by this little thing that it was impossible to tell what could control such a man. He never gave that secret away. Perhaps there was nothing within him. Such a suspicion made one pause—for out there there were no external checks. Once when various tropical diseases had laid low almost every 'agent' in the station, he was heard to say, 'Men who come out here should have no entrails.' He sealed the utterance with that smile of his, as though it had been a door opening into a darkness he had in his keeping. You fancied you had seen things—but the seal was on. When annoyed at meal-times by the constant quarrels of the white men about precedence, he ordered an immense round table to be made, for which a special house had to be built. This was the station's mess-room. Where he sat was the first place—the rest were nowhere. One felt this to be his unalterable conviction. He was neither civil or uncivil. He was quiet. He allowed his 'boy'—an overfed young negro from the coast—to treat the white men, under his very eyes, with provoking insolence.

"He began to speak as soon as he saw me. I had been very long on the road. He could not wait. Had to start without me. The up-river stations had to be relieved. There had been so many delays already that he did not know who was dead and who was alive, and how they got on—and so on, and so on. He paid no attention to my explanations, and, playing with a stick of sealing-wax, repeated several times that the situation was 'very grave, very grave.' There were rumours that a very important station was in jeopardy, and its chief, Mr. Kurtz, was ill. Hoped it was not true. Mr. Kurtz was ... I felt weary and irritable. Hang Kurtz, I thought. I interrupted him by saying I had heard of Mr. Kurtz on the coast. 'Ah! So they talk of him down there,' he murmured to himself. Then he began again, assuring me Mr. Kurtz was the best agent he had, an exceptional man, of the greatest importance to the Company; therefore I could understand his anxiety. He was, he said, 'very, very uneasy.' Certainly he fidgeted on his chair a good deal, exclaimed, 'Ah, Mr. Kurtz!' broke the stick of sealing-wax and seemed dumbfounded by the accident. Next thing he wanted to know 'how long it would take to' ... I interrupted him again. Being hungry, you know, and kept on my feet too, I was getting savage. 'How can I tell?' I said. 'I haven't even seen the wreck yet—some months, no doubt.' All this talk seemed to me so futile. 'Some months,' he said. 'Well, let us say three months before we can make a start. Yes. That ought to do the affair.' I flung out of his hut (he lived all alone in a clay hut with a sort of verandah) muttering to myself my opinion of him. He was a chattering idiot. Afterwards I took it back when it was borne in upon me startlingly with what extreme nicety he had estimated the time requisite for the 'affair.'

"I went to work the next day, turning, so to speak, my back on that station. In that way only it seemed to me I could keep my hold on the redeeming facts of life. Still, one must look about sometimes; and then I saw this station, these men strolling aimlessly about in the sunshine of the yard. I asked myself sometimes what it all meant. They wandered here and there with their absurd long staves in their hands, like a lot of faithless pilgrims bewitched inside a rotten fence. The word 'ivory' rang in the air, was whispered, was sighed. You would think they were praying to it. A taint of imbecile rapacity blew through it all, like a whiff from some corpse. By Jove! I've never seen anything so unreal in my life. And outside, the silent wilderness surrounding this cleared speck on the earth struck me as something great and invincible, like evil or truth, waiting patiently for the passing away of this fantastic invasion.

"Oh, those months! Well, never mind. Various things happened. One evening a grass shed full of calico, cotton prints, beads, and I don't know what else, burst into a blaze so suddenly that you would have thought the earth had opened to let an avenging fire consume all that trash. I was smoking my pipe quietly by my dismantled steamer, and saw them all cutting capers in the light, with their arms lifted high, when the stout man with moustaches came tearing down to the river, a tin pail in his hand, assured me that everybody was 'behaving splendidly, splendidly,' dipped about a quart of water and tore back again. I noticed there was a hole in the bottom of his pail.

"I strolled up. There was no hurry. You see the thing had gone off like a box of matches. It had been hopeless from the very first. The flame had leaped high, driven everybody back, lighted up everything—and collapsed. The shed was already a heap of embers glowing fiercely. A nigger was being beaten near by. They said he had caused the fire in some way; be that as it may, he was screeching most horribly. I saw him, later, for several days, sitting in a bit of shade looking very sick and trying to recover himself: afterwards he arose and went out—and the wilderness without a sound took him into its bosom again. As I approached the glow from the dark I found myself at the back of two men, talking. I heard the name of Kurtz pronounced, then the words, 'take advantage of this unfortunate accident.' One of the men was the manager. I wished him a good evening. 'Did you ever see anything like it—eh? it is incredible,' he said, and walked off. The other man remained. He was a first-class agent, young, gentlemanly, a bit reserved, with a forked little beard and a hooked nose. He was stand-offish with the other agents, and they on their side said he was the manager's spy upon them. As to me, I had hardly ever spoken to him before. We got into talk, and by and by we strolled away from the hissing ruins. Then he asked me to his room, which was in the main building of the station. He struck a match, and I perceived that this young aristocrat had not only a silver-mounted dressing-case but also a whole candle all to himself. Just at that time the manager was the only man supposed to have any right to candles. Native mats covered the clay walls; a collection of spears, assegais, shields, knives, was hung up in trophies. The business entrusted to this fellow was the making of bricks—so I had been informed; but there wasn't a fragment of a brick anywhere in the station, and he had been there more than a year—waiting. It seems he could not make bricks without something, I don't know what—straw maybe. Anyway, it could not be found there, and as it was not likely to be sent from Europe, it did not appear clear to me what he was waiting for. An act of special creation perhaps. However, they were all waiting—all the sixteen or twenty pilgrims of them—for something; and upon my word it did not seem an uncongenial occupation, from the way they took it, though the only thing that ever came to them was disease—as far as I could see. They beguiled the time by backbiting and intriguing against each other in a foolish kind of way. There was an air of plotting about that station, but nothing came of it, of course. It was as unreal as everything else—as the philanthropic pretence of the whole concern, as their talk, as their government, as their show of work. The only real feeling was a desire to get appointed to a trading-post where ivory was to be had, so that they could earn percentages. They intrigued and slandered and hated each other only on that account—but as to effectually lifting a little finger—oh no. By Heavens! there is something after all in the world allowing one man to steal a horse while another must not look at a halter. Steal a horse straight out. Very well. He has done it. Perhaps he can ride. But there is a way of looking at a halter that would provoke the most charitable of saints into a kick.

"I had no idea why he wanted to be sociable, but as we chatted in there it suddenly occurred to me the fellow was trying to get at something—in fact, pumping me. He alluded constantly to Europe, to the people I was supposed to know there—putting leading questions as to my acquaintances in the sepulchral city, and so on. His little eyes glittered like mica discs—with curiosity—though he tried to keep up a bit of superciliousness. At first I was astonished, but very soon I became awfully curious to see what he would find out from me. I couldn't possibly imagine what I had in me to make it worth his while. It was very pretty to see how he baffled himself, for in truth my body was full only of chills, and my head had nothing in it but that wretched steamboat business. It was evident he took me for a perfectly shameless prevaricator. At last he got angry, and, to conceal a movement of furious annoyance, he yawned. I rose. Then I noticed a small sketch in oils, on a panel, representing a woman, draped and blindfolded, carrying a lighted torch. The background was sombre—almost black. The movement of the woman was stately, and the effect of the torchlight on the face was sinister.

"It arrested me, and he stood by civilly, holding an empty half-pint champagne bottle (medical comforts) with the candle stuck in it. To my question he said Mr. Kurtz had painted this—in this very station more than a year ago—while waiting for means to go to his trading-post. 'Tell me, pray,' said I, 'who is this Mr. Kurtz?'

"'The chief of the Inner Station,' he answered in a short tone, looking away. 'Much obliged,' I said, laughing. 'And you are the brickmaker of the Central Station. Every one knows that.' He was silent for a while. 'He is a prodigy,' he said at last. 'He is an emissary of pity, and science, and progress, and devil knows what else. We want,' he began to declaim suddenly, 'for the guidance of the cause entrusted to us by Europe, so to speak, higher intelligence, wide sympathies, a singleness of purpose.' 'Who says that?' I asked. 'Lots of them,' he replied. 'Some even write that; and so *he* comes here, a special being, as you ought to know.' 'Why ought I to know?' I interrupted, really surprised. He paid no attention. 'Yes. To-day he is chief of the best station, next year he will be assistant-manager, two years more and ... but I daresay you know what he will be in two years' time. You are of the new gang—the gang of virtue. The same people who sent him specially also recommended you. Oh, don't say no. I've my own eyes to trust.' Light dawned upon me. My dear aunt's influential acquaintances were producing an unexpected effect upon that young man. I nearly burst into a laugh. 'Do you read the Company's confidential correspondence?' I asked. He hadn't a word to say. It was great fun. 'When Mr. Kurtz,' I continued severely, 'is General Manager, you won't have the opportunity.'

"He blew the candle out suddenly, and we went outside. The moon had risen. Black figures strolled about listlessly, pouring water on the glow, whence proceeded a sound of hissing; steam ascended in the moonlight; the beaten nigger groaned somewhere. 'What a row the brute makes!' said the indefatigable man with the moustaches, appearing near us. 'Serve him right. Transgression—punishment—bang! Pitiless, pitiless. That's the only way. This will prevent all conflagrations for the future. I was just telling the manager ...' He noticed my companion, and became crestfallen all at once. 'Not in bed yet,' he said, with a kind of servile heartiness; 'it's so natural. Ha! Danger—agitation.' He vanished. I went on to the river-side, and the other followed me. I heard a scathing murmur at my ear, 'Heaps of muffs—go to.' The pilgrims could be seen in knots gesticulating, discussing. Several had still their staves in their hands. I verily believe they took these sticks to bed with them. Beyond the fence the forest stood up spectrally in the moonlight, and through the dim stir, through the faint sounds of that lamentable courtyard, the silence of the land went home to one's very heart—its mystery, its greatness, the amazing reality of its concealed life. The hurt nigger moaned feebly somewhere near by, and then fetched a deep sigh that made me mend my pace away from there. I felt a hand introducing itself under my arm. 'My dear sir,' said the fellow, 'I don't want to be misunderstood, and especially by you, who will see Mr. Kurtz long before I can have that pleasure. I wouldn't like him to get a false idea of my disposition. ...'

"I let him run on, this papier-mâché Mephistopheles, and it seemed to me that if I tried I could poke my forefinger through him, and would find nothing inside but a little loose dirt, maybe. He, don't you see, had been planning to be assistant-manager by and by under the present man, and I could see that the coming of that Kurtz had upset them both not a little. He talked precipitately, and I did not try to stop him. I had my shoulders against the wreck of my steamer, hauled up on the slope like a carcass of some big river animal. The smell of mud, of primeval mud, by Jove! was in my nostrils, the high stillness of primeval forest was before my eyes; there were shiny patches on the black creek. The moon had spread over everything a thin layer of silver—over the rank grass, over the mud, upon the wall of matted vegetation standing higher than the wall of a temple, over the great river I could see through a sombre gap glittering, glittering, as it flowed broadly by without a murmur. All this was great, expectant, mute, while the man jabbered about himself. I wondered whether the stillness on the face of the immensity looking at us two were meant as an appeal or as a menace. What were we who had strayed in here? Could we handle that dumb thing, or would it handle us? I felt how big, how confoundedly big, was that thing that couldn't talk and perhaps was deaf as well. What was in there? I could see a little ivory coming out from there, and I had heard Mr. Kurtz was in there. I had heard enough about it too—God knows! Yet somehow it didn't bring any image with it—no more than if I had been told an angel or a fiend was in there. I believed it in the same way one of you might believe there are inhabitants in the planet Mars. I knew once a Scotch sailmaker who was certain, dead sure, there were people in Mars. If you asked him for some idea how they looked and behaved, he would get shy and mutter something about 'walking on all-fours.' If you as much as smiled, he would—though a man of sixty—offer to fight you. I would not have gone so far as to fight for Kurtz, but I went for him near enough to a lie. You know I hate, detest, and can't bear a lie, not because I am straighter than the rest of us, but simply because it appals me. There is a taint of death, a flavour of mortality in lies—which is exactly what I hate and detest in the world—what I want to forget. It makes me miserable and sick, like biting something rotten would do. Temperament, I suppose. Well, I went near enough to it by letting the young fool there believe anything he liked to imagine as to my influence in Europe. I became in an instant as much of a pretence as the rest of the bewitched pilgrims. This simply because I had a notion it somehow would be of help to that Kurtz whom at the time I did not see—you understand. He was just a word for me. I did not see the man in the name any more than you do. Do you see him? Do you see the story? Do you see anything? It seems to me I am trying to tell you a dream—making a vain attempt, because no relation of a dream can convey the dream-sensation, that commingling of absurdity, surprise, and bewilderment in a tremor of struggling revolt, that notion of being captured by the incredible which is of the very essence of dreams. ..."

He was silent for a while.

"... No, it is impossible; it is impossible to convey the life-sensation of any given epoch of one's existence—that which makes its truth, its meaning—its subtle and penetrating essence. It is impossible. We live, as we dream—alone. ..."

He paused again as if reflecting, then added:

"Of course in this you fellows see more than I could then. You see me, whom you know. ..."

It had become so pitch dark that we listeners could hardly see one another. For a long time already he, sitting apart, had been no more to us than a voice. There was not a word from anybody. The others might have been asleep, but I was awake. I listened, I listened on the watch for the sentence, for the word, that would give me the clue to the faint uneasiness inspired by this narrative that seemed to shape itself without human lips in the heavy night-air of the river.

"... Yes—I let him run on," Marlow began again, "and think what he pleased about the powers that were behind me. I did! And there was nothing behind me! There was nothing but that wretched, old, mangled steamboat I was leaning against, while he talked fluently about 'the necessity for every man to get on.' 'And when one comes out here, you conceive, it is not to gaze at the moon.' Mr. Kurtz was a 'universal genius,' but even a genius would find it easier to work with 'adequate tools—intelligent men.' He did not make bricks—why, there was a physical impossibility in the way—as I was well aware; and if he did secretarial work for the manager, it was because 'no sensible man rejects wantonly the confidence of his superiors.' Did I see it? I saw it. What more did I want? What I really wanted was rivets, by Heaven! Rivets. To get on with the work—to stop the hole. Rivets I wanted. There were cases of them down at the coast—cases—piled up—burst—split! You kicked a loose rivet at every second step in that station yard on the hillside. Rivets had rolled into the grove of death. You could fill your pockets with rivets for the trouble of stooping down—and there wasn't one rivet to be found where it was wanted. We had plates that would do, but nothing to fasten them with. And every week the messenger, a lone negro, letter-bag on shoulder and staff in hand, left our station for the coast. And several times a week a coast caravan came in with trade goods—ghastly glazed calico that made you shudder only to look at it, glass beads value about a penny a quart, confounded spotted cotton handkerchiefs. And no rivets. Three carriers could have brought all that was wanted to set that steamboat afloat.

"He was becoming confidential now, but I fancy my unresponsive attitude must have exasperated him at last, for he judged it necessary to inform me he feared neither God nor devil, let alone any mere man. I said I could see that very well, but what I wanted was a certain quantity of rivets—and rivets were what really Mr. Kurtz wanted, if he had only known it. Now letters went to the coast every week. ... 'My dear sir,' he cried, 'I write from dictation.' I demanded rivets. There was a way—for an intelligent man. He changed his manner; became very cold, and suddenly began to talk about a hippopotamus; wondered whether sleeping on board the steamer (I stuck to my salvage night and day) I wasn't disturbed. There was an old hippo that had the bad habit of getting out on the bank and roaming at night over the station grounds. The pilgrims used to turn out in a body and empty every rifle they could lay hands on at him. Some even had sat up o' nights for him. All this energy was wasted, though. 'That animal has a charmed life,' he said; 'but you can say this only of brutes in this country. No man—you apprehend me?—no man here bears a charmed life.' He stood there for a moment in the moonlight with his delicate hooked nose set a little askew, and his mica eyes glittering without a wink, then, with a curt Good-night, he strode off. I could see he was disturbed and considerably puzzled, which made me feel more hopeful than I had been for days. It was a great comfort to turn from that chap to my influential friend, the battered, twisted, ruined, tin-pot steamboat. I clambered on board. She rang under my feet like an empty Huntley & Palmer biscuit-tin kicked along a gutter; she was nothing so solid in make, and rather less pretty in shape, but I had expended enough hard work on her to make me love her. No influential friend would have served me better. She had given me a chance to come out a bit—to find out what I could do. No, I don't like work. I had rather laze about and think of all the fine things that can be done. I don't like work—no man does—but I like what is in the work—the chance to find yourself. Your own reality—for yourself, not for others—what no other man can ever know. They can only see the mere show, and never can tell what it really means.

"I was not surprised to see somebody sitting aft, on the deck, with his legs dangling over the mud. You see I rather chummed with the few mechanics there were in that station, whom the other pilgrims naturally despised—on account of their imperfect manners, I suppose. This was the foreman—a boiler-maker by trade—a good worker. He was a lank, bony, yellow-faced man, with big intense eyes. His aspect was worried, and his head was as bald as the palm of my hand; but his hair in falling seemed to have stuck to his chin, and had prospered in the new locality, for his beard hung down to his waist. He was a widower with six young children (he had left them in charge of a sister of his to come out there), and the passion of his life was pigeon-flying. He was an enthusiast and a connoisseur. He would rave about pigeons. After work hours he used sometimes to come over from his hut for a talk about his children and his pigeons; at work, when he had to crawl in the mud under the bottom of the steamboat, he would tie up that beard of his in a kind of white serviette he brought for the purpose. It had loops to go over his ears. In the evening be could be seen squatted on the bank rinsing that wrapper in the creek with great care, then spreading it solemnly on a bush to dry.

"I slapped him on the back and shouted 'We shall have rivets!' He scrambled to his feet exclaiming 'No! Rivets!' as though he couldn't believe his ears. Then in a low voice, 'You ... eh?' I don't know why we behaved like lunatics. I put my finger to the side of my nose and nodded mysteriously. 'Good for you!' he cried, snapped his fingers above his head, lifting one foot. I tried a jig. We capered on the iron deck. A frightful clatter came out of that hulk, and the virgin forest on the other bank of the creek sent it back in a thundering roll upon the sleeping station. It must have made some of the pilgrims sit up in their hovels. A dark figure obscured the lighted doorway of the manager's hut, vanished, then, a second or so after, the doorway itself vanished too. We stopped, and the silence driven away by the stamping of our feet flowed back again from the recesses of the land. The great wall of vegetation, an exuberant and entangled mass of trunks, branches, leaves, boughs, festoons, motionless in the moonlight, was like a rioting invasion of soundless life, a rolling wave of plants, piled up, crested, ready to topple over the creek, to sweep every little man of us out of his little existence. And it moved not. A deadened burst of mighty splashes and snorts reached us from afar, as though an ichthyosaurus had been taking a bath of glitter in the great river. 'After all,' said the boiler-maker in a reasonable tone, 'why shouldn't we get the rivets?' Why not, indeed! I did not know of any reason why we shouldn't. 'They'll come in three weeks,' I said confidently.

"But they didn't. Instead of rivets there came an invasion, an infliction, a visitation. It came in sections during the next three weeks, each section headed by a donkey carrying a white man in new clothes and tan shoes, bowing from that elevation right and left to the impressed pilgrims. A quarrelsome band of footsore sulky niggers trod on the heels of the donkey; a lot of tents, camp-stools, tin boxes, white cases, brown bales would be shot down in the courtyard, and the air of mystery would deepen a little over the muddle of the station. Five such instalments came, with their absurd air of disorderly flight with the loot of innumerable outfit shops and provision stores, that, one would think, they were lugging, after a raid, into the wilderness for equitable division. It was an inextricable mess of things decent in themselves but that human folly made look like the spoils of thieving.

"This devoted band called itself the Eldorado Exploring Expedition, and I believe they were sworn to secrecy. Their talk, however, was the talk of sordid buccaneers: it was reckless without hardihood, greedy without audacity, and cruel without courage; there was not an atom of foresight or of serious intention in the whole batch of them, and they did not seem aware these things are wanted for the work of the world. To tear treasure out of the bowels of the land was their desire, with no more moral purpose at the back of it than there is in burglars breaking into a safe. Who paid the expenses of the noble enterprise I don't know; but the uncle of our manager was leader of that lot.

"In exterior he resembled a butcher in a poor neighbourhood, and his eyes had a look of sleepy cunning. He carried his fat paunch with ostentation on his short legs, and during the time his gang infested the station spoke to no one but his nephew. You could see these two roaming about all day long with their heads close together in an everlasting confab.

"I had given up worrying myself about the rivets. One's capacity for that kind of folly is more limited than you would suppose. I said Hang!—and let things slide. I had plenty of time for meditation, and now and then I would give some thought to Kurtz. I wasn't very interested in him. No. Still, I was curious to see whether this man, who had come out equipped with moral ideas of some sort, would climb to the top after all, and how he would set about his work when there."

II

"One evening as I was lying flat on the deck of my steamboat, I heard voices approaching—and there were the nephew and the uncle strolling along the bank. I laid my head on my arm again, and had nearly lost myself in a doze, when somebody said in my ear, as it were: 'I am as harmless as a little child, but I don't like to be dictated to. Am I the manager—or am I not? I was ordered to send him there. It's incredible.' ... I became aware that the two were standing on the shore alongside the forepart of the steamboat, just below my head. I did not move; it did not occur to me to move: I was sleepy. 'It *is* unpleasant,' grunted the uncle. 'He has asked the Administration to be sent there,' said the other, 'with the idea of showing what he could do; and I was instructed accordingly. Look at the influence that man must have. Is it not frightful?' They both agreed it was frightful, then made several bizarre remarks: 'Make rain and fine weather—one man—the Council—by the nose'—bits of absurd sentences that got the better of my drowsiness, so that I had pretty near the whole of my wits about me when the uncle said, 'The climate may do away with this difficulty for you. Is he alone there?' 'Yes,' answered the manager; 'he sent his assistant down the river with a note to me in these terms: "Clear this poor devil out of the country, and don't bother sending more of that sort. I had rather be alone than have the kind of men you can dispose of with me." It was more than a year ago. Can you imagine such impudence?' 'Anything since then?' asked the other hoarsely. 'Ivory,' jerked the nephew; 'lots of it—prime sort—lots—most annoying, from him.' 'And with that?' questioned the heavy rumble. 'Invoice,' was the reply fired out, so to speak. Then silence. They had been talking about Kurtz.

"I was broad awake by this time, but, lying perfectly at ease, remained still, having no inducement to change my position. 'How did that ivory come all this way?' growled the elder man, who seemed very vexed. The other explained that it had come with a fleet of canoes in charge of an English half-caste clerk Kurtz had with him; that Kurtz had apparently intended to return himself, the station being by that time bare of goods and stores, but after coming three hundred miles, had suddenly decided to go back, which he started to do alone in a small dugout with four paddlers, leaving the half-caste to continue down the river with the ivory. The two fellows there seemed astounded at anybody attempting such a thing. They were at a loss for an adequate motive. As for me, I seemed to see Kurtz for the first time. It was a distinct glimpse: the dugout, four paddling savages, and the lone white man turning his back suddenly on the headquarters, on relief, on thoughts of home—perhaps; setting his face towards the depths of the wilderness, towards his empty and desolate station. I did not know the motive. Perhaps he was just simply a fine fellow who stuck to his work for its own sake. His name, you understand, had not been pronounced once. He was 'that man.' The half-caste, who, as far as I could see, had conducted a difficult trip with great prudence and pluck, was invariably alluded to as 'that scoundrel.' The 'scoundrel' had reported that the 'man' had been very ill—had recovered imperfectly. … The two below me moved away then a few paces, and strolled back and forth at some little distance. I heard: 'Military post—doctor—two hundred miles—quite alone now—unavoidable delays—nine months—no news—strange rumours.' They approached again, just as the manager was saying, 'No one, as far as I know, unless a species of wandering trader—a pestilential fellow, snapping ivory from the natives.' Who was it they were talking about now? I gathered in snatches that this was some man supposed to be in Kurtz's district, and of whom the manager did not approve. 'We will not be free from unfair competition till one of these fellows is hanged for an example,' he said. 'Certainly,' grunted the other; 'get him hanged! Why not? Anything—anything can be done in this country. That's what I say; nobody here, you understand, *here*, can endanger your position. And why? You stand the climate—you outlast them all. The danger is in Europe; but there before I left I took care to——' They moved off and whispered, then their voices rose again. 'The extraordinary series of delays is not my fault. I did my possible.' The fat man sighed, 'Very sad.' 'And the pestiferous absurdity of his talk,' continued the other; 'he bothered me enough when he was here. "Each station should be like a beacon on the road towards better things, a centre for trade of course, but also for humanising, improving, instructing." Conceive you—that ass! And he wants to be manager! No, it's——' Here he got choked by excessive indignation, and I lifted my head the least bit. I was surprised to see how near they were—right under me. I could have spat upon their hats. They were looking on the ground, absorbed in thought. The manager was switching his leg with a slender twig: his sagacious relative lifted his head. 'You have been well since you came out this time?' he asked. The other gave a start. 'Who? I? Oh! Like a charm—like a charm. But the rest—oh, my goodness! All sick. They die so quick, too, that I haven't the time to send them out of the country—it's incredible!' 'H'm. Just so,' grunted the uncle. 'Ah! my boy, trust to this—I say, trust to this.' I saw him extend his short flipper of an arm for a gesture that took in the forest, the creek, the mud, the river—seemed to beckon with a dishonouring flourish before the sunlit face of the land a treacherous appeal to the lurking death, to the hidden evil, to the profound darkness of its heart. It was so startling that I leaped to my feet and looked back at the edge of the forest, as though I had expected an answer of some sort to that black display of confidence. You know the foolish notions that come to one sometimes. The high stillness confronted these two figures with its ominous patience, waiting for the passing away of a fantastic invasion.

"They swore aloud together—out of sheer fright, I believe—then, pretending not to know anything of my existence, turned back to the station. The sun was low; and leaning forward side by side, they seemed to be tugging painfully uphill their two ridiculous shadows of unequal length, that trailed behind them slowly over the tall grass without bending a single blade.

"In a few days the Eldorado Expedition went into the patient wilderness, that closed upon it as the sea closes over a diver. Long afterwards the news came that all the donkeys were dead. I know nothing as to the fate of the less valuable animals. They, no doubt, like the rest of us, found what they deserved. I did not inquire. I was then rather excited at the prospect of meeting Kurtz very soon. When I say very soon I mean it comparatively. It was just two months from the day we left the creek when we came to the bank below Kurtz's station.

"Going up that river was like travelling back to the earliest beginnings of the world, when vegetation rioted on the earth and the big trees were kings. An empty stream, a great silence, an impenetrable forest. The air was warm, thick, heavy, sluggish. There was no joy in the brilliance of sunshine. The long stretches of the waterway ran on, deserted, into the gloom of overshadowed distances. On silvery sandbanks hippos and alligators sunned themselves side by side. The broadening waters flowed through a mob of wooded islands; you lost your way on that river as you would in a desert, and butted all day long against shoals, trying to find the channel, till you thought yourself bewitched and cut off for ever from everything you had known once—somewhere—far away—in another existence perhaps. There were moments when one's past came back to one, as it will sometimes when you have not a moment to spare to yourself; but it came in the shape of an unrestful and noisy dream, remembered with wonder amongst the overwhelming realities of this strange world of plants, and water, and silence. And this stillness of life did not in the least resemble a peace. It was the stillness of an implacable force brooding over an inscrutable intention. It looked at you with a vengeful aspect. I got used to it afterwards; I did not see it any more; I had no time. I had to keep guessing at the channel; I had to discern, mostly by inspiration, the signs of hidden banks; I watched for sunken stones; I was learning to clap my teeth smartly before my heart flew out, when I shaved by a fluke some infernal sly old snag that would have ripped the life out of the tin-pot steamboat and drowned all the pilgrims; I had to keep a look-out for the signs of dead wood we could cut up in the night for next day's steaming. When you have to attend to things of that sort, to the mere incidents of the surface, the reality—the reality, I tell you—fades. The inner truth is hidden—luckily, luckily. But

I felt it all the same; I felt often its mysterious stillness watching me at my monkey tricks, just as it watches you fellows performing on your respective tight-ropes for—what is it? half a crown a tumble——"

"Try to be civil, Marlow," growled a voice, and I knew there was at least one listener awake besides myself.

"I beg your pardon. I forgot the heartache which makes up the rest of the price. And indeed what does the price matter, if the trick be well done? You do your tricks very well. And I didn't do badly either, since I managed not to sink that steamboat on my first trip. It's a wonder to me, yet. Imagine a blindfolded man set to drive a van over a bad road. I sweated and shivered over that business considerably, I can tell you. After all, for a seaman, to scrape the bottom of the thing that's supposed to float all the time under his care is the unpardonable sin. No one may know of it, but you never forget the thump—eh? A blow on the very heart. You remember it, you dream of it, you wake up at night and think of it—years after—and go hot and cold all over. I don't pretend to say that steamboat floated all the time. More than once she had to wade for a bit, with twenty cannibals splashing around and pushing. We had enlisted some of these chaps on the way for a crew. Fine fellows—cannibals—in their place. They were men one could work with, and I am grateful to them. And, after all, they did not eat each other before my face: they had brought along a provision of hippo-meat which went rotten, and made the mystery of the wilderness stink in my nostrils. Phoo! I can sniff it now. I had the manager on board and three or four pilgrims with their staves—all complete. Sometimes we came upon a station close by the bank, clinging to the skirts of the unknown, and the white men rushing out of a tumble-down hovel, with great gestures of joy and surprise and welcome, seemed very strange—had the appearance of being held there captive by a spell. The word 'ivory' would ring in the air for a while—and on we went again into the silence, along empty reaches, round the still bends, between the high walls of our winding way, reverberating in hollow claps the ponderous beat of the stern-wheel. Trees, trees, millions of trees, massive, immense, running up high; and at their foot, hugging the bank against the stream, crept the little begrimed steamboat, like a sluggish beetle crawling on the floor of a lofty portico. It made you feel very small, very lost, and yet it was not altogether depressing, that feeling. After all, if you were small, the grimy beetle crawled on—which was just what you wanted it to do. Where the pilgrims imagined it crawled to I don't know. To some place where they expected to get something, I bet! For me it crawled towards Kurtz—exclusively; but when the steam-pipes started leaking we crawled very slow. The reaches opened before us and closed behind, as if the forest had stepped leisurely across the water to bar the way for our return. We penetrated deeper and deeper into the heart of darkness. It was very quiet there. At night sometimes the roll of drums behind the curtain of trees would run up the river and remain sustained faintly, as if hovering in the air high over our heads, till the first break of day. Whether it meant war, peace, or prayer we could not tell. The dawns were heralded by the descent of a chill stillness; the woodcutters slept, their fires burned low; the snapping of a twig would make you start. We were wanderers on a prehistoric earth, on an earth that wore the aspect of an unknown planet. We could have fancied ourselves the first of men taking possession of an accursed inheritance, to be subdued at the cost of profound anguish and of excessive toil. But suddenly, as we struggled round a bend, there would be a glimpse of rush walls, of peaked grass-roofs, a burst of yells, a whirl of black limbs, a mass of hands clapping, of feet stamping, of bodies swaying, of eyes rolling, under the droop of heavy and motionless foliage. The steamer toiled along slowly on the edge of a black and incomprehensible frenzy. The prehistoric man was cursing us, praying to us, welcoming us—who could tell? We were cut off from the comprehension of our surroundings; we glided past like phantoms, wondering and secretly appalled, as sane men would be before an enthusiastic outbreak in a madhouse. We could not understand because we were too far and could not remember, because we were travelling in the night of first ages, of those ages that are gone, leaving hardly a sign—and no memories.

"The earth seemed unearthly. We are accustomed to look upon the shackled form of a conquered monster, but there—there you could look at a thing monstrous and free. It was unearthly, and the men were—No, they were not inhuman. Well, you know, that was the worst of it—this suspicion of their not being inhuman. It would come slowly to one. They howled and leaped, and spun, and made horrid faces; but what thrilled you was just the thought of their humanity—like yours—the thought of your remote kinship with this wild and passionate uproar. Ugly. Yes, it was ugly enough; but if you were man enough you would admit to yourself that there was in you just the faintest trace of a response to the terrible frankness of that noise, a dim suspicion of there being a meaning in it which you—you so remote from the night of first ages—could comprehend. And why not? The mind of man is capable of anything—because everything is in it, all the past as well as all the future. What was there after all? Joy, fear, sorrow, devotion, valour, rage—who can tell?—but truth—truth stripped of its cloak of time. Let the fool gape and shudder—the man knows, and can look on without a wink. But he must at least be as much of a man as these on the shore. He must meet that truth with his own true stuff—with his own inborn strength. Principles? Principles won't do. Acquisitions, clothes, pretty rags—rags that would fly off at the first good shake. No; you want a deliberate belief. An appeal to me in this fiendish row—is there? Very well; I hear; I admit, but I have a voice too, and for good or evil mine is the speech that cannot be silenced. Of course, a fool, what with sheer fright and fine sentiments, is always safe. Who's that grunting? You wonder I didn't go ashore for a howl and a dance? Well, no—I didn't. Fine sentiments, you say? Fine sentiments be hanged! I had no time. I had to mess about with white-lead and strips of woollen blanket helping to put bandages on those leaky steam-pipes—I tell you. I had to watch the steering, and circumvent those snags, and get the tin-pot along by hook or by crook. There was surface-truth enough in these things to save a wiser man. And between whiles I had to look after the savage who was fireman. He was an improved specimen; he could fire up a vertical boiler. He was there below me, and, upon my word, to look at him was as edifying as seeing a dog in a parody of breeches and a feather hat, walking on his hind legs. A few months of training had done for that really fine chap. He squinted at the steam-gauge and at the water-gauge with an evident effort of intrepidity—and he had filed teeth too, the poor devil, and the wool of his pate shaved into queer patterns, and three ornamental scars on each of his cheeks. He ought to have been clapping his hands and stamping his feet on the bank, instead of which he was hard at work, a thrall to strange witchcraft, full of improving knowledge. He was useful because he had been instructed; and what he knew was this—that should the water in that transparent thing disappear, the evil spirit inside the boiler would get angry through the greatness of his thirst, and take a terrible vengeance. So he sweated and fired up and watched the glass fearfully (with an impromptu charm, made of rags, tied to his arm, and a piece of polished bone, as big as a watch, stuck flatways through his lower lip), while the wooded banks slipped past us slowly, the short noise was left behind, the interminable miles of silence—and we crept on, towards Kurtz. But the snags were thick, the water was treacherous and shallow, the boiler seemed indeed to have a sulky devil in it, and thus neither that fireman nor I had any time to peer into our creepy thoughts.

"Some fifty miles below the Inner Station we came upon a hut of reeds, an inclined and melancholy pole, with the unrecognisable tatters of what had been a flag of some sort flying from it, and a neatly stacked wood-pile. This was unexpected. We came to the bank, and on the stack of firewood found a flat piece of board with some faded pencil-writing on it. When deciphered it said: 'Wood for you. Hurry up. Approach cautiously.' There was a signature, but it was illegible—not Kurtz—a much longer word. 'Hurry up.' Where? Up the river? 'Approach cautiously.' We had not done so. But the warning could not have been meant for the place where it could be only found after approach. Something was wrong above. But what—and how much? That was the question. We commented adversely upon the imbecility of that telegraphic style. The bush around said nothing, and would not let us look very far, either. A torn curtain of red twill hung in the doorway of the hut, and flapped sadly in our faces. The dwelling was dismantled; but we could see a white man had lived there not very long ago. There remained a rude table—a plank on two posts; a heap of rubbish reposed in a dark corner, and by the door I picked up a book. It had lost its covers, and the pages had been thumbed into a state of extremely dirty softness; but the back had been lovingly stitched afresh with white cotton thread, which looked clean yet. It was an extraordinary find. Its title was, *An Inquiry into some Points of Seamanship*, by a man Towser, Towson—some such name—Master in His Majesty's Navy. The matter looked dreary reading enough, with illustrative diagrams and repulsive tables of figures, and the copy was sixty years old. I handled this amazing antiquity with the greatest possible tenderness, lest it should dissolve in my hands. Within, Towson or Towser was inquiring earnestly into the breaking strain of ships' chains and tackle, and other such matters. Not a very enthralling book; but at the first glance you could see there a singleness of intention, an honest concern for the right way of going to work, which made these humble pages, thought out so many years ago, luminous with another than a professional light. The simple old sailor, with his talk of chains and purchases, made me forget the jungle and the pilgrims in a delicious sensation of having come upon something unmistakably real. Such a book being there was wonderful enough; but still more astounding were the notes pencilled in the margin, and plainly referring to the text. I couldn't believe my eyes! They were in cipher! Yes, it looked like cipher. Fancy a man lugging with him a book of that description into this nowhere and studying it—and making notes—in cipher at that! It was an extravagant mystery.

"I had been dimly aware for some time of a worrying noise, and when I lifted my eyes I saw the wood-pile was gone, and the manager, aided by all the pilgrims, was shouting at me from the river-side. I slipped the book into my pocket. I assure you to leave off reading was like tearing myself away from the shelter of an old and solid friendship.

"I started the lame engine ahead. 'It must be this miserable trader—this intruder,' exclaimed the manager, looking back malevolently at the place we had left. 'He must be English,' I said. 'It will not save him from getting into trouble if he is not careful,' muttered the manager darkly. I observed with assumed innocence that no man was safe from trouble in this world.

"The current was more rapid now, the steamer seemed at her last gasp, the stern-wheel flopped languidly, and I caught myself listening on tiptoe for the next beat of the float, for in sober truth I expected the wretched thing to give up every moment. It was like watching the last flickers of a life. But still we crawled. Sometimes I would pick out a tree a little way ahead to measure our progress towards Kurtz by, but I lost it invariably before we got abreast. To keep the eyes so long on one thing was too much for human patience. The manager displayed a beautiful resignation. I fretted and fumed and took to arguing with myself whether or no I would talk openly with Kurtz; but before I could come to any conclusion it occurred to me that my speech or my silence, indeed any action of mine, would be a mere futility. What did it matter what any one knew or ignored? What did it matter who was manager? One gets sometimes such a flash of insight. The essentials of this affair lay deep under the surface, beyond my reach, and beyond my power of meddling.

"Towards the evening of the second day we judged ourselves about eight miles from Kurtz's station. I wanted to push on; but the manager looked grave, and told me the navigation up there was so dangerous that it would be advisable, the sun being very low already, to wait where we were till next morning. Moreover, he pointed out that if the warning to approach cautiously were to be followed, we must approach in daylight—not at dusk, or in the dark. This was sensible enough. Eight miles meant nearly three hours' steaming for us, and I could also see suspicious ripples at the upper end of the reach. Nevertheless, I was annoyed beyond expression at the delay, and most unreasonably too, since one night more could not matter much after so many months. As we had plenty of wood, and caution was the word, I brought up in the middle of the stream. The reach was narrow, straight, with high sides like a railway cutting. The dusk came gliding into it long before the sun had set. The current ran smooth and swift, but a dumb immobility sat on the banks. The living trees, lashed together by the creepers and every living bush of the undergrowth, might have been changed into stone, even to the slenderest twig, to the lightest leaf. It was not sleep—it seemed unnatural, like a state of trance. Not the faintest sound of any kind could be heard. You looked on amazed, and began to suspect yourself of being deaf—then the night came suddenly, and struck you blind as well. About three in the morning some large fish leaped, and the loud splash made me jump as though a gun had been fired. When the sun rose there was a white fog, very warm and clammy, and more blinding than the night. It did not shift or drive; it was just there, standing all round you like something solid. At eight or nine, perhaps, it lifted as a shutter lifts. We had a glimpse of the towering multitude of trees, of the immense matted jungle, with the blazing little ball of the sun hanging over it—all perfectly still—and then the white shutter came down again, smoothly, as if sliding in greased grooves. I ordered the chain, which we had begun to heave in, to be paid out again. Before it stopped running with a muffled rattle, a cry, a very loud cry, as of infinite desolation, soared slowly in the opaque air. It ceased. A complaining clamour, modulated in savage discords, filled our ears. The sheer unexpectedness of it made my hair stir under my cap. I don't know how it struck the others: to me it seemed as though the mist itself had screamed, so suddenly, and apparently from all sides at once, did this tumultuous and mournful uproar arise. It culminated in a hurried outbreak of almost intolerably excessive shrieking, which stopped short, leaving us stiffened in a variety of silly attitudes, and obstinately listening to the nearly as appalling and excessive silence. 'Good God! What is the meaning——?' stammered at my elbow one of the pilgrims—a little fat man, with sandy hair and red whiskers, who wore side-spring boots, and pink pyjamas tucked into his socks. Two others remained open-mouthed a whole minute, then dashed into the little cabin, to rush out incontinently and stand darting scared glances, with Winchesters at 'ready' in their hands. What we could see was just the steamer we were on, her outlines blurred as though she had been on the point of dissolving, and a misty strip of water, perhaps two feet broad, around her—and that was all. The rest of the world was nowhere, as far as our eyes and ears were concerned. Just nowhere. Gone, disappeared; swept off without leaving a whisper or a shadow behind.

"I went forward, and ordered the chain to be hauled in short, so as to be ready to trip the anchor and move the steamboat at once if necessary. 'Will they attack?' whispered an awed voice. 'We will all be butchered in this fog,' murmured another. The faces twitched with the strain, the hands trembled slightly, the eyes forgot to wink. It was very curious to see the contrast of expressions of the white men and of the black fellows of our crew, who were as much strangers to that part of the river as we, though their homes were only eight hundred miles away. The whites, of course greatly discomposed, had besides a curious look of being painfully shocked by such an outrageous row. The others had an alert, naturally interested expression; but their faces were essentially quiet, even those of the one or two who grinned as they hauled at the chain. Several exchanged short, grunting phrases, which seemed to settle the matter to their satisfaction. Their head-man, a young, broad-chested black, severely draped in dark-blue fringed cloths, with fierce nostrils and his hair all done up artfully in oily ringlets, stood near me. 'Aha!' I said, just for good fellowship's sake. 'Catch 'im,' he snapped, with a bloodshot widening of his eyes and a flash of sharp teeth—'catch 'im. Give 'im to us.' 'To you, eh?' I asked; 'what would you do with them?' 'Eat 'im!' he said curtly, and, leaning his elbow on the rail, looked out into the fog in a dignified and profoundly pensive attitude. I would no doubt have been properly horrified, had it not occurred to me that he and his chaps must be very hungry: that they must have been growing increasingly hungry for at least this month past. They had been engaged for six months (I don't think a single one of them had any clear idea of time, as we at the end of countless ages have. They still belonged to the beginnings of time—had no inherited experience to teach them, as it were), and of course, as long as there was a piece of paper written over in accordance with some farcical law or other made down the river, it didn't enter anybody's head to trouble how they would live. Certainly they had brought with them some rotten hippo-meat, which couldn't have lasted very long, anyway, even if the pilgrims hadn't, in the midst of a shocking hullabaloo, thrown a considerable quantity of it overboard. It looked like a high-handed proceeding; but it was really a case of legitimate self-defence. You can't breathe dead hippo waking, sleeping, and eating, and at the same time keep your precarious grip on existence. Besides that, they had given them every week three pieces of brass wire, each about nine inches long; and the theory was they were to buy their provisions with that currency in river-side villages. You can see how *that* worked. There were either no villages, or the people were hostile, or the director, who like the rest of us fed out of tins, with an occasional old he-goat thrown in, didn't want to stop the steamer for some more or less recondite reason. So, unless they swallowed the wire itself, or made loops of it to snare the fishes with, I don't see what good their extravagant salary could be to them. I must say it was paid with a regularity worthy of a large and honourable trading company. For the rest, the only thing to eat—though it didn't look eatable in the least—I saw in their possession was a few lumps of some stuff like half-cooked dough, of a dirty lavender colour, they kept wrapped in leaves, and now and then swallowed a piece of, but so small that it seemed done more for the look of the thing than for any serious purpose of sustenance. Why in the name of all the gnawing devils of hunger they didn't go for us—they were thirty to five—and have a good tuck-in for once, amazes me now when I think of it. They were big powerful men, with not much capacity to weigh the consequences, with courage, with strength, even yet, though their skins were no longer glossy and their muscles no longer hard. And I saw that something restraining, one of those human secrets that baffle probability, had come into play there. I looked at them with a swift quickening of interest—not because it occurred to me I might be eaten by them before very long, though I own to you that just then I perceived—in a new light, as it were—how unwholesome the pilgrims looked, and I hoped, yes, I positively hoped, that my aspect was not so—what shall I say?—so—unappetising: a touch of fantastic vanity which fitted well with the dream-sensation that pervaded all my days at that time. Perhaps I had a little fever too. One can't live with one's finger everlastingly on one's pulse. I had often 'a little fever,' or a little touch of other things—the playful paw-strokes of the wilderness, the preliminary trifling before the more serious onslaught which came in due course. Yes; I looked at them as you would on any human being, with a curiosity of their impulses, motives, capacities, weaknesses, when brought to the test of an inexorable physical necessity. Restraint! What possible restraint? Was it superstition, disgust, patience, fear—or some kind of primitive honour? No fear can stand up to hunger, no patience can wear it out, disgust simply does not exist where hunger is; and as to superstition, beliefs, and what you may call principles, they are less than chaff in a breeze. Don't you know the devilry of lingering starvation, its exasperating torment, its black thoughts, its sombre and brooding ferocity? Well, I do. It takes a man all his inborn strength to fight hunger properly. It's really easier to face bereavement, dishonour, and the perdition of one's soul—than this kind of prolonged hunger. Sad, but true. And these chaps too had no earthly reason for any kind of scruple. Restraint! I would just as soon have expected restraint from a hyena prowling amongst the corpses of a battlefield. But there was the fact facing me—the fact dazzling, to be seen, like the foam on the depths of the sea, like a ripple on an unfathomable enigma, a mystery greater—when I thought of it—than the curious, inexplicable note of desperate grief in this savage clamour that had swept by us on the river-bank, behind the blind whiteness of the fog.

"Two pilgrims were quarrelling in hurried whispers as to which bank. 'Left.' 'No, no; how can you? Right, right, of course.' 'It is very serious,' said the manager's voice behind me; 'I would be desolated if anything should happen to Mr. Kurtz before we came up.' I looked at him, and had not the slightest doubt he was sincere. He was just the kind of man who would wish to preserve appearances. That was his restraint. But when he muttered something about going on at once, I did not even take the trouble to answer him. I knew, and he knew, that it was impossible. Were we to let go our hold of the bottom, we would be absolutely in the air—in space. We wouldn't be able to tell where we were going to—whether up or down stream, or across—till we fetched against one bank or the other—and then we wouldn't know at first which it was. Of course I made no move. I had no mind for a smash-up. You couldn't imagine a more deadly place for a shipwreck. Whether drowned at once or not, we were sure to perish speedily in one way or another. 'I authorise you to take all the risks,' he said, after a short silence. 'I refuse to take any,' I said shortly; which was just the answer he expected, though its tone might have surprised him. 'Well, I must defer to your judgment. You are captain,' he said, with marked civility. I turned my shoulder to him in sign of my appreciation, and looked into the fog. How long would it last? It was the most hopeless look-out. The approach to this Kurtz grubbing for ivory in the wretched bush was beset by as many dangers as though he had been an enchanted princess sleeping in a fabulous castle. 'Will they attack, do you think?' asked the manager, in a confidential tone.

"I did not think they would attack, for several obvious reasons. The thick fog was one. If they left the bank in their canoes they would get lost in it, as we would be if we attempted to move. Still, I had also judged the jungle of both banks quite impenetrable—and yet eyes were in it, eyes that had seen us. The river-side bushes were certainly very thick; but the undergrowth behind was evidently penetrable. However, during the short lift I had seen no canoes anywhere in the reach—certainly not abreast of the steamer. But what made the idea of attack inconceivable to me was the nature of the noise—of the cries we had heard. They had not the fierce character boding of immediate hostile intention. Unexpected, wild, and violent as they had been, they had given me an irresistible impression of sorrow. The glimpse of the steamboat had for some reason filled those savages with unrestrained grief. The danger, if any, I expounded, was from our proximity to a great human passion let loose. Even extreme grief may ultimately vent itself in violence—but more generally takes the form of apathy. ...

"You should have seen the pilgrims stare! They had no heart to grin, or even to revile me; but I believe they thought me gone mad—with fright, maybe. I delivered a regular lecture. My dear boys, it was no good bothering. Keep a lookout? Well, you may guess I watched the fog for the signs of lifting as a cat watches a mouse; but for anything else our eyes were of no more use to us than if we had been buried miles deep in a heap of cotton-wool. It felt like it too—choking, warm, stifling. Besides, all I said, though it sounded extravagant, was absolutely true to fact. What we afterwards alluded to as an attack was really an attempt at repulse. The action was very far from being aggressive—it was not even defensive, in the usual sense: it was undertaken under the stress of desperation, and in its essence was purely protective.

"It developed itself, I should say, two hours after the fog lifted, and its commencement was at a spot, roughly speaking, about a mile and a half below Kurtz's station. We had just floundered and flopped round a bend, when I saw an islet, a mere grassy hummock of bright green, in the middle of the stream. It was the only thing of the kind; but as we opened the reach more, I perceived it was the head of a long sandbank, or rather of a chain of shallow patches stretching down the middle of the river. They were discoloured, just awash, and the whole lot was seen just under the water, exactly as a man's backbone is seen running down the middle of his back under the skin. Now, as far as I did see, I could go to the right or to the left of this. I didn't know either channel, of course. The banks looked pretty well alike, the depth appeared the same; but as I had been informed the station was on the west side, I naturally headed for the western passage.

"No sooner had we fairly entered it than I became aware it was much narrower than I had supposed. To the left of us there was the long uninterrupted shoal, and to the right a high steep bank heavily overgrown with bushes. Above the bush the trees stood in serried ranks. The twigs overhung the current thickly, and from distance to distance a large limb of some tree projected rigidly over the stream. It was then well on in the afternoon, the face of the forest was gloomy, and a broad strip of shadow had already fallen on the water. In this shadow we steamed up—very slowly, as you may imagine. I sheered her well inshore—the water being deepest near the bank, as the sounding-pole informed me.

"One of my hungry and forbearing friends was sounding in the bows just below me. This steamboat was exactly like a decked scow. On the deck there were two little teak-wood houses, with doors and windows. The boiler was in the fore-end, and the machinery right astern. Over the whole there was a light roof, supported on stanchions. The funnel projected through that roof, and in front of the funnel a small cabin built of light planks served for a pilot-house. It contained a couch, two camp-stools, a loaded Martini-Henry leaning in one corner, a tiny table, and the steering-wheel. It had a wide door in front and a broad shutter at each side. All these were always thrown open, of course. I spent my days perched up there on the extreme fore-end of that roof, before the door. At night I slept, or tried to, on the couch. An athletic black belonging to some coast tribe, and educated by my poor predecessor, was the helmsman. He sported a pair of brass earrings, wore a blue cloth wrapper from the waist to the ankles, and thought all the world of himself. He was the most unstable kind of fool I had ever seen. He steered with no end of a swagger while you were by; but if he lost sight of you, he became instantly the prey of an abject funk, and would let that cripple of a steamboat get the upper hand of him in a minute.

"I was looking down at the sounding-pole, and feeling much annoyed to see at each try a little more of it stick out of that river, when I saw my poleman give up the business suddenly, and stretch himself flat on the deck, without even taking the trouble to haul his pole in. He kept hold on it though, and it trailed in the water. At the same time the fireman, whom I could also see below me, sat down abruptly before his furnace and ducked his head. I was amazed. Then I had to look at the river mighty quick, because there was a snag in the fairway. Sticks, little sticks, were flying about—thick: they were whizzing before my nose, dropping below me, striking behind me against my pilot-house. All this time the river, the shore, the woods, were very quiet—perfectly quiet. I could only hear the heavy splashing thump of the stern-wheel and the patter of these things. We cleared the snag clumsily. Arrows, by Jove! We were being shot at! I stepped in quickly to close the shutter on the land-side. That fool-helmsman, his hands on the spokes, was lifting his knees high, stamping his feet, champing his mouth, like a reined-in horse. Confound him! And we were staggering within ten feet of the bank. I had to lean right out to swing the heavy shutter, and I saw a face amongst the leaves on the level with my own, looking at me very fierce and steady; and then suddenly, as though a veil had been removed from my eyes, I made out, deep in the tangled gloom, naked breasts, arms, legs, glaring eyes—the bush was swarming with human limbs in movement, glistening, of bronze colour. The twigs shook, swayed, and rustled, the arrows flew out of them, and then the shutter came to. 'Steer her straight,' I said to the helmsman. He held his head rigid, face forward; but his eyes rolled, he kept on lifting and setting down his feet gently, his mouth foamed a little. 'Keep quiet!' I said in a fury. I might just as well have ordered a tree not to sway in the wind. I darted out. Below me there was a great scuffle of feet on the iron deck; confused exclamations; a voice screamed, 'Can you turn back?' I caught sight of a V-shaped ripple on the water ahead. What? Another snag! A fusillade burst out under my feet. The pilgrims had opened with their Winchesters, and were simply squirting lead into that bush. A deuce of a lot of smoke came up and drove slowly forward. I swore at it. Now I couldn't see the ripple or the snag either. I stood in the doorway, peering, and the arrows came in swarms. They might have been poisoned, but they looked as though they wouldn't kill a cat. The bush began to howl. Our woodcutters raised a warlike whoop; the report of a rifle just at my back deafened me. I glanced over my shoulder, and the pilot-house was yet full of noise and smoke when I made a dash at the wheel. The fool-nigger had dropped everything, to throw the shutter open and let off that Martini-Henry. He stood before the wide opening, glaring, and I yelled at him to come back, while I straightened the sudden twist out of that steamboat. There was no room to turn even if I had wanted to, the snag was somewhere very near ahead in that confounded smoke, there was no time to lose, so I just crowded her into the bank—right into the bank, where I knew the water was deep.

"We tore slowly along the overhanging bushes in a whirl of broken twigs and flying leaves. The fusillade below stopped short, as I had foreseen it would when the squirts got empty. I threw my head back to a glinting whiz that traversed the pilot-house, in at one shutter-hole and out at the other. Looking past that mad helmsman, who was shaking the empty rifle and yelling at the shore, I saw vague forms of men running bent double, leaping, gliding, distinct, incomplete, evanescent. Something big appeared in the air before the shutter, the rifle went overboard, and the man stepped back swiftly, looked at me over his shoulder in an extraordinary, profound, familiar manner, and fell upon my feet. The side of his head hit the wheel twice, and the end of what appeared a long cane clattered round and knocked over a little camp-stool. It looked as though after wrenching that thing from somebody ashore he had lost his balance in the effort. The thin smoke had blown away, we were clear of the snag, and looking ahead I could see that in another hundred yards or so I would be free to sheer off, away from the bank; but my feet felt so very warm and wet that I had to look down. The man had rolled on his back and stared straight up at me; both his hands clutched that cane. It was the shaft of a spear that, either thrown or lunged through the opening, had caught him in the side just below the ribs; the blade had gone in out of sight, after making a frightful gash; my shoes were full; a pool of blood lay very still, gleaming dark-red under the wheel; his eyes shone with an amazing lustre. The fusillade burst out again. He looked at me anxiously, gripping the spear like something precious, with an air of being afraid I would try to take it away from him. I had to make an effort to free my eyes from his gaze and attend to the steering. With one hand I felt above my head for the line of the steam whistle, and jerked out screech after screech hurriedly. The tumult of angry and warlike yells was checked instantly, and then from the depths of the woods went out such a tremulous and prolonged wail of mournful fear and utter despair as may be imagined to follow the flight of the last hope from the earth. There was a great commotion in the bush; the shower of arrows stopped, a few dropping shots rang out sharply—then silence, in which the languid beat of the stern-wheel came plainly to my ears. I put the helm hard a-starboard at the moment when the pilgrim in pink pyjamas, very hot and agitated, appeared in the doorway. 'The manager sends me——' he began in an official tone, and stopped short. 'Good God!' he said, glaring at the wounded man.

"We two whites stood over him, and his lustrous and inquiring glance enveloped us both. I declare it looked as though he would presently put to us some question in an understandable language; but he died without uttering a sound, without moving a limb, without twitching a muscle. Only in the very last moment, as though in response to some sign we could not see, to some whisper we could not hear, he frowned heavily, and that frown gave to his black death-mask an inconceivably sombre, brooding, and menacing expression. The lustre of inquiring glance faded swiftly into vacant glassiness. 'Can you steer?' I asked the agent eagerly. He looked very dubious; but I made a grab at his arm, and he understood at once I meant him to steer whether or no. To tell you the truth, I was morbidly anxious to change my shoes and socks. 'He is dead,' murmured the fellow, immensely impressed. 'No doubt about it,' said I, tugging like mad at the shoe-laces. 'And by the way, I suppose Mr. Kurtz is dead as well by this time.'

"For the moment that was the dominant thought. There was a sense of extreme disappointment, as though I had found out I had been striving after something altogether without a substance. I couldn't have been more disgusted if I had travelled all this way for the sole purpose of talking with Mr. Kurtz. Talking with ... I flung one shoe overboard, and became aware that that was exactly what I had been looking forward to—a talk with Kurtz. I made the strange discovery that I had never imagined him as doing, you know, but as discoursing. I didn't say to myself, 'Now I will never see him,' or 'Now I will never shake him by the hand,' but, 'Now I will never hear him.' The man presented himself as a voice. Not of course that I did not connect him with some sort of action. Hadn't I been told in all the tones of jealousy and admiration that he had collected, bartered, swindled, or stolen more ivory than all the other agents together? That was not the point. The point was in his being a gifted creature, and that of all his gifts the one that stood out pre-eminently, that carried with it a sense of real presence, was his ability to talk, his words—the gift of expression, the bewildering, the illuminating, the most exalted and the most contemptible, the pulsating stream of light, or the deceitful flow from the heart of an impenetrable darkness.

"The other shoe went flying unto the devil-god of that river. I thought, By Jove! it's all over. We are too late; he has vanished—the gift has vanished, by means of some spear, arrow, or club. I will never hear that chap speak after all—and my sorrow had a startling extravagance of emotion, even such as I had noticed in the howling sorrow of these savages in the bush. I couldn't have felt more of lonely desolation somehow, had I been robbed of a belief or had missed my destiny in life. ... Why do you sigh in this beastly way, somebody? Absurd? Well, absurd. Good Lord! mustn't a man ever—— Here, give me some tobacco." ...

There was a pause of profound stillness, then a match flared, and Marlow's lean face appeared, worn, hollow, with downward folds and dropped eyelids, with an aspect of concentrated attention; and as he took vigorous draws at his pipe, it seemed to retreat and advance out of the night in the regular flicker of the tiny flame. The match went out.

"Absurd!" he cried. "This is the worst of trying to tell ... Here you all are, each moored with two good addresses, like a hulk with two anchors, a butcher round one corner, a policeman round another, excellent appetites, and temperature normal—you hear—normal from year's end to year's end. And you say, Absurd! Absurd be—exploded! Absurd! My dear boys, what can you expect from a man who out of sheer nervousness had just flung overboard a pair of new shoes? Now I think of it, it is amazing I did not shed tears. I am, upon the whole, proud of my fortitude. I was cut to the quick at the idea of having lost the inestimable privilege of listening to the gifted Kurtz. Of course I was wrong. The privilege was waiting for me. Oh yes, I heard more than enough. And I was right, too. A voice. He was very little more than a voice. And I heard—him—it—this voice—other voices—all of them were so little more than voices—and the memory of that time itself lingers around me, impalpable, like a dying vibration of one immense jabber, silly, atrocious, sordid, savage, or simply mean, without any kind of sense. Voices, voices—even the girl herself—now—"

He was silent for a long time.

"I laid the ghost of his gifts at last with a lie," he began suddenly. "Girl! What? Did I mention a girl? Oh, she is out of it—completely. They—the women I mean—are out of it—should be out of it. We must help them to stay in that beautiful world of their own, lest ours gets worse. Oh, she had to be out of it. You should have heard the disinterred body of Mr. Kurtz saying, 'My Intended.' You would have perceived directly then how completely she was out of it. And the lofty frontal bone of Mr. Kurtz! They say the hair goes on growing sometimes, but this—ah—specimen was impressively bald. The wilderness had patted him on the head, and, behold, it was like a ball—an ivory ball; it had caressed him, and—lo!—he had withered; it had taken him, loved him, embraced him, got into his veins, consumed his flesh, and sealed his soul to its own by the inconceivable ceremonies of some devilish initiation. He was its spoiled and pampered favourite. Ivory? I should think so. Heaps of it, stacks of it. The old mud shanty was bursting with it. You would think there was not a single tusk left either above or below the ground in the whole country. 'Mostly fossil,' the manager had remarked disparagingly. It was no more fossil than I am; but they call it fossil when it is dug up. It appears these niggers do bury the tusks sometimes—but evidently they couldn't bury this parcel deep enough to save the gifted Mr. Kurtz from his fate. We filled the steamboat with it, and had to pile a lot on the deck. Thus he could see and enjoy as long as he could see, because the appreciation of this favour had remained with him to the last. You should have heard him say, 'My ivory.' Oh yes, I heard him. 'My Intended, my ivory, my station, my river, my——' everything belonged to him. It made me hold my breath in expectation of hearing the wilderness burst into a prodigious peal of laughter that would shake the fixed stars in their places. Everything belonged to him—but that was a trifle. The thing was to know what he belonged to, how many powers of darkness claimed him for their own. That was the reflection that made you creepy all over. It was impossible—it was not good for one either—trying to imagine. He had taken a high seat amongst the devils of the land—I mean literally. You can't understand. How could you?—with solid pavement under your feet, surrounded by kind neighbours ready to cheer you or to fall on you, stepping delicately between the butcher and the policeman, in the holy terror of scandal and gallows and lunatic asylums—how can you imagine what particular region of the first ages a man's untrammelled feet may take him into by the way of solitude—utter solitude without a policeman—by the way of silence—utter silence, where no warning voice of a kind neighbour can be heard whispering of public opinion? These little things make all the great difference. When they are gone you must fall back upon your own innate strength, upon your own capacity for faithfulness. Of course you may be too much of a fool to go wrong—too dull even to know you are being assaulted by the powers of darkness. I take it, no fool ever made a bargain for his soul with the devil: the fool is too much of a fool, or the devil too much of a devil—I don't know which. Or you may be such a thunderingly exalted creature as to be altogether deaf and blind to anything but heavenly sights and sounds. Then the earth for you is only a standing place—and whether to be like this is your loss or your gain I won't pretend to say. But most of us are neither one nor the other. The earth for us is a place to live in, where we must put up with sights, with sounds, with smells, too, by Jove!—breathe dead hippo, so to speak, and not be contaminated. And there, don't you see? your strength comes in, the faith in your ability for the digging of unostentatious holes to bury the stuff in—your power of devotion, not to yourself, but to an obscure, back-breaking business. And that's difficult enough. Mind, I am not trying to excuse or even explain—I am trying to account to myself for—for—Mr. Kurtz—for the shade of Mr. Kurtz. This initiated wraith from the back of Nowhere honoured me with its amazing confidence before it vanished altogether. This was because it could speak English to me. The original Kurtz had been educated partly in England, and—as he was good enough to say himself—his sympathies were in the right place. His mother was half-English, his father was half-French. All Europe contributed to the making of Kurtz; and by and by I learned that, most appropriately, the International Society for the Suppression of Savage Customs had entrusted him with the making of a report, for its future guidance. And he had written it too. I've seen it. I've read it. It was eloquent, vibrating with eloquence, but too high-strung, I think. Seventeen pages of close writing he had found time for! But this must have been before his—let us say—nerves went wrong, and caused him to preside at certain midnight dances ending with unspeakable rites, which—as far as I reluctantly gathered from what I heard at various times—were offered up to him—do you understand?—to Mr. Kurtz himself. But it was a beautiful piece of writing. The opening paragraph, however, in the light of later information, strikes me now as ominous. He began the argument that we whites, from the point of development we had arrived at, 'must necessarily appear to them [savages] in the nature of supernatural beings—we approach them with the might as of a deity,' and so on, and so on. 'By the simple exercise of our will we can exert a power for good practically unbounded,' etc. etc. From that point he soared and took me with him. The peroration was magnificent, though difficult to remember, you know. It gave me the notion of an exotic Immensity ruled by an august Benevolence. It made me tingle with enthusiasm. This was the unbounded power of eloquence—of words—of burning noble words. There were no practical hints to interrupt the magic current of phrases, unless a kind of note at the foot of the last page, scrawled evidently much later, in an unsteady hand, may be regarded as the exposition of a method. It was very simple, and at the end of that moving appeal to every altruistic sentiment it blazed at you, luminous and terrifying, like a flash of lightning in a serene sky: 'Exterminate all the brutes!' The curious part was that he had apparently forgotten all about that valuable postscriptum, because, later on, when he in sense came to himself, he repeatedly entreated me to take good care of 'my pamphlet' (he called it), as it was sure to have in the future a good influence upon his career. I had full information about all these things, and, besides, as it turned out, I was to have the care of his memory. I've done enough for it to give me the indisputable right to lay it, if I choose, for an everlasting rest in the dust-bin of progress, amongst all the sweepings and, figuratively speaking, all the dead cats of civilisation. But then, you see, I can't choose. He won't be forgotten. Whatever he was, he was not common. He had the power to charm or frighten rudimentary souls into an aggravated witch-dance in his honour; he could also fill the small souls of the pilgrims with bitter misgivings: he had one devoted friend at least, and he had conquered one soul in the world that was neither rudimentary nor tainted with self-seeking. No; I can't forget him, though I am not prepared to affirm the fellow was exactly worth the life we lost in getting to him. I missed my late helmsman awfully—I missed him even while his body was still lying in the pilot-house. Perhaps you will think it passing strange this regret for a savage who was no more account than a grain of sand in a black Sahara. Well, don't you see, he had done something, he had steered; for months I had him at my back—a help—an instrument. It was a kind of partnership. He steered for me—I had to look after him, I worried about his deficiencies, and thus a subtle bond had been created, of which I only became aware when it was suddenly broken. And the intimate profundity of that look he gave me when he received his hurt remains to this day in my memory—like a claim of distant kinship affirmed in a supreme moment.

"Poor fool! If he had only left that shutter alone. He had no restraint, no restraint—just like Kurtz—a tree swayed by the wind. As soon as I had put on a dry pair of slippers, I dragged him out, after first jerking the spear out of his side, which operation I confess I performed with my eyes shut tight. His heels leaped together over the little door-step; his shoulders were pressed to my breast; I hugged him from behind desperately. Oh! he was heavy, heavy; heavier than any man on earth, I should imagine. Then without more ado I tipped him overboard. The current snatched him as though he had been a wisp of grass, and I saw the body roll over twice before I lost sight of it for ever. All the pilgrims and the manager were then congregated on the awning-deck about the pilot-house, chattering at each other like a flock of excited magpies, and there was a scandalised murmur at my heartless promptitude. What they wanted to keep that body hanging about for I can't guess. Embalm it, maybe. But I had also heard another, and a very ominous, murmur on the deck below. My friends the wood-cutters were likewise scandalised, and with a better show of reason—though I admit that the reason itself was quite inadmissible. Oh, quite! I had made up my mind that if my late helmsman was to be eaten, the fishes alone should have him. He had been a very second-rate helmsman while alive, but now he was dead he might have become a first-class temptation, and possibly cause some startling trouble. Besides, I was anxious to take the wheel, the man in pink pyjamas showing himself a hopeless duffer at the business.

"This I did directly the simple funeral was over. We were going half-speed, keeping right in the middle of the stream, and I listened to the talk about me. They had given up Kurtz, they had given up the station; Kurtz was dead, and the station had been burnt—and so on, and so on. The red-haired pilgrim was beside himself with the thought that at least this poor Kurtz had been properly revenged. 'Say! We must have made a glorious slaughter of them in the bush. Eh? What do you think? Say?' He positively danced, the bloodthirsty little gingery beggar. And he had nearly fainted when he saw the wounded man! I could not help saying, 'You made a glorious lot of smoke, anyhow.' I had seen, from the way the tops of the bushes rustled and flew, that almost all the shots had gone too high. You can't hit anything unless you take aim and fire from the shoulder; but these chaps fired from the hip with their eyes shut. The retreat, I maintained—and I was right—was caused by the screeching of the steam-whistle. Upon this they forgot Kurtz, and began to howl at me with indignant protests.

"The manager stood by the wheel murmuring confidentially about the necessity of getting well away down the river before dark at all events, when I saw in the distance a clearing on the river-side and the outlines of some sort of building. 'What's this?' I asked. He clapped his hands in wonder. 'The station!' he cried. I edged in at once, still going half-speed.

"Through my glasses I saw the slope of a hill interspersed with rare trees and perfectly free from undergrowth. A long decaying building on the summit was half buried in the high grass; the large holes in the peaked roof gaped black from afar; the jungle and the woods made a background. There was no enclosure or fence of any kind; but there had been one apparently, for near the house half a dozen slim posts remained in a row, roughly trimmed, and with their upper ends ornamented with round carved balls. The rails, or whatever there had been between, had disappeared. Of course the forest surrounded all that. The river-bank was clear, and on the water side I saw a white man under a hat like a cart-wheel beckoning persistently with his whole arm. Examining the edge of the forest above and below, I was almost certain I could see movements—human forms gliding here and there. I steamed past prudently, then stopped the engines and let her drift down. The man on the shore began to shout, urging us to land. 'We have been attacked,' screamed the manager. 'I know—I know. It's all right,' yelled back the other, as cheerful as you please. 'Come along. It's all right. I am glad.'

"His aspect reminded me of something I had seen—something funny I had seen somewhere. As I manoeuvred to get alongside, I was asking myself, 'What does this fellow look like?' Suddenly I got it. He looked like a harlequin. His clothes had been made of some stuff that was brown holland probably, but it was covered with patches all over, with bright patches, blue, red, and yellow—patches on the back, patches on the front, patches on elbows, on knees; coloured binding round his jacket, scarlet edging at the bottom of his trousers; and the sunshine made him look extremely gay and wonderfully neat withal, because you could see how beautifully all this patching had been done. A beardless, boyish face, very fair, no features to speak of, nose peeling, little blue eyes, smiles and frowns chasing each other over that open countenance like sunshine and shadow on a wind-swept plain. 'Look out, captain!' he cried; 'there's a snag lodged in here last night.' What! Another snag? I confess I swore shamefully. I had nearly holed my cripple, to finish off that charming trip. The harlequin on the bank turned his little pug-nose up to me. 'You English?' he asked, all smiles. 'Are you?' I shouted from the wheel. The smiles vanished, and he shook his bead as if sorry for my disappointment. Then he brightened up. 'Never mind!' he cried encouragingly. 'Are we in time?' I asked. 'He is up there,' he replied, with a toss of the head up the hill, and becoming gloomy all of a sudden. His face was like the autumn sky, overcast one moment and bright the next.

"When the manager, escorted by the pilgrims, all of them armed to the teeth, had gone to the house, this chap came on board. 'I say, I don't like this. These natives are in the bush,' I said. He assured me earnestly it was all right. 'They are simple people,' he added; 'well, I am glad you came. It took me all my time to keep them off.' 'But you said it was all right,' I cried. 'Oh, they meant no harm,' he said; and as I stared he corrected himself, 'Not exactly.' Then vivaciously, 'My faith, your pilot-house wants a clean-up!' In the next breath he advised me to keep enough steam on the boiler to blow the whistle in case of any trouble. 'One good screech will do more for you than all your rifles. They are simple people,' he repeated. He rattled away at such a rate he quite overwhelmed me. He seemed to be trying to make up for lots of silence, and actually hinted, laughing, that such was the case. 'Don't you talk with Mr. Kurtz?' I said. 'You don't talk with that man—you listen to him,' he exclaimed with severe exaltation. 'But now——' He waved his arm, and in the twinkling of an eye was in the uttermost depths of despondency. In a moment he came up again with a jump, possessed himself of both my hands, shook them continuously, while he gabbled: 'Brother sailor ... honour ... pleasure ... delight ... introduce myself ... Russian ... son of an arch-priest ... Government of Tambov ... What? Tobacco! English tobacco; the excellent English tobacco! Now, that's brotherly. Smoke? Where's a sailor that does not smoke?'

"The pipe soothed him, and gradually I made out he had run away from school, had gone to sea in a Russian ship; ran away again; served some time in English ships; was now reconciled with the arch-priest. He made a point of that. 'But when one is young one must see things, gather experience, ideas; enlarge the mind.' 'Here!' I interrupted. 'You can never tell! Here I met Mr. Kurtz,' he said, youthfully solemn and reproachful. I held my tongue after that. It appears he had persuaded a Dutch trading-house on the coast to fit him out with stores and goods, and had started for the interior with a light heart, and no more idea of what would happen to him than a baby. He had been wandering about that river for nearly two years alone, cut off from everybody and everything. 'I am not so young as I look. I am twenty-five,' he said. 'At first old Van Shuyten would tell me to go to the devil,' he narrated with keen enjoyment; 'but I stuck to him, and talked and talked, till at last he got afraid I would talk the hind-leg off his favourite dog, so he gave me some cheap things and a few guns, and told me he hoped he would never see my face again. Good old Dutchman, Van Shuyten. I sent him one small lot of ivory a year ago, so that he can't call me a little thief when I get back. I hope he got it. And for the rest, I don't care. I had some wood stacked for you. That was my old house. Did you see?'

"I gave him Towson's book. He made as though he would kiss me, but restrained himself. 'The only book I had left, and I thought I had lost it,' he said, looking at it ecstatically. 'So many accidents happen to a man going about alone, you know. Canoes get upset sometimes—and sometimes you've got to clear out so quick when the people get angry.' He thumbed the pages. 'You made notes in Russian?' I asked. He nodded. 'I thought they were written in cipher,' I said. He laughed, then became serious. 'I had lots of trouble to keep these people off,' he said. 'Did they want to kill you?' I asked. 'Oh no!' he cried, and checked himself. 'Why did they attack us?' I pursued. He hesitated, then said shamefacedly, 'They don't want him to go.' 'Don't they?' I said curiously. He nodded a nod full of mystery and wisdom. 'I tell you,' he cried, 'this man has enlarged my mind.' He opened his arms wide, staring at me with his little blue eyes that were perfectly round."

III

"I looked at him, lost in astonishment. There he was before me, in motley, as though he had absconded from a troupe of mimes, enthusiastic, fabulous. His very existence was improbable, inexplicable, and altogether bewildering. He was an insoluble problem. It was inconceivable how he had existed, how he had succeeded in getting so far, how he had managed to remain—why he did not instantly disappear. 'I went a little farther,' he said, 'then still a little farther—till I had gone so far that I don't know how I'll ever get back. Never mind. Plenty time. I can manage. You take Kurtz away quick—quick—I tell you.' The glamour of youth enveloped his parti-coloured rags, his destitution, his loneliness, the essential desolation of his futile wanderings. For months—for years—his life hadn't been worth a day's purchase; and there he was gallantly, thoughtlessly alive, to all appearance indestructible solely by the virtue of his few years and of his unreflecting audacity. I was seduced into something like admiration—like envy. Glamour urged him on, glamour kept him unscathed. He surely wanted nothing from the wilderness but space to breathe in and to push on through. His need was to exist, and to move onwards at the greatest possible risk, and with a maximum of privation. If the absolutely pure, uncalculating, unpractical spirit of adventure had ever ruled a human being, it ruled this be-patched youth. I almost envied him the possession of this modest and clear flame. It seemed to have consumed all thought of self so completely, that, even while he was talking to you,

you forgot that it was he—the man before your eyes—who had gone through these things. I did not envy him his devotion to Kurtz, though. He had not meditated over it. It came to him, and he accepted it with a sort of eager fatalism. I must say that to me it appeared about the most dangerous thing in every way he had come upon so far.

"They had come together unavoidably, like two ships becalmed near each other, and lay rubbing sides at last. I suppose Kurtz wanted an audience, because on a certain occasion, when encamped in the forest, they had talked all night, or more probably Kurtz had talked. 'We talked of everything,' he said, quite transported at the recollection. 'I forgot there was such a thing as sleep. The night did not seem to last an hour. Everything! Everything! ... Of love too.' 'Ah, he talked to you of love!' I said, much amused. 'It isn't what you think,' he cried, almost passionately. 'It was in general. He made me see things—things.'

"He threw his arms up. We were on deck at the time, and the head-man of my wood-cutters, lounging near by, turned upon him his heavy and glittering eyes. I looked around, and I don't know why, but I assure you that never, never before, did this land, this river, this jungle, the very arch of this blazing sky, appear to me so hopeless and so dark, so impenetrable to human thought, so pitiless to human weakness. 'And, ever since, you have been with him, of course?' I said.

"On the contrary. It appears their intercourse had been very much broken by various causes. He had, as he informed me proudly, managed to nurse Kurtz through two illnesses (he alluded to it as you would to some risky feat), but as a rule Kurtz wandered alone, far in the depths of the forest. 'Very often coming to this station, I had to wait days and days before he would turn up,' he said. 'Ah, it was worth waiting for!—sometimes.' 'What was be doing? exploring or what?' I asked. 'Oh yes, of course'; he had discovered lots of villages, a lake too—he did not know exactly in what direction; it was dangerous to inquire too much—but mostly his expeditions had been for ivory. 'But he had no goods to trade with by that time,' I objected. 'There's a good lot of cartridges left even yet,' he answered, looking away. 'To speak plainly, he raided the country,' I said. He nodded. 'Not alone, surely!' He muttered something about the villages round that lake. 'Kurtz got the tribe to follow him, did he?' I suggested. He fidgeted a little. 'They adored him,' he said. The tone of these words was so extraordinary that I looked at him searchingly. It was curious to see his mingled eagerness and reluctance to speak of Kurtz. The man filled his life, occupied his thoughts, swayed his emotions. 'What can you expect?' he burst out; 'he came to them with thunder and lightning, you know—and they had never seen anything like it—and very terrible. He could be very terrible. You can't judge Mr. Kurtz as you would an ordinary man. No, no, no! Now—just to give you an idea—I don't mind telling you, he wanted to shoot me too one day—but I don't judge him.' 'Shoot you!' I cried. 'What for?' 'Well, I had a small lot of ivory the chief of that village near my house gave me. You see I used to shoot game for them. Well, he wanted it, and wouldn't hear reason. He declared he would shoot me unless I gave him the ivory and then cleared out of the country, because he could do so, and had a fancy for it, and there was nothing on earth to prevent him killing whom he jolly well pleased.

And it was true too. I gave him the ivory. What did I care! But I didn't clear out. No, no. I couldn't leave him. I had to be careful, of course, till we got friendly again for a time. He had his second illness then. Afterwards I had to keep out of the way; but I didn't mind. He was living for the most part in those villages on the lake. When he came down to the river, sometimes he would take to me, and sometimes it was better for me to be careful. This man suffered too much. He hated all this, and somehow he couldn't get away. When I had a chance I begged him to try and leave while there was time; I offered to go back with him. And he would say yes, and then he would remain; go off on another ivory hunt; disappear for weeks; forget himself amongst these people—forget himself—you know.' 'Why! he's mad,' I said. He protested indignantly. Mr. Kurtz couldn't be mad. If I had heard him talk, only two days ago, I wouldn't dare hint at such a thing. ... I had taken up my binoculars while we talked, and was looking at the shore, sweeping the limit of the forest at each side and at the back of the house. The consciousness of there being people in that bush, so silent, so quiet—as silent and quiet as the ruined house on the hill—made me uneasy. There was no sign on the face of nature of this amazing tale that was not so much told as suggested to me in desolate exclamations, completed by shrugs, in interrupted phrases, in hints ending in deep sighs. The woods were unmoved, like a mask—heavy, like the closed door of a prison—they looked with their air of hidden knowledge, of patient expectation, of unapproachable silence. The Russian was explaining to me that it was only lately that Mr. Kurtz had come down to the river, bringing along with him all the fighting men of that lake tribe. He had been absent for several months—getting himself adored, I suppose—and had come down unexpectedly, with the intention to all appearance of making a raid either across the river or down stream. Evidently the appetite for more ivory had got the better of the—what shall I say?—less material aspirations. However, he had got much worse suddenly. 'I heard he was lying helpless, and so I came up—took my chance,' said the Russian. 'Oh, he is bad, very bad.' I directed my glass to the house. There were no signs of life, but there were the ruined roof, the long mud wall peeping above the grass, with three little square window-holes, no two of the same size; all this brought within reach of my hand, as it were. And then I made a brusque movement, and one of the remaining posts of that vanished fence leaped up in the field of my glass. You remember I told you I had been struck at the distance by certain attempts at ornamentation, rather remarkable in the ruinous aspect of the place. Now I had suddenly a nearer view, and its first result was to make me throw my head back as if before a blow. Then I went carefully from post to post with my glass, and I saw my mistake. These round knobs were not ornamental but symbolic; they were expressive and puzzling, striking and disturbing—food for thought and also for vultures if there had been any looking down from the sky; but at all events for such ants as were industrious enough to ascend the pole. They would have been even more impressive, those heads on the stakes, if their faces had not been turned to the house. Only one, the first I had made out, was facing my way. I was not so shocked as you may think. The start back I had given was really nothing but a movement of surprise.

I had expected to see a knob of wood there, you know. I returned deliberately to the first I had seen—and there it was, black, dried, sunken, with closed eyelids—a head that seemed to sleep at the top of that pole, and, with the shrunken dry lips showing a narrow white line of the teeth, was smiling too, smiling continuously at some endless and jocose dream of that eternal slumber.

"I am not disclosing any trade secrets. In fact the manager said afterwards that Mr. Kurtz's methods had ruined the district. I have no opinion on that point, but I want you to clearly understand that there was nothing exactly profitable in these heads being there. They only showed that Mr. Kurtz lacked restraint in the gratification of his various lusts, that there was something wanting in him—some small matter which, when the pressing need arose, could not be found under his magnificent eloquence. Whether he knew of this deficiency himself I can't say. I think the knowledge came to him at last—only at the very last. But the wilderness had found him out early, and had taken on him a terrible vengeance for the fantastic invasion. I think it had whispered to him things about himself which he did not know, things of which he had no conception till he took counsel with this great solitude—and the whisper had proved irresistibly fascinating. It echoed loudly within him because he was hollow at the core. ... I put down the glass, and the head that had appeared near enough to be spoken to seemed at once to have leaped away from me into inaccessible distance.

"The admirer of Mr. Kurtz was a bit crestfallen. In a hurried, indistinct voice he began to assure me he had not dared to take these—say, symbols—down. He was not afraid of the natives; they would not stir till Mr. Kurtz gave the word. His ascendancy was extraordinary. The camps of these people surrounded the place, and the chiefs came every day to see him. They would crawl ... 'I don't want to know anything of the ceremonies used, when approaching Mr. Kurtz,' I shouted. Curious, this feeling that came over me that such details would be more intolerable than those heads drying on the stakes under Mr. Kurtz's windows. After all, that was only a savage sight, while I seemed at one bound to have been transported into some lightless region of subtle horrors, where pure, uncomplicated savagery was a positive relief, being something that had a right to exist—obviously—in the sunshine. The young man looked at me with surprise. I suppose it did not occur to him that Mr. Kurtz was no idol of mine. He forgot I hadn't heard any of these splendid monologues on, what was it? on love, justice, conduct of life—or what not. If it had come to crawling before Mr. Kurtz, he crawled as much as the veriest savage of them all. I had no idea of the conditions, he said: these heads were the heads of rebels. I shocked him excessively by laughing. Rebels! What would be the next definition I was to hear? There had been enemies, criminals, workers—and these were rebels. Those rebellious heads looked very subdued to me on their sticks. 'You don't know how such a life tries a man like Kurtz,' cried Kurtz's last disciple. 'Well, and you?' I said. 'I! I! I am a simple man. I have no great thoughts. I want nothing from anybody. How can you compare me to ...?' His feelings were too much for speech, and suddenly he broke down. 'I don't understand,' he groaned. 'I've been doing my best to keep him alive, and that's enough. I had no hand in all this. I have no abilities. There hasn't been a drop of medicine or a mouthful of invalid food for months here. He was shamefully abandoned. A man like this, with such ideas. Shamefully! Shamefully! I—I—haven't slept for the last ten nights. ...'

"His voice lost itself in the calm of the evening. The long shadows of the forest had slipped downhill while we talked, had gone far beyond the ruined hovel, beyond the symbolic row of stakes. All this was in the gloom, while we down there were yet in the sunshine, and the stretch of the river abreast of the clearing glittered in a still and dazzling splendour, with a murky and overshadowed bend above and below. Not a living soul was seen on the shore. The bushes did not rustle.

"Suddenly round the corner of the house a group of men appeared, as though they had come up from the ground. They waded waist-deep in the grass, in a compact body, bearing an improvised stretcher in their midst. Instantly, in the emptiness of the landscape, a cry arose whose shrillness pierced the still air like a sharp arrow flying straight to the very heart of the land; and, as if by enchantment, streams of human beings—of naked human beings—with spears in their hands, with bows, with shields, with wild glances and savage movements, were poured into the clearing by the dark-faced and pensive forest. The bushes shook, the grass swayed for a time, and then everything stood still in attentive immobility.

"'Now, if he does not say the right thing to them we are all done for,' said the Russian at my elbow. The knot of men with the stretcher had stopped too, halfway to the steamer, as if petrified. I saw the man on the stretcher sit up, lank and with an uplifted arm, above the shoulders of the bearers. 'Let us hope that the man who can talk so well of love in general will find some particular reason to spare us this time,' I said. I resented bitterly the absurd danger of our situation, as if to be at the mercy of that atrocious phantom had been a dishonouring necessity. I could not hear a sound, but through my glasses I saw the thin arm extended commandingly, the lower jaw moving, the eyes of that apparition shining darkly far in its bony head that nodded with grotesque jerks. Kurtz—Kurtz—that means 'short' in German—don't it? Well, the name was as true as everything else in his life—and death. He looked at least seven feet long. His covering had fallen off, and his body emerged from it pitiful and appalling as from a winding-sheet. I could see the cage of his ribs all astir, the bones of his arm waving. It was as though an animated image of death carved out of old ivory had been shaking its hand with menaces at a motionless crowd of men made of dark and glittering bronze. I saw him open his mouth wide—it gave him a weirdly voracious aspect, as though he had wanted to swallow all the air, all the earth, all the men before him. A deep voice reached me faintly. He must have been shouting. He fell back suddenly. The stretcher shook as the bearers staggered forward again, and almost at the same time I noticed that the crowd of savages was vanishing without any perceptible movement of retreat, as if the forest that had ejected these beings so suddenly had drawn them in again as the breath is drawn in a long aspiration.

"Some of the pilgrims behind the stretcher carried his arms—two shot-guns, a heavy rifle, and a light revolver-carbine—the thunderbolts of that pitiful Jupiter. The manager bent over him murmuring as he walked beside his head.

They laid him down in one of the little cabins—just a room for a bed-place and a camp-stool or two, you know. We had brought his belated correspondence, and a lot of torn envelopes and open letters littered his bed. His hand roamed feebly amongst these papers. I was struck by the fire of his eyes and the composed languor of his expression. It was not so much the exhaustion of disease. He did not seem in pain. This shadow looked satiated and calm, as though for the moment it had had its fill of all the emotions.

"He rustled one of the letters, and looking straight in my face said, 'I am glad.' Somebody had been writing to him about me. These special recommendations were turning up again. The volume of tone he emitted without effort, almost without the trouble of moving his lips, amazed me. A voice! a voice! It was grave, profound, vibrating, while the man did not seem capable of a whisper. However, he had enough strength in him—factitious no doubt—to very nearly make an end of us, as you shall hear directly.

"The manager appeared silently in the doorway; I stepped out at once and he drew the curtain after me. The Russian, eyed curiously by the pilgrims, was staring at the shore. I followed the direction of his glance.

"Dark human shapes could be made out in the distance, flitting indistinctly against the gloomy border of the forest, and near the river two bronze figures, leaning on tall spears, stood in the sunlight under fantastic head-dresses of spotted skins, warlike and still in statuesque repose. And from right to left along the lighted shore moved a wild and gorgeous apparition of a woman.

"She walked with measured steps, draped in striped and fringed cloths, treading the earth proudly, with a slight jingle and flash of barbarous ornaments. She carried her head high; her hair was done in the shape of a helmet; she had brass leggings to the knees, brass wire gauntlets to the elbow, a crimson spot on her tawny cheek, innumerable necklaces of glass beads on her neck; bizarre things, charms, gifts of witch-men, that hung about her, glittered and trembled at every step. She must have had the value of several elephant tusks upon her. She was savage and superb, wild-eyed and magnificent; there was something ominous and stately in her deliberate progress. And in the hush that had fallen suddenly upon the whole sorrowful land, the immense wilderness, the colossal body of the fecund and mysterious life seemed to look at her, pensive, as though it had been looking at the image of its own tenebrous and passionate soul.

"She came abreast of the steamer, stood still, and faced us. Her long shadow fell to the water's edge. Her face had a tragic and fierce aspect of wild sorrow and of dumb pain mingled with the fear of some struggling, half-shaped resolve. She stood looking at us without a stir, and like the wilderness itself, with an air of brooding over an inscrutable purpose. A whole minute passed, and then she made a step forward. There was a low jingle, a glint of yellow metal, a sway of fringed draperies, and she stopped as if her heart had failed her. The young fellow by my side growled. The pilgrims murmured at my back. She looked at us all as if her life had depended upon the unswerving steadiness of her glance. Suddenly she opened her bared arms and threw them up rigid above her head, as though in an uncontrollable desire to touch the sky, and at the same time the swift shadows darted out on the earth, swept around on the river, gathering the steamer in a shadowy embrace. A formidable silence hung over the scene.

"She turned away slowly, walked on, following the bank, and passed into the bushes to the left. Once only her eyes gleamed back at us in the dusk of the thickets before she disappeared.

"'If she had offered to come aboard I really think I would have tried to shoot her,' said the man of patches nervously. 'I had been risking my life every day for the last fortnight to keep her out of the house. She got in one day and kicked up a row about those miserable rags I picked up in the storeroom to mend my clothes with. I wasn't decent. At least it must have been that, for she talked like a fury to Kurtz for an hour, pointing at me now and then. I don't understand the dialect of this tribe. Luckily for me, I fancy Kurtz felt too ill that day to care, or there would have been mischief. I don't understand. ... No—it's too much for me. Ah, well, it's all over now.'

"At this moment I heard Kurtz's deep voice behind the curtain: 'Save me!—save the ivory, you mean. Don't tell me. Save *me*! Why, I've had to save you. You are interrupting my plans now. Sick! Sick! Not so sick as you would like to believe. Never mind. I'll carry my ideas out yet—I will return. I'll show you what can be done. You with your little peddling notions—you are interfering with me. I will return. I ...'

"The manager came out. He did me the honour to take me under the arm and lead me aside. 'He is very low, very low,' he said. He considered it necessary to sigh, but neglected to be consistently sorrowful. 'We have done all we could for him—haven't we? But there is no disguising the fact, Mr. Kurtz has done more harm than good to the Company. He did not see the time was not ripe for vigorous action. Cautiously, cautiously—that's my principle. We must be cautious yet. The district is closed to us for a time. Deplorable! Upon the whole, the trade will suffer. I don't deny there is a remarkable quantity of ivory—mostly fossil. We must save it, at all events—but look how precarious the position is—and why? Because the method is unsound.' 'Do you,' said I, looking at the shore, 'call it "unsound method"?' 'Without doubt,' he exclaimed hotly. 'Don't you?' ... 'No method at all,' I murmured after a while. 'Exactly,' he exulted. 'I anticipated this. Shows a complete want of judgment. It is my duty to point it out in the proper quarter.' 'Oh,' said I, 'that fellow—what's his name?—the brickmaker, will make a readable report for you.' He appeared confounded for a moment. It seemed to me I had never breathed an atmosphere so vile, and I turned mentally to Kurtz for relief—positively for relief. 'Nevertheless, I think Mr. Kurtz is a remarkable man,' I said with emphasis. He started, dropped on me a cold heavy glance, said very quietly, 'He *was*,' and turned his back on me. My hour of favour was over; I found myself lumped along with Kurtz as a partisan of methods for which the time was not ripe: I was unsound! Ah! but it was something to have at least a choice of nightmares.

"I had turned to the wilderness really, not to Mr. Kurtz, who, I was ready to admit, was as good as buried. And for a moment it seemed to me as if I also were buried in a vast grave full of unspeakable secrets. I felt an intolerable weight oppressing my breast, the smell of the damp earth, the unseen presence of victorious corruption, the darkness of an impenetrable night. … The Russian tapped me on the shoulder. I heard him mumbling and stammering something about 'brother seaman—couldn't conceal—knowledge of matters that would affect Mr. Kurtz's reputation.' I waited. For him evidently Mr. Kurtz was not in his grave; I suspect that for him Mr. Kurtz was one of the immortals. 'Well!' said I at last, 'speak out. As it happens, I am Mr. Kurtz's friend—in a way.'

"He stated with a good deal of formality that had we not been 'of the same profession,' he would have kept the matter to himself without regard to consequences. He suspected 'there was an active ill-will towards him on the part of these white men that——' 'You are right,' I said, remembering a certain conversation I had overheard. 'The manager thinks you ought to be hanged.' He showed a concern at this intelligence which amused me at first. 'I had better get out of the way quietly,' he said earnestly. 'I can do no more for Kurtz now, and they would soon find some excuse. What's to stop them? There's a military post three hundred miles from here.' 'Well, upon my word,' said I, 'perhaps you had better go if you have any friends amongst the savages near by.' 'Plenty,' he said. 'They are simple people—and I want nothing, you know.' He stood biting his lip, then: 'I don't want any harm to happen to these whites here, but of course I was thinking of Mr. Kurtz's reputation—but you are a brother seaman and——' 'All right,' said I, after a time. 'Mr. Kurtz's reputation is safe with me.' I did not know how truly I spoke.

"He informed me, lowering his voice, that it was Kurtz who had ordered the attack to be made on the steamer. 'He hated sometimes the idea of being taken away—and then again … But I don't understand these matters. I am a simple man. He thought it would scare you away—that you would give it up, thinking him dead. I could not stop him. Oh, I had an awful time of it this last month.' 'Very well,' I said. 'He is all right now.' 'Ye-e-es,' he muttered, not very convinced apparently. 'Thanks,' said I; 'I shall keep my eyes open.' 'But quiet—eh?' he urged anxiously. 'It would be awful for his reputation if anybody here—' I promised a complete discretion with great gravity. 'I have a canoe and three black fellows waiting not very far. I am off. Could you give me a few Martini-Henry cartridges?' I could, and did, with proper secrecy. He helped himself, with a wink at me, to a handful of my tobacco. 'Between sailors—you know—good English tobacco.' At the door of the pilot-house he turned round—'I say haven't you a pair of shoes you could spare?' He raised one leg. 'Look.' The soles were tied with knotted strings sandal-wise under his bare feet. I rooted out an old pair, at which he looked with admiration before tucking it under his left arm. One of his pockets (bright red) was bulging with cartridges, from the other (dark blue) peeped 'Towson's Inquiry,' etc. etc. He seemed to think himself excellently well equipped for a renewed encounter with the wilderness. 'Ah! I'll never, never meet such a man again. You ought to have heard him recite poetry—his own too it was, he told me. Poetry!' He rolled his eyes at the recollection of these delights. 'Oh, he enlarged my mind!'—'Good-bye,' said I. He shook hands and vanished in the night. Sometimes I ask myself whether I had ever really seen him—whether it was possible to meet such a phenomenon! …

"When I woke up shortly after midnight his warning came to my mind with its hint of danger that seemed, in the starred darkness, real enough to make me get up for the purpose of having a look round. On the hill a big fire burned, illuminating fitfully a crooked corner of the station-house. One of the agents with a picket of a few of our blacks, armed for the purpose, was keeping guard over the ivory; but deep within the forest, red gleams that wavered, that seemed to sink and rise from the ground amongst confused columnar shapes of intense blackness, showed the exact position of the camp where Mr. Kurtz's adorers were keeping their uneasy vigil. The monotonous beating of a big drum filled the air with muffled shocks and a lingering vibration. A steady droning sound of many men chanting each to himself some weird incantation came out from the black, flat wall of the woods as the humming of bees comes out of a hive, and had a strange narcotic effect upon my half-awake senses. I believe I dozed off leaning over the rail, till an abrupt burst of yells, an overwhelming outbreak of a pent-up and mysterious frenzy, woke me up in a bewildered wonder. It was cut short all at once, and the low droning went on with an effect of audible and soothing silence. I glanced casually into the little cabin. A light was burning within, but Mr. Kurtz was not there.

"I think I would have raised an outcry if I had believed my eyes. But I didn't believe them at first—the thing seemed so impossible. The fact is, I was completely unnerved by a sheer blank fright, pure abstract terror, unconnected with any distinct shape of physical danger. What made this emotion so overpowering was—how shall I define it?—the moral shock I received, as if something altogether monstrous, intolerable to thought and odious to the soul, had been thrust upon me unexpectedly. This lasted of course the merest fraction of a second, and then the usual sense of commonplace, deadly danger, the possibility of a sudden onslaught and massacre, or something of the kind, which I saw impending, was positively welcome and composing. It pacified me, in fact, so much, that I did not raise an alarm.

"There was an agent buttoned up inside an ulster and sleeping on a chair on deck within three feet of me. The yells had not awakened him; he snored very slightly; I left him to his slumbers and leaped ashore. I did not betray Mr. Kurtz—it was ordered I should never betray him—it was written I should be loyal to the nightmare of my choice. I was anxious to deal with this shadow by myself alone—and to this day I don't know why I was so jealous of sharing with any one the peculiar blackness of that experience.

"As soon as I got on the bank I saw a trail—a broad trail through the grass. I remember the exultation with which I said to myself, 'He can't walk—he is crawling on all-fours—I've got him.' The grass was wet with dew. I strode rapidly with clenched fists. I fancy I had some vague notion of falling upon him and giving him a drubbing. I don't know. I had some imbecile thoughts. The knitting old woman with the cat obtruded herself upon my memory as a most improper person to be sitting at the other end of such an affair. I saw a row of pilgrims squirting lead in the air out of Winchesters held to the hip. I thought I would never get back to the steamer, and imagined myself living alone and unarmed in the woods to an advanced age. Such silly things—you know. And I remember I confounded the beat of the drum with the beating of my heart, and was pleased at its calm regularity.

"I kept to the track though—then stopped to listen. The night was very clear; a dark blue space, sparkling with dew and starlight, in which black things stood very still. I thought I could see a kind of motion ahead of me. I was strangely cocksure of everything that night. I actually left the track and ran in a wide semicircle (I verily believe chuckling to myself) so as to get in front of that stir, of that motion I had seen—if indeed I had seen anything. I was circumventing Kurtz as though it had been a boyish game.

"I came upon him, and, if he had not heard me coming, I would have fallen over him too, but he got up in time. He rose, unsteady, long, pale, indistinct, like a vapour exhaled by the earth, and swayed slightly, misty and silent before me; while at my back the fires loomed between the trees, and the murmur of many voices issued from the forest. I had cut him off cleverly; but when actually confronting him I seemed to come to my senses, I saw the danger in its right proportion. It was by no means over yet. Suppose he began to shout? Though he could hardly stand, there was still plenty of vigour in his voice. 'Go away—hide yourself,' he said, in that profound tone. It was very awful. I glanced back. We were within thirty yards from the nearest fire. A black figure stood up, strode on long black legs, waving long black arms, across the glow. It had horns—antelope horns, I think—on its head. Some sorcerer, some witch-man, no doubt: it looked fiend-like enough. 'Do you know what you are doing?' I whispered. 'Perfectly,' he answered, raising his voice for that single word: it sounded to me far off and yet loud, like a hail through a speaking-trumpet. If he makes a row we are lost, I thought to myself. This clearly was not a case for fisticuffs, even apart from the very natural aversion I had to beat that Shadow—this wandering and tormented thing. 'You will be lost,' I said—'utterly lost.' One gets sometimes such a flash of inspiration, you know. I did say the right thing, though indeed he could not have been more irretrievably lost than he was at this very moment, when the foundations of our intimacy were being laid—to endure—to endure—even to the end—even beyond.

"'I had immense plans,' he muttered irresolutely. 'Yes,' said I; 'but if you try to shout I'll smash your head with——' There was not a stick or a stone near. 'I will throttle you for good,' I corrected myself. 'I was on the threshold of great things,' he pleaded, in a voice of longing, with a wistfulness of tone that made my blood run cold. 'And now for this stupid scoundrel——' 'Your success in Europe is assured in any case,' I affirmed steadily. I did not want to have the throttling of him, you understand—and indeed it would have been very little use for any practical purpose. I tried to break the spell—the heavy, mute spell of the wilderness—that seemed to draw him to its pitiless breast by the awakening of forgotten and brutal instincts, by the memory of gratified and monstrous passions. This alone, I was convinced, had driven him out to the edge of the forest, to the bush, towards the gleam of fires, the throb of drums, the drone of weird incantations; this alone had beguiled his unlawful soul beyond the bounds of permitted aspirations. And, don't you see, the terror of the position was not in being knocked on the head—though I had a very lively sense of that danger too—but in this, that I had to deal with a being to whom I could not appeal in the name of anything high or low. I had, even like the niggers, to invoke him—himself—his own exalted and incredible degradation. There was nothing either above or below him, and I knew it. He had kicked himself loose of the earth. Confound the man! he had kicked the very earth to pieces. He was alone, and I before him did not know whether I stood on the ground or floated in the air. I've been telling you what we said—repeating the phrases we pronounced—but what's the good? They were common everyday words—the familiar, vague sounds exchanged on every waking day of life. But what of that? They had behind them, to my mind, the terrific suggestiveness of words heard in dreams, of phrases spoken in nightmares. Soul! If anybody had ever struggled with a soul, I am the man. And I wasn't arguing with a lunatic either. Believe me or not, his intelligence was perfectly clear—concentrated, it is true, upon himself with horrible intensity, yet clear; and therein was my only chance—barring, of course, the killing him there and then, which wasn't so good, on account of unavoidable noise. But his soul was mad. Being alone in the wilderness, it had looked within itself, and, by Heavens! I tell you, it had gone mad. I had—for my sins, I suppose, to go through the ordeal of looking into it myself. No eloquence could have been so withering to one's belief in mankind as his final burst of sincerity. He struggled with himself too. I saw it—I heard it. I saw the inconceivable mystery of a soul that knew no restraint, no faith, and no fear, yet struggling blindly with itself. I kept my head pretty well; but when I had him at last stretched on the couch, I wiped my forehead, while my legs shook under me as though I had carried half a ton on my back down that hill. And yet I had only supported him, his bony arm clasped round my neck—and he was not much heavier than a child.

"When next day we left at noon, the crowd, of whose presence behind the curtain of trees I had been acutely conscious all the time, flowed out of the woods again, filled the clearing, covered the slope with a mass of naked, breathing, quivering, bronze bodies. I steamed up a bit, then swung down-stream, and two thousand eyes followed the evolutions of the splashing, thumping, fierce river-demon beating the water with its terrible tail and breathing black smoke into the air. In front of the first rank, along the river, three men, plastered with bright red earth from head to foot, strutted to and fro restlessly. When we came abreast again, they faced the river, stamped their feet, nodded their horned heads, swayed their scarlet bodies; they shook towards the fierce river-demon a bunch of black feathers, a mangy skin with a pendent tail—something that looked like a dried gourd; they shouted periodically together strings of amazing words that resembled no sounds of human language; and the deep murmurs of the crowd, interrupted suddenly, were like the responses of some satanic litany.

"We had carried Kurtz into the pilot-house: there was more air there. Lying on the couch, he stared through the open shutter. There was an eddy in the mass of human bodies, and the woman with helmeted head and tawny cheeks rushed out to the very brink of the stream. She put out her hands, shouted something, and all that wild mob took up the shout in a roaring chorus of articulated, rapid, breathless utterance.

"'Do you understand this?' I asked.

"He kept on looking out past me with fiery, longing eyes, with a mingled expression of wistfulness and hate. He made no answer, but I saw a smile, a smile of indefinable meaning, appear on his colourless lips that a moment after twitched convulsively. 'Do I not?' he said slowly, gasping, as if the words had been torn out of him by a supernatural power.

"I pulled the string of the whistle, and I did this because I saw the pilgrims on deck getting out their rifles with an air of anticipating a jolly lark. At the sudden screech there was a movement of abject terror through that wedged mass of bodies. 'Don't! don't you frighten them away,' cried some one on deck disconsolately. I pulled the string time after time. They broke and ran, they leaped, they crouched, they swerved, they dodged the flying terror of the sound. The three red chaps had fallen flat, face down on the shore, as though they had been shot dead. Only the barbarous and superb woman did not so much as flinch, and stretched tragically her bare arms after us over the sombre and glittering river.

"And then that imbecile crowd down on the deck started their little fun, and I could see nothing more for smoke.

"The brown current ran swiftly out of the heart of darkness, bearing us down towards the sea with twice the speed of our upward progress; and Kurtz's life was running swiftly too, ebbing, ebbing out of his heart into the sea of inexorable time. The manager was very placid, he had no vital anxieties now, he took us both in with a comprehensive and satisfied glance: the 'affair' had come off as well as could be wished. I saw the time approaching when I would be left alone of the party of 'unsound method.' The pilgrims looked upon me with disfavour. I was, so to speak, numbered with the dead. It is strange how I accepted this unforeseen partnership, this choice of nightmares forced upon me in the tenebrous land invaded by these mean and greedy phantoms.

"Kurtz discoursed. A voice! a voice! It rang deep to the very last. It survived his strength to hide in the magnificent folds of eloquence the barren darkness of his heart. Oh, he struggled! he struggled! The wastes of his weary brain were haunted by shadowy images now—images of wealth and fame revolving obsequiously round his unextinguishable gift of noble and lofty expression. My Intended, my station, my career, my ideas—these were the subjects for the occasional utterances of elevated sentiments. The shade of the original Kurtz frequented the bedside of the hollow sham, whose fate it was to be buried presently in the mould of primeval earth. But both the diabolic love and the unearthly hate of the mysteries it had penetrated fought for the possession of that soul satiated with primitive emotions, avid of lying fame, of sham distinction, of all the appearances of success and power.

"Sometimes he was contemptibly childish. He desired to have kings meet him at railway stations on his return from some ghastly Nowhere, where be intended to accomplish great things. 'You show them you have in you something that is really profitable, and then there will be no limits to the recognition of your ability,' he would say. 'Of course you must take care of the motives—right motives—always.' The long reaches that were like one and the same reach, monotonous bends that were exactly alike, slipped past the steamer with their multitude of secular trees looking patiently after this grimy fragment of another world, the forerunner of change, of conquest, of trade, of massacres, of blessings. I looked ahead—piloting. 'Close the shutter,' said Kurtz suddenly one day; 'I can't bear to look at this.' I did so. There was a silence. 'Oh, but I will wring your heart yet!' he cried at the invisible wilderness.

"We broke down—as I had expected—and had to lie up for repairs at the head of an island. This delay was the first thing that shook Kurtz's confidence. One morning he gave me a packet of papers and a photograph—the lot tied together with a shoe-string. 'Keep this for me,' he said. 'This noxious fool' (meaning the manager) 'is capable of prying into my boxes when I am not looking.' In the afternoon I saw him. He was lying on his back with closed eyes, and I withdrew quietly, but I heard him mutter, 'Live rightly, die, die ...' I listened. There was nothing more. Was he rehearsing some speech in his sleep, or was it a fragment of a phrase from some newspaper article? He had been writing for the papers and meant to do so again, 'for the furthering of my ideas. It's a duty.'

"His was an impenetrable darkness. I looked at him as you peer down at a man who is lying at the bottom of a precipice where the sun never shines. But I had not much time to give him, because I was helping the engine-driver to take to pieces the leaky cylinders, to straighten a bent connecting-rod, and in other such matters. I lived in an infernal mess of rust, filings, nuts, bolts, spanners, hammers, ratchet-drills—things I abominate, because I don't get on with them. I tended the little forge we fortunately had aboard; I toiled wearily in a wretched scrap-heap—unless I had the shakes too bad to stand.

"One evening coming in with a candle I was startled to hear him say a little tremulously, 'I am lying here in the dark waiting for death.' The light was within a foot of his eyes. I forced myself to murmur, 'Oh, nonsense!' and stood over him as if transfixed.

"Anything approaching the change that came over his features I have never seen before, and hope never to see again. Oh, I wasn't touched. I was fascinated. It was as though a veil had been rent. I saw on that ivory face the expression of sombre pride, of ruthless power, of craven terror—of an intense and hopeless despair. Did he live his life again in every detail of desire, temptation, and surrender during that supreme moment of complete knowledge? He cried in a whisper at some image, at some vision—he cried out twice, a cry that was no more than a breath:

"'The horror! The horror!'

"I blew the candle out and left the cabin. The pilgrims were dining in the mess-room, and I took my place opposite the manager, who lifted his eyes to give me a questioning glance, which I successfully ignored. He leaned back, serene, with that peculiar smile of his sealing the unexpressed depths of his meanness. A continuous shower of small flies streamed upon the lamp, upon the cloth, upon our hands and faces. Suddenly the manager's boy put his insolent black head in the doorway, and said in a tone of scathing contempt:

"'Mistah Kurtz—he dead.'

"All the pilgrims rushed out to see. I remained, and went on with my dinner. I believe I was considered brutally callous. However, I did not eat much. There was a lamp in there—light, don't you know—and outside it was so beastly, beastly dark. I went no more near the remarkable man who had pronounced a judgment upon the adventures of his soul on this earth. The voice was gone. What else had been there? But I am of course aware that next day the pilgrims buried something in a muddy hole.

"And then they very nearly buried me.

"However, as you see, I did not go to join Kurtz there and then. I did not. I remained to dream the nightmare out to the end, and to show my loyalty to Kurtz once more. Destiny. My destiny! Droll thing life is—that mysterious arrangement of merciless logic for a futile purpose. The most you can hope from it is some knowledge of yourself—that comes too late—a crop of unextinguishable regrets. I have wrestled with death. It is the most unexciting contest you can imagine. It takes place in an impalpable greyness, with nothing underfoot, with nothing around, without spectators, without clamour, without glory, without the great desire of victory, without the great fear of defeat; in a sickly atmosphere of tepid scepticism, without much belief in your own right, and still less in that of your adversary. If such is the form of ultimate wisdom, then life is a greater riddle than some of us think it to be. I was within a hair's-breadth of the last opportunity for pronouncement, and I found with humiliation that probably I would have nothing to say. This is the reason why I affirm that Kurtz was a remarkable man. He had something to say. He said it. Since I had peeped over the edge myself, I understand better the meaning of his stare, that could not see the flame of the candle, but was wide enough to embrace the whole universe, piercing enough to penetrate all the hearts that beat in the darkness. He had summed up—he had judged. 'The horror!' He was a remarkable man. After all, this was the expression of some sort of belief; it had candour, it had conviction, it had a vibrating note of revolt in its whisper, it had the appalling face of a glimpsed truth—the strange commingling of desire and hate. And it is not my own extremity I remember best—a vision of greyness without form filled with physical pain, and a careless contempt for the evanescence of all things—even of this pain itself. No! It is his extremity that I seem to have lived through. True, he had made that last stride, he had stepped over the edge, while I had been permitted to draw back my hesitating foot. And perhaps in this is the whole difference; perhaps all the wisdom, and all truth, and all sincerity, are just compressed into that inappreciable moment of time in which we step over the threshold of the invisible. Perhaps! I like to think my summing-up would not have been a word of careless contempt. Better his cry—much better. It was an affirmation, a moral victory paid for by innumerable defeats, by abominable terrors, by abominable satisfactions. But it was a victory! That is why I have remained loyal to Kurtz to the last, and even beyond, when a long time after I heard once more, not his own voice, but the echo of his magnificent eloquence thrown to me from a soul as translucently pure as a cliff of crystal.

"No, they did not bury me, though there is a period of time which I remember mistily, with a shuddering wonder, like a passage through some inconceivable world that had no hope in it and no desire. I found myself back in the sepulchral city resenting the sight of people hurrying through the streets to filch a little money from each other, to devour their infamous cookery, to gulp their unwholesome beer, to dream their insignificant and silly dreams. They trespassed upon my thoughts. They were intruders whose knowledge of life was to me an irritating pretence, because I felt so sure they could not possibly know the things I knew. Their bearing, which was simply the bearing of commonplace individuals going about their business in the assurance of perfect safety, was offensive to me like the outrageous flauntings of folly in the face of a danger it is unable to comprehend. I had no particular desire to enlighten them, but I had some difficulty in restraining myself from laughing in their faces, so full of stupid importance. I daresay I was not very well at that time. I tottered about the streets—there were various affairs to settle—grinning bitterly at perfectly respectable persons. I admit my behaviour was inexcusable, but then my temperature was seldom normal in these days. My dear aunt's endeavours to 'nurse up my strength' seemed altogether beside the mark. It was not my strength that wanted nursing, it was my imagination that wanted soothing. I kept the bundle of papers given me by Kurtz, not knowing exactly what to do with it. His mother had died lately, watched over, as I was told, by his Intended. A clean-shaved man, with an official manner and wearing gold-rimmed spectacles, called on me one day and made inquiries, at first circuitous, afterwards suavely pressing, about what he was pleased to denominate certain 'documents.' I was not surprised, because I had had two rows with the manager on the subject out there. I had refused to give up the smallest scrap out of that package, and I took the same attitude with the spectacled man. He became darkly menacing at last, and with much heat argued that the Company had the right to every bit of information about its 'territories.' And, said he, 'Mr. Kurtz's knowledge of unexplored regions must have been necessarily extensive and peculiar—owing to his great abilities and to the deplorable circumstances in which he had been placed: therefore——' I assured him Mr. Kurtz's knowledge, however extensive, did not bear upon the problems of commerce or administration. He invoked then the name of science. 'It would be an incalculable loss if,' etc. etc. I offered him the report on the 'Suppression of Savage Customs,' with the postscriptum torn off. He took it up eagerly, but ended by sniffing at it with an air of contempt. 'This is not what we had a right to expect,' he remarked. 'Expect nothing else,' I said. 'There are only private letters.' He withdrew upon some threat of legal proceedings, and I saw him no more; but another fellow, calling himself Kurtz's cousin, appeared two days later, and was anxious to hear all the details about his dear relative's last moments. Incidentally he gave me to understand that Kurtz had been essentially a great musician. 'There was the making of an immense success,' said the man, who was an organist, I believe, with lank grey hair flowing over a greasy coat-collar. I had no reason to doubt his statement; and to this day I am unable to say what was Kurtz's profession, whether he ever had any—which was the greatest of his talents. I had taken him for a painter who wrote for the papers, or else for a journalist who could paint—but even the cousin (who took snuff during the interview) could not tell me what he had been—exactly. He was a universal genius—on that point I agreed with the old chap, who thereupon blew his nose noisily into a large cotton handkerchief and withdrew in senile agitation, bearing off some family letters and memoranda without importance. Ultimately a journalist anxious to know something of the fate of his 'dear colleague' turned up. This visitor informed me Kurtz's proper sphere ought to have been politics 'on the popular side.' He had furry straight eyebrows, bristly hair cropped short, an eyeglass on a broad ribbon, and, becoming expansive, confessed his opinion that Kurtz really couldn't write a bit—' but Heavens! how that man could talk! He electrified large meetings. He had faith—don't you see?—he had the faith. He could get himself to believe anything—anything. He would have been a splendid leader of an extreme party.' 'What party?' I asked. 'Any party,' answered the other. 'He was an—an—extremist.' Did I not think so? I assented. Did I know, he asked, with a sudden flash of curiosity, 'what it was that had induced him to go out there?' 'Yes,' said I, and forthwith handed him the famous Report for publication, if he thought fit. He glanced through it hurriedly, mumbling all the time, judged 'it would do,' and took himself off with this plunder.

"Thus I was left at last with a slim packet of letters and the girl's portrait. She struck me as beautiful—I mean she had a beautiful expression. I know that the sunlight can be made to lie too, yet one felt that no manipulation of light and pose could have conveyed the delicate shade of truthfulness upon those features. She seemed ready to listen without mental reservation, without suspicion, without a thought for herself. I concluded I would go and give her back her portrait and those letters myself. Curiosity? Yes; and also some other feeling perhaps. All that had been Kurtz's had passed out of my hands: his soul, his body, his station, his plans, his ivory, his career. There remained only his memory and his Intended—and I wanted to give that up too to the past, in a way—to surrender personally all that remained of him with me to that oblivion which is the last word of our common fate. I don't defend myself. I had no clear perception of what it was I really wanted. Perhaps it was an impulse of unconscious loyalty, or the fulfilment of one of those ironic necessities that lurk in the facts of human existence. I don't know. I can't tell. But I went.

"I thought his memory was like the other memories of the dead that accumulate in every man's life—a vague impress on the brain of shadows that had fallen on it in their swift and final passage; but before the high and ponderous door, between the tall houses of a street as still and decorous as a well-kept alley in a cemetery, I had a vision of him on the stretcher, opening his mouth voraciously, as if to devour all the earth with all its mankind. He lived then before me; he lived as much as he had ever lived—a shadow insatiable of splendid appearances, of frightful realities; a shadow darker than the shadow of the night, and draped nobly in the folds of a gorgeous eloquence. The vision seemed to enter the house with me—the stretcher, the phantom-bearers, the wild crowd of obedient worshippers, the gloom of the forests, the glitter of the reach between the murky bends, the beat of the drum, regular and muffled like the beating of a heart—the heart of a conquering darkness. It was a moment of triumph for the wilderness, an invading and vengeful rush which, it seemed to me, I would have to keep back alone for the salvation of another soul. And the memory of what I had heard him say afar there, with the horned shapes stirring at my back, in the glow of fires, within the patient woods, those broken phrases came back to me, were heard again in their ominous and terrifying simplicity. I remembered his abject pleading, his abject threats, the colossal scale of his vile desires, the meanness, the torment, the tempestuous anguish of his soul. And later on I seemed to see his collected languid manner, when he said one day, 'This lot of ivory now is really mine. The Company did not pay for it. I collected it myself at a very great personal risk. I am afraid they will try to claim it as theirs though. H'm. It is a difficult case. What do you think I ought to do—resist? Eh? I want no more than justice.' ... He wanted no more than justice—no more than justice. I rang the bell before a mahogany door on the first floor, and while I waited he seemed to stare at me out of the glassy panel—stare with that wide and immense stare embracing, condemning, loathing all the universe. I seemed to hear the whispered cry, 'The horror! The horror!'

"The dusk was falling. I had to wait in a lofty drawing-room with three long windows from floor to ceiling that were like three luminous and bedraped columns. The bent gilt legs and backs of the furniture shone in indistinct curves. The tall marble fireplace had a cold and monumental whiteness. A grand piano stood massively in a corner; with dark gleams on the flat surfaces like a sombre and polished sarcophagus. A high door opened—closed. I rose.

"She came forward, all in black, with a pale head, floating towards me in the dusk. She was in mourning. It was more than a year since his death, more than a year since the news came; she seemed as though she would remember and mourn for ever. She took both my hands in hers and murmured, 'I had heard you were coming.' I noticed she was not very young—I mean not girlish. She had a mature capacity for fidelity, for belief, for suffering. The room seemed to have grown darker, as if all the sad light of the cloudy evening had taken refuge on her forehead. This fair hair, this pale visage, this pure brow, seemed surrounded by an ashy halo from which the dark eyes looked out at me. Their glance was guileless, profound, confident, and trustful. She carried her sorrowful head as though she were proud of that sorrow, as though she would say, I—I alone know how to mourn for him as he deserves. But while we were still shaking hands, such a look of awful desolation came upon her face that I perceived she was one of those creatures that are not the playthings of Time. For her he had died only yesterday. And, by Jove! the impression was so powerful that for me too he seemed to have died only yesterday—nay, this very minute. I saw her and him in the same instant of time—his death and her sorrow—I saw her sorrow in the very moment of his death. Do you understand? I saw them together—I heard them together. She had said, with a deep catch of the breath, 'I have survived';

while my strained ears seemed to hear distinctly, mingled with her tone of despairing regret, the summing-up whisper of his eternal condemnation. I asked myself what I was doing there, with a sensation of panic in my heart as though I had blundered into a place of cruel and absurd mysteries not fit for a human being to behold. She motioned me to a chair. We sat down. I laid the packet gently on the little table, and she put her hand over it. ... 'You knew him well,' she murmured, after a moment of mourning silence.

"'Intimacy grows quickly out there,' I said. 'I knew him as well as it is possible for one man to know another.'

"'And you admired him,' she said. 'It was impossible to know him and not to admire him. Was it?'

"'He was a remarkable man,' I said unsteadily. Then before the appealing fixity of her gaze, that seemed to watch for more words on my lips, I went on, 'It was impossible not to——'

"'Love him,' she finished eagerly, silencing me into an appalled dumbness. 'How true! how true! But when you think that no one knew him so well as I! I had all his noble confidence. I knew him best.'

"'You knew him best,' I repeated. And perhaps she did. But with every word spoken the room was growing darker, and only her forehead, smooth and white, remained illumined by the unextinguishable light of belief and love.

"'You were his friend,' she went on. 'His friend,' she repeated, a little louder. 'You must have been, if he had given you this, and sent you to me. I feel I can speak to you—and oh! I must speak. I want you—you who have heard his last words—to know I have been worthy of him. ... It is not pride. ... Yes! I am proud to know I understood him better than any one on earth—he told me so himself. And since his mother died I have had no one—no one—to—to——'

"I listened. The darkness deepened. I was not even sure whether he had given me the right bundle. I rather suspect he wanted me to take care of another batch of his papers which, after his death, I saw the manager examining under the lamp. And the girl talked, easing her pain in the certitude of my sympathy; she talked as thirsty men drink. I had heard that her engagement with Kurtz had been disapproved by her people. He wasn't rich enough or something. And indeed I don't know whether he had not been a pauper all his life. He had given me some reason to infer that it was his impatience of comparative poverty that drove him out there.

"'... Who was not his friend who had heard him speak once?' she was saying. 'He drew men towards him by what was best in them.' She looked at me with intensity. 'It is the gift of the great,' she went on, and the sound of her low voice seemed to have the accompaniment of all the other sounds, full of mystery, desolation, and sorrow, I had ever heard—the ripple of the river, the soughing of the trees swayed by the wind, the murmurs of the crowds, the faint ring of incomprehensible words cried from afar, the whisper of a voice speaking from beyond the threshold of an eternal darkness. 'But you have heard him! You know!' she cried.

"'Yes, I know,' I said with something like despair in my heart, but bowing my head before the faith that was in her, before that great and saving illusion that shone with an unearthly glow in the darkness, in the triumphant darkness from which I could not have defended her—from which I could not even defend myself.

"'What a loss to me—to us!'—she corrected herself with beautiful generosity; then added in a murmur, 'To the world.' By the last gleams of twilight I could see the glitter of her eyes, full of tears—of tears that would not fall.

"'I have been very happy—very fortunate—very proud,' she went on. 'Too fortunate. Too happy for a little while. And now I am unhappy for—for life.'

"She stood up; her fair hair seemed to catch all the remaining light in a glimmer of gold. I rose too.

"'And of all this,' she went on mournfully, 'of all his promise, and of all his greatness, of his generous mind, of his noble heart, nothing remains—nothing but a memory. You and I——'

"'We shall always remember him,' I said hastily.

"'No!' she cried. 'It is impossible that all this should be lost—that such a life should be sacrificed to leave nothing—but sorrow. You know what vast plans he had. I knew of them too—I could not perhaps understand—but others knew of them. Something must remain. His words, at least, have not died.'

"'His words will remain,' I said.

"'And his example,' she whispered to herself. 'Men looked up to him—his goodness shone in every act. His example——'

"'True,' I said; 'his example too. Yes, his example. I forgot that.'

"'But I do not. I cannot—I cannot believe—not yet. I cannot believe that I shall never see him again, that nobody will see him again, never, never, never.'

"She put out her arms as if after a retreating figure, stretching them back and with clasped pale hands across the fading and narrow sheen of the window. Never see him! I saw him clearly enough then. I shall see this eloquent phantom as long as I live, and I shall see her too, a tragic and familiar Shade, resembling in this gesture another one, tragic also, and bedecked with powerless charms, stretching bare brown arms over the glitter of the infernal stream, the stream of darkness. She said suddenly very low, 'He died as he lived.'

"'His end,' said I, with dull anger stirring in me, 'was in every way worthy of his life.'

"'And I was not with him,' she murmured. My anger subsided before a feeling of infinite pity.

"'Everything that could be done——' I mumbled.

"'Ah, but I believed in him more than any one on earth—more than his own mother, more than—himself. He needed me! Me! I would have treasured every sigh, every word, every sign, every glance.'

"I felt like a chill grip on my chest. 'Don't,' I said, in a muffled voice.

"'Forgive me. I—I—have mourned so long in silence—in silence. ... You were with him—to the last? I think of his loneliness. Nobody near to understand him as I would have understood. Perhaps no one to hear ...'

"'To the very end,' I said shakily. 'I heard his very last words. ...' I stopped in a fright.

"'Repeat them,' she murmured in a heart-broken tone. 'I want—I want—something—something—to—to live with.'

"I was on the point of crying at her, 'Don't you hear them?' The dusk was repeating them in a persistent whisper all around us, in a whisper that seemed to swell menacingly like the first whisper of a rising wind. 'The horror! The horror!'

"'His last word—to live with,' she insisted. 'Don't you understand I loved him—I loved him—I loved him!'

"I pulled myself together and spoke slowly.

"'The last word he pronounced was—your name.'

"I heard a light sigh and then my heart stood still, stopped dead short by an exulting and terrible cry, by the cry of inconceivable triumph and of unspeakable pain. 'I knew it—I was sure!' ... She knew. She was sure. I heard her weeping; she had hidden her face in her hands. It seemed to me that the house would collapse before I could escape, that the heavens would fall upon my head. But nothing happened. The heavens do not fall for such a trifle. Would they have fallen, I wonder, if I had rendered Kurtz that justice which was his due? Hadn't he said he wanted only justice? But I couldn't. I could not tell her. It would have been too dark—too dark altogether. ..."

Marlow ceased, and sat apart, indistinct and silent, in the pose of a meditating Buddha. Nobody moved for a time. "We have lost the first of the ebb," said the Director suddenly. I raised my head. The offing was barred by a black bank of clouds, and the tranquil waterway leading to the uttermost ends of the earth flowed sombre under an overcast sky—seemed to lead into the heart of an immense darkness.

William Faulkner

William Faulkner was born in New Albany, Mississippi, in 1897 and raised in Oxford, where he spent most of his life, except for a brief stint in the Royal Canadian Air Force in World War I, six months as a rum-runner and beginning novelist in New Orleans, where he met and befriended Sherwood Anderson and wrote *Soldier's Pay* (1926), and some months as a scriptwriter in Hollywood. He worked at odd jobs, including that of a coal porter in a power plant, where he wrote *As I Lay Dying* (1930) in his spare hours during a six-week period. Faulkner attended the University of Mississippi, but never completed a degree and never pursued a public, or literary, life; he wrote sketches and stories for the New Orleans *Times-Picayune* and *The Toronto Star* early in his career, but was very reclusive and resistant to playing the role of artist; only after winning the Nobel Prize for Literature in 1950 did he consent regularly to make himself available for speeches and interviews. Faulkner's reticence may have something to do with the anti-intellectual environment from which he emerged, as this comment from his essay "On Privacy" suggests: "America has not yet found any place for him who deals only in things of the human spirit except to use his notoriety to sell soap or cigarettes or fountain pens or to advertise automobiles and cruises and resort hotels (or if he can be taught to contort fast enough to meet the standards) in radio and moving pictures where he can produce enough income tax to be worth attention."

Although he wrote nothing extensive on the art of fiction and was often deliberately vague or devious in his interviews, Faulkner did, however, offer a few clues concerning his aims and strategies in fiction. He considered language "the damndest clumsiest frailest awkwardest tool" he could have been given, yet one that might reveal something of man's soul, his divinity. His letters to publishers' editors reveal his intense interest in all matters of style, including punctuation, typography, how to telegraph the shift from an objective to a subjective mode, and so on; yet he declared style to be "unimportant": "I think that if one spends too much time bothering too much about his style, he'll finish with having nothing left but style." Faulkner considered that each new work "demands its own style"; beyond that, he felt style to be more a matter of temperament, impinged on, for Americans, by a Puritan sense of urgency and the culture of mass production. While Hemingway forged an "undeviable style," Faulkner claimed that he and Thomas Wolfe did not have that kind of instinct: "We tried to crowd and cram everything, all experience, into each paragraph, to get the whole complete nuance of the moment's experience, all of the recaptured light rays, into each paragraph. That's why it's clumsy and hard to read. ... We just couldn't help it." More likely, he needed his long, labyrinthine sentences and shifting points of view to accommodate the range and complexity of his materials.

"A writer needs 3 things: experience, observation, imagination, any two of which, at times any one of which, can supply the lack of the others," Faulkner wrote. "With me, a story usually begins with a single idea or memory or mental picture. The writing of the story is simply a matter of working up to that moment, to explain why it happened or what it caused to follow. A writer is trying to create credible people in credible moving situations in the most moving way he can." He stressed understatement as the best means of drawing character: "Remember, all Tolstoy said about Anna Karenina was that she was beautiful and could see in the dark like a cat. That's all he ever said to describe her. ... And it's best to take the gesture, the shadow of the branch and let the mind create the tree."

Faulkner often described himself as a failed poet, but his real aim seems to have been to draw attention to the poetic nature of both his prose and his narrative structures. Plot, for him, was "anything that moves you enough to keep working on it. A story usually makes its own plot, works itself out as you go." In other words, the action derives from the intersection of character and context, or situation. His knowledge of human nature and his close reading of his society meant that he had to invent very little: "Beginning with *Sartoris*, I discovered that my own little postage stamp of native soil was worth writing about and that I would never live long enough to exhaust it, and by sublimating the actual into the apocryphal I would have complete liberty to use whatever talent I might have to its absolute top."

By this, he did not mean that he only needed to report or record the events of his time. "Just to report facts, to report injustice sometimes, is not enough. That doesn't move people. The writer's got to add the gift of his talent; he has got to take the truth and set it on fire so that people will remember it." Music, he thought, would be an easier, more satisfying medium through which to give imaginative expression to feelings, to catch the fire; however, as a story-teller, a man of words, he had to accept that "the thunder and the music of prose take place in silence."

In many of his public statements, Faulkner appears cautious and conservative, nowhere more so than in his pronouncements on racial integration, where he was an advocate of gradualism. However, in a handful of novels, including *The Sound and the Fury* (1929), *Light in August* (1932), and *Absolom, Absolom!* (1936), and a gathering of short stories—available in *Collected Stories* (1950) and *Go Down, Moses* (1942)—few twentieth-century writers have come closer to capturing both the fire and the thunder of our racially and morally turbulent times.

A Rose for Emily

I

When Miss Emily Grierson died, our whole town went to her funeral: the men through a sort of respectful affection for a fallen monument, the women mostly out of curiosity to see the inside of her house, which no one save an old manservant—a combined gardener and cook—had seen in at least ten years.

It was a big, squarish frame house that had once been white, decorated with cupolas and spires and scrolled balconies in the heavily lightsome style of the seventies, set on what had once been our most select street. But garages and cotton gins had encroached and obliterated even the august names of that neighborhood; only Miss Emily's house was left, lifting its stubborn and coquettish decay above the cotton wagons and the gasoline pumps—an eyesore among eyesores. And now Miss Emily had gone to join the representatives of those august names where they lay in the cedar-bemused cemetery among the ranked and anonymous graves of Union and Confederate soldiers who fell at the battle of Jefferson.

Alive, Miss Emily had been a tradition, a duty, and a care; a sort of hereditary obligation upon the town, dating from that day in 1894 when Colonel Sartoris, the mayor—he who fathered the edict that no Negro woman should appear on the streets without an apron—remitted her taxes, the dispensation dating from the death of her father on into perpetuity. Not that Miss Emily would have accepted charity. Colonel Sartoris invented an involved tale to the effect that Miss Emily's father had loaned money to the town, which the town, as a matter of business, preferred this way of repaying. Only a man of Colonel Sartoris' generation and thought could have invented it, and only a woman could have believed it.

When the next generation, with its more modern ideas, became mayors and aldermen, this arrangement created some little dissatisfaction. On the first of the year they mailed her a tax notice. February came, and there was no reply. They wrote her a formal letter, asking her to call at the sheriff's office at her convenience. A week later the mayor wrote her himself, offering to call or to send his car for her, and received in reply a note on paper of an archaic shape, in a thin, flowing calligraphy in faded ink, to the effect that she no longer went out at all. The tax notice was also enclosed, without comment.

They called a special meeting of the Board of Aldermen. A deputation waited upon her, knocked at the door through which no visitor had passed since she ceased giving china-painting lessons eight or ten years earlier. They were admitted by the old Negro into a dim hall from which a stairway mounted into still more shadow. It smelled of dust and disuse—a close, dank smell. The Negro led them into the parlor. It was furnished in heavy, leather-covered furniture. When the Negro opened the blinds of one window, they could see that the leather was cracked; and when they sat down, a faint dust rose sluggishly about their thighs, spinning with slow motes in the single sun-ray. On a tarnished gilt easel before the fireplace stood a crayon portrait of Miss Emily's father.

They rose when she entered—a small, fat woman in black, with a thin gold chain descending to her waist and vanishing into her belt, leaning on an ebony cane with a tarnished gold head. Her skeleton was small and spare; perhaps that was why what would have been merely plumpness in another was obesity in her. She looked bloated, like a body long submerged in motionless water, and of that pallid hue. Her eyes, lost in the fatty ridges of her face, looked like two small pieces of coal pressed into a lump of dough as they moved from one face to another while the visitors stated their errand.

She did not ask them to sit. She just stood in the door and listened quietly until the spokesman came to a stumbling halt. Then they could hear the invisible watch ticking at the end of the gold chain.

Her voice was dry and cold. "I have no taxes in Jefferson. Colonel Sartoris explained it to me. Perhaps one of you can gain access to the city records and satisfy yourselves."

"But we have. We are the city authorities, Miss Emily. Didn't you get a notice from the sheriff, signed by him?"

"I received a paper, yes," Miss Emily said. "Perhaps he considers himself the sheriff ... I have no taxes in Jefferson."

"But there is nothing on the books to show that, you see. We must go by the—"

"See Colonel Sartoris. I have no taxes in Jefferson."

"But, Miss Emily—"

"See Colonel Sartoris." (Colonel Sartoris had been dead almost ten years.) "I have no taxes in Jefferson. Tobe!" The Negro appeared. "Show these gentlemen out."

II

So she vanquished them, horse and foot, just as she had vanquished their fathers thirty years before about the smell. That was two years after her father's death and a short time after her sweetheart—the one we believed would marry her—had deserted her. After her father's death she went out very little; after her sweetheart went away, people hardly saw her at all. A few of the ladies had the temerity to call, but were not received, and the only sign of life about the place was the Negro man—a young man then—going in and out with a market basket.

"Just as if a man—any man—could keep a kitchen properly," the ladies said; so they were not surprised when the smell developed. It was another link between the gross, teeming world and the high and mighty Griersons.

A neighbor, a woman, complained to the mayor, Judge Stevens, eighty years old.

"But what will you have me do about it, madam?" he said.

"Why, send her word to stop it," the woman said. "Isn't there a law?"

"I'm sure that won't be necessary," Judge Stevens said. "It's probably just a snake or a rat that nigger of hers killed in the yard. I'll speak to him about it."

The next day he received two more complaints, one from a man who came in diffident deprecation. "We really must do something about it, Judge. I'd be the last one in the world to bother Miss Emily, but we've got to do something." That night the Board of Aldermen met—three graybeards and one younger man, a member of the rising generation.

"It's simple enough," he said. "Send her word to have her place cleaned up. Give her a certain time to do it in, and if she don't ..."

"Dammit, sir," Judge Stevens said, "will you accuse a lady to her face of smelling bad?"

So the next night, after midnight, four men crossed Miss Emily's lawn and slunk about the house like burglars, sniffing along the base of the brickwork and at the cellar openings while one of them performed a regular sowing motion with his hand out of a sack slung from his shoulder. They broke open the cellar door and sprinkled lime there, and in all the outbuildings. As they recrossed the lawn, a window that had been dark was lighted and Miss Emily sat in it, the light behind her, and her upright torso motionless as that of an idol. They crept quietly across the lawn and into the shadow of the locusts that lined the street. After a week or two the smell went away.

That was when people had begun to feel really sorry for her. People in our town, remembering how old lady Wyatt, her great-aunt, had gone completely crazy at last, believed that the Griersons held themselves a little too high for what they really were. None of the young men were quite good enough to Miss Emily and such. We had long thought of them as a tableau; Miss Emily a slender figure in white in the background, her father a spraddled silhouette in the foreground, his back to her and clutching a horsewhip, the two of them framed by the back-flung front door. So when she got to be thirty and was still single, we were not pleased exactly, but vindicated; even with insanity in the family she wouldn't have turned down all of her chances if they had really materialized.

When her father died, it got about that the house was all that was left to her; and in a way, people were glad. At last they could pity Miss Emily. Being left alone, and a pauper, she had become humanized. Now she too would know the old thrill and the old despair of a penny more or less.

The day after his death all the ladies prepared to call at the house and offer condolence and aid, as is our custom. Miss Emily met them at the door, dressed as usual and with no trace of grief on her face. She told them that her father was not dead. She did that for three days, with the ministers calling on her, and the doctors, trying to persuade her to let them dispose of the body. Just as they were about to resort to law and force, she broke down, and they buried her father quickly.

We did not say she was crazy then. We believed she had to do that. We remembered all the young men her father had driven away, and we knew that with nothing left, she would have to cling to that which had robbed her, as people will.

III

She was sick for a long time. When we saw her again, her hair was cut short, making her look like a girl, with a vague resemblance to those angels in colored church windows—sort of tragic and serene.

The town had just let the contracts for paving the sidewalks, and in the summer after her father's death they began the work. The construction company came with niggers and mules and machinery, and a foreman named Homer Barron, a Yankee—a big, dark, ready man, with a big voice and eyes lighter than his face. The little boys would follow in groups to hear him cuss the niggers, and the niggers singing in time to the rise and fall of picks. Pretty soon he knew everybody in town. Whenever you heard a lot of laughing anywhere about the square, Homer Barron would be in the center of the group. Presently we began to see him and Miss Emily on Sunday afternoons driving in the yellow-wheeled buggy and the matched team of bays from the livery stable.

At first we were glad that Miss Emily would have an interest, because the ladies all said, "Of course a Grierson would not think seriously of a Northerner, a day laborer." But there were still others, older people, who said that even grief could not cause a real lady to forget *noblesse oblige*—without calling it *noblesse oblige*. They just said, "Poor Emily. Her kinsfolk should come to her." She had some kin in Alabama; but years ago her father had fallen out with them over the estate of old lady Wyatt, the crazy woman, and there was no communication between the two families. They had not even been represented at the funeral.

And as soon as the old people said, "Poor Emily," the whispering began. "Do you suppose it's really so?" they said to one another. "Of course it is. What else could ..." This behind their hands; rustling of craned silk and satin behind jalousies closed upon the sun of Sunday afternoon as the thin, swift clop-clop-clop of the matched team passed: "Poor Emily."

She carried her head high enough—even when we believed that she was fallen. It was as if she demanded more than ever the recognition of her dignity as the last Grierson; as if it had wanted that touch of earthiness to reaffirm her imperviousness. Like when she bought the rat poison, the arsenic. That was over a year after they had begun to say "Poor Emily," and while the two female cousins were visiting her.

"I want some poison," she said to the druggist. She was over thirty then, still a slight woman, though thinner than usual, with cold, haughty black eyes in a face the flesh of which was strained across the temples and about the eye-sockets as you imagine a lighthouse-keeper's face ought to look. "I want some poison," she said.

"Yes, Miss Emily. What kind? For rats and such? I'd recom—"

"I want the best you have. I don't care what kind."

The druggist named several. "They'll kill anything up to an elephant. But what you want is—"

"Arsenic," Miss Emily said. "Is that a good one?"

"Is ... arsenic? Yes, ma'am. But what you want—"

"I want arsenic."

The druggist looked down at her. She looked back at him, erect, her face like a strained flag. "Why, of course," the druggist said. "If that's what you want. But the law requires you to tell what you are going to use it for."

Miss Emily just stared at him, her head tilted back in order to look him eye for eye, until he looked away and went and got the arsenic and wrapped it up. The Negro delivery boy brought her the package; the druggist didn't come back. When she opened the package at home there was written on the box, under the skull and bones: "For rats."

IV

So the next day we all said, "She will kill herself"; and we said it would be the best thing. When she had first begun to be seen with Homer Barron, we had said, "She will marry him." Then we said, "She will persuade him yet," because Homer himself had remarked—he liked men, and it was known that he drank with the younger men in the Elks' Club—that he was not a marrying man. Later we said, "Poor Emily" behind the jalousies as they passed on Sunday afternoon in the glittering buggy, Miss Emily with her head high and Homer Barron with his hat cocked and a cigar in his teeth, reins and whip in a yellow glove.

Then some of the ladies began to say that it was a disgrace to the town and a bad example to the young people. The men did not want to interfere, but at last the ladies forced the Baptist minister—Miss Emily's people were Episcopal—to call upon her. He would never divulge what happened during that interview, but he refused to go back again. The next Sunday they again drove about the streets, and the following day the minister's wife wrote to Miss Emily's relations in Alabama.

So she had blood-kin under her roof again and we sat back to watch developments. At first nothing happened. Then we were sure that they were to be married. We learned that Miss Emily had been to the jeweler's and ordered a man's toilet set in silver, with the letters H. B. on each piece. Two days later we learned that she had bought a complete outfit of men's clothing, including a nightshirt, and we said, "They are married." We were really glad. We were glad because the two female cousins were even more Grierson than Miss Emily had ever been.

So we were not surprised when Homer Barron—the streets had been finished some time since—was gone. We were a little disappointed that there was not a public blowing-off, but we believed that he had gone on to prepare for Miss Emily's coming, or to give her a chance to get rid of the cousins. (By that time it was a cabal, and we were all Miss Emily's allies to help circumvent the cousins.) Sure enough, after another week they departed. And, as we had expected all along, within three days Homer Barron was back in town. A neighbor saw the Negro man admit him at the kitchen door at dusk one evening.

And that was the last we saw of Homer Barron. And of Miss Emily for some time. The Negro man went in and out with the market basket, but the front door remained closed. Now and then we would see her at a window for a moment, as the men did that night when they sprinkled the lime, but for almost six months she did not appear on the streets. Then we knew that this was to be expected too; as if that quality of her father which had thwarted her woman's life so many times had been too virulent and too furious to die.

When we next saw Miss Emily, she had grown fat and her hair was turning gray. During the next few years it grew grayer and grayer until it attained an even pepper-and-salt iron-gray, when it ceased turning. Up to the day of her death at seventy-four it was still that vigorous iron-gray, like the hair of an active man.

From that time on her front door remained closed, save for a period of six or seven years, when she was about forty, during which she gave lessons in china-painting. She fitted up a studio in one of the downstairs rooms, where the daughters and granddaughters of Colonel Sartoris' contemporaries were sent to her with the same regularity and in the same spirit that they were sent to church on Sundays with a twenty-five cent piece for the collection plate. Meanwhile her taxes had been remitted.

Then the newer generation became the backbone and the spirit of the town, and the painting pupils grew up and fell away and did not send their children to her with boxes of color and tedious brushes and pictures cut from the ladies' magazines. The front door closed upon the last one and remained closed for good. When the town got free postal delivery, Miss Emily alone refused to let them fasten the metal numbers above her door and attach a mailbox to it. She would not listen to them.

Daily, monthly, yearly we watched the Negro grow grayer and more stooped, going in and out with the market basket. Each December we sent her a tax notice, which would be returned by the post office a week later, unclaimed. Now and then we would see her in one of the downstairs windows—she had evidently shut up the top floor of the house—like the carven torso of an idol in a niche, looking or not looking at us, we could never tell which. Thus she passed from generation to generation—dear, inescapable, impervious, tranquil, and perverse.

And so she died. Fell ill in the house filled with dust and shadows, with only a doddering Negro man to wait on her. We did not even know she was sick; we had long since given up trying to get any information from the Negro. He talked to no one, probably not even to her, for his voice had grown harsh and rusty, as if from disuse.

She died in one of the downstairs rooms, in a heavy walnut bed with a curtain, her gray head propped on a pillow yellow and moldy with age and lack of sunlight.

V

The Negro met the first of the ladies at the front door and let them in, with their hushed, sibilant voices and their quick, curious glances, and then he disappeared. He walked right through the house and out the back and was not seen again.

The two female cousins came at once. They held the funeral on the second day, with the town coming to look at Miss Emily beneath a mass of bought flowers, with the crayon face of her father musing profoundly above the bier and the ladies sibilant and macabre; and the very old men—some in their brushed Confederate uniforms—on the porch and the lawn, talking of Miss Emily as if she had been a contemporary of theirs, believing that they had danced with her and courted her perhaps, confusing time with its mathematical progression, as the old do, to whom all the past is not a diminishing road but, instead, a huge meadow which no winter ever quite touches, divided from them now by the narrow bottle-neck of the most recent decade of years.

Already we knew that there was one room in that region above stairs which no one had seen in forty years, and which would have to be forced. They waited until Miss Emily was decently in the ground before they opened it.

The violence of breaking down the door seemed to fill this room with pervading dust. A thin, acrid pall as of the tomb seemed to lie everywhere upon this room decked and furnished as for a bridal: upon the valence curtains of faded rose color, upon the rose-shaded lights, upon the dressing table, upon the delicate array of crystal and the man's toilet things backed with tarnished silver, silver so tarnished that the monogram was obscured. Among them lay a collar and tie, as if they had just been removed, which, lifted, left upon the surface a pale crescent in the dust. Upon a chair hung the suit, carefully folded; beneath it the two mute shoes and the discarded socks.

The man himself lay in the bed.

For a long while we just stood there, looking down at the profound and fleshless grin. The body had apparently once lain in the attitude of an embrace, but now the long sleep that outlasts love, that conquers even the grimace of love, had cuckolded him. What was left of him, rotted beneath what was left of the nightshirt, had become inextricable from the bed in which he lay; and upon him and upon the pillow beside him lay that even coating of the patient and biding dust.

Then we noticed that in the second pillow was the indentation of a head. One of us lifted something from it, and leaning forward, that faint and invisible dust dry and acrid in the nostrils, we saw a long strand of iron-gray hair.

Mavis Gallant

Mavis de Trafford Young was born in Montreal in 1922 and attended schools there and in the eastern U.S. She worked at the National Film Board and as a feature writer at the *Montreal Standard*, and was married briefly to John Gallant, before leaving for Paris in 1950. Her first publication in *The New Yorker* appeared in 1951. Apart from frequent visits to Canada and a stint as writer-in-residence at the University of Toronto in 1983, she has lived most of her adult life in Paris, which accounts for the tardiness with which Canadians have recognized her prodigious talent. Her publications include two novels, *Green Water, Green Sky* (1959) and *A Fairly Good Time* (1970), and various books of stories: *The Other Paris* (1956), *My Heart Is Broken* (1959), *The Peignitz Junction* (1973), *From the Fifteenth District* (1979), which won the Governor General's Award, *Home Truths* (1981), *In Transit* (1988), *The Moselm Wife and Other Stories* (1994), *The Collected Stories of Mavis Gallant* (1996), and *Across the Bridge* (1997). She was awarded the Molson Prize in 1996. She is also the author of *Paris Notebooks: Essays and Reviews* (1986) and two books of non-fiction, one on the Dreyfus affair and the other a study of the public response to a French schoolteacher's love affair with an adolescent student, *The Affair of Gabrielle Russier* (1971).

In the introduction to *Home Truths*, Gallant objects strongly to the notion that she or anyone else should have to "paint Canadian": to the critic who demands this, she claims a "wider allegiance," the freedom of the imagination. "He thinks there is more than meets the eye, and in a sense he is right: fiction, like painting, consists entirely of more than meets the eye; otherwise it is not worth a second's notice." Gallant rejects political fashions and tub-thumping nationalism in favour of a centre of gravity to be found in those childhood experiences that "give rise to a national consciousness": "A deeper culture is contained in memory. Memory is something that cannot be subsidized or ordained. It can, however, be destroyed; and it is inseparable from language."

Gallant has been a faithful student of both language and memory since she made the decision to write full time. "My goal was to get free and write. The only thing I don't know is why I waited so long. I never sent a story anywhere until I was twenty-seven years old. I don't know why. I had piles of stories. Then suddenly I decided this was it. Twenty-seven is, I think, a watershed age." In an interview with Alan Twigg (*Strong Voices*) conducted in 1981, she describes her typical process of creation as follows:

"I begin in pencil. It's usually a visual image in a situation. Sometimes the first image isn't even in the story at the end. I start in longhand. Then for the next few days there are bits of the story that come. It's almost as if the story already existed and I was getting scraps of it. It just comes. And I don't know where from. I don't mean I'm a mystic. I don't mean it comes from the planet Venus or anything.

"You get an accumulation of things. Written on buses, I'm not joking. Even on match-covers. Once I had a story written on a metro ticket. A little bit of dialogue. Then I type it. Then I make all the corrections. The form then is very clear. Once it's typed there's no doubt that that's the beginning and that's the end of it and the story does this. Then I correct in pencil again and it's all around the edges. Then I type it all again to get it clean. Then I think it's no good."

Gallant insists that plausibility, not experience, is what matters in fiction.

"Even if a thing happened, if it's completely eccentric, there's no point writing about it. If it isn't plausible, it doesn't matter." In response to Twigg's remark that "In the Tunnel," though grossly comic, was entirely plausible, Gallant said: "That's barely caricature, believe me. I was at a dinner party of Brits in exile in the south of France. The man across from me leaned over with those light eyes. He leaned across and said: 'Don't you think there are people so rotten that they have to be killed?' I remember thinking, rotten for what kind of world? Suppose I was an African, brought up with completely different legends, gods, realities, and that man with his very light eyes said this. The story began out of that."

Gallant's whimsical account of the mechanics of the creative process and her insistence upon plausibility cannot hide the fact that she is a painstaking stylist, attentive to her characters' every nuance of gesture and speech and how these might best be rendered in words on the page. She considers style to be "not a last minute addition to prose, a charming and universal slip-cover, a coat of paint used to mask the failings of a structure," but, rather, the "author's thumbprint": "Style is inseparable from structure, part of the conformation of whatever the author has to say. What he says—this is what fiction is about—is that something is taking place and that nothing lasts. Against the sustained tick of a watch, fiction takes the measure of a life, a season, a look exchanged, the turning point, desire as brief as a dream, the grief and terror that after childhood we cease to express. The life, the look, the grief are without permanence. The watch continues to tick where the story stops."

Rue de Lille

My second wife, Juliette, died in the apartment on Rue de Lille, where she had lived—at first alone, more or less, then with me—since the end of the war. All the rooms gave onto the ivy-hung well of a court, and were for that reason dark. We often talked about looking for a brighter flat, on a top floor with southern exposure and a wide terrace, but Parisians seldom move until they're driven to. "We know the worst of what we've got," we told each other. "It's better than a bad surprise."

"And what about your books?" Juliette would add. "It would take you months to get them packed, and in the new place you'd never get them sorted." I would see myself as Juliette saw me, crouched over a slanting, shaking stack of volumes piled on a strange floor, cursing and swearing, as I tried to pry out a dictionary. "Just the same, I don't intend to die here," she also said.

I once knew someone who believed drowning might be easy, even pleasant, until he almost drowned by accident. Juliette's father was a colonel who expected to die in battle or to be shot by a German firing squad, but he died of typhus in a concentration camp. I had once, long ago, imagined for myself a clandestine burial with full honors after some Resistance feat, but all I got out of the war was a few fractures and a broken nose in a motorcycle accident.

Juliette had thirty-seven years of blacked-out winter mornings in Rue de Lille. She was a few days short of her sixtieth birthday when I found her stretched out on the floor of our bedroom, a hand slackened on a flashlight. She had been trying to see under a chest of drawers, and her heart stopped. (Later, I pulled the chest away from the wall and discovered a five-franc coin.) Her gray-and-dark hair, which had grown soft and wayward with age, was tied back with a narrow satin ribbon. She looked more girlish than at any time since I'd first met her. (She fell in love with me young.) She wore a pleated flannel skirt, a tailored blouse, and one of the thick cardigans with gilt buttons she used to knit while watching television. She had been trained to believe that to look or to listen quietly is to do nothing; she would hum along with music, to show she wasn't idle. She was discreet, she was generous to a sensible degree, she was anything but contentious. I often heard her remark, a trifle worriedly, that she was never bored. She was faithful, if "faithful" means avoiding the acknowledged forms of trouble. She was patient. I know she was good. Any devoted male friend, any lover, any husband would have shown up beside her as selfish, irritable, even cruel. She displayed so little of the ordinary kinds of jealousy, the plain marital do-you-often-have-lunch-with-her? sort, that I once asked her if she had a piece missing.

"Whoever takes this place over," she said, when we spoke of moving, "will be staggered by the size of the electricity bills." (Juliette paid them; I looked after a number of other things.) We had to keep the lights turned on all day in winter. The apartment was L-shaped, bent round two sides of a court, like a train making a sharp turn. From our studies, at opposite ends of the train, we could look out and see the comforting glow of each other's working life, a lamp behind a window. Juliette would be giving some American novel a staunch, steady translation; I might be getting into shape my five-hour television series, *Stendhal and the Italian Experience*, which was to win an award in Japan.

We were together for a duration of time I daren't measure against the expanse of Juliette's life; it would give me the feeling that I had decamped to a height of land, a survivor's eminence, so as to survey the point at which our lives crossed and mingled and began to move in the same direction: a long, narrow reach of time in the Rue de Lille. It must be the washy, indefinite colorations of blue that carpeted, papered, and covered floors, walls, and furniture and shaded our lamps which cast over that reach the tone of a short season. I am thinking of the patches of distant, neutral blue that appear over Paris in late spring, when it is still wet and cold in the street and tourists have come too early. The tourists shelter in doorways, trying to read their soaked maps, perennially unprepared in their jeans and thin jackets. Overhead, there are scrapings of a color that carries no threat and promises all.

That choice, Juliette's preference, I sometimes put down to her Calvinist sobriety—call it a temperament—and sometimes to a refinement of her Huguenot taste. When I was feeling tired or impatient, I complained that I had been consigned to a Protestant Heaven by an arbitrary traffic cop, and that I was better suited to a pagan Hell. Again, as I looked round our dining-room table at the calm, clever faces of old friends of Juliette's family, at their competent and unassuming wives, I saw what folly it might be to set such people against a background of buttercup yellow or apple green. The soft clicking of their upper-class

Protestant consonants made conversation distant and neutral, too. It was a voice that had puzzled me the first time I'd heard it from Juliette. I had supposed, mistakenly, that she was trying it on for effect; but she was wholly natural.

The sixteenth-century map of Paris I bought for her birthday is still at the framer's; I sent a check but never picked it up. I destroyed her private correspondence without reading it, and gave armfuls of clothes away to a Protestant charity. To the personal notice of her death in *Le Monde* was attached a brief mention of her father, a hero of the Resistance for whom suburban streets are named; and of her career as a respected translator, responsible for having introduced postwar American literature to French readers; and of her husband, the well-known radio and television interviewer and writer, who survived her.

Another person to survive her was my first wife. One night when Juliette and I were drinking coffee in the little sitting room where she received her women friends, and where we watched television, Juliette said, again, "But how much of what she says does she believe? About her Catholicism, and all those fantasies running round in her head—that she is your true and only wife, that your marriage is registered in Heaven, that you and she will be together in another world?"

"Those are things people put in letters," I said. "They sit down alone and pour it out. It's sincere at that moment. I don't know why she would suddenly be *in*sincere."

"After all the trouble she's made," said Juliette. She meant that for many years my wife would not let me divorce.

"She couldn't help that," I said.

"How do you know?"

"I don't know. It's what I think. I hardly knew her."

"You must have known *something*."

"I haven't seen her more than three or four times in the last thirty-odd years, since I started living with you."

"What do you mean?" said Juliette. "You saw her just once, with me. We had lunch. You backed off asking for the divorce."

"You can't ask for a divorce at lunch. It had to be done by mail."

"And since then she hasn't stopped writing," said Juliette. "Do you mean three or four times, or do you mean once?"

I said, "Once, probably. Probably just that once."

Viewing me at close range, as if I were a novel she had to translate, Juliette replied that one ought to be spared unexpected visions. Just now, it was as if three walls of the court outside had been bombed flat. Through a bright new gap she saw straight through to my first marriage. We—my first wife and I—postured in the distance, like characters in fiction.

I had recently taken part in a panel discussion, taped for television, on the theme "What Literature, for Which Readers, at Whose Price?" I turned away from Juliette and switched on the set, about ten minutes too early. Juliette put the empty cups and the coffeepot on a tray she had picked up in Milan, the summer I was researching the Stendhal, and carried the tray down the dim passage to the kitchen. I watched the tag end of the late news. It must have been during the spring of 1976. Because of the energy crisis, daylight saving had been established. Like any novelty, it was deeply upsetting. People said they could no longer digest their food or be nice to their children, and that they needed sedation to help them through the altered day. A doctor was interviewed; he advised a light diet and early bed until mind and body adjusted to the change.

I turned, smiling, to where Juliette should have been. My program came on then, and I watched myself making a few points before I got up and went to find her. She was in the kitchen, standing in the dark, clutching the edge of the sink. She did not move when I turned the light on. I put my arms around her, and we came back to her sitting room and watched the rest of the program together. She was knitting squares of wool to be sewn together to make a blanket; there was always, somewhere, a flood or an earthquake or a flow of refugees, and those who outlasted jeopardy had to be covered.

Gabriel García Márquez

Gabriel García Márquez was born in 1928 in Aracataca, a small town in Colombia surrounded by banana plantations. He has lived in Mexico since 1961, supporting himself by journalism until fiction brought him fame. He has published numerous novels, including *No One Writes to the Colonel* (1961), *Evil Hour* (1962), *The Autumn of the Patriarch* (1975), *Love in the Time of Cholera* (1988), and *The General in His Labyrinth* (1990), but it is *One Hundred Years of Solitude* (1967) that brought his work international recognition. He has written several volumes of short stories, including *No One Writes to the Colonel and Other Stories* (1968), *Leaf Storm and Other Stories* (1972), *Innocente Eréndira and Other Stories* (1978), *Collected Stories* (1984), and *Love and Other Demons* (1995). He received the Nobel Prize for Literature in 1982.

García Márquez says, in *The Paris Review* interview with Peter H. Stone, that he started his creative activities as a child by drawing cartoons. Although he had a reputation in school as a writer, he said he did not actually do anything serious until reading Kafka's story "The Metamorphosis: "When I read the line ["As Gregor Samsa awoke that morning from uneasy dreams, he found himself transformed in his bed into a gigantic insect. ..."] I thought to myself that I didn't know anyone was allowed to write things like that. If I had known, I would have started writing a long time ago. So I immediately started writing stories." He claims to have learned the technique of interior monologue from reading Joyce's *Ulysses*. What allowed him to progress beyond the writing of stories that were intellectual exercises to work that had a deeper "relationship with life" were three things: reading writers of the American Lost Generation, such as Hemingway and Fitzgerald; experiencing the riots of April 9, 1948, when the political leader Gaitan was shot and the people of Bogotá went on a rampage in the streets; and returning with his mother to sell the childhood home in Aracataca: "When I got there it was at first quite shocking because I was now twenty-two and hadn't been there since the age of eight. Nothing had really changed, but I felt that I wasn't really looking at the village, but I was *experiencing* it as if I were reading it. It was as if everything I saw had already been written, and all I had to do was to sit down and copy what was already there and what I was just reading. For all practical purposes everything had evolved into literature: the houses, the people, and the memories." It was after this experience that he wrote his first short novel, *Leaf Storm* (1953).

"It always amuses me," García Márquez says, "that the biggest praise for my work comes for the imagination, while the truth is that there's not a single line in all my work that does not have a basis in reality. The problem is that Caribbean reality resembles the wildest imagination." In terms of audience, he claims that "in the end all books are written for your friends." The evolution of his literary style was influenced by his journalism, his nostalgia, and the struggle to work out the relationship between literature and politics; still, he felt something was missing: "I was not sure what it was until one day I discovered the right tone—the tone that I eventually used in *One Hundred Years of Solitude*. It was based on the way my grandmother used to tell her stories. She told things that sounded supernatural and fantastic, but she told them with complete naturalness. When I finally discovered the tone I had to use, I sat down for eighteen months and worked every day."

When asked to elaborate on how he was able to give his fantastical material such a sense of reality, García Márquez says: "That's a journalistic trick which you can also apply to literature. For example, if you say that there are elephants flying in the sky, people are not going to believe you. But if you say that there are four hundred and twenty-five elephants in the sky, people will probably believe you. ... The problem for every writer is credibility. Anybody can write anything so long as it's believed."

García Márquez makes the point that a writer must be disciplined, not only in terms of keeping to a schedule, but also in terms of the specifics of the craft: "One of the most difficult things is the first paragraph. I have spent many months on a first paragraph, and once I get it, the rest just comes out very easily. In the first paragraph you solve most of the problems with your book. The theme is defined, the style, the tone. At least in my case, the first paragraph is a kind of sample of what the rest of the book is going to be. That's why writing a book of short stories is much more difficult than writing a novel. Every time you write a short story, you have to begin all over again."

"Ultimately, literature is nothing but carpentry," García Márquez says. "Both are very hard work. Writing something is almost as hard as making a table. With both you are working with reality, a material just as hard wood. Both are full of tricks and techniques. Basically very little magic and a lot of hard work are involved. And as Proust, I think, said, it takes ten percent inspiration and ninety percent perspiration. I never have done any carpentry but it's the job I admire most, especially because you can never find anyone to do it for you."

In response to a question about the solitude of the writer, García Márquez says: "It has a lot to do with the solitude of power. The writer's very attempt to portray reality often leads him to a distorted view of it. In trying to transpose reality he can end up losing contact with it, in an ivory tower, as they say. Journalism is a very good guard against that. That's why I have always tried to keep on doing journalism, because it keeps me in contact with the real world, particularly political journalism and politics."

Asked if he feels there are things the novel or fiction can do that journalism can't, García Márquez says: "Nothing. I don't think there is any difference. The sources are the same, the material is the same, the resources and the language are the same. *The Journal of the Plague Year* by Daniel Defoe is a great novel and *Hiroshima* [by John Hersey] is a great work of journalism. ... In journalism just one fact that is false prejudices the entire work. In contrast, in fiction one single fact that is true gives legitimacy to the entire work. That's the only difference, and it lies in the commitment of the writer. A novelist can do anything he wants so long as he makes people believe in it."

One of These Days

Monday dawned warm and rainless. Aurelio Escovar, a dentist without a degree, and a very early riser, opened his office at six. He took some false teeth, still mounted in their plaster mould, out of the glass case and put on the table a fistful of instruments which he arranged in size order, as if they were on display. He wore a collarless striped shirt, closed at the neck with a golden stud, and pants held up by suspenders. He was erect and skinny, with a look that rarely corresponded to the situation, the way deaf people have of looking.

When he had things arranged on the table, he pulled the drill toward the dental chair and sat down to polish the false teeth. He seemed not to be thinking about what he was doing, but worked steadily, pumping the drill with his feet, even when he didn't need it.

After eight he stopped for a while to look at the sky through the window, and he saw two pensive buzzards who were drying themselves in the sun on the ridgepole of the house next door. He went on working with the idea that before lunch it would rain again. The shrill voice of his eleven-year-old son interrupted his concentration.

"Papá."

"What?"

"The Mayor wants to know if you'll pull his tooth."

"Tell him I'm not here."

He was polishing a gold tooth. He held it at arm's length, and examined it with his eyes half closed. His son shouted again from the little waiting room.

"He says you are, too, because he can hear you."

The dentist kept examining the tooth. Only when he had put it on the table with the finished work did he say:

"So much the better."

He operated the drill again. He took several pieces of a bridge out of a cardboard box where he kept the things he still had to do and began to polish the gold.

"Papá."

"What?"

He still hadn't changed his expression.

"He says if you don't take out his tooth, he'll shoot you."

Without hurrying, with an extremely tranquil movement, he stopped pedaling the drill, pushed it away from the chair, and pulled the lower drawer of the table all the way out. There was a revolver. "O.K.," he said. "Tell him to come and shoot me."

He rolled the chair over opposite the door, his hand resting on the edge of the drawer. The Mayor appeared at the door. He had shaved the left side of his face, but the other side, swollen and in pain, had a five-day-old beard. The dentist saw many nights of desperation in his dull eyes. He closed the drawer with his fingertips and said softly:

"Sit down."

"Good morning," said the Mayor.

"Morning," said the dentist.

While the instruments were boiling, the Mayor leaned his skull on the headrest of the chair and felt better. His breath was icy. It was a poor office: an old wooden chair, the pedal drill, a glass case with ceramic bottles. Opposite the chair was a window with a shoulder-high cloth curtain. When he felt the dentist approach, the Mayor braced his heels and opened his mouth.

Aurelio Escovar turned his head toward the light. After inspecting the infected tooth, he closed the Mayor's jaw with a cautious pressure of his fingers.

"It has to be without anesthesia," he said.

"Why?"

"Because you have an abscess."

The Mayor looked him in the eye. "All right," he said, and tried to smile. The dentist did not return the smile. He brought the basin of sterilized instruments to the worktable and took them out of the water with a pair of cold tweezers, still without hurrying. Then he pushed the spittoon with the tip of his shoe, and went to wash his hands in the washbasin. He did all this without looking at the Mayor. But the Mayor didn't take his eyes off him.

It was a lower wisdom tooth. The dentist spread his feet and grasped the tooth with the hot forceps. The Mayor seized the arms of the chair, braced his feet with all his strength, and felt an icy void in his kidneys, but didn't make a sound. The dentist moved only his wrist. Without rancor, rather with a bitter tenderness, he said:

"Now you'll pay for our twenty dead men."

The Mayor felt the crunch of bones in his jaw, and his eyes filled with tears. But he didn't breathe until he felt the tooth come out. Then he saw it through his tears. It seemed so foreign to his pain that he failed to understand his torture of the five previous nights.

Bent over the spittoon, sweating, panting, he unbuttoned his tunic and reached for the handkerchief in his pants pocket. The dentist gave him a clean cloth.

"Dry your tears," he said.

The Mayor did. He was trembling. While the dentist washed his hands, he saw the crumbling ceiling and a dusty spider web with spider's eggs and dead insects. The dentist returned, drying his hands. "Go to bed," he said, "and gargle with salt water." The Mayor stood up, said goodbye with a casual military salute, and walked toward the door, stretching his legs, without buttoning up his tunic.

"Send the bill," he said.

"To you or the town?"

The Mayor didn't look at him. He closed the door and said through the screen:

"It's the same damn thing."

Nadine Gordimer

Nadine Gordimer, who won the Nobel Prize for Literature in 1991, was born in 1923 in a small mining town called Spring in Transvaal, South Africa, to an English mother and a Latvian father, who was a watchmaker and later a jeweller. She had dreamed of being a dancer, but a minor heart ailment in childhood resulted in her being withdrawn from physical activities and acquiring much of her education by way of private tutoring; as a result, her energies were diverted into reading and writing. She published her first story at age fifteen, attended Witwatersrand University briefly, and established herself early as a writer of short stories, publishing her first book in 1949 and selling fiction to *The New Yorker*. She describes her gradual awareness and breaking out of the colour bar as a second birth, which gave her writing depth and focus. Many of her books were banned in South Africa for their frank and unrelenting portrait of apartheid, but she refused to go into exile and has continued to support the idea of black majority rule. She did not travel outside South Africa until she was thirty, but has since been very much in demand for lectures and public appearances, winning numerous international awards for her more than twenty-seven books. Her first book of stories, *Face to Face*, was published in 1949; this was followed by *The Soft Voice of the Serpent* (1952), *Friday's Footprint and Other Stories* (1960), *Not for Publication and Other Stories* (1965), *Livingstone's Companion* (1971), *Selected Stories* (1976), *Jump and Other Stories* (1991), *Crimes of Conscience: Selected Short Stories* (1991), and many novels, the best known of which are *A World of Strangers* (1958), *Occasion for Loving* (1963), *The Conservationist* (1974), *Burger's Daughter* (1979), *July's People* (1981), *A Sport of Nature* (1987), *My Son's Story* (1990), *The Lying Days* (1994), and *The Gun House* (1998). Her ideas on the craft of fiction and the world of South African politics are available in *Conversations with Nadine Gordimer* (1990), edited by Nancy Topping Bazin and Marilyn Dallman Seymour, and in *Three in a Bed: Fiction, Morals, and Politics* (1991). She was awarded the Nobel Prize for Literature in 1991. Gordimer has one daughter and one son and lives in Johannesburg with her second husband, Reinhold Cassirer, an art dealer.

Gordimer believes that "the function of the writer is to make sense of life." She describes herself as a "natural writer," who came to politics by looking clearly at her own society: "I began writing out of a sense of wonder about life, a sense of its mystery, and also out of a sense of its chaos." However, harsh reality soon invaded her life and work: "I have come to the abstractions of politics through the flesh and blood of individual behaviour. I didn't know what politics was about until I saw it all happening to people," she said to Alan Ross in 1965. Although she suggests that "character is politics in South Africa," Gordimer claims never to have written for any specific audience: "My eyes are not out there; my struggle is with the material. It's like a net that you keep putting down into these mysterious waters of life around you, and you are struggling to bring up what is there, what is there in the depths, and of course you're also struggling with yourself because you're also down there." Gordimer distinguishes between art and propaganda, insisting that "the protest can only be as good as the writing." She advises writing posthumously: "The ideal way to write is as if you were dead and will be unaffected by any repercussions."

As she said to interviewer Pat Schwartz in 1977, Gordimer considers the matter of technique "a very delicate and complex question." "For me it is a matter of finding the approach that will release the most from the subject. The form is dictated by the subject. In some people's writing you are very conscious of the writer—the writer is between you and the subject all the time. My own aim is to be invisible and to make the identification for the reader with what is being written about and with the people in the work—not to distance the reader." She regards the creation of character as a "subconscious process," which includes a blending of everything a writer knows with much that is revealed only in the process of writing: "My method is to let the general seep up through the individual, whether or not the theme can be summed up afterwards as 'Jealousy,' 'Racial Conflict' or what have you." As she says to Jill Fullerton-Smith, "Yes, I do use descriptions sparingly, because I think it's very difficult to describe people's physical characteristics. I prefer to let the reader imagine them from the way the person speaks, moves, reacts and from a few little clues if they have some outstanding physical characteristics one way or another. I think this comes from having started as a short-story writer. ... In a short story you've got to find significant detail. You're not going to describe a person from head to foot, so just maybe the way they sit, some little tic that they have is going to create a line from which the reader can build up the whole picture. And I don't think it should be done all at once as was done in a nineteenth-century novel. ... I prefer to drop these little sketches or hints through the work as it goes along, so that readers can build up their own picture of what this person looks like."

In a fascinating comment to Alan Ross, Gordimer describes the conception of much of her work: "My stories often originate in what might be called the tail-tip of a situation as it is whisked out of sight. A look, a sentence hanging in mid-air (I'm a great unconscious eavesdropper, always have been, on street corners, in restaurants, planes, etc.). A train of associations begins to play out; the story begins to form about the fragment. When stories arise out of actual experiences of my own, there is usually a lapse of months or even years between the happening and the writing, a lapse during which the experience lies dormant, gathers like a magnet those characters, phrases, ideas, ancillary events, that belong with it in kind, and will transform it. Time means nothing in that part of the mind where this takes place; something that happened ten years ago on the other side of the world coexists with something observed yesterday."

In terms of structure, Gordimer prefers the musical analogy. "A story to me is like a piece of music," she said to John Barkham in 1962, "with its distinctive movements, rhythms, and cadences. Only when I have worked these out to my satisfaction do I write them down, and, once on paper, I rarely have to change anything. Every story presents its own technical problems, and I confess that I enjoy grappling with them." In 1986, she reasserted her interest in formal complexity and suggested to interviewers Marchant, Kitchen, and Rubin why she sometimes feels pushed towards longer forms such as the novel: "No, it's a matter of thematic layers. Even in my stories, I'm not satisfied with one layer. It's really like peeling an onion: once you begin to invent an alternative life for others, once you begin to find out why they are as they are, you just go deeper and deeper and deeper, and sometimes it seems the story doesn't give enough space to do that."

The Ultimate Safari

'The African adventure lives on ... You can do it! The ultimate safari or expedition with leaders who know Africa.'
—Travel advertisement, *Observer*, 27 November 1988

That night our mother went to the shop and she didn't come back. Ever. What happened? I don't know. My father also had gone away one day and never come back; but he was fighting in the war. We were in the war, too, but we were children, we were like our grandmother and grandfather, we didn't have guns. The people my father was fighting—the bandits, they are called by our government—ran all over the place and we ran away from them like chickens chased by dogs. We didn't know where to go. Our mother went to the shop because someone said you could get some oil for cooking. We were happy because we hadn't tasted oil for a long time; perhaps she got the oil and someone knocked her down in the dark and took that oil from her. Perhaps she met the bandits. If you meet them, they will kill you. Twice they came to our village and we ran and hid in the bush and when they'd gone we came back and found they had taken everything; but the third time they came back there was nothing to take, no oil, no food, so they burned the thatch and the roofs of our houses fell in. My mother found some pieces of tin and we put those up over part of the house. We were waiting there for her that night she never came back.

We were frightened to go out, even to do our business, because the bandits did come. Not into our house—without a roof it must have looked as if there was no one in it, everything gone—but all through the village. We heard people screaming and running. We were afraid even to run, without our mother to tell us where. I am the middle one, the girl, and my little brother clung against my stomach with his arms round my neck and his legs round my waist like a baby monkey to its mother. All night my first-born brother kept in his hand a broken piece of wood from one of our burnt house-poles. It was to save himself if the bandits found him.

We stayed there all day. Waiting for her. I don't know what day it was; there was no school, no church any more in our village, so you didn't know whether it was a Sunday or a Monday.

When the sun was going down, our grandmother and grandfather came. Someone from our village had told them we children were alone, our mother had not come back. I say 'grandmother' before 'grandfather' because it's like that: our grandmother is big and strong, not yet old, and our grandfather is small, you don't know where he is, in his loose trousers, he smiles but he hasn't heard what you're saying, and his hair looks as if he's left it full of soap suds. Our grandmother took us—me, the baby, my first-born brother, our grandfather—back to her house and we were all afraid (except the baby, asleep on our grandmother's back) of meeting the bandits on the way. We waited a long time at our grandmother's place. Perhaps it was a month. We were hungry. Our mother never came. While we were waiting for her to fetch us, our grandmother had no food for us, no food for our grandfather and herself. A woman with milk in her breasts gave us some for my little brother, although at our house he used to eat porridge, same as we did. Our grandmother took us to look for wild spinach but everyone else in the village did the same and there wasn't a leaf left.

Our grandfather, walking a little behind some young men, went to look for our mother but didn't find her. Our grandmother cried with other women and I sang the hymns with them. They brought a little food—some beans—but after two days there was nothing again. Our grandfather used to have three sheep and a cow and a vegetable garden but the bandits had long ago taken the sheep and the cow, because they were hungry, too; and when planting time came our grandfather had no seed to plant.

So they decided—our grandmother did; our grandfather made little noises and rocked from side to side, but she took no notice—we would go away. We children were pleased. We wanted to go away from where our mother wasn't and where we were hungry. We wanted to go where there were no bandits and there was food. We were glad to think there must be such a place; away.

Our grandmother gave her church clothes to someone in exchange for some dried mealies and she boiled them and tied them in a rag. We took them with us when we went and she thought we would get water from the rivers but we didn't come to any river and we got so thirsty we had to turn back. Not all the way to our grandparents' place but to a village where there was a pump. She opened the basket where she carried some clothes and the mealies and she sold her shoes to buy a big plastic container for water. I said, *Gogo*, how will you go to church now even without shoes, but she said we had a long journey and too much to carry. At that village we met other people who were also going away. We joined them because they seemed to know where that was better than we did.

To get there we had to go through the Kruger Park. We knew about the Kruger Park. A kind of whole country of animals—elephants, lions, jackals, hyenas, hippos, crocodiles, all kinds of animals. We had some of them in our own country, before the war (our grandfather remembers; we children weren't born yet) but the bandits kill the elephants and sell their tusks, and the bandits and our soldiers have eaten all the buck. There was a man in our village without legs—a crocodile took them off, in our river; but all the same our country is a country of people, not animals. We knew about the Kruger Park because some of our men used to leave home to work there in the places where white people came to stay and look at the animals.

So we started to go away again. There were women and other children like me who had to carry the small ones on their backs when the women got tired. A man led us into the Kruger Park: are we there yet, are we there yet, I kept asking our grandmother. Not yet, the man said, when she asked him for me. He told us we had to take a long way to get round the fence, which he explained would kill you, roast off your skin the moment you touched it, like the wires high up on poles that give electric light in our towns. I've seen that sign of a head without ears or skin or hair on an iron box at the mission hospital we used to have before it was blown up.

When I asked the next time, they said we'd been walking in the Kruger Park for an hour. But it looked just like the bush we'd been walking through all day, and we hadn't seen any animals except the monkeys and birds which live around us at home, and a tortoise that, of course, couldn't get away from us. My first-born brother and the other boys brought it to the man so it could be killed and we could cook and eat it. He let it go because he told us we could not make a fire; all the time we were in the Park we must not make a fire because the smoke would show we were there. Police, wardens, would come and send us back where we came from. He said we must move like animals among the animals, away from the roads, away from the white people's camps. And at that moment I heard—I'm sure I was the first to hear—cracking branches and the sound of something parting grasses and I almost squealed because I thought it was the police, wardens—the people he was telling us to look out for—who had found us already. And it was an elephant, and another elephant, and more elephants, big blots of dark moved wherever you looked between the trees. They were curling their trunks round the red leaves of the mopane trees and stuffing them into their mouths. The babies leaned against their mothers. The almost grown-up ones wrestled like my first-born brother with his friends—only they used trunks instead of arms. I was so interested I forgot to be afraid. The man said we should just stand still and be quiet while the elephants passed. They passed very slowly because elephants are too big to need to run from anyone.

The buck ran from us. They jumped so high they seemed to fly. The wart-hogs stopped dead, when they heard us, and swerved off the way a boy in our village used to zigzag on the bicycle his father had brought back from the mines. We followed the animals to where they drank. When they had gone, we went to their waterholes. We were never thirsty without finding water, but the animals ate, ate all the time. Whenever you saw them they were eating, grass, trees, roots. And there was nothing for us. The mealies were finished. The only food we could eat was what the baboons ate, dry little figs full of ants, that grow along the branches of the trees at the rivers. It was hard to be like the animals.

When it was very hot during the day we would find lions lying asleep. They were the colour of the grass and we didn't see them at first but the man did, and he led us back and a long way round where they slept. I wanted to lie down like the lions. My little brother was getting thin but he was very heavy. When our grandmother looked for me, to put him on my back, I tried not to see. My first-born brother stopped talking; and when we rested he had to be shaken to get up again, as if he was just like our grandfather, he couldn't hear. I saw flies crawling on our grandmother's face and she didn't brush them off; I was frightened. I picked up a palm leaf and chased them.

We walked at night as well as by day. We could see the fires where the white people were cooking in the camps and we could smell the smoke and the meat. We watched the hyenas with their backs that slope as if they're ashamed, slipping through the bush after the smell. If one turned its head, you saw it had big brown shining eyes like our own, when we looked at each other in the dark. The wind brought voices in our own language from the compounds where the people who work in the camps live. A woman among us wanted to go to them at night and ask them to help us. They can give us the food from the dustbins, she said, she started wailing and our grandmother had to grab her and put a hand over her mouth. The men who led us had told us that we must keep out of the way of our people who worked at the Kruger Park; if they helped us they would lose their work. If they saw us, all they could do was pretend we were not there; they had seen only animals.

Sometimes we stopped to sleep for a little while at night. We slept close together. I don't know which night it was—because we were walking, walking, any time, all the time—we heard the lions very near. Not groaning loudly the way they did far off. Panting, like we do when we run, but it's a different kind of panting: you can hear they're not running, they're waiting, somewhere near. We all rolled closer together, on top of each other, the ones on the edge fighting to get into the middle. I was squashed against a woman who smelled bad because she was afraid but I was glad to hold tight on to her. I prayed to God to make the lions take someone on the edge and go. I shut my eyes not to see the tree from which a lion might jump right into the middle of us, where I was. The man who led us jumped up instead, and beat on the tree with a dead branch. He had taught us never to make a sound but he shouted. He shouted at the lions like a drunk man shouting at nobody in our village. The lions went away. We heard them groaning, shouting back at him from far off.

We were tired, so tired. My first-born brother and the man had to lift our grandfather from stone to stone where we found places to cross the rivers. Our grandmother is strong but her feet were bleeding. We could not carry the basket on our heads any longer, we couldn't carry anything except my little brother. We left our things under a bush. As long as our bodies get there, our grandmother said. Then we ate some wild fruit we didn't know from home and our stomachs ran. We were in the grass called elephant grass because it is nearly as tall as an elephant, that day we had those pains, and our grandfather couldn't just get down in front of people like my little brother, he went off into the grass to be on his own. We had to keep up, the man who led us always kept telling us, we must catch up, but we asked him to wait for our grandfather.

So everyone waited for our grandfather to catch up. But he didn't. It was the middle of the day; insects were singing in our ears and we couldn't hear him moving through the grass. We couldn't see him because the grass was so high and he was so small. But he must have been somewhere there inside his loose trousers and his shirt that was torn and our grandmother couldn't sew because she had no cotton. We knew he couldn't have gone far because he was weak and slow. We all went to look for him, but in groups, so we too wouldn't be hidden from each other in that grass. It got into our eyes and noses; we called him softly but the noise of the insects must have filled the little space left for hearing in his ears. We looked and looked but we couldn't find him. We stayed in that long grass all night. In my sleep I found him curled round in a place he had tramped down for himself, like the places we'd seen where the buck hide their babies.

When I woke up he still wasn't anywhere. So we looked again, and by now there were paths we'd made by going through the grass many times, it would be easy for him to find us if we couldn't find him. All that day we just sat and waited. Everything is very quiet when the sun is on your head, inside your head, even if you lie, like the animals, under the trees. I lay on my back and saw those ugly birds with hooked beaks and plucked necks flying round and round above us. We had passed them often where they were feeding on the bones of dead animals, nothing was ever left there for us to eat. Round and round, high up and then lower down and then high again. I saw their necks poking to this side and that. Flying round and round. I saw our grandmother, who sat up all the time with my little brother on her lap, was seeing them, too.

In the afternoon the man who led us came to our grandmother and told her the other people must move on. He said, If their children don't eat soon they will die.

Our grandmother said nothing.

I'll bring you water before we go, he told her.

Our grandmother looked at us, me, my first-born brother, and my little brother on her lap. We watched the other people getting up to leave. I didn't believe the grass would be empty, all around us, where they had been. That we would be alone in this place, the Kruger Park, the police or the animals would find us. Tears came out of my eyes and nose on to my hands but our grandmother took no notice. She got up, with her feet apart the way she puts them when she is going to lift firewood, at home in our village, she swung my little brother on to her back, tied him in her cloth—the top of her dress was torn and her big breasts were showing but there was nothing in them for him. She said, Come.

So we left the place with the long grass. Left behind. We went with the others and the man who led us. We started to go away, again.

There's a very big tent, bigger than a church or a school, tied down to the ground. I didn't understand that was what it would be, when we got there, away. I saw a thing like that the time our mother took us to the town because she heard our soldiers were there and she wanted to ask them if they knew where our father was. In that tent, people were praying and singing. This one is blue and white like that one but it's not for praying and singing, we live in it with other people who've come from our country. Sister from the clinic says we're 200 without counting the babies, and we have new babies, some were born on the way through the Kruger Park.

Inside, even when the sun is bright it's dark and there's a kind of whole village in there. Instead of houses each family has a little place closed off with sacks or cardboard from boxes—whatever we can find to show the other families it's yours and they shouldn't come in even though there's no door and no windows and no thatch, so that if you're standing up and you're not a small child you can see into everybody's house. Some people have even made paint from ground rocks and drawn designs on the sacks.

Of course, there really is a roof—the tent is the roof, far, high up. It's like a sky. It's like a mountain and we're inside it; through the cracks paths of dust lead down, so thick you think you could climb them. The tent keeps off the rain overhead but the water comes in at the sides and in the little streets between our places you can only move along them one person at a time—the small kids like my little brother play in the mud. You have to step over them. My little brother doesn't play. Our grandmother takes him to the clinic when the doctor comes on Mondays. Sister says there's something wrong with his head, she thinks it's because we didn't have enough food at home. Because of the war. Because our father wasn't there. And then because he was so hungry in the Kruger Park. He likes just to lie about on our grandmother all day, on her lap or against her somewhere and he looks at us and looks at us. He wants to ask something but you can see he can't. If I tickle him he may just smile. The clinic gives us special powder to make into porridge for him and perhaps one day he'll be all right.

When we arrived we were like him—my first-born brother and I. I can hardly remember. The people who lived in the village near the tent took us to the clinic, it's where you have to sign that you've come—away, through the Kruger Park. We sat on the grass and everything was muddled. One Sister was pretty with her hair straightened and beautiful high-heeled shoes and she brought us the special powder. She said we must mix it with water and drink it slowly. We tore the packets open with our teeth and licked it all up, it stuck round my mouth and I sucked it from my lips and fingers. Some other children who had walked with us vomited. But I only felt everything in my belly moving, the stuff going down and around like a snake, and hiccups hurt me. Another Sister called us to stand in line on the veranda of the clinic but we couldn't. We sat all over the place there, falling against each other: the Sisters helped each of us up by the arm and then stuck a needle in it. Other needles drew our blood into tiny bottles. This was against sickness, but I didn't understand, every time my eyes dropped closed I thought I was walking, the grass was long. I saw the elephants, I didn't know we were away.

But our grandmother was still strong, she could still stand up, she knows how to write and she signed for us. Our grandmother got us this place in the tent against one of the sides, it's the best kind of place there because although the rain comes in, we can lift the flap when the weather is good and then the sun shines on us, the smells in the tent go out. Our grandmother knows a woman here who showed her where there is good grass for sleeping mats, and our grandmother made some for us. Once every month the food truck comes to the clinic. Our grandmother takes along one of the cards she signed and when it has been punched we get a sack of mealie meal. There are wheelbarrows to take it back to the tent: my first-born brother does this for her and then he and the other boys have races, steering the empty wheelbarrows back to the clinic. Sometimes he's lucky and a man who's bought beer in the village gives him money to deliver it—though that's not allowed, you're supposed to take that wheelbarrow straight back to the Sisters. He buys a cold drink and shares it with me if I catch him. On another day, every month, the church leaves a pile of old clothes in the clinic yard. Our grandmother has another card to get punched, and then we can choose something: I have two dresses, two pants and a jersey, so I can go to school.

The people in the village have let us join their school. I was surprised to find they speak our language; our grandmother told me, That's why they allow us to stay on their land. Long ago, in the time of our fathers, there was no fence that kills you, there was no Kruger Park between them and us, we were the same people under our own king, right from our village we left to this place we've come to.

Now that we've been in the tent so long—I have turned eleven and my little brother is nearly three although he is so small, only his head is big, he's not come right in it yet—some people have dug up the bare ground around the tent and planted beans and mealies and cabbage. The old men weave branches to put up fences round their gardens. No one is allowed to look for work in the towns but some of the women have found work in the village and can buy things. Our grandmother, because she's still strong, finds work where people are building houses—in this village the people build nice houses with bricks and cement, not mud like we used to have at our home. Our grandmother carries bricks for these people and fetches baskets of stones on her head. And so she has money to buy sugar and tea and milk and soap. The store gave her a calendar she has hung up on our flap of the tent. I am clever at school and she collected advertising paper people throw away outside the store and covered my school-books with it. She makes my first-born brother and me do our homework every afternoon before it gets dark because there is no room except to lie down, close together, just as we did in the Kruger Park, in our place in the tent, and candles are expensive. Our grandmother hasn't been able to buy herself a pair of shoes for church yet, but she has bought black school shoes and polish to clean them with for my first-born brother and me. Every morning, when people are getting up in the tent, the babies are crying, people are pushing each other at the taps outside and some children are already pulling the crusts of porridge off the pots we ate from last night, my first-born brother and I clean our shoes. Our grandmother makes us sit on our mats with our legs straight out so she can look carefully at our shoes to make sure we have done it properly. No other children in the tent have real school shoes. When we three look at them it's as if we are in a real house again, with no war, no away.

Some white people came to take photographs of our people living in the tent—they said they were making a film, I've never seen what that is though I know about it. A white woman squeezed into our space and asked our grandmother questions which were told to us in our language by someone who understands the white woman's.

'How long have you been living like this?'

'She means here?' Our grandmother said. 'In this tent, two years and one month.'

'And what do you hope for the future?'

'Nothing. I'm here.'

'But for your children?'

'I want them to learn so that they can get good jobs and money.'

'Do you hope to go back to your own country?'

'I will not go back.'

'But when the war is over—you won't be allowed to stay here? Don't you want to go home?'

I didn't think our grandmother wanted to speak again. I didn't think she was going to answer the white woman. The white woman put her head on one side and smiled at us.

Our grandmother looked away from her and spoke. 'There is nothing. No home.'

Why does our grandmother say that? Why? I'll go back. I'll go back through that Kruger Park. After the war, if there are no bandits any more, our mother may be waiting for us. And maybe when we left our grandfather, he was only left behind, he found his way somehow, slowly, through the Kruger Park, and he'll be there. They'll be home, and I'll remember them.

Ernest Hemingway

Ernest Hemingway was born in Oak Park, Illinois, in 1899. He graduated from high school in 1917 and went to work for the *Kansas City Star*. He was an ambulance driver for the Red Cross in Italy in the later stages of World War I and was seriously wounded. He was a foreign correspondent briefly for *The Toronto Star*, before leaving for Paris where he joined the so-called Lost Generation of expatriate writers and artists. His first book of stories, *In Our Time*, was published in 1925, followed by two novels, *The Sun Also Rises* (1926) and *A Farewell to Arms* (1929). He served as a correspondent on the Loyalist side in the Spanish Civil War, from which grew *For Whom the Bell Tolls* (1940), and then as a foreign correspondent in Europe and Asia during World War II. Of his formal training, he said: "I went to war instead of college. When I came back from the war it was too late to go to college." Asked if there are any tricks to writing, he replied: "No. The hardest trade in the world to do is the writing of straight, honest prose about human beings." He lived in Cuba until the Revolution and was awarded the Nobel Prize for Literature in 1954. In poor health and unable to write, he shot himself in 1961 at his hunting lodge in Ketchum, Idaho.

"Every man should have a built-in crap detector operating inside him," Hemingway said. "It also should have a manual drill and crank handle in case the machine breaks down." In almost all of his conversations and public pronouncements about writing, the words *truth* and *honesty* are to be found. As he explains in *A Moveable Feast*, an account of his early years in Paris, when he was a guest at 27 rue de Fleurus, where Gertrude Stein held court, there was one thing he had to remind himself of when starting a new story: "'All you have to do is write one true sentence. Write the truest sentence that you know.' So finally I would write one true sentence, and then go on from there. It was easy then because there was always one true sentence that I knew or had seen or had heard someone say. If I started to write elaborately, or like someone introducing or presenting something, I found that I could cut that scroll-work or ornament out and throw it away and start with the first true simple declarative sentence I had written."

For writing, he recommended curiosity and training in recall: "When you walk into a room and you get a certain feeling or emotion, remember back until you see exactly what it was that gave you the emotion. Remember what the noises and smells were and what was said. Then write it down, making it clear so the reader will see it too and have the same feeling you had. And watch people, observe, try to put yourself in somebody else's head. If two men argue, don't just think who is right and who is wrong. Think what both their sides are. As a man, you know who is right and who is wrong; you have to judge. As a writer, you should not judge, you should understand."

"What a writer must try to do," Hemingway said, "is to write as truly as he can. For a writer of fiction has to invent out of what he knows in order to make something not photographic, or naturalistic, or realistic, which will be something entirely new and invented out of his own knowledge. ... A writer should try ... to make something which will be so written that it will become a part of the experience of those who read him." He claims to have struggled "to break down all my writing and get rid of all facility and try to make instead of describe." Asked how he would define his style, Hemingway told his interviewer: "In stating as fully as I could how things really were, it was often very difficult and I wrote awkwardly and the awkwardness is what they called my style."

Asked in *The Paris Review* interview what the technical problem was that made him rewrite the last page of *A Farewell to Arms* thirty-nine times, he replied, simply: "Getting the words right. ... I always try to write on the principle of the iceberg. There is seven-eighths of it underwater for every part that shows. Anything you know you can eliminate and it only strengthens your iceberg. It is the part that doesn't show. If a writer omits something because he does not know it then there is a hole in the story. ... In writing you are limited by what has already been done satisfactorily [by other writers]. So I have tried to learn to do something else. First I have tried to eliminate everything unnecessary to conveying experience. ... A writer, if he is any good, does not describe. He invents or *makes* out of knowledge personal and impersonal and sometimes he seems to have unexplained knowledge which could come from forgotten racial or family experience. Who teaches the homing pigeon to fly as he does; where does a fighting bull get his bravery, or a hunting dog his nose?"

Hills Like White Elephants

The hills across the valley of the Ebro were long and white. On this side there was no shade and no trees and the station was between two lines of rails in the sun. Close against the side of the station there was the warm shadow of the building and a curtain, made of strings of bamboo beads, hung across the open door into the bar, to keep out flies. The American and the girl with him sat at a table in the shade outside the building. It was very hot and the express from Barcelona would come in forty minutes. It stopped at this junction for two minutes and went on to Madrid.

"What should we drink?" the girl asked. She had taken off her hat and put it on the table.

"It's pretty hot," the man said.

"Let's drink beer."

"Dos cervezas," the man said into the curtain.

"Big ones?" a woman asked from the doorway.

"Yes. Two big ones."

The woman brought two glasses of beer and two felt pads. She put the felt pads and the beer glasses on the table and looked at the man and the girl. The girl was looking off at the line of hills. They were white in the sun and the country was brown and dry.

"They look like white elephants," she said.

"I've never seen one," the man drank his beer.

"No, you wouldn't have."

"I might have," the man said. "Just because you say I wouldn't have doesn't prove anything."

The girl looked at the bead curtain. "They've painted something on it," she said. "What does it say?"

"Anis del Toro. It's a drink."

"Could we try it?"

The man called "Listen" through the curtain. The woman came out from the bar.

"Four reales."

"We want two Anis del Toro."

"With water?"

"Do you want it with water?"

"I don't know," the girl said. "Is it good with water?"

"It's all right."

"You want them with water?" asked the woman.

"Yes, with water."

"It tastes like licorice," the girl said and put the glass down.

"That's the way with everything."

"Yes," said the girl. "Everything tastes of licorice. Especially all the things you've waited so long for, like absinthe."

"Oh, cut it out."

"You started it," the girl said. "I was being amused. I was having a fine time."

"Well, let's try and have a fine time."

"All right. I was trying. I said the mountains looked like white elephants. Wasn't that bright?"

"That was bright."

"I wanted to try this new drink. That's all we do, isn't it—look at things and try new drinks?"

"I guess so."

The girl looked across at the hills.

"They're lovely hills," she said. "They don't really look like white elephants. I just meant the coloring of their skin through the trees."

"Should we have another drink?"

"All right."

The warm wind blew the bead curtain against the table.

"The beer's nice and cool," the man said.

"It's lovely," the girl said.

"It's really an awfully simple operation, Jig," the man said. "It's not really an operation at all."

The girl looked at the ground the table legs rested on.

"I know you wouldn't mind it, Jig. It's really not anything. It's just to let the air in."

The girl did not say anything.

"I'll go with you and I'll stay with you all the time. They just let the air in and then it's all perfectly natural."

"Then what will we do afterward?"

"We'll be fine afterward. Just like we were before."

"What makes you think so?"

"That's the only thing that bothers us. It's the only thing that's made us unhappy."

The girl looked at the bead curtain, put her hand out and took hold of two of the strings of heads.

"And you think then we'll be all right and be happy."

"I know we will. You don't have to be afraid. I've known lots of people that have done it."

"So have I," said the girl. "And afterward they were all so happy."

"Well," the man said, "if you don't want to you don't have to. I wouldn't have you do it if you didn't want to. But I know it's perfectly simple."

"And you really want to?"

"I think it's the best thing to do. But I don't want you to do it if you don't really want to."

"And if I do it you'll be happy and things will be like they were and you'll love me?"

"I love you now. You know I love you."

"I know. But if I do it, then it will be nice again if I say things are like white elephants, and you'll like it?"

"I'll love it. I love it now but I just can't think about it. You know how I get when I worry."

"If I do it you won't ever worry?"

"I won't worry about that because it's perfectly simple."

"Then I'll do it. Because I don't care about me."

"What do you mean?"

"I don't care about me."

"Well, I care about you."

"Oh, yes. But I don't care about me. And I'll do it and then everything will be fine."

"I don't want you to do it if you feel that way."

The girl stood up and walked to the end of the station. Across, on the other side, were fields of grain and trees along the banks of the Ebro. Far away, beyond the river, were mountains. The shadow of a cloud moved across the field of grain and she saw the river through the trees.

"And we could have all this," she said. "And we could have everything and every day we make it more impossible."

"What did you say?"

"I said we could have everything."

"We can have everything."

"No, we can't."

"We can have the whole world."

"No, we can't."

"We can go everywhere."

"No, we can't. It isn't ours any more."

"It's ours."

"No, it isn't. And once they take it away, you never get it back."

"But they haven't taken it away."

"We'll wait and see."

"Come on back in the shade," he said. "You mustn't feel that way."

"I don't feel any way," the girl said. "I just know things."

"I don't want you to do anything that you don't want to do—"

"Nor that isn't good for me," she said. "I know. Could we have another beer?"

"All right. But you've got to realize—"

"I realize," the girl said. "Can't we maybe stop talking?"

They sat down at the table and the girl looked across at the hills on the dry side of the valley and the man looked at her and at the table.

"You've got to realize," he said, "that I don't want you to do it if you don't want to. I'm perfectly willing to go through with it if it means anything to you."

"Doesn't it mean anything to you? We could get along."

"Of course it does. But I don't want anybody but you. I don't want any one else. And I know it's perfectly simple."

"Yes, you know it's perfectly simple."

"It's all right for you to say that, but I do know it."

"Would you do something for me now?"

"I'd do anything for you."

"Would you please please please please please please please stop talking?"

He did not say anything but looked at the bags against the wall of the station. There were labels on them from all the hotels where they had spent nights.

"But I don't want you to," he said, "I don't care anything about it."

"I'll scream," the girl said.

The woman came out through the curtains with two glasses of beer and put them down on the damp felt pads. "The train comes in five minutes," she said.

"What did she say?" asked the girl.

"That the train is coming in five minutes."

The girl smiled brightly at the woman, to thank her.

"I'd better take the bags over to the other side of the station," the man said. She smiled at him.

"All right. Then come back and we'll finish the beer."

He picked up the two heavy bags and carried them around the station to the other tracks. He looked up the tracks but could not see the train. Coming back, he walked through the barroom, where people waiting for the train were drinking. He drank an Anis at the bar and looked at the people. They were all waiting reasonably for the train. He went out through the bead curtain. She was sitting at the table and smiled at him.

"Do you feel better?" he asked.

"I feel fine," she said. "There's nothing wrong with me. I feel fine."

Amy Hempel

Amy Hempel was born in Chicago in 1951, but moved to Denver in the third grade, and to San Francisco when she was in high school. In spite of the suicide of her mother when Hempel was only eighteen, she attributes to her mother her own love of words: "About the only time we really talked and got along was when we were talking about books. I read above my level because my mother was a real, real reader. How we communicated, when we did, was to talk about the books we read. I read as a way to talk to her. She'd always use words I didn't know and she wouldn't tell me what they meant. I had to read the dictionary to look up the words. I read it the way you'd read a book, just to keep up with her." She attended Whittier College in California, studied journalism, worked as a veterinarian's assistant, as publicist at Putnam's, and as an editorial assistant at Crown Publishers; later, she participated in writing workshops at Breadloaf and Columbia University, where she studied with Gordon Lish and wrote the much-anthologized story "In the Cemetery Where Al Jolson Is Buried" as an assignment to write about personal failure. Although she has chosen to live in New York, Hempel writes almost exclusively about California, where, she says, "It's very easy to have your worst fears made tangible in the form of natural disaster. Every year, they'll have these fires. And then there are the floods and mudslides and the quakes. I've been through all that." Hempel is a contributing editor to *Vanity Fair*. Her first collection of stories, *Reasons to Live*, was published in 1985; it was followed in 1990 by *At the Gates of the Animal Kingdom*. *Tumble Home*, a novella and short stories, appeared in 1997.

While she is often linked to the minimalists in fiction, Hempel rejects the designation, arguing that a story should only be as long as it needs to be. "I think that what I'm doing, because of the compression and phrasing, has more to do with poetry than with conventional short stories. ... Someone recently asked me if I was looking forward to writing a novel or longer work, and I said that I was looking forward to writing *shorter* work." Her thoughts on editing and brevity in fiction are to be found in the first issue of *The Quarterly*, where she discusses her story "The Harvest," based on her own experience of being in a serious accident. "The trick," she says in an interview with Michael Schumacher in *Reasons to Believe: New Voices in American Fiction*, "is to find a tiny way into a huge subject. In my case, it's loss. Every story in this book [*Reasons to Live*] has to do with some kind of loss. As I was writing these stories, I discovered that the way I write was like piecing a crazy quilt. I'd have these scraps and little bits of information and phrases and so on, and I'd kind of piece them together. If I did it right, they accumulated and signified by the end of the story. This ties in with the notion I got from my editor, Gordon Lish, who was also my writing teacher: he used to say 'Do it right in the small and the large will take care of itself.'"

Pondering the choice of the writer's material, and why she does not write about sex, Hempel suggests that she prefers to avoid what everyone is writing about, and not very well: "Then, too, one of my favorite lines in all of literature is one that's never been published. My little brother once tried to write an erotic story when he was about twelve. When I read this piece of erotica by my twelve-year-old brother, it contained the line: 'Then he unzipped her negligee.' That just stayed with me forever. If I ever write about sex, it will sound like 'and then he unzipped her negligee.' I just know it would. It's like this sign that comes up when I get toward that territory."

Although she strives in her work to touch readers, to enable them to move towards affirmation, Hempel rejects the notion of fiction as mere confession or therapy. "Looking for catharsis or a way to salve pain is a bad reason to go into fiction, but it's a good reason to keep a journal. ... Extremity—that's what I respond to. I'm endlessly, endlessly interested in people who have *come through* something, and the more they have come through, the more interested I am in them and their stories. That's what it's all about: How do you get through?"

The Harvest

The year I began to say *vahz* instead of *vase*, a man I barely knew nearly accidentally killed me.

The man was not hurt when the other car hit ours. The man I had known for one week held me in the street in a way that meant I couldn't see my legs. I remember knowing that I shouldn't look, and knowing that I *would* look if it wasn't that I couldn't.

My blood was on the front of this man's clothes.

He said, "You'll be okay, but this sweater is ruined."

I screamed from the fear of pain. But I did not feel any pain. In the hospital, after injections, I knew there was pain in the room—I just didn't know whose pain it was.

What happened to one of my legs required four hundred stitches, which, when I told it, became five hundred stitches, because nothing is ever quite as bad as it *could* be.

The five days they didn't know if they could save my leg or not I stretched to ten.

The lawyer was the one who used the word. But I won't get around to that until a couple of paragraphs.

We were having the looks discussion—how important *are* they. Crucial is what I had said.

I think looks are crucial.

But this guy was a lawyer. He sat in an aqua vinyl chair drawn up to my bed. What he meant by looks was how much my loss of them was worth in a court of law.

I could tell that the lawyer liked to say *court of law*. He told me he had taken the bar three times before he had passed. He said that his friends had given him handsomely embossed business cards, but where these lovely cards were supposed to say *Attorney-at-Law*, his cards said *Attorney-at-Last*.

He had already covered loss of earnings, that I could not now become an airline stewardess. That I had never considered becoming one was immaterial, he said, legally.

"There's another thing," he said. "We have to talk here about marriageability."

The tendency was to say marriage-a-*what*? although I knew what he meant the first time I heard it.

I was eighteen years old. I said, "First, don't we talk about *date*ability?"

The man of a week was already gone, the accident driving him back to his wife.

"Do you think looks are important?" I asked the man before he left.

"Not at first," he said.

In my neighborhood there is a fellow who was a chemistry teacher until an explosion took his face and left what was left behind. The rest of him is neatly dressed in dark suits and shined shoes. He carries a briefcase to the college campus. What a comfort—his family, people said—until his wife took the kids and moved out.

In the solarium, a woman showed me a snapshot. She said, "This is what my son used to look like."

I spent my evenings in Dialysis. They didn't mind when a lounger was free. They had wide-screen color TV, better than they had in Rehab. Wednesday nights we watched a show where women in expensive clothes appeared on lavish sets and promised to ruin one another.

On one side of me was a man who spoke only in phone numbers. You would ask him how he felt, he would say, "924-3130." Or he would say, "757-1366." We guessed what these numbers might be, but nobody spent the dime.

There was sometimes, on the other side of me, a twelve-year-old boy. His lashes were thick and dark from blood-pressure medication. He was next on the transplant list, as soon as—the word they used was *harvest*—as soon as a kidney was harvested.

The boy's mother prayed for drunk drivers.

I prayed for men who were not discriminating.

Aren't we all, I thought, somebody's harvest?

The hour would end, and a floor nurse would wheel me back to my room. She would say, "Why watch that trash? Why not just ask me how my day went?"

I spent fifteen minutes before going to bed squeezing rubber grips. One of the medications was making my fingers stiffen. The doctor said he'd give it to me till I couldn't button my blouse—a figure of speech to someone in a cotton gown.

The lawyer said, "Charitable works."

He opened his shirt and showed me where an acupuncture person had dabbed at his chest with cola syrup, sunk four needles, and told him that the real cure was charitable works.

I said, "Cure for what?"

The lawyer said, "Immaterial."

As soon as I knew that I would be all right, I was sure that I was dead and didn't know it. I moved through the days like a severed head that finishes a sentence. I waited for the moment that would snap me out of my seeming life.

The accident happened at sunset, so that is when I felt this way the most. The man I had met the week before was driving me to dinner when it happened. The place was at the beach, a beach on a bay that you can look across and see the city lights, a place where you can see everything without having to listen to any of it.

A long time later I went to that beach myself. *I* drove the car. It was the first good beach day; I wore shorts.

At the edge of the sand I unwound the elastic bandage and waded into the surf. A boy in a wet suit looked at my leg. He asked me if a shark had done it; there were sightings of great whites along that part of the coast.

I said that, yes, a shark had done it.

"And you're going back in?" the boy asked.

I said, "And I'm going back in."

I leave a lot out when I tell the truth. The same when I write a story. I'm going to start now to tell you what I left out of "The Harvest," and maybe begin to wonder why I had to leave it out.

There was no other car. There was only the one car, the one that hit me when I was on the back of the man's motorcycle. But think of the awkward syllables when you have to say *motorcycle.*

The driver of the car was a newspaper reporter. He worked for a local paper. He was young, a recent graduate, and he was on his way to a labor meeting to cover a threatened strike. When I say I was then a journalism student, it is something you might not have accepted in "The Harvest."

In the years that followed, I watched for the reporter's byline. He broke the People's Temple story that resulted in Jim Jones's flight to Guyana. Then he covered Jonestown. In the city room of the San Francisco *Chronicle*, as the death toll climbed to nine hundred, the numbers were posted like donations on pledge night. Somewhere in the hundreds, a sign was fixed to the wall that said JUAN CORONA, EAT YOUR HEART OUT.

In the emergency room, what happened to one of my legs required not four hundred stitches but just over three hundred stitches. I exaggerated even before I began to exaggerate, because it's true—nothing *is* ever quite as bad as it could be.

My lawyer was no attorney-at-last. He was a partner in one of the city's oldest law firms. He would never have opened his shirt to reveal the site of acupuncture, which is something that he never would have had.

"Marriageability" was the original title of "The Harvest."

The damage to my leg was considered cosmetic although I am still, fifteen years later, unable to kneel. In an out-of-court settlement the night before the trial, I was awarded nearly $100,000. The reporter's car insurance went up $12.43 per month.

It had been suggested that I rub my leg with ice, to bring up the scars, before I hiked my skirt three years later for the court. But there was no ice in the judge's chambers, so I did not get a chance to pass or fail that moral test.

The man of a week, whose motorcycle it was, was not a married man. But when you thought he had a wife, wasn't I liable to do anything? And didn't I have it coming?

After the accident, the man got married. The girl he married was a fashion model. ("Do you think looks are important?" I asked the man before he left. "Not at first," he said.)

In addition to being a beauty, the girl was worth millions of dollars. Would you have accepted this in "The Harvest"—that the model was also an heiress?

It is true we were headed for dinner when it happened. But the place where you can see everything without having to listen to any of it was not a beach on a bay—it was the top of Mount Tamalpais. We had the dinner with us as we headed up the twisting mountain road. This is the version that has room for perfect irony, so you won't mind when I say that for the next several months, from my hospital bed, I had a dead-on spectacular view of that very mountain.

I would have written this next part into the story if anybody would have believed it. But who would have? I was there and I didn't believe it.

On the day of my third operation, there was an attempted breakout in the Maximum Security Adjustment Center, adjacent to Death Row, at San Quentin prison. "Soledad Brother" George Jackson, a twenty-nine-year-old black man, pulled out a smuggled-in .38 caliber pistol, yelled, "This is it!" and opened fire. Jackson was killed; so were three guards and two "tier-tenders," inmates who bring other prisoners their meals.

Three other guards were stabbed in the neck. The prison is a five-minute drive from Marin General, so that is where the injured guards were taken. The people who brought them were three kinds of police, including California Highway Patrol and Marin County sheriff's deputies, heavily armed.

Police were stationed on the roof of the hospital with rifles; they were posted in the hallways, waving patients and visitors back into their rooms.

When I was wheeled out of Recovery later that day, bandaged waist to ankle, three officers and an armed sheriff frisked me.

On the news that night, there was footage of the riot.

They showed my surgeon talking to reporters, indicating, with a finger to his throat, how he had saved one of the guards by sewing up a slice from ear to ear.

I watched this on television, and because it was my doctor, and because hospital patients are self-absorbed, and because I was drugged, I thought the surgeon was talking about me. I thought that he was saying, "Well, she's dead. I'm announcing it to her in her bed."

The psychiatrist I saw at the surgeon's referral said that the feeling was a common one. She said that victims of trauma who have not yet assimilated the trauma often believe they are dead and do not know it.

The great white sharks in the waters near my home attack one to seven people a year. Their primary victim is the abalone diver. With abalone steaks at thirty-five dollars a pound and going up, the Department of Fish and Game expects the shark attacks to show no slackening.

James Joyce

James Joyce was born in 1882 near Dublin, Ireland. He was educated at Conglowes Wood College from age six to nine, until his parents fell on difficult times financially. Later he was educated by the Jesuits at Bellevedere and University College, Dublin. His love affair with and self-imposed exile from Ireland, which he described as "an old sow that eats its farrow," was one of poverty and hardships, and included a ten-year struggle to find a publisher for *Dubliners* (1914), which sold fewer than five hundred copies. The book was savagely attacked by publishers and editors; even the plates themselves were destroyed at the printer's. *A Portrait of the Artist as a Young Man* had a more immediate success and won the approval of T. S. Eliot and Ezra Pound, both of whom helped garner support for his two major works, *Ulysses* (1922) and *Finnegan's Wake* (1939). His survival in Trieste, Zurich, and Paris was, at best, precarious, with occasional teaching, commissions, and handouts from family and friends.

Joyce wrote very little about the art of fiction that was not, finally, incorporated into the fabric of his novels, particularly in the aesthetic ascribed to Stephen Dedalus in *A Portrait of the Artist as a Young Man*. However, there are in the letters a number of comments about fiction that are worthy of mention. Of *Dubliners*, he said: "My intention was to write a chapter of the moral history of my country and I chose Dublin for the scene because that city seemed to me the centre of paralysis. I have tried to present it to the indifferent public under four of its aspects: childhood, adolescence, maturity and public life. The stories are arranged in this order. I have written it for the most part in a style of scrupulous meanness and with the conviction that he is a very bold man who dares to alter in the presentment, still more to deform, whatever he has seen and heard. I cannot do any more than this. I cannot alter what I have written."

Joyce was preoccupied with attacks from editors, printers, and the public over many aspects of his work: "I have come to the conclusion that I cannot write without offending people. The printer denounces *Two Gallants* and *Counterparts*. A Dubliner would denounce *Ivy Day in the Committee-Room*. The more subtle inquisitor will denounce *An Encounter*, the enormity of which the printer cannot see because he is, as I said, a plain blunt man. The Irish priest will denounce *The Sisters*. The Irish boarding-house keeper will denounce *The Boarding-House*. Do not let the printer imagine, for goodness' sake, that he is going to have all the barking to himself."

The letters reveal him to be extremely scrupulous about the physical details of his stories, writing to friends in Dublin to ask them to check the name of a street, whether municipal elections can take place in October, and whether the police are supplied with provisions by government or private contacts. There is a wonderful letter from Joyce to Grant Richards, whose firm had contracted to publish *Dubliners*, but who had written to Joyce to say: "If I had written your stories I should certainly wish to be able to afford your attitude; but as I stand on the publisher's side, I feel most distinctly that for more than one reason you cannot afford it. ... You won't get a publisher—a real publisher—to issue it as it stands. ... After all, remember, *it is only words and sentences that have to be altered* [italics added]; and it seems to me that the man who cannot convey his meaning by more than one set of words and sentences has not yet realized the possibilities of the English language." Apparently, the publisher and his reader took exception to, among other things, use of the word *bloody* and the phrase *she changed the position of her legs often.*

To this Joyce responded: "The first passage I could alter. The second passage (with infinite regret) I could alter by omitting the word simply. But the third passage I absolutely could not alter. Read *The Boarding-House* yourself and tell me frankly what you think. The word, the exact expression I have used ["he'd bloody well put his teeth down his throat, so he would"], is in my opinion the one expression in the English language which can create on the reader the effect which I wish to create. Surely you can see this for yourself? And if the word appears once in the book it may as well appear three times. Is it not ridiculous that my book cannot be published because it contains this one word which is neither indecent nor blasphemous?" Joyce's reply barely veils his anger and justified contempt. "The objections raised against *Counterparts* seem to me equally trivial. Is it possible that at this age of the world in the country which the ingenuous Latins are fond of calling 'the home of liberty' an allusion to 'two establishments' cannot appear in print or that I cannot write the phrase 'she changed the position of her legs often?' To invoke the name of Areopagitica in this connection would be to render the artist as absurd as the printer.

"You say it is a small thing I am asked to do, to efface a word here and there. But do you not see clearly that in a short story above all such effacement may be fatal. You cannot say that the phrases objected to are gratuitous and impossible to print and at the same time approve of the tenor of the book. Granted this latter as legitimate I cannot see how anyone can consider these minute and necessary details illegitimate." The argument that you cannot divorce content from the form it acquires, or assumes, seems to have escaped the publisher.

Even when he managed to overcome difficulties in the way of publication, Joyce lived on the razor's edge financially, as a letter to Ezra Pound explains: "I live in a flat with eleven other people and have had great difficulty in securing time and peace enough to write those two chapters." He claimed to have no money to buy adequate clothes and to have to wear his son's shoes and castoff suit; he read newspapers and returned them for a refund, spending "the greatest part of my time sprawled across two beds surrounded by mountains of notes." His labours with *Ulysses* seem, appropriately, to have been Herculean; the book, which had begun as a short story for *Dubliners*, was abandoned and later grew to be "a kind of encyclopaedia." Among the many misconceptions people had of him, Joyce found most amusing the idea that he was lazy: "I calculate I have spent nearly 20,000 hours in writing *Ulysses*. ... The task I set myself technically in writing a book from eighteen different points of view and in as many different styles, all apparently unknown or undiscovered by my fellow tradesmen, that and the nature of the legend chosen would be enough to upset anyone's mental balance. I want to finish the book and try to settle my entangled material affairs definitely one way or the other (somebody here said of me: 'They call him a poet. He appears to be interested chiefly in mattresses'). And in fact, I was. After that I want a good long rest in which to forget *Ulysses* completely."

Clay

The matron had given her leave to go out as soon as the women's tea was over and Maria looked forward to her evening out. The kitchen was spick and span: the cook said you could see yourself in the big copper boilers. The fire was nice and bright and on one of the side-tables were four very big barmbracks. These barmbracks seemed uncut; but if you went closer you would see that they had been cut into long thick even slices and were ready to be handed round at tea. Maria had cut them herself.

Maria was a very, very small person indeed but she had a very long nose and a very long chin. She talked a little through her nose, always soothingly: *Yes, my dear*, and *No, my dear*. She was always sent for when the women quarrelled over their tubs and always succeeded in making peace. One day the matron had said to her:

—Maria, you are a veritable peace-maker!

And the sub-matron and two of the Board ladies had heard the compliment. And Ginger Mooney was always saying what she wouldn't do to the dummy who had charge of the irons if it wasn't for Maria. Everyone was so fond of Maria.

The women would have their tea at six o'clock and she would be able to get away before seven. From Ballsbridge to the Pillar, twenty minutes; from the Pillar to Drumcondra, twenty minutes; and twenty minutes to buy the things. She would be there before eight. She took out her purse with the silver clasps and read again the words *A Present from Belfast*. She was very fond of that purse because Joe had brought it to her five years before when he and Alphy had gone to Belfast on a Whit-Monday trip. In the purse were two half-crowns and some coppers. She would have five shillings clear after paying tram fare. What a nice evening they would have, all the children singing! Only she hoped that Joe wouldn't come in drunk. He was so different when he took any drink.

Often he had wanted her to go and live with them; but she would have felt herself in the way (though Joe's wife was ever so nice with her) and she had become accustomed to the life of the laundry. Joe was a good fellow. She had nursed him and Alphy too; and Joe used often say:

—Mamma is mamma but Maria is my proper mother.

After the break-up at home the boys had got her that position in the *Dublin by Lamplight* laundry, and she liked it. She used to have such a bad opinion of Protestants but now she thought they were very nice people, a little quiet and serious, but still very nice people to live with. Then she had her plants in the conservatory and she liked looking after them. She had lovely ferns and wax-plants and, whenever anyone came to visit her, she always gave the visitor one or two slips from her conservatory. There was one thing she didn't like and that was the tracts on the walls; but the matron was such a nice person to deal with, so genteel.

When the cook told her everything was ready she went into the women's room and began to pull the big bell. In a few minutes the women began to come in by twos and threes, wiping their steaming hands in their petticoats and pulling down the sleeves of their blouses over their red steaming arms. They settled down before their huge mugs which the cook and the dummy filled up with hot tea, already mixed with milk and sugar in huge tin cans. Maria superintended the distribution of the barmbrack and saw that every woman got her four slices. There was a great deal of laughing and joking during the meal. Lizzie Fleming said Maria was sure to get the ring and, though Fleming had said that for so many Hallow Eves, Maria had to laugh and say she didn't want any ring or man either; and when she laughed her grey-green eyes sparkled with disappointed shyness and the tip of her nose nearly met the tip of her chin. Then Ginger Mooney lifted up her mug of tea and proposed Maria's health while all the other women clattered with their mugs on the table, and said she was sorry she hadn't a sup of porter to drink it in. And Maria laughed again till the tip of her nose nearly met the tip of her chin and till her minute body nearly shook itself asunder because she knew that Mooney meant well though, of course, she had the notions of a common woman.

But wasn't Maria glad when the women had finished their tea and the cook and the dummy had begun to clear away the tea-things! She went into her little bedroom and, remembering that the next morning was a mass morning, changed the hand of the alarm from seven to six. Then she took off her working skirt and her house-boots and laid her best skirt out on the bed and her tiny dress-boots beside the foot of the bed. She changed her blouse too and, as she stood before the mirror, she thought of how she used to dress for mass on Sunday morning when she was a young girl; and she looked with quaint affection at the diminutive body which she had so often adorned. In spite of its years she found it a nice tidy little body.

When she got outside the streets were shining with rain and she was glad of her old brown raincloak. The tram was full and she had to sit on the little stool at the end of the car, facing all the people, with her toes barely touching the floor. She arranged in her mind all she was going to do and thought how much better it was to be independent and to have your own money in your pocket. She hoped they would have a nice evening. She was sure they would but she could not help thinking what a pity it was Alphy and Joe were not speaking. They were always falling out now but when they were boys together they used to be the best of friends: but such was life.

She got out of her tram at the Pillar and ferreted her way quickly among the crowds. She went into Downes's cake-shop but the shop was so full of people that it was a long time before she could get herself attended to. She bought a dozen of mixed penny cakes, and at last came out of the shop laden with a big bag. Then she thought what else would she buy: she wanted to buy something really nice. They would be sure to have plenty of apples and nuts. It was hard to know what to buy and all she could think of was cake. She decided to buy some plumcake but Downes's plumcake had not enough almond icing on top of it so she went over to a shop in Henry Street. Here she was a long time in suiting herself and the stylish young lady behind the counter, who was evidently a little annoyed by her, asked her was it wedding-cake she wanted to buy. That made Maria blush and smile at the young lady; but the young lady took it all very seriously and finally cut a thick slice of plumcake, parcelled it up and said:

—Two-and-four, please.

She thought she would have to stand in the Drumcondra tram because none of the young men seemed to notice her but an elderly gentleman made room for her. He was a stout gentleman and he wore a brown hard hat; he had a square red face and a greying moustache. Maria thought he was a colonel-looking gentleman and she reflected how much more polite he was than the young men who simply stared straight before them. The gentleman began to chat with her about Hallow Eve and the rainy weather. He supposed the bag was full of good things for the little ones and said it was only right that the youngsters should enjoy themselves while they were young. Maria agreed with him and favoured him with demure nods and hems. He was very nice with her, and when she was getting out at the Canal Bridge she thanked him and bowed, and he bowed to her and raised his hat and smiled agreeably; and while she was going up along the terrace, bending her tiny head under the rain, she thought how easy it was to know a gentleman even when he has a drop taken.

Everybody said: *O, here's Maria!* when she came to Joe's house. Joe was there, having come home from business, and all the children had their Sunday dresses on. There were two big girls in from next door and games were going on. Maria gave the bag of cakes to the eldest boy, Alphy, to divide and Mrs Donnelly said it was too good of her to bring such a big bag of cakes and made all the children say:

—Thanks, Maria.

But Maria said she had brought something special for papa and mamma, something they would be sure to like, and she began to look to for her plumcake. She tried in Downes's bag and then in the pockets of her raincloak and then on the hallstand but nowhere could she find it. Then she asked all the children had any of them eaten it—by mistake, of course—but the children all said no and looked as if they did not like to eat cakes if they were to be accused of stealing. Everybody had a solution for the mystery and Mrs Donnelly said it was plain that Maria had left it behind her in the tram. Maria, remembering how confused the gentleman with the greyish moustache had made her, coloured with shame and vexation and disappointment. At the thought of the failure of her little surprise and of the two and fourpence she had thrown away for nothing she nearly cried outright.

But Joe said it didn't matter and made her sit down by the fire. He was very nice with her. He told her all that went on in his office, repeating for her a smart answer which he had made to the manager. Maria did not understand why Joe laughed so much over the answer he had made but she said that the manager must have been a very overbearing person to deal with. Joe said he wasn't so bad when you knew how to take him, that he was a decent sort so long as you didn't rub him the wrong way. Mrs Donnelly played the piano for the children and they danced and sang. Then the two next-door girls handed round the nuts.

Nobody could find the nutcrackers and Joe was nearly getting cross over it and asked how did they expect Maria to crack nuts without a nutcracker. But Maria said she didn't like nuts and that they weren't to bother about her. Then Joe asked would she take a bottle of stout and Mrs Donnelly said there was port wine too in the house if she would prefer that. Maria said she would rather they didn't ask her to take anything: but Joe insisted.

So Maria let him have his way and they sat by the fire talking over old times and Maria thought she would put in a good word for Alphy. But Joe cried that God might strike him stone dead if ever he spoke a word to his brother again and Maria said she was sorry she had mentioned the matter. Mrs Donnelly told her husband it was a great shame for him to speak that way of his own flesh and blood but Joe said that Alphy was no brother of his and there was nearly being a row on the head of it. But Joe said he would not lose his temper on account of the night it was and asked his wife to open some more stout. The two next-door girls had arranged some Hallow Eve games and soon everything was merry again. Maria was delighted to see the children so merry and Joe and his wife in such good spirits. The next-door girls put some saucers on the table and then led the children up to the table, blindfold. One got the prayer book and the other three got the water; and when one of the next-door girls got the ring Mrs Donnelly shook her finger at the blushing girl as much as to say: *O, I know all about it!* They insisted then on blindfolding Maria and leading her up to the table to see what she would get; and, while they were putting on the bandage, Maria laughed and laughed again till the top of her nose nearly met the tip of her chin.

They led her up to the table amid laughing and joking and she put her hand out in the air as she was told to do. She moved her hand about here and there in the air and descended on one of the saucers. She felt a soft wet substance with her fingers and was surprised that nobody spoke or took off her bandage. There was a pause for a few seconds; and then a great deal of scuffling and whispering. Somebody said something about the garden, and at last Mrs Donnelly said something very cross to one of the next-door girls and told her to throw it out at once: that was no play. Maria understood that it was wrong that time and so she had to do it over again: and this time she got the prayer-book.

After that Mrs Donnelly played Miss McCloud's Reel for the children and Joe made Maria take a glass of wine. Soon they were all quite merry again and Mrs Donnelly said Maria would enter a convent before the year was out because she had got the prayer-book. Maria had never seen Joe so nice to her as he was that night, so full of pleasant talk and reminiscences. She said they were all very good to her.

At last the children grew tired and sleepy and Joe asked Maria would she not sing some little song before she went, one of the old songs. Mrs Donnelly said *Do, please, Maria!* and so Maria had to get up and stand beside the piano. Mrs Donnelly bade the children be quiet and listen to Maria's song. Then she played the prelude and said *Now, Maria!* and Maria, blushing very much, began to sing in a tiny quavering voice. She sang *I Dreamt that I Dwelt*, and when she came to the second verse she sang again:

I dreamt that I dwelt in marble halls
With vassals and serfs at my side
And of all who assembled within those walls
That I was the hope and the pride.
I had riches too great to count, could boast
Of a high ancestral name,
But I also dreamt, which pleased me most,
That you loved me still the same.

But no one tried to show her her mistake; and when she had ended her song Joe was very much moved. He said that there was no time like the long ago and no music for him like poor old Balfe, whatever other people might say; and his eyes filled up so much with tears that he could not find what he was looking for and in the end he had to ask his wife to tell him where the corkscrew was.

Thomas King

Thomas King is a writer of mixed Cherokee, German, and Greek descent. He was born in Roseville, California, in 1943 and, although his story "Borders" may make saying so seem rather ironic, he has dual Canadian and American citizenship. He has taught in the Native Studies Department at the University of Lethbridge and is currently teaching in the American Studies Department at the University of Minnesota. He co-edited a volume of critical essays on Native literature and has edited an issue of *Canadian Fiction Magazine* (No. 60, 1987) on Native fiction that provided the groundwork for his anthology of contemporary Canadian Native fiction, *All My Relations* (1990). His poems and short stories have appeared widely in magazines in Canada and the U.S. His first novel, *Medicine River*, appeared in 1990; his second, *Green Grass Running Water*, in 1993. He also writes and performs in "The Mad Dog Café," satirical sketches featured irregularly on CBC radio.

In the Introduction to *All My Relations*, King stresses the centrality of the idea of family, or community—"intricate webs of kinship"—in Native culture. "'All my relations' is at first a reminder of who we are and of our relationship with both our family and our relatives. It also reminds us of the extended relationship we share with all human beings. But the relationships that Native people see go further, the web of kinship extending to the animals, to the birds, to the fish, to the plants, to all the animate and inanimate forms that can be seen or imagined. More than that, 'all my relations' is an encouragement for us to accept the responsibilities we have within this universal family by living our lives in a harmonious and moral manner (a common admonishment is to say of someone that they act as if they have no relations)." While there is, as yet, no clear definition of Native literature, King accepts the view that it is "literature produced by Natives and not by non-Natives, recognizing that being Native is a matter of race rather than something more transitory such as nationality."

In response to the question of why Native writers avoid historical settings, particularly the nineteenth century, King says: "Some of the reasons for this avoidance are obvious. The literary stereotypes and clichés for which the period is famous have been, I think, a deterrent to many of us. Feathered warriors on Pinto ponies, laconic chiefs in full regalia, dusky raven-haired maidens, demonic shamans with eagle-claw rattles and scalping knives are all picturesque and exciting images, but they are, more properly, servants of a non-Native imagination. Rather than try to unravel the complex relationship between the nineteenth-century Indian and the white mind, or to craft a new set of images that still reflects the time but avoids the flat, static depiction of the Native and the two-dimensional quality of the culture, most of us have consciously set our literature in the present, a period that is reasonably free of literary monoliths and which allows for greater latitude in the creation of characters and situations, and, more important, allows us the opportunity to create for ourselves and our respective cultures both a present and a future."

In an interview conducted by Ray Beauchemin, where he suggests that there is no border between past and present for Native writers, King tries to explain in greater detail the Native writer's relation to the past. "In my own fiction that's absolutely true. I don't make any designation between the past and the present. I am always very happy to bring what appears to be older materials forward and present them in a contemporary context. A lot of my coyote stories do that, they mix the past and the present, and so they're filled with what we in the 'biz' call anachronisms—things that just don't go together, because of the time period in which they exist. I feel comfortable talking about when the world was created and throwing in a couple of television sets along with everything else that gets created at that period of time. It doesn't rest too easily [with some], but to me the connections are quite easy to make."

King emphasizes the orality of Native fiction, suggesting that he and many other Native writers try to maintain in their written fiction as much of the character of oral story-telling as possible. While he admits that most of his stories "start off with a piece of oral literature or a title or a character," he occasionally starts with an idea, as in "Borders." "The philosophical stuff is just a small percentage," he says. "It's always hardest to make sure that the message doesn't get in the way of the story, that it doesn't stick its nose out from behind the curtain. If it does that, people see it and it ruins the fiction, it ruins the moment."

Regarding the current debate about the appropriation of voice, King admits that he would expect to learn more about Native experience from reading Native writers, just as he would expect to learn more about women's experience by reading women writers, though he acknowledges that there are exceptional cases where non-Natives write insightfully about Native experience and men write well about women. However, he suggests a political consideration worth noting: "I don't think that you can be successful writing about an oppressed people if you are one of the oppressors. The societal set, the mindset that you have, is very different from the person who has to suffer under that oppression."

Borders

When I was twelve, maybe thirteen, my mother announced that we were going to go to Salt Lake City to visit my sister who had left the reserve, moved across the line, and found a job. Laetitia had not left home with my mother's blessing, but over time my mother had come to be proud of the fact that Laetitia had done all of this on her own.

"She did real good," my mother would say.

Then there were the fine points to Laetitia's going. She had not, as my mother liked to tell Mrs. Manyfingers, gone floating after some man like a balloon on a string. She hadn't snuck out of the house, either, and gone to Vancouver or Edmonton or Toronto to chase rainbows down alleys. And she hadn't been pregnant.

"She did real good."

I was seven or eight when Laetitia left home. She was seventeen. Our father was from Rocky Boy on the American side.

"Dad's American," Laetitia told my mother, "so I can go and come as I please."

"Send us a postcard."

Laetitia packed her things, and we headed for the border. Just outside of Milk River, Laetitia told us to watch for the water tower.

"Over the next rise. It's the first thing you see."

"We got a water tower on the reserve," my mother said. "There's a big one in Lethbridge, too."

"You'll be able to see the tops of the flagpoles, too. That's where the border is."

When we got to Coutts, my mother stopped at the convenience store and bought her and Laetitia a cup of coffee. I got an Orange Crush.

"This is real lousy coffee."

"You're just angry because I want to see the world."

"It's the water. From here on down, they got lousy water."

"I can catch the bus from Sweetgrass. You don't have to lift a finger."

"You're going to have to buy your water in bottles if you want good coffee."

There was an old wooden building about a block away, with a tall sign in the yard that said "Museum." Most of the roof had been blown away. Mom told me to go and see when the place was open. There were boards over the windows and doors. You could tell that the place was closed, and I told Mom so, but she said to go and check anyway. Mom and Laetitia stayed by the car. Neither one of them moved. I sat down on the steps of the museum and watched them, and I don't know that they ever said anything to each other. Finally, Laetitia got her bag out of the trunk and gave Mom a hug.

I wandered back to the car. The wind had come up, and it blew Laetitia's hair across her face. Mom reached out and pulled the strands out of Laetitia's eyes, and Laetitia let her.

"You can still see the mountain from here," my mother told Laetitia in Blackfoot.

"Lots of mountains in Salt Lake," Laetitia told her in English.

"The place is closed," I said. "Just like I told you."

Laetitia tucked her hair into her jacket and dragged her bag down the road to the brick building with the American flag flapping on a pole. When she got to where the guards were waiting, she turned, put the bag down, and waved to us. We waved back. Then my mother turned the car around, and we came home.

We got postcards from Laetitia regular, and, if she wasn't spreading jelly on the truth, she was happy. She found a good job and rented an apartment with a pool.

"And she can't even swim," my mother told Mrs. Manyfingers.

Most of the postcards said we should come down and see the city, but whenever I mentioned this, my mother would stiffen up.

So I was surprised when she bought two new tires for the car and put on her blue dress with the green and yellow flowers. I had to dress up, too, for my mother did not want us crossing the border looking like Americans. We made sandwiches and put them in a big box with pop and potato chips and some apples and bananas and a big jar of water.

"But we can stop at one of those restaurants, too, right?"

"We maybe should take some blankets in case you get sleepy."

"But we can stop at one of those restaurants, too, right?"

The border was actually two towns, though neither one was big enough to amount to anything. Coutts was on the Canadian side and consisted of the convenience store and gas station, the museum that was closed and boarded up, and a motel. Sweetgrass was on the American side, but all you could see was an overpass that arched across the highway and disappeared into the prairies. Just hearing the names of these towns, you would expect that Sweetgrass, which is a nice name and sounds like it is related to other places such as Medicine Hat and Moose Jaw and Kicking Horse Pass, would be on the Canadian side, and that Coutts, which sounds abrupt and rude, would be on the American side. But this was not the case.

Between the two borders was a duty-free shop where you could buy cigarettes and liquor and flags. Stuff like that.

We left the reserve in the morning and drove until we got to Coutts.

"Last time we stopped here," my mother said, "you had an Orange Crush. You remember that?"

"Sure," I said. "That was when Laetitia took off."

"You want another Orange Crush?"

"That means we're not going to stop at a restaurant, right?"

My mother got a coffee at the convenience store, and we stood around and watched the prairies move in the sunlight. Then we climbed back in the car. My mother straightened the dress across her thighs, leaned against the wheel, and drove all the way to the border in first gear, slowly, as if she were trying to see through a bad storm or riding high on black ice.

The border guard was an old guy. As he walked to the car, he swayed from side to side, his feet set wide apart, the holster on his hip pitching up and down. He leaned into the window, looked into the back seat, and looked at my mother and me.

"Morning, ma'am."

"Good morning."

"Where you heading?"

"Salt Lake City."

"Purpose of your visit?"

"Visit my daughter."

"Citizenship?"

"Blackfoot," my mother told him.

"Ma'am?"

"Blackfoot," my mother repeated.

"Canadian?"

"Blackfoot."

It would have been easier if my mother had just said "Canadian" and been done with it, but I could see she wasn't going to do that. The guard wasn't angry or anything. He smiled and looked towards the building. Then he turned back and nodded.

"Morning, ma'am."

"Good morning."

"Any firearms or tobacco?"

"No."

"Citizenship?"

"Blackfoot."

He told us to sit in the car and wait, and we did. In about five minutes, another guard came out with the first man. They were talking as they came, both men swaying back and forth like two cowboys headed for a bar or a gunfight.

"Morning, ma'am."

"Good morning."

"Cecil tells me you and the boy are Blackfoot."

"That's right."

"Now, I know that we got Blackfeet on the American side and the Canadians got Blackfeet on their side. Just so we can keep our records straight, what side do you come from?"

I knew exactly what my mother was going to say, and I could have told them if they had asked me.

"Canadian side or American side?" asked the guard.

"Blackfoot side," she said.

It didn't take them long to lose their sense of humour, I can tell you that. The one guard stopped smiling altogether and told us to park our car at the side of the building and come in.

We sat on a wood bench for about an hour before anyone came over to talk to us. This time it was a woman. She had a gun, too.

"Hi," she said. "I'm Inspector Pratt. I understand there is a little misunderstanding."

"I'm going to visit my daughter in Salt Lake City," my mother told her. "We don't have any guns or beer."

"It's a legal technicality, that's all."

"My daughter's Blackfoot, too."

The woman opened a briefcase and took out a couple of forms and began to write on one of them. "Everyone who crosses our border has to declare their citizenship. Even Americans. It helps us keep track of the visitors we get from the various countries."

She went on like that for maybe fifteen minutes, and a lot of the stuff she told us was interesting.

"I can understand how you feel about having to tell us your citizenship, and here's what I'll do. You tell me, and I won't put it down on the form. No-one will know but you and me."

Her gun was silver. There were several chips in the wood handle and the name "Stella" was scratched into the metal butt.

We were in the border office for about four hours, and we talked to almost everyone there. One of the men bought me a Coke. My mother brought a couple of sandwiches in from the car. I offered part of mine to Stella, but she said she wasn't hungry.

I told Stella that we were Blackfoot and Canadian, but she said that that didn't count because I was a minor. In the end, she told us that if my mother didn't declare her citizenship, we would have to go back to where we came from. My mother stood up and thanked Stella for her time. Then we got back in the car and drove to the Canadian border, which was only about a hundred yards away.

I was disappointed. I hadn't seen Laetitia for a long time, and I had never been to Salt Lake City. When she was still at home, Laetitia would go on and on about Salt Lake City. She had never been there, but her boyfriend Lester Tallbull had spent a year in Salt Lake at a technical school.

"It's a great place," Lester would say. "Nothing but blondes in the whole state."

Whenever he said that, Laetitia would slug him on his shoulder hard enough to make him flinch. He had some brochures on Salt Lake and some maps, and every so often the two of them would spread them out on the table.

"That's the temple. It's right downtown. You got to have a pass to get in."

"Charlotte says anyone can go in and look around."

"When was Charlotte in Salt Lake? Just when the hell was Charlotte in Salt Lake?"

"Last year."

"This is Liberty Park. It's got a zoo. There's good skiing in the mountains."

"Got all the skiing we can use," my mother would say. "People come from all over the world to ski at Banff. Cardston's got a temple, if you like those kinds of things."

"Oh, this one is real big," Lester would say. "They got armed guards and everything."

"Not what Charlotte says."

"What does she know?"

Lester and Laetitia broke up, but I guess the idea of Salt Lake stuck in her mind.

The Canadian border guard was a young woman, and she seemed happy to see us. "Hi," she said. "You folks sure have a great day for a trip. Where are you coming from?"

"Standoff."

"Is that in Montana?"

"No."

"Where are you going?"

"Standoff."

The woman's name was Carol and I don't guess she was any older than Laetitia. "Wow, you both Canadians?"

"Blackfoot."

"Really? I have a friend I went to school with who is Blackfoot. Do you know Mike Harley?"

"No."

"He went to school in Lethbridge, but he's really from Browning."

It was a nice conversation and there were no cars behind us, so there was no rush.

"You're not bringing any liquor back, are you?"

"No."

"Any cigarettes or plants or stuff like that?"

"No."

"Citizenship?"

"Blackfoot."

"I know," said the woman, "and I'd be proud of being Blackfoot if I were Blackfoot. But you have to be American or Canadian."

When Laetitia and Lester broke up, Lester took his brochures and maps with him, so Laetitia wrote to someone in Salt Lake City, and, about a month later, she got a big envelope of stuff. We sat at the table and opened up all the brochures, and Laetitia read each one out loud.

"Salt Lake City is the gateway to some of the world's most magnificent skiing.

"Salt Lake City is the home of one of the newest professional basketball franchises, the Utah Jazz.

"The Great Salt Lake is one of the natural wonders of the world."

It was kind of exciting seeing all those colour brochures on the table and listening to Laetitia read all about how Salt Lake City was one of the best places in the entire world.

"That Salt Lake City place sounds too good to be true," my mother told her. "It has everything."

"We got everything right here."

"It's boring here."

"People in Salt Lake City are probably sending away for brochures of Calgary and Lethbridge and Pincher Creek right now."

In the end, my mother would say that maybe Laetitia should go to Salt Lake City, and Laetitia would say that maybe she would.

We parked the car to the side of the building and Carol led us into a small room on the second floor. I found a comfortable spot on the couch and flipped through some back issues of *Saturday Night* and *Alberta Report*.

When I woke up, my mother was just coming out of another office. She didn't say a word to me. I followed her down the stairs and out to the car. I thought we were going home, but she turned the car around and drove back towards the American border, which made me think we were going to visit Laetitia in Salt Lake City after all. Instead she pulled into the parking lot of the duty-free store and stopped.

"We going to see Laetitia?"

"No."

"We going home?"

Pride is a good thing to have, you know. Laetitia had a lot of pride, and so did my mother. I figured that someday, I'd have it, too.

"So where are we going?"

Most of that day, we wandered around the duty-free store, which wasn't very large. The manager had a name tag with a tiny American flag on one side and a tiny Canadian flag on the other. His name was Mel. Towards evening, he began suggesting that we should be on our way. I told him we had nowhere to go, that neither the Americans nor the Canadians would let us in. He laughed at that and told us that we should buy something or leave.

The car was not very comfortable, but we did have all that food and it was April, so even if it did snow as it sometimes does on the prairies, we wouldn't freeze. The next morning my mother drove to the American border.

It was a different guard this time, but the questions were the same. We didn't spend as much time in the office as we had the day before. By noon, we were back at the Canadian border. By two we were back in the duty-free shop parking lot.

The second night in the car was not as much fun as the first, but my mother seemed in good spirits, and, all in all, it was as much an adventure as an inconvenience. There wasn't much food left and that was a problem, but we had lots of water as there was a faucet at the side of the duty-free shop.

One Sunday, Laetitia and I were watching television. Mom was over at Mrs. Manyfingers's. Right in the middle of the programme, Laetitia turned off the set and said she was going to Salt Lake City, that life around here was too boring. I had wanted to see the rest of the programme and really didn't care if Laetitia went to Salt Lake City or not. When Mom got home, I told her what Laetitia had said.

What surprised me was how angry Laetitia got when she found out that I had told Mom.

"You got a big mouth."

"That's what you said."

"What I said is none of your business."

"I didn't say anything."

"Well, I'm going for sure, now."

That weekend, Laetitia packed her bags, and we drove her to the border.

Mel turned out to be friendly. When he closed up for the night and found us still parked in the lot, he came over and asked us if our car was broken down or something. My mother thanked him for his concern and told him that we were fine, that things would get straightened out in the morning.

"You're kidding," said Mel. "You'd think they could handle the simple things."

"We got some apples and a banana," I said, "but we're all out of ham sandwiches."

"You know, you read about these things, but you just don't believe it."

"Hamburgers would be even better because they got more stuff for energy."

My mother slept in the back seat. I slept in the front because I was smaller and could lie under the steering wheel. Late that night, I heard my mother open the car door. I found her sitting on her blanket leaning against the bumper of the car.

"You see all those stars," she said. "When I was a little girl, my grandmother used to take me and my sisters out on the prairies and tell us stories about all the stars."

"Do you think Mel is going to bring us any hamburgers?"

"Every one of those stars has a story. You see that bunch of stars over there that look like a fish?"

"He didn't say no."

"Coyote went fishing, one day. That's how it all started." We sat out under the stars that night, and my mother told me all sorts of stories. She was serious about it, too. She'd tell them slow, repeating parts as she went, as if she expected me to remember each one.

Early the next morning, the television vans began to arrive, and guys in suits and women in dresses came trotting over to us, dragging microphones and cameras and lights behind them. One of the vans had a table set up with orange juice and sandwiches and fruit. It was for the crew, but when I told them we hadn't eaten for a while, a really skinny blonde woman told us we could eat as much as we wanted.

They mostly talked to my mother. Every so often one of the reporters would come over and ask me questions about how it felt to be an Indian without a country. I told them we had a nice house on the reserve and that my cousins had a couple of horses we rode when we went fishing. Some of the television people went over to the American border, and then they went to the Canadian border.

Around noon, a good-looking guy in a dark blue suit and an orange tie with little ducks on it drove up in a fancy car. He talked to my mother for a while, and, after they were done talking, my mother called me over, and we got into our car. Just as my mother started the engine, Mel came over and gave us a bag of peanut brittle and told us that justice was a damn hard thing to get, but that we shouldn't give up.

I would have preferred lemon drops, but it was nice of Mel anyway.

"Where are we going now?"

"Going to visit Laetitia."

The guard who came out to our car was all smiles. The television lights were so bright they hurt my eyes, and, if you tried to look through the windshield in certain directions, you couldn't see a thing.

"Morning, ma'am."

"Good morning."

"Where you heading?"

"Salt Lake City."

"Purpose of your visit?"

"Visit my daughter."

"Any tobacco, liquor, or firearms?"

"Don't smoke."

"Any plants or fruit?"

"Not any more."

"Citizenship?"

"Blackfoot."

The guard rocked back on his heels and jammed his thumbs into his gun belt. "Thank you," he said, his fingers patting the butt of the revolver. "Have a pleasant trip."

My mother rolled the car forward, and the television people had to scramble out of the way. They ran alongside the car as we pulled away from the border, and, when they couldn't run any farther, they stood in the middle of the highway and waved and waved and waved.

We got to Salt Lake City the next day. Laetitia was happy to see us, and, that first night, she took us out to a restaurant that made really good soups. The list of pies took up a whole page. I had cherry. Mom had chocolate. Laetitia said that she saw us on television the night before and, during the meal, she had us tell her the story over and over again.

Laetitia took us everywhere. We went to a fancy ski resort. We went to the temple. We got to go shopping in a couple of large malls, but they weren't as large as the one in Edmonton, and Mom said so.

After a week or so, I got bored and wasn't at all sad when my mother said we should be heading back home. Laetitia wanted us to stay longer, but Mom said no, that she had things to do back home and that next time, Laetitia should come up and visit. Laetitia said she was thinking about moving back, and Mom told her to do as she pleased, and Laetitia said that she would.

On the way home, we stopped at the duty-free shop, and my mother gave Mel a green hat that said "Salt Lake" across the front. Mel was a funny guy. He took the hat and blew his nose and told my mother that she was an inspiration to us all. He gave us some more peanut brittle and came out into the parking lot and waved at us all the way to the Canadian border.

It was almost evening when we left Coutts. I watched the border through the rear window until all you could see were the tops of the flagpoles and the blue water tower, and then they rolled over a hill and disappeared.

Margaret Laurence

Jean Margaret Wemyss (pronounced Weems) was born in Neepawa, Manitoba, in 1926. Her mother died when she was four, her father when she was ten, and she was raised by one of her aunts. Her difficult childhood years, spent in the sphere of a dominating grandfather, are explored in a collection of stories called *A Bird in the House* (1970). Laurence attended United College and received her B.A. from the University of Winnipeg in 1947, the same year she married civil engineer Jack Laurence. She did short stints writing for the Winnipeg *Citizen* and working as a registrar at the YWCA before moving for seven years to Africa, where she spent two years in the Haud desert of Somaliland, an account of which appears in *The Prophet's Camel Bell* (1963). She edited and translated for the Somali government a collection of poems and fables called *A Tree for Poverty* (1954). Laurence lived in Vancouver from 1957 to 1962, where she completed her first novel, *This Side Jordan* (1960), while gathering the impressions for a later work, *The Fire-Dwellers* (1969). When she and her husband separated, Laurence moved to England, to Elm Cottage, High Wycombe, not far from London, where much of her best work was written: *The Stone Angel* (1964), *The Tomorrow-Tamers and Other Stories* (1964), *A Jest of God* (1966, made into a Warner Bros. film called *Rachel, Rachel*), *Long Drums and Cannons: Nigerian Dramatists and Novelists, 1952–1966* (1968), and *The Diviners* (1974). She was writer-in-residence at the University of Toronto in 1968–69 and returned to Canada in 1974, settling in Lakefield, Ontario. Her memoir, *Dance on the Earth* (1989), was published after her death in January 1987, at age sixty.

Laurence holds a special place in the imagination of Canadians for her work on behalf of her "tribe" of fellow writers. Although she was a deeply religious and moral person, she was vigorously persecuted by self-righteous religious bigots in Peterborough County who managed to have her books removed from the shelves of schools and libraries. This persecution exacted a great cost, emotionally and artistically, but it did not stop her from taking up causes such as racial equality, freedom of the press, disarmament, human rights, and Canadian independence. "It is my feeling," she says in "My Final Hour," an address to the Trent University Philosophy Society, on March 29, 1983 (published in *Canadian Literature*, 50), "that as we grow older we should become not less radical but more so." She believed in the social gospel, which puts the central premises of Christianity into practice; and, as an artist, she believed that art "is, deeply, an honouring of the past, a perception of the present in one way or another and a looking towards the future. ... Art, by its very nature of necessary expression, is an act of faith, an acknowledgement of the profound mystery at the core of life."

While she is a passionate advocate of human rights, Laurence rejects the use of art for partisan purposes. As she said to writer Barry Callaghan, in an interview published in *Books in Canada* (Vol. 16, No. 2, 1987), "I think very few writers, maybe none, can be novelists and political propagandists at the same time. I think they find themselves writing propaganda. It becomes propaganda rather than a novel because when a writer becomes highly political, he thinks he knows the answers and wants to make you hold the same political point of view, whereas a novel is almost always a kind of discovery. I don't think the writer herself knows entirely what's going to happen, or what's going to emerge, and she has to be prepared for the unexpected. In fact, you partly write to discover something you didn't know before."

As for experimental writing, she confesses, "Well, sometimes I see my work in terms of deep Celtic gloom, to tell you the truth. I think maybe some of those writers are too far out, and I say to myself, 'Margaret, you're too far in'—but I can't help it. The fact is, I know that my prose style is essentially a traditional one, but for me to try to change simply for the sake of changing, or for the sake of trying to be more 'with it' ... this would be so phony, nothing would happen—except disaster. So all I can really do is to try and put down things according to my own way of seeing, and if the style changes naturally, by itself, and develops, well ... well and good, and if it doesn't, I'm stuck with the idiom of myself ... The only thing, really, that concerns me is to try to put down things as I see them, because it is all you've got. You've got your own pair of eyes, that's all, and the thing I would like to be able to do more than anything else is to create characters that step off the page, because this is what really obsesses me. This is still what I look for in a novel. What I'm interested in more than anything else is character."

Laurence made no distinction between formal problems and concerns of the novel and short story, except to say that in the short story she may focus on a single theme, or dilemma, whereas, in the novel, she may be able to handle many.

Laurence is equally adamant about form and links her problems once again to the creation of character. "Generally speaking, I believe that most writers work out their own forms and means of expression through a strong compulsion to get closer to their material, to express it more fully. ... I have never thought of forms and means of expression (I refuse to use that odious word 'style') as having any meaning in themselves. ... Form for its own sake is an abstraction which carries no allure for me. I do not make this as a qualitative statement—I only say that it happens to be true for myself. I am concerned mainly, I think, with finding a form which will enable a novel [or story] to reveal itself, a form through which the characters can breathe. When I try to think of form by itself, I have to put it in visual terms—I see it not like a house or a cathedral or any enclosing edifice, but rather as a forest, through which one can see outward, in which the shapes of trees do not prevent air and sun, and in which the trees themselves are growing structures, something alive. That is, of course, an ideal, not something that can ever be achieved." Laurence concludes her address, "Gadgetry or Growing: Form and Voice in the Novel," given at the University of Toronto in 1969 and reprinted in *The Journal of Canadian Fiction*, with this statement: "What I'm looking for, which—as far as form in writing is concerned—is the kind of vehicle capable of risking that peculiar voyage of exploration which constitutes a novel [or story]."

The Loons

Just below Manawaka, where the Wachakwa River ran brown and noisy over the pebbles, the scrub oak and grey-green willow and chokecherry bushes grew in a dense thicket. In a clearing at the centre of the thicket stood the Tonnerre family's shack. The basis of this dwelling was a small square cabin made of poplar poles and chinked with mud, which had been built by Jules Tonnerre some fifty years before, when he came back from Batoche with a bullet in his thigh, the year that Riel was hung and the voices of the Metis entered their long silence. Jules had only intended to stay the winter in the Wachakwa Valley, but the family was still there in the thirties, when I was a child. As the Tonnerres had increased, their settlement had been added to, until the clearing at the foot of the town hill was a chaos of lean-tos, wooden packing cases, warped lumber, discarded car tires, ramshackle chicken coops, tangled strands of barbed wire and rusty tin cans.

The Tonnerres were French half-breeds, and among themselves they spoke a *patois* that was neither Cree nor French. Their English was broken and full of obscenities. They did not belong among the Cree of the Galloping Mountain reservation, further north, and they did not belong among the Scots-Irish and Ukrainians of Manawaka, either. They were, as my Grandmother MacLeod would have put it, neither flesh, fowl, nor good salt herring. When their men were not working at odd jobs or as section hands on the C.P.R., they lived on relief. In the summers, one of the Tonnerre youngsters, with a face that seemed totally unfamiliar with laughter, would knock at the doors of the town's brick houses and offer for sale a lard-pail full of bruised wild strawberries, and if he got as much as a quarter he would grab the coin and run before the customer had time to change her mind. Sometimes old Jules, or his son Lazarus, would get mixed up in a Saturday-night brawl, and would hit out at whoever was nearest, or howl drunkenly among the offended shoppers on Main Street, and then the Mountie would put them for the night in the barred cell underneath the Court House, and the next morning they would be quiet again.

Piquette Tonnerre, the daughter of Lazarus, was in my class at school. She was older than I, but she had failed several grades, perhaps because her attendance had always been sporadic and her interest in school-work negligible. Part of the reason she had missed a lot of school was that she had had tuberculosis of the bone, and had once spent many months in hospital. I knew this because my father was the doctor who had looked after her. Her sickness was almost the only thing I knew about her, however. Otherwise, she existed for me only as a vaguely embarrassing presence, with her hoarse voice and her clumsy limping walk and her grimy cotton dresses that were always miles too long. I was neither friendly nor unfriendly towards her. She dwelt and moved somewhere within my scope of vision, but I did not actually notice her very much until that peculiar summer when I was eleven.

'I don't know what to do about that kid,' my father said at dinner one evening. 'Piquette Tonnerre, I mean. The damn bone's flared up again. I've had her in hospital for quite a while now, and it's under control all right, but I hate like the dickens to send her home again.'

'Couldn't you explain to her mother that she has to rest a lot?' my mother said.

'The mother's not there,' my father replied. 'She took off a few years back. Can't say I blame her. Piquette cooks for them, and she says Lazarus would never do anything for himself as long as she's there. Anyway, I don't think she'd take much care of herself, once she got back. She's only thirteen, after all. Beth, I was thinking—what about taking her up to Diamond Lake with us this summer? A couple of months rest would give that bone a much better chance.'

My mother looked stunned.

'But Ewen—what about Roddie and Vanessa?'

'She's not contagious,' my father said. 'And it would be company for Vanessa.'

'Oh dear,' my mother said in distress, 'I'll bet anything she has nits in her hair.'

'For Pete's sake,' my father said crossly, 'do you think Matron would let her stay in the hospital for all this time like that? Don't be silly, Beth.'

Grandmother MacLeod, her delicately featured face as rigid as a cameo, now brought her mauve-veined hands together as though she were about to begin a prayer.

'Ewen, if that half-breed youngster comes along to Diamond Lake, I'm not going,' she announced. 'I'll go to Morag's for the summer.'

I had trouble in stifling my urge to laugh, for my mother brightened visibly and quickly tried to hide it. If it came to a choice between Grandmother MacLeod and Piquette, Piquette would win hands down, nits or not.

'It might be quite nice for you, at that,' she mused. 'You haven't seen Morag for over a year, and you might enjoy being in the city for a while. Well, Ewen dear, you do what you think best. If you think it would do Piquette some good, then we'll be glad to have her, as long as she behaves herself.'

So it happened that several weeks later, when we all piled into my father's old Nash, surrounded by suitcases and boxes of provisions and toys for my ten-month-old brother, Piquette was with us and Grandmother MacLeod, miraculously, was not. My father would only be staying at the cottage for a couple of weeks, for he had to get back to his practice, but the rest of us would stay at Diamond Lake until the end of August.

Our cottage was not named, as many were, 'Dew Drop Inn' or 'Bide-a-Wee,' or 'Bonnie Doon.' The sign on the roadway bore in austere letters only our name, MacLeod. It was not a large cottage, but it was on the lakefront. You could look out the windows and see, through the filigree of the spruce trees, the water glistening greenly as the sun caught it. All around the cottage were ferns, and sharp-branched raspberry bushes, and moss that had grown over fallen tree trunks. If you looked carefully among the weeds and grass, you could find wild strawberry plants which were in white flower now and in another month would bear fruit, the fragrant globes hanging like miniature scarlet lanterns on the thin hairy stems. The two grey squirrels were still there, gossiping at us from the tall spruce beside the cottage, and by the end of the summer they would again be tame enough to take pieces of crust from my hands. The broad moose antlers that hung above the back door were a little more bleached and fissured after the winter, but otherwise everything was the same. I raced joyfully around my kingdom, greeting all the places I had not seen for a year. My brother, Roderick, who had not been born when we were here last summer, sat on the car rug in the sunshine and examined a brown spruce cone, meticulously turning it round and round in his small and curious hands. My mother and father toted the luggage from car to cottage, exclaiming over how well the place had wintered, no broken windows, thank goodness, no apparent damage from storm-felled branches or snow.

Only after I had finished looking around did I notice Piquette. She was sitting on the swing, her lame leg held stiffly out, and her other foot scuffing the ground as she swung slowly back and forth. Her long hair hung black and straight around her shoulders, and her broad coarse-featured face bore no expression—it was blank, as though she no longer dwelt within her own skull, as though she had gone elsewhere. I approached her very hesitantly.

'Want to come and play?'

Piquette looked at me with a sudden flash of scorn.

'I ain't a kid,' she said.

Wounded, I stamped angrily away, swearing I would not speak to her for the rest of the summer. In the days that followed, however, Piquette began to interest me, and I began to want to interest her. My reasons did not appear bizarre to me. Unlikely as it may seem, I had only just realized that the Tonnerre family, whom I had always heard called half-breeds, were actually Indians, or as near as made no difference. My acquaintance with Indians was not extensive. I did not remember ever having seen a real Indian, and my new awareness that Piquette sprang from the people of Big Bear and Poundmaker, of Tecumseh, of the Iroquois who had eaten Father Brebeuf's heart—all this gave her an instant attraction in my eyes. I was a devoted reader of Pauline Johnson at this age, and sometimes would orate aloud and in an exalted voice, *West Wind, blow from your prairie nest; Blow from the mountains, blow from the west*—and so on. It seemed to me that Piquette must be in some way a daughter of the forest, a kind of junior prophetess of the wilds who might impart to me, if I took the right approach, some of the secrets which she undoubtedly knew—where the whippoorwill made her nest, how the coyote reared her young, or whatever it was that it said in *Hiawatha*.

I set about gaining Piquette's trust. She was not allowed to go swimming, with her bad leg, but I managed to lure her down to the beach—or rather she came because there was nothing else to do. The water was always icy, for the lake was fed by springs, but I swam like a dog, thrashing my arms and legs around at such speed and with such an output of energy that I never grew cold. Finally, when I had had enough, I came out and sat beside Piquette on the sand. When she saw me approaching, her hand squashed flat the sand castle she had been building, and she looked at me sullenly, without speaking.

'Do you like this place?' I asked, after a while, intending to lead on from there into the question of forest lore.

Piquette shrugged. 'It's okay. Good as anywhere.'

'I love it,' I said. 'We come here every summer.'

'So what?' Her voice was distant, and I glanced at her uncertainly, wondering what I could have said wrong.

'Do you want to come for a walk?' I asked her. 'We wouldn't need to go far.

If you walk just around the point there, you come to a bay where great big reeds grow in the water, and all kinds of fish hang around there. Want to? Come on.'

She shook her head.

'Your dad said I ain't supposed to do no more walking than I got to.'

I tried another line.

'I bet you know a lot about the woods and all that, eh?' I began respectfully.

Piquette looked at me from her large dark unsmiling eyes.

'I don't know what in hell you're talkin' about,' she replied. 'You nuts or somethin'? If you mean where my old man, and me, and all them live, you better shut up, by Jesus, you hear?'

I was startled and my feelings were hurt, but I had a kind of dogged perseverance. I ignored her rebuff.

'You know something, Piquette? There's loons here, on this lake. You can see their nests just up the shore there, behind those logs. At night, you can hear them even from the cottage, but it's better to listen from the beach. My dad says we should listen and try to remember how they sound, because in a few years when more cottages are built at Diamond Lake and more people come in, the loons will go away.'

Piquette was picking up stones and snail shells and then dropping them again.

'Who gives a good goddamn?' she said.

It became increasingly obvious that, as an Indian, Piquette was a dead loss. That evening I went out by myself, scrambling through the bushes that overhung the steep path, my feet slipping on the fallen spruce needles that covered the ground. When I reached the shore, I walked along the firm damp sand to the small pier that my father had built, and sat down there. I heard someone else crashing through the undergrowth and the bracken, and for a moment I thought Piquette had changed her mind, but it turned out to be my father. He sat beside me on the pier and we waited, without speaking.

At night the lake was like black glass with a streak of amber which was the path of the moon. All around, the spruce trees grew tall and close-set, branches blackly sharp against the sky, which was lightened by a cold flickering of stars. Then the loons began their calling. They rose like phantom birds from the nests on the shore, and flew out onto the dark still surface of the water.

No one can ever describe that ululating sound, the crying of the loons, and no one who has heard it can ever forget it. Plaintive, and yet with a quality of chilling mockery, those voices belonged to a world separated by aeons from our neat world of summer cottages and the lighted lamps of home.

'They must have sounded just like that,' my father remarked, 'before any person ever set foot here.'

Then he laughed. 'You could say the same, of course, about sparrows, or chipmunks, but somehow it only strikes you that way with the loons.'

'I know,' I said.

Neither of us suspected that this would be the last time we would ever sit here together on the shore, listening. We stayed for perhaps half an hour, and then we went back to the cottage. My mother was reading beside the fireplace. Piquette was looking at the burning birch log, and not doing anything.

'You should have come along,' I said, although in fact I was glad she had not.

'Not me,' Piquette said. 'You wouldn' catch me walkin' way down there jus' for a bunch of squawkin' birds.'

Piquette and I remained ill at ease with one another. I felt I had somehow failed my father, but I did not know what was the matter, nor why she would not or could not respond when I suggested exploring the woods or playing house. I thought it was probably her slow and difficult walking that held her back. She stayed most of the time in the cottage with my mother, helping her with the dishes or with Roddie, but hardly ever talking. Then the Duncans arrived at their cottage, and I spent my days with Mavis, who was my best friend. I could not reach Piquette at all, and I soon lost interest in trying. But all that summer she remained as both a reproach and a mystery to me.

That winter my father died of pneumonia, after less than a week's illness. For some time I saw nothing around me, being completely immersed in my own pain and my mother's. When I looked outward once more, I scarcely noticed that Piquette Tonnerre was no longer at school. I do not remember seeing her at all until four years later, one Saturday night when Mavis and I were having Cokes in the Regal Café. The jukebox was booming like tuneful thunder, and beside it, leaning lightly on its chrome and its rainbow glass, was a girl.

Piquette must have been seventeen then, although she looked about twenty. I stared at her, astounded that anyone could have changed so much. Her face, so stolid and expressionless before, was animated now with a gaiety that was almost violent. She laughed and talked very loudly with the boys around her. Her lipstick was bright carmine, and her hair was cut short and frizzily permed. She had not been pretty as a child, and she was not pretty now, for her features were still heavy and blunt. But her dark and slightly slanted eyes were beautiful, and her skin-tight skirt and orange sweater displayed to enviable advantage a soft and slender body.

She saw me, and walked over. She teetered a little, but it was not due to her once-tubercular leg, for her limp was almost gone.

'Hi, Vanessa.' Her voice still had the same hoarseness. 'Long time no see, eh?'

'Hi,' I said. 'Where've you been keeping yourself, Piquette?'

'Oh, I been around,' she said. 'I been away almost two years now. Been all over the place—Winnipeg, Regina, Saskatoon. Jesus, what I could tell you! I come back this summer, but I ain't stayin'. You kids goin' to the dance?'

'No,' I said abruptly, for this was a sore point with me. I was fifteen, and thought I was old enough to go to the Saturday-night dances at the Flamingo. My mother, however, thought otherwise.

'Y'oughta come,' Piquette said. 'I never miss one. It's just about the on'y thing in this jerkwater town that's any fun. Boy, you couldn' catch me stayin' here. I don't give a shit about this place. It stinks.'

She sat down beside me, and I caught the harsh over-sweetness of her perfume.

'Listen, you wanna know something, Vanessa?' she confided, her voice only slightly blurred. 'Your dad was the only person in Manawaka that ever done anything good to me.'

I nodded speechlessly. I was certain she was speaking the truth. I knew a little more than I had that summer at Diamond Lake, but I could not reach her now any more than I had then. I was ashamed, ashamed of my own timidity, the frightened tendency to look the other way. Yet I felt no real warmth towards her—I only felt that I ought to, because of that distant summer and because my father had hoped she would be company for me, or perhaps that I would be for her, but it had not happened that way. At this moment, meeting her again, I had to admit that she repelled and embarrassed me, and I could not help despising the self-pity in her voice. I wished she would go away. I did not want to see her. I did not know what to say to her. It seemed that we had nothing to say to one another.

'I'll tell you something else,' Piquette went on. 'All the old bitches an' biddies in this town will sure be surprised. I'm gettin' married this fall—my boyfriend, he's an English fella, works in the stockyards in the city there, a very tall guy, got blond wavy hair. Gee, is he ever handsome. Got this real classy name. Alvin Gerald Cummings—some handle, eh? They call him Al.'

For the merest instant, then, I saw her. I really did see her, for the first and only time in all the years we had both lived in the same town. Her defiant face, momentarily, became unguarded and unmasked, and in her eyes there was a terrifying hope.

'Gee, Piquette—' I burst out awkwardly, 'that's swell. That's really wonderful. Congratulations—good luck—I hope you'll be happy—'

As I mouthed the conventional phrases, I could only guess how great her need must have been, that she had been forced to seek the very things she so bitterly rejected.

When I was eighteen, I left Manawaka and went away to college. At the end of my first year, I came back home for the summer. I spent the first few days in talking non-stop with my mother, as we exchanged all the news that somehow had not found its way into letters—what had happened in my life and what had happened here in Manawaka while I was away. My mother searched her memory for events that concerned people I knew.

'Did I ever write you about Piquette Tonnerre, Vanessa?' she asked one morning.

'No I don't think so,' I replied. 'Last I heard of her, she was going to marry some guy in the city. Is she still there?'

My mother looked perturbed, and it was a moment before she spoke, as though she did not know how to express what she had to tell and wished she did not need to try.

'She's dead,' she said at last. Then, as I stared at her, 'Oh, Vanessa, when it happened, I couldn't help thinking of her as she was that summer—so sullen and gauche and badly dressed. I couldn't help wondering if we could have done something more at that time—but what could we do? She used to be around in the cottage there with me all day, and honestly, it was all I could do to get a word out of her. She didn't even talk to your father very much, although I think she liked him, in her way.'

'What happened?' I asked.

'Either her husband left her, or she left him,' my mother said. 'I don't know which. Anyway, she came back here with two youngsters, both only babies—they must have been born very close together. She kept house, I guess, for Lazarus and her brothers, down in the valley there, in the old Tonnerre place. I used to see her on the street sometimes, but she never spoke to me. She'd put on an awful lot of weight, and she looked a mess, to tell you the truth, a real slattern, dressed any old how. She was up in court a couple of times—drunk and disorderly, of course. One Saturday night last winter, during the coldest weather, Piquette was alone in the shack with the children. The Tonnerres made home brew all the time, so I've heard, and Lazarus said later she'd been drinking most of the day when he and the boys went out that evening. They had an old woodstove there—you know the kind, with exposed pipes. The shack caught fire. Piquette didn't get out, and neither did the children.'

I did not say anything. As so often with Piquette, there did not seem to be anything to say. There was a kind of silence around the image in my mind of the fire and the snow, and I wished I could put from my memory the look that I had seen once in Piquette's eyes.

I went up to Diamond Lake for a few days that summer, with Mavis and her family. The MacLeod cottage had been sold after my father's death, and I did not even go to look at it, not wanting to witness my long-ago kingdom possessed now by strangers. But one evening I went down to the shore by myself.

The small pier which my father had built was gone, and in its place there was a large and solid pier built by the government, for Galloping Mountain was now a national park, and Diamond Lake had been re-named Lake Wapakata, for it was felt that an Indian name would have a greater appeal to tourists. The one store had become several dozen, and the settlement had all the attributes of a flourishing resort—hotels, a dance-hall, cafés with neon signs, the penetrating odours of potato chips and hot dogs.

I sat on the government pier and looked out across the water. At night the lake at least was the same as it had always been, darkly shining and bearing within its black glass the streak of amber that was the path of the moon. There was no wind that evening, and everything was quiet all around me. It seemed too quiet, and then I realized that the loons were no longer here. I listened for some time, to make sure, but never once did I hear that long-drawn call, half mocking and half plaintive, spearing through the stillness across the lake.

I did not know what had happened to the birds. Perhaps they had gone away to some far place of belonging. Perhaps they had been unable to find such a place, and had simply died out, having ceased to care any longer whether they lived or not.

I remembered how Piquette had scorned to come along, when my father and I sat there and listened to the lake birds. It seemed to me now that in some unconscious and totally unrecognized way, Piquette might have been the only one, after all, who had heard the crying of the loons.

D. H. Lawrence

David Herbert Lawrence was born in 1885 in Eastwood, Nottinghamshire, England. Some of the flavour of his childhood and adolescence, as the son of a miner and an overly possessive middle-class mother, is recorded in his novel *Sons and Lovers* (1913). Lawrence obtained his teacher's certificate from Nottingham University College, but ill-health (subsequently diagnosed as tuberculosis) forced him to cut short his teaching career. He first appeared in print as a poet in the *English Review* in 1909, the same year that his first novel, *The White Peacock*, was published. Lawrence met Frieda von Richthoffen, the wife of a former professor, and they left for the Continent, but returned to England prior to the outbreak of World War I. They married, but were never comfortable in England, because of persecution and censorship, and became voluntary wanderers in Italy, Australia, New Mexico, and Mexico, seeking a dry, healthy climate and, it seems, a refuge that might offer both freedom and security. While he is best known for his novels, including *Women in Love* (1920) and *Lady Chatterley's Lover* (1928), Lawrence also published several collections of stories: *The Prussian Officer* (1914), *England, My England* (1922), *The Ladybird* (1923), *Glad Ghosts* (1926), and *The Woman Who Rode Away* (1928). He returned to Europe in 1929, a year before his death.

As a victim of censorship, Lawrence, not surprisingly, had something to say on the subject. As he says in a letter to Morris Ernst in 1928, "Myself, I believe censorship helps nobody; and hurts many. Our civilisation cannot afford to let the censor-moron loose. The censor-moron does not really hate anything but the living and growing human consciousness. It is our developing and extending consciousness that he threatens—and our consciousness in its newest, most sensitive activity, its vital growth. To arrest or circumscribe the vital consciousness is to produce morons, and nothing but a moron would wish to do it."

Lawrence, using a metaphor appropriate to his upbringing, called literature "a mine of practical truth." He was a social critic and visionary, who called into question the rules of conventional morality and sexual etiquette, as is evident in his famous statement: "The business of art is to reveal the relation between man and his circumambient universe, at the living moment. As mankind is always struggling in the toils of old relationships, art is always ahead of the 'times,' which themselves are always far in the rear of the living moment." In the same essay, called "Morality and the Novel," Lawrence claims fiction has become immoral by being forced to dictate on ethical issues: "The novel is the highest example of subtle interrelatedness that man has discovered. Everything is true in its own time, place, circumstance, and untrue outside its own place, time, circumstance. If you try to nail anything down, in the novel, either it kills the novel, or the novel gets up and walks away with the nail." While he was reluctant to prescribe for the novel or the story, Lawrence was not averse to making pronouncements about life itself. "The great relationship, for humanity, will always be the relation between man and woman. And the relation between man and woman will change for ever, and will for ever be the new central clue to human life. It is the relation itself which is the quick and the central clue to life."

In a letter to his agent, Edward Garnet, Lawrence tried to explain his conception of character in fiction. He dismissed the "old-fashioned" approach to character, "which causes one to conceive a character in a certain moral scheme and make him consistent. The certain moral scheme is what I object to. ... You mustn't look in my novel for the old stable ego—of the character. There is another ego, according to whose action the individual is unrecognizable, and passes through, as it were, allotropic states which it needs in a deeper sense than any we've been used to exercise, to discover are states of the same single radically unchanged element. ... Don't look for the development of the novel to follow the lines of certain characters: the characters fall into the form of some other rhythmic form, as when one draws a fiddle-bow across a fine tray delicately sanded, the sand takes lines unknown."

Although he is speaking here of the novel, Lawrence's comments on character apply equally well to the short story, which, unless it is mere imitation, will have its own rules of construction. He was constantly struggling to refine his own techniques to enable him to explore experience more deeply, as this letter to a young writer, Kyle Crichton, suggests: "You are too journalistic, too much concerned with facts. You don't concern yourself with the human inside at all, only with the insides of steel works. It's the sort of consciousness the working man has: but at the same time he's got a passionate sub-conscious. And it's the sub-conscious which makes the story: otherwise you have journalism. Now you want to be an artist, so you've got to use the artist's faculty of making the sub-conscious conscious. Take your Andy, a boy as blank as most American boys. ... What was there in the mines that held the boy's feelings? The darkness, the mystery, the other-worldliness, the peculiar camaraderie, the sort of naked intimacy: men as gods in the underworld, or as elementals. Create *that* in a picture."

The Horse Dealer's Daughter

'Well, Mabel, and what are you going to do with yourself?' asked Joe, with foolish flippancy. He felt quite safe himself. Without listening for an answer, he turned aside, worked a grain of tobacco to the tip of his tongue, and spat it out. He did not care about anything, since he felt safe himself.

The three brothers and the sister sat round the desolate breakfast-table, attempting some sort of desultory consultation. The morning's post had given the final tap to the family fortunes, and all was over. The dreary dining-room itself, with its heavy mahogany furniture, looked as if it were waiting to be done away with.

But the consultation amounted to nothing. There was a strange air of ineffectuality about the three men, as they sprawled at table, smoking and reflecting vaguely on their own condition. The girl was alone, a rather short, sullen-looking young woman of twenty-seven. She did not share the same life as her brothers. She would have been good-looking, save for the impressive fixity of her face, 'bull-dog', as her brothers called it.

There was a confused tramping of horses' feet outside. The three men all sprawled round in their chairs to watch. Beyond the dark holly bushes that separated the strip of lawn from the high road, they could see a cavalcade of shire horses swinging out of their own yard, being taken for exercise. This was the last time. These were the last horses that would go through their hands. The young men watched with critical, callous look. They were all frightened at the collapse of their lives, and the sense of disaster in which they were involved left them no inner freedom.

Yet they were three fine, well-set fellows enough. Joe, the eldest, was a man of thirty-three, broad and handsome in a hot, flushed way. His face was red, he twisted his black moustache over a thick finger, his eyes were shallow and restless. He had a sensual way of uncovering his teeth when he laughed, and his bearing was stupid. Now he watched the horses with a glazed look of helplessness in his eyes, a certain stupor of downfall.

The great draught-horses swung past. They were tied head to tail, four of them, and they heaved along to where a lane branched off from the high-road, planting their great hoofs floutingly in the fine black mud, swinging their great rounded haunches sumptuously, and trotting a few sudden steps as they were led into the lane, round the corner. Every movement showed a massive, slumbrous strength, and a stupidity which held them in subjection. The groom at the head looked back, jerking the leading rope. And the cavalcade moved out of sight up the lane, the tail of the last horse, bobbed up tight and stiff, held out taut from the swinging great haunches as they rocked behind the hedges in a motion-like sleep.

Joe watched with glazed hopeless eyes. The horses were almost like his own body to him. He felt he was done for now. Luckily he was engaged to a woman as would provide him with a job. He would marry and go into harness. His life was over, he would be a subject animal now.

He turned uneasily aside, the retreating steps of the horses echoing in his ears. Then, with foolish restlessness, he reached for the scraps of bacon-rind from the plates, and making a faint whistling sound, flung them to the terrier that lay against the fender. He watched the dog swallow them, and waited till the creature looked into his eyes. Then a faint grin came on his face, and in a high, foolish voice he said:

'You won't get much more bacon, shall you, you little b—?'

The dog faintly and dismally wagged its tail, then lowered its haunches, circled round, and lay down again.

There was another helpless silence at the table. Joe sprawled uneasily in his seat, not willing to go till the family conclave was dissolved. Fred Henry, the second brother, was erect, clean-limbed, alert. He had watched the passing of the horses with more *sang-froid*. If he was an animal, like Joe, he was an animal which controls, not one which is controlled. He was master of any horse, and he carried himself with a well-tempered air of mastery. But he was not master of the situations of life. He pushed his coarse brown moustache upwards, off his lip, and glanced irritably at his sister, who sat impassive and inscrutable.

'You'll go and stop with Lucy for a bit, shan't you?' he asked. The girl did not answer.

'I don't see what else you can do,' persisted Fred Henry.

'Go as a skivvy,' Joe interpolated laconically.

The girl did not move a muscle.

'If I was her, I should go in training for a nurse,' said Malcolm, the youngest of them all. He was the baby of the family, a young man of twenty-two, with a fresh, jaunty *museau*.

But Mabel did not take any notice of him. They had talked at her and round her for so many years, that she hardly heard them at all.

The marble block on the mantelpiece softly chimed the half-hour, the dog rose uneasily from the hearth-rug and looked at the party at the breakfast-table. But still they sat on in ineffectual conclave.

'Oh, all right,' said Joe suddenly, apropos of nothing. 'I'll get a move on.'

He pushed back his chair, straddled his knees with a downward jerk, to get them free, in horsey fashion, and went to the fire. Still he did not go out of the room; he was curious to know what the others would do or say. He began to charge his pipe, looking down at the dog and saying in a high, affected voice:

'Going wi' me? Going wi' me are ter? Tha'rt goin' further than tha counts on just now, dost hear?'

The dog faintly wagged its tail, the man stuck out his jaw and covered his pipe with his hands, and puffed intently, losing himself in the tobacco, looking down all the while at the dog with an absent brown eye. The dog looked up at him in mournful distrust. Joe stood with his knees stuck out, in real horsey fashion.

'Have you had a letter from Lucy?' Fred Henry asked of his sister.

'Last week,' came the neutral reply.

'And what does she say?'

There was no answer.

'Does she *ask* you to go and stop there?' persisted Fred Henry.

'She says I can if I like.'

'Well, then, you'd better. Tell her you'll come on Monday.'

This was received in silence.

'That's what you'll do then, is it?' said Fred Henry, in some exasperation.

But she made no answer. There was a silence of futility and irritation in the room. Malcolm grinned fatuously.

'You'll have to make up your mind between now and next Wednesday,' said Joe loudly, 'or else find yourself lodgings on the kerbstone.'

The face of the young woman darkened, but she sat on immutable.

'Here's Jack Fergusson!' exclaimed Malcolm, who was looking aimlessly out of the window.

'Where?' exclaimed Joe loudly.

'Just gone past.'

'Coming in?'

Malcolm craned his neck to see the gate.

'Yes,' he said.

There was a silence. Mabel sat on like one condemned, at the head of the table. Then a whistle was heard from the kitchen. The dog got up and barked sharply. Joe opened the door and shouted:

'Come on.'

After a moment a young man entered. He was muffled up in overcoat and a purple woollen scarf, and his tweed cap, which he did not remove, was pulled down on his head. He was of medium height, his face was rather long and pale, his eyes looked tired.

'Hello, Jack! Well, Jack!' exclaimed Malcolm and Joe. Fred Henry merely said: 'Jack.'

'What's doing?' asked the newcomer, evidently addressing Fred Henry.

'Same. We've got to be out by Wednesday. Got a cold?'

'I have—got it bad, too.'

'Why don't you stop in?'

'*Me* stop in? When I can't stand on my legs, perhaps I shall have a chance.' The young man spoke huskily. He had a slight Scotch accent.

'It's a knock-out isn't it,' said Joe, boisterously, 'if a doctor goes round croaking with a cold. Looks bad for the patients, doesn't it?'

The young doctor looked at him slowly.

'Anything the matter with *you*, then?' he asked sarcastically.

'Not as I know of. Damn your eyes, I hope not. Why?'

'I thought you were very concerned about the patients, wondered if you might be one yourself.'

'Damn it, no, I've never been patient to no flaming doctor, and hope I never shall be,' returned Joe.

At this point Mabel rose from the table, and they all seemed to become aware of her existence. She began putting the dishes together. The young doctor looked at her, but did not address her. He had not greeted her. She went out of the room with the tray, her face impassive and unchanged.

'When are you off then, all of you?' asked the doctor.

'I'm catching the eleven-forty,' replied Malcolm. 'Are you goin' down wi' th' trap, Joe?'

'Yes, I've told you I'm going down wi' the' trap, haven't I?'

'We'd better be getting her in then. So long, Jack, if I don't see you before I go,' said Malcolm, shaking hands.

He went out, followed by Joe, who seemed to have his tail between his legs.

'Well, this is the devil's own,' exclaimed the doctor, when he was left alone with Fred Henry. 'Going before Wednesday, are you?'

'That's the orders,' replied the other.

'Where, to Northampton?'

'That's it.'

'The devil!' exclaimed Fergusson, with quiet chagrin.

And there was silence between the two.

'All settled up, are you?' asked Fergusson.

'About.'

There was another pause.

'Well, I shall miss yer, Freddy, boy,' said the young doctor.

'And I shall miss thee, Jack,' returned the other.

'Miss you like hell,' mused the doctor.

Fred Henry turned aside. There was nothing to say. Mabel came in again, to finish clearing the table.

'What are *you* going to do, then, Miss Pervin?' asked Fergusson. 'Going to your sister's, are you?'

Mabel looked at him with her steady, dangerous eyes, that always made him uncomfortable, unsettling his superficial ease.

'No,' she said.

'Well, what in the name of fortune *are* you going to do? Say what you mean to do,' cried Fred Henry, with futile intensity.

But she only averted her head, and continued her work. She folded the white tablecloth, and put on the chenille cloth.

'The sulkiest bitch that ever trod!' muttered her brother.

But she finished her task with perfectly impassive face, the young doctor watching her interestedly all the while. Then she went out.

Fred Henry stared after her, clenching his lips, his blue eyes fixing in sharp antagonism, as he made a grimace of sour exasperation.

'You could bray her into bits, and that's all you'd get out of her,' he said, in a small, narrowed tone.

The doctor smiled faintly.

'What's she *going* to do, then?' he asked.

'Strike me if *I* know!' returned the other.

There was a pause. Then the doctor stirred.

'I'll be seeing you to-night, shall I?' he said to his friend.

'Ay—where's it to be? Are we going over to Jessdale?'

'I don't know. I've got such a cold on me. I'll come round to the "Moon and Stars", anyway.'

'Let Lizzie and May miss their night for once, eh?'

'That's it—if I feel as I do now.'

'All's one—'

The two young men went through the passage and down to the back door together. The house was large, but it was servantless now, and desolate. At the back was a small bricked house-yard and beyond that a big square, gravelled fine and red, and having stables on two sides. Sloping, dank, winter-dark fields stretched away on the open sides.

But the stables were empty. Joseph Pervin, the father of the family, had been a man of no education, who had become a fairly large horse dealer. The stables had been full of horses, there was a great turmoil and come-and-go of horses and of dealers and grooms. Then the kitchen was full of servants. But of late things had declined. The old man had married a second time, to retrieve his fortunes. Now he was dead and everything was gone to the dogs, there was nothing but debt and threatening.

For months, Mabel had been servantless in the big house, keeping the home together in penury for her ineffectual brothers. She had kept house for ten years. But previously it was with unstinted means. Then, however brutal and coarse everything was, the sense of money had kept her proud, confident. The men might be foul-mouthed, the women in the kitchen might have bad reputations, her brothers might have illegitimate children. But so long as there was money, the girl felt herself established, and brutally proud, reserved.

No company came to the house, save dealers and coarse men. Mabel had no associates of her own sex, after her sister went away. But she did not mind. She went regularly to church, she attended to her father. And she lived in the memory of her mother, who had died when she was fourteen, and whom she had loved. She had loved her father, too, in a different way, depending upon him, and feeling secure in him, until at the age of fifty-four he married again. And then she had set hard against him. Now he had died and left them all hopelessly in debt.

She had suffered badly during the period of poverty. Nothing, however, could shake the curious, sullen, animal pride that dominated each member of the family. Now, for Mabel, the end had come. Still she would not cast about her. She would follow her own way just the same. She could always hold the keys of her own situation. Mindless and persistent, she endured from day to day. Why should she think? Why should she answer anybody? It was enough that this was the end, and there was no way out. She need not pass any more darkly along the main street of the small town, avoiding every eye. She need not demean herself any more, going into the shops and buying the cheapest food. This was at an end. She thought of nobody, not even of herself. Mindless and persistent, she seemed in a sort of ecstasy to be coming nearer to her fulfilment, her own glorification, approaching her dead mother, who was glorified.

In the afternoon she took a little bag, with shears and sponge and a small scrubbing-brush, and went out. It was a grey, wintry day, with saddened, dark green fields and an atmosphere blackened by the smoke of foundries not far off. She went quickly, darkly along the causeway, heeding nobody, through the town to the churchyard.

There she always felt secure, as if no one could see her, although as a matter of fact she was exposed to the stare of everyone who passed along under the churchyard wall. Nevertheless, once under the shadow of the great looming church, among the graves, she felt immune from the world, reserved within the thick churchyard wall as in another country.

Carefully she clipped the grass from the grave, and arranged the pinky white, small chrysanthemums in the tin cross. When this was done, she took an empty jar from a neighbouring grave, brought water, and carefully, most scrupulously sponged the marble headstone and the coping-stone.

It gave her sincere satisfaction to do this. She felt in immediate contact with the world of her mother. She took minute pains, went through the park in a state bordering on pure happiness, as if in performing this task she came into a subtle, intimate connection with her mother. For the life she followed here in the world was far less real than the world of death she inherited from her mother.

The doctor's house was just by the church. Fergusson, being a mere hired assistant, was slave to the country-side. As he hurried now to attend to the outpatients in the surgery, glancing across the graveyard with his quick eye, he saw the girl at her task at the grave. She seemed so intent and remote, it was like looking into another world. Some mystical element was touched in him. He slowed down as he walked, watching her as if spellbound.

She lifted her eyes, feeling him looking. Their eyes met. And each looked again at once, each feeling, in some way, found out by the other. He lifted his cap and passed on down the road. There remained distinct in his consciousness, like a vision, the memory of her face, lifted from the tombstone in the churchyard and looking at him with slow, large, portentous eyes. It *was* portentous, her face. It seemed to mesmerize him. There was a heavy power in her eyes which laid hold of his whole being, as if he had drunk some powerful drug. He had been feeling weak and done before. Now the life came back into him, he felt delivered from his own fretted, daily self.

He finished his duties at the surgery as quickly as might be, hastily filling up the bottles of the waiting people with cheap drugs. Then, in perpetual haste, he set off again to visit several cases in another part of his round, before tea-time. At all times he preferred to walk if he could, but particularly when he was not well. He fancied the motion restored him.

The afternoon was falling. It was grey, deadened, and wintry, with a slow, moist, heavy coldness sinking in and deadening all the faculties. But why should he think or notice? He hastily climbed the hill and turned across the dark green fields, following the black cinder-track. In the distance, across a shallow dip in the country, the small town was clustered like smouldering ash, a tower, a spire, a heap of low, raw, extinct houses. And on the nearest fringe of the town, sloping into the dip, was Oldmeadow, the Pervins' house. He could see the stables and the outbuildings distinctly, as they lay towards him on the slope. Well, he would not go there many more times! Another resource would be lost to him, another place gone: the only company he cared for in the alien, ugly little town he was losing. Nothing but work, drudgery, constant hastening from dwelling to dwelling among the colliers and the iron-workers. It wore him out, but at the same time he had a craving for it. It was a stimulant to him to be in the homes of the working people, moving, as it were, through the innermost body of their life. His nerves were excited and gratified. He could come so near, into the very lives of the rough, inarticulate, powerfully emotional men and women. He grumbled, he said he hated the hellish hole. But as a matter of fact it excited him, the contact with the rough, strongly-feeling people was a stimulant applied direct to his nerves.

Below Oldmeadow, in the green, shallow, soddened hollow of fields, lay a square, deep pond. Roving across the landscape, the doctor's quick eye detected a figure in black passing through the gate of the field, down towards the pond. He looked again. It would be Mabel Pervin. His mind suddenly became alive and attentive.

Why was she going down there? He pulled up on the path on the slope above, and stood staring. He could just make sure of the small black figure moving in the hollow of the failing day. He seemed to see her in the midst of such obscurity, that he was like a clairvoyant, seeing rather with the mind's eye than with ordinary sight. Yet he could see her positively enough, whilst he kept his eye attentive. He felt, if he looked away from her, in the thick, ugly falling dusk, he would lose her altogether.

He followed her minutely as she moved, direct and intent, like something transmitted rather than stirring in voluntary activity, straight down the field towards the pond. There she stood on the bank for a moment. She never raised her head. Then she waded slowly into the water.

He stood motionless as the small black figure walked slowly and deliberately towards the centre of the pond, very slowly, gradually moving deeper into the motionless water, and still moving forward as the water got up to her breast. Then he could see her no more in the dusk of the dead afternoon.

'There!' he exclaimed. 'Would you believe it?'

And he hastened straight down, running over the wet, soddened fields, pushing through the hedges, down into the depression of callous wintry obscurity. It took him several minutes to come to the pond. He stood on the bank, breathing heavily. He could see nothing. His eyes seemed to penetrate the dead water. Yes, perhaps that was the dark shadow of her black clothing beneath the surface of the water.

He slowly ventured into the pond. The bottom was deep, soft clay, he sank in, and the water clasped dead cold round his legs. As he stirred he could smell the cold, rotten clay that fouled up into the water. It was objectionable in his lungs. Still, repelled and yet not heeding, he moved deeper into the pond. The cold water rose over his thighs, over his loins, upon his abdomen. The lower part of his body was all sunk in the hideous cold element. And the bottom was so deeply soft and uncertain, he was afraid of pitching with his mouth underneath. He could not swim, and was afraid.

He crouched a little, spreading his hands under the water and moving them round, trying to feel for her. The dead cold pond swayed upon his chest. He moved again, a little deeper, and again, with his hands underneath, he felt all around under the water. And he touched her clothing. But it evaded his fingers. He made a desperate effort to grasp it.

And so doing he lost his balance and went under, horribly, suffocating in the foul earthy water, struggling madly for a few moments. At last, after what seemed an eternity, he got his footing, rose again into the air and looked around. He gasped, and knew he was in the world. Then he looked at the water. She had risen near him. He grasped her clothing, and drawing her nearer, turned to take his way to land again.

He went very slowly, carefully, absorbed in the slow progress. He rose higher, climbing out of the pond. The water was now only about his legs; he was thankful, full of relief to be out of the clutches of the pond. He lifted her and staggered on to the bank, out of the horror of wet, grey clay.

He laid her down on the bank. She was quite unconscious and running with water. He made the water come from her mouth, he worked to restore her. He did not have to work very long before he could feel the breathing begin again in her; she was breathing naturally. He worked a little longer. He could feel her live beneath his hands; she was coming back. He wiped her face, wrapped her in his overcoat, looked round into the dim, dark grey world, then lifted her and staggered down the bank and across the fields.

It seemed an unthinkably long way, and his burden so heavy he felt he would never get to the house. But at last he was in the stable-yard, and then in the house-yard. He opened the door and went into the house. In the kitchen he laid her down on the hearth rug and called. The house was empty. But the fire was burning in the grate.

Then again he kneeled to attend to her. She was breathing regularly, her eyes were wide open and as if conscious, but there seemed something missing in her look. She was conscious in herself, but unconscious of her surroundings.

He ran upstairs, took blankets from a bed, and put them before the fire to warm. Then he removed her saturated, earthy-smelling clothing, rubbed her dry with a towel, and wrapped her naked in the blankets. Then he went into the dining-room, to look for spirits. There was a little whisky. He drank a gulp himself, and put some into her mouth.

The effect was instantaneous. She looked full into his face, as if she had been seeing him for some time, and yet had only just become conscious of him.

'Dr. Fergusson?' she said.

'What?' he answered.

He was divesting himself of his coat, intending to find some dry clothing upstairs. He could not bear the smell of the dead, clayey water, and he was mortally afraid for his own health.

'What did I do?' she asked.

'Walked into the pond,' he replied. He had begun to shudder like one sick, and could hardly attend to her. Her eyes remained full on him, he seemed to be going dark in his mind, looking back at her helplessly. The shuddering became quieter in him, his life came back to him, dark and unknowing, but strong again.

'Was I out of my mind?' she asked, while her eyes were fixed on him all the time.

'Maybe, for the moment,' he replied. He felt quiet, because his strength had come back. The strange fretful strain had left him.

'Am I out of my mind now?' she asked.

'Are you?' he reflected a moment. 'No,' he answered truthfully. 'I don't see that you are.' He turned his face aside. He was afraid now, because he felt dazed, and felt dimly that her power was stronger than his, in this issue. And she continued to look at him fixedly all the time. 'Can you tell me where I shall find some dry things to put on?' he asked.

'Did you dive into the pond for me?' she asked.

'No,' he answered. 'I walked in. But I went in overhead as well.'

There was silence for a moment. He hesitated. He very much wanted to go upstairs to get into dry clothing. But there was another desire in him. And she seemed to hold him. His will seemed to have gone to sleep, and left him, standing there slack before her. But he felt warm inside himself. He did not shudder at all, though his clothes were sodden on him.

'Why did you?' she asked.

'Because I didn't want you to do such a foolish thing,' he said.

'It wasn't foolish,' she said, still gazing at him as she lay on the floor, with a sofa cushion under her head. 'It was the right thing to do. I knew best, then.'

'I'll go and shift these wet things,' he said. But still he had not the power to move out of her presence, until she sent him. It was as if she had the life of his body in her hands, and he could not extricate himself. Or perhaps he did not want to.

Suddenly she sat up. Then she became aware of her own immediate condition. She felt the blankets about her, she knew her own limbs. For a moment it seemed as if her reason were going. She looked round, with wild eye, as if seeking something. He stood still with fear. She saw her clothing lying scattered.

'Who undressed me?' she asked, her eyes resting full and inevitable on his face.

'I did,' he replied, 'to bring you round.'

For some moments she sat and gazed at him awfully, her lips parted.

'Do you love me, then?' she asked.

He only stood and stared at her, fascinated. His soul seemed to melt.

She shuffled forward on her knees, and put her arms round him, round his legs, as he stood there, pressing her breasts against his knees and thighs, clutching him with strange, convulsive certainty, pressing his thighs against her, drawing him to her face, her throat, as she looked up at him with flaring, humble eyes of transfiguration, triumphant in first possession.

'You love me,' she murmured, in strange transport, yearning and triumphant and confident. 'You love me. I know you love me, I know.'

And she was passionately kissing his knees, through the wet clothing, passionately and indiscriminately kissing his knees, his legs, as if unaware of everything.

He looked down at the tangled wet hair, the wild, bare, animal shoulders. He was amazed, bewildered, and afraid. He had never thought of loving her. He had never wanted to love her. When he rescued her and restored her, he was a doctor, and she was a patient. He had had no single personal thought of her. Nay, this introduction of the personal element was very distasteful to him, a violation of his professional honour. It was horrible to have her there embracing his knees. It was horrible. He revolted from it, violently. And yet—and yet—he had not the power to break away.

She looked at him again, with the same supplication of powerful love, and that same transcendent, frightening light of triumph. In view of the delicate flame which seemed to come from her face like a light, he was powerless. And yet he had never intended to love her. He had never intended. And something stubborn in him could not give way.

'You love me,' she repeated, in a murmur of deep, rhapsodic assurance. 'You love me.'

Her hands were drawing him, drawing him down to her. He was afraid, even a little horrified. For he had, really, no intention of loving her. Yet her hands were drawing him towards her. He put out his hand quickly to steady himself and grasped her bare shoulder. A flame seemed to burn the hand that grasped her soft shoulder. He had no intention of loving her: his whole will was against his yielding. It was horrible. And yet wonderful was the touch of her shoulders, beautiful the shining of her face. Was she perhaps mad? He had a horror of yielding to her. Yet something in him ached also.

He had been staring away at the door, away from her. But his hand remained on her shoulder. She had gone suddenly very still. He looked down at her. Her eyes were now wide with fear, with doubt, the light was dying from her face, a shadow of terrible greyness was returning. He could not bear the touch of her eyes' question upon him, and the look of death behind the question.

With an inward groan he gave way and let his heart yield towards her. A sudden gentle smile came on his face. And her eyes, which never left his face, slowly, slowly filled with tears. He watched the strange water rise in her eyes, like some slow fountain coming up. And his heart seemed to burn and melt away in his breast.

He could not bear to look at her any more. He dropped on his knees and caught her head with his arms and pressed her face against his throat. She was very still. His heart, which seemed to have broken, was burning with a kind of agony in his breast. And he felt her slow, hot tears wetting his throat. But he could not move.

He felt the hot tears wet his neck and the hollows of his neck, and he remained motionless, suspended through one of man's eternities. Only now it had become indispensable to him to have her face pressed close to him; he could never let her go again. He could never let her head go away from the close clutch of his arm. He wanted to remain like that for ever, with his heart hurting him in a pain that was also life to him. Without knowing, he was looking down on her damp, soft brown hair.

Then, as it were suddenly, he smelt the horrid stagnant smell of that water. And at the same moment she drew away from him and looked at him. Her eyes were wistful and unfathomable. He was afraid of them, and he fell to kissing her, not knowing what he was doing. He wanted her eyes not to have that terrible, wistful, unfathomable look.

When she turned her face to him again, a faint delicate flush was glowing, and there was again dawning that terrible shining of joy in her eyes, which really terrified him, and yet which he now wanted to see, because he feared the look of doubt still more.

'You love me?' she said, rather faltering.

'Yes.' The word cost him a painful effort. Not because it wasn't true. But because it was too newly true, the saying seemed to tear open again his newly-torn heart. And he hardly wanted it to be true, even now.

She lifted her face to him, and he bent forward and kissed her on the mouth, gently, with the one kiss that is an eternal pledge. And as he kissed her his heart strained again in his breast. He never intended to love her. But now it was over. He had crossed over the gulf to her, and all that he had left behind had shrivelled and become void.

After the kiss, her eyes again slowly filled with tears. She sat still, away from him, with her face drooped aside, and her hands folded in her lap. The tears fell very slowly. There was complete silence. He too sat there motionless and silent on the hearth-rug. The strange pain of his heart that was broken seemed to consume him. That he should love her? That this was love! That he should be ripped open in this way! Him, a doctor! How they would all jeer if they knew! It was agony to him to think they might know.

In the curious naked pain of the thought he looked again to her. She was sitting there drooped into a muse. He saw a tear fall, and his heart flared hot. He saw for the first time that one of her shoulders was quite uncovered, one arm bare, he could see one of her small breasts; dimly, because it had become almost dark in the room.

'Why are you crying?' he asked, in an altered voice.

She looked up at him, and behind her tears the consciousness of her situation for the first time brought a dark look of shame to her eyes.

'I'm not crying, really,' she said, watching him, half frightened.

He reached his hand, and softly closed it on her bare arm.

'I love you! I love you!' he said in a soft, low vibrating voice, unlike himself.

She shrank, and dropped her head. The soft, penetrating grip of his hand on her arm distressed her. She looked up at him.

'I want to go,' she said. 'I want to go and get you some dry things.'

'Why?' he said. 'I'm all right.'

'But I want to go,' she said. 'And I want you to change your things.'

He released her arm, and she wrapped herself in the blanket, looking at him rather frightened. And still she did not rise.

'Kiss me,' she said wistfully.

He kissed her, but briefly, half in anger.

Then, after a second, she rose nervously, all mixed up in the blanket. He watched her in her confusion as she tried to extricate herself and wrap herself up so that she could walk. He watched her relentlessly, as she knew. And as she went, the blanket trailing, and as he saw a glimpse of her feet and her white leg, he tried to remember her as she was when he had wrapped her in the blanket. But then he didn't want to remember, because she had been nothing to him then, and his nature revolted from remembering her as she was when she was nothing to him.

A tumbling, muffled noise from within the dark house startled him. Then he heard her voice: 'There are clothes.' He rose and went to the foot of the stairs, and gathered up the garments she had thrown down. Then he came back to the fire, to rub himself down and dress. He grinned at his own appearance when he had finished.

The fire was sinking, so he put on coal. The house was now quite dark, save for the light of a street-lamp that shone in faintly from beyond the holly trees. He lit the gas with matches he found on the mantelpiece. Then he emptied the pockets of his own clothes, and threw all his wet things in a heap into the scullery. After which he gathered up her sodden clothes, gently, and put them in a separate heap on the copper-top in the scullery.

It was six o'clock on the clock. His own watch had stopped. He ought to go back to the surgery. He waited, and still she did not come down. So he went to the foot of the stairs and called:

'I shall have to go.'

Almost immediately he heard her coming down. She had on her best dress of black voile, and her hair was tidy, but still damp. She looked at him—and in spite of herself, smiled.

'I don't like you in those clothes,' she said.

'Do I look a sight?' he answered.

They were shy of one another.

'I'll make you some tea,' she said.

'No, I must go.'

'Must you?' And she looked at him again with the wide, strained, doubtful eyes. And again, from the pain of his breast, he knew how he loved her. He went and bent to kiss her, gently, passionately, with his heart's painful kiss.

'And my hair smells so horrible,' she murmured in distraction. 'And I'm so awful, I'm so awful. Oh, no, I'm too awful.' And she broke into bitter, heart-broken sobbing. 'You can't want to love me, I'm horrible.'

'Don't be silly, don't be silly,' he said, trying to comfort her, kissing her, holding her in his arms. 'I want you, I want to marry you, we're going to be married, quickly, quickly—tomorrow if I can.'

But she only sobbed terribly, and cried:

'I feel awful, I feel awful. I feel I'm horrible to you.'

'No, I want you, I want you,' was all he answered, blindly, with that terrible intonation which frightened her almost more than her horror lest he should *not* want her.

Alistair MacLeod

Alistair MacLeod was born in 1936 in North Battleford, Saskatchewan, to Cape Breton parents. He was raised in Alberta and Inverness, Nova Scotia, and educated at Nova Scotia Teachers' College, St. Francis Xavier University, and Notre Dame University. He has worked as a labourer, milkman, miner, public relations man, and teacher, from a one-room school to the Universities of New Brunswick, Indiana, and Windsor, where, since 1969, he has taught English and Creative Writing. MacLeod is not a prolific writer, but has had considerable recognition for his painstaking craftsmanship, his work having been included in *Best American Stories* and numerous anthologies. His books include *The Lost Salt Gift of Blood* (1976) and *As Birds Bring Forth the Sun and Other Stories* (1986).

MacLeod writes primarily about the families of miners and fishermen in Cape Breton, their confrontation with the land and with changing conditions in the world around them. There is a stark, almost mythic quality to his writing, as if the characters have stepped outside of contemporary history, or conventional reality as we know it, and are seen moving against the backdrop of eternity. As he says in an interview with Mark Fortier (*Books in Canada*, Aug./Sept. 1986), "I like to think of myself as basically a kind of realistic writer, not steeped in pessimism. I like to think of myself as telling the truth as I see it. What else can I do? In an urbanized world there is more of a chance to escape death, because you don't have to see it. But if you grow up in a rural world, where the animals are always being killed, that is part of your reality. I don't think that's pessimistic."

Writing in the tradition of Faulkner and Flannery O'Connor, MacLeod is a regional writer whose work has a universal appeal. He quotes T. S. Eliot's comment in *The Four Quartets* that home is where we start from; and yet, he does not deny the power of ancient, tribal memory at work in his characters. "Well, the world that we live in is not necessarily all that we have. And the world that we comprehend intellectually is not all that we have either. A lot of these characters are not instant North Americans. They go back a long way, and, whether this is any good or not, they have no choice. You cannot not know what you do know."

MacLeod is committed, imaginatively, to his small piece of turf, but would not wish to be described as "the voice of Cape Breton." He prefers to think of himself, this time quoting Elizabeth Spencer, as inscribing a "landscape of the heart." "I write about what I want to write about, which I think is a good way to write. I think of that material almost as you think of someone you love. If I were free to spend all my time with someone, who would I spend it with? That material is who—or what—I want to spend my time with. What's happened over the years is that I've come to think of it as being more worthwhile—this is as good a way to spend your life as any other. Why not do it? Alice Munro has said about her own work, 'Everything I do is an offering, and people can take from it what they wish.' That's all I can do, is put it out as well as I possibly can. That's all you can do."

In a brief statement entitled "A Voice from Rural Canada" (*Transitions II*, 1978), MacLeod tries to articulate his sense of the depth of experience that lies in often remote rural communities: "In the older, more isolated communities the patterns are more firmly established. There is a weight of history behind the traditions and the occupations associated with them. Such 'narrowness' as it might be called is often a 'deepness' as well; what is lost in breadth is compensated for in depth. For many people this results in a fierce intensity that has to do with where they stand in place and time and how they spend their allotted years. What they have learned and what they possess to pass on is often personal and almost physical. You cannot learn to be a good trapper or a good fisherman by going to university, and The Flying Wallendas do not run ads in Help Wanted columns."

In an interview with Andrew Garrod (*Speaking for Myself: Canadian Writers in Interview*, 1986), MacLeod justifies his sometimes long descriptive passages on the grounds that "my description is the whereness against which events take place." He also links his commitment to the short story to its potential for intensity: "I like to write in a kind of intense manner, and you can only be intense for so long." This process, which may resemble the hundred-yard dash but which is by no means quick and easy, involves rigorous rewriting, reading the work aloud to see if it works orally, and attention to linguistic devices such as repetition, which "obviously gives you emphasis, and if it's not overdone, I think it has a sort of oral appeal. I write for sound as well as for sense. This is why in medieval literature or ballad literature or whatever, refrain is very important. This is ritual."

MacLeod is interested in the "great prices paid" by the isolated protagonists in his stories for whatever they accept or reject in their lives. He has, as a writer, paid a price, in popularity and immediate recognition, for his decision to limit his focus and to carve his stories so carefully and lovingly. However, as he suggests in the Afterwords included in this anthology, the great writer must keep his eye on eternity, not on the stock market or the best-seller list. As a teacher of writing and as fiction editor of the *University of Windsor Review*, he insists that "I'm looking for whether I care about what happens, whether I care about the people. I also look to see if the language is beautiful, whether what is described is done so with beauty. I don't care what the subjects are. The office is full of manuscripts from everywhere. I read them and see whether they make my heart beat faster or something like that."

As Birds Bring Forth the Sun

Once there was a family with a Highland name who lived beside the sea. And the man had a dog of which he was very fond. She was large and grey, a sort of staghound from another time. And if she jumped up to lick his face, which she loved to do, her paws would jolt against his shoulders with such force that she would come close to knocking him down and he would be forced to take two or three backward steps before he could regain his balance. And he himself was not a small man, being slightly over six feet and perhaps one hundred and eighty pounds.

She had been left, when a puppy, at the family's gate in a small handmade box and no one knew where she had come from or that she would eventually grow to such a size. Once, while still a small pup, she had been run over by the steel wheel of a horse-drawn cart which was hauling kelp from the shore to be used as fertilizer. It was in October and the rain had been falling for some weeks and the ground was soft. When the wheel of the cart passed over her, it sunk her body into the wet earth as well as crushing some of her ribs; and apparently the silhouette of her small crushed body was visible in the earth after the man lifted her to his chest while she yelped and screamed. He ran his fingers along her broken bones, ignoring the blood and urine which fell upon his shirt, trying to soothe her bulging eyes and her scrabbling front paws and her desperately licking tongue.

The more practical members of his family, who had seen run-over dogs before, suggested that her neck be broken by his strong hands or that he grasp her by the hind legs and swing her head against a rock, thus putting an end to her misery. But he would not do it.

Instead, he fashioned a small box and lined it with woollen remnants from a sheep's fleece and one of his old and frayed shirts. He placed her within the box and placed the box behind the stove and then he warmed some milk in a small saucepan and sweetened it with sugar. And he held open her small and trembling jaws with his left hand while spooning in the sweetened milk with his right, ignoring the needlelike sharpness of her small teeth. She lay in the box most of the remaining fall and into the early winter, watching everything with her large brown eyes.

Although some members of the family complained about her presence and the odour from the box and the waste of time she involved, they gradually adjusted to her: and as the weeks passed by, it became evident that her ribs were knitting together in some form or other and that she was recovering with the resilience of the young. It also became evident that she would grow to a tremendous size, as she outgrew one box and then another and the grey hair began to feather from her huge front paws. In the spring she was outside almost all of the time and followed the man everywhere; and when she came inside during the following months, she had grown so large that she would no longer fit into her accustomed place behind the stove and was forced to lie beside it. She was never given a name but was referred to in Gaelic as *cù mòr glas*, the big grey dog.

By the time she came into her first heat, she had grown to a tremendous height, and although her signs and her odour attracted many panting and highly aroused suitors, none was big enough to mount her and the frenzy of their disappointment and the longing of her unfulfillment were more than the man could stand. He went, so the story goes, to a place where he knew there was a big dog. A dog not as big as she was, but still a big dog, and he brought him home with him. And at the proper time he took the *cù mòr glas* and the big dog down to the sea where he knew there was a hollow in the rock which appeared only at low tide. He took some sacking to provide footing for the male dog and he placed the *cù mòr glas* in the hollow of the rock and knelt beside her and steadied her with his left arm under her throat and helped position the male dog above her and guided his blood-engorged penis. He was a man used to working with the breeding of animals, with the guiding of rams and bulls and stallions and often with the funky smell of animal semen heavy on his large and gentle hands.

The winter that followed was a cold one and ice formed on the sea and frequent squalls and blizzards obliterated the offshore islands and caused the people to stay near their fires much of the time, mending clothes and nets and harness and waiting for the change in season. The *cù mòr glas* grew heavier and even more huge until there was hardly room for her around the stove or even under the table. And then one morning, when it seemed that spring was about to break, she was gone.

The man and even his family, who had become more involved than they cared to admit, waited for her but she did not come. And as the frenzy of spring wore on, they busied themselves with readying their land and their fishing gear and all of the things that so desperately required their attention. And then they were into summer and fall and winter and another spring which saw the birth of the man and his wife's twelfth child. And then it was summer again.

That summer the man and two of his teenaged sons were pulling their herring nets about two miles offshore when the wind began to blow off the land and the water began to roughen. They became afraid that they could not make it safely back to shore, so they pulled in behind one of the offshore islands, knowing that they would be sheltered there and planning to outwait the storm. As the prow of their boat approached the gravelly shore, they heard a sound above them, and looking up they saw the *cù mòr glas* silhouetted on the brow of the hill which was the small island's highest point.

"*M'eudal cù mòr glas*" shouted the man in his happiness—*m'eudal* meaning something like dear or darling; and as he shouted, he jumped over the side of his boat into the waist-deep water, struggling for footing on the rolling gravel as he waded eagerly and awkwardly towards her and the shore. At the same time, the *cù mòr glas* came hurtling down towards him in a shower of small rocks dislodged by her feet; and just as he was emerging from the water, she met him as she used to, rearing up on her hind legs and placing her huge front paws on his shoulders while extending her eager tongue.

The weight and speed of her momentum met him as he tried to hold his balance on the sloping angle and the water rolling gravel beneath his feet, and he staggered backwards and lost his footing and fell beneath her force. And in that instant again, as the story goes, there appeared over the brow of the hill six more huge grey dogs hurtling down towards the graveled strand. They had never seen him before; and seeing him stretched prone beneath their mother, they misunderstood, like so many armies, the intention of their leader.

They fell upon him in a fury, slashing his face and tearing aside his lower jaw and ripping out his throat, crazed with blood-lust or duty or perhaps starvation. The *cù mòr glas* turned on them in her own savagery, slashing and snarling and, it seemed, crazed by their mistake; driving them bloodied and yelping before her, back over the brow of the hill where they vanished from sight but could still be heard screaming in the distance. It all took perhaps little more than a minute.

The man's two sons, who were still in the boat and had witnessed it all, ran sobbing through the salt water to where their mauled and mangled father lay; but there was little they could do other than hold his warm and bloodied hands for a few brief moments. Although his eyes "lived" for a small fraction of time, he could not speak to them because his face and throat had been torn away, and of course there was nothing they could do except to hold and be held tightly until that too slipped away and his eyes glazed over and they could no longer feel his hands holding theirs. The storm increased and they could not get home and so they were forced to spend the night huddled beside their father's body. They were afraid to try to carry the body to the rocking boat because he was so heavy and they were afraid that they might lose even what little of him remained and they were afraid also, huddled on the rocks, that the dogs might return. But they did not return at all and there was no sound from them, no sound at all, only the moaning of the wind and the washing of the water on the rocks.

In the morning they debated whether they should try to take his body with them or whether they should leave it and return in the company of older and wiser men. But they were afraid to leave it unattended and felt that the time needed to cover it with protective rocks would be better spent in trying to get across to their home shore. For a while they debated as to whether one should go in the boat and the other remain on the island, but each was afraid to be alone and so in the end they managed to drag and carry and almost float him towards the bobbing boat. They laid him face down and covered him with what clothes there were and set off across the still-rolling sea. Those who waited on the shore missed the large presence of the man within the boat and some of them waded into the water and others rowed out in skiffs, attempting to hear the tearful messages called out across the rolling waves.

The *cù mòr glas* and her six young dogs were never seen again, or perhaps I should say they were never seen again in the same way. After some weeks, a group of men circled the island tentatively in their boats but they saw no sign. They went again and then again but found nothing. A year later, and grown much braver, they beached their boats and walked the island carefully, looking into the small sea caves and the hollows at the base of the wind-ripped trees, thinking perhaps that if they did not find the dogs, they might at least discover their whitened bones; but again they discovered nothing.

The *cù mòr glas*, though, was supposed to be sighted here and there for a number of years. Seen on a hill in one region or silhouetted on a ridge in another or loping across the valleys or glens in the early morning or the shadowy evening. Always in the area of the half perceived. For a while she became rather like the Loch Ness monster or the Sasquatch on a smaller scale. Seen but not recorded. Seen when there were no cameras. Seen but never taken.

The mystery of where she went became entangled with the mystery of whence she came. There was increased speculation about the handmade box in which she had been found and much theorizing as to the individual or individuals who might have left it. People went to look for the box but could not find it. It was felt she might have been part of a *buidseachd* or evil spell cast on the man by some mysterious enemy. But no one could go much further than that. All of his caring for her was recounted over and over again and nobody missed any of the ironies.

What seemed literally known was that she had crossed the winter ice to have her pups and had been unable to get back. No one could remember ever seeing her swim; and in the early months at least, she could not have taken her young pups with her.

The large and gentle man with the smell of animal semen often heavy on his hands was my great-great-great-grandfather, and it may be argued that he died because he was too good at breeding animals or that he cared too much about their fulfillment and well-being. He was no longer there for his own child of the spring who, in turn, became my great-great-grandfather, and he was perhaps too much there in the memory of his older sons who saw him fall beneath the ambiguous force of the *cù mòr glas*. The youngest boy in the boat was haunted and tormented by the awfulness of what he had seen. He would wake at night screaming that he had seen the *cù mòr glas á bhàis*, the big grey dog of death, and his screams filled the house and the ears and minds of the listeners, bringing home again and again the consequences of their loss. One morning, after a night in which he saw the *cù mòr glas á bhàis* so vividly that his sheets were drenched with sweat, he walked to the high cliff which faced the island and there he cut his throat with a fish knife and fell into the sea.

The other brother lived to be forty, but, again so the story goes, he found himself in a Glasgow pub one night, perhaps looking for answers, deep and sodden with the whisky which had become his anaesthetic. In the half darkness he saw a large, grey-haired man sitting by himself against the wall and mumbled something to him. Some say he saw the *cù mòr glas á bhàis* or uttered the name. And perhaps the man heard the phrase through ears equally affected by drink and felt he was being called a dog or a son of a bitch or something of that nature. They rose to meet one another and struggled outside into the cobblestoned passageway behind the pub where, most improbably, there were supposed to be six other large, grey-haired men who beat him to death on the cobblestones, smashing his bloodied head into the stone again and again before vanishing and leaving him to die with his face turned to the sky. The *cù mòr glas á bhàis* had come again, said his family, as they tried to piece the tale together.

This is how the *cù mòr glas á bhàis* came into our lives, and it is obvious that all of this happened a long, long time ago. Yet with succeeding generations it seemed the spectre had somehow come to stay and that it had become *ours*—not in the manner of an unwanted skeleton in the closet from a family's ancient past but more in the manner of something close to a genetic possibility. In the deaths of each generation, the grey dog was seen by some—by women who were to die in childbirth; by soldiers who went forth to the many wars but did not return; by those who went forth to feuds or dangerous love affairs; by those who answered mysterious midnight messages; by those who swerved on the highway to avoid the real or imagined grey dog and ended in masses of crumpled steel. And by one professional athlete who, in addition to his ritualized athletics superstitions, carried another fear or belief as well. Many of the man's descendants moved like careful hemophiliacs, fearing that they carried unwanted possibilities deep within them. And others, while they laughed, were like members of families in which there is a recurrence over the generations of repeated cancer or the diabetes which comes to those beyond middle age. The feeling of those who may say little to others but who may say often and quietly to themselves, "It has not happened to me," while adding always the cautionary "*yet*".

I am thinking all of this now as the October rain falls on the city of Toronto and the pleasant, white-clad nurses pad confidently in and out of my father's room. He lies quietly amidst the whiteness, his head and shoulders elevated so that he is in that hospital position of being neither quite prone nor yet sitting. His hair is white upon his pillow and he breathes softly and sometimes unevenly, although it is difficult ever to be sure.

My five grey-haired brothers and I take turns beside his bedside, holding his heavy hands in ours and feeling their response, hoping ambiguously that he will speak to us, although we know that it may tire him. And trying to read his life and ours into his eyes when they are open. He has been with us a long time, well into our middle age. Unlike those boys in that boat of so long ago, we did not see him taken from us in our youth. And unlike their youngest brother who, in turn, became our great-great-grandfather, we did not grow into a world in which there was no father's touch. We have been lucky to have this large and gentle man so deep into our lives.

No one in this hospital has mentioned the *cù mòr glas á bhàis*. Yet as my mother said ten years ago, before slipping into her own death as quietly as a grown-up child who leaves or enters her parents' house in the early hours, "It is hard to *not* know what you do know."

Even those who are most sceptical, like my oldest brother who has driven here from Montreal, betray themselves by their nervous actions. "I avoided the Greyhound bus stations in both Montreal and Toronto," he smiled upon his arrival, and then added, "Just in case."

He did not realize how ill our father was and has smiled little since then. I watch him turning the diamond ring upon his finger, knowing that he hopes he will not hear the Gaelic phrase he knows too well. Not having the luxury, as he once said, of some who live in Montreal and are able to pretend they do not understand the "other" language. You cannot *not* know what you do know.

Sitting here, taking turns holding the hands of the man who gave us his life, we are afraid for him and for ourselves. We are afraid of what he may see and we are afraid to hear the phrase born of the vision. We are aware that it may become confused with what the doctors call "the will to live" and we are aware that some beliefs are what others would dismiss as "garbage". We are aware that there are men who believe the earth is flat and that the birds bring forth the sun.

Bound here in our own peculiar mortality, we do not wish to see or see others see that which signifies life's demise. We do not want to hear the voice of our father, as did those other sons, calling down his own particular death upon him.

We would shut our eyes and plug our ears, even as we know such actions to be of no avail. Open still and fearful to the grey hair rising on our necks if and when we hear the scrabble of the paws and the scratching at the door.

Katherine Mansfield

Born in Wellington, New Zealand, in 1888, Katherine Mansfield Beauchamp was educated in the village school in Karori and a private school for girls before completing four years at Queen's College, London. At the age of nineteen, she persuaded her merchant father to permit her to return to London, on a continuing allowance to pursue a career as a writer. She became pregnant that first year in London, married a man who was not the father of the child, had a miscarriage, and lived briefly in Germany. This restless period was followed by a number of happy years married to critic and journalist John Middleton Murry, marred only by the death of her younger brother in World War I and her gradually failing health. She was influenced by the work of Chekhov, diminishing the importance of plot and letting small, seemingly insignificant details carry the emotional weight of her stories: "an overheard word can bring down the empire of the self." Her first book of stories, *In a German Pension*, was published in 1911; *Bliss and Other Stories* appeared in 1920; and *The Garden Party and Other Stories* in 1922. She died of tuberculosis in 1923 at the age of thirty-four, while in pursuit of physical and spiritual relief at the Gurdjieff Institute in France.

Mansfield seems to have considered character to be less central to the short story than other matters: "The short story, by reason of its aesthetics, is not, and is not intended to be, the medium either for the exploration or long-term development of character. Character cannot be more than *shown—it is there for use, the use is dramatic. Foreshortening is not only unavoidable, it is right.*" Colour, tone, verbal texture seem more important to her. In a letter to S. S. Koteliansky, she writes about how she even dreams of the "smallest details": "Do you, too feel an infinite delight and value in *detail*—not for the sake of detail but for the life *in* the life of it. I never can express myself (and you can laugh as much as you please). But do you ever feel as though the Lord threw you into eternity—into the very exact centre of eternity, and even as you plunged you felt every ripple that flowed out from your plunging—every single ripple floating away and touching and drawing into its circle every slightest thing it touched."

In a letter to Richard Murry, she writes: "It's a very queer thing how *craft* comes into writing. I mean down to details. Par exemple. In Miss Brill I chose not only the length of every sentence, but even the sound of every sentence—I chose the rise and fall of every paragraph to fit her—and to fit her on that day at that very moment. After I'd written it I read it aloud—numbers of times—just as one would *play over* a musical composition, trying to get it nearer and nearer to the expression of Miss Brill—until it fitted her. ... I often wonder whether other writers do the same. If a thing has really come off it seems to me there mustn't be one single word out of place or one word that could be taken out. That's how I AIM at writing. It will take some time to get anywhere near there."

Mansfield kept journals—she called them "minute notebooks"—which are chock-full of poems, story ideas, plans, personal pep talks. She claimed to be "always trembling on the brink of poetry," yet, strangely, often unable to write: "I pose myself, yet once more, *my* Eternal Question. What is it that makes the moment of delivery so difficult for me? If I were to sit down—now—and just to write out, plain, some of the stories—all written, all ready, in my mind 'twould take me days. There are so many of them. I sit and *think* them out, and if I overcome my lassitude and *do* take the pen they ought (they are so word perfect) to write themselves. But it's the activity. I haven't a place to write in or on—the chair isn't comfortable—yet even as I complain *this* seems the place and *this* the chair. And don't I want to write them? Lord! Lord! it's my only desire—my one *happy issue*."

In words that recall the letters of Flaubert and Conrad, she addresses the issue of writing as work, as a religious vocation: "Work. Shall I be able to express, one day, my love of work—my desire to be a better writer—my longing to take greater pains. And the passion I feel. It takes the place of religion—it *is* my religion—of people—I create my people: of 'life'—it *is* Life. The temptation is to kneel before it, to adore, to prostrate myself, to stay too long in a state of ecstasy before the *idea* of it. I must be more busy about my master's business."

Mansfield's struggles are fascinating, the ecstasy and the hard labour of creation, the difficult mixture of self-congratulation and self-doubt, the fear of literary pride that "interferes very much with work. One can't be calm, clear, good as one must be, while it goes on. I look at the mountains, I try to pray and I think of something *clever*. It's a kind of excitement within one, which shouldn't be there. Calm yourself. Clear yourself. And anything that I write in this mood will be no good; it will be full of *sediment*. If I were well, I would go off by myself somewhere and sit under a tree. One must learn, one must practise, to *forget* oneself. I can't tell the truth about Aunt Anne unless I am free to enter into her life without selfconsciousness. Oh God! I am divided still, I am bad. I fail in my personal life. I lapse into impatience, temper, vanity, and so I fail as thy priest. Perhaps poetry will help."

A Dill Pickle

And then, after six years, she saw him again. He was seated at one of those little bamboo tables decorated with a Japanese vase of paper daffodils. There was a tall plate of fruit in front of him, and very carefully, in a way she recognized immediately as his 'special' way, he was peeling an orange.

He must have felt that shock of recognition in her for he looked up and met her eyes. Incredible! He didn't know her! She smiled; he frowned. She came towards him. He closed his eyes an instant, but opening them his face lit up as though he had struck a match in a dark room. He laid down the orange and pushed back his chair, and she took her little warm hand out of her muff and gave it to him.

'Vera!' he exclaimed. 'How strange. Really, for a moment I didn't know you. Won't you sit down? You've had lunch? Won't you have some coffee?'

She hesitated, but of course she meant to.

'Yes, I'd like some coffee.' And she sat down opposite him.

'You've changed. You've changed very much,' he said, staring at her with that eager, lighted look. 'You look so well. I've never seen you look so well before.'

'Really?' She raised her veil and unbuttoned her high fur collar. 'I don't feel very well. I can't bear this weather, you know.'

'Ah, no. You hate the cold. ...'

'Loathe it.' She shuddered. 'And the worst of it is that the older one grows ...'

He interrupted her. 'Excuse me,' and tapped on the table for the waitress. 'Please bring some coffee and cream.' To her: 'You are sure you won't eat anything? Some fruit, perhaps. The fruit here is very good.'

'No, thanks. Nothing.'

'Then that's settled.' And smiling just a hint too broadly he took up the orange again. 'You were saying—the older one grows—'

'The colder,' she laughed. But she was thinking how well she remembered that trick of his—the trick of interrupting her—and of how it used to exasperate her six years ago. She used to feel then as though he, quite suddenly, in the middle of what she was saying, put his hand over her lips, turned from her, attended to something different, and then took his hand away, and with just the same slightly too broad smile, gave her his attention again. ... Now we are ready. That is settled.

'The colder!' He echoed her words, laughing too. 'Ah, ah. You still say the same things. And there is another thing about you that is not changed at all—your beautiful voice your beautiful way of speaking.' Now he was very grave; he leaned towards her, and she smelled the warm, stinging scent of the orange peel. 'You have only to say one word and I would know your voice among all other voices. I don't know what it is—I've often wondered—that makes your voice such a—haunting memory. ... Do you remember that first afternoon we spent together at Kew Gardens? You were so surprised because I did not know the names of any flowers. I am still just as ignorant for all your telling me. But whenever it is very fine and warm, and I see some bright colours—it's awfully strange—I hear your voice saying: "Geranium, marigold, and verbena." And I feel those three words are all I recall of some forgotten, heavenly language. ... You remember that afternoon?'

'Oh, yes, very well.' She drew a long, soft breath, as though the paper daffodils between them were almost too sweet to bear. Yet, what had remained in her mind of that particular afternoon was an absurd scene over the tea table. A great many people taking tea in a Chinese pagoda, and he behaving like a maniac about the wasps—waving them away, flapping at them with his straw hat, serious and infuriated out of all proportion to the occasion. How delighted the sniggering tea drinkers had been. And how she had suffered.

But now, as he spoke, that memory faded. His was the truer. Yes, it had been a wonderful afternoon, full of geranium and marigold and verbena, and—warm sunshine. Her thoughts lingered over the last two words as though she sang them.

In the warmth, as it were, another memory unfolded. She saw herself sitting on a lawn. He lay beside her, and suddenly, after a long silence, he rolled over and put his head in her lap.

'I wish,' he said, in a low, troubled voice, 'I wish that I had taken poison and were about to die—here now!'

At that moment a little girl in a white dress, holding a long, dripping water lily, dodged from behind a bush, stared at them, and dodged back again. But he did not see. She leaned over him.

'Ah, why do you say that? I could not say that.'

But he gave a kind of soft moan, and taking her hand he held it to his cheek.

'Because I know I am going to love you too much—far too much. And I shall suffer so terribly, Vera, because you never, never will love me.'

He was certainly far better looking now than he had been then. He had lost all that dreamy vagueness and indecision. Now he had the air of a man who has found his place in life, and fills it with a confidence and an assurance which was, to say the least, impressive. He must have made money, too. His clothes were admirable, and at that moment he pulled a Russian cigarette case out of his pocket.

'Won't you smoke?'

'Yes, I will.' She hovered over them. 'They look very good.'

'I think they are. I get them made for me by a little man in St James's Street. I don't smoke very much. I'm not like you—but when I do, they must be delicious, very fresh cigarettes. Smoking isn't a habit with me; it's a luxury—like perfume. Are you still so fond of perfumes? Ah, when I was in Russia ...'

She broke in: 'You've really been to Russia?'

'Oh, yes. I was there for over a year. Have you forgotten how we used to talk of going there?'

'No, I've not forgotten.'

He gave a strange half laugh and leaned back in his chair. 'Isn't it curious. I have really carried out all those journeys that we planned. Yes, I have been to all those places that we talked of, and stayed in them long enough to—as you used to say, "air oneself" in them. In fact, I have spent the last three years of my life travelling all the time. Spain, Corsica, Siberia, Russia, Egypt. The only country left is China, and I mean to go there, too, when the war is over.'

As he spoke, so lightly, tapping the end of his cigarette against the ash-tray, she felt the strange beast that had slumbered so long within her bosom stir, stretch itself, yawn, prick up its ears, and suddenly bound to its feet, and fix its longing, hungry stare upon those far away places. But all she said was, smiling gently: 'How I envy you.'

He accepted that. 'It has been,' he said, 'very wonderful—especially Russia. Russia was all that we had imagined, and far, far more. I even spent some days on a river boat on the Volga. Do you remember that boatman's song that you used to play?'

'Yes.' It began to play in her mind as she spoke.

'Do you ever play it now?'

'No, I've no piano.'

He was amazed at that. 'But what has become of your beautiful piano?'

She made a little grimace. 'Sold. Ages ago.'

'But you were so fond of music,' he wondered.

'I've no time for it now,' said she.

He let it go at that. 'That river life,' he went on, 'is something quite special. After a day or two you cannot realize that you have ever known another. And it is not necessary to know the language—the life of the boat creates a bond between you and the people that's more than sufficient. You eat with them, pass the day with them, and in the evening there is that endless singing.'

She shivered, hearing the boatman's song break out again loud and tragic, and seeing the boat floating on the darkening river with melancholy trees on either side. ... 'Yes, I should like that,' said she, stroking her muff.

'You'd like almost everything about Russian life,' he said warmly. 'It's so informal, so impulsive, so free without question. And then the peasants are so splendid. They are such human beings—yes, that is it. Even the man who drives your carriage has—has some real part in what is happening. I remember the evening a party of us, two friends of mine and the wife of one of them, went for a picnic by the Black Sea. We took supper and champagne and ate and drank on the grass. And while we were eating the coachman came up. "Have a dill pickle," he said. He wanted to share with us. That seemed to me so right, so—you know what I mean?'

And she seemed at that moment to be sitting on the grass beside the mysteriously Black Sea, black as velvet, and rippling against the banks in silent, velvet waves. She saw the carriage drawn up to one side of the road, and the little group on the grass, their faces and hands white in the moonlight. She saw the pale dress of the woman outspread and her folded parasol, lying on the grass like a huge pearl crochet hook. Apart from them, with his supper in a cloth on his knees, sat the coachman. 'Have a dill pickle,' said he, and although she was not certain what a dill pickle was, she saw the greenish glass jar with a red chili like a parrot's beak glimmering through. She sucked in her cheeks; the dill pickle was terribly sour. ...

'Yes, I know perfectly what you mean,' she said.

In the pause that followed they looked at each other. In the past when they had looked at each other like that they had felt such a boundless understanding between them that their souls had, as it were, put their arms round each other and dropped into the same sea, content to be drowned, like mournful lovers. But now, the surprising thing was that it was he who held back. He who said:

'What a marvelous listener you are. When you look at me with those wild eyes I feel that I could tell you things that I would never breathe to another human being.'

Was there just a hint of mockery in his voice or was it her fancy? She could not be sure.

'Before I met you,' he said, 'I had never spoken of myself to anybody. How well I remember one night, the night that I brought you the little Christmas tree, telling you all about my childhood. And of how I was so miserable that I ran away and lived under a cart in our yard for two days without being discovered. And you listened, and your eyes shone, and I felt that you had even made the little Christmas tree listen too, as in a fairy story.'

But of that evening she had remembered a little pot of caviare. It had cost seven and sixpence. He could not get over it. Think of it—a tiny jar like that costing seven and sixpence. While she ate it he watched her, delighted and shocked.

'No, really, that is eating money. You could not get seven shillings into a little pot that size. Only think of the profit they must make. ...' And he had begun some immensely complicated calculations. ... But now good-bye to the caviare. The Christmas tree was on the table, and the little boy lay under the cart with his head pillowed on the yard dog.

'The dog was called Bosun,' she cried delightedly.

But he did not follow. 'Which dog? Had you a dog? I don't remember a dog at all.'

'No, no. I meant the yard dog when you were a little boy.' He laughed and snapped the cigarette case to.

'Was he? Do you know I had forgotten that. It seems such ages ago. I cannot believe that it is only six years. After I had recognized you today—I had to take such a leap—I had to take a leap over my whole life to get back to that time. I was such a kid then.' He drummed on the table. 'I've often thought how I must have bored you. And now I understand so perfectly why you wrote to me as you did—although at the time that letter nearly finished my life. I found it again the other day, and I couldn't help laughing as I read it. It was so clever—such a true picture of me.' He glanced up. 'You're not going?'

She had buttoned her collar again and drawn down her veil.

'Yes, I am afraid I must,' she said, and managed a smile. Now she knew that he had been mocking.

'Ah, no, please,' he pleaded. 'Don't go just for a moment,' and he caught up one of her gloves from the table and clutched at it as if that would hold her. 'I see so few people to talk to nowadays, that I have turned into a sort of barbarian,' he said. 'Have I said something to hurt you?'

'Not a bit,' she lied. But as she watched him draw her glove through his fingers, gently, gently, her anger really did die down, and besides, at the moment he looked more like himself of six years ago. ...

'What I really wanted then,' he said softly, 'was to be a sort of carpet—to make myself into a sort of carpet for you to walk on so that you need not be hurt by the sharp stones and the mud that you hated so. It was nothing more positive than that—nothing more selfish. Only I did desire, eventually, to turn into a magic carpet and carry you away to all those lands you longed to see.'

As he spoke she lifted her head as though she drank something; the strange beast in her bosom began to purr. ...

'I felt that you were more lonely than anybody else in the world,' he went on, 'and yet, perhaps, that you were the only person in the world who was really, truly alive. Born out of your time,' he murmured, stroking the glove, 'fated.'

Ah, God! What had she done! How had she dared to throw away her happiness like this. This was the only man who had ever understood her. Was it too late? Could it be too late? *She* was that glove that he held in his fingers. ...

'And then the fact that you had no friends and never had made friends with people. How I understood that, for neither had I. Is it just the same now?'

'Yes,' she breathed. 'Just the same. I am as alone as ever.'

'So am I,' he laughed gently, 'just the same.'

Suddenly with a quick gesture he handed her back the glove and scraped his chair on the floor. 'But what seemed to me so mysterious then is perfectly plain to me now. And to you, too, of course. ... It simply was that we were such egoists, so self-engrossed, so wrapped up in ourselves that we hadn't a corner in our hearts for anybody else. Do you know,' he cried, naïve and hearty, and dreadfully like another side of that old self again, 'I began studying a Mind System when I was in Russia, and I found that we were not peculiar at all. It's quite a well known form of ...'

She had gone. He sat there, thunder-struck, astounded beyond words. ... And then he asked the waitress for his bill.

'But the cream has not been touched,' he said. 'Please do not charge me for it.'

Alice Munro

Alice Munro was born in Wingham, Ontario, in 1931 and grew up in a Huron County farming community, where her father raised silver foxes. After two years at the University of Western Ontario, she married and moved to Vancouver and then Victoria, where raising children and working in a bookstore left little time for writing. In 1968, at the age of thirty-seven, she published *Dance of the Happy Shades*, which won the Governor General's Award for fiction. This was followed by a collection of interlocking short stories called *Lives of Girls and Women* (1971), *Something I've Been Meaning to Tell You* (1974), *Who Do You Think You Are?* (1978), *The Moons of Jupiter* (1982), *The Progress of Love* (1986), *Friend of My Youth* (1990), *Open Secrets* (1994), *Selected Stories* (1996), and *The Love of a Good Woman* (1998), for which she won the Giller Prize. Her stories, which have won numerous awards, share certain affinities with the work of such Southern writers as Eudora Welty and Flannery O'Connor: "It was nothing ... definite," Munro says. "It was more like a way you could see ordinary life. A way of seeing perhaps grotesque things, comic things. It wasn't anything technical, though I imitate techniques without thinking about it. ..."

There is a paragraph at the end of "Who Do You Think You Are?" that seems to embody a central concern in Munro's fiction—the relation of verisimilitude to moral sympathy. The central figure, Rose, feels a certain shame for her acting talents, a shame that, perhaps, she has, in her devotion to surface and gesture—to appearances—missed the essence of a character: "The thing she was ashamed of, in acting, was that she might he paying attention to the wrong things, reporting antics, when there was always something further, a tone, a depth, a light, that she couldn't get and wouldn't get." Rose's dilemma is also the dilemma of her creator, whose concern for both accuracy and depth keeps her on the trail of a character or story or situation when most authors would lay down their pens, satisfied with a minor victory or revelation. That urgency to know all—not necessarily to tell all, of course—informs all her work.

In an interview with Geoff Hancock, published in *Canadian Fiction Magazine*, Munro dismisses both plot and setting as essential ingredients in fiction. "What happens as event doesn't really matter much. When the event becomes the thing that matters, the story isn't working too well." Feeling, she says, must predominate over both plot and setting. "I don't think the setting matters at all. A lot of people think I'm a regional writer. And I use the region where I grew up a lot. But I don't have any idea of writing to show the kind of things that happen in a certain place. These things happen and the place is part of it. But, in a way, it's incidental."

In order to create a feeling, or climate, in a story, Munro depends on her eye for texture and detail. "I know I get excited by ordinary things," Munro says. "Even totally commonplace things like a shopping centre and a supermarket and things like that are just sort of endlessly interesting in their physical reality. I find them that way. That they seem to mean something beyond themselves. But I can't explain much more than that." She differentiates between the person she is, who would lament the destruction of woodland to put up a service station, and the writer in her, who would find the comings and goings at that station endlessly fascinating.

On the genesis and gestation of stories, Munro's observations are fascinating. "I have this picture. It generates some other images and attracts them like a magnet." She describes herself as a juggler, trying to keep these images and anecdotes in the air; then, as an architect without a blueprint, striving to discover the structure or form that will house the feeling, the "soul of the story," that has been building up in her. "A story must be made in the same way our dreams are made, truth in them being cast, with what seems to us often a rather high-handed frivolity, in any kind of plausible, implausible, giddy, strange, humdrum terms at all. This is the given story ... and from that I work, getting no more help, doing the hard repetitive work of putting it in words that are hardly any good at all, then a little better, then quite a bit better, at times satisfactory."

"I love doing things right. All that accuracy," Munro says, even if doing things right involves making the story deliberately grainy or awkward. In an interview with Alan Twigg in *Strong Voices*, Munro admits her lack of sympathy for literary expressionism, the free-fall and let-it-all-hang-out school of writing: "It's as if I must take great care of everything. Instead of splashing the colours off and trusting that they will all come together." Her concern for accuracy extends not only to language and form, but also to the desire for psychological realism that drives her writing. As she explains to Hancock: "I like to look at people's lives over a number of years, without continuity. Like catching them in snapshots. And I like the way people relate, or don't relate, to the people they were earlier. This is the sense of life that interests me a lot. ... I think this is why I'm not drawn to writing novels. Because I don't see that people develop and arrive somewhere. I just see people living in flashes."

The Shining Houses

Mary sat on the back steps of Mrs. Fullerton's house, talking—or really listening—to Mrs. Fullerton, who sold her eggs. She had come in to pay the egg money, on her way to Edith's Debbie's birthday party. Mrs. Fullerton did not pay calls herself and she did not invite them, but, once a business pretext was established, she liked to talk. And Mary found herself exploring her neighbour's life as she had once explored the lives of grandmothers and aunts—by pretending to know less than she did, asking for some story she had heard before; this way, remembered episodes emerged each time with slight differences of content, meaning, colour, yet with a pure reality that usually attaches to things which are at least part legend. She had almost forgotten that there are people whose lives can be seen like this. She did not talk to many old people any more. Most of the people she knew had lives like her own, in which things were not sorted out yet, and it is not certain if this thing, or that, should be taken seriously. Mrs. Fullerton had no doubts or questions of this kind. How was it possible, for instance, not to take seriously the broad blithe back of Mr. Fullerton, disappearing down the road on a summer day, not to return?

"I didn't know that," said Mary. "I always thought Mr. Fullerton was dead."

"He's no more dead than I am," said Mrs. Fullerton, sitting up straight. A bold Plymouth Rock walked across the bottom step and Mary's little boy, Danny, got up to give rather cautious chase. "He's just gone off on his travels, that's what he is. May of gone up north, may of gone to the States, I don't know.

But he's not dead. I would of felt it. He's not old neither, you know, not old like I am. He was my second husband, he was younger. I never made any want of it. I had this place and raised my children and buried my first husband, before ever Mr. Fullerton came upon the scene. Why, one time down in the post office we was standing together by the wicket and I went over to put a letter in the box and left my bag behind me, and Mr. Fullerton turns to go after me and the girl calls to him, she says, here, your mother's left her purse!"

Mary smiled, answering Mrs. Fullerton's high-pitched and not trustful laughter. Mrs. Fullerton was old, as she had said—older than you might think, seeing her hair still fuzzy and black, her clothes slatternly-gay, dime-store brooches pinned to her ravelling sweater. Her eyes showed it, black as plums, with a soft inanimate sheen; things sank into them and they never changed. The life in her face was all in the nose and mouth, which were always twitching, fluttering, drawing tight grimace-lines down her cheeks. When she came around every Friday on her egg deliveries her hair was curled, her blouse held together by a bunch of cotton flowers, her mouth painted, a spidery and ferocious line of red; she would not show herself to her new neighbours in any sad old-womanish disarray.

"Thought I was his mother," she said. "I didn't care. I had a good laugh. But what I was telling you," she said, "a day in summer, he was off work. He had the ladder up and he was picking me the cherries off of my black-cherry tree. I came out to hang my clothes and there was this man I never seen before in my life, taking the pail of cherries my husband hands down to him. Helping himself, too, not backward, he sat down and ate cherries out of my pail. Who's that, I said to my husband, and he says, just a fellow passing. If he's a friend of yours, I said, he's welcome to stay for supper. What are you talking about, he says, I never seen him before. So I never said another thing. Mr. Fullerton went and talked to him, eating my cherries I intended for a pie, but that man would talk to anybody, tramp, Jehovah's Witness, anybody—that didn't need to mean anything."

"And half an hour after that follow went off," she said, "Mr. Fullerton comes out in his brown jacket and his hat on. I have to meet a man downtown. How long will you be, I said. Oh, not long. So off he goes down the road, down to where the old tram went—we was all in the bush then—and something made me look after him. He must be hot in that coat, I said. And that's when I knew he wasn't coming back. Yet I couldn't've expected it, he liked it here. He was talking about putting chinchillas in the back yard. What's in a man's mind even when you're living with him you will never know."

"Was it long ago?" said Mary.

"Twelve years. My boys wanted me to sell then and go and live in rooms. But I said no. I had my hens and a nanny goat too at that time. More or less a pet. I had a pet coon too for a while, used to feed him chewing gum. Well, I said, husbands maybe come and go, but a place you've lived fifty years is something else. Making a joke of it with my family. Besides, I thought, if Mr. Fullerton was to come back, he'd come back here, not knowing where else to go. Of course he'd hardly know where to find me, the way it's changed now. But I always had the idea he might of suffered a loss of memory and it might come back. That has happened.

"I'm not complaining. Sometimes it seems to me about as reasonable a man should go as stay. I don't mind changes, either, that helps out my egg business. But this baby-sitting. All the time one or the other is asking me about baby-sitting. I tell them I got my own house to sit in and I raised my share of children."

Mary, remembering the birthday party, got up and called to her little boy. "I thought I might offer my black cherries for sale next summer," Mrs. Fullerton said. "Come and pick your own and they're fifty cents a box. I can't risk my old bones up a ladder no more."

"That's too much," Mary said, smiling. "They're cheaper than that at the supermarket." Mrs. Fullerton already hated the supermarket for lowering the price of eggs. Mary shook out her last cigarette and left it with her, saying she had another package in her purse. Mrs. Fullerton was fond of a cigarette but would not accept one unless you took her by surprise. Baby-sitting would pay for them, Mary thought. At the same time she was rather pleased with Mrs. Fullerton for being so unaccommodating. When Mary came out of this place, she always felt as if she were passing through barricades. The house and its surroundings were so self-sufficient, with their complicated and seemingly unalterable layout of vegetables and flower beds, apple and cherry trees, wired chicken-run, berry patch and wooden walks, woodpile, a great many roughly built dark little sheds, for hens or rabbits or a goat. Here was no open or straightforward plan, no order that an outsider could understand; yet what was haphazard time had made final. The place had become fixed, impregnable, all its accumulations necessary, until it seemed that even the washtubs, mops, couch springs and stacks of old police magazines on the back porch were there to stay.

Mary and Danny walked down the road that had been called, in Mrs. Fullerton's time, Wicks Road, but was now marked on the maps of the subdivision as Heather Drive. The name of the subdivision was Garden Place, and its streets were named for flowers. On either side of the road the earth was raw; the ditches were running full. Planks were laid across the open ditches, planks approached the doors of the newest houses. The new, white and shining houses, set side by side in long rows in the wound of the earth. She always thought of them as white houses, though of course they were not entirely white. They were stucco and siding, and only the stucco was white; the siding was painted in shades of blue, pink, green and yellow, all fresh and vivid colours. Last year, just at this time, in March, the bulldozers had come in to clear away the brush and second-growth and great trees of the mountain forest; in a little while the houses were going up among the boulders, the huge torn stumps, the unimaginable upheavals of that earth. The houses were frail at first, skeletons of new wood standing up in the dusk of the cold spring days. But the roofs went on, black and green, blue and red, and the stucco, the siding; the windows were put in, and plastered with signs that said, Murry's Glass, French's Hardwood Floors; it could be seen that the houses were real. People who would live in them came out and tramped around in the mud on Sundays. They were for people like Mary and her husband and their child, with not much money but expectations of more; Garden Place was already put down, in the minds of people who understood addresses, as less luxurious than Pine Hills but more desirable than Wellington Park. The bathrooms were beautiful, with three-part mirrors, ceramic tile, and coloured plumbing. The cupboards in the kitchen were light birch or mahogany, and there were copper lighting fixtures there and in the dining ells. Brick planters, matching the fireplaces, separated the living rooms and halls. The rooms were all large and light and the basements dry, and all this soundness and excellence seemed to be clearly, proudly indicated on the face of each house—those ingenuously similar houses that looked calmly out at each other, all the way down the street.

Today, since it was Saturday, all the men were out working around their houses. They were digging drainage ditches and making rookeries and clearing off and burning torn branches and brush. They worked with competitive violence and energy, all this being new to them; they were not men who made their livings by physical work. All day Saturday and Sunday they worked like this, so that in a year or two there should be green terraces, rock walls, shapely flower beds and ornamental shrubs. The earth must be heavy to dig now; it had been raining last night and this morning. But the day was brightening; the clouds had broken, revealing a long thin triangle of sky, its blue still cold and delicate, a winter colour. Behind the houses on one side of the road were pine trees, their ponderous symmetry not much stirred by any wind. These were to be cut down any day now, to make room for a shopping centre, which had been promised when the houses were sold.

And under the structure of this new subdivision, there was still something else to be seen; that was the old city, the old wilderness city that had lain on the side of the mountain. It had to be called a city because there were tramlines running into the woods, the houses had numbers and there were all the public buildings of a city, down by the water. But houses like Mrs. Fullerton's had been separated from each other by uncut forest and a jungle of wild blackberry and salmonberry bushes; these surviving houses, with thick smoke coming out of their chimneys, walls unpainted and patched and showing different degrees of age and darkening, rough sheds and stacked wood and compost heaps and grey board fences around them—these appeared every so often among the large new houses of Mimosa and Marigold and Heather Drive—enclosed, expressing something like savagery in their disorder and the steep, unmatched angles of roofs and lean-tos; not possible on these streets, but there.

"What are they saying," said Edith, putting on more coffee. She was surrounded in her kitchen by the ruins of the birthday party—cake and molded jellies and cookies with animal faces. A balloon rolled underfoot. The children had been fed, had posed for flash cameras and endured the birthday games; now they were playing in the back bedrooms and the basement, while their parents had coffee. "What are they saying in there?" said Edith.

"I wasn't listening," Mary said, holding the empty cream pitcher in her hand. She went to the sink window. The rent in the clouds had been torn wide open and the sun was shining. The house seemed too hot.

"Mrs. Fullerton's house," said Edith, hurrying back to the living-room. Mary knew what they were talking about. Her neighbours' conversation, otherwise not troubling, might at any moment snag itself on this subject and eddy menacingly in familiar circles of complaint, causing her to look despairingly out of windows, or down into her lap, trying to find some wonderful explanatory word to bring it to a stop; she did not succeed. She had to go back; they were waiting for cream.

A dozen neighbourhood women sat around the living room, absently holding the balloons they had been given by their children. Because the children on the street were so young, and also because any gathering-together of the people who lived there was considered a healthy thing in itself, most birthday parties were attended by mothers as well as children. Women who saw each other every day met now in earrings, nylons and skirts, with their hair fixed and faces applied. Some of the men were there too—Steve, who was Edith's husband, and others he had invited in for beer; they were all in their work clothes. The subject just introduced was one of the few on which male and female interest came together.

"I tell you what I'd do if I was next door to it," Steve said, beaming good-naturedly in expectation of laughter. "I'd send my kids over there to play with matches."

"Oh, funny," Edith said. "It's past joking. You joke, I try to do something. I even phoned the Municipal Hall."

"What did they say?" said Mary Lou Ross.

"Well *I* said couldn't they get her to paint it, at least, or pull down some of the shacks, and they said no they couldn't. I said I thought there must be some kind of ordinance applied to people like that and they said they knew how I *felt* and they were very *sorry*—"

"But no?"

"But no."

"But what about the chickens, I thought—"

"Oh, they wouldn't let you or me keep chickens, but she has some special dispensation about that too, I forgot how it goes."

"I'm going to stop buying them," Janie Inger said. "The supermarket's cheaper and who cares that much about fresh? And my God, the smell. I said to Carl I knew we were coming to the sticks but I somehow didn't picture us next door to a barnyard."

"Across the street is worse than next door. It makes me wonder why we ever bothered with a picture window, whenever anybody comes to see us I want to draw the drapes so they won't see what's across from us."

"Okay, okay," Steve said, cutting heavily through these female voices. "What Carl and I started out to tell you was that, if we can work this lane deal, she has got to go. It's simple and it's legal. That's the beauty of it."

"What lane deal?"

"We are getting to that. Carl and I been cooking this for a couple of weeks, but we didn't like to say anything in case it didn't work out. Take it, Carl."

"Well she's on the lane allowance, that's all," Carl said. He was a real estate salesman, stocky, earnest, successful. "I had an idea it might be that way, so I went down to the Municipal Hall and looked it up."

"What does that mean, dear?" said Janie, casual, wifely.

"This is it," Carl said. "There's an allowance for a lane, there always has been, the idea being if the area ever got built up they would put a lane through. But they never thought that would happen, people just built where they liked. She's got part of her house and half a dozen shacks sitting right where the lane has to go through. So what we do now, we get the municipality to put through a lane. We need a lane anyway. Then she has to get out. It's the law."

"It's the law," said Steve, radiating admiration. "What a smart boy. These real estate operators are smart boys."

"Does she get anything?" said Mary Lou. "I'm sick of looking at it and all but I don't want to see anybody in the poorhouse."

"Oh, she'll get paid. More than it's worth. Look, it's to her advantage. She'll get paid for it, and she couldn't sell it, she couldn't give it away."

Mary set her coffee cup down before she spoke and hoped her voice would sound all right, not emotional or scared. "But remember she's been here a long time," she said. "She was here before most of us were born," She was trying desperately to think of other words, words more sound and reasonable than these; she could not expose to this positive tide any notion that they might think flimsy and romantic, or she would destroy her argument. But she had no argument. She could try all night and never find any words to stand up to their words, which came at her now invincibly from all sides: *shack*, *eyesore*, *filth*, *property*, *value*.

"Do you honestly think that people who let their property get so rundown have that much claim to our consideration?" Janie said, feeling her husband's plan was being attacked.

"She's been here forty years, now we're here," Carl said. "So it goes. And whether you realize it or not, just standing there that house is bringing down the resale value of every house on this street. I'm in the business, I know."

And these were joined by other voices; it did not matter much what they said as long as they were full of self-assertion and anger. That was their strength, proof of their adulthood, of themselves and their seriousness. The spirit of anger rose among them, bearing up their young voices, sweeping them together as on a flood of intoxication, and they admired each other in this new behaviour as property-owners as people admire each other for being drunk.

"We might as well get everybody now," Steve said. "Save going around to so many places."

It was supper time, getting dark out. Everybody was preparing to go home, mothers buttoning their children's coats, children clutching, without much delight, their balloons and whistles and paper baskets full of jelly beans. They had stopped fighting, almost stopped noticing each other; the party had disintegrated. The adults too had grown calmer and felt tired.

"Edith! Edith, have you got a pen?"

Edith brought a pen and they spread the petition for the lane, which Carl had drawn up, on the dining-room table, clearing away the paper plates with smears of dried ice cream. People began to sign mechanically as they said goodbye. Steve was still scowling slightly; Carl stood with one hand on the paper, businesslike, but proud. Mary knelt on the floor and struggled with Danny's zipper. She got up and put on her own coat, smoothed her hair, put on her gloves and took them off again. When she could not think of anything else to do she walked past the dining-room table on her way to the door. Carl held out the pen.

"I can't sign that," she said. Her face flushed up, at once, her voice was trembling. Steve touched her shoulder.

"What's the matter, honey?"

"I don't think we have the right. We haven't the right."

"Mary, don't you care how things look? You live here too."

"No, I—I don't care." Oh, wasn't it strange, how in your imagination, when you stood up for something, your voice rang, people started, abashed; but in real life they all smiled in rather a special way and you saw that what you had really done was serve yourself up as a conversational delight for the next coffee party.

"Don't worry, Mary, she's got money in the bank," Janie said. "She must have. I asked her to baby-sit for me once and she practically spit in my face. She isn't exactly a charming old lady, you know."

"I know she isn't a charming old lady," Mary said.

Steve's hand still rested on her shoulder. "Hey what do you think we are, a bunch of ogres?"

"Nobody wants to turn her out just for the fun of it," Carl said. "Its unfortunate. We all know that. But we have to think of the community."

"Yes," said Mary. But she put her hands in the pockets of her coat and to say thank you to Edith, thank you for the birthday party. It occurred to her that they were right, for themselves, for whatever it was they had to be. And Mrs. Fullerton was old, she had dead eyes, nothing could touch her. Mary went out and walked with Danny up the street. She saw the curtains being drawn across living-room windows; cascades of flowers, of leaves, of geometrical designs, shut off these rooms from the night. Outside it was quite dark, the white houses were growing dim, the clouds breaking and breaking, and smoke blowing from Mrs. Fullerton's chimney. The pattern of Garden Place, so assertive in the daytime, seemed to shrink at night into the raw black mountainside.

The voices in the living room have blown away, Mary thought. If they would blow away and their plans be forgotten, if one thing could be left alone. But these are people who win, and they are good people; they want homes for their children, they help each other when there is trouble, they plan a community—saying that word as if they found a modern and well-proportioned magic in it, and no possibility anywhere of a mistake.

There is nothing you can do at present but put your hands in your pockets and keep a disaffected heart.

Vladimir Nabokov

Vladimir Nabokov was born in 1899 in St. Petersburg to a family of liberal landowners who fell afoul of both the Czar and the Bolsheviks and were forced to flee Russia in 1919. He completed his formal education at Cambridge University in 1922, the same year his father was assassinated in Berlin. He supported himself by teaching languages and tennis while pursuing his lifelong interests in butterflies, chess, and writing in German, French, and Russian. When the Germans invaded France, Nabokov emigrated with his Jewish wife to the United States, where he became a citizen, translated more of his work into English, and taught at Wellesley, Cornell, and Stanford Universities. He described himself in an interview as "an American writer born in Russia and educated in England where I studied French literature before spending fifteen years in Germany." According to Nabokov, writing in English "was exceedingly painful, like learning anew to handle things after losing seven or eight fingers in an explosion." He is best known for his novel *Lolita* (1955), about the love of an older man for a young girl, but he has written many other volumes of fiction including *Laughter in the Dark* (1938), *Pnin* (1957), portions of which appeared in *The New Yorker*, *Nabokov's Dozen* (1958), *Pale Fire* (1962), *Nabokov's Quartet* (1966), *Ada: Or, Ardor: A Family Chronicle* (1969) He retired to Montreux, Switzerland, in 1962 and died there in 1977.

Like so many of his favourite writers, including Pushkin, Tolstoy, Gogol, and Chekhov, Nabokov was fascinated by that "sudden slanting of the rational plane of life" which reveals us in all our glory and absurdity. He admired the richness of detail in Chekhov's "quiet" stories, as well as the subtle transitions, and the way the stories fade away without offering any final solution. About Chekhov's "The Lady with the Pet Dog," he writes: "All the traditional rules of story telling have been broken in this wonderful short story of twenty or so pages. There is no problem, no regular climax, no point at the end. And it is one of the greatest stories ever written."

Nabokov was described by Ihab Hassan as having "an antic and subversive disposition." He is a great wit and parodist who loves verbal play, including puns, irrational twists, and the principle of disorganization, most of his books consisting of various literary tricks with mirrors, a combination of effects not always praised by the critics. While granting him the most allusive prose style since James Joyce, Anthony Burgess nevertheless complains that "There is something in Nabokov's vocabulary that is contemptuous of the ordinary reader's difficulties ... just as there is something in his approach to the America of *Lolita* that is supercilious, world-weary, cynically 'European.'" His later work, particularly *Ada*, was attacked by critics in the *Yale Review* as pedantic and overdecorated. According to Mary Ellmann, Nabokov "is subject to the same disjunctive sense of words in the present as of objects in the past, but while all the returns to the concrete are humid, these excursions into the abstract are arid. ... It is all evidently intended to be a perilous, marvelous balance, in the end, of lust and lucubration, a linguist's love-nest."

Nabokov struggled between the man and the "fictionist" in himself, the individual who recalls and the writer who creates. One of the most useful works for students of his fiction is his autobiography, *Speak, Memory* (1947, revised 1966), which contains delightful insights into his recollective and creative processes. For Nabokov, as for Conrad, writing was a means of taking hold of and preserving the past, as is evident in this memory of his uncle "gloating over a tattered book. A sense of security, of well-being, of summer warmth pervades my memory. That robust reality makes a ghost of the present. The mirror brims with brightness; a bumblebee has entered the room and bumps against the ceiling. Everything is as it should be, nothing will ever change, nobody will ever die." Of course the boundaries between life and art occasionally blur, as they do when he thinks of precious objects from years past: "Somewhere, in the apartment house of a chapter, in the hired rooms of a paragraph, I have also placed that tilted mirror, and the lamp, and the chandelier drops." In this process of recall, or rescue, the self dissolves; so, too, does time.

"I confess I do not believe in time. I like to fold my magic carpet, after use, in such a way as to superimpose one part of the pattern upon another. Let visitors trip. And the highest enjoyment of timelessness—in a landscape selected at random—is when I stand among rare butterflies and their food plants. This is ecstacy, and behind the ecstacy is something else, which is hard to explain. It is like a momentary vacuum into which rushes all that I love. A sense of oneness with sun and stone. A thrill of gratitude to whom it may concern—to the contrapuntal genius of human fate or to tender ghosts humoring a lucky mortal."

The task of the writer is not, after all, unlike that of the lover and the lepidopterist, whose jobs are to recognize, or be open to the discovery of, patterns in nature, the beloved, and everyday experience: "It occurs to me that the closest reproduction of the mind's birth obtainable is the stab of wonder that accompanies the precise moment when, gazing at a tangle of twigs and leaves, one suddenly realizes that what had seemed a natural component of that tangle is a marvelously disguised insect or bird."

Signs and Symbols

I

For the fourth time in as many years they were confronted with the problem of what birthday present to bring a young man who was incurably deranged in his mind. He had no desires. Man-made objects were to him either hives of evil, vibrant with a malignant activity that he alone could perceive, or gross comforts for which no use could be found in his abstract world. After eliminating a number of articles that might offend him or frighten him (anything in the gadget line for instance was taboo), his parents chose a dainty and innocent trifle: a basket with ten different fruit jellies in ten little jars.

At the time of his birth they had been married already for a long time; a score of years had elapsed, and now they were quite old. Her drab gray hair was done anyhow. She wore cheap black dresses. Unlike other women of her age (such as Mrs. Sol, their next-door neighbor, whose face was all pink and mauve with paint and whose hat was a cluster of brookside flowers), she presented a naked white countenance to the fault-finding light of spring days. Her husband, who in the old country had been a fairly successful businessman, was now wholly dependent on his brother Isaac, a real American of almost forty years standing. They seldom saw him and had nicknamed him "the Prince."

That Friday everything went wrong. The underground train lost its life current between two stations, and for a quarter of an hour one could hear nothing but the dutiful beating of one's heart and the rustling of newspapers. The bus they had to take next kept them waiting for ages; and when it did come, it was crammed with garrulous high school children. It was raining hard as they walked up the brown path leading to the sanatorium. There they waited again; and instead of their boy shuffling into the room as he usually did (his poor face botched with acne, ill-shaven, sullen, and confused), a nurse they knew, and did not care for, appeared at last and brightly explained that he had again attempted to take his life. He was all right, she said, but a visit might disturb him. The place was so miserably understaffed, and things got mislaid or mixed up so easily, that they decided not to leave their present in the office but to bring it to him next time they came.

She waited for her husband to open his umbrella and then took his arm. He kept clearing his throat in a special resonant way he had when he was upset. They reached the bus-stop shelter on the other side of the street and he closed his umbrella. A few feet away, under a swaying and dripping tree, a tiny half-dead unfledged bird was helplessly twitching in a puddle.

During the long ride to the subway station, she and her husband did not exchange a word; and every time she glanced at his old hands (swollen veins, brown-spotted skin), clasped and twitching upon the handle of his umbrella, she felt the mounting pressure of tears. As she looked around trying to hook her mind onto something, it gave her a kind of soft shock, a mixture of compassion and wonder, to notice that one of the passengers, a girl with dark hair and grubby red toenails, was weeping on the shoulder of an older woman. Whom did that woman resemble? She resembled Rebecca Borisovna, whose daughter had married one of the Soloveichiks—in Minsk, years ago.

The last time he had tried to do it, his method had been, in the doctor's words, a masterpiece of inventiveness; he would have succeeded, had not an envious fellow patient thought be was learning to fly—and stopped him. What he really wanted to do was to tear a hole in his world and escape.

The system of his delusions had been the subject of an elaborate paper in a scientific monthly, but long before that she and her husband had puzzled it out for themselves. "Referential mania," Herman Brink had called it. In these very rare cases the patient imagines that everything happening around him is a veiled reference to his personality and existence. He excludes real people from the conspiracy—because he considers himself to be so much more intelligent than other men. Phenomenal nature shadows him wherever he goes. Clouds in the staring sky transmit to one another, by means of slow signs, incredibly detailed information regarding him. His inmost thoughts are discussed at nightfall, in manual alphabet, by darkly gesticulating trees. Pebbles or stains or sun flecks form patterns representing in some awful way messages which he must intercept. Everything is a cipher and of everything he is the theme. Some of the spies are detached observers, such as glass surfaces and still pools; others, such as coats in store windows, are prejudiced witnesses, lynchers at heart; others again (running water, storms) are hysterical to the point of insanity, have a distorted opinion of him, and grotesquely misinterpret his actions. He must be always on his guard and devote every minute and module of life to the decoding of the undulation of things. The very air he exhales is indexed and filed away. If only the interest he provokes were limited to his immediate surroundings—but alas it is not! With distance the torrents of wild scandal increase in volume and volubility. The silhouettes of his blood corpuscles, magnified a million times, flit over vast plains; and still farther, great mountains of unbearable solidity and height sum up in terms of granite and groaning firs the ultimate truth of his being.

II

When they emerged from the thunder and foul air of the subway, the last dregs of the day were mixed with the streetlights. She wanted to buy some fish for supper, so she handed him the basket of jelly jars, telling him to go home. He walked up to the third landing and then remembered he had given her his keys earlier in the day.

In silence he sat down on the steps and in silence rose when some ten minutes later she came, heavily trudging upstairs, wanly smiling, shaking her head in deprecation of her silliness. They entered their two-room flat and he at once went to the mirror. Straining the corners of his mouth apart by means of his thumbs, with a horrible masklike grimace, he removed his new hopelessly uncomfortable dental plate and severed the long tusks of saliva connecting him to it. He read his Russian-language newspaper while she laid the table. Still reading, he ate the pale victuals that needed no teeth. She knew his moods and was also silent.

When he had gone to bed, she remained in the living room with her pack of soiled cards and her old albums. Across the narrow yard where the rain tinkled in the dark against some battered ash cans, windows were blandly alight and in one of them a black-trousered man with his bare elbows raised could be seen lying supine on an untidy bed. She pulled the blind down and examined the photographs. As a baby he looked more surprised than most babies. From a fold in the album, a German maid they had had in Leipzig and her fat-faced fiancé fell out. Minsk, the Revolution, Leipzig, Berlin, Leipzig, a slanting housefront badly out of focus. Four years old, in a park: moodily, shyly, with puckered forehead, looking away from an eager squirrel as he would from any other stranger. Aunt Rosa, a fussy, angular, wild-eyed old lady, who had lived in a tremulous world of bad news, bankruptcies, train accidents, cancerous growths—until the Germans put her to death, together with all the people she had worried about. Age six—that was when he drew wonderful birds with human hands and feet, and suffered from insomnia like a grown-up man. His cousin, now a famous chess player. He again, aged about eight, already difficult to understand, afraid of the wallpaper in the passage, afraid of a certain picture in a book which merely showed an idyllic landscape with rocks on a hillside and an old cart wheel hanging from the branch of a leafless tree. Aged ten: the year they left Europe. The shame, the pity, the humiliating difficulties, the ugly, vicious, backward children he was with in that special school. And then came a time in his life, coinciding with a long convalescence after pneumonia, when those little phobias of his which his parents had stubbornly regarded as the eccentricities of a prodigiously gifted child hardened as it were into a dense tangle of logically interacting illusions, making him totally inaccessible to normal minds.

This, and much more, she accepted—for after all living did mean accepting the loss of one joy after another, not even joys in her case—mere possibilities of improvement. She thought of the endless waves of pain that for some reason or other she and her husband had to endure; of the invisible giants hurting her boy in some unimaginable fashion; of the incalculable amount of tenderness contained in the world; of the fate of this tenderness, which is either crushed, or wasted, or transformed into madness; of neglected children humming to themselves in unswept corners; of beautiful weeds that cannot hide from the farmer and helplessly have to watch the shadow of his simian stoop leave mangled flowers in its wake, as the monstrous darkness approaches.

III

It was past midnight when from the living room she heard her husband moan; and presently he staggered in, wearing over his nightgown the old overcoat with astrakhan collar which he much preferred to the nice blue bathrobe he had.

"I can't sleep," he cried.

"Why," she asked, "why can't you sleep? You were so tired."

"I can't sleep because I am dying," he said and lay down on the couch.

"Is it your stomach? Do you want me to call Dr. Solov?"

"No doctors, no doctors," he moaned. "To the devil with doctors! We must get him out of there quick. Otherwise we'll be responsible. Responsible!" he repeated and hurled himself into a sitting position, both feet on the floor, thumping his forehead with his clenched fist.

"All right," she said quietly, "we shall bring him home tomorrow morning."

"I would like some tea," said her husband, and retired to the bathroom.

Bending with difficulty, she retrieved some playing cards and a photograph or two that had slipped from the couch to the floor: knave of hearts, nine of spades, ace of spades, Elsa and her bestial beau.

He returned in high spirits, saying in a loud voice, "I have it all figured out. We will give him the bedroom. Each of us will spend part of the night near him and the other part on this couch. By turns. We will have the doctor see him at least twice a week. It does not matter what the Prince says. He won't have to say much anyway because it will come out cheaper."

The telephone rang. It was an unusual hour for their telephone to ring. His left slipper had come off and he groped for it with his heel and toe as he stood in the middle of the room, and childishly, toothlessly, gaped at his wife. Having more English than he did, it was she who attended to calls.

"Can I speak to Charlie," said a girl's dull little voice.

"What number you want? No. That is not the right number."

The receiver was gently cradled. Her hand went to her old tired heart.

"It frightened me," she said.

He smiled a quick smile and immediately resumed his excited monologue. They would fetch him as soon as it was day. Knives would have to be kept in a locked drawer. Even at his worst he presented no danger to other people.

The telephone rang a second time. The same toneless anxious young voice asked for Charlie.

"You have the incorrect number. I will tell you what you are doing: you are turning the letter O instead of the zero."

They sat down to their unexpected festive midnight tea. The birthday present stood on the table. He sipped noisily; his face was flushed; every now and then he imparted a circular motion to his raised glass so as to make the sugar dissolve more thoroughly. The vein on the side of his bald head where there was a large birthmark stood out conspicuously and, although he had shaved that morning, a silvery bristle showed on his chin. While she poured him another glass of tea, he put on his spectacles and reexamined with pleasure the luminous yellow, green, red little jars. His clumsy moist lips spelled out their eloquent labels: apricot, grape, beech plum, quince. He had got to crab apple, when the telephone rang again.

Flannery O'Connor

Flannery O'Connor was born in 1925 in Savannah, Georgia, but her father's affliction with disseminated lupus forced the family to move back to the security of Milledgeville, where her ancestors had lived since prior to the Civil War. Her rigorous Catholic upbringing did not prevent her from pursuing her literary interests in high school and then at Georgia State College for Women. A literary fellowship took her to the Writers' Workshop at the University of Iowa, where she earned her M.F.A. in 1946 and sold her first story. She attended the Yaddo writers' colony in Saratoga Springs, New York, where she made various contacts that helped her towards the publication of her work. In 1950, she became ill with the same disease that had killed her father, so she moved from New York back to the family dairy farm in Milledgeville, where she wrote and raised peacocks and from whence, while her health permitted, she made frequent sallies to teach, lecture, and serve as writer-in-residence. Before her death in 1964, she had published two novels, *Wise Blood* (1952) and *The Violent Bear It Away* (1960), and written thirty-one short stories, collected in *A Good Man Is Hard to Find* (1955) and in the posthumous volume, *Everything That Rises Must Converge* (1965). Her *Complete Stories* won the National Book Award for fiction in 1972.

Readers are fortunate to have not only O'Connor's fiction, but also her remarkable observations on the creative process in *Mystery and Manners* (1969), particularly on the relation between craft and vision. She once said, "The only way, I think, to learn to write stories is to write them and then try to discover what you have done," but she had some very practical statements to make as well. She had no use for thematic criticism and used to bristle at the mention of the word *theme*; her own work was a struggle for what she called *meaning*, but she felt that meaning was inseparable from the words themselves. "A story isn't any good unless it successfully resists paraphrase, unless it hangs on and expands in the mind." She felt that a good story was likely to be regional, literal, and rooted in the senses. "A good story is literal in the same sense that a child's drawing is literal. When a child draws, he doesn't intend to distort what he sees, and as his gaze is direct, he sees the lines that create motion. Now the lines of motion that interest the writer are usually invisible. They are the lines of spiritual motion."

By regional writing, she meant not parochialism or local colour, but "reading a small history in a universal light." "It is the knowledge that the writer finds in his community. When he ceases to find it there, he will cease to write, or at least he will cease to write anything enduring. The writer operates at a peculiar crossroads where time and place and eternity somehow meet. His problem is to find that location." Like the work of Faulkner and Margaret Laurence and Alice Munro, her so-called regional stories are universal precisely because they put down a taproot that reaches to the wellsprings of human emotion.

Although she is a Christian writer, O'Connor never uses religious dogma or ideas as props in her fiction. Her primary concern in terms of craft, which she shares with Conrad, is to reach the reader through sensory images: "Fiction begins where human knowledge begins—with the senses—and every fiction writer is bound by this fundamental aspect of his medium." "He appeals through the senses, and you cannot appeal to the senses through abstractions." She aims for a gradual accumulation of detail, slower in the novel than in the story. "It's always necessary to remember that the fiction writer is much less immediately concerned with grand ideas and bristling emotions than he is with putting list slippers on clerks."

The accretions of detail that interest her are most often the dress, habits, and patterns of speech of her characters. "If you start with a real personality, a real character, then something is bound to happen; and you don't know what before you begin. In fact, it may be better if you don't know what before you begin. You ought to be able to discover something from your stories. If you don't, probably nobody else will." There are two qualities, she says, that make good fiction: "One is the sense of mystery and the other is the sense of manners. You get the manners from the texture of existence that surrounds you."

And where do you get the mystery? Probably not from teachers: "the teacher's work is largely negative ... largely a matter of saying 'This doesn't work because ...' or 'This does work because.' The *because* is very important ... So many people can now write competent stories that the short story is in danger of dying of competence. We want competence, but competence by itself is deadly. What is needed is the vision to go with it, and you do not get this from a writing class." In the end, craft alone is not enough. "The peculiar problem of the short story writer is how to make the action he describes reveal as much of the mystery of existence as possible."

For O'Connor art is a form of revelation, but one that mirrors the revelation of fallen man raised again by Christ's redemptive act. So the stories themselves are not so much realistic portraits of life seen, as parables of life experienced, by the visionary artist or prophet: "The prophet is a *realist of distances*, and it is this kind of realism that you find in the best modern instances of the grotesque" (italics added).

Good Country People

Besides the neutral expression that she wore when she was alone, Mrs. Freeman had two others, forward and reverse, that she used for all her human dealings. Her forward expression was steady and driving like the advance of a heavy truck. Her eyes never swerved to left or right but turned as the story turned as if they followed a yellow line down the center of it. She seldom used the other expression because it was not often necessary for her to retract a statement, but when she did, her face came to a complete stop, there was an almost imperceptible movement of her black eyes, during which they seemed to be receding, and then the observer would see that Mrs. Freeman, though she might stand there as real as several grain sacks thrown on top of each other, was no longer there in spirit. As for getting anything across to her when this was the case, Mrs. Hopewell had given it up. She might talk her head off. Mrs. Freeman could never be brought to admit herself wrong on any point. She would stand there and if she could be brought to say anything, it was something like, "Well, I wouldn't of said it was and I wouldn't of said it wasn't," or letting her gaze range over the top kitchen shelf where there was an assortment of dusty bottles, she might remark, "I see you ain't ate many of them figs you put up last summer."

They carried on their most important business in the kitchen at breakfast. Every morning Mrs. Hopewell got up at seven o'clock and lit her gas heater and Joy's. Joy was her daughter, a large blonde girl who had an artificial leg. Mrs. Hopewell thought of her as a child though she was thirty-two years old and highly educated. Joy would get up while her mother was eating and lumber into the bathroom and slam the door, and before long, Mrs. Freeman would arrive at the back door. Joy would hear her mother call, "Come on in," and then they would talk for a while in low voices that were indistinguishable in the bathroom. By the time Joy came in, they had usually finished the weather report and were on one or the other of Mrs. Freeman's daughters, Glynese or Carramae. Joy called them Glycerin and Caramel. Glynese, a redhead, was eighteen and had many admirers; Carramae, a blonde, was only fifteen but already married and pregnant. She could not keep anything on her stomach. Every morning Mrs. Freeman told Mrs. Hopewell how many times she had vomited since the last report.

Mrs. Hopewell liked to tell people that Glynese and Carramae were two of the finest girls she knew and that Mrs. Freeman was a *lady* and that she was never ashamed to take her anywhere or introduce her to anybody they might meet. Then she would tell how she had happened to hire the Freemans in the first place and how they were a godsend to her and how she had had them four years. The reason for her keeping them so long was that they were not trash. They were good country people. She had telephoned the man whose name they had given as a reference and he had told her that Mr. Freeman was a good farmer but that his wife was the nosiest woman ever to walk the earth. "She's got to be into everything," the man said. "If she don't get there before the dust settles, you can bet she's dead, that's all. She'll want to know all your business. I can stand him real good," he had said, "but me nor my wife neither could have stood that woman one more minute on this place." That had put Mrs. Hopewell off for a few days.

She had hired them in the end because there were no other applicants but she had made up her mind beforehand exactly how she would handle the woman. Since she was the type who had to be into everything, then, Mrs. Hopewell had decided, she would not only let her be into everything, she would *see to it* that she was into everything—she would give her the responsibility of everything, she would put her in charge. Mrs. Hopewell had no bad qualities of her own but she was able to use other people's in such a constructive way that she never felt the lack. She had hired the Freemans and she had kept them four years.

Nothing is perfect. This was one of Mrs. Hopewell's favorite sayings. Another was: that is life! And still another, the most important, was: well, other people have their opinions too. She would make these statements, usually at the table, in a tone of gentle insistence as if no one held them but her, and the large hulking Joy, whose constant outrage had obliterated every expression from her face, would stare just a little to the side of her, her eyes icy blue, with the look of someone who had achieved blindness by an act of will and means to keep it.

When Mrs. Hopewell said to Mrs. Freeman that life was like that, Mrs. Freeman would say, "I always said so myself." Nothing had been arrived at by anyone that had not first been arrived at by her. She was quicker than Mr. Freeman. When Mrs. Hopewell said to her after they had been on the place a while, "You know, you're the wheel behind the wheel," and winked, Mrs. Freeman had said, "I know it, I've always been quick. It's some that are quicker than others."

"Everybody is different," Mrs. Hopewell said.

"Yes, most people is," Mrs. Freeman said.

"It takes all kinds to make the world."

"I always said it did myself."

The girl was used to this kind of dialogue for breakfast and more of it for dinner; sometimes they had it for supper too. When they had no guest they ate in the kitchen because that was easier. Mrs. Freeman always managed to arrive at some point during the meal and to watch them finish it. She would stand in the doorway if it were summer but in the winter she would stand with one elbow on top of the refrigerator and look down on them, or she would stand by the gas heater, lifting the back of her skirt slightly. Occasionally she would stand against the wall and roll her head from side to side. At no time was she in any hurry to leave. All this was very trying on Mrs. Hopewell but she was a woman of great patience. She realized that nothing is perfect and that in the Freemans she had good country people and that if, in this day and age, you get good country people, you had better hang onto them.

She had had plenty of experience with trash. Before the Freemans she had averaged one tenant family a year. The wives of these farmers were not the kind you would want to be around you for very long. Mrs. Hopewell, who had divorced her husband long ago, needed someone to walk over the fields with her; and when Joy had to be impressed for these services, her remarks were usually so ugly and her face so glum that Mrs. Hopewell would say, "If you can't come pleasantly, I don't want you at all," to which the girl, standing square and rigid-shouldered with her neck thrust slightly forward, would reply, "If you want me, here I am—LIKE I AM."

Mrs. Hopewell excused this attitude because of the leg (which had been shot off in a hunting accident when Joy was ten). It was hard for Mrs. Hopewell to realize that her child was thirty-two now and that for more than twenty years she had had only one leg. She thought of her still as a child because it tore her heart to think instead of the poor stout girl in her thirties who had never danced a step or had any *normal* good times. Her name was really Joy but as soon as she was twenty-one and away from home, she had had it legally changed. Mrs. Hopewell was certain that she had thought and thought until she had hit upon the ugliest name in any language. Then she had gone and had the beautiful name, Joy, changed without telling her mother until after she had done it. Her legal name was Hulga.

When Mrs. Hopewell thought the name, Hulga, she thought of the broad blank hull of a battleship. She would not use it. She continued to call her Joy to which the girl responded but in a purely mechanical way.

Hulga had learned to tolerate Mrs. Freeman who saved her from taking walks with her mother. Even Glynese and Carramae were useful when they occupied attention that might otherwise have been directed at her. At first she had thought she could not stand Mrs. Freeman for she had found that it was not possible to be rude to her. Mrs. Freeman would take on strange resentments and for days together she would be sullen but the source of her displeasure was always obscure; a direct attack, a positive leer, blatant ugliness to her face—these never touched her. And without warning one day, she began calling her Hulga.

She did not call her that in front of Mrs. Hopewell who would have been incensed but when she and the girl happened to be out of the house together, she would say something and add the name Hulga to the end of it, and the big spectacled Joy-Hulga would scowl and redden as if her privacy had been intruded upon. She considered the name her personal affair. She had arrived at it first purely on the basis of its ugly sound and then the full genius of its fitness had struck her. She had a vision of the name working like the ugly sweating Vulcan who stayed in the furnace and to whom, presumably, the goddess had to come when called. She saw it as the name of her highest creative act. One of her major triumphs was that her mother had not been able to turn her dust into Joy, but the greater one was that she had been able to turn it herself into Hulga. However, Mrs. Freeman's relish for using the name only irritated her. It was as if Mrs. Freeman's beady steel-pointed eyes had penetrated far enough behind her face to reach some secret fact. Something about her seemed to fascinate Mrs. Freeman and then one day Hulga realized that it was the artificial leg. Mrs. Freeman had a special fondness for the details of secret infections, hidden deformities, assaults upon children. Of diseases, she preferred the lingering or incurable. Hulga had heard Mrs. Hopewell give her the details of the hunting accident, how the leg had been literally blasted off, how she had never lost consciousness. Mrs. Freeman could listen to it any time as if it had happened an hour ago.

When Hulga stumped into the kitchen in the morning (she could walk without making the awful noise but she made it—Mrs. Hopewell was certain—because it was ugly-sounding), she glanced at them and did not speak. Mrs. Hopewell would be in her red kimono with her hair tied around her head in rags. She would be sitting at the table, finishing her breakfast and Mrs. Freeman would be hanging by her elbow outward from the refrigerator, looking down at the table. Hulga always put her eggs on the stove to boil and then stood over them with her arms folded, and Mrs. Hopewell would look at her—a kind of indirect gaze divided between her and Mrs. Freeman—and would think that if she would only keep herself up a little, she wouldn't be so bad looking. There was nothing wrong with her face that a pleasant expression wouldn't help. Mrs. Hopewell said that people who looked on the bright side of things would be beautiful even if they were not.

Whenever she looked at Joy this way, she could not help but feel that it would have been better if the child had not taken the Ph.D. It had certainly not brought her out any and now that she had it, there was no more excuse for her to go to school again. Mrs. Hopewell thought it was nice for girls to go to school to have a good time but Joy had "gone through." Anyhow, she would not have been strong enough to go again. The doctors had told Mrs. Hopewell that with the best of care, Joy might see forty-five. She had a weak heart. Joy had made it plain that if it had not been for this condition, she would be far from these red hills and good country people. She would be in a university lecturing to people who knew what she was talking about. And Mrs. Hopewell could very well picture her there, looking like a scarecrow and lecturing to more of the same. Here she went about all day in a six-year-old skirt and a yellow sweat shirt with a faded cowboy on a horse embossed on it. She thought this was funny; Mrs. Hopewell thought it was idiotic and showed simply that she was still a child. She was brilliant but she didn't have a grain of sense. It seemed to Mrs. Hopewell that every year she grew less like other people and more like herself—bloated, rude, and squint-eyed. And she said such strange things! To her own mother she had said—without warning, without excuse, standing up in the middle of a meal with her face purple and her mouth half full—"Woman! do you ever look inside? Do you ever look inside and see what you are *not*? God!" she had cried sinking down again and staring at her plate, "Malebranche was right: we are not our own light. We are not our own light!" Mrs. Hopewell had no idea to this day what brought that on. She had only made the remark, hoping Joy would take it in, that a smile never hurt anyone.

The girl had taken the Ph.D. in philosophy and this left Mrs. Hopewell at a complete loss. You could say, "My daughter is a nurse," or "My daughter is a school teacher," or even, "My daughter is a chemical engineer." You could not say, "My daughter is a philosopher." That was something that had ended with the Greeks and Romans. All day Joy sat on her deck in a deep chair, reading. Sometimes she went for walks but she didn't like dogs or cats or birds or flowers or nature or nice young men. She looked at nice young men as if she could smell their stupidity.

One day Mrs. Hopewell had picked up one of the books the girl had just put down and opening it at random, she read, "Science, on the other hand, has to assert its soberness and seriousness afresh and declare that it is concerned solely with what-is. Nothing—how can it be for science anything but a horror and a phantasm? If science is right, then one thing stands firm: science wishes to know nothing of nothing. Such is after all the strictly scientific approach to Nothing. We know it by wishing to know nothing of Nothing." These words had been underlined with a blue pencil and they worked on Mrs. Hopewell like some evil incantation in gibberish. She shut the book quickly and went out of the room as if she were having a chill.

This morning when the girl came in, Mrs. Freeman was on Carramae. "She's thrown up four times after supper," she said, "and was up twice in the night after three o'clock. Yesterday she didn't do nothing but ramble in the bureau drawer. All she did. Stand up there and see what she could run up on."

"She's got to eat," Mrs. Hopewell muttered, sipping her coffee, while she watched Joy's back at the stove. She was wondering what the child had said to the Bible salesman. She could not imagine what kind of a conversation she could possibly have had with him.

He was a tall gaunt hatless youth who had called yesterday to sell them a Bible. He had appeared at the door, carrying a large black suitcase that weighted him so heavily on one side that he had to brace himself against the door facing. He seemed on the point of collapse but he said in a cheerful voice, "Good morning, Mrs. Cedars!" and set the suitcase down on the mat. He was not a bad-looking young man though he had on a bright blue suit and yellow socks that were not pulled up far enough. He had prominent face bones and a streak of sticky-looking brown hair falling across his forehead.

"I'm Mrs. Hopewell," she said.

"Oh!" he said, pretending to look puzzled but with his eyes sparkling, "I saw it said 'The Cedars,' on the mailbox so I thought you was Mrs. Cedars!" and he burst out in a pleasant laugh. He picked up the satchel and under cover of a pant, he fell forward into her hall. It was rather as if the suitcase had moved first, jerking him after it. "Mrs. Hopewell!" he said and grabbed her hand. "I hope you are well!" and he laughed again and then all at once his face sobered completely. He paused and gave her a straight earnest look and said, "Lady, I've come to speak of serious things."

"Well, come in," she muttered, none too pleased because her dinner was almost ready. He came into the parlor and sat down on the edge of a straight chair and put the suitcase between his feet and glanced around the room as if he were sizing her up by it. Her silver gleamed on the two sideboards; she decided he had never been in a room as elegant as this.

"Mrs. Hopewell," he began, using her name in a way that sounded almost intimate, "I know you believe in Chrustian service."

"Well, yes," she murmured.

"I know," he said and paused, looking very wise with his head cocked on one side, "that you're a good woman. Friends have told me."

Mrs. Hopewell never liked to be taken for a fool. "What are you selling?" she asked.

"Bibles," the young man said and his eye raced around the room before he added, "I see you have no family Bible in your parlor, I see that is the one lack you got!"

Mrs. Hopewell could not say, "My daughter is an atheist and won't let me keep the Bible in the parlor." She said, stiffening slightly, "I keep my Bible by my bedside." This was not the truth. It was in the attic somewhere.

"Lady," he said, "the word of God ought to be in the parlor."

"Well, I think that's a matter of taste," she began. "I think ..."

"Lady," he said, "for a Chrustian, the word of God ought to be in every room in the house besides in his heart. I know you're a Chrustian because I can see it in every line of your face."

She stood up and said, "Well, young man, I don't want to buy a Bible and I smell my dinner burning."

He didn't get up. He began to twist his hands and looking down at them, he said softly, "Well lady, I'll tell you the truth—not many people want to buy one nowadays and besides, I know I'm real simple. I don't know how to say a thing but to say it. I'm just a country boy." He glanced up into her unfriendly face. "People like you don't like to fool with country people like me!"

"Why!" she cried, "good country people are the salt of the earth! Besides, we all have different ways of doing, it takes all kinds to make the world go 'round. That's life!"

"You said a mouthful," he said.

"Why, I think there aren't enough good country people in the world!" she said, stirred. "I think that's what's wrong with it!"

His face had brightened. "I didn't inraduce myself," he said. "I'm Manley Pointer from out in the country around Willohobie, not even from a place, just from near a place."

"You wait a minute," she said. "I have to see about my dinner." She went out to the kitchen and found Joy standing near the door where she had been listening.

"Get rid of the salt of the earth," she said, "and let's eat."

Mrs. Hopewell gave her a pained look and turned the heat down under the vegetables. "*I* can't be rude to anybody," she murmured and went back into the parlor.

He had opened the suitcase and was sitting with a Bible on each knee.

"You might as well put those up," she told him. "I don't want one."

"I appreciate your honesty," he said. "You don't see any more real honest people unless you go way out in the country."

"I know," she said, "real genuine folks!" Through the crack in the door she heard a groan.

"I guess a lot of boys come telling you they're working their way through college," he said, "but I'm not going to tell you that. Somehow," he said, "I don't want to go to college. I want to devote my life to Chrustian service. See," he said, lowering his voice, "I got this heart condition. I may not live long. When you know it's something wrong with you and you may not live long, well then, lady ..." He paused, with his mouth open, and stared at her.

He and Joy had the same condition! She knew that her eyes were filling with tears but she collected herself quickly and murmured, "Won't you stay for dinner? We'd love to have you!" and was sorry the instant she heard herself say it.

"Yes mam," he said in an abashed voice, "I would sher love to do that!"

Joy had given him one look on being introduced to him and then throughout the meal had not glanced at him again. He had addressed several remarks to her, which she had pretended not to hear. Mrs. Hopewell could not understand deliberate rudeness, although she lived with it, and she felt she had always to overflow with hospitality to make up for Joy's lack of courtesy. She urged him to talk about himself and he did. He said he was the seventh child of twelve and that his father had been crushed under a tree when he himself was eight year old. He had been crushed very badly, in fact, almost cut in two and was practically not recognizable. His mother had got along the best she could by hard working and she had always seen that her children went to Sunday School and that they read the Bible every evening. He was now nineteen year old and he had been selling Bibles for four months. In that time he had sold seventy-seven Bibles and had the promise of two more sales. He wanted to become a missionary because he thought that was the way you could do most for people. "He who losest his life shall find it," he said simply and he was so sincere, so genuine and earnest that Mrs. Hopewell would not for the world have smiled. He prevented his peas from sliding onto the table by blocking them with a piece of bread which he later cleaned his plate with. She could see Joy observing sidewise how he handled his knife and fork and she saw too that every few minutes, the boy would dart a keen appraising glance at the girl as if he were trying to attract her attention.

After dinner Joy cleared the dishes off the table and disappeared and Mrs. Hopewell was left to talk with him. He told her again about his childhood and his father's accident and about various things that had happened to him. Every five minutes or so she would stifle a yawn. He sat for two hours until finally she told him she must go because she had an appointment in town. He packed his Bibles and thanked her and prepared to leave, but in the doorway he stopped and wrung her hand and said that not on any of his trips had he met a lady as nice as her and he asked if he could come again. She had said she would always be happy to see him.

Joy had been standing in the road, apparently looking at something in the distance, when he came down the steps toward her, bent to the side with his heavy valise. He stopped where she was standing and confronted her directly. Mrs. Hopewell could not hear what he said but she trembled to think what Joy would say to him. She could see that after a minute Joy said something and that then the boy began to speak again, making an excited gesture with his free hand. After a minute Joy said something else at which the boy began to speak once more. Then to her amazement, Mrs. Hopewell saw the two of them walk off together, toward the gate. Joy had walked all the way to the gate with him and Mrs. Hopewell could not imagine what they had said to each other, and she had not yet dared to ask.

Mrs. Freeman was insisting upon her attention. She had moved from the refrigerator to the heater so that Mrs. Hopewell had to turn and face her in order to seem to be listening. "Glynese gone out with Harvey Hill again last night," she said. "She had this sty."

"Hill," Mrs. Hopewell said absently, "is that the one who works in the garage?"

"Nome, he's the one that goes to chiropracter school," Mrs. Freeman said. "She had this sty. Been had it two days. So she says when he brought her in the other night he says, 'Lemme get rid of that sty for you,' and she says, 'How?' and he says, 'You just lay yourself down across the seat of that car and I'll show you.' So she done it and he popped her neck. Kept on a-popping it several times until she made him quit. This morning," Mrs. Freeman said, "she ain't got no sty. She ain't got no traces of a sty."

"I never heard of that before," Mrs. Hopewell said.

"He ast her to marry him before the Ordinary," Mrs. Freeman went on, "and she told him she wasn't going to be married in no *office*."

"Well, Glynese is a fine girl," Mrs. Hopewell said. "Glynese and Carramae are both fine girls."

"Carramae said when her and Lyman was married Lyman said it sure felt sacred to him. She said he said he wouldn't take five hundred dollars for being married by a preacher."

"How much would he take?" the girl asked from the stove.

"He said he wouldn't take five hundred dollars," Mrs. Freeman repeated.

"Well we all have work to do," Mrs. Hopewell said.

"Lyman said it just felt more sacred to him," Mrs. Freeman said. "The doctor wants Carramae to eat prunes. Says instead of medicine. Says them cramps is coming from pressure. You know where I think it is?"

"She'll be better in a few weeks," Mrs. Hopewell said.

"In the tube," Mrs. Freeman said. "Else she wouldn't be as sick as she is."

Hulga had cracked her two eggs into a saucer and was bringing them to the table along with a cup of coffee that she had filled too full. She sat down carefully and began to eat, meaning to keep Mrs. Freeman there by questions if for any reason she showed an inclination to leave. She could perceive her mother's eye on her. The first roundabout question would be about the Bible salesman and she did not wish to bring it on. "How did he pop her neck?" she asked.

Mrs. Freeman went into a description of how he had popped her neck. She said he owned a '55 Mercury but that Glynese said she would rather marry a man with only a '36 Plymouth who would be married by a preacher. The girl asked what if he had a '32 Plymouth and Mrs. Freeman said what Glynese had said was a '36 Plymouth.

Mrs. Hopewell said there were not many girls with Glynese's common sense. She said what she admired in those girls was their common sense. She said that reminded her that they had had a nice visitor yesterday, a young man selling Bibles. "Lord," she said, "he bored me to death but he was so sincere and genuine I couldn't be rude to him. He was just good country people, you know," she said, "—just the salt of the earth."

"I seen him walk up," Mrs. Freeman said, "and then later—I seen him walk off," and Hulga could feel the slight shift in her voice, the slight insinuation, that he had not walked off alone, had he? Her face remained expressionless but the color rose into her neck and she seemed to swallow it down with the next spoonful of egg. Mrs. Freeman was looking at her as if they had a secret together.

"Well, it takes all kinds of people to make the world go 'round," Mrs. Hopewell said. "It's very good we aren't all alike."

"Some people are more alike than others," Mrs. Freeman said.

Hulga got up and stumped, with about twice the noise that was necessary, into her room and locked the door. She was to meet the Bible salesman at ten o'clock at the gate. She had thought about it half the night. She had started thinking of it as a great joke and then she had begun to see profound implications in it. She had lain in bed imagining dialogues for them that were insane on the surface but that reached below to depths that no Bible salesman would be aware of. Their conversation yesterday had been of this kind.

He had stopped in front of her and had simply stood there. His face was bony and sweaty and bright, with a little pointed nose in the center of it, and his look was different from what it had been at the dinner table. He was gazing at her with open curiosity, with fascination, like a child watching a new fantastic animal at the zoo, and he was breathing as if he had run a great distance to reach her. His gaze seemed somehow familiar but she could not think where she had been regarded with it before. For almost a minute he didn't say anything. Then on what seemed an insuck of breath, he whispered "You ever ate a chicken that was two days old?"

The girl looked at him stonily. He might have just put this question up for consideration at the meeting of a philosophical association. "Yes," she presently replied as if she had considered it from all angles.

"It must have been mighty small!" he said triumphantly and shook all over with little nervous giggles, getting very red in the face, and subsiding finally into his gaze of complete admiration, while the girl's expression remained exactly the same.

"How old are you?" he asked softly.

She waited some time before she answered. Then in a flat voice she said, "Seventeen."

His smiles came in succession like waves breaking on the surface of a little lake. "I see you got a wooden leg," he said. "I think you're real brave. I think you're real sweet."

The girl stood blank and solid and silent.

"Walk to the gate with me," he said. "You're a brave sweet little thing and I liked you the minute I seen you walk in the door."

Hulga began to move forward.

"What's your name?" he asked, smiting down on the top of her head.

"Hulga," she said.

"Hulga," he murmured, "Hulga. Hulga. I never heard of anybody name Hulga before. You're shy, aren't you, Hulga?" he asked.

She nodded, watching his large red hand on the handle of the giant valise.

"I like girls that wear glasses," he said. "I think a lot. I'm not like these people that a serious thought don't ever enter their heads. It's because I may die."

"I may die too," she said suddenly and looked up at him. His eyes were very small and brown, glittering feverishly.

"Listen," he said, "don't you think some people was meant to meet on account of what all they got in common and all? Like they both think serious thoughts and all?" He shifted the valise to his other hand so that the hand nearest her was free. He caught hold of her elbow and shook it a little. "I don't work on Saturday," he said. "I like to walk in the woods and see what Mother Nature is wearing. O'er the hills and far away. Pic-nics and things. Couldn't we go on a pic-nic tomorrow? Say yes, Hulga," he said and gave her a dying look as if he felt his insides about to drop out of him. He had even seemed to sway slightly toward her.

During the night she had imagined that she seduced him. She imagined that the two of them walked on the place until they came to the storage barn beyond the two back fields and there, she imagined, that things came to such a pass that she very easily seduced him and that then, of course, she had to reckon with his remorse. True genius can get an idea across even to an inferior mind. She imagined that she took his remorse in hand and changed it into a deeper understanding of life. She took all his shame away and turned it into something useful.

She set off for the gate at exactly ten o'clock, escaping without drawing Mrs. Hopewell's attention. She didn't take anything to eat, forgetting that food is usually taken on a picnic. She wore a pair of slacks and a dirty white shirt, and as an afterthought, she had put some Vapex on the collar of it since she did not own any perfume. When she reached the gate no one was there.

She looked up and down the empty highway and had the furious feeling that she had been tricked, that he had only meant to make her walk to the gate after the idea of him. Then suddenly he stood up, very tall, from behind a bush on the opposite embankment. Smiling, he lifted his hat which was new and wide-brimmed. He had not worn it yesterday and she wondered if he had bought it for the occasion. It was toast-colored with a red and white band around it and was slightly too large for him. He stepped from behind the bush still carrying the black valise. He had on the same suit and the same yellow socks sucked down in his shoes from walking. He crossed the highway and said, "I knew you'd come!"

The girl wondered acidly how he had known this. She pointed to the valise and asked, "Why did you bring your Bibles?"

He took her elbow, smiling down on her as if he could not stop. "You can never tell when you'll need the word of God, Hulga," he said. She had a moment in which she doubted that this was actually happening and then they began to climb the embankment. They went down into the pasture toward the woods. The boy walked lightly by her side, bouncing on his toes. The valise did not seem to be heavy today; he even swung it. They crossed half the pasture without saying anything and then, putting his hand easily on the small of her back, he asked softly, "Where does your wooden leg join on?"

She turned an ugly red and glared at him and for an instant the boy looked abashed. "I didn't mean you no harm," he said. "I only meant you're so brave and all. I guess God takes care of you."

"No," she said, looking forward and walking fast, "I don't even believe in God."

At this he stopped and whistled. "No!" he exclaimed as if he were too astonished to say anything else.

She walked on and in a second he was bouncing at her side, fanning with his hat. "That's very unusual for a girl," he remarked, watching her out of the corner of his eye. When they reached the edge of the wood, he put his hand on her back again and drew her against him without a word and kissed her heavily.

The kiss, which had more pressure than feeling behind it, produced that extra surge of adrenalin in the girl that enables one to carry a packed trunk out of a burning house, but in her, the power went at once to the brain. Even before he released her, her mind, clear and detached and ironic anyway, was regarding him from a great distance, with amusement but with pity. She had never been kissed before and she was pleased to discover that it was an unexceptional experience and all a matter of the mind's control. Some people might enjoy drain water if they were told it was vodka. When the boy, looking expectant but uncertain, pushed her gently away, she turned and walked on, saying nothing as if such business, for her, were common enough.

He came along panting at her side, trying to help her when he saw a root that she might trip over. He caught and held back the long swaying blades of thorn vine until she had passed beyond them. She led the way and he came breathing heavily behind her. Then they came out on a sunlit hillside, sloping softly into another one a little smaller. Beyond, they could see the rusted top of the old barn where the extra hay was stored.

The hill was sprinkled with small pink weeds. "Then you ain't saved?" he asked suddenly, stopping.

The girl smiled. It was the first time she had smiled at him at all. "In my economy," she said, "I'm saved and you are damned but I told you I didn't believe in God."

Nothing seemed to destroy the boy's look of admiration. He gazed at her now as if the fantastic animal at the zoo had put its paw through the bars and given him a loving poke. She thought he looked as if he wanted to kiss her again and she walked on before he had the chance.

"Ain't there somewheres we can sit down sometime?" he murmured, his voice softening toward the end of the sentence.

"In that barn," she said.

They made for it rapidly as if it might slide away like a train. It was a large two-story barn, cool and dark inside. The boy pointed up the ladder that led into the loft and said, "It's too bad we can't go up there."

"Why can't we?" she asked.

"Yer leg," he said reverently.

The girl gave him a contemptuous look and putting both hands on the ladder, she climbed it while he stood below apparently awestruck. She pulled herself expertly through the opening and then looked down at him and said, "Well, come on if you're coming," and he began to climb the ladder, awkwardly bringing the suitcase with him.

"We won't need the Bible," she observed.

"You never can tell," he said, panting. After he had got into the loft, he was a few seconds catching his breath. She had sat down in a pile of straw. A wide sheath of sunlight, filled with dust particles, slanted over her. She lay back against a bale, her face turned away, looking out the front opening of the barn where hay was thrown from a wagon into the loft. The two pink-speckled hillsides lay back against a dark ridge of woods. The sky was cloudless and cold blue. The boy dropped down by her side and put one arm under her and the other over her and began methodically kissing her face, making little noises like a fish. He did not remove his hat but it was pushed far enough back not to interfere. When her glasses got in his way, he took them off of her and slipped them into his pocket.

The girl at first did not return any of the kisses but presently she began to and after she had put several on his cheek, she reached his lips and remained there, kissing him again and again as if she were trying to draw all the breath out of him. His breath was clear and sweet like a child's and the kisses were sticky like a child's. He mumbled about loving her and about knowing when he first seen her that he loved her, but the mumbling was like the sleepy fretting of a child being put to sleep by his mother. Her mind, throughout this, never stopped or lost itself for a second to her feelings. "You ain't said you loved me none," he whispered finally, pulling back from her. "You got to say that."

She looked away from him off into the hollow sky and then down at a black ridge and then down farther into what appeared to be two green swelling lakes. She didn't realize he had taken her glasses but this landscape could not seem exceptional to her for she seldom paid any close attention to her surroundings.

"You got to say it," he repeated. "You got to say you love me."

She was always careful how she committed herself. "In a sense," she began, "if you use the word loosely, you might say that. But it's not a word I use. I don't have illusions. I'm one of those people who see *through* to nothing."

The boy was frowning. "You got to say it. I said it and you got to say it," he said.

The girl looked at him almost tenderly. "You poor baby," she murmured. "It's just as well you don't understand," and she pulled him by the neck, face-down, against her. "We are all damned," she said, "but some of us have taken off our blindfolds and see that there's nothing to see. It's a kind of salvation."

The boy's astonished eyes looked blankly through the ends of her hair. "Okay," he almost whined, "but do you love me or don'tcher?"

"Yes," she said and added, "in a sense. But I must tell you something. There mustn't be anything dishonest between us." She lifted his head and looked him in the eye. "I am thirty years old," she said. "I have a number of degrees."

The boy's look was irritated but dogged. "I don't care," he said. "I don't care a thing about what all you done. I just want to know if you love me or don'tcher?" and he caught her to him and wildly planted her face with kisses until she said, "Yes, yes."

"Okay then," he said, letting her go. "Prove it."

She smiled, looking dreamily out on the shifty landscape. She had seduced him without even making up her mind to try. "How?" she asked, feeling that he should be delayed a little.

He leaned over and put his lips to her ear. "Show me where your wooden leg joins on," he whispered.

The girl uttered a sharp little cry and her face instantly drained of color. The obscenity of the suggestion was not what shocked her. As a child she had sometimes been subject to feelings of shame but education had removed the last traces of that as a good surgeon scrapes for cancer; she would no more have felt it over what he was asking than she would have believed in his Bible. But she was as sensitive about the artificial leg as a peacock about his tail. No one ever touched it but her. She took care of it as someone else would his soul in private and almost with her own eyes turned away. "No," she said.

"I known it," he muttered, sitting up. "You're just playing me for a sucker."

"Oh no no!" she cried. "It joins on at the knee. Only at the knee. Why do you want to see it?"

The boy gave her a long penetrating look. "Because," he said, "it's what makes you different. You ain't like anybody else."

She sat staring at him. There was nothing about her face or her round freezing-blue eyes to indicate that this had moved her; but she felt as if her heart had stopped and left her mind to pump her blood. She decided that for the first time in her life she was face to face with real innocence. This boy, with an instinct that came from beyond wisdom, had touched the truth about her. When after a minute, she said in a hoarse high voice, "All right," it was like surrendering to him completely. It was like losing her own life and finding it again, miraculously, in his.

Very gently he began to roll the slack leg up. The artificial limb, in a white sock and brown flat shoe, was bound in a heavy material like canvas and ended in an ugly jointure where it was attached to the stump. The boy's face and his voice were entirely reverent as he uncovered it and said, "Now show me how to take it off and on."

She took it off for him and put it back on again and then he took it off himself, handling it as tenderly as if it were a real one. "See!" he said with a delighted child's face. "Now I can do it myself!"

"Put it back on," she said. She was thinking that she would run away with him and that every night he would take the leg off and every morning put it back on again. "Put it back on," she said.

"Not yet," he murmured, setting it on its foot out of her reach. "Leave it off for a while. You got me instead."

She gave a little cry of alarm but he pushed her down and began to kiss her again. Without the leg she felt entirely dependent on him. Her brain seemed to have stopped thinking altogether and to be about some other function that it was not very good at. Different expressions raced back and forth over her face. Every now and then the boy, his eyes like two steel spikes, would glance behind him where the leg stood. Finally she pushed him off and said, "Put it back on me now."

"Wait," he said. He leaned the other way and pulled the valise toward him and opened it. It had a pale blue spotted lining and there were only two Bibles in it. He took one of these out and opened the cover of it. It was hollow and contained a pocket flask of whiskey, a pack of cards, and a small blue box with printing on it. He laid these out in front of her one at a time in an evenly-spaced row, like one presenting offerings at the shrine of a goddess. He put the blue box in her hand. THIS PRODUCT TO BE USED ONLY FOR THE PREVENTION OF DISEASE, she read, and dropped it. The boy was unscrewing the top of the flask. He stopped and pointed, with a smile, to the deck of cards. It was not an ordinary deck but one with an obscene picture on the back of each card. "Take a swig," he said, offering her the bottle first. He held it in front of her, but like one mesmerized, she did not move.

Her voice when she spoke had an almost pleading sound. "Aren't you," she murmured, "aren't you just good country people?"

The boy cocked his head. He looked as if he were just beginning to understand that she might be trying to insult him. "Yeah," he said, curling his lip slightly, "but it ain't held me back none. I'm as good as you any day in the week."

"Give me my leg," she said.

He pushed it farther away with his foot. "Come on now, let's begin to have us a good time," he said coaxingly. "We ain't got to know one another good yet."

"Give me my leg!" she screamed and tried to lunge for it but he pushed her down easily.

"What's the matter with you all of a sudden?" he asked, frowning as he screwed the top on the flask and put it quickly back inside the Bible. "You just a while ago said you didn't believe in nothing. I thought you was some girl!"

Her face was almost purple. "You're a Christian!" she hissed. "You're a fine Christian! You're just like them all—say one thing and do another. You're a perfect Christian, you're ..."

The boy's mouth was set angrily. "I hope you don't think," he said in a lofty indignant tone, "that I believe in that crap! I may sell Bibles but I know which end is up and I wasn't born yesterday and I know where I'm going!"

"Give me my leg!" she screeched. He jumped up so quickly that she barely saw him sweep the cards and the blue box back into the Bible and throw the Bible into the valise. She saw him grab the leg and then she saw it for an instant slanted forlornly across the inside of the suitcase with a Bible at either side of its opposite ends. He slammed the lid shut and snatched up the valise and swung it down the hole and then stepped through himself.

When all of him had passed but his head, he turned and regarded her with a look that no longer had any admiration in it. "I've gotten a lot of interesting things," he said. "One time I got a woman's glass eye this way. And you needn't to think you'll catch me because Pointer ain't really my name. I use a different name at every house I call at and don't stay nowhere long. And I'll tell you another thing, Hulga," he said, using the name as if he didn't think much of it, "you ain't so smart. I been believing in nothing ever since I was born!" and then the toast-colored hat disappeared down the hole and the girl was left, sitting on the straw in the dusty sunlight. When she turned her churning face toward the opening, she saw his blue figure struggling successfully over the green speckled lake.

Mrs. Hopewell and Mrs. Freeman, who were in the back pasture, digging up onions, saw him emerge a little later from the woods and head across the meadow toward the highway. "Why, that looks like that nice dull young man that tried to sell me a Bible yesterday," Mrs. Hopewell said, squinting. "He must have been selling them to the Negroes back in there. He was so simple," she said, "but I guess the world would be better off if we were all that simple."

Mrs. Freeman's gaze drove forward and just touched him before he disappeared under the hill. Then she returned her attention to the evil-smelling onion shoot she was lifting from the ground. "Some can't be that simple," she said. "I know I never could."

Tillie Olsen

Born in Omaha, Nebraska, in 1913, Tillie Olsen has become a touchstone in feminist literary circles, not only for her determination to write, but also for her painful articulation of the difficulties women face when they try to combine art, motherhood, and full-time paid employment. The daughter of Russian refugees from Czarist repression, Olsen was a high school drop-out by age fifteen. She lived through the Depression of the thirties, working in factories and offices, trying to raise her children properly and keep alive the creative spark that had started her writing a novel at age nineteen. She and her child were abandoned by her first husband. She was a member of the Young Communist League and had been jailed briefly for her activities on behalf of the packing-house workers in Kansas City, so it is not surprising that she later married Jack Olsen, a political activist. Three more children, a job, and pressing political causes left her no time to write. Although she had published a chapter of her unfinished novel in *Partisan Review* in 1934, her first book, a collection of four stories called *Tell Me a Riddle*, was not published until 1961, after she had enrolled in a fiction writing class at San Francisco State College and been awarded a Stanford University writing fellowship in the mid-fifties. In 1974, she published *Yonnondio*, from what she had been able to reconstruct of the novel started forty-three years earlier. *Silences*, a collection of essays, appeared in 1978; *Mothers and Daughters: That Special Quality*, in 1987.

In *Silences*, her moving account of the obstacles women face in trying to create, Tillie Olsen takes up the theme Virginia Woolf first addressed in *A Room of One's Own*. She speaks of Balzac's claim that there is something about the creative process that recalls motherhood: "Yes, in intelligent passionate motherhood there are similarities, and in more than the toil and patience. The calling upon total capacities; the reliving and new using of the past; the comprehensions; the fascination, absorption, intensity. All almost certain death to creation—(so far).

"Not because the capacities to create no longer exist, or the need (though for a while, as in any fullness of life, the need may be obscured), but because the circumstances for sustained creation have been almost impossible. The need cannot be first. It can have, at best, only part self, part time. (Unless someone else does the nurturing. Read Dorothy Fisher's 'Babushka Farnham' in *Fables for Parents*.) More than in any other human relationship, overwhelmingly more, motherhood means being instantly interruptible, responsive, responsible. Children need one *now* (and remember, in our society, the family must often try to be the centre for love and health the outside world is not). The very fact that these are real needs, that one feels them as one's own (love, not duty); *that there is no one else responsible for these needs*, gives them primacy. It is distraction, not meditation, that becomes habitual; interruption, not continuity; spasmodic, not constant toil. The rest has been said here. Work interrupted, deferred, relinquished, makes blockage—at best, less accomplishment. Unused capacities atrophy, cease to be."

This discussion, which is continued in a larger extract from *Silences* in the Afterwords section, helps to suggest why Olsen's work has been the subject of such keen interest—Margaret Atwood uses the term *reverence*—and why it has been translated into many languages. Her exploration of the riddles and enigmas of existence, her unique fictionalizing of autobiographical materials, and her use of stream-of-consciousness techniques give her stories a timeless, deceptively simple, resonance and appeal.

I Stand Here Ironing

I stand here ironing, and what you asked me moves tormented back and forth with the iron.

"I wish you would manage the time to come in and talk with me about your daughter. I'm sure you can help me understand her. She's a youngster who needs help and whom I'm deeply interested in helping."

"Who needs help." ... Even if I came, what good would it do? You think because I am her mother I have a key, or that in some way you could use me as a key? She has lived for nineteen years. There is all that life that has happened outside of me, beyond me.

And when there is time to remember, to sift, to weigh, to estimate, to total? I will start and there will be an interruption and I will have to gather together again. Or I will become engulfed with all I did or did not do, with what should have been and what cannot be helped.

She was a beautiful baby. The first and only one of our five that was beautiful at birth. You do not guess how new and uneasy her tenancy in her now-loveliness. You did not know her all those years she was thought homely, or see her poring over her baby pictures, making me tell her over and over how beautiful she had been—and would be, I would tell her—and was now, to the seeing eye. But the seeing eyes were few or nonexistent. Including mine.

I nursed her. They feel that's important nowadays. I nursed all the children, but with her, with all the fierce rigidity of first motherhood, I did like books then said. Though her cries battered me to trembling and my breasts ached with swollenness, I waited till the clock decreed.

Why do I put that first? I do not even know if it matters, or if it explains anything.

She was a beautiful baby. She blew shining bubbles of sound. She loved motion, loved light, loved color and music and textures. She would lie on the floor in her blue overalls patting the surface so hard in ecstasy her hands and feet would blur. She was a miracle to me, but when she was eight months old I had to leave her daytimes with the woman downstairs to whom she was no miracle at all, for I worked or looked for work and for Emily's father, who "could no longer endure" (he wrote in his good-bye note) "sharing want with us."

I was nineteen. It was the pre-relief, pre-WPA world of the depression. I would start running as soon as I got off the streetcar, running up the stairs, the place smelling sour, and awake or asleep to startle awake, when she saw me she would break into a clogged weeping that could not be comforted, a weeping I can hear yet.

After a while I found a job hashing at night so I could be with her days, and it was better. But it came to where I had to bring her to his family and leave her.

It took a long time to raise the money for her fare back. Then she got chicken pox and I had to wait longer. When she finally came, I hardly knew her, walking quick and nervous like her father, looking like her father, thin, and dressed in a shoddy red that yellowed her skin and glared at the pockmarks. All the baby loveliness gone.

She was two. Old enough for nursery school they said, and I did not know then what I know now—the fatigue of the long day, and the lacerations of group life in the kinds of nurseries that are only parking places for children.

Except that it would have made no difference if I had known. It was the only place there was. It was the only way we could be together, the only way I could hold a job.

And even without knowing, I knew. I knew the teacher that was evil because all these years it has curdled into my memory, the little boy hunched in the corner, her rasp, "why aren't you outside, because Alvin hits you? that's no reason, go out, scaredy." I knew Emily hated it even if she did not clutch and implore "don't go Mommy" like the other children, mornings.

She always had a reason why we should stay home. Momma, you look sick. Momma, I feel sick. Momma, the teachers aren't there today, they're sick. Momma, we can't go, there was a fire last night. Momma, it's a holiday today, no school, they told me.

But never a direct protest, never rebellion. I think of our others in their three-, four-year-oldness—the explosions, the tempers, the denunciations, the demands—and I feel suddenly ill. I put the iron down. What in me demanded that goodness in her? And what was the cost, the cost to her of such goodness?

The old man living in the back once said in his gentle way: "You should smile at Emily more when you look at her." What *was* in my face when I looked at her? I loved her. There were all the acts of love.

It was only with the others I remembered what he said, and it was the face of joy, and not of care or tightness or worry I turned to them—too late for Emily. She does not smile easily, let alone almost always as her brothers and sisters do. Her face is closed and sombre, but when she wants, how fluid. You must have seen it in her pantomimes, you spoke of her rare gift for comedy on the stage that rouses laughter out of the audience so dear they applaud and applaud and do not want to let her go.

Where does it come from, that comedy? There was none of it in her when she came back to me that second time, after I had to send her away again. She had a new daddy now to learn to love, and I think perhaps it was a better time.

Except when we left her alone nights, telling ourselves she was old enough.

"Can't you go some other time, Mommy, like tomorrow?" she would ask. "Will it be just a little while you'll be gone? Do you promise?"

The time we came back, the front door open, the clock on the floor in the hall. She rigid awake. "It wasn't just a little while. I didn't cry. Three times I called you, just three times, and then I ran downstairs to open the door so you could come faster. The clock talked loud. I threw it away, it scared me what it talked."

She said the clock talked loud again that night I went to the hospital to have Susan. She was delirious with the fever that comes before red measles, but she was fully conscious all the week I was gone and the week after we were home when she could not come near the new baby or me.

She did not get well. She stayed skeleton thin, not wanting to eat, and night after night she had nightmares. She would call for me, and I would rouse from exhaustion to sleepily call back: "You're all right, darling, go to sleep, it's just a dream," and if she still called, in a sterner voice, "now go to sleep, Emily, there's nothing to hurt you." Twice, only twice, when I had to get up for Susan anyhow, I went in to sit with her.

Now when it is too late (as if she would let me hold her and comfort her like I do the others) I get up and go to her at once at her moan or restless stirring. "Are you awake, Emily? Can I get you something?" And the answer is always the same: "No, I'm all right, go back to sleep, Mother."

They persuaded me at the clinic to send her away to a convalescent home in the country where "she can have the kind of food and care you can't manage for her, and you'll be free to concentrate on the new baby." They still send children to that place. I see pictures on the society page of sleek young women planning affairs to raise money for it, or dancing at the affairs, or decorating Easter eggs or filling Christmas stockings for the children.

They never have a picture of the children so I do not know if the girls still wear those gigantic red bows and the ravaged looks on the every other Sunday when parents can come to visit "unless otherwise notified"—as we were notified the first six weeks.

Oh it is a handsome place, green lawns and tall trees and fluted flower beds. High up on the balconies of each cottage the children stand, the girls in their red bows and white dresses, the boys in white suits and giant red ties. The parents stand below shrieking up to be heard and the children shriek down to be heard, and between them the invisible wall "Not to Be Contaminated by Parental Germs or Physical Affection."

There was a tiny girl who always stood hand in hand with Emily. Her parents never came. One visit she was gone. "They moved her to Rose Cottage" Emily shouted in explanation. "They don't like you to love anybody here."

She wrote once a week, the labored writing of a seven-year-old. "I am fine. How is the baby. If I write my leter nicly I will have a star. Love." There never was a star. We wrote every other day, letters she could never hold or keep but only hear read—once. "We simply do not have room for children to keep any personal possessions," they patiently explained when we pieced one Sunday's shrieking together to plead how much it would mean to Emily, who loved so to keep things, to be allowed to keep her letters and cards.

Each visit she looked frailer. "She isn't eating," they told us.

(They had runny eggs for breakfast or mush with lumps, Emily said later, I'd hold it in my mouth and not swallow. Nothing ever tasted good, just when they had chicken.)

It took us eight months to get her released home, and only the fact that she gained back so little of her seven lost pounds convinced the social worker.

I used to try to hold and love her after she came back, but her body would stay stiff, and after a while she'd push away. She ate little. Food sickened her, and I think much of life too. Oh she had physical lightness and brightness, twinkling by on skates, bouncing like a ball up and down up and down over the jump rope, skimming over the hill; but these were momentary.

She fretted about her appearance, thin and dark and foreign-looking at a time when every little girl was supposed to look or thought she should look a chubby blonde replica of Shirley Temple. The doorbell sometimes rang for her, but no one seemed to come and play in the house or to be a best friend. Maybe because we moved so much.

There was a boy she loved painfully through two school semesters. Months later she told me how she had taken pennies from my purse to buy him candy. "Licorice was his favorite and I brought him some every day but he still liked Jennifer better'n me. Why, Mommy?" The kind of question for which there is no answer.

School was a worry for her. She was not glib or quick in a world where glibness and quickness were easily confused with ability to learn. To her overworked and exasperated teachers she was an overconscientious "slow learner" who kept trying to catch up and was absent entirely too often.

I let her be absent, though sometimes the illness was imaginary. How different from my now-strictness about attendance with the others. I wasn't working. We had a new baby. I was home anyhow. Sometimes, after Susan grew old enough, I would keep her home from school, too, to have them together.

Mostly Emily had asthma, and her breathing, harsh and labored, would fill the house with a curiously tranquil sound. I would bring the two old dresser mirrors and her boxes of collections to her bed. She would select beads and single earrings, bottle tops and shells, dried flowers and pebbles, old postcards and scraps, all sorts of oddments; then she and Susan would play Kingdom, setting up landscapes and furniture, peopling them with action.

Those were the only times of peaceful companionship between her and Susan. I have edged away from it, that poisonous feeling between them, that terrible balancing of hurts and needs I had to do between the two, and did so badly, those earlier years.

Oh there were conflicts between the others too, each one human, needing, demanding, hurting, taking—but only between Emily and Susan, no, Emily toward Susan that corroding resentment. It seems so obvious on the surface, yet it is not obvious. Susan, the second child, Susan, golden- and curly-haired and chubby, quick and articulate and assured, everything in appearance and manner Emily was not; Susan, not able to resist Emily's precious things, losing or sometimes clumsily breaking them; Susan telling jokes and riddles to company for applause while Emily sat silent (to say to me later: that was *my* riddle, Mother, I told it to Susan); Susan, who for all the five years' difference in age was just a year behind Emily in developing physically.

I am glad for that slow physical development that widened the difference between her and her contemporaries, though she suffered over it. She was too vulnerable for that terrible world of youthful competition, of preening and parading, of constant measuring of yourself against every other, of envy, "if I had that copper hair," "If I had that skin. ..." She tormented herself enough about not looking like the others, there was enough of unsureness, the having to be conscious of words before you speak, the constant caring—what are they thinking of me? without having it all magnified by the merciless physical drives.

Ronnie is calling. He is wet and I change him. It is rare there is such a cry now. That time of motherhood is almost behind me when the ear is not one's own but must always be racked and listening for the child cry, the child call. We sit for a while and I hold him, looking out over the city spread in charcoal with its soft aisles of light. "*Shoogily*," he breathes and curls closer. I carry him back to bed, asleep. *Shoogily.* A funny word, a family word, inherited from Emily, invented by her to say: *comfort.*

In this and other ways she leaves her seal, I say aloud. And startle at my saying it. What do I mean? What did I start to gather together, to try and make coherent? I was at the terrible, growing years. War years. I do not remember them well. I was working, there were four smaller ones now, there was not time for her. She had to help be a mother, and housekeeper, and shopper. She had to get her seal. Mornings of crisis and near hysteria trying to get lunches packed, hair combed, coats and shoes found, everyone to school or Child Care on time, the baby ready for transportation. And always the paper scribbled on by a smaller one, the book looked at by Susan then mislaid, the homework not done. Running out to that huge school where she was one, she was lost, she was a drop; suffering over the unpreparedness, stammering and unsure in her classes.

There was so little time left at night after the kids were bedded down. She would struggle over books, always eating (it was in those years she developed her enormous appetite that is legendary in our family) and I would be ironing, or preparing food for the next day, or writing V-mail to Bill, or tending the baby. Sometimes, to make me laugh, or out of her despair, she would imitate happenings or types at school.

I think I said once: "Why don't you do something like this in the school amateur show?" One morning she phoned me at work, hardly understandable through the weeping: "Mother, I did it. I won, I won; they gave me first prize; they clapped and clapped and wouldn't let me go."

Now suddenly she was Somebody, and as imprisoned in her difference as she had been in anonymity.

She began to be asked to perform at other high schools, even in colleges, then at city and statewide affairs. The first one we went to, I only recognized her that first moment when thin, shy, she almost drowned herself into the curtains. Then: Was this Emily? The control, the command, the convulsing and deadly clowning, the spell, then the roaring, stamping audience, unwilling to let this rare and precious laughter out of their lives.

Afterwards: You ought to do something about her with a gift like that—but without money or knowing how, what does one do? We have left it all to her, and the gift has so often eddied inside, clogged and clotted, as been used and growing.

She is coming. She runs up the stairs two at a time with her light graceful step, and I know she is happy tonight. Whatever it was that occasioned your call did not happen today.

"Aren't you ever going to finish the ironing, Mother? Whistler painted his mother in a rocker. I'd have to paint mine standing over an ironing board." This is one of her communicative nights and she tells me everything and nothing as she fixes herself a plate of food out of the icebox.

She is so lovely. Why did you want me to come in at all? Why were you concerned? She will find her way.

She starts up the stairs to bed. "Don't get me up with the rest in the morning." "But I thought you were having midterms." "Oh, those," she comes back in, kisses me, and says quite lightly, "in a couple of years when we'll all be atom-dead they won't matter a bit."

She has said it before. She *believes* it. But because I have been denying the past, and all that compounds a human being is so heavy and meaningful in me, I cannot endure it tonight.

I will never total it all. I will never come in to say: She was a child seldom smiled at. Her father left me before she was a year old. I had to work her first six years when there was work, or I sent her home and to his relatives. There were years she had care she hated. She was dark and thin and foreign-looking in a world where the prestige went to blondeness and curly hair and dimples, she was slow where glibness was prized. She was a child of anxious, not proud, love. We were poor and could not afford for her the soil of easy growth. I was a young mother, I was a distracted mother. There were other children pushing up, demanding. Her younger sister seemed all that she was not. There were years she did not want me to touch her. She kept too much in herself, her life was such she had to keep too much in herself. My wisdom came too late. She has much to her and probably little will come of it. She is a child of her age, of depression, of war, of fear.

Let her be. So all that is in her will not bloom—but in how many does it? There is still enough left to live by. Only help her to know—help make it so there is cause for her to know—that she is more than this dress on the ironing board, helpless before the iron.

Jayne Anne Phillips

Jayne Anne Phillips was born in Buckhannon, West Virginia, in 1952. She supported herself through the University of West Virginia by working in the home improvement business, then travelled across the U.S. working as a waitress. At age twenty-four, she was accepted into the University of Iowa writing program for the M.F.A. on the strength of poems and two short stories. She published her first book of short prose pieces, *Sweethearts*, with a small press in 1976; this was followed by *Counting* (1978), *Black Tickets* (1979), which won the Sue Kaufman Award for First Fiction from the American Academy and Institute for Arts and Letters, the novel *Machine Dreams* (1984), and *Shelter* (1994). Her work has appeared in *Fiction*, *Redbook*, *Iowa Review*, and *Fiction International*. She lives in Cambridge, Massachusetts.

In an interview with *Newsweek* (No. 94, Oct. 22, 1979), Phillips describes writing as "almost a metaphysical process." She goes on to explain by saying that "it's a privilege to have a passion. Real writers serve their material. They allow it to pass through them and have the opportunity to move beyond the daily limitations of being inside themselves. It's like being led by a whisper." Phillips is speaking here of more than Byron's and Camus's idea of creating as living doubly, though, of course, that meaning is also intended; she is saying something about the artist as a vehicle, a mouthpiece, through which the community guarantees, if not its survival, at least a record of its passage through time. Whether it is the collective unconscious or tribal memory, the whisper makes itself felt in the mind of the story-teller, like Shelley's west wind or Auden's intolerable neural itch.

Phillips has an amazing ear for the nuances and idioms of ordinary speech; her strippers, seamstresses, and drug addicts are drawn deftly and convincingly. Many of these characters, who step precariously along the razor's edge of sanity, remain in the reader's mind primarily as voices; others, who struggle to survive poverty or social disadvantage, are remembered for a single detail, such as cracked lipstick or a "pale strand of scalp." Phillips turns the same discerning eye on personal relationships, frustration, domestic violence, and betrayal, reminding one of her acknowledged debt to Faulkner, Welty, and Flannery O'Connor. "I'm interested in what homes consist of," she says. "Because we move around so much, families are forced to be immediate; they must stand on their relationships, rather than on stereotypes or assumptions or a common history."

Phillips's work stems as much from a commitment to process, rather than to theory or traditional forms and ideas, as it does from close observation. "I believe that you are led to discover what things mean and how things are related to each other through the process of doing the work." Her training as a poet has no doubt influenced her strategies as a prose writer. Many of her shortest stories are less than a page in length and even the longer pieces are imbued with a sense of verbal economy. "I became more challenged by the difficulty of writing fiction," she said. "I was really attracted by the subversive look of the paragraph. In a poem you're always having to confront the identity of the writer. In fiction the reader becomes less defended against that identity and more open to the text."

The Stripper

When I was fifteen back in Charleston, my cousin Phoebe taught me to strip. She was older than my mother but she had some body. When I watched her she'd laugh, say That's all right Honey sex is sex. It don't matter if you do it with monkeys. Yeah she said, You're white an dewy an tickin like a time bomb an now's the time to learn. With that long blond hair you can't lose. An don't you paint your face till you have to, every daddy wants his daughter. That's what she said. The older dancers wear makeup an love the floor, touchin themselves. The men get scared an cluster round, smokin like paper on a slow fire. Once in Laramie I was in one of those spotted motels after a show an a man's shadow fell across the window. I could smell him past the shade, hopeless an cracklin like a whip. He scared me, like I had a brother who wasn't right found a bullwhip in the shed. He used to take it out some days and come back with such a look on his face. I don't wanna know what they know. I went into the bathroom an stood in the fluorescent light. Those toilets have a white strip across em that you have to rip off. I left it on an sat down. I brushed my hair an counted. Counted till he walked away kickin gravel in the parkin lot. Now I'm feelin his shadow fall across stages in Denver an Cheyenne. I close my eyes an dance faster, like I used to dance blind an happy in Pop's closet. His suits hangin faceless on the racks with their big woolly arms empty. I play five clubs a week, $150 first place. I dance three sets each against five other girls. We pick jukebox songs while the owner does his gig on the mike. Now Marlene's gonna slip ya into a little darkness Let's get her up there with a big hand. The big hands clap an I walk the bar all shaven an smooth, rhinestoned velvet on my crotch. Don't ever show em a curly hair Phoebe told me, Angels don't have no curly hair. That's what she said. Beggin, they're starin up my white legs. That jukebox is cookin an they feel their fingers in me. Honey you know it ain't fair what you do Oh tell me why love is a lie jus like a ball an chain. Yeah I'm a white leather dream in a cowboy hat, a ranger with fringed breasts. Baby stick em up Baby don't touch Baby I'm a star an you are dyin. Better find a soft blond god to take you down. I got you Baby I got you Let go.

Edgar Allan Poe

Edgar Allan Poe was born in 1809 to itinerant actors in Boston and orphaned before the age of three. He became the ward of a Richmond, Virginia, couple, John and Francis Allan, whose name he adopted. Poe travelled with the Allans to Scotland and England in 1815. His studies at the University of Virginia were terminated as a result of his drinking and carousing, a pattern that would plague his life. A brief military career was followed by dismissal from West Point and various short-lived jobs, including the editorship of the Richmond *Southern Literary Messenger*. Marriage to his thirteen-year-old cousin, Virginia Clemm, ended with her death in 1847, after which he became engaged to a wealthy widow. However, a celebratory binge left him unconscious in a Baltimore street; he died three days later in 1849. A legendary Romantic figure, who is credited with inventing the detective story, Poe won a number of literary prizes and left an impressive body of poetry, fiction, and criticism; however, the fame, mostly posthumous, which came to him for his Gothic horror tales and literary sorties with the supernatural was never far removed from poverty and personal disaster. His stories were collected in *Tales of the Grotesque and Arabesque* (1840) and *Tales by Edgar A. Poe* (1845).

Poe made a major contribution to the development of the short story, both as a writer and as a theorist. What he called *ratiocination* is operative in the detective stories, such as "The Purloined Letter," where the reader is caught up in the various mental processes of C. Auguste Dupin trying to unravel the crime. Poe's horror stories, such as "The Fall of the House of Usher" and "The Cask of Amontillado," achieve their power by objectifying extreme psychological states, as D. H. Lawrence points out in *Studies in Classic American Literature* (1923), so that the unconscious desire to possess, or be possessed, utterly is projected in the images of burying, or being buried, alive.

Poe's reviews of the work of Nathaniel Hawthorne reveal a first-rate critical mind at work, trying to describe, much as Aristotle did for Greek drama in his *Poetics,* the nature of literary composition in fiction. Poe rejects superficial notions of originality and novelty for something that is deeper, involving both the mind that writes and the mind that reads. "But the true originality—true in respect of its purposes—is that which, in bringing out the half-formed, the reluctant, or the unexpressed fancies of mankind, or in exciting the more delicate pulses of the heart's passion, or in giving birth to some universal sentiment or instinct in embryo, thus combines with the pleasurable effect of apparent novelty, a real egoistic delight. The reader, in the case first supposed (that of the absolute novelty) is excited, but embarrassed, disturbed, in some degree even pained at his own want of perception, at his own folly in not having himself hit upon the idea. In the second case, his pleasure is doubled. He is filled with an intrinsic and extrinsic delight. He feels and intensely enjoys the seeming novelty of the thought, enjoys it as really novel, as absolutely original with the writer—and himself. They two, he fancies, have, alone of all men, thought thus. They two have, together, created this thing. Henceforward there is a bond of sympathy between them, a sympathy which irradiates every subsequent page of the book."

Many of Poe's major critical statements originated as reviews of the work of other writers. In a review of Nathaniel Parker Willis, for example, Poe tried to define style, dismissing mere experiment, or what he called "sleight-of-pen trickeries." He considered the work of art a technical challenge, "a difficulty happily overcome," and attributed the success of a work to imaginative genius, rather than to the fanciful scribblings or games of "all the little frisky men, personally considered." In the 1847 review of Hawthorne, Poe simplifies his thoughts by stating that originality in fiction is a matter of *tone*, not just content. He also repeats his famous remarks about the importance of a single, unified effect in the short story, or tale, which have been excerpted for inclusion in the Afterwords.

Perhaps Poe's insistence on thought and design in the creative process was consciously or unconsciously intended not only to help him set himself apart from the ordinary pack of scribblers, but also to distract readers from the deeply disturbing content of much of his work. In a moving letter to James R. Lowell, he acknowledges those elements in his character that proved to be self-destructive: "I have thus rambled and dreamed away whole months and awake, at last, to a sort of mania for composition. Then I scribble all day, and read all night, so long as the disease endures. ... I live continually in a reverie of the future. I have no faith in human perfectibility. I think that human exertion will have no appreciable effect upon humanity. Man is now only more active—not more happy—than he was 6000 years ago. ... I have been too deeply conscious of the mutability and evanescence of temporal things, to give any continuous effort to anything—to be consistent in anything. My life has been whim—impulse—passion—a longing for solitude—a scorn of all things present, in an earnest desire for the future." And yet, for all his scepticism and personal misgivings, his work has endured and created for him a lasting legacy.

The Cask of Amontillado

The thousand injuries of Fortunato I had borne as I best could; but when he ventured upon insult, I vowed revenge. You, who so well know the nature of my soul, will not suppose, however, that I gave utterance to a threat. *At length* I would be avenged; this was a point definitely settled—but the very defectiveness with which it was resolved precluded the idea of risk. I must not only punish, but punish with impunity. A wrong is unredressed when retribution overtakes its redresser. It is equally unredressed when the avenger fails to make himself felt as such to him who has done the wrong.

It must be understood that neither by word nor deed had I given Fortunato cause to doubt my good will. I continued, as was my wont, to smile in his face, and he did not perceive that my smile *now* was at the thought of his immolation.

He had a weak point—this Fortunato—although in other regards he was a man to be respected and even feared. He prided himself on his connoisseurship in wine. Few Italians have the true virtuoso spirit. For the most part their enthusiasm is adopted to suit the time and opportunity—to practise imposture upon the British and Austrian *millionaires*. In painting and gemmary Fortunato, like his countrymen, was a quack—but in the matter of old wines he was sincere. In this respect I did not differ from him materially; I was skilful in the Italian vintages myself, and bought largely whenever I could.

It was about dusk, one evening during the supreme madness of the carnival season, that I encountered my friend. He accosted me with excessive warmth, for he had been drinking much. The man wore motley. He had on a tight-fitting parti-striped dress, and his head was surmounted by the conical cap and bells. I was so pleased to see him that I thought I should never have done wringing his hand.

I said to him—'My dear Fortunato, you are luckily met. How remarkably well you are looking to-day! But I have received a pipe of what passes for Amontillado, and I have my doubts.'

'How?' said he. 'Amontillado? A pipe? Impossible! And in the middle of the carnival!'

'I have my doubts', I replied; 'and I was silly enough to pay the full Amontillado price without consulting you in the matter. You were not to be found, and I was fearful of losing a bargain.'

'Amontillado!'

'I have my doubts.'

'Amontillado!'

'And I must satisfy them.'

'Amontillado!'

'As you are engaged, I am on my way to Luchesi. If any one has a critical turn, it is he. He will tell me—'

'Luchesi cannot tell Amontillado from Sherry.'

'And yet some fools will have it that his taste is a match for your own.'

'Come, let us go.'

'Wither?'

'To your vaults.'

'My friend, no; I will not impose upon your good nature. I perceive you have an engagement. Luchesi—'

'I have no engagement;—come.'

'My friend, no. It is not the engagement, but the severe cold with which I perceive you are afflicted. The vaults are insufferably damp. They are encrusted with nitre.'

'Let us go, nevertheless. The cold is merely nothing. Amontillado! You have been imposed upon. And as for Luchesi, he cannot distinguish Sherry from Amontillado.'

Thus speaking, Fortunato possessed himself of my arm. Putting on a mask of black silk, and drawing a *roquelaire* closely about my person, I suffered him to hurry me to my palazzo.

There were no attendants at home; they had absconded to make merry in honor of the time. I had told them that I should not return until the morning, and had given them explicit orders not to stir from the house. These orders were sufficient, I well knew, to insure their immediate disappearance, one and all, as soon as my back was turned.

I took from their sconces two flambeaux, and giving one to Fortunato, bowed him through several suites of rooms to the archway that led into the vaults. I passed down a long and winding staircase, requesting him to be cautious as he followed. We came at length to the foot of the descent, and stood together on the damp ground of the catacombs of the Montresors.

The gait of my friend was unsteady, and the bells upon his cap jingled as he strode.

'The pipe,' said he.

'It is farther on,' said I; 'but observe the white web-work which gleams from these cavern walls.'

He turned towards me, and looked into my eyes with two filmy orbs that distilled the rheum of intoxication.

'Nitre?' he asked, at length.

'Nitre,' I replied. 'How long have you had that cough?'

'Ugh! ugh! ugh!—ugh! ugh! ugh!—ugh! ugh! ugh!—ugh! ugh! ugh!—ugh! ugh! ugh!'

My poor friend found it impossible to reply for many minutes.

'It is nothing', he said, at last.

'Come', I said, with decision, 'we will go back; your health is precious. You are rich, respected, admired, beloved; you are happy, as once I was. You are a man to be missed. For me it is no matter. We will go back; you will be ill, and I cannot be responsible. Besides, there is Luchesi—'

'Enough,' he said; 'the cough is a mere nothing; it will not kill me. I shall not die of a cough.'

'True—true,' I replied; 'and, indeed, I had no intention of alarming you unnecessarily—but you should use all proper caution. A draught of this Medoc will defend us from the damps.'

Here I knocked off the neck of a bottle which I drew from a long row of its fellows that lay upon the mould.

'Drink,' I said, presenting him the wine.

He raised it to his lips with a leer. He paused and nodded to me familiarly, while his bells jingled.

'I drink,' he said, 'to the buried that repose around us.'

'And I to your long life.'

He again took my arm, and we proceeded.

'These vaults,' he said, 'are extensive.'

'The Montresors,' I replied, 'were a great and numerous family.'

'I forget your arms.'

'A huge human foot d'or, in a field azure; the foot crushes a serpent rampant whose fangs are imbedded in the heel.'

'And the motto?'

'*Nemo me inpune lacessit.*'

'Good,' he said.

The wine sparkled in his eyes and bells jingled. My own fancy grew warm with the Medoc. We had passed through walls of piled bones, with casks and puncheons intermingling, into the inmost recesses of the catacombs. I paused again, and this time I made bold to seize Fortunato by an arm above the elbow.

'The nitre!' I said; 'see, it increases. It hangs like moss upon the vaults. We are below the river's bed. The drops of moisture trickle among the bones. Come, we will go back ere it is too late. Your cough—'

'It is nothing,' he said; 'let us go on. But first, another draught of the Medoc.'

I broke and reached him a flaçon of De Grâve. He emptied it at a breath. His eyes flashed with a fierce light. He laughed and threw the bottle upwards with a gesticulation I did not understand.

I looked at him in surprise. He repeated the movement—a grotesque one.

'You do not comprehend?' he said.

'Not I,' I replied.

'Then you are not of the brotherhood.'

'How?'

'You are not of the masons.'

'Yes, yes,' I said, 'yes, yes.'

'You? Impossible! A mason?'

'A mason,' I replied.

'A sign,' he said.

'It is this,' I answered, producing a trowel from beneath the folds of my *roquelaire*.

'You jest,' he exclaimed, recoiling a few paces. 'But let us proceed to the Amontillado.'

'Be it so,' I said, replacing the tool beneath the cloak, and again offering him my arm. He leaned upon it heavily. We continued our route in search of the Amontillado. We passed through a range of low arches, descended, passed on, and descending again, arrived at a deep crypt, in which the foulness of the air caused our flambeaux rather to glow than flame.

At the most remote end of the crypt there appeared another less spacious. Its walls had been lined with human remains, piled to the vault overhead, in the fashion of the great catacombs of Paris. Three sides of this interior crypt were still ornamented in this manner. From the fourth the bones had been thrown down, and lay promiscuously upon the earth, forming at one point a mound of some size. Within the wall thus exposed by the displacing of the bones, we perceived a still interior recess, in depth about four feet, in width three, in height six or seven. It seemed to have been constructed for no especial use within itself, but formed merely the interval between two of the colossal supports of the roof of the catacombs, and was backed by one of their circumscribing walls of solid granite.

It was in vain that Fortunato, uplifting his dull torch, endeavored to pry into the depth of the recess. Its termination the feeble light did not enable us to see.

'Proceed,' I said; 'herein is the Amontillado. As for Luchesi—'

'He is an ignoramus,' interrupted my friend, as he stepped unsteadily forward, while I followed immediately at his heels. In an instant he had reached the extremity of the niche, and finding his progress arrested by the rock, stood stupidly bewildered. A moment more and I had fettered him to the granite. In its surface were two iron staples, distant from each other about two feet, horizontally. From one of these depended a short chain, from the other a padlock. Throwing the links about his waist, it was but the work of a few seconds to secure it. He was too much astounded to resist. Withdrawing the key I stepped back from the recess.

'Pass your hand,' I said, 'over the wall; you cannot help feeling the nitre. Indeed it is *very* damp. Once more let me *implore* you to return. No? Then I must positively leave you. But I must first render you all the little attentions in my power.'

'The Amontillado!' ejaculated my friend, not yet recovered from his astonishment.

'True,' I replied; 'the Amontillado.'

As I said these words I busied myself among the pile of bones of which I have before spoken. Throwing them aside, I soon uncovered a quantity of building stone and mortar. With these materials and with the aid of my trowel, I began vigorously to wall up the entrance of the niche.

I had scarcely laid the first tier of the masonry when I discovered that the intoxication of Fortunato had in a great measure worn off. The earliest indication I had of this was a low moaning cry from the depth of the recess. It was *not* the cry of a drunken man. There was then a long and obstinate silence. I laid the second tier, and the third, and the fourth; and then I heard the furious vibrations of the chain. The noise lasted for several minutes, during which, that I might hearken to it with the more satisfaction, I ceased my labors and sat down upon the bones. When at last the clanking subsided, I resumed the trowel, and finished without interruption the fifth, the sixth, and the seventh tier. The wall was now nearly upon a level with my breast. I again paused, and holding the flambeaux over the masonwork, threw a few feeble rays upon the figure within.

A succession of loud and shrill screams, bursting suddenly from the throat of the chained form, seemed to thrust me violently back. For a brief moment I hesitated—I trembled. Unsheathing my rapier, I began to grope with it about the recess: but the thought of an instant reassured me. I placed my hand upon the solid fabric of the catacombs, and felt satisfied. I reapproached the wall. I replied to the yells of him who clamored. I re-echoed—I aided—I surpassed them in volume and in strength. I did this, and the clamorer grew still.

It was now midnight, and my task was drawing to a close. I had completed the eighth, the ninth, and the tenth tier. I had finished a portion of the last and the eleventh; there remained but a single stone to be fitted and plastered in. I struggled with its weight; I placed it partially in its destined position. But now there came from out the niche a low laugh that erected the hairs upon my head. It was succeeded by a sad voice, which I had difficulty in recognising as that of the noble Fortunato. The voice said—

'Ha! ha! ha!—he! he!—a very good joke indeed—an excellent jest. We will have many a rich laugh about it at the palazzo—he! ho! he!—over our wine—he! he! he!'

'The Amontillado!' I said.

'He! he! he!—he! he! he!—yes, the Amontillado. But is it not getting late? Will not they be awaiting us at the palazzo, the Lady Fortunato and the rest? Let us be gone.'

'Yes,' I said, 'let us be gone.'

'For the love of God, Montresor!'

'Yes,' I said, 'for the love of God!'

But to these words I hearkened in vain for a reply. I grew impatient. I called aloud—

'Fortunato!'

No answer. I called again—

'Fortunato!'

No answer still. I thrust a torch through the remaining aperture and let it fall within. There came forth in return only a jingling of the bells. My heart grew sick—on account of the dampness of the catacombs. I hastened to make an end of my labor. I forced the last stone into its position; I plastered it up. Against the new masonry I re-erected the old rampart of bones. For the half of a century no mortal has disturbed them. *In pace requiescat!*

Katherine Anne Porter

Katherine Anne Porter was born in 1890 in Indian Creek, Texas, and educated in schools in Texas and Louisiana. She ran away from New Orleans to get married at age sixteen; the union did not last. At twenty-one, she took off for Chicago where she did newspaper work and, on assignment, inadvertently found herself in a line-up for movie auditions. She sang Scottish ballads in costume, spent time in a sanatorium, and did more newspaper work in Denver, all the while writing. Towards the end of World War I, she almost died from influenza, like Miranda in *Pale Horse, Pale Rider*; the experience profoundly altered her life: "It simply just divided my life, cut across it like that. So that everything before that was just getting ready, and after that I was in some strange way altered, ready. It took me a long time to go out and live in the world again. I was really 'alienated' in the pure sense. It was, I think, the fact that I really had participated in death, that I knew what death was, and had almost experienced it. I had what the Christians call the 'beatific vision,' and the Greeks called the 'happy day,' the happy vision just before death. Now if you have had that, and survived it, come back from it, you are no longer like other people, and there's no use deceiving yourself that you are. But you see, I did: I made the mistake of thinking I was quite like everybody else, of trying to live like other people. It took me a long time to realize that that simply wasn't true, that I had my own needs and that I had to live like me."

Living "like me" involved taking off to Mexico, ostensibly to study Aztec and Mayan art designs, and becoming involved in the Obrégon Revolution of 1921; it also involved resisting conventional roles for women and harnessing her energies to write. "You're brought up with the notion of feminine chastity and inaccessibility, yet with the curious idea of feminine availability in all spiritual ways, and in giving service to anyone who demands it. And I suppose that's why it has taken me twenty years to write this novel [*Ship of Fools*]; it's been interrupted by just anyone who could jimmy his way into my life." Her first collection of stories, *Flowering Judas*, was published in 1930. A Guggenheim Fellowship took her to Berlin, Basel, and Madrid; her return to the U.S. was marked by numerous awards, periods of teaching and lecturing, and the publication of *Hacienda* (1934), *Noon Wine* (1937), *Pale Horse, Pale Rider* (1939), *The Leaning Tower and Other Stories* (1944), a book of essays called *The Days Before* (1952), *Ship of Fools* (1962), and *The Collected Essays and Occasional Writings of Katherine Anne Porter* (1970). She died in 1980.

Writing, Porter says, in *The Paris Review* interview, "is an act of faith. But one of the marks of a gift is to have the courage of it." "Art is a vocation as much as anything in this world. For the real artist, it is the most natural thing in the world, not as necessary as air and water, perhaps, but as food and water. But we really do lead almost a monastic life, you know; to follow it you very often have to give up something."

"So, I shall tell the truth," Porter says in "My First Speech," discussing the origin of her characters, "but the result will be fiction. It is a curious long process, roundabout to the last degree, like a slow chemical change, and I believe it holds true as much when one is not recreating one's own life and past but the life-history of another person. I think there are very few living characters in fiction who were not founded on a real living original. ... I should dare say that none of these characters so living in fiction would have recognized their own portraits, for if the transformation is successful the character becomes something else in its own right, as alive as the person who posed for the portrait."

Porter rejects nihilism and cultivated violence in art just as readily as she rejects the autobiographical: "Human life itself may be almost pure chaos, but the work of the artist—the only thing he's good for—is to take these handfuls of confusion and disparate things, things that seem to be irreconcilable, and put them together in a frame to give them some kind of shape and meaning." However, this does not mean that she thinks art must please or prettify: "artists do not always create a pleasant world, because that is not their business. If they do that, you will be right not to trust them in anything. We must all leave that to people whose affair it is to smooth our daily existence a little. Great art is hardly ever agreeable; the artist should remind you that, for some, experience is a horror in this world, and that the human imagination also knows horror. He should direct you to points of view you have not examined before, or cause you to comprehend, even if you do not sympathize with predicaments not your own, ways of life, manners of speech, even of dress, above all of the unique human heart, outside of your normal experience. And this can better be done by presentation than by argument. This presentation must be real, with a truth beyond the artist's own prejudices, loves, hates; I mean his personal ones. The outright propagandist sets up in me such a fury of opposition I am not apt to care much whether he has got his facts straight or not."

She was a firm advocate of craftsmanship and more than once described herself as a worker, a carpenter, even a bricklayer: "In the work of art, nothing can be accidental: the sprawling, chaotic sense of that word as we use it in everyday life, where so many things happen to us that we by no means plan, it takes craftsmanship quite often beyond our powers to manage to plan even a short day for ourselves. The craftsmanship of the artist can make what he wishes of anything that excites his imagination. Craftsmanship is a homely, workaday thing. It is a little like making shoes, or weaving cloth. A writer may be inspired occasionally: that's his good luck; but he doesn't learn to write by inspiration: he works at it. In that sense the writer is a worker, a workingman, a workingwoman. Writing is not an elegant pastime, it is a sober and hardworked trade, which gives great joy to the worker. The artist is first a worker. He must roll up his sleeves and get to work like a bricklayer." In a similar letter to Edward Schwartz, she says that one of her works "was written in one single sitting in a great burst of emotional recollection yet with my mind working soberly as a carpenter at his bench, choosing the right pieces and cutting them to shape and scale—this is not duality, not really, but we have many faculties material and immaterial and they work together harmoniously sometimes. ..."

Porter, in "No Plot, My Dear, No Story," says, "Except in emergencies, when you are trying to manufacture a quick tale and make some easy money, you don't really need a plot." She claims to "love the purity of language ... the basic pure human speech that exists in every langauge" but to detest the abuses language has undergone, the jargon of trades, professions, and vested interests. In response to a question about style, however, she says: "I've been called a stylist until I really could tear my hair out. And I simply don't believe in style. The style is you. ... You do not create a style. You work, and develop yourself; your style is an emanation from your own being."

Flowering Judas

Braggioni sits heaped upon the edge of a straight-backed chair much too small for him, and sings to Laura in a furry, mournful voice. Laura has begun to find reasons for avoiding her own house until the latest possible moment, for Braggioni is there almost every night. No matter how late she is, he will be sitting there with a surly, waiting expression, pulling at his kinky yellow hair, thumbing the strings of his guitar, snarling a tune under his breath. Lupe the Indian maid meets Laura at the door, and says with a flicker of a glance towards the upper room, "He waits."

Laura wishes to lie down, she is tired of her hairpins and the feel of her long tight sleeves, but she says to him, "Have you a new song for me this evening?" If he says yes, she asks him to sing it. If he says no, she remembers his favorite one, and asks him to sing it again. Lupe brings her a cup of chocolate and a plate of rice, and Laura eats at the small table under the lamp, first inviting Braggioni, whose answer is always the same: "I have eaten, and besides, chocolate thickens the voice."

Laura says, "Sing, then," and Braggioni heaves himself into song. He scratches the guitar familiarly as though it were a pet animal, and sings passionately off key, taking the high notes in a prolonged painful squeal. Laura, who haunts the markets listening to the ballad singers, and stops every day to hear the blind boy playing his reed-flute in Sixteenth of September Street, listens to Braggioni with pitiless courtesy, because she dares not smile at his miserable performance. Nobody dares to smile at him. Braggioni is cruel to everyone, with a kind of specialized insolence, but he is so vain of his talents, and so sensitive to slights, it would require a cruelty and vanity greater than his own to lay a finger on the vast cureless wound of his self-esteem. It would require courage, too, for it is dangerous to offend him, and nobody has this courage.

Braggioni loves himself with such tenderness and amplitude and eternal charity that his followers—for he is a leader of men, a skilled revolutionist, and his skin has been punctured in honorable warfare—warm themselves in the reflected glow, and say to each other: "He has a real nobility, a love of humanity raised above mere personal affections." The excess of this self-love has flowed out, inconveniently for her, over Laura, who, with so many others, owes her comfortable situation and her salary to him. When he is in a very good humor, he tells her, "I am tempted to forgive you for being a *gringa. Gringita!*" and Laura, burning, imagines herself leaning forward suddenly, and with a sound backhanded slap wiping the suety smile from his face. If he notices her eyes at these moments he gives no sign.

She knows what Braggioni would offer her, and she must resist tenaciously without appearing to resist, and if she could avoid it she would not admit even to herself the slow drift of his intention. During these long evenings which have spoiled a long month for her, she sits in her deep chair with an open book on her knees, resting her eyes on the consoling rigidity of the printed page when the sight and sound of Braggioni singing threaten to identify themselves with all her remembered afflictions and to add their weight to her uneasy premonitions of the future. The gluttonous bulk of Braggioni has become a symbol of her many disillusions, for a revolutionist should be lean, animated by heroic faith, a vessel of abstract virtues. This is nonsense, she knows it now and is ashamed of it. Revolution must have leaders, and leadership is a career for energetic men. She is, her comrades tell her, full of romantic error, for what she defines as cynicism in them is merely "a developed sense of reality." She is almost too willing to say, "I am wrong, I suppose I don't really understand the principles," and afterward she makes a secret truce with herself, determined not to surrender her will to such expedient logic. But she cannot help feeling that she has been betrayed irreparably by the disunion between her way of living and her feeling of what life should be, and at times she is almost contented to rest in this sense of grievance as a private store of consolation. Sometimes she wishes to run away, but she stays. Now she longs to fly out of this room, down the narrow stairs, and into the street where the houses lean together like conspirators under a single mottled lamp, and leave Braggioni singing to himself.

Instead she looks at Braggioni, frankly and clearly, like a good child who understands the rules of behavior. Her knees cling together under sound blue serge, and her round white collar is not purposely nun-like. She wears the uniform of an idea, and has renounced vanities. She was born Roman Catholic, and in spite of her fear of being seen by someone who might make a scandal of it, she slips now and again into some crumbling little church, kneels on the chilly stone, and says a Hail Mary on the gold rosary she bought in Tehuantepec. It is no good and she ends by examining the altar with its tinsel flowers and ragged brocades, and feels tender about the battered doll-shape of some male saint whose white, lace-trimmed drawers hang limply around his ankles below the hieratic dignity of his velvet robe. She has encased herself in a set of principles derived from her early training, leaving no detail of gesture or of personal taste untouched, and for this reason she will not wear lace made on machines. This is her private heresy, for in her special group the machine is sacred, and will be the salvation of the workers. She loves fine lace, and there is a tiny edge of fluted cobweb on this collar, which is one of twenty precisely alike, folded in blue tissue paper in the upper drawer of her clothes chest.

Braggioni catches her glance solidly as if he had been waiting for it, leans forward, balancing his paunch between his spread knees, and sings with tremendous emphasis, weighing his words. He has, the song relates, no father and no mother, nor even a friend to console him; lonely as a wave of the sea he comes and goes, lonely as a wave. His mouth opens round and yearns sideways, his balloon cheeks grow oily with the labor of song. He bulges marvelously in his expensive garments. Over his lavender collar, crushed upon a purple necktie, held by a diamond hoop: over his ammunition belt of tooled leather worked in silver, buckled cruelly around his gasping middle: over the tops of his glossy yellow shoes Braggioni swells with ominous ripeness, his mauve silk hose stretched taut, his ankles bound with the stout leather thongs of his shoes.

When he stretches his eyelids at Laura she notes again that his eyes are the true tawny yellow cat's eyes. He is rich, not in money, he tells her, but in power, and this power brings with it the blameless ownership of things, and the right to indulge his love of small luxuries. "I have a taste for the elegant refinements," he said once, flourishing a yellow silk handkerchief before her nose. "Smell that? It is Jockey Club, imported from New York." Nonetheless he is wounded by life. He will say so presently. "It is true everything turns to dust in the hand, to gall on the tongue." He sighs and his leather belt creaks like a saddle girth. "I am disappointed in everything as it comes. Everything." He shakes his head. "You, poor thing, you will be disappointed too. You are born for it. We are more alike than you realize in some things. Wait and see. Some day you will remember what I have told you, you will know that Braggioni was your friend."

Laura feels a slow chill, a purely physical sense of danger, a warning in her blood that violence, mutilation, a shocking death, wait for her with lessening patience. She has translated this fear into something homely, immediate, and sometimes hesitates before crossing the street. "My personal fate is nothing, except as the testimony of a mental attitude," she reminds herself, quoting from some forgotten philosophic primer, and is sensible enough to add, "Anyhow, I shall not be killed by an automobile if I can help it."

"It may be true I am as corrupt, in another way, as Braggioni," she thinks in spite of herself, "as callous, as incomplete," and if this is so, any kind of death seems preferable. Still she sits quietly, she does not run. Where could she go? Uninvited she has promised herself to this place; she can no longer imagine herself as living in another country, and there is no pleasure in remembering her life before she came here.

Precisely what is the nature of this devotion, its true motives, and what are its obligations? Laura cannot say. She spends part of her days in Xochimilco, near by, teaching Indian children to say in English, "The cat is on the mat." When she appears in the classroom they crowd about her with smiles on their wise, innocent, clay-colored faces, crying, "Good morning, my titcher!" in immaculate voices, and they make of her desk a fresh garden of flowers every day.

During her leisure she goes to union meetings and listens to busy important voices quarreling over tactics, methods, internal politics. She visits the prisoners of her own political faith in their cells, where they entertain themselves with counting cockroaches, repenting of their indiscretions, composing their memoirs, writing out manifestoes and plans for their comrades who are still walking about free, hands in pockets, sniffing fresh air. Laura brings them food and cigarettes and a little money, and she brings messages disguised in equivocal phrases from the men outside who dare not set foot in the prison for fear of disappearing into the cells kept empty for them. If the prisoners confuse night and day, and complain, "Dear little Laura, time doesn't pass in this infernal hole, and I won't know when it is time to sleep unless I have a reminder," she brings them their favorite narcotics, and says in a tone that does not wound them with pity, "Tonight will really be night for you," and though her Spanish amuses them, they find her comforting, useful. If they lose patience and all faith, and curse the slowness of their friends in coming to their rescue with money and influence, they trust her not to repeat everything, and if she inquires, "Where do you think we can find money, or influence?" they are certain to answer, "Well, there is Braggioni, why doesn't he do something?"

She smuggles letters from headquarters to men hiding from firing squads in back streets in mildewed houses, where they sit in tumbled beds and talk bitterly as if all Mexico were at their heels, when Laura knows positively they might appear at the band concert in the Alameda on Sunday morning, and no one would notice them. But Braggioni says, "Let them sweat a little. The next time they may be careful. It is very restful to have them out of the way for a while." She is not afraid to knock on any door in any street after midnight, and enter in the darkness, and say to one of these men who is really in danger: "They will be looking for you—seriously—tomorrow morning after six. Here is some money from Vicente. Go to Vera Cruz and wait."

She borrows money from the Roumanian agitator to give to his bitter enemy the Polish agitator. The favor of Braggioni is their disputed territory, and Braggioni holds the balance nicely, for he can use them both. The Polish agitator talks love to her over café tables, hoping to exploit what he believes is her secret sentimental preference for him, and he gives her misinformation which he begs her to repeat as the solemn truth to certain persons. The Roumanian is more adroit. He is generous with his money in all good causes, and lies to her with an air of ingenuous candor, as if he were her good friend and confidant. She never repeats anything they may say. Braggioni never asks questions. He has other ways to discover all that he wishes to know about them.

Nobody touches her, but all praise her gray eyes, and the soft, round under lip which promises gayety, yet is always grave, nearly always firmly closed: and they cannot understand why she is in Mexico. She walks back and forth on her errands, with puzzled eyebrows, carrying her little folder of drawings and music and school papers. No dancer dances more beautifully than Laura walks, and she inspires some amusing, unexpected ardors, which cause little gossip, because nothing comes of them. A young captain who had been a soldier in Zapata's army attempted, during a horseback ride near Cuernavaca, to express his desire for her with the noble simplicity befitting a rude folk-hero: but gently, because he was gentle. This gentleness was his defeat, for when he alighted, and removed her foot from the stirrup, and essayed to draw her down into his arms, her horse, ordinarily a tame one, shied fiercely, reared and plunged away. The young hero's horse careered blindly after his stable-mate, and the hero did not return to the hotel until rather late that evening. At breakfast he came to her table in full charro dress, gray buckskin jacket and trousers with strings of silver buttons down the leg, and he was in a humorous, careless mood. "May I sit with you?" and "You are a wonderful rider. I was terrified that you might be thrown and dragged. I should never have forgiven myself. But I cannot admire you enough for your riding!"

"I learned to ride in Arizona," said Laura.

"If you will ride with me again this morning, I promise you a horse that will not shy with you," he said. But Laura remembered that she must return to Mexico City at noon.

Next morning the children made a celebration and spent their playtime writing on the blackboard, "We lov ar ticher," and with tinted chalks they drew wreaths of flowers around the words. The young hero wrote her a letter: "I am a very foolish, wasteful, impulsive man. I should have first said I love you, and then you would not have run away. But you shall see me again." Laura thought, "I must send him a box of colored crayons," but she was trying to forgive herself for having spurred her horse at the wrong moment.

A brown, shock-haired youth came and stood in her patio one night and sang like a lost soul for two hours, but Laura could think of nothing to do about it. The moonlight spread a wash of gauzy silver over the clear spaces of the garden, and the shadows were cobalt blue. The scarlet blossoms of the Judas tree were dull purple, and the names of the colors repeated themselves automatically in her mind, while she watched not the boy, but his shadow, fallen like a dark garment across the fountain rim, trailing in the water. Lupe came silently and whispered expert counsel in her ear: "If you will throw him one little flower, he will sing another song or two and go away." Laura threw the flower, and he sang a last song and went away with the flower tucked in the band of his hat. Lupe said, "He is one of the organizers of the Typographers Union, and before that he sold corridos in the Merced market, and before that, he came from Guanajuato, where I was born. I would not trust any man, but I trust least those from Guanajuato."

She did not tell Laura that he would be back again the next night, and the next, nor that he would follow her at a certain fixed distance around the Merced market, through the Zócolo, up Francisco I. Madero Avenue, and so along the Paseo de la Reforma to Chapultepec Park, and into the Philosopher's Footpath, still with that flower withering in his hat, and an indivisible attention in his eyes.

Now Laura is accustomed to him, it means nothing except that he is nineteen years old and is observing a convention with all propriety, as though it were founded on a law of nature, which in the end it might well prove to be. He is beginning to write poems which he prints on a wooden press, and he leaves them stuck like handbills in her door. She is pleasantly disturbed by the abstract, unhurried watchfulness of his black eyes which will in time turn easily towards another object. She tells herself that throwing the flower was a mistake, for she is twenty-two years old and knows better; but she refuses to regret it, and persuades herself that her negation of all external events as they occur is a sign that she is gradually perfecting herself in the stoicism she strives to cultivate against that disaster she fears, though she cannot name it.

She is not at home in the world. Every day she teaches children who remain strangers to her, though she loves their tender round hands and their charming opportunist savagery. She knocks at unfamiliar doors not knowing whether a friend or a stranger shall answer, and even if a known face emerges from the sour gloom of that unknown interior, still it is the face of a stranger. No matter what this stranger says to her, nor what her message to him, the very cells of her flesh reject knowledge and kinship in one monotonous word. No. No. No. She draws her strength from this one holy talismanic word which does not suffer her to be led into evil. Denying everything, she may walk anywhere in safety, she looks at everything without amazement.

No, repeats this firm unchanging voice of her blood; and she looks at Braggioni without amazement. He is a great man, he wishes to impress this simple girl who covers her great round breasts with thick dark cloth, and who hides long, invaluably beautiful legs under a heavy skirt. She is almost thin except for the incomprehensible fullness of her breasts, like a nursing mother's, and Braggioni, who considers himself a judge of women, speculates again on the puzzle of her notorious virginity, and takes the liberty of speech which she permits without a sign of modesty, indeed, without any sort of sign, which is disconcerting.

"You think you are so cold, *gringita!* Wait and see. You will surprise yourself some day! May I be there to advise you!" He stretches his eyelids at her, and his ill-humored cat's eyes waver in a separate glance for the two points of light marking the opposite ends of a smoothly drawn path between the swollen curve of her breasts. He is not put off by that blue serge, nor by her resolutely fixed gaze. There is all the time in the world. His cheeks are bellying with the wind of song. "O girl with the dark eyes," he sings, and reconsiders. "But yours are not dark. I can change all that. O girl with the green eyes, you have stolen my heart away!" then his mind wanders to the song, and Laura feels the weight of his attention being shifted elsewhere. Singing thus, he seems harmless, he is quite harmless, there is nothing to do but sit patiently and say "No," when the moment comes. She draws a full breath, and her mind wanders also, but not far. She dares not wander too far.

Not for nothing has Braggioni taken pains to be a good revolutionist and a professional lover of humanity. He will never die of it. He has the malice, the cleverness, the wickedness, the sharpness of wit, the hardness of heart, stipulated for loving the world profitably. *He will never die of it.* He will live to see himself kicked out from his feeding trough by other hungry world-saviors. Traditionally he must sing in spite of his life which drives him to bloodshed, he tells Laura, for his father was a Tuscany peasant who drifted to Yucatan and married a Maya woman: a woman of race, an aristocrat. They gave him the love and knowledge of music, thus: and under the rip of his thumbnail, the strings of the instrument complain like exposed nerves.

Once he was called Delgadito by all the girls and married women who ran after him; he was so scrawny all his bones showed under his thin cotton clothing, and he could squeeze his emptiness to the very backbone with his two hands. He was a poet and the revolution was only a dream then; too many women loved him and sapped away his youth, and he could never find enough to eat anywhere, anywhere! Now he is a leader of men, crafty men who whisper in his ear, hungry men who wait for hours outside his office for a word with him, emaciated men with wild faces who waylay him at the street gate with a timid, "Comrade, let me tell you ..." and they blow the foul breath from their empty stomachs in his face.

He is always sympathetic. He gives them handfuls of small coins from his own pocket, he promises them work, there will be demonstrations, they must join the unions and attend the meetings, above all they must be on the watch for spies. They are closer to him than his own brothers, without them he can do nothing—until tomorrow, comrade!

Until tomorrow. "They are stupid, they are lazy, they are treacherous, they would cut my throat for nothing," he says to Laura. He has good food and abundant drink, he hires an automobile and drives in the Paseo on Sunday morning, and enjoys plenty of sleep in a soft bed beside a wife who dares not disturb him; and he sits pampering his bones in easy billows of fat, singing to Laura, who knows and thinks these things about him. When he was fifteen, he tried to drown himself because he loved a girl, his first love, and she laughed at him. "A thousand women have paid for that," and his tight little mouth turns down at the corners. Now he perfumes his hair with Jockey Club, and confides to Laura: "One woman is really as good as another for me, in the dark. I prefer them all."

His wife organizes unions among the girls in the cigarette factories, and walks in picket lines, and even speaks at meetings in the evening. But she cannot be brought to acknowledge the benefits of true liberty. "I tell her I must have my freedom, net. She does not understand my point of view." Laura has heard this many times. Braggioni scratches the guitar and meditates. "She is an instinctively virtuous woman, pure gold, no doubt of that. If she were not, I should lock her up, and she knows it."

His wife, who works so hard for the good of the factory girls, employs part of her leisure lying on the floor weeping because there are so many women in the world, and only one husband for her, and she never knows where nor when to look for him. He told her: "Unless you can learn to cry when I am not here, I must go away for good." That day he went away and took a room at the Hotel Madrid.

It is this month of separation for the sake of higher principles that has been spoiled not only for Mrs. Braggioni, whose sense of reality is beyond criticism, but for Laura, who feels herself bogged in a nightmare. Tonight Laura envies Mrs. Braggioni, who is alone, and free to weep as much as she pleases about a concrete wrong. Laura has just come from a visit to the prison, and she is waiting for tomorrow with a bitter anxiety as if tomorrow may not come, but time may be caught immovably in this hour, with herself transfixed, Braggioni singing on forever, and Eugenio's body not yet discovered by the guard.

Braggioni says: "Are you going to sleep?" Almost before she can shake her head, he begins telling her about the May-day disturbances coming on in Morelia, for the Catholics hold a festival in honor of the Blessed Virgin, and the Socialists celebrate their martyrs on that day. "There will be two independent processions, starting from either end of town, and they will march until they meet, and the rest depends ..." He asks her to oil and load his pistols. Standing up, he unbuckles his ammunition belt, and spreads it laden across her knees. Laura sits with the shells slipping through the cleaning cloth dipped in oil, and he says again he cannot understand why she works so hard for the revolutionary idea unless she loves some man who is in it. "Are you not in love with someone?" "No," says Laura. "And no one is in love with you?" "No." "Then it is your own fault. No woman need go begging. Why, what is the matter with you? The legless beggar woman in the Alameda has a perfectly faithful lover. Did you know that?"

Laura peers down the pistol barrel and says nothing, but a long, slow faintness rises and subsides in her; Braggioni curves his swollen fingers around the throat of the guitar and softly smothers the music out of it, and when she hears him again he seems to have forgotten her, and is speaking in the hypnotic voice he uses when talking in small rooms to a listening, close-gathered crowd. Some day this world, now seemingly so composed and eternal, to the edges of every sea shall be merely a tangle of gaping trenches, of crashing walls and broken bodies. Everything must be torn from its accustomed place where it has rotted for centuries, hurled skyward and distributed, cast down again clean as rain, without separate identity. Nothing shall survive that the stiffened hands of poverty have created for the rich and no one shall be left alive except the elect spirits destined to procreate a new world cleansed of cruelty and injustice, ruled by benevolent anarchy: "Pistols are good, I love them, cannon are even better, but in the end I pin my faith to good dynamite," he concludes, and strokes the pistol lying in her hands. "Once I dreamed of destroying this city, in case it offered resistance to General Ortíz, but it fell into his hands like an overripe pear."

He is made restless by his own words, rises and stands waiting. Laura holds up the belt to him: "Put that on, and go kill somebody in Morelia, and you will be happier," she says softly. The presence of death in the room makes her bold. "Today, I found Eugenio going into a stupor. He refused to allow me to call the prison doctor. He had taken all the tablets I brought him yesterday. He said he took them because he was bored."

"He is a fool, and his death is his own business," says Braggioni, fastening his belt carefully.

"I told him if he had waited only a little while longer, you would have got him set free," says Laura. "He said he did not want to wait."

"He is a fool and we are well rid of him," says Braggioni, reaching for his hat.

He goes away. Laura knows his mood has changed, she will not see him any more for a while. He will send word when he needs her to go on errands into strange streets, to speak to the strange faces that will appear, like clay masks with the power of human speech, to mutter their thanks to Braggioni for his help. Now she is free, and she thinks, I must run while there is time. But she does not go.

Braggioni enters his own house where for a month his wife has spent many hours every night weeping and tangling her hair upon her pillow. She is weeping now, and she weeps more at the sight of him, the cause of all her sorrows. He looks about the room. Nothing is changed, the smells are good and familiar, he is well acquainted with the woman who comes toward him with no reproach except grief on her face. He says to her tenderly: "You are so good, please don't cry any more, you dear good creature." She says, "Are you tired, my angel? Sit here and I will wash your feet." She brings a bowl of water, and kneeling, unlaces his shoes, and when from her knees she raises her sad eyes under her blackened lids, he is sorry for everything, and bursts into tears. "Ah, yes, I am hungry, I am tired, let us eat something together," he says, between sobs. His wife leans her head on his arm and says, "Forgive me!" and this time he is refreshed by the solemn, endless rain of her tears.

Laura takes off her serge dress and puts on a white linen nightgown and goes to bed. She turns her head a little to one side, and lying still, reminds herself that it is time to sleep. Numbers tick in her brain like little clocks, soundless doors close of themselves around her. If you would sleep, you must not remember anything, the children will say tomorrow, good morning, my teacher, the poor prisoners who come every day bringing flowers to their jailor. 1-2-3-4-5—it is monstrous to confuse love with revolution, night with day, life with death—ah, Eugenio!

The tolling of the midnight bell is a signal, but what does it mean? Get up, Laura, and follow me: come out of your sleep, out of your bed, out of this strange house. What are you doing in this house? Without a word, without fear she rose and reached for Eugenio's hand, but he eluded her with a sharp, sly smile and drifted away. This is not all, you shall see—Murderer, he said, follow me, I will show you a new country, but it is far away and we must hurry. No, said Laura, not unless you take my hand, no; and she clung first to the stair rail, and then to the topmost branch of the Judas tree that bent down slowly and set her upon the earth, and then to the rocky ledge of a cliff, and then to the jagged wave of a sea that was not water but a desert of crumbling stone. Where are you taking me, she asked in wonder but without fear. To death, and it is a long way off, and we must hurry, said Eugenio. No, said Laura, not unless you take my hand. Then eat these flowers, poor prisoner, said Eugenio in a voice of pity, take and eat: and from the Judas tree he stripped the warm bleeding flowers, and held them to her lips. She saw that his hand was fleshless, a cluster of small white petrified branches, and his eye sockets were without light, but she ate the flowers greedily for they satisfied both hunger and thirst. Murderer! said Eugenio, and Cannibal! This is my body and my blood. Laura cried No! and at the sound of her own voice, she awoke trembling, and was afraid to sleep again.

Audrey Thomas

Audrey Thomas was born in 1935 in Binghamton, New York, and educated at Smith College in the U.S. and St. Andrews University in Scotland. She and her former husband immigrated to Canada in 1958, where he taught in Vancouver, and she completed her M.A. at the University of British Columbia in 1963. They spent two years in Ghana in the mid-sixties. Thomas says she left the United States partly for political reasons (she was a student during the McCarthy hearings and saw what happened to writers who were "on trial" then) and has remained active in Amnesty International, PEN, and the Writers' Union of Canada. She lives on Galiano Island, not far from Vancouver, and has taught intermittently at the universities of Victoria, British Columbia, and Concordia. She published her first collection of stories, *Ten Green Bottles*, in 1967. This was followed by several novels, *Mrs. Blood* (1970), *Songs My Mother Taught Me* (1973), *Blown Figures* (1974), *Latakia* (1979), and *Intertidal Life* (1984), two short novels in a single volume, *Munchmeyer* and *Prospero on the Island* (1971), *Coming Down from WA* (1995), and several collections of stories: *Ladies & Escorts* (1977), *Real Mothers* (1981), *Two in the Bush and Other Stories* (1981), *Goodbye Harold, Good Luck* (1986), and *Wild Blue Yonder* (1990). An issue of the literary quarterly *Room of One's Own*, (Vol. 10, No. 3 and 4, 1986), is devoted to the work of Thomas and contains critical commentary, a selected bibliography, and an interview.

Some of her more interesting statements about fiction are quoted in an article by Liam Lacey for *The Globe and Mail* (Saturday, Nov. 3, 1990). Writing a short story "is a frame of mind. I'm sure the image isn't original, but I like to compare it to skipping a stone across a pond. Each place it touches the water, it sets off circles of ripples, and those circles overlap with each other. It's all the same stone, though." When asked specifically about technique, Thomas is cagey: "It sounds a bit like something you'd pick up in a sex shop, doesn't it?" However, she is very innovative and conscientious about matters of craft, mocking the idea that "stories write themselves." "I violently disagree with the idea that you don't know what you're doing as a writer. You don't pre-plan every detail, but you're more or less in control. I liken it to taking a puppy for a walk. It's going to go on the walk you decide, although not perhaps the way you planned. Sometimes the puppy stops and drags behind. Sometimes it worries this twig for longer than you'd care to, and that twig turns out to be the central symbol of your story. Sometimes you drag that puppy gasping back home with you and sometimes the puppy dies. But you're still the one determining where the walk goes." In response to one of her creative writing students asking what, basically, she wanted in a story, Thomas replied: "Basically, I'm looking for perfection; it never goes out of style."

Thomas sees herself in the mainstream of twentieth-century short fiction. "Nothing has really changed in the short story. It's always about the human heart. Alice Munro, Flannery O'Connor, Eudora Welty, William Trevor all write from the heart. The other thing is they all write from their neighbourhoods, either physically or spiritually. It's true I don't feel rooted in one place, but most of the places I write about I've lived in, shopped there, that sort of thing. The short story is like a little black dress: it's very versatile. No one should be without one." However, her work is much more verbally playful, and linguistically textured, than that of many of her contemporaries. "I like to use humour in my stories, but I'm not really doing those things with language as jokes. It's about language and its power. It's what T. S. Eliot's Sweeney said: 'I gotta use words when I talk to you.' Words aren't like those little letter puzzles, where you fit the letters L-O-V-E into the puzzle, and they fit right into the same slots. This is where men and women get into trouble, I think—they think they mean the same things by the same words when they really don't. I don't have any answers for this. Chekhov said in one of his letters that the role of the artist was to state the question correctly, and I think that's all I can do."

As these comments about language (and those in her essay "Basmati Rice") suggest, Thomas is interested in prose that maintains open borders with poetry. She acknowledges, in an interview with Allen Twigg (*Strong Voices*), having first learned from Australian novelist Patrick White about breaking sentences and using fragmentation for emphasis. When asked by Twigg about the unconventional quality of her prose, Thomas replies: "Well, the novel is essentially a middle-class form. I know I'm not unique in saying that. The novel has a tradition of received morality behind it. And if you no longer believe in that—or if you believe there isn't any such collective morality in the society in which you live—then the novel is about breaking down all that. And the minute your novel is about breaking down, it's not a novel anymore. It's a book. I write books."

Mothering Sunday

Hail Mary, Wounded art Thou among Women. That's what it means, doesn't it? Still, there in the French: *blesser:* to harm, to hurt, to injure, to wound. "*C'était une blessure grave.*" *Se blesser*, to wound oneself. In English we can trace the word back to *blōd*. Hail Mary, Blessed art Thou among Women. All the Marys bleed.

I am sitting here in this elegant French restaurant, surrounded by mothers and daughters, mothers and sons, mothers and sons and daughters-in-law (who probably rang up and made the reservations and arranged for the corsage). Not many children around but then, this is not the kind of restaurant where one takes young children, not North American children. Families with young children are no doubt celebrating at McDonalds or Smitty's Pancake House. I had forgotten it was Mother's Day when I arranged to meet Lydia at this restaurant and I, as usual, was early. She, as usual, is very late. Perhaps she missed her train connection and will not show up at all. I'd hate to miss her—I'm hardly ever in Toronto—but sitting here surrounded by all these mothers is dreadful. Should I hold up a sign: I AM A MOTHER TOO or stand up and show my stretch marks? But then they would think—if she is a mother where are her children. Why is she sitting alone, corsageless, with no one to buy her an "Anna M" cocktail, concocted in honour of Anna M. Jarvis, the founder, foundress, of Mother's Day in America. A little card on the table explains the whole thing. Anna M. never had children of her own and died penniless and almost sightless, in a quiet sanitorium in Pennsylvania at the age of eighty-four. She devoted her life to Mother's Day and to her blind sister Elsinore. I wonder about Anna M.'s mother, naming a daughter Elsinore, especially when the other gets a common-garden name like Anna M. Something rotten in the State of Pennsylvania! "In a quiet sanitorium in Pennsylvania." I've worked in those places. Hardly quiet. Noisy and rowdy and the old ladies coming out with words you could hardly believe, throwing balls of shit at one another, puddles forming under their chairs. I didn't mind. I was young; it would never happen to me. I wonder if there were at least two pennies in her purse, to shut her eyes.

Several of the mothers are sipping their Anna M. cocktails—they look like Harvey Wallbangers. I am sipping white wine. I wish Lydia would hurry up; she and I are good together, we make each other laugh, egg each other on to say more and more outrageous things. The young no-hipped waiter (imagine *him* giving birth to anything bigger than a jelly baby) would be very quickly demolished by a combination of Lydia and myself. When he suggested an Anna M. cocktail Lydia would ask for a Bloody Mary or a glass of milk, as being more appropriate for the occasion. Who first came up with *that* name, Bloody Mary? Businessmen ordering it on airplanes without batting an eye, if you gave them a glass of blood they'd reach for the sick-bags pretty quickly. Or Bloody Caesar, who, like MacDuff was from his mother's womb untimely ripp'd. No blood, no bloody Mary in the nativity accounts. Immaculate conception, immaculate delivery. We mothers know better, sitting here with our legs underneath the table, sitting here sipping our drinks, picking at the expensive food. Blood. A heavy word. No blood for months and then a lot. All cleaned up, fresh straw, fresh clothes, by the time the Wise Men came. In our church there was always a Christmas pageant and a white gift service on a Sunday near to Christmas. Children playing Mary, Joseph, Angels, Shepherds, Wise Men. "Gifts" for the poor children wrapped in white tissue paper and laid in front of the *tableau vivant*. All the parents loved it, especially the mothers. All the mothers wanted their daughters to be Mary.

The other day a young woman told me that, if you have the sperm, you can impregnate yourself with a turkey baster. I laughed and laughed and she was hurt. It was the turkey baster that made me laugh. Birds still involved in immaculate conceptions. Turkeys, such large, stupid delicate birds. Raised to be devoured at times of Thanksgiving and praise. Hail turkey, blessed art thou amongst birds. Turkeys didn't come completely dressed (meaning undressed) when I was a kid; my mother sat in the kitchen pulling out pin feathers after she had singed the bird, holding it over a candle, turning it. The kitchen smelled of burning feathers.

What do you do? Squirt the turkey-baster up you and then stand on your head for half an hour? (I don't really want to know.)

Where is Lydia? She knows the name of the restaurant, why hasn't she phoned? I could leave and go back to my hotel and wait for her there I guess; but I'm hungry and it's Sunday. We can't buy a bottle of wine and take it up to my room.

There are two carnations, one red, one white, in a crystal vase at each table. I wonder why it's always carnations—something to do with incarnate perhaps? The Word made flesh? That's another memory from my childhood, women standing on the church steps after the Mother's Day service, women wearing corsages of white or red carnations. White if the mother were dead, red if she were alive. But I don't remember us ever giving our mother a corsage of carnations. She probably told us not to. She had a habit of telling us not to do things: not to give her candy on Valentine's Day, not to give her birthday presents. I think now it was her way of asking for them but I didn't understand then. I understand, now, a great deal more about mothers. How they weren't, perhaps still aren't, supposed to ask for things. Unless they are useful of course—washing machines or microwave ovens.

Was Jesus a difficult child? Did he have tantrums, nightmares? Did he wet the bed? The Holy Ghost, the Original Big Bird, descends on her while she is sleeping and she wakes up pregnant.

(Lydia would probably add, "with maybe a spot of bird shit on the sheet.")

The original surrogate mother, and she doesn't even get to name the child. I wonder if he was a cult figure after he started preaching, he and his gang of twelve. We know that Mary and the other women followed him and the apostles "ministering" to them. But did the women steal bits of his clothes or snippets of hair, did they fight over who was going to bake the bread or hand him the honeycomb?

I think I'm a little oppressed by all this Mother's Day stuff, special drinks, special flowers. Shall I stay or shall I go? I don't feel neglected. When I get back home next week there will be cards and probably flowers, promises of breakfast in bed. But just now, alone in a room full of mothers and children I have some sense of what it must be like for those who never had children, never had that clear proof of their femaleness. See! See! I'm a mother; at least I've done something with my life. "Ocular proof."

Lydia's mother died when Lydia was fifteen. We talked about it once, whether that affected her and if so in what ways. Lydia ran the house for her father and younger brothers and sisters. She remembers her mother in a red-checked housedress with a big white collar. And a bib-apron over that. She was English and she wrote a lot of letters home. In England Mother's Day is called Mothering Sunday. She always wanted to send flowers to England on Mothering Sunday but never had the money. She died without ever seeing England or her mother again.

Lydia remembers that her mother cut out poems by Edna Jacques and stuck them on the ice-box. Lydia was very funny about Edna Jacques the Poet Laureate of the Kitchen. Even Nellie McClung admired her. The poems had titles like "A Mother at Night," "Small Deeds" and "A Mother at Christmas." I grew up in the States and had never heard of Edna Jacques. I think we had a similar person called Audrey Alexandra Brown. Last year Lydia found a copy of one of Edna Jacques's books in a second-hand store and gave it to me for my birthday. It's full of words like *bounteous* and *mayhap* and *laughter-tinted song*. The trouble is that although I laugh at Edna Jacques she does understand something about the wonder of watching little children. I've saved locks of "golden" hair, and early drawings, even a Mother's Day card from one of them

HAPY M
OTHERS DAY

I have no right to laugh at Edna Jacques.

I grew up during the Second World War. Mothers hung little silk flags in the front-room windows: a blue star on the flag if your son was fighting overseas, a gold star if he were killed or missing in action. Gold stars, in elementary school, were given for the very best, perfect or nearly perfect work. The teacher hung gold-star papers around the room. So gold-star mothers, and they were called that reverently, "Gold Star Mothers" were the perfect mothers, who had given up their sons to make the world safe for democracy. They would not have seen how they were part of the great myth, the old lie.

(I have just ordered another carafe of the house wine and some pâté and bread. "My friend has been delayed," I said brightly to my pretty no-hipped waiter. He doesn't believe me; he thinks I am a rejected Mother. He frowned when I ordered more wine. "It's all right," I said. "I'm not an alcoholic, I'm a drinker." Lydia will be here soon—she has never let me down. None of her children are at home any more, but perhaps she had an unexpected long distance call and missed the train. You can't cut people off when they've taken the trouble to phone you long distance.)

I went to see my mother last week. She is eighty-nine years old and lives in a cosy apartment in a senior citizens' complex near Boston. Every time I visit now she gives me something or shows me something that is "coming to me" after she dies. This time it was two lovely fans, one red silk and lace, one black, which had belonged to her mother. They are very fragile and I shall have to open them out, mount them and then frame them. Very fragile and very exotic, from a time when women carried fans on special occasions. We looked at old photographs and talked a bit, drank tea. Then in one box of bits and pieces which are to go to my sister and me my eye lit on a large oval frame, of some beautiful dark wood, cherry wood perhaps. I asked her what had been in it—I didn't remember it at all. She said, "Oh, do you want it? I was going to throw that away." I asked again whose picture the frame had been for. She said, "My mother." I asked her where the picture was now. She said, "I tore it up." Then she took the frame out of my hands and put it away in a drawer. She didn't offer the frame to me again.

Why? What had her mother done? I had always thought she loved her mother. I couldn't ask. It was something terrible and private, something between mothers and daughters, something Edna Jacques would never write about, the dark side of all this, the wounds as well as blessings.

"Well," I said, "I must be going now." I could see that she was tired, that we had run out of safe things to talk about. I have wounded her many times; she has wounded me. We don't talk about this. We send each other letters and greeting cards and presents; we worry about one another. We wonder.

"Well," I said, putting on my coat, "I'll write to you soon." We kissed the air and then she walked me to the front entrance. She looks twenty years younger than she really is. Women her age move through the overheated halls pushing walkers or shaking with those hidden winds of extreme age.

"Goodbye," we call to one another through the glass door. "Goodbye, goodbye."

Here's Lydia coming in, shaking her umbrella, laughing. She sees me and waves.

"Don't have the Anna M. Jarvis cocktail," I say as she sits down, breathless and laughing. She smiles up at the waiter.

"What about a Bloody Mary?" and winks at me.

One of the mothers is celebrating her birthday. Her waiter is bringing in a cake. The whole restaurant starts singing, takes up the tune.

"Happy Birthday, Dear Mother, Happy Birthday to you."

"I missed the train," Lydia says, then looks around. "My God, look at all the mothers!"

"Did you bronze your children's baby shoes?"

"No, no. We didn't have the money. But I was definitely of the bronzed shoe school."

"Me too. Did you save things?"

"Boxes and boxes of things. But I wasn't as bad as a woman up the street. She saved all her children's milk teeth in a glass jar on the kitchen counter."

"Listen Lydia, I want to tell you something that just happened with my mother. Only let's order first. I'm starving."

We signal the waiter to bring the menus. I pour another glass of wine and begin.

José Leandro Urbina

José Leandro Urbina was born in Chile in 1949. He studied literature at the University of Chile, but was forced into exile by the 1973 military coup. He fled to Argentina for three years, but a coup d'état in that country set him in motion again and he arrived in Canada in 1977. He continued his studies at Carleton University in Ottawa and became a Canadian citizen. He was one of the founding editors of the publishing company Cordillera. His stories have appeared in magazines and anthologies around the world and he has been the recipient of various arts grants from the Canada Council and the Ontario Arts Council. Urbina's first collection of stories, *Las malas juntas*, was published in Spanish in 1978; the English version, *Lost Causes*, appeared in 1987 in a translation by Urbina's wife, Christina Shantz. Urbina has lived in New York, working as a free-lance writer and film-maker, and, most recently, in Bethesda, Maryland, from where his wife commutes to work in Washington, D.C., and he pursues his doctorate at the Catholic University of the Americas on the relationship between fiction and history in four novels about the discovery of America. In 1992 he published a novel in Spanish, *Cobro revertido* (Collect Call), which was short-listed in the prestigious Planeta competition in Spain.

Urbina's ideas on brevity in fiction are intimately linked with his political experiences in Chile and Argentina. As he says in a statement prepared for this anthology, "Outrageous as it may seem, my notion of brevity in the short story has to do with my understanding and experience of the joke, as a narrative structure and in its social and cultural function.

"The day after the military coup d'état in Chile in 1973 and Allende's death in the presidential palace, there were already jokes circulating in Santiago about the dead President. Most of them didn't perform the function attributed to the joke by Bergson, of shaming people who oppose a flexible social order. Most of them seemed funny to the people who supported the army's violence, and offensive to the supporters of the former President. Some of those jokes were failures because of their stupidity. Some of them, funny in retrospect, were sickening in the circumstances.

"Then the opposition created their own repertory of jokes, and the generals were not amused.

"Later, in Argentina, my contacts with the cruel humour of Buenos Aires and the people's somewhat cynical attitude towards politics after years of military dictatorship led me to use the very short story, similar to the joke in its dual status, to express aspects of the painful Chilean experience without being unbearably sentimental or pitiful.

"As well as their narrative effectiveness, short short stories have the advantage of being easy to circulate and turn into anecdotes. This can broaden the scope of the political story, even though it may strip it of literary values. My short story, 'Our father who art in heaven,' was photocopied and circulated widely during the Pinochet regime, even though the book was semi-available. Many people have told me that they know of a case 'in real life' just like the one in the story I wrote around the theme of the involuntary or innocent traitor and the 'comic' possibilities of the title (may God forgive)."

Our Father Who Art in Heaven

While the sergeant was interrogating his mother and sister, the captain took the child by the hand to the other room.

—Where is your father? he asked.

—He's in heaven, whispered the boy.

—What's that? Is he dead? asked the captain, surprised.

—No, said the child. Every night he comes down from heaven to eat with us.

The captain raised his eyes and discovered the little door in the ceiling.

Portrait of a Lady

In the light of dawn that filtered timidly through the window, she smoothed her dress carefully. One of her fingernails cleaned the others. She moistened her fingertips with saliva and smoothed her eyebrows. As she finished arranging her hair, she heard the jailers coming along the passageway.

In front of the interrogation room, remembering the pain, her legs trembled. Then they put a hood on her and she crossed the threshold. Inside was the same voice as the day before. The same footsteps as the day before came over to her chair, bringing the damp voice right up her ear.

—Where were we yesterday, Miss Jimenez?

—We were saying that you should remember you're dealing with a lady, she said.

A blow smashed into her face. She felt her jawbone crack.

—Where were we, Miss Jimenez?

—We were saying that you should remember you're dealing with a lady, she said.

W. D. Valgardson

William Dempsey Valgardson was born of Irish and Icelandic parents in Winnipeg in 1939 and raised in Gimli, an Icelandic fishing community on Lake Winnipeg. He studied at the United College and taught school for several years before completing his M.F.A. at the University of Iowa. He teaches Creative Writing at the University of Victoria. His publications include several collections of short stories—*Bloodflowers* (1973), *God Is Not a Fish Inspector* (1975), *Red Dust* (1978), *What Can't Be Changed Shouldn't Be Mourned* (1990), *Garbage Creek and Other Stories* (1995), and a children's book, *Winter Rescue* (1995). He has also published two novels, *Gentle Sinners* (1980), which won the *Books in Canada* First Novel Award and was made into a film, and *The Girl with the Botticelli Face* (1992), as well as a book of poems, *The Gutting Shed* (1976).

Valgardson has said in an interview in 1981 with Alan Twigg (*Strong Voices*) that he feels himself capable of any crime. "I tell my students that there are two journeys every writer must take. The first journey is into the lives of others. But the second journey is the most terrifying. It is the journey into the self. I think what happens with a lot of people is that they turn away. They suddenly become aware of their motivations and they realize some of the things they are capable of. They don't understand that just because they're capable of something they don't have to do it."

When he talks about becoming a writer, Valgardson speaks of his skill with words as a compensation for being small and not having the physical skills valued in his community as a youth. "I was a dreamer and a reader. At some stage I obviously learned that you can fight with words. You can lay people wide open with words! You might have to learn to run like hell after you've said what you said ... but I think there's a lot of people who become lawyers for that reason. And politicians. And writers." He speaks of the discovery of Al Purdy's *The Cariboo Horses* as an empowering experience, giving him the confidence to write as a Canadian. "For me writing is like an Eskimo carving. The form is in the stone. The trick is for me to find the form. And so it's a case of exploration. I write to discover what I think. I don't think and then write. If you think and then write, you often get propaganda. For instance, I think the worst thing any writer can do is impose symbols. That's a dreadful thing, to nail them on. It should be like driftwood. You don't nail the knots on. The water washes and erodes and what's left are those hard knobs. That is the way that symbols should be. They should rise out of the material naturally. Then go back over your material and see what you've got. Then heighten it. You see connections. Because one's genius is in spots. It's not necessarily coherent all the way through. So you try to make it coherent. It's like painting. You add touches."

In an interview with Geoff Hancock in *Canadian Fiction Magazine* (No. 32/33, 1979), he claims to write mainly out of "a mood, a feeling, an emotion" and to force his stories through many drafts. "I never work from a plot. I don't know who said a plot is the last refuge of a hack, but I firmly believe it. I'm far more concerned with theme. Every story has to tell at least two stories and if you're capable, if you have the skill, hopefully your story is multi-layered and therefore will continue to have interest for a long time. Writers and readers enjoy the kinds of secrets that lie within a story, in the explorations."

In discussing structure and design, Valgardson favours the unfamiliar and the unexpected: "One critic said he had the feeling that so far into my stories he felt he was on firm ground and then the sand turned and he felt as if he was sliding and he didn't know what happened to him. There is that kind of quality there sometimes." "I think open-ended stories are much more intriguing than closed stories. Certainly, I wouldn't want to opt for one kind or another. It depends on the story itself as to what form it's going to take. The needs of the theme. Myself, I really admire 'The Lady or the Tiger?' and have admired it ever since I was a very small child. It is a story that people want to talk about five minutes after, a day after, a year after they've read it. A lot of stories with severely closed endings cease to be of interest once the endings have been read."

Valgardson claims to have learned from Hemingway to love the simple sentence; and from Jane Austen, complexity of structure. He also singles out Barthelme, Coover, and Europeans such as Ilse Aischinger, author of *The Bound Man*. However, he seems most profoundly influenced by writers of the Deep South, particularly Flannery O'Connor, for both moral vision and the starkness and elemental nature of the human encounters in his stories. Setting is very important in Valgardson's work. However, when accused of exaggerating the harshness of the Canadian scene for dramatic effect, he laughs: "One of the people I know went looking for her husband one day. He was late coming home for supper. He was a farmer. She found him with his tractor fallen over on him in a pool of water. He was pinned beneath the tractor and couldn't move and could just barely hold his head above the surface. She was faced with a dilemma. As long as she held his head up, he wouldn't drown. But if she stayed with him, he was going to die slowly from his injuries. I didn't make that up. That's the way life is. She had to make the best decision she could. Maybe some day, I'll write this in a fiction. But that's reality. The land is not malevolent. It's just simply there. In the Interlake area of Manitoba, and in Northern Manitoba, it's a very harsh environment. Have your car break down when it's thirty below with wind, as has happened to me, and have suddenly to walk five miles to the closest house, and then say to yourself, 'Valgardson makes up a stark land.' No way. The stark land is just there."

Celebration

While Mabel fried the potatoes, she watched Eric out of the corner of her left eye. He was stretched precariously over a kitchen chair, the sharp points of his shoulder blades pressed against the high wooden back, his spine resting on the edge of the wooden seat. The heavy lids of his eyes were nearly closed but she knew that he was only feigning sleep and that beneath the wrinkled skin and thin lashes, his eyes were constantly shifting, following her every move. The last time she had taken her eyes off him, he had kicked her in the back of the leg.

She saw Eric's hands tense. He started to ease himself toward her.

"I've got a pan of hot grease," she warned. As she spoke, she lifted the pan from the stove.

"Lousy bitch," he replied, just barely moving his lips. "Lousy bitch."

The windows were feathered with frost and, in the corners of the frames, ice had gathered in thick knots. Cold drafts swirled under the door. It was only four o'clock but, already, outside the windows, it was as black as if the sky had been drenched in tar. The darkness had forced its way into the corners of the room and under the furniture. Here, it lay like a silent animal, ready to pounce at the first opportunity. Outside, a blizzard tore at the frozen land.

"We need more wood," she said, rattling the cast-iron pan against the stove to emphasize her point. "We gotta keep up the heat."

There was a space-heater sitting mutely in the middle of the floor. It worked but they had been unable to pay their last year's fuel bill and the deliveryman had cut them off. They had to depend on wood for both cooking and heating.

"Get it yourself," he replied at last.

Mabel seldom spoke. Now, because she had been drinking, she shifted her wide hips and said, with the studied seriousness of someone who has come to a conclusion after long thought, "You're ugly when you're drunk."

Eric snorted. "You're ugly all the time."

On the table, there was an open quart jar. It was a third full of homebrew. Eric's arm, as though it had a life of its own, snaked across the table, picked up the jar and brought it to his mouth. He drank without taking his eyes from Mabel, put the jar back and wiped his mouth with his sleeve. The social worker had said she thought she could get them onto welfare and they were celebrating. Eric had walked five miles to buy the liquor from a pulp cutter. Mabel and he had shared the first half but then, seeing how quickly it was being used up, he had decided to keep the rest for himself.

"Don't be so cheap," she said. She let go of the pan and pushed her red sweater up over her elbows. She had short arms and legs and her clothes were always too long for her. "Gimme a drink."

When he was sober, Eric was generous, letting her have money for mail-order clothes and, when they went into town, buying her french fries and taking her to bingo. When he drank, he was different. He sat and brooded about how little he had, listing a life's accumulation of grievances. It was then that they fought. Mostly, it was kicks and slaps but, sometimes, when she turned on him, they fought with fists and feet, teeth and nails. Once, he had broken her arm with a piece of stovewood and, once, she had cut open his thigh with an axe.

She was short, shorter than he was, with straight dark hair hacked off at the shoulders. Her body was round, with three large rolls of fat between her hips and her large breasts. Eric had found her in the Eddyville beer parlour. They had not married but, despite their differences, had stayed together for ten years.

Mabel turned the potatoes over, checking to see that they were brown and crisp, then skidded the pan to the edge of the stove.

"Feed them kids," Eric said. They both spoiled the children but they were his particular pets. He never denied them anything. He fed them jawbreakers and raspberry drops and potato chips and bought them plastic dolls with pink cheeks. Even when he was drunk, he did no more than brush them out of his way.

"That's what I'm doing."

Incensed by her answering back, he opened his eyes. They were as pale as shallow water in harsh sunlight.

"No-damn-good hotel trash. Lying under a table with your skirt over your head, that's you."

"I ain't been in a hotel for over a year and when I was, I walked out on my own two feet. Nobody had to carry me." She turned her head just enough to watch half his face purse with annoyance.

With a hint of satisfaction, she dumped a portion of the potatoes into a foil pie pan and placed it on the floor beside the couch. The four-year-old's brown arm darted out and dragged the pan into the shadows. Right away, the two-year-old began a broken cry of despair. It started slowly at first with spaces in between each cry but the spaces quickly became shorter. It was as though she was winding up a spring. If it was not stopped, her cry would become an endless wail.

"Josie, you give her some or I'll give you the broom," her mother threatened. There was the shuffling of aluminum on wood. The crying stopped.

Whenever their parents fought, the children hid under the Toronto couch, lying absolutely still, making no sound for hours on end. They were like two small animals hiding in a cave; only their large, dark eyes moved. A stranger might have spent an hour or more in the room and never known they were there.

Mabel dug in the bottom of the woodbox. The box was high, with a lid that folded back. It was large enough to contain two grown people. The top half of her body disappeared over the edge so that all that was visible was the wide expanse of her buttocks in a voluminous blue dress, men's grey wool socks and snow boots, one brown, one black. She heaved herself back up and held three sticks out so that Eric could see them. Her face was bright red from the effort of nearly standing on her head.

"That's all there is. We gotta have more."

His eyes regarded her with the distant blankness they assumed when he dealt with anyone in authority. Deliberately, he picked at his teeth before saying, "Get it yourself."

She filled the stove, then skidded his plate over the pink oilcloth. Although he was hungry, he let it sit.

"You've done nothing all day," she said.

Angered by the truth of her statement, he struck the table with his fist. He accidentally hit the rim of the pan. Potatoes were catapulted across the room.

"See what you made me do," he squawked. He had wanted the potatoes. In his surprise, he pushed his chair backward until it was resting on its rear legs.

Mabel moved her plate out of his reach.

"Pick that up," he ordered, swallowing three times as he thought about his lost supper.

She remained where she was, stuffing her mouth with potatoes.

"Whore! That's all you are."

Emboldened by the liquor, she retorted, "That's all you could get."

He lashed out with his boot but she was too far away. He lost his precarious balance. For a moment, he hung suspended, one leg stuck straight out, one foot on the floor, one hand flung out as though to grab the air and hold him in place. He fell flat on his back. Startled, he lay while his wife finished another mouthful of potatoes. Without changing position, he slowly raised his fist toward the open beams of the ceiling and shook it in silent rage as though to challenge a host of malevolent gods secreted among the rafters.

His eyes travelled across the smoke-darkened ceiling, down the wall, over Mabel's moon-like face and locked on her vigorously chewing mouth.

"I got nothin'," he shouted, "I never had nothin' and what I had, you eat."

The two-year-old, seeing that no-one was looking her way, crept out from under the couch and began to gather slices of fried potato, cramming them into her mouth until her cheeks bulged. She had on a pink sweater, green corduroy overalls and knitted slippers with felt rabbit's ears on the toes. When her mouth and hands could hold no more, she scurried back to the safety of the couch.

Gazing down upon her husband as he lay with his clenched fist raised stiffly toward heaven, Mabel said, without any change of expression, "We gotta have more wood." Her arm curved around her aluminum foil plate, cradling it so carefully that it might have been made of beaten silver.

"Is that all you can think about? Your own comfort?" Eric's face had grown mottled. "I might have injured a vital element," he paused to add weight to his statement, then added, "fatally." He saw in that instant the tragedy of his own death and was overwhelmed by it. To impress upon her what might have been, he let his arms fall to his side and rolled his eyes back into his head. In his raw, red face, they looked like eggs that had been boiled and peeled.

Mabel wasn't impressed. "We gotta have more wood," she repeated.

"You," Eric screeched, his voice thin and high, "have no respect." His upper body popped up as though it was attached to his hips by a suddenly released spring. "No respect."

He was slight, with a long face and hardly any chin. When he got dressed up in his grey suit, he looked distinguished in a minor way like a failed bookkeeper. He had cut pulp and hired out as a shorehand all his life but, because of his drinking, had never been able to hold a job more than six months. It was one of his grievances and it made him sensitive to slights, both imagined and real.

"You don't care what happens to me," he said with the hurt voice of a child. "I might as well be alone."

The thought had not occurred to him before. Normally he lived in the present, accepting it as unchangeable. The future was a mystery, revealed only when it became the present. Now, his idea, falling on fertile soil, sprouted and immediately blossomed. He saw himself unencumbered with Mabel. His face took on a settled look.

"You might as well get going," he said, as if something had been concluded. "You can take your clothes and five dollars."

Mabel looked away. In spite of all their disputes, they had never done two things: laid charges against one another or walked out on one another. The morning after she had hit Eric with an axe, Mabel had sat at his bedside, giving him sips of Pepsi and vodka from a soft-drink bottle.

"I got no place to go," she replied in a quiet, defeated voice.

He paid no attention. "I'll get somebody else. I've made up my mind."

His attention had wandered from her. Groping behind himself, he found the chair, righted it and, lost in thought, lifted himself backward up the rungs until he was seated in his former position. He stared at the ceiling.

"I'll get the wood," Mabel said, her face averted.

Ten feet from the front door, wood was stacked in rows. A narrow, waist-high path had been dug so that they could get to the woodpile and beyond. Normally, it was kept clear but, now, the path was five inches deep in loose snow.

The woodpile was so close that Mabel didn't bother to put on a jacket. Because of the draft on the floor, she was wearing fleece-lined boots. As she stepped outside, blown snow rose as thickly as smoke from damp leaves. She hurried, running to the woodpile, pulling a stick loose, then using it to knock three more pieces free. Before she had the wood stacked in her arms, the layer of heat next to her skin had been swept away. Particles of dry snow struck her skin as sharply as sand. She gave a violent shiver.

She would have stacked more wood in her arms but the wind beat against her, drawing tears from her eyes. Squeezing her head down into her shoulders, keeping her face turned away from the wind, she struggled back. The white layer of frost that covered the wood burned the soft flesh of her bare hands. By the time she reached the door, she was desperate to get inside. She bent to grasp the latch. Lifting it, she pushed. The door did not open. Often, because of ice forming on the frame, the door stuck. She gave it a push with her knee. It still did not budge.

"Eric," she yelled. "The door's stuck." She kicked against the rough boards.

"Open the door, Eric." She thought for a moment that he might not be able to hear her over the wind but she knew immediately that that could not be. However, he did not hold his liquor well and it was possible he had passed out.

She dropped the wood, caught the handle and jerked up. She threw her body against the door but the door did not move.

Pounding with the flat of one hand, she yelled, "Let me in. I'm freezing."

When there was no response, she picked up one of the sticks and began to beat on the door but it was made of birch slabs and did no more than shiver. At first, she held the stick like a bat. When that did not work, she changed her tactics, holding the log like a ram and concentrating her blows on the latch. The metal handle buckled, then broke but the door did not give way. She knew then that Eric had to have set the wooden bar in place. Years before, she had been nervous about his being away at night so he had bolted angle-iron to each side of the frame. With a two-by-four set across the door, nothing short of an axe would be sufficient to break in.

She dropped the log. Her anger and the exertion had combined to stave off the effects of the cold but now, as she stood panting, her entire body began to shake. Snow had sifted into her boots, collecting in a cold band around her ankles. Crouching awkwardly to gain the protection of the snowdrifts, she instinctively made her body as small as possible to preserve her warmth. Her hands were shaking so much that she crossed them tightly over her breasts. For the first time, as she squatted, helpless, she realized that Eric might not let her in and that, if he didn't, she would die. The anger that had sprung up only a short time before was swept away by fear.

Turning to the door, she placed her face against it and called out plaintively, "Eric, please let me in." When there was no reply, she began to plead in a loud, anguished voice, saying *please* over and over again. Fear cleared her mind, dispelling the blurred confusion of the liquor. It was as though her mind had expanded, become a vast plain on which there was no light but over which she could see with perfect clarity.

She needed shelter. Unable to find it where she was, she had to seek it elsewhere. She saw, as plainly as if she was looking at it from an airplane, the stretch of road that led to the next camp. She thought of trying to reach it, then gave up the idea. On the open road, the wind would be unobstructed and would sweep down on her with its full fury. The trip would take her three hours. Dressed the way she was, she wouldn't get past the first mile.

The cabin was long and low. Snow drifts rose nearly to the eaves. The side windows were partially hidden. Shivering so hard that she had a difficult time making her hands obey, she left the protection of the doorway and crawled onto the drift. The bank was steep and she had to dig her bare hands into the snow so that she could pull herself forward. On top of the drift, she rose into a crouching position. She took two steps. The brittle crust gave way beneath her. Her right leg plunged down past the knee and she pitched forward.

The shock of falling and the painful wrench of her knee made her lie still for a full minute before the cold forced her to lift one stiff hand, dig it into the snow and pull herself forward. She reached out with the other hand. Her leg felt as though it had been broken. The ice had made a shallow but painful gash from her ankle to her knee. When her leg came free, her boot remained trapped at the bottom of the hole. She did not try to retrieve it but floundered ahead, half-crawling, half-swimming, muttering, "Oh God. Oh, God." Snow pushed past the neck of her dress and up the sleeves of her sweater.

Lying flat, she pressed her face to the window. Her hair and eyebrows were crusted with snow, the round flesh of her face was white and drawn. She tried to see inside but the glass was so thickly covered with ice that the warmth and light were reduced to no more than an orange glow.

Using her hands like claws, she tapped at the window. There was no answer. She tried to make a fist. Her fingers would not close.

Desperately, she struck at the glass. The window broke.

Pressing her face to the hole, she called, "Eric, let me in."

A shadow obscured the light, then a board covered the hole and she knew that Eric was barring the window with a fishbox lid. She could hear him hammering nails. In a frenzy, she flailed at the glass, cutting her hands. She felt nothing. Blood ran over her fingers and immediately congealed.

She began to cry then. Her tears froze on her face. Defeated, she twisted her heavy body away from the window and began crawling back to the door. Her mind, only a short time before had been clear and immense. Now, it began to contract as it started to close off everything except the instinct for survival.

When she reached the path, she slid down to the bottom of the trail and crouched in the doorway. Blowing snow curled over the lip of the drift and settled on her like confetti. The small, remaining part of her conscious thought would have kept her there, straining helplessly at the heat which was such a short distance away. Instinct made her get up to begin an awkward, relentless pacing.

She walked as far as the woodpile, returned, beating her arms on her body. Because of her wrenched knee and her missing boot, she limped as badly as a cripple. Sometimes, she stumbled and fell but, always, she got up. For a time, she increased her pace until she was nearly running. Occasionally, she stopped and stood helplessly, as though she had forgotten what it was that she was doing. Her eyes became unfocused, staring directly ahead of her. All the time she walked, her body jerked and shook and from her mouth there came a steady, unceasing moan.

The door opened. Light spilled onto the path and great gusts of steam billowed upward. Leaning heavily on the doorframe, engulfed in light and steam, Eric might have been standing at the entrance to hell.

"Had enough?" he called belligerently, his head waving from side to side, his words slurred.

Mabel was at the farthest point of her journey. Turning, she stumbled back along the trail she had ploughed in the snow, her legs rising and falling in the jerky, unco-ordinated movements of a spastic.

"You had ..." Eric began again but Mabel, her eyes staring as though they had been frozen in their sockets, her face burned white, her hair thick with snow, pushed past him, nearly knocking him down. She staggered clumsily across the room, pieces of caked snow falling from her. In front of the stove, she slipped to her knees.

Eric watched her, then with stiff, exaggerated care, bent and picked up the pieces of wood she had dropped in front of the door. Shutting the door behind him, he closed one eye, sighted the stove like he was going to shoot it and crossed the room, his body teetering this way and that, constantly on the verge of falling. He managed to stuff the wood into the stove.

"You're okay," he said. His speech was slurred, indefinite. "I decided to keep you." He staggered sideways for two steps. "That'll teach you to mind your mouth."

When Mabel did not reply but remained huddled as close to the stove as she could get, he steadied himself by catching hold of the back of a chair and leaned over her. Water streamed down her face and body and gathered in a pool around her. Her eyes were shut; her mouth gaped open. As he hung over her, she slumped to the floor and lay on her right side.

"I'll get you a drink. That's all you need." She made no indication she had heard him. He went to the table and his skinny red hands tipped the jar up, spilling the last of the homebrew into a fish-paste glass. He picked up the glass and held it out to her back. She did not move. His hand turned in a constant, unsteady circle.

Unable to keep the floor from tipping first one way, then the other, he got down on his knees and walked on them to her.

"Have a drink," he said. The liquor slopped over his fingers.

Mabel began to cough. Her cough was shallow and persistent, as though a piece of dry bread had caught in her windpipe.

Eric pushed his face up to hers. Even through his drunkenness, what he saw worried him. He tried to put the glass on the stove and failed. It fell to the floor and rolled away.

He pushed himself to his feet, staggered to the washstand for the basin, then continued to the door.

It was while he was on his knees in the doorway, scraping snow into the washbasin that she screamed. Her scream, high and unbroken, filled the room. At the same time, she began to twist about as if to escape from pain inflicted upon her by some unseen tormentor.

Eric looked at her uncomprehendingly. Snow blew over him in a twisting funnel. In the brief time he had the door open, twin fingers of snow had formed at each corner of the sill.

He brought the half-filled pan of snow to her, setting it on the floor. Not knowing how to deal with her writhing, he sat back, his legs tucked under him, staring at her with the puzzled, stupid expression of a cat seeing something it is curious about but does not understand. He reached a handful of snow toward her but she cried, "Get away. Get away." She crawled to the far end of the stove.

Unable to stand her screaming and afraid of what he had done, he said, "I'll go for help."

It took him ten minutes to get dressed. He found his flashlight tucked in a rubber boot, tested it, then staggered outside. Negotiating the path was not too difficult. Its narrowness guided him and the high banks gave him support. The cold helped clear his head but the wind, driving full into his face, made him retch. After he had thrown up, he felt more in control of himself but his co-ordination was still so poor that when he fell into the snow, he had to make three attempts to get to his feet. The wind and the darkness confused him.

By the time he reached the highway, he was breathing so hard that he had to rest. The snow had drifted in places until it rose to his crotch. There was no way that a vehicle could get in or out of the access road. For a time, he leaned against a tree trunk, his back to the wind, waiting for someone to come by. There was nothing but the roar of the wind in the frozen trees. His feet started to get cold so he decided to start walking to the next camp. He knew that there was a truck with chains there.

He had stumbled along for half an hour when the snow turned milky, then began to sparkle. He moved onto the shoulder of the road and waved his flashlight in an arc. The pale light divided. A truck pulled up beside him.

He climbed into the cab. When he had caught his breath, he said, "My wife got lost in the storm and got herself frozen. I gotta get her to town."

There was no place to turn around. The road had narrowed to one lane and even this was deep in loose snow. The truck driver was tall and had a long, untidy beard. He peered through the windshield. There was nothing to see but the snow that slanted across the twin beams of light. It was obvious that he was anxious to keep going.

"Bad?" he asked.

Eric nodded.

They started back. Eric walked behind and to one side of the truck, marking the edge of the road with his flashlight. There was hardly any shoulder before a deep ditch began. With snow blanketing everything, it would be easy to put a wheel off the road. If that happened, they would need a tractor to free the truck.

Their progress was slow. Three times, Eric thought he had found the access road. The first two times, he was wrong. The third time, he waded into the snow to identify a tree stump that marked the corner. They left the truck with its lights on and its flashers going.

As they opened the door, they could hear Mabel screaming.

"Leave me alone," she yelled when she saw them. "Don't touch me." Her flesh, thawing, felt as though it had swollen to four times its normal size and as if the skin had been roughly cut from it with a piece of broken glass.

Spreading their arms wide, they herded her into a corner. They pinned her there, one holding her arms, the other her legs, then rolled her in a quilt so that she was completely covered. To keep her from tearing off the quilt, they wound it with sideline. The wind tore at them; the snow blinded them. Mabel was short and heavy. They floundered through the snow. The quilt sagged awkwardly in the middle, frequently slipping out of their mittened hands. They lost their footing time and again. When they finally reached the truck, they were both so winded that they had to lay Mabel on the road and lean against the truck to rest before they could lift her inside.

The ride was a nightmare of noise and motion. Snow engulfed them, blinding them with its whiteness. Wind tore at the truck. They skidded time and again, sometimes ploughing down the road sideways. When that happened, they both sat rigid, holding their breath, waiting for the wheels to catch on a rut and overturn them.

When they reached curves where snow had drifted into banks, the truck driver, not daring to slow down, sped up, racing at the white barriers. When they struck, snow flew up in a solid wall, completely covering the windshield until the wipers cleared it away. At such times, the truck shuddered as though under repeated blows. Once, they did not make it all the way through a drift and Eric plunged into the storm, wrenched a shovel from the side of the truck and attacked the snow in a frenzy.

As soon as the wheels were clear, he threw his shoulder against the tailgate, straining until he felt his body would crack. Slowly, inch by inch, the truck moved ahead. Once the wheels caught, the driver did not dare stop and Eric, with one hand on the box, ran to reach the door. He pulled himself inside and then sagged against the dashboard, sucking in gusts of warm air.

Whenever they were tempted to slow down, Mabel's cries and groans spurred them on.

It took them two hours before the faint glow of streetlights appeared on either side of them. The town itself was lost in the blizzard.

The driver flung the truck recklessly toward the hospital. It swayed, skidded, bounced like it was a duck boat in a choppy sea. Without warning, the hospital loomed out of the snow. The truck driver jammed on the brakes and the truck spun in two complete circles before stopping with its rear wheels on the lower step.

They half-dragged and half-carried Mabel in through the entrance and laid her on the floor in front of the receptionist's desk. Little strangled cries rose from the quilt. The receptionist rang for the doctor, then wheeled in a bed. They heaved Mabel onto it.

The doctor appeared. He was a brisk little man with grey hair cut close to his head to make him look younger. He had been a doctor in Eddyville for twenty years and nothing surprised him any longer.

"What," he said, studying the wet quilt wrapped with rope, "have we here?"

"Mabel," Eric answered. "She froze herself so bad she might die."

"It looks," the doctor replied, "more like she might be smothered." He treated their injuries every time they went on a drunk and he was prepared for anything. He reached into his pocket, took out a pair of curved surgical scissors and cut the rope.

When they pulled the quilt free, he inspected Mabel's face and hands and feet. She lay on her back, twitching and gasping like a beached fish.

"Get her into a room," he said to a nurse who had materialized at the end of the bed.

"How bad is she?" the truck driver asked.

"We'll see tomorrow morning. She'll probably lose some toes and fingers." He scowled at Eric. "If you're going to kill each other, why don't you get it over with?"

The receptionist, an elderly lady with blue-tinged hair, was more sympathetic. "You were lucky to get here," she said.

The truck driver smiled. He was relieved that the trip was over. "And how. Half an hour more of this and nothing will move, not even the snowplows." To Eric, he said, "You got anywhere to stay? You can sleep at my place."

"I'll stay at the hotel," Eric replied. Now that the trip was over, his head ached fiercely and he wanted a drink. A fast beer, then two slow ones would drive the pain away. He felt in his pockets. "Oh, hell," he said, "I forgot my wallet."

"That's okay," the truck driver replied. "My old lady'll give you some supper, then we'll get some sleep. You can have the kids' bed. They can sleep on the couch."

At these last words, Eric gave a sudden start and his eyes widened as if, without warning, a terrible vision had been thrust upon him. He took a step toward the door, then stopped. Snow and darkness beat against the glass. His tongue pressed against the back of his teeth, forming a single word, but he made no sound.

Alice Walker

Alice Walker was born to a family of sharecroppers in Eatonton, Georgia, in 1944. She is the author of numerous books of poems, short stories (see *In Love & Trouble: Stories of Black Women*, 1973, *You Can't Keep a Good Woman Down*, 1981, and *Everyday Use*, 1994), nonfiction, and novels, including *The Third Life of Grange Copeland* (1970), *The Color Purple* (1982), which won an American Book Award and the Pulitzer Prize and has been made into a film, *Possessing the Secret of Joy* (1992), and *By the Light of My Father's Smile* (1998), which expands on the themes of "The Child Who Favored Daughter.". She attended Spelman College in Atlanta for two and a half years, then, as she explains, *fled* to Sarah Lawrence College in 1964, where "I found all that I was looking for at the time—freedom to come and go, to read leisurely, to go my own way, dress my own way, and conduct my personal life as I saw fit." She was deeply involved in the civil rights movement in the 1960s; then, while still committed to her interracial marriage to her Jewish husband, a civil rights lawyer, wrote a letter to *Ms.* magazine, protesting Israel's annexation of the Golan Heights and the resultant suffering of Palestinians for whom this was the only homeland. Walker now lives in northern California. *Living by the Word: Selected Writings, 1973–1987* appeared in 1988.

In her book of essays, *In Search of Our Mothers' Gardens: Womanist Prose* (1983), Alice Walker gives eloquent expression to her primary concerns: the fight for racial equality, women's rights, and social change. The mood of the book is upbeat, although she does not hide the anger that is the legacy of her heritage; she suggests that while white American writers tend to be gloomy and defeatist in their works, black writers "seem always involved in a moral and/or physical struggle, the result of which is expected to be some kind of larger freedom. Perhaps this is because our literary tradition is based on slave narratives, where escape for the body and freedom for the soul went together, or perhaps this is because black people have never felt themselves guilty of global, cosmic sins."

Although black writers Toni Morrison and James Baldwin have written fiction that is as bleak and guilt-ridden as any, Walker does put her finger on a fundamental concern of all writers: "It is, in the end, the saving of lives that we writers are about. ... We do it because we care." Such a statement is even more poignant in her own case, since she writes elsewhere of her suicide attempts, of having grown up conditioned to think of herself as unlovely and inferior. In her essay "The Black Writer and the Southern Experience," she partially attributes the sense of affirmation in the black writer to "a religion that had been given to pacify him as a slave but which he soon transformed into an antidote against bitterness."

In a convocation address, Walker advised her largely female audience to read recent women's liberation literature. "For you will find, as women have found through the ages, that changing the world requires a lot of free time. Requires a lot of mobility. Requires money, and, as Virginia Woolf put it so well, 'a room of one's own,' preferably with a key and a lock. Which means that women must be prepared to think for themselves, which means, undoubtedly, trouble with boyfriends, lovers, and husbands, which means all kinds of heartache and misery, and times when you will wonder if independence, freedom of thought, or your own work is worth it all."

Walker lost her respect for Faulkner, she says, because of his gradualism and lack of leadership in the struggle for racial equality. But she maintained a high regard for Flannery O'Connor: "That she retained a certain distance (only, however, in her later, mature work) from the inner workings of her black characters seems to me all to her credit, since, by deliberately limiting her treatment of them to cover their observable demeanor and actions, she leaves them free, in the reader's imagination, to inhabit another landscape, another life, than the one she creates for them. This is a kind of grace many writers do not have when dealing with representatives of an oppressed people within a story, and their insistence on knowing everything, on being God, in fact, has burdened us with more stereotypes than we can ever hope to shed."

About her own writing, Walker says: "One thing I try to have in my life and my fiction is an awareness of and openness to mystery, which, to me, is deeper than any politics, race, or geographical location." "I like those of my short stories," she says, "that show the plastic, shaping, almost painting quality of words. In 'Roselily' and 'The Child Who Favored Daughter' the prose is poetry, or, prose and poetry run together to add a new dimension to the language. But the most I would say about where I am trying to go is this: I am trying to arrive at that place where black music already is; to arrive at that unself-conscious sense of collective oneness; that naturalness, that (even when anguished) grace." And in her provocative essay "The Unglamorous but Worthwhile Duties of the Black Revolutionary Artist, or of the Black Writer Who Simply Works and Writes," Walker lists the humble tasks of becoming informed, cherishing the old and the heritage passed down to you, offering guidance for living to those who need it, and, above all, writing, keeping the record.

The Child Who Favored Daughter

That my daughter should
fancy herself in love
with any man!
How can this be?

—Anonymous

I

She knows he has read the letter. He is sitting on the front porch watching her make the long trek from the school bus down the lane into the front yard. *Father, judge, giver of life.* Shadowy clouds indicating rain hang low on either side of the four o'clock sun and she holds her hand up to her eyes and looks out across the rows of cotton that stretch on one side of her from the mailbox to the house in long green hedges. After an initial shutting off of breath caused by fear, a calm numbness sets in and as she makes her way slowly down the lane she shuffles her feet in the loose red dust and tries to seem unconcerned. But she wonders how he knows about the letter. Her lover has a mother who dotes on the girl he married. It could have been her, preserving the race. Or the young bride herself, brittled to ice to find a letter from her among keepsakes her husband makes no move to destroy. Or—? But that notion does not develop in her mind. She loves him.

Fire of earth
Lure of flower smells
The sun

Down the lane with slow deliberate steps she walks in the direction of the house, toward the heavy silent man on the porch. The heat from the sun is oppressively hot but she does not feel its heat so much as its warmth, for there is a cold spot underneath the hot skin of her back that encloses her heart and reaches chilled arms around the bottom cages of her ribs.

Lure of flower smells
The sun

She stops to gaze intently at a small wild patch of black-eyed Susans and a few stray buttercups. Her fingers caress lightly the frail petals and she stands a moment wondering.

The lure of flower smells
The sun
Softly the scent of—
Softly the scent of flowers
And petals
Small, bright last wishes

II

He is sitting on the porch with his shotgun leaning against the banister within reach. If he cannot frighten her into chastity with his voice he will threaten her with the gun. He settles tensely in the chair and waits. He watches her from the time she steps from the yellow bus. He sees her shade her eyes from the hot sun and look widely over the rows of cotton running up, nearly touching him where he sits. He sees her look, knows its cast through any age and silence, knows she knows he has the letter.

Above him among the rafters in a half-dozen cool pots shielded from the afternoon sun the sound of dirt daubers. And busy wasps building onto their paper houses a dozen or more cells. Late in the summer, just as the babies are getting big enough to fly he will have to light paper torches and burn the paper houses down, singeing the wings of the young wasps before they get a chance to fly or to sting him as he sits in the cool of the evening reading his Bible.

Through eyes half closed he watches her come, her feet ankle deep in the loose red dust. Slowly, to the droning of the enterprising insects overhead, he counts each step, surveys each pause. He sees her looking closely at the bright patch of flowers. She is near enough for him to see clearly the casual slope of her arm that holds the schoolbooks against her hip. The long dark hair curls in bits about her ears and runs in corded plainness down her back. Soon he will be able to see her eyes, perfect black-eyed Susans. Flashing back fragmented bits of himself. Reflecting his mind.

Memories of years
Unknowable women—
sisters
spouses
illusions of soul

When he was a boy he had a sister called "Daughter." She was like honey, tawny, wild, and sweet. She was a generous girl and pretty, and he could not remember a time when he did not love her intensely, with his whole heart. She would give him anything she had, give anybody anything she had. She could not keep money, clothes, health. Nor did she seem to care for the love that came to her too easily. When he begged her not to go out, to stay with him, she laughed at him and went her way, sleeping here, sleeping there. Wherever she was needed, she would say, and laugh. But this could not go on forever; coming back from months with another woman's husband, her own mind seemed to have struck her down. He was struck down, too, and cried many nights on his bed; for she had chosen to give her love to the very man in whose cruel, hot, and lonely fields he, her brother, worked. Not treated as a man, scarcely as well as a poor man treats his beast.

Memories of years
Unknowable women—
sisters
spouses
illusions of soul

When she came back all of her long strong hair was gone, her teeth wobbled in her gums when she ate, and she recognized no one. All day and all night long she would sing and scream and tell them she was on fire. He was still a boy when she began playing up to him in her cunning way, exploiting again his love. And he, tears never showing on his face, would let her bat her lashless eyes at him and stroke his cheeks with her frail, clawlike hands. Tied on the bed as she was she was at the mercy of everyone in the house. They threw her betrayal at her like sharp stones, until they satisfied themselves that she could no longer feel their ostracism or her own pain. Gradually, as it became apparent she was not going to die, they took to flinging her food to her as if she were an animal and at night when she howled at the shadows thrown over her bed by the moon his father rose up and lashed her into silence with his belt.

On a day when she seemed nearly her old self she begged him to let her loose from the bed. He thought that if he set her free she would run away into the woods and never return. His love for her had turned into a dull ache of constant loathing, and he dreamed vague fearful dreams of a cruel revenge on the white lover who had shamed them all. But Daughter, climbing out of bed like a wary animal, knocked him unconscious to the floor and night found her impaled on one of the steel-spike fence posts near the house.

That she had given herself to the lord of his own bondage was what galled him! And that she was cut down so! He could not forgive her the love she gave that knew nothing of master and slave. For though her own wound was a bitter one and in the end fatal, he bore a hurt throughout his life that slowly poisoned him. In a world where innocence and guilt became further complicated by questions of color and race, he felt hesitant and weary of living as though all the world were out to trick him. His only guard against the deception he believed life had in store for him was a knowledge that evil and deception *would come* to him; and a readiness to provide them with a match.

The women in his life faced a sullen barrier of distrust and hateful mockery. He could not seem to help hating even the ones who loved him, and laughed loudest at the ones who cared for him, as if they were fools. His own wife, beaten into a cripple to prevent her from returning the imaginary overtures of the white landlord, killed herself while she was still young enough and strong enough to escape him. But she left a child, a girl, a daughter; a replica of Daughter, his dead sister. A replica in every way.

Memories of once
like a mirror reflecting—
all hope, all loss

His hands are not steady and he makes a clawing motion across the air in front of his face. She is walking, a vivid shape in blue and white, across the yard, underneath the cedar trees. She pauses at the low limb of the big magnolia and seems to contemplate the luminous gloss of the cone-shaped flowers beyond her reach. In the hand away from the gun is the open letter. He holds it tightly by a corner. The palms of his hands are sweating, his throat is dry. He swallows compulsively and rapidly bats his eyes. The slight weight of her foot sends vibrations across the gray boards of the porch. Her eyes flicker over him and rest on the open letter. Automatically his hand brings the letter upward a little although he finds he cannot yet, facing her strange familiar eyes, speak.

With passive curiosity the girl's eyes turn from the letter to the gun leaning against the banister to his face, which he feels growing blacker and tighter as if it is a mask that, when it is completely hardened, will drop off. Almost casually she sways back against the porch post, looking at him and from time to time looking over his head at the brilliant afternoon sky. Without wanting it his eyes travel heavily down the slight, roundly curved body and rest on her offerings to her lover in the letter. He is a black man but he blushes, the red underneath his skin glowing purple, and the coils of anger around his tongue begin to loosen.

"White man's slut!" he hisses at her through nearly sealed lips and clenched teeth. Her body reacts as if hit by a strong wind and lightly she sways on her slender legs and props herself more firmly against the post. At first she gazes directly into his eyes as if there is nowhere else to look. Soon she drops her head.

She leads the way to the shed behind the house. She is still holding her books loosely against her thigh and he makes his eyes hard as they cover the small light tracks made in the dust. The brown of her skin is full of copper tints and her arms are like long golden fruits that take in and throw back the hues of the sinking sun. Relentlessly he hurries her steps through the sagging door of boards, with hardness he shoves her down into the dirt. She is like a young willow without roots under his hands and as she does not resist he beats her for a long time with a harness from the stable and where the buckles hit there is a welling of blood which comes to be level with the tawny skin then spills over and falls curling into the dust of the floor.

Stumbling weakly toward the house through the shadows of the trees, he tries to look up beseechingly to the stars, but the sky is full of clouds and rain beats down around his ears and drenches him by the time he reaches the back steps. The dogs run excitedly and hungry around the damp reaches of the back porch and although he feeds them not one will stand unmoving beneath his quickscratching fingers. Dully he watches them eat and listens to the high winds in the trees. Shuddering with chill he walks through the house to the front porch and picks up the gun that is getting wet and sits with it across his lap, rocking it back and forth on his knees like a baby.

It is rainsoaked, but he can make out "I love you" written in a firm hand across the blue face of the letter. He hates the very paper of the letter and crumples it in his fist. A wet storm wind lifts it lightly and holds it balled up against the taut silver screen on the side of the porch. He is glad when the wind abandons it and leaves it sodden and limp against the slick wet boards under his feet. He rests his neck heavily on the back of his chair. Words of the letter—her letter to the white devil who has disowned her to marry one of his own kind—are running on a track in his mind. "Jealousy is being nervous about something that has never, and probably won't ever, belong to you." A wet waning moon fills the sky before he nods.

III

No amount of churchgoing changed her ways. Prayers offered nothing to quench her inner thirst. Silent and lovely, but barren of essential hope if not of the ability to love, hers was a world of double images, as if constantly seen through tears. It was Christianity as it invaded her natural wanderings that threw color into high and fast relief, but its hard Southern rudeness fell flat outside her house, its agony of selfishness failed completely to pervade the deep subterranean country of her mind. When asked to abandon her simple way of looking at simple flowers, she could only yearn the more to touch those glowing points of bloom that lived and died away among the foliage over there, rising and fading like certain stars of which she was told, coming and being and going on again, always beyond her reach. Staring often and intently into the ivory hearts of fallen magnolia blossoms she sought the answer to the question that had never really been defined for her, although she was expected to know it, but she only learned from this that it is the fallen flower most earnestly hated, most easily bruised.

The lure of flowersmells
The sun

In the morning, finding the world newly washed but the same, he rises from stiff-jointed sleep and wanders through the house looking at old photographs. In a frame of tarnish and gilt, her face forming out of the contours of a peach, the large dead eyes of beautiful Daughter, his first love. For the first time he turns it upside down then makes his way like a still sleeping man, wonderingly, through the house. At the back door he runs his fingers over the long blade of his pocketknife and puts it, with gentleness and resignation, into his pocket. He knows that as one whose ultimate death must conform to an aged code of madness, resignation is a kind of dying. A preparation for the final event. He makes a step in the direction of the shed. His eyes hold the panicked calm of fishes taken out of water, whose bodies but not their eyes beat a frantic maneuver over dry land.

In the shed he finds her already awake and for a long time she lies as she was, her dark eyes reflecting the sky through the open door. When she looks at him it is not with hate, but neither is it passivity he reads in her face. Gone is the silent waiting of yesterday, and except for the blood she is strong looking and the damp black hair trailing loose along the dirt floor excites him and the terror she has felt in the night is nothing to what she reads now in his wide-stretched eyes.

He begs her hoarsely, when it clears for him that she is his daughter, and not Daughter, his first love, if she will deny the letter. Deny the letter; the paper eaten and the ink drunk, the words never wrung from the air. Her mouth curls into Daughter's own hilarity. She says quietly no. No, with simplicity, a shrug, finality. No. Her slow tortured rising is a strong advance and scarcely bothering to look at him, she reflects him silently, pitilessly with her black-pond eyes.

"Going," she says, as if already there, and his heart buckles. He can only strike her with his fist and send her sprawling once more into the dirt. She gazes up at him over her bruises and he sees her blouse, wet and slippery from the rain, has slipped completely off her shoulders and her high young breasts are bare. He gathers their fullness in his fingers and begins a slow twisting. The barking of the dogs creates a frenzy in his ears and he is suddenly burning with unnamable desire. In his agony he draws the girl away from him as one pulling off his own arm and with quick slashes of his knife leaves two bleeding craters the size of grapefruits on her bare bronze chest and flings what he finds in his hands to the yelping dogs.

Memories of once
constant and silent
lie a mirror
reflecting

Today he is slumped in the same chair facing the road. The yellow school bus sends up clouds of red dust on its way. If he stirs it may be to Daughter shuffling lightly along the red dirt road, her dark hair down her back and her eyes looking intently at buttercups and stray black-eyed Susans along the way. If he stirs it may be he will see his own child, a black-eyed Susan from the soil on which she walks. A slight, pretty flower that grows on any ground; and flowers pledge no allegiance to banners of any man. If he stirs he might see the perfection of an ancient dream, his own nightmare; the answer to the question still whispered about, undefined. If he stirs he might feel the energetic whirling of wasps about his head and think of ripe late-summer days and time when scent makes a garden of the air. If he stirs he might wipe the dust from the dirt daubers out of his jellied eyes. If he stirs he might take up the heavy empty shotgun and rock it back and forth on his knees, like a baby.

Eudora Welty

Eudora Welty was born in 1909 in Jackson, Mississippi. After studying at Mississippi State College for Women and the University of Wisconsin and working for various newspapers and radio stations in Mississippi, she began to write fiction in the 1930s, publishing her first collection, *A Curtain of Green*, in 1941. This was followed by other collections of stories, *The Wide Net* (1943), *The Golden Apples* (1949), *The Bride of Innisfallen* (1955), and *Thirteen Stories* (1965), and two novels, *Delta Wedding* (1946) and *The Ponder Heart* (1956). *The Collected Stories of Eudora Welty* appeared in 1980. She seems to have begun writing at a very early age, publishing in her mid-twenties, but did not publish in a wide circulation magazine such as *The Atlantic Monthly* until 1941. She places little importance on the details of her own upbringing (her mother's milk cow or her father's insurance company), but does admit that she was a voracious reader.

Welty is admired for her quiet celebration of the lives of ordinary people and for her ear for the rhythms of colloquial speech. In the preface to her *Collected Stories*, she admits to a love for all her characters, whatever their sex or race, and considers the author's leap into another skin the most important work of the imagination. Alice Munro describes "A Worn Path" as an almost perfect story; Katherine Anne Porter has praised its dream-like quality, where external act and internal reality merge so powerfully.

A Writer's Eye: Collected Book Reviews (1994), other non-fiction writings, gathered into *The Eye of the Storm* (1977), and *Conversations with Eudora Welty* (1985) are storehouses of useful and provocative statements about the craft of fiction. One of her critical preoccupations has been with the difficulty of defining, or coming to terms with, structure in fiction: "The first thing we notice about our story is that we can't really see the solid outlines of it—it seems bathed in something of its own. It is wrapped in an atmosphere. This is what makes it shine, perhaps, as well as what initially obscures its plain, real shape." Hemingway, she says, specializes in action that produces a kind of "dazzling light," while Faulkner's stories are "comet-like ... wildly careening"; D. H. Lawrence, on the other hand, has sometimes no obvious plot or shape at all, yet his stories have a marvellous "cloak of self-luminous air."

Welty insists on the temperamental basis of art: "For the source of the short story is lyrical. And all writers speak from, and speak to, emotions eternally the same in all of us: love, pity, terror do not show favorites or leave any of us out." Consequently, atmosphere, or mystery, replaces plot as the central concern of the story. "So, the first thing we see about a story is its mystery. And in the best stories, we return at last to see mystery again. Every good story has mystery—not the puzzle kind, but the mystery of allurement. As we understand the story better, it is likely that the mystery does not necessarily decrease; rather it simply grows more beautiful."

According to Welty, "Plot is what we see *with*. What's *seen* is what we are interested in" (italics added). She defines form as "the residue, the thrown-off shape, of the very act of writing. ... From the writer's point of view, we might say that form is somehow connected with the process of the story's work—that form *is* the work. From the reader's point of view, we might say that form is connected with recognition; it is what makes us know, in a story, what we are looking at, what unique thing we are for a length of time contemplating. It does seem that the part of the mind which form speaks to and reaches is memory."

"A narrative line," she says, "is in its deeper sense, of course, the tracing out of a meaning, and the real continuity of a story lies in this probing forward. The real dramatic force of a story depends on the strength of the emotion that has set it going. The emotional value is the measure of the reach of the story."

In her fascinating essay called "Writing and Analyzing a Story," Welty suggests that writing each story poses a new technical problem. All the wrestling a writer indulges in to find the right shape for her fiction, Welty says, does not explain the element of mystery at work in the creative process: "I think it goes to show, all the same, that subject, method, form, style, all wait upon—indeed hang upon—a sort of double thunderclap at the author's ears: the break of the living world upon what is already stirring inside the mind, and the answering impulse that in a moment of high consciousness fuses impact and image and fires them off together. ... Between the writer and the story he writes, *there* is the undying third character."

Welty is, like Faulkner and Flannery O'Connor, a regionalist, her stories rooted in the talk and in the social and geographical particulars of the South. Although "touched off by place," she is equally determined to see through the particulars to the essential truth, the universality, of her materials. In speaking of the incident—seeing an old woman crossing a winter landscape—which inspired her to write "A Worn Path," Welty says: "The sight of her made me write the story. I invented an errand for her, but that only seemed a living part of the figure she was herself ... her going was the first thing, her persisting in her landscape was the real thing. ... I brought her up close enough, by imagination, to describe her face, make her present to the eyes, but the full-length figure moving across the winter fields was the indelible one and the image to keep, and the perspective extending into the vanishing distance the true one to hold in mind."

A Worn Path

It was December—a bright frozen day in the early morning. Far out in the country there was an old Negro woman with her head tied in a red rag, coming along a path through the pinewoods. Her name was Phoenix Jackson. She was very old and small and she walked slowly in the dark pine shadows, moving a little from side to side in her steps, with the balanced heaviness and lightness of a pendulum in a grandfather clock. She carried a thin, small cane made from an umbrella, and with this she kept tapping the frozen earth in front of her. This made a grave and persistent noise in the still air, that seemed meditative like the chirping of a solitary little bird.

She wore a dark striped dress reaching down to her shoe tops, and an equally long apron of bleached sugar sacks, with a full pocket: all neat and tidy, but every time she took a step she might have fallen over her shoelaces, which dragged from her unlaced shoes. She looked straight ahead. Her eyes were blue with age. Her skin had a pattern all its own of numberless branching wrinkles and as though a whole little tree stood in the middle of her forehead, but a golden color ran underneath, and the two knobs of her cheeks were illumined by a yellow burning under the dark. Under the red rag her hair came down on her neck in the frailest of ringlets, still black, and with an odor like copper.

Now and then there was a quivering in the thicket. Old Phoenix said, "Out of my way, all you foxes, owls, beetles, jack rabbits, coons and wild animals! ... Keep out from under these feet, little bobwhites. ... Keep the big wild hogs out of my path. Don't let none of those come running my direction. I got a long way." Under her small black-freckled hand her cane, limber as a buggy whip, would switch at the brush as if to rouse up any hiding things.

On she went. The woods were deep and still. The sun made the pine needles almost too bright to look at, up where the wind rocked. The cones dropped as light as feathers. Down in the hollow was the mourning dove—it was not too late for him.

The path ran up a hill. "Seem like there is chains about my feet, time I get this far," she said, in the voice of argument old people keep to use with themselves. "Something always take a hold of me on this hill—pleads I should stay."

After she got to the top she turned and gave a full, severe look behind her where she had come. "Up through pines," she said at length. "Now down through oaks."

Her eyes opened their widest, and she started down gently. But before she got to the bottom of the hill a bush caught her dress.

Her fingers were busy and intent, but her skirts were full and long, so that before she could pull them free in one place they were caught in another. It was not possible to allow the dress to tear. "I in the thorny bush," she said. "Thorns, you doing your appointed work. Never want to let folks pass, no sir. Old eyes thought you was a pretty little *green* bush."

Finally, trembling all over, she stood free, and after a moment dared to stoop for her cane.

"Sun so high!" she cried, leaning back and looking, while the thick tears went over her eyes. "The time getting all gone here."

At the foot of this hill was a place where a log was laid across the creek.

"Now comes the trial," said Phoenix.

Putting her right foot out, she mounted the log and shut her eyes. Lifting her skirt, leveling her cane fiercely before her, like a festival figure in some parade, she began to march across. Then she opened her eyes and she was safe on the other side.

"I wasn't as old as I thought," she said.

But she sat down to rest. She spread her skirts on the bank around her and folded her hands over her knees. Up above her was a tree in a pearly cloud of mistletoe. She did not dare to close her eyes, and when a little boy brought her a plate with a slice of marble-cake on it she spoke to him. "That would be acceptable," she said. But when she went to take it there was just her own hand in the air.

So she left that tree, and had to go through a barbed-wire fence. There she had to creep and crawl, spreading her knees and stretching her fingers like a baby trying to climb the steps. But she talked loudly to herself: she could not let her dress be torn now, so late in the day, and she could not pay for having her arm or her leg sawed off if she got caught fast where she was.

At last she was safe through the fence and risen up out in the clearing.

Big dead trees, like black men with one arm, were standing in the purple stalks of the withered cotton field. There sat a buzzard.

"Who you watching?"

In the furrow she made her way along.

"Glad this not the season for bulls," she said, looking sideways, "and the good Lord made his snakes to curl up and sleep in the winter. A pleasure I don't see no two-headed snake coming around that tree, where it come once. It took a while to get by him, back in the summer."

She passed through the old cotton and went into a field of dead corn. It whispered and shook and was taller than her head. "Through the maze now," she said, for there was no path.

Then there was something tall, black, and skinny there, moving before her.

At first she took it for a man. It could have been a man dancing in the field. But she stood still and listened, and it did not make a sound. It was as silent as a ghost.

"Ghost," she said sharply, "who be you the ghost of? For I have heard of nary death close by."

But there was no answer—only the ragged dancing in the wind.

She shut her eyes, reached out her hand, and touched a sleeve. She found a coat and inside that an emptiness, cold as ice.

"You scarecrow," she said. Her face lighted. "I ought to be shut up for good," she said with laughter. "My senses is gone. I too old. I the oldest people I ever know. Dance, old scarecrow," she said, "while I dancing with you."

She kicked her foot over the furrow, and with mouth drawn down, shook her head once or twice in a little strutting way. Some husks blew down and whirled in streamers about her skirts.

Then she went on, parting her way from side to side with the cane, through the whispering field. At last she came to the end, to a wagon track where the silver grass blew between the red ruts. The quail were walking around like pullets, seeming all dainty and unseen.

"Walk pretty," she said. "This the easy place. This the easy going."

She followed the track, swaying through the quiet bare fields, through the little strings of trees silver in their dead leaves, past cabins silver from weather, with the doors and windows boarded shut, all like old women under a spell sitting there. "I walking in their sleep," she said, nodding her head vigorously.

In a ravine she went where a spring was silently flowing through a hollow log. Old Phoenix bent and drank. "Sweet-gum makes the water sweet," she said, and drank more. "Nobody know who made this well, for it was here when I was born."

The track crossed a swampy part where the moss hung as white as lace from every limb. "Sleep on, alligators, and blow your bubbles." Then the track went into the road.

Deep, deep the road went down between the high green-colored banks. Overhead the live-oaks met, and it was as dark as a cave.

A black dog with a lolling tongue came up out of the weeds by the ditch. She was meditating, and not ready, and when he came at her she only hit him a little with her cane. Over she went in the ditch, like a little puff of milkweed.

Down there, her senses drifted away. A dream visited her, and she reached her hand up, but nothing reached down and gave her a pull. So she lay there and presently went to talking. "Old woman," she said to herself, "that black dog come up out of the weeds to stall you off, and now there he sitting on his fine tail, smiling at you."

A white man finally came along and found her—a hunter, a young man, with his dog on a chain.

"Well, Granny!" he laughed. "What are you doing there?"

"Lying on my back like a June-bug waiting to be turned over, mister," she said, reaching up her hand.

He lifted her up, gave her a swing in the air, and set her down. "Anything broken, Granny?"

"No sir, them old dead weeds is springy enough," said Phoenix, when she had got her breath. "I thank you for your trouble."

"Where do you live, Granny?" he asked, while the two dogs were growling at each other.

"Away back yonder, sir, behind the ridge. You can't even see it from here."

"On your way home?"

"No sir, I going to town."

"Why, that's too far! That's as far as I walk when I come out myself, and I get something for my trouble." He patted the stuffed bag he carried, and there hung down a little closed claw. It was one of the bobwhites, with its beak hooked bitterly to show it was dead. "Now you go on home, Granny!"

"I bound to go to town, mister," said Phoenix. "The time come around."

He gave another laugh, filling the whole landscape. "I know you old colored people! Wouldn't miss going to town to see Santa Claus!"

But something held old Phoenix very still. The deep lines in her face went into a fierce and different radiation. Without warning, she had seen with her own eyes a flashing nickel fall out of the man's pocket onto the ground.

"How old are you, Granny?" he was saying.

"There is no telling, mister," she said, "no telling."

Then she gave a little cry and clapped her hands and said, "Git away from here, dog! Look! Look at that dog!" She laughed as if in admiration. "He ain't scared of nobody. He a big black dog." She whispered, "Sic him!"

"Watch me get rid of that cur," said the man. "Sic him, Pete! Sic him!"

Phoenix heard the dogs fighting, and heard the man running and throwing sticks. She even heard a gunshot. But she was slowly bending forward by that time, further and further forward, the lid stretched down over her eyes, as if she were doing this in her sleep. Her chin was lowered almost to her knees. The yellow palm of her hand came out from the fold of her apron. Her fingers slid down and along the ground under the piece of money with the grace and care they would have in lifting an egg from under a setting hen. Then she slowly straightened up, she stood erect, and the nickel was in her apron pocket. A bird flew by. Her lips moved. "God watching me the whole time. I come to stealing."

The man came back, and his own dog panted about them. "Well, I scared him off that time," he said, and then he laughed and lifted his gun and pointed it at Phoenix.

She stood straight and faced him.

"Doesn't the gun scare you?" he said, still pointing it.

"No, sir, I seen plenty go off closer by, in my day, and for less than what I done," she said, holding utterly still.

He smiled, and shouldered the gun. "Well, Granny," he said, "you must be a hundred years old, and scared of nothing. I'd give you a dime if I had any money with me. But you take my advice and stay home, and nothing will happen to you."

"I bound to go on my way, mister," said Phoenix. She inclined her head in the red rag. Then they went in different directions, but she could hear the gun shooting again and again over the hill.

She walked on. The shadows hung from the oak trees to the road like curtains. Then she smelled wood-smoke, and smelled the river, and she saw a steeple and the cabins on their steep steps. Dozens of little black children whirled around her. There ahead was Natchez shining. Bells were ringing. She walked on.

In the paved city it was Christmas time. There were red and green electric lights strung and crisscrossed everywhere, and all turned on in the daytime. Old Phoenix would have been lost if she had not distrusted her eyesight and depended on her feet to know where to take her.

She paused quietly on the sidewalk where people were passing by. A lady came along in the crowd, carrying an armful of red-, green-, and silver-wrapped presents; she gave off perfume like the red roses in hot summer, and Phoenix stopped her.

"Please, missy, will you lace up my shoe?" She held up her foot.

"What do you want, Grandma?"

"See my shoe," said Phoenix. "Do all right for out in the country, but wouldn't look right to go in a big building."

"Stand still then, Grandma," said the lady. She put her packages down on the sidewalk beside her and laced and tied both shoes tightly.

"Can't lace 'em with a cane," said Phoenix. "Thank you, missy. I doesn't mind asking a nice lady to tie up my shoe, when I gets out on the street."

Moving slowly and from side to side, she went into the big building, and into a tower of steps, where she walked up and around and around until her feet knew to stop.

She entered a door, and there she saw nailed up on the wall the document that had been stamped with the gold seal and framed in the gold frame, which matched the dream that was hung up in her head.

"Here I be," she said. There was a fixed and ceremonial stiffness over her body.

"A charity case, I suppose," said an attendant who sat at the desk before her.

But Phoenix only looked above her head. There was sweat on her face, the wrinkles in her skin shone like a bright net.

"Speak up, Grandma," the woman said. "What's your name? We must have your history, you know. Have you been here before? What seems to be the trouble with you?"

Old Phoenix only gave a twitch to her face as if a fly were bothering her.

"Are you deaf?" cried the attendant.

But then the nurse came in.

"Oh, that's just old Aunt Phoenix," she said. "She doesn't come for herself—she has a little grandson. She makes these trips just as regular as clockwork. She lives away back off the Old Natchez Trace." She bent down. "Well, Aunt Phoenix, why don't you just take a seat? We won't keep you standing after your long trip." She pointed.

The old woman sat down, bolt upright in the chair.

"Now, how is the boy?" asked the nurse.

Old Phoenix did not speak.

"I said, how is the boy?"

But Phoenix only waited and stared straight ahead, her face very solemn and withdrawn into rigidity.

"Is his throat any better?" asked the nurse. "Aunt Phoenix, don't you hear me? Is your grandson's throat any better since the last time you came for the medicine?"

With her hands on her knees, the old woman waited, silent, erect and motionless, just as if she were in armor.

"You mustn't take up our time this way, Aunt Phoenix," the nurse said. "Tell us quickly about your grandson, and get it over. He isn't dead, is he?"

At last there came a flicker and then a flame of comprehension across her face, and she spoke.

"My grandson. It was my memory had left me. There I sat and forgot why I made my long trip."

"Forgot?" The nurse frowned. "After you came so far?"

Then Phoenix was like an old woman begging a dignified forgiveness for waking up frightened in the night. "I never did go to school, I was too old at the Surrender," she said in a soft voice. "I'm an old woman without an education. It was my memory fail me. My little grandson, he is just the same, and I forgot it in the coming."

"Throat never heals, does it?" said the nurse, speaking in a loud, sure voice to old Phoenix. By now she had a card with something written on it, a little list. "Yes. Swallowed lye. When was it?—January—two, three years ago—"

Phoenix spoke unasked now. "No, missy, he not dead, he just the same. Every little while his throat begin to close up again, and he not able to swallow. He not get his breath. He not able to help himself. So the time come around, and I go on another trip for the soothing medicine."

"All right. The doctor said as long as you came to get it, you could have it," said the nurse. "But it's an obstinate case."

"My little grandson, he sit up there in the house all wrapped up, waiting by himself," Phoenix went on. "We is the only two left in the world. He suffer and it don't seem to put him back at all. He got a sweet look. He going to last. He wear a little patch quilt and peep out holding his mouth open like a little bird. I remembers so plain now. I not going to forget him again, no, the whole enduring time. I could tell him from all the others in creation."

"All right." The nurse was trying to hush her now. She brought her a bottle of medicine. "Charity," she said, making a check mark in a book.

Old Phoenix held the bottle close to her eyes, and then carefully put it into her pocket.

"I thank you," she said.

"It's Christmas time, Grandma," said the attendant. "Could I give you a few pennies out of my purse?"

"Five pennies is a nickel," said Phoenix stiffly.

"Here's a nickel," said the attendant.

Phoenix rose carefully and held out her hand. She received the nickel and then fished the other nickel out of her pocket and laid it beside the new one. She stared at her palm closely, with her head on one side.

Then she gave a tap with her cane on the floor.

"This is what come to me to do," she said. "I going to the store and buy my child a little windmill they sells, made out of paper. He going to find it hard to believe there such a thing in the world. I'll march myself back where he waiting, holding it straight up in this hand."

She lifted her free hand, gave a little nod, turned around, and walked out of the doctor's office. Then her slow step began on the stairs, going down.

Virginia Woolf

Virginia Stephen was born in 1882 in London, where she was educated in the library of her father, Sir Leslie Stephen, a well-known scholar and editor of the *Dictionary of National Biography*. She married Leonard Woolf, a journalist and political philosopher, in 1912. The couple settled in fashionable Bloomsbury, where they started The Hogarth Press, which published Katherine Mansfield, E. M. Forster, T. S. Eliot, and a number of Virginia's own works, including the stories in *Monday and Tuesday* (1921) and the following novels: *Jacob's Room* (1922), *Mrs. Dalloway* (1925), *To the Lighthouse* (1927), and *The Waves* (1931). Woolf's physical and emotional condition was fragile at the best of times and compounded, it is now believed, by possible abuse as a child and by being unfairly denied the formal education allowed her half brothers. Her non-fiction writings, particularly *A Room of One's Own* (1929) and *Three Guineas* (1938), provide a moving record of her intellectual courage and her struggles on behalf of women's rights. Fearing another severe mental breakdown, she took her own life by drowning in 1941.

The Common Reader (1925; second series, 1932) contains many of her reviews and pronouncements on the art of fiction, including the famous manifesto of psychological realism, "Modern Fiction," in which she makes her case against the realistic novels of H. G. Wells, Arnold Bennett, and John Galsworthy, whose works, she felt, ignored "the dark places of psychology" and were obsessed with surfaces, with action, manners, and materiality: "Look within and life, it seems, is very far from being 'like this.' Examine for a moment an ordinary mind on an ordinary day. The mind receives a myriad of impressions—trivial, fantastic, evanescent, or engraved with the sharpness of steel. From all sides they come, an incessant shower of innumerable atoms; and as they fall, as they shape themselves into the life of Monday or Tuesday, the accent falls differently from of old; the moment of importance came not here but there; so that, if a writer were a free man and not a slave, if he could write what he chose, not what he must, if he could base his work upon his own feeling and not upon convention, there would be no plot, no comedy, no tragedy, no love interest or catastrophe in the accepted style, and perhaps not a single button sewn on as the Bond Street tailors would have it. Life is not a series of gig lamps symmetrically arranged; life is a luminous halo, a semi-transparent envelope surrounding us from the beginning of consciousness to the end. Is it not the task of the novelist to convey this varying, this unknown and uncircumscribed spirit, whatever aberration or complexity it may display, with as little mixture of the alien and external as possible? We are not pleading merely for courage and sincerity; we are suggesting that the proper stuff of fiction is a little other than custom would have us believe it."

As she suggests in *Books and Portraits*, "We are by this time alive to the fact that inconclusive stories are legitimate; that is to say, though they leave us feeling melancholy and perhaps uncertain, yet somehow they provide a resting-point for the mind—a solid object casting its shade of reflection and speculation. The fragments of which it is composed may have the air of having come together by chance."

Woolf's letters and diaries record her efforts to "grope and experiment" with new forms, for a work with "no scaffolding; scarcely a brick to be seen; all crepuscular, but the heart, the passion, humour, everything as bright as fire in the mist." She rejected traditional notions of character, arguing that "characters are to be merely views: personality must be avoided at all costs. I'm sure my Conrad adventure taught me this. Directly you specify hair, age, etc. something frivolous, or irrelevant, gets into the book." Part of her plan was to "dig out beautiful caves behind my characters: I think that gives exactly what I want; humanity, humour, depth. The idea is that the caves shall connect and each comes to daylight at the present moment." Subterranean imagery abounds in the diaries, not only caves, but also the image of the fiction writing "tunnelling," "deep in the richest strata," boring down to the deep wells (not the H. G. Wells!) of feeling.

To achieve her desired effects, what has come to be called stream of consciousness, Woolf needed to rework the medium of prose fiction. She dispensed, to a large extent, with dialogue and conventional action. "I can make up situations, but I cannot make up plots," she said. "That is: if I pass a lame girl I can, without knowing I do it, instantly make up a scene. ... This is the germ of such fictitious gifts as I have." To render the inner life of these situations, she had "to break up, dig deep, make prose move—yes I swear—as prose has never moved before; from the chuckle, the babble, to the rhapsody." The greatest book in the world, she said, "would be one that was made entirely solely and with integrity of one's thoughts. Suppose one could catch them before they became 'works of art'? Catch them hot and sudden as they rise in the mind—walking up Asheham hill for instance. Of course one cannot; for the process of language is slow and deluding. One must stop to find a word. Then, there is the form of the sentence, soliciting one to fill it."

In a letter to Vita Sackville-West, Woolf tries to define style: "As for the *mot juste*, you are quite wrong. Style is a very simple matter; it is all rhythm. Once you get that, you can't use the wrong words. But on the other hand here am I sitting after half the morning, crammed with ideas, and visions, and so on, and can't dislodge them, for lack of the right rhythm. Now this is very profound, what rhythm is, and goes far deeper than words. A sight, an emotion, creates this wave in the mind, long before it makes words to fit it; and in writing (such is my present belief) one has to recapture this, and set this working (which has nothing apparently to do with words) and then, as it breaks and tumbles in the mind, it makes words to fit it: But no doubt I shall think differently next year." Woolf related her method to painting and music, talking about the text as a canvas, or score, and writing as a process of composition and layering: "I should like to write four lines at a time, describing the same feeling, as a musician does; because it always seems to me that things are going on at so many different levels simultaneously."

Moments of Being: 'Slater's Pins Have No Points'

'Slater's pins have no points—don't you always find that?' said Miss Craye, turning round as the rose fell out of Fanny Wilmot's dress, and Fanny stooped with her ears full of the music, to look for the pin on the floor.

The words gave her an extraordinary shock, as Miss Craye struck the last chord of the Bach fugue. Did Miss Craye actually go to Slater's and buy pins then, Fanny Wilmot asked herself, transfixed for a moment? Did she stand at the counter waiting like anybody else, and was she given a bill with coppers wrapped in it, and did she slip them into her purse and then, an hour later, stand by her dressing table and take out the pins? What need had she of pins? For she was not so much dressed as cased, like a beetle compactly in its sheath, blue in winter, green in summer. What need had she of pins—Julia Craye—who lived, it seemed, in the cool, glassy world of Bach fugues, playing to herself what she liked and only consenting to take one or two pupils at the Archer Street College of Music (so the Principal, Miss Kingston said) as a special favour to herself, who had 'the greatest admiration for her in every way'. Miss Crave was left badly off, Miss Kingston was afraid, at her brother's death. Oh, they used to have such lovely things, when they lived at Salisbury and her brother Julius was, of course, a very well-known man: a famous archaeologist. It was a great privilege to stay with them, Miss Kingston said ('My family had always known them—they were regular Salisbury people,' Miss Kingston said), but a little frightening for a child; one had to be careful not to slam the door or bounce into the room unexpectedly. Miss Kingston, who gave little character sketches like this on the first day of term while she received cheques and wrote out receipts for them, smiled here. Yes, she had been rather a tomboy; she had bounced in and set all those green Roman glasses and things jumping in their case. The Crayes were none of them married. The Crayes were not used to children. They kept cats. The cats, one used to feel, knew as much about the Roman urns and things as anybody.

'Far more than I did!' said Miss Kingston brightly, writing her name across the stamp, in her dashing, cheerful, full-bodied hand, for she had always been practical.

Perhaps then, Fanny Wilmot thought, looking for the pin, Miss Craye said that about 'Slater's pins having no points', at a venture. None of the Crayes had ever married. She knew nothing about pins—nothing whatever. But she wanted to break the spell that had fallen on the house; to break the pane of glass which separated them from other people. When Polly Kingston, that merry little girl, had slammed the door and made the Roman vases jump, Julius, seeing that no harm was done (that would be his first instinct) looked, for the case was stood in the window, at Polly skipping home across the fields; looked with the look his sister often had, that lingering, desiring look.

'Stars, sun, moon,' it seemed to say, 'the daisy in the grass, fires, frost on the window pane, my heart goes out to you. But,' it always seemed to add, 'you break, you pass, you go.' And simultaneously it covered the intensity of both these states of mind with 'I can't reach you—I can't get at you,' spoken wistfully, frustratedly. And the stars faded, and the child went.

That was the kind of spell, that was the glassy surface that Miss Craye wanted to break by showing, when she had played Bach beautifully as a reward to a favourite pupil (Fanny Wilmot knew that she was Miss Craye's favourite pupil) that she too felt as other people felt about pins. Slater's pins had no points.

Yes, the 'famous archaeologist' had looked like that, too. The famous archaeologist'—as she said that endorsing cheques, ascertaining the day of the month, speaking so brightly and frankly, there was in Miss Kingston's voice an indescribable tone which hinted at something odd, something queer, in Julius Craye. It was the very same thing that was odd perhaps in Julia too. One could have sworn, thought Fanny Wilmot, as she looked for the pin, that at parties, meetings (Miss Kingston's father was a clergyman) she had picked up some piece of gossip, or it might only have been a smile, or a tone when his name was mentioned, which had given her 'a feeling' about Julius Craye. Needless to say, she had never spoken about it to anybody. Probably she scarcely knew what she meant by it. But whenever she spoke of Julius, or heard him mentioned, that was the first thought that came to mind: there was something odd about Julius Craye.

It was so that Julia looked too, as she sat half turned on the music stool, smiling. It's on the field, it's on the pane, it's in the sky—beauty; and I can't get at it; I can't have it—I, she seemed to add, with that little clutch of the hand which was so characteristic, who adore it so passionately, would give the whole world to possess it! And she picked up the carnation which had fallen on the floor, while Fanny searched for the pin. She crushed it, Fanny felt, voluptuously in her smooth, veined hands stuck about with water-coloured rings set in pearls. The pressure of her fingers seemed to increase all that was most brilliant in the flower; to set it off; to make it more frilled, fresh, immaculate. What was odd in her, and perhaps in her brother too, was that this crush and grasp of the fingers was combined with a perpetual frustration. So it was even now with the carnation. She had her hands on it; she pressed it; but she did not possess it, enjoy it, not altogether.

None of the Crayes had married, Fanny Wilmot remembered. She had in mind how one evening when the lesson had lasted longer than usual and it was dark, Julia Craye had said, 'It's the use of men, surely, to protect us,' smiling at her that same odd smile, as she stood fastening her cloak, which made her, like the flower, conscious to her finger tips of youth and brilliance, but, like the flower too, Fanny suspected, inhibited.

'Oh, but I don't want protection,' Fanny had laughed, and when Julia Craye, fixing on her that extraordinary look, had said she was not so sure of that, Fanny positively blushed under the admiration in her eyes.

It was the only use of men, she had said. Was it for that reason then, Fanny wondered, with her eyes on the floor, that she had never married? After all, she had not lived all her life in Salisbury. 'Much the nicest part of London,' she had said once, (but I'm speaking of fifteen or twenty years ago) is Kensington. One was in the Gardens in ten minutes—it was like the heart of the country. One could dine out in one's slippers without catching cold. 'Kensington—it was like a village then, you know,' she had said.

Here she had broken off, to denounce acridly, the draughts in the Tubes.

'It was the use of men,' she had said, with a queer, wry acerbity. Did that throw any light on the problem why she had not married? One could imagine every sort of scene in her youth, when with her good, blue eyes, her straight, firm nose, her piano playing, her rose flowering with chaste passion in the bosom of her muslin dress, she had attracted first the young men to whom such things, and the china tea-cups and the silver candlesticks, and the inlaid tables (for the Crayes had such nice things) were wonderful; young men not sufficiently distinguished; young men of the Cathedral town with ambitions. She had attracted them first, and then her brother's friends from Oxford or Cambridge. They would come down in the summer, row her up the river, continue the argument about Browning by letter, and arrange perhaps on the rare occasions when she stayed in London to show her—Kensington Gardens?

'Much the nicest part of London—Kensington. I'm speaking of fifteen or twenty years ago,' she had said once. 'One was in the Gardens in ten minutes—in the heart of the country.' One could make that yield what one liked, Fanny Wilmot thought, single out for instance, Mr Sherman, the painter, an old friend of hers; make him call for her by appointment one sunny day in June; take her to have tea under the trees. (They had met, too, at those parties to which one tripped in slippers without fear of catching cold.) The aunt or other elderly relative was to wait there while they looked at the Serpentine. They looked at the Serpentine. He may have rowed her across. They compared it with the Avon. She would have considered the comparison very seriously, for views of rivers were important to her. She sat hunched a little, a little angular, though she was graceful then, steering. At the critical moment, for he had determined that he must speak now—it was his only chance of getting her alone—he was speaking with his head turned at an absurd angle, in his great nervousness, over his shoulder—at that very moment she interrupted fiercely. He would have them into the Bridge, she cried. It was a moment of horror, of disillusionment, of revelation for both of them. I can't have it, I can't possess it, she thought. He could not see why she had come then. With a great splash of his oar he pulled the boat round. Merely to snub him? He rowed her back and said good-bye to her.

The setting of that scene could be varied as one chose, Fanny Wilmot reflected. (Where had that pin fallen?) It might be Ravenna—or Edinburgh, where she had kept house for her brother. The scene could be changed and the young man and the exact manner of it all; but one thing was constant—her refusal and her frown and her anger with herself afterwards and her argument, and her relief—yes, certainly her immense relief. The very next day perhaps she would get up at six, put on her cloak, and walk all the way from Kensington to the river. She was so thankful that she had not sacrificed her right to go and look at things when they are at their best—before people are up, that is to say. She could have her breakfast in bed if she liked. She had not sacrificed her independence.

Yes, Fanny Wilmot smiled, Julia had not endangered her habits. They remained safe, and her habits would have suffered if she had married. 'They're ogres,' she had said one evening, half laughing, when another pupil, a girl lately married, suddenly bethinking her that she would miss her husband, had rushed off in haste.

'They're ogres,' she had said, laughing grimly. An ogre would have interfered perhaps with breakfast in bed; with walks at dawn down to the river. What would have happened (but one could hardly conceive this) had she had children? She took astonishing precautions against chills, fatigue, rich food, the wrong food, draughts, heated rooms, journeys in the Tube, for she could never determine which of these it was exactly that brought on those terrible headaches that gave her life the semblance of a battlefield. She was always engaged in outwitting the enemy, until it seemed as if the pursuit had its interest; could she have beaten the enemy finally she would have found life a little dull. As it was, the tug-of-war was perpetual—on one side the nightingale or the view which she loved with passion—yes, for views and birds she felt nothing less than passion; on the other, the damp path or the horrid long drag up a steep hill which would certainly make her good for nothing next day and bring on one of her headaches. When, therefore, from time to time, she managed her forces adroitly and brought off a visit to Hampton Court the week the crocuses (those glossy bright flowers were her favourites) were at their best, it was a victory. It was something that lasted; something that mattered for ever. She strung the afternoon on the necklace of memorable days, which was not too long for her to be able to recall this one or that one; this view, that city; to finger it, to feel it, to savour, sighing, the quality that made it unique.

'It was so beautiful last Friday,' she said, 'that I determined I must go there.' So she had gone off to Waterloo on her great undertaking—to visit Hampton Court—alone. Naturally, but perhaps foolishly, one pitied her for the thing she never asked pity for (indeed she was reticent habitually, speaking of her health only as a warrior might speak of his foe)—one pitied her for always doing everything alone. Her brother was dead. Her sister was asthmatic. She found the climate of Edinburgh good for her. It was too bleak for Julia. Perhaps too she found the associations painful, for her brother, the famous archaeologist, had died there; and she had loved her brother. She lived in a little house off the Brompton Road entirely alone.

Fanny Wilmot saw the pin on the carpet; she picked it up. She looked at Miss Craye. Was Miss Craye so lonely? No, Miss Craye was steadily, blissfully, if only for a moment, a happy woman. Fanny had surprised her in a moment of ecstasy. She sat there, half turned away from the piano, with her hands clasped in her lap holding the carnation upright, while behind her was the sharp square of the window, uncurtained, purple in the evening, intensely purple after the brilliant electric lights which burnt unshaded in the bare music room. Julia Craye sitting hunched and compact holding her flower seemed to emerge out of the London night, seemed to fling it like a cloak behind her. It seemed in its bareness and intensity the effluence of her spirit, something she had made which surrounded her, which was her. Fanny stared.

All seemed transparent for a moment to the gaze of Fanny Wilmot, as if looking through Miss Craye, she saw the very fountain of her being spurt up in pure, silver drops. She saw back and back into the past behind her. She saw the green Roman vases stood in their case; heard the choristers playing cricket; saw Julia quietly descend the curving steps on to the lawn; saw her pour out tea beneath the cedar tree; softly enclose the old man's hand in hers; saw her going round and about the corridors of that ancient Cathedral dwelling place with towels in her hand to mark them; lamenting as she went the pettiness of daily life; and slowly ageing, and putting away clothes when summer came, because at her age they were too bright to wear; and tending her father's sickness; and cleaving her way ever more definitely as her will stiffened towards her solitary goal; travelling frugally; counting the cost and measuring out of her tight shut purse the sum needed for this journey, or for that old mirror; obstinately adhering whatever people might say in choosing her pleasures for herself. She saw Julia—

She saw Julia open her arms; saw her blaze; saw her kindle. Out of the night she burnt like a dead white star. Julia kissed her. Julia possessed her.

'Slater's pins have no points,' Miss Craye said, laughing queerly and relaxing her arms, as Fanny Wilmot pinned the flower to her breast with trembling fingers.

The Fascination of the Pool

It may have been very deep—certainly one could not see to the bottom of it. Round the edge was so thick a fringe of rushes that their reflections made a darkness like the darkness of very deep water. However in the middle was something white. The big farm a mile off was to be sold and some zealous person, or it may have been a joke on the part of a boy, had stuck one of the posters advertising the sale, with farm horses, agricultural implements, and young heifers, on a tree stump by the side of the pool. The centre of the water reflected the white placard and when the wind blew the centre of the pool seemed to flow and ripple like a piece of washing. One could trace the big red letters in which Romford Mill was printed in the water. A tinge of red was in the green that rippled from bank to bank.

But if one sat down among the rushes and watched the pool—pools have some curious fascination, one knows not what—the red and black letters and the white paper seemed to lie very thinly on the surface, while beneath went on some profound under-water life like the brooding, the ruminating of a mind. Many, many people must have come there alone, from time to time, from age to age, dropping their thoughts into the water, asking it some question, as one did oneself this summer evening. Perhaps that was the reason of its fascination—that it held in its waters all kinds of fancies, complaints, confidences, not printed or spoken aloud, but in a liquid state, floating one on top of another, almost disembodied. A fish would swim through them, be cut in two by the blade of a reed; or the moon would annihilate them with its great white plate. The charm of the pool was that thoughts had been left there by people who had gone away and without their bodies their thoughts wandered in and out freely, friendly and communicative, in the common pool.

Among all these liquid thoughts some seemed to stick together and to form recognizable people—just for a moment. And one saw a whiskered red face formed in the pool leaning low over it, drinking it. I came here in 1851 after the heat of the Great Exhibition. I saw the Queen open it. And the voice chuckled liquidly, easily, as if he had thrown off his elastic side boots and put his top hat on the edge of the pool. Lord, how hot it was! and now all gone, all crumbled, of course, the thoughts seemed to say, swaying among the reeds. But I was a lover, another thought began, sliding over the other silently and orderly as fish not impeding each other. A girl; we used to come down from the farm (the placard of its sale was reflected on the top of the water) that summer, 1662. The soldiers never saw us from the road. It was very hot. We lay here. She was lying hidden in the rushes with her lover, laughing into the pool and slipping into it, thoughts of eternal love, of fiery kisses and despair. And I was very happy, said another thought glancing briskly over the girl's despair (for she had drowned herself). I used to fish here. We never caught the giant carp but we saw him once—the day Nelson fought at Trafalgar. We saw him under the willow—my word! what a great brute he was! They say he was never caught. Alas, alas, sighed a voice, slipping over the boy's voice. So sad a voice must come from the very bottom of the pool. It raised itself under the others as a spoon lifts all the things in a bowl of water. This was the voice we all wished to listen to. All the voices slipped gently away to the side of the pool to listen to the voices which so sad it seemed—it must surely know the reason of all this. For they all wished to know.

One drew closer to the pool and parted the reeds so that one could see deeper, through the reflections, through the faces, through the voices to the bottom. But there under the man who had been to the Exhibition; and the girl who had drowned herself and the boy who had seen the fish; and the voice which cried alas alas! yet there was always something else. There was always another face, another voice. One thought came and covered another. For though there are moments when a spoon seems about to lift all of us, and our thoughts and longings and questions and confessions and disillusions into the light of day, somehow the spoon always slips beneath and we flow back again over the edge into the pool. And once more the whole of its centre is covered over with the reflection of the placard which advertises the sale of Romford Mill Farm. That perhaps is why one loves to sit and look into pools.

Afterwords

Writings on the Art of Fiction and the Act of Critical Reading

As I said in the Introduction, writers are not always the most accurate and reliable guides to their own work. Flannery O'Connor admitted to an audience that "your asking me to talk about story-writing is just like asking a fish to lecture on swimming." And yet, she went on to write and talk brilliantly and movingly about the craft of story-writing. While her comments are often not as flashy and self-assured—or so full of fashionable jargon—as the essays of her critics, O'Connor's common-sense ideas about writing and reading stories are well worth considering. Although she was conscious of the need for critical terminology, she preferred to keep the discussion as simple as possible.

In the essay in this anthology, she says that describing a story in terms of plot, character, and theme is "like trying to describe the expression on a face by saying where the eyes, nose, and mouth are." Instead of theme, she proposes talking about a story's *meaning*, which is less easily extractable and which is likely to emerge only from a consideration of the story in its entirety; she also draws attention to the importance of *idiom*, or local speech patterns, suggesting that idiom "characterizes a society" and that "our history lives in our talk." In her view, a storywriter is more in need of a good ear than a dictionary or thesaurus.

I have deliberately chosen statements about the craft of fiction that are, for the most part, quite general and can be used in thinking about any of the stories included here. Most writers don't want to talk about what they are trying to do in a specific story, especially in terms that will limit the story to a single interpretation or interfere with the pleasure and excitement of a reader's first encounter with the text. However, they can be very insightful when talking generally about the aims and techniques of fiction.

The point of considering these diverse statements on short fiction is that they will help you develop your own critical approaches and your own working vocabulary. If you take the time to read through the controversial statements, most of which are written in an engaging, conversational style, and through the mélange of brief quotations in the Notes on the Authors, you will have treated yourself to a painless but instructive crash course in how to read and how to begin to talk about—perhaps even how to write—the short story.

IAN REID

Problems of Definition

From *The Short Story*

CRITICAL NEGLECT

Over the last 150 years the short story has come to figure conspicuously in the literature of several countries. Appearing in diverse periodicals as well as in books, it is probably the most widely read of all modern genres, and not only light-weight entertainers but also many distinguished fiction-writers during this period have found it congenial. Yet even now it seldom receives serious critical attention commensurate with that importance. Not until the OED Supplement of 1933 did the term 'short story' itself, designating a particular kind of literary product, gain formal admittance into the vocabulary of English readers. Theoretical discussion of the form had begun nearly a century before that tardy christening with some essays by Edgar Allan Poe, but was slow to develop and is still in an immature state. It seems to be impeded especially by problems connected with the popularity of the short-story genre.

Slightness and slickness, for instance, while not invariably resulting from brevity, do often infect the short story when it is adapting itself to market requirements. Magazine publication expanded hugely during the nineteenth century, tending to encourage stereotypes, mannerisms, gimmickry and the like. Consequently critics are sometimes reluctant to take the short story seriously as a substantial genre in its own right. Bernard Bergonzi, for one, thinks that 'the modern short-story writer is bound to see the world in a certain way' because the form he is using has an insidiously reductive effect: it is disposed 'to filter down experience to the prime elements of defeat and alienation.' More satirically, Howard Nemerov applies these belittling strictures:

> Short stories amount for the most part to parlor tricks, party favors with built-in snappers, gadgets for inducing recognitions and reversals: a small pump serves to build up the pressure, a tiny trigger releases it, there follows a puff and a flash as freedom and necessity combine; finally a celluloid doll drops from the muzzle and descends by parachute to the floor. These things happen, but they happen to no-one in particular.

There are indeed many magazine stories that one could justly dismiss in such terms, and it may well be true that even the acme of short fiction hardly matches the greatest novels in depicting the complex and wide-ranging nature of much human experience. Complexity and breadth, however, are not always the most central or interesting features of our lives. Only a naive reader would confuse significance with bulk. The lyric is by no means less potent and meaningful, inherently, than a discursive poem, and the short story can move us by an intensity which the novel is unable to sustain.

Small-scale prose fiction deserves much more careful criticism, theoretical and practical, than it has usually had. It gets elbowed out of curricula at the universities and elsewhere by its heftier relatives, novel, poetry and drama; and of the countless academic journals very few regularly give space to essays on this neglected genre. Good books about the novel are legion; good books about the short story are extremely scarce. Most of those in English were written on the side by practitioners such as H. E. Bates, Frank O'Connor and Sean O'Faolain. Germany has produced numerous scholarly studies of short fiction, but these are frequently impaired by a finicky taxonomic purism which would set the *Novelle* in contradistinction to the *Kurzgeschichte*, each regarded as a discrete type, whereas in English usage 'short story' is an inclusive concept. The Russian school of formalist criticism, flourishing in the 1920s, generated sound work on theoretical aspects of the short story (notably essays by Boris Eichenbaum and Victor Shklovsky) and of its ancestor the *Märchen* (Vladimir Propp's classic account of 'The Morphology of the Folktale'), but permutations in the genre during the last half-century have outdated some of their findings. Those formalist investigations have recently been extended somewhat by the analytical 'narratology' of French structuralists such as Tzvetan Todorov and Claude Bremond, who however have not yet attended closely to any compositional principles which might be said to set the short story apart from the novel.

Protean Variety

If on the one hand their popularity has tempted short stories towards the reductive formulae of merchandise, on the other hand it has sometimes encouraged protean variety. The tale-telling impulse is too irrepressibly fecund to be confined within any single narrative pattern. Therefore the history of the modern short story embraces diverse tendencies, some of which have stretched, shrunk or otherwise altered previous conceptions of the nature of the genre. Ideas once proposed as definitive about the proper structure and subject material of the short story have needed revising to meet the facts of literary evolution. For example, nineteenth-century critics frequently insisted on the need for a firmly developed plot design in any 'true' short story; this was part of their effort to make the form respectable in terms of current taste, to lift it beyond its lowly origins. Some modern writers have undermined that principle of neat plot-making, both by bringing their fictions back in contact with various prototypical modes and by moving away from narrative techniques used in the novel towards the methods both of poetry (in their language, which is often more figurative and rhythmic than was usual in nineteenth-century prose) and of drama (in their tendency to keep the narrator's voice out and rely on direct presentation of character and situation).

While it may be a sign of vigour, this variegated development is not conducive to establishing a precise descriptive vocabulary which would satisfy all critics. Yet if perfect consensus is lacking, adequate working definitions are nevertheless possible and helpful provided one recognizes that they must refer to predominant norms rather than all-inclusive categories, to evolving features rather than fixities and definites. At risk of eroding completely any idea of an essential generic type, a quasi-Platonic form of the short story, we need to be empirically mindful of changes undergone by short prose fiction before and since its widespread acceptance in the Romantic period as a field of serious literary activity. If the New Testament parable, medieval French *fabliau*, seventeenth-century Chinese *p'ing-hua*, nineteenth-century American tall tale or recent experimental prose poem are to be regarded as outside the pale, they should still provide reference points for us in delimiting the territory of the short story proper. Accordingly the following chapters will examine some 'primitive' and proximate varieties of fiction, and look into the possibility that there may be certain formal properties which distinguish *the* short story ('Short-story', as Brander Matthews and others wanted to call it) from stories that just happen to be short.

When Is a Story Not a Story?

The simple term 'story' itself needs some preliminary attention. How strictly should one interpret it? Does it imply at least some plot, some sequence of narrated actions, or can a 'story' be purely descriptive in a static way?

E. M. Forster once represented himself as saying, in 'a sort of drooping regretful voice, "Yes—oh dear yes—the novel tells a story".' And the short story, we might think, can hardly justify its name if, on a smaller scale, it does not do likewise. Herbert Gold, contributing to an 'International Symposium on the Short Story' in the *Kenyon Review* (XXX, 4, 1968), asserts that 'the story-teller must have a story to tell, not merely some sweet prose to take out for a walk'. That seems reasonable as far as it goes. There remains, however, the fundamental question: what does 'story' mean? Few critics deign to examine such a rudimentary concept. We all know (it is ordinarily supposed) what a story is: a recital of events. But what constitutes an event? How many events go to make up a minimal story? Need they all be logically related to one another? Gerald Prince pursues these questions in his recent study *A Grammar of Stories*, using transformational principles derived from linguistics to account for the nature of tacit rules operating in various kinds of narrative. An event, he remarks, is a structural unit that can be summarized by a sentence of the simple kind which, in linguistic parlance, is the transform of less than two discrete elementary strings. Thus, 'Adam said that it was all Eve's fault' records a single event, whereas 'Adam blamed Eve, who had initially encouraged him to eat the apple' records two events, being derived from the transforms of two discrete elementary strings. At any rate, neither of these examples is a story in the proper sense. No story exists, says Prince, until three or more events are conjoined, with at least two of them occurring at different times and being causally linked. Other theorists have made similar observations: Claude Bremond, for instance, calls the requisite group of three events or stages of development *une séquence élémentaire*. 'Eve took a bite of the apple and then Adam did so too': that does not amount to even a skeletal story. But this does: 'Eve took a bite of the apple and then, at her urging, Adam did so too, as a result of which they became crazy and bit each other.' Temporal movement and logical linkage are just enough to make it a story, though no doubt insufficient to make it an interesting one.

We might ask in passing why a three-phase action is generally accepted as basic. Prince and others say nothing to explain this; it is adduced axiomatically, since it probably lies (though they do not admit as much) outside the scope of their strictly objective method, in the field of affective aesthetics. There may well be a connection here with Aristotle's sage remark, in the seventh chapter of his *Poetics*, that a plot must have beginning, middle and end in order to be a whole. And the same aesthetic pattern is evinced in that incremental trebling of actions which recurs in so many durably appealing tales. Our sense of shapeliness would not be satisfied if the poor woodcutter had only two magic wishes, or if four billy goats gruff crossed the troll's bridge, or if Goldilocks found five plates of porridge in the bears' cottage. (Indeed, in the latter story, there are not only three items in each bearish set but three sets too: only after the intruder has tried food, chairs and beds is it timely for the owners to return.) That there are seven dwarfs in Snow White's tale, that the valiant tailor kills seven flies with one blow—these and other numerical formulae are of a different sort, since they do not produce a structure of incremental narration. And besides, the point is not that a tripartite sequence is invariable in simple stories, just that its frequency seems to support the idea that a deep-rooted aesthetic preference is behind it.

We might also ask how important, or narrow, are the principles of temporal ordering and causal connectivity on which Prince insists. He is not alone in that insistence; most generalizations about the nature of narrative are to the same effect and beg the same question. Arthur C. Danto, in his *Analytical Philosophy of History* (Cambridge, 1965), proposes that 'narratives are forms of explanation' (p. 233); accordingly, 'to tell a story is to exclude *some* happenings. ... Stories, to be stories, must leave things out' (pp. 11–12). But how much can be left out? For Danto, 'explanation' means a delineated pattern of causation, and he expects this to involve a temporal process, a change of situation. Must every story be rationally coherent in those ways? Help with the problem could perhaps have been expected from the contemporary linguists who pursue under such various banners as discourse analysis or *Textgrammatik* or *translinguistique* the aim of distinguishing between a succession of sentences which are intelligibly connected and a succession of sentences which are randomly jumbled. But actually this kind of linguistic inquiry proves too inflexible to be applied usefully to literary narrative, which sometimes allows events to become unbonded while still retaining the reader's interest in the 'story'. Fiction can be as disjunctive, yet as emotionally compelling, as a weird dream; and not to let 'story' cover such cases would be to make the generic category more constricted than some modern story-tellers wish it to be. At a time when the border-lines of definition are in practice shifting outwards, an inclusive theoretical view has to be taken. To begin with, at least, let us regard almost any piece of brief fictional prose as a short story provided that, while it may lack a coherently sequential plot, it retains some clear formal relation to plotted stories. It may for instance present a surrealistic counterpart to any cause-and-effect organization of material, as in Sylvia Plath's 'Johnny Panic and the Bible of Dreams', Jan Gerhard Toonder's 'The Spider', or Franz Kafka's 'Ein Landarzt'. Or it may leave the reader to elicit a plot from disconnected data; Robert Coover's 'The

Babysitter' offers a variety of alternative developments from the initial situation, each of these being a more or less credible fulfilment of fantasies in the minds of the characters. There is no defined story of an orthodox sort in 'The Babysitter', no single arrangement of happenings in whose actuality the author solicits our conventional belief. But psychological action is certainly there, and we may select a story from the available possibilities if we wish. More subversive still, yet parodically relevant to the tradition of plotted stories, is Jorge Luis Borges' 'El jardin de los senderos que se bifurcan' (The Garden of Forking Paths), which collapses normal distinctions between the veracious and the invented and which itself splits into several incompatible plot-paths so as to undermine the premise of causality on which narrative has usually depended. We can call these 'anti-stories' *if* we like, but that is implicitly to concede that they need to be seen in relation to the mainstream. Seemingly adversative developments often come to be absorbed within a generic tradition.

Having extended the concept 'short story' in certain respects, let us now venture some delimiting comments. For while narrowly prescriptive definitions will not do, since it is already clear that this genre has no monotypic purity, it would be useless to go to the latitudinarian extreme of including in it every kind of brief prose fiction. For instance, as Alfred G. Engstrom observes, 'legends of demons, saints, gods and the like and tales of outright wizardry' seldom have a claim to be considered short stories. They do not focus, as a rule, on human affairs and at any rate are not primarily intended as fictions. Thus we can discard the sort of thing recounted by Yeats in *The Celtic Twilight*, a scrapbook of local superstitions and spooky gossip, or material such as that collected by Martin Buber in *Tales of the Hasidim*, consisting largely of legendary anecdotes. But it is important to emphasize that what disqualifies such pieces is not the subject matter in itself, because that can give rise to admissible stories like Flaubert's 'La Légende de Saint Julien L'Hospitalier' which are shaped with artistry so as to convey a fully human dimension. The point is that unless there is something more than a fragmentary or an episodic structure, something more than a pious or a credulous tone, the potential interest of character in action will hardly be realized. This does not contradict the previous point that some apparently disjointed narratives may qualify as short stories. In particular instances it is usually easy to recognize sub-literary material by its lack of either formal poise or psychological cogency. *Exempla* about tediously saintly figures, snippets of legend about marvels and eerie occurrences: such things differ quite patently from those tales that are imaginatively cohesive even when fantastic and elliptical, or from tales that explore a mental and moral dimension by evoking the preternatural, as in Hawthorne's 'Young Goodman Brown' with its symbols of devilry and witchcraft.

How Long Is Short?

With the kind of reservation just noted, one can say that in current usage 'short story' is generally applied to almost any kind of fictitious prose narrative briefer than a novel. This, however, needs further refining. What range of sizes does the term cover? How much contraction or protraction is allowable? Presumably the lower limit comes down in theory to a mere sentence, of the sort exemplified earlier, though in practice it is hard to imagine how anything under a page or two can offer more than a skinny outline of happenings (as with Hemingway's stringently abbreviated piece 'A Short Story') or a diminutive gesture towards some narrative possibilities (as with Fielding Dawson's 'Thunder Road'). The upper limit is less clear, and its demarcation will depend partly on whether author, reader or middleman is made the primary point of reference. Poe said that a 'tale' (which for the moment can be taken as a synonym; this and related designations will be discussed in later chapters) is capable of being perused at one sitting. The trouble with that idea, as William Saroyan once remarked, is that some people can sit for longer than others. Shifting the pragmatic focus, one may choose to let the matter of length be decided not by the reader's span of concentration so much as by editorial exigencies; Henry James mentions the 'hard-and-fast rule' among contemporary magazines of keeping inside the range of between six and eight thousand words. But of course such rules vary from time to time and magazine to magazine, so that a single piece of writing may fall within the bounds according to one editor yet be out of bounds according to another; generic lines need to be less arbitrarily drawn. An alternative possibility is to accept as short stories whatever an author wishes to nominate—or allows to be nominated—as such. Somerset Maugham notes in the preface to his *Complete Short Stories* that the smallest item there comes to about 1,600 words in all, the longest to about 20,000, and that is approximately the median range—though some authors would include briefer and longer work: in Frank Sargeson's *Collected Stories* a few pieces are less than 500 words, while one runs to about 32,000.

None of these alternatives seems wholly adequate. There is, however, no need to choose between them, because at any rate it would be unsatisfactory to make a word-count the sole criterion. Genre is not arithmetically defined. Aristotle could say that a tragic plot must have 'a certain magnitude', yet he made no attempt to measure that magnitude precisely; and while it can be said incontrovertibly that a short story must have a certain brevity, confining it within specific dimensions is futile. But if structural considerations, tectonic elements, are more important, they must nevertheless bear a relation to sheer size. That Sargeson story of 32,000 words, for instance, approaches in scale some other works of his which have been announced and accepted as 'novels'. What length can a short story reach without becoming a short novel? Is there indeed an intermediate category, as the increasingly frequent use in English criticism of the Italian word *novella* appears to suggest? This brings us up against another obstacle: the lack of a precise trans-lingual vocabulary for comparative purposes.

Translating Terms

Generic definition becomes considerably more awkward once we extend the inquiry beyond literature and criticism in English. There is no exact equivalent to 'short story' in the usage of other European languages, only a cluster of like terms, most of which are confusingly cognate with the English word 'novel'. This difficulty needs clarifying historically. (The following paragraph is indebted to Gerald Gillespie's review of the terminological problem in *Neophilologus* for 1967.)

'Novel', from the sixteenth to the eighteenth centuries, had a meaning which, like the French *nouvelle*, stemmed from Italian *novella* and Spanish *novela*; it was applied, usually in the plural, to tales or short stories of the type contained in such works as Boccaccio's *Decameron*, the *Heptaméron* of Marguerite de Navarre, Cervantes' *Novelas Ejemplares* or Pettie's *Petite Pallace*. It referred to a fictitious prose narrative with characters or actions representing everyday life (sometimes in the past but more often in the present—hence 'new', a matter of novelty, a *novella*); and as such it stood in contrast to the traditional 'romance', which was less realistic and longer. As late as 1774 'novel' was still being regarded as a narrative of small compass: Chesterfield in his *Letters* described it as 'a kind of abbreviation of a Romance'. Only in the nineteenth century, when the old romance had declined further as a genre, did the concept of the novel expand to fill the space available. By then the word 'novel' had lost its original associations. But on the Continent its cognates, especially the German *Novelle*, continued to be linked in many writers' minds with the Renaissance *novella* despite an increasing disparity in size between much of their work and that small-scale prototype. In Boccaccio's hands the *novella* was very succinct, seldom extending to more than about ten pages. This was one of the ways in which it opposed the medieval romance, a diffuse form. But it did normally delineate a completed span of action (such as the full course of love intrigue), and hence nineteenth-century writers could claim to be working within a tradition that stemmed from the *Decameron* even when their own narratives stretched to 150 pages. The process of expansion was in fact already under way in the *Novelas Ejemplares* (1613) of Cervantes, perhaps as important a progenitor as Boccaccio himself. A few critics, however, look sceptically at the idea of a tradition reaching from those earlier figures down into modern literature, and argue that the Italian term *novella* should not be applied to post-Renaissance forms; with works like Kleist's 'Michael Kohlhaas' or Mérimée's 'Carmen' or Conrad's 'The Secret Sharer' or Lawrence's 'The Virgin and the Gipsy' we no longer have (these rigorists point out) the kind of economy, narrative frame, light tone, and so forth, that Boccaccio established. But that view is too fastidious. Every literary genre continually alters its shape, and due weight should be given to the fact that many writers did see themselves as belonging to a certain tradition.

In France a distinction between *nouvelle* and *conte* was available but not consistently observed. In 1664 La Fontaine entitled a collection of his verse tales (some of them derived from Boccaccio) *Nouvelles*; but a second series of the same works, issued the next year, was called *Contes et Nouvelles*. Even in the Romantic period these two terms were sometimes indiscriminately used, by de Musset and Nodier for instance, but around the mid-nineteenth century a distinction began to emerge: as Albert J. George observes in his study *Short Fiction in France, 1800–1850*, 'the word *conte* was assuming a meaning that differentiated it from *nouvelle*, the former accepted as more concentrated, with one major episode, the latter more complex and consisting of several scenes' (p. 234).

Conte, like the English 'tale', implied a narrative manner reminiscent of oral delivery, and frequently contained an element of fantasy; a *nouvelle*, on the other hand, 'included a series of incidents for the analysis and development of character or motive' (George, p. 9), and—after Mérimée—tended towards an objective tone. But confusion remained; later in the century, works of this latter sort were often labelled *contes*, by Maupassant for instance.

In Germany, over that same period, classification was taken more seriously. Exactly what constituted a true *Novelle* was not a matter of complete agreement, but no-one doubted that it was a distinct and important genre. Various structural theories had their day, with Ludwig Tieck asserting that the action of a *Novelle* must have a 'curious, striking turning-point' (*sonderbaren, auffallenden Wendepunkt*), Paul Heyse that it must have a quintessential silhouette, others that it must have a linear development, still others that it should follow a concentric path, and so forth. One fairly consistent tendency, however, among *Novelle* practitioners was to extend their compositions substantially. Consequently, when some German writers in recent times started to produce much more compressed stories, a different word had to be coined to distinguish these: *Kurzgeschichte*. This directly translates the English 'short story'—but its usage is narrowly confined to stories of a few pages only, whereas 'short story' is normally more flexible. Moreover, such had been the prestige of the *Novelle* that the *Kurzgeschichte* came to be regarded by some as an essentially inferior form: 'an illegitimate child of the *Novelle*', in Johannes Klein's words (*ein illegitimes Kind der Novelle*). But even those German critics who do view the *Kurzgeschichte* without such prejudice have usually regarded it as something to be set in firm contradistinction to the *Novelle*. Thus Ruth J. Kilchenmann declares that the *Kurzgeschichte* presents 'a fragment of extracted experience' (*ein Stück herausgerissenes Leben*) while the *Novelle* is 'constructed around a crisis' (*auf einen Höhepunkt zu konstruiert*); that the plot of the *Kurzgeschichte* consists of 'netlike interweaving' (*netzhafte Verflechtung*) while that of the *Novelle* follows a 'rising and sharply falling curve' (*aufsteigende und scharf abfallende Kurve*); and that, in general, 'the compact, causally and logically built up form of the *Novelle* is in distinct contrast with the often desultorily, often arabesquely extended or concentrated and elliptical configuration of the *Kurzgeschichte*' (*Die dichte, kausal und logisch aufgebaute Form der Novelle hebt sich deutlich ab von der oft sprunghaften, oft arabeskenhaft erweiterten oder gerafften und aussparenden Gestaltung der Kurzgeschichte*). This impressionistic scheme is attractive in its tidiness. Unfortunately short fiction, even in Germany, is too perversely untidy to conform to any such contrast.

What all this terminological flux indicates is a simple principle of literary evolution which was previously exemplified by the linked histories of the words 'novel' and 'romance'. As described by the Russian formalist Jurij Tynjanov half a century ago, this principle is based on the recognition that at any given time literature as a whole consists of a complex system of interrelated variable elements, including generic concepts. These concepts change as their context in the system changes. Thus, as we have seen, the scope of the 'novel' in eighteenth-century English literature became altered in direct proportion to a corresponding shift in the scope of the 'romance'. And similarly, 'short story' and novella are relative, even symbiotic, categories, sharing space as components in a total literary system which from time to time undergoes mutations:

> The size of a thing, the quantity of verbal material, is not an indifferent feature; we cannot, however, define the genre of a work if it is isolated from the system ... The study of isolated genres outside the features characteristic of the genre system with which they are related is impossible.

We shall need to return to the question whether the field of the short story is contiguous with that of the novel, or should be separated from it by an intermediate field. But these fields exist temporally as well as spatially, and in order to clarify our terms further we must now trace in broader outline the antecedents and emergence of what is usually meant by the 'modern short story'.

GARY GEDDES

Doing the Four-Brick Cross: Or, How to Read and Write About the Short Story

When I was a small boy, my grandfather used to ply me with stories about his youth in Jefferson, Wisconsin, the most repeated being the one about how he quit school in grade six after a teacher accused him of something he did not do. He would describe how he opened the classroom window and stepped (is this why he was a step-grandparent?) into the schoolyard. He was twelve years old. He was afraid to go home and tell his parents what he'd done, so he walked downtown and hung around a construction site, watching the men work while he ate the lunch he'd had the good sense to grab before putting an end to his formal education. Two boys not much older than himself were carrying bricks from the horsedrawn wagon to the masons, bent under the weight. The muscles in their necks bulged like knots in a rope. The upshot of this story was, of course, that my grandfather joined those boys, carrying more than a million bricks, a load not nearly so light or so useful as school learning.

Since I'd heard the story so many times I could have told it myself, what interested me most was my grandfather's body language, the way his eyes rolled and his shoulders twitched when he mentioned the weight of the bricks. His huge, gnarled fingers had their own story to tell, a choreography of gestures which were always the prelude to his famous demonstration of the four-brick cross. I say famous, because my grandfather would challenge house guests, even perfect strangers, to pick up those four brick (he never used the plural form *bricks*) with one hand and see how far they could carry them. In his prime, he was reputed to have carried them around the bases in a ballpark in Yorkton, Saskatchewan. Most conscripts would be unable to lift the bricks at all; occasionally someone would raise and carry the crossed bricks a few feet before they came crashing to the ground, to my grandfather's delight.

There was a trick, of course, in knowing just how to grip the bricks, which I managed to observe and execute at the same age though without having to quit school. What I am trying to suggest here is that writing about the short story may not be so foreign or difficult a task as you may think. You're already a seasoned analyst of stories. When your friend at the mall starts in—"You should've seen what happened last night outside The Cess Pool"—all your critical receptors kick in to help you piece together not only the basic events (plot), but also the underlying psychology (character), and your friend's relation to the situation she is describing (tone, point of view). If she was directly involved, chances are she'll be telling the story from a first-person point of view ("I was lighting a smoke, minding my own business, when"); if she was a casual observer or is reporting the story from hearsay, she might use the third-person omniscient point of view ("The sun had just set when this rusted black Land Rover pulled alongside the ..."). You're probably thinking, my friend wouldn't talk like that. If so, congratulations; that means you're paying attention to the words, the idiom, deciding whether the choice of word and phrase is formal, grammatically correct, or some kind of vaguely dated street lingo: "Ya, man, I was, like, toked to the rafters, orbiting. And dark? The day was toast when these two Nerds rolled up in a burb-boat. ..."

While you are busy soaking up the local lore and gossip, you'll have noticed your friend's tone: admiration, disapproval, irony, contempt, perhaps all of these in varying degrees. At some level, too, you'll be wondering whether she's telling you this story to impress, entertain, shock, or irritate you. Whatever our motivations for telling them, sharing stories is an essential ingredient of daily living; it's the way we organize and make sense of the strange world we inhabit, our means of constructing a coherent version of who we are and where we fit into the scheme of things. While you're reading a short story, underline the images (of things, events, people) that seem particularly striking, words and phrases that are somehow memorable or thought-provoking. Looking over these underlinings or marginal notes later, you may notice a pattern emerging, certain recurrences or variations on a theme. In thinking about motivation, ask yourself whether the cause of the character's downfall or malaise is internal (some personal flaw or shortcoming) or external (social forces beyond his or her control). A fictional character is rendered by way of his or her actions, gestures, speech, and by direct comments made by the narrator and other characters. In longer forms such as the novel, characters may form part of a larger structure of meaning, so that the character relations (the configuration of actions and values) in a given work may be said to constitute the author's view of human nature. Traditionally, the short story has a shorter arc of action than the novel and employs a more simplified psychology. To achieve this kind of economy, the writer has to develop a kind of verbal and emotional shorthand that gives us the bare minimum of information—but just enough. An art of brush-strokes, to refer again to Nadine Gordimer's wonderfully apt term.

The figures in fiction don't exist in a vacuum. They are found in certain places (rooms, vehicles, towns, landscapes). Whether the setting is "realistic" or fantastical, we find characters more interesting and—yes—credible, if they inhabit settings that have recognizable features: taps, doorknobs, windows, cellars, eating utensils. A preposterous creature from outer space with huge fungus-like growths on its forehead will be more deeply rooted in our senses by giving it a lisp, a wart on the nose, a particular odour, as well as certain recognizable drives and neuroses. Nothing in the world of fiction is real, of course—that is, identical with what it tries to represent. The word *tree* bears no relation to that complex of branches, trunk, limbs, and leaves that we see outside the window, but words have the power to remind us of a world experienced through the senses. They are useful signs, or signifiers, vehicles through which an author calls before our minds a certain vision. Nothing is more awesome and exciting than this power of words to create an illusion of reality that holds us in thrall and shapes the way we see and understand the world.

How, exactly, is this illusion of reality created in a short story? Well, for one thing, by creating the illusion of time passing. In addition to character and setting, stories create the illusion of time. It's not for nothing that the traditional story begins "Once upon a time ...." Our awareness of time and its passage is central to the artistic process; art is the record of our brief passage through time, an elegant graffiti that announces KILROY WAS HERE. Like ourselves, fictional characters are creatures of time, whether the fleeting present or the recent or remote past. As such, they enjoy our curiosity and sympathy. We marvel at their antics and at the amazing authorial shorthand which allows us in half an hour of reading to experience events that cover an hour, a day, a month, or several years of fictional time. As much as being an excellent yarn-spinner, the writer of short fiction must be a master of the art of illusion, of finding the telling detail and leaving the rest unsaid.

To understand how the illusion of time is created in fiction, consider briefly the range of devices used in cinema, from the printed indicator saying **Montreal, August 1939**, which tells the alert reader that events are taking place on the eve of World War II, to more sophisticated jump-cuts that shift us back and forth between several characters, settings, and points in time or reveal to us the same character at different points in his or her life. In their earliest, most primitive forms these shifts in time may have been signaled by a close-up of the principal character suddenly looking pensive, the images on screen becoming blurry and impressionistic until—presto!—there is Angie at half the age and twice the size. These are all techniques adapted from fiction, the subtlest ones from Virginia Woolf and other stream-of-consciousness writers who were quite adept at creating in words a sense of the mind's workings, that marvelous interface between present event and distant memory. Proust, who predates and is in a category of his own, described the game in the title of his novel *À la recherche du temps perdu*, appallingly translated into English as *Remembrance of Things Past*.

If you think of words and phrases and the images they deliver as stopped-frames in a moving-picture, you will come close to understanding how fiction is created. As in the case of film, where a thousand frames of footage may end up on the cutting-room floor for every ten frames that are used, at the moving edge of every sentence, every thought, a writer is faced with an infinite number of choices. What should so-and-so say next? Would her reaction more likely be silence, followed by the hurling of a beer bottle? Should this emotion be stated bluntly, embodied in some action or gesture (showing versus telling)? What difference would it make if I used the word *mechanical*, rather than *stunned*, to describe her physical reactions at this point? Is it more powerful, in this instance, to imply rather than state, to employ understatement as they did in the Israeli pavilion at Expo 67 in Montreal, where the vast library of atrocities associated with the Holocaust was depicted only by a child's single shoe on a low pedestal at the centre of the pavilion? Like the maker of an animated film, the writer must breathe life into the clay of words to make his figures weep, laugh, and dance in our mind's eye.

If you pay attention to some of these elements of the craft of fiction while you read a story, you'll soon find something that interests you enough to talk or write about. You could do worse than ask yourself: what feelings does this story evoke in me—sadness, fear, joy, anger, resentment, desire, envy? This is a tremendously important stage to acknowledge, since the critical experience of a work of art begins in the emotions of the reader, viewer, or listener just as surely as the work emerges from some deep well of feeling in the creator. Once you've tried to articulate how you feel about a story, the most natural, and useful, question to ask is: how did the writer create these feelings in me, what techniques did she use to make me think and feel so deeply about a fictional character, a mere creature of words on the page? The HOW of a story will lead you back to the specifics of the story, words, phrases, images, descriptions, events, evocations of place and mood, strategies for moving a character through fictional space and time. Just as cooks have to employ many ingredients and be masters of timing in order to make all the parts of a meal ready at just the right moment, without burnt beans, rock-hard potatoes, or spongy broccoli, so, too, the writer of fiction has to have a superb sense of taste and timing to hold our attention, especially in this age of competing visual media.

In the notes on each author, in the other essays in this section, and in the Glossary, you'll find lots of material to guide you in preparing an essay. Chekhov advises a fellow-writer to focus on specific details, not on vague emotions. Alice Munro dismisses plot and setting and insists instead on the importance of feeling. As for the role of so-called reality in her stories, Munro describes it as starter dough: "So when I write a story I want a certain kind of structure and I know the feeling I want to get from being inside that structure. ... Then I start accumulating the material and putting it together. Some of the material I may have lying around already, in memories and observations, and some I invent, and some I have to go diligently looking for (factual details), while some is dumped in my lap (anecdotes, bits of speech). I see how this material might go together to make the shape I need, and I try it. I keep trying and seeing where I went wrong and trying again."

Use these materials to write your essay rather than secondary sources. Some enrollees (I won't call them students) in universities, out of laziness, malice, or insecurity, don't bother reading primary sources. Instead, they ransack the libraries and cribs for interpretations they can offer up as their own. Plagiarism, the unacknowledged use of another's ideas and words, is dishonest and bad enough in its own right; worse, in my view, is giving up the chance to test your mettle, to discover something new and exciting and to try your best to understand and explain how it works. Your own interpretation, however simple or limited it might feel at first, is what's important. Nobody expects an undergraduate to be a critical whiz-kid, capable of matching the analytical skills of a seasoned critic. A good professor will prefer to see evidence of thinking and close-reading and intellectual struggle rather than the aping of professionals. The word "essay" comes from the French verb *essayer*, meaning *to try*. Your essay is an effort to construct an argument, a thesis, beginning with an assertion about the story, perhaps even identifying a problem you've encountered in reading the text. This assertion is usually followed by a number of sections in which you try to approach the problem from different angles, learning to elaborate, to expand on a point, even to admit to certain difficulties or potential contradictions. In other words, the stages and development of the argument, not the assertion itself, are what matter most.

For example, I may have noticed that there are birds everywhere in a particular story—they're perched on fences, flying out of cupboards, showing up in the oddest places, including a children's book left open on the coffee table at The Briars Motel in Perth. When I re-read the story, I notice that the main character is a civil servant who works all day in the bowels of the Parliamentary library, sorting books and dreaming of a more interesting life. At night, he retreats to his basement apartment to read books about aviation. This makes me think, hey, I'm beginning to see a pattern here: entrapment and the dream of escape. And then (a key moment) a young woman named Robin moves into the same building, inadvertently stirring and putting to test his dreams of flight and escape. Robin is enchanting; she seems to represent all that our clerk dreams of, yet she also seems beyond his reach. I'm beginning to wonder if this isn't going to be a story about the impossibility of escape. If so, I'll want to flesh out my argument over several paragraphs (or sections, each containing a number of paragraphs), quoting relevant passages from the text to make a point and elaborating on other material in the story that supports my thesis.

Reading the story several times, I may decide, after all, that what is most interesting is not the subject or theme that could be extracted from it, but rather the way in which certain scenes are set up, the descriptive detail, the kinds of words (diction) used to create a mood or impression. There are, in fact, though I had not noticed before, two distinct kinds of birds represented in the story: birds of prey, with characteristics not unlike those of our librarian's crude and ruthless associates in the sorting department at work; then there are the more gentle domestic variety of birds that offer beauty and comfort and delight to our ordinary lives. So a polarity has been introduced that seems to be structurally important: our hero has to move between two extremes of behaviour and possibility, neither of which may be quite to his liking. I noticed, then, that different settings are used to highlight these different values. The Briars Motel, where our librarian takes Robin for a romantic evening has a rapacious landlord and a noisy bar called—who's surprised by anything at this stage of shameless invention?—The Bird's Nest. Some peculiar things are happening in the story, too, in terms of the handling of time. It's certainly not presented in a straightforward linear or chronological fashion. In fact, there are jumps back and forth in time and several difficult bits that seem to come from right out of the blue, including a prosaic, almost academic section on the iconography of angels in medieval times. What's the point of this intrusive objective material? Does it work? How do I explain this and what does it do to the shape and design of the story?

There's also an old man who seems a little dazed standing on the sidewalk outside the medical clinic in Perth. He's carrying something in a brown gunnysack that must be heavy because it gives his body a slight list to starboard. Or more likely to port—port wine, that is—at least that's what our young librarian thinks as he sees the old man lurch towards him. He's already shaken as he ushers his female companion towards a waiting taxi, her arm and its freshly made plaster cast cradled in a sling, so he's in no mood for drunks or panhandlers. He extracts a loonie from his pocket and thrusts it in the old man's face.

"Take this and leave us alone."

He tries to avoid eye contact with this intruder, but has miscalculated both the distance and his audience. The old man is already on his knees, a red and black chequered flannel shirttail hanging out of his pants. He's placing four dull terracotta building bricks on the sidewalk so they form a perfect cross, then locking his huge knuckles strategically in place on top. Before the young man can register a protest or deliver his girlfriend with her injured wing into the safety of the open car-door, the old man has lifted the four-brick cross and is making a circle around them, after which he makes a second circuit, this time around the entire perimeter of the taxi.

"There now, you try it." He flashes the young couple a lopsided grin and eases the four bricks, still intact, to the ground. The civil servant half expects to see a bird nesting among the white hairs protruding from the old man's pendulous ears. Cuckoo, he thinks. Absolutely cuckoo.

But Robin, his wounded companion, has taken the old man's gnarled fingers in her good hand. The three of them stand mesmerized by the contrast in shape and delicacy as she slowly rotates the old man's hand with her own. Between the callouses and liver-spots, the skin has separated in four places, the first thin lines of blood beginning to form in the cracks. Without hesitation she presses the open palm gently to her cheek and begins to cry.

Making. That's what it's all about, writing a story or, as reader, describing your experience of reading and thinking about the shape and meaning of a story. Writing and reading are interdependent, as Jean-Paul Sartre suggests in his essay "Why Write?" Literature, he says, involves "a pact of generosity between writer and reader." The gift of creation on the one hand is repaid by the gift of attention on the other, a collaboration in credulity, a sharing of imaginative freedoms. Writers and their readers/critics are a lot like bricklayers. They find the right words, put them together just so, using events, ideas, psychology, as well as patterns of image and sound, as the mortar that holds them together, that creates a dynamic of desire to keep us reading, attending closely and expectantly to each nuance from sentence to sentence and paragraph to paragraph.

It's like doing the four-brick cross. If you study the texture and patterning of the bricks, look closely at how they are placed, at the points where the fingers apply most pressure, eventually you'll raise them off the ground, maybe even get them to first-base; if you're determined, and enjoy a challenge, you might even make it to home-plate, though not without losing a bit of skin around the knuckles.

GARY GEDDES

Some Notes on the Novella

1. According to Martin Swales in *The German Novelle*, "The novelle is not a leisurely form in an interpretive sense; it does not have the breadth to allow for detailed and expansive exposition. It works by intense concentration: by focussing on one event or cluster of events, and by suggesting that its intense selectivity is justified by one over-riding interpretive issue. The exposition of many novellen is, then, interpretive, rather than descriptive; we begin with the immediate posing of a problem rather than with the spacious documentation of a given world" (25).

"I would argue that the mainspring of much novelle writing is the contact between an ordered and reliably interpreted human universe on the one hand and an experience or set of experiences that would appear to conflict utterly with any notion of order or manageable interpretation on the other. Hence, the novelle derives its peculiar and insistent energy from what one can best describe as a hermeneutic gamble, as a shock confrontation with marginal events. Implicitly, the attempt to make an ordered statement of that which by definition resists the ordering intention is one of the central undertakings within the narrative universe of the novelle" (28).

"Friedrich Schlegel insists on an inherent irony in the novelle, and in his view, this irony springs from the intrinsic discrepancy between what is being narrated and the way in which it is narrated ... the tension between the societal expectation of reader (and narrator) and the fact that the material stands outside that expectation and has to be interpreted, mediated via the narrative voice, before it can have meaning for that societal universe. It is the measure of the discrepancy this undertaking seeks to overcome that the form itself, for Friedrich Schlegel, is by definition ironic" (31).

"It could, then, be said that while the genre is inherently subjective, it distrusts its own subjectivity, even resents it. The attempt at objectivity is not just a trick, an artistic tour de force; it is a desperately serious gamble—and nowhere more so, of course, than when it fails" (38).

2. Judith Liebowitz, in *Narrative Purpose in the Novella* (1974), says that the novella's distinction lies in its "double effect of intensity and expansion."

3. Mark Schorer: "It aims at something like the concentration of the short story at the same time that it employs the complexities of the novel."

4. Irving Howe describes the novella (he prefers the term *short novel*) as a "happy hybrid" in which "The sense of performance becomes central."

5. In *Forms of the Modern Novella* (1975), Mary Doyle Springer reminds us that Henry James, who was pleased to find magazine editors enlightened enough to free him from short magazine stories, which he said were characterized by a "rude prescription of brevity at any cost," opted instead for "our ideal, the beautiful and blest nouvelle", a form which he loved for its *shapeliness*.

6. Howard Nemerov has written a wonderful essay called "Composition and Fate in the Short Novel" (*Graduate Journal* 2, Winter 1963, 375–91; reprinted in Nemerov's *Poetry and Fiction: Essays*, 1963), in which he sets out ten features of the novella, or short novel, including a stress on depth rather than length; compression allied to rhythmic intensification; a delicate balancing of event and circumstance; a rootedness in authorial fantasies, if not psychoses, which explains its preoccupation with the forbidden, the extravagant, the illicit; and poetic or symbolic patterning that goes hand in hand with a temporal succession of events. Short novels, he says, are characterized by their "outright concentration upon traditional problems of philosophy, boldness of their venture into generality, the evidence they give of profound moral concern ... acute awareness of themselves as parables, as philosophic myths, and almost invariably announce and demonstrate the intention of discursive profundity—the intention, it is not too much to say, of becoming sacred books."

Writers on Writing

MARGARET ATWOOD

From *An End to Audience?*

I believe that poetry is the heart of the language, the activity through which language is renewed and kept alive. I believe that fiction writing is the guardian of the moral and ethical sense of the community. Especially now that organized religion is scattered and in disarray, and politicians have, Lord knows, lost their credibility, fiction is one of the few forms left through which we may examine our society not in its particular but in its typical aspects; through which we can see ourselves and the ways in which we behave towards each other, through which we can see others and judge them and ourselves.

Writing is a craft, true, and discussions of the position of colons and the rhyming of *plastic* and *spastic* have some place in it. You cannot be a concert pianist without having first learned the scales, you cannot throw a porcelain vase without having put in a good number of hours at the wheel. But writing is also a vocation. By *vocation* I mean a lifetime pursuit to which you feel called. There is a big difference between a doctor who goes into medicine because he wants to cure people and one who goes into it because that's where he thinks the money is. They may both be able to fix your broken leg, technically just as well; but there is a difference.

Under the right conditions, the first may turn into Norman Bethune. The second never will. If you want to be a writer, you should go into the largest library you can find and stand there contemplating the books that have been written. Then you should ask yourself, "Do I really have anything to add?" If you have the arrogance or the humility to say yes, you will know you have the vocation.

Writing is also a profession, and, at its best, an honorable one. It has been made honorable by those who have already been members of it. Whether you like it or not, every time you set pen to paper you're staring at the same blank space that confronted Milton, Melville, Emily Brontë, Dostoevsky and George Eliot, George Orwell and William Faulkner and Virginia Woolf and William Carlos Williams, not to mention the latest hero, Gabriel García Márquez. Imitation is not emulation; nobody expects you to write the books of these writers over again. But unless you're trying to do as well, unless you're trying to do as well as you can, you are not worthy of the profession. There's a certain amount of cynicism among writers, just as there is among doctors. But if all doctors were hacking off legs with septic instruments in barber shops and losing sponges inside people's lungs because they're drunk during the operation, we would not think of medicine as an honorable profession but as a game played for money by charlatans and quacks, and doctors would still quite rightly be known as leeches.

Writing can also be an art, and one of the reasons that so many writers dodge this on television talk shows is that art is hard to define or describe. Money is easier to talk about, so we talk about money. Nevertheless, art happens. It happens when you have the craft and the vocation and are waiting for something else, something extra, or maybe not waiting; in any case it happens. It's the extra rabbit coming out of the hat, the one you didn't put there. It's Odysseus standing by the blood-filled trench, except that the blood is his own. It is bringing the dead to life and giving voices to those who lack them so that they may speak for themselves. It is not "expressing yourself." It is opening yourself, discarding your *self*, so that the language and the world may be evoked through you. *Evocation* is quite different from *expression*. Because we are so fixated on the latter, we forget that writing also does the former. Maybe the writer expresses; but evocation, calling up, is what writing does for the reader. Writing is also a kind of soothsaying, a truth-telling. It is a naming of the world, a reverse incarnation: the flesh becoming word. It's also a witnessing. *Come with me*, the writer is saying to the reader. *There is a story I have to tell you, there is something you need to know.* The writer is both an eye-witness and I-witness, the one to whom personal experience happens and the one who makes experience personal for others. The writer *bears witness*. Bearing witness is not the same as self-expression.

There's something compulsive about the act of writing. All writers play Ancient Mariner at times to the reader's Wedding Guest, hoping that they are holding the reader with their glittering eye, at least long enough so he'll turn the next page. The tale the Mariner tells is partly about himself, true, but it's partly about the universe and partly about something the Wedding Guest needs to know; or at least, that's what the story tells us.

Jacob, so one of the stories goes, wrestled with an angel all night, neither prevailing against the other; and he would not let go until the angel blessed him. *What is your name?* said the angel, unable to give the blessing until the name was spoken. When the angel gave the blessing, it was not for Jacob alone but for his people. There is not a writer alive who would fail to interpret this story as a parable of his own relationship with his art. The encounter with language is a struggle in which each side is equally active, for what writer has not felt the language taking him over at times, blocking him at others? We all hope for the blessing; we all hope finally to be able to speak our name. And, we hope that if we receive the blessing it will not be for ourselves alone.

ANTON CHEKHOV

The Matter of Technique in Short-Story Writing

You underscore trifles in your writings, and yet you are not a subjective writer by nature; it is an acquired trait in you. To give up this acquired subjectivity is as easy as to take a drink. One needs only to be more honest, to throw oneself overboard everywhere, not to obtrude oneself into the hero of one's own novel, to renounce oneself for at least a half hour. You have a story in which a young wedded couple kiss all through dinner, grieve without cause, weep oceans of tears. Not a single sensible word; nothing but *sentimentality*. And you did not write for the reader. You wrote because *you* like that sort of chatter. But suppose you were to describe the dinner, how they ate, what they ate, what the cook was like, how insipid your hero is, how content with his lazy happiness, how insipid your heroine is, how funny is her love for this napkin-bound, sated, overfed goose,—we all like to see happy, contented people, that is true,—but to describe them, what they said and how many times they kissed is not enough—you need something else: to free yourself from the personal expression that a placid honey-happiness produces upon everybody. … Subjectivity is a terrible thing. It is bad in this alone, that it reveals the author's hands and feet. I'll bet that all priests' daughters and clerks' wives who read your works are in love with you, and if you were a German you would get free beer in all the Bierhalle where the German women serve. If it were not for this subjectivity you would be the best of artists. You know how to laugh, sting and ridicule, you possess a rounded style, you have experienced much, have seen so much,—alas! The material is all wasted. …

> From a letter to Alexander P. Chekhov, April 1883. Reprinted here from *Letters on the Short Story, the Drama, and Other Literary Topics* by Anton Chekhov, ed. Louis S. Friedland, trans. Constance Garnett (New York: Minton, Balch and Co., 1924), pp. 69–70.

In my opinion a true description of Nature should be very brief and have a character of relevance. Commonplaces such as, "the setting sun bathing in the waves of the darkening sea, poured its purple gold, etc."—"the swallows flying over the surface of the water twittered merrily,"—such commonplaces one ought to abandon. In descriptions of Nature one ought to seize upon the little particulars, grouping them in such a way that, in reading, when you shut your eyes, you get a picture.

For instance, you will get the full effect of a moonlight night if you write that on the mill-dam a little glowing star-point flashed from the neck of a broken bottle, and the round, black shadow of a dog, or a wolf, emerged and ran, etc. Nature becomes animated if you are not squeamish about employing comparisons of her phenomena with ordinary human activities, etc.

In the sphere of psychology, details are also the thing. God preserve us from commonplaces. Best of all is it to avoid depicting the hero's state of mind; you ought to try to make it clear from the hero's actions. It is not necessary to portray many characters. The centre of gravity should be in two persons: him and her. …

I write this to you as a reader having a definite taste. Also, in order that you, when writing, may not feel alone. To be alone in work is a hard thing. Better poor criticism than none at all. Is it not so?

From a letter to Alexander P. Chekhov, May 10, 1886. Reprinted here from *Letters*, pp. 70–71.

Oh, you of little faith,—you are interested to know what flaws I found in your "Mignon." Before I point them out I warn you that they have a technical rather than a critico-literary interest. Only a writer can appreciate them, but a reader not at all. Here they are. ... I think that you, an author scrupulous and untrusting, afraid that your characters will not stand out clearly enough, are too much given to thoroughly detailed description. The result is an overwrought "motleyness" of effect that impairs the general impression.

In order to show how powerfully music can affect one at times, but distrustful of the reader's ability to understand you readily, you zealously set forth the psychology of your Feodrik; the psychology is successful, but then the interval between two such moments as "amari, morire" and the pistol-shot, is dragged out unduly, and the reader, before he reaches the suicide-scene, has had time to recover from the pain of "amari, morire." But you must give the reader no chance to recover: he must always be kept in suspense. These remarks would not apply if "Mignon" were a novel. Long, detailed works have their own peculiar aims, which require a most careful execution regardless of the total impression. But in short stories it is better to say not enough than to say too much, because,—because—I don't know why!. ...

From a letter to I. L. Shcheglov, January 22, 1888. Reprinted here from *Letters*, p. 106.

... I read your story with great pleasure. Your hand is acquiring firmness, and your ... style is improving. I like the whole story, except the ending, which appears to me to lack force. ... But this is a matter of taste and not so important. If one is to talk about flaws one should not confine oneself to details. You have a defect and a very serious one. In my opinion it is this: you do not polish your things, and hence they seem frequently to be florid and overloaded. Your works lack the compactness that makes short things alive. There is skill in your stories; there is talent, literary sense, but very slight art. You put your characters together in the right way, but not plastically. You are either too lazy or you do not wish to slough off at one stroke all that is useless. To make a face from marble means to remove from the slab everything that is not the face. Do I make myself clear? Do you understand? There are two or three awkward expressions which I underlined.

From a letter to E. M. Sh——, November 17, 1895. Reprinted here from *Letters*, pp. 82–83.

... More advice: when reading the proofs, cross out a host of concrete nouns and other words. You have so many such nouns that the reader's mind finds it a task to concentrate on them, and he soon grows tired. You understand it at once when I say, "The man sat on the grass;" you understand it because it is clear and makes no demands on the attention. On the other hand, it is not easily understood, and it is difficult for the mind, if I write, "A tall, narrow-chested, middle-sized man, with a red beard, sat on the green grass, already trampled by pedestrians, sat silently, shyly, and timidly looked about him." That is not immediately grasped by the mind, whereas good writing should be grasped at once,—in a second. ...

From a letter to Maxim Gorky, September 3, 1899. Reprinted here from *Letters*, p. 88.

JOSEPH CONRAD

The Creative Process

1. A ROMANTIC REALIST

I have not sought for special imaginative freedom or a larger play of fancy in my choice of characters and subjects. The nature of the knowledge, suggestions or hints used in my imaginative work has depended directly on the conditions of my active life. It depended more on contacts, and very slight contacts at that, than on actual experience; because my life as a matter of fact was far from being adventurous in itself. Even now when I look back on it with a certain regret (who would not regret his youth?) and positive affection, its colouring wears the sober hue of hard work and exacting calls of duty, things which in themselves are not much charged with a feeling of romance. If these things appeal strongly to me even in retrospect it is, I suppose, because the romantic feeling of reality was in me an inborn faculty. This in itself may be a curse but when disciplined by a sense of personal responsibility and a recognition of the hard facts of existence shared with the rest of mankind becomes but a point of view from which the very shadows of life appear endowed with an internal glow. And such romanticism is not a sin. It is none the worse for the knowledge of truth. It only tries to make the best of it, hard as it may be; and in this hardness discovers a certain aspect of beauty.

I am speaking here of romanticism in relation to life, not of romanticism in relation to imaginative literature, which, in its early days, was associated simply with medieval subjects sought for in a remote past. My subjects are not medieval and I have a natural right to them because my past is very much my own. If their course lie out of the beaten path of organized social life, it is, perhaps, because I myself did in a short break away from it early in obedience to an impulse which must have been very genuine since it has sustained me through all the dangers of disillusion. But that origin of my literary work was very far from giving a larger scope to my imagination. On the contrary, the mere fact of dealing with matters outside the general run of everyday experience laid me under the obligation of a more scrupulous fidelity to the truth of my own sensations. The problem was to make unfamiliar things credible. To do that I had to create for them, to reproduce for them, to envelop them in their proper atmosphere of actuality. This was the hardest task of all and the most important, in view of that conscientious rendering of truth in thought and fact which has always been my aim.

Preface to *Within the Tides* (1915)

2. Cherishing Undying Hope

... It must not be supposed that I claim for the artist in fiction the freedom of moral Nihilism. I would require from him many acts of faith of which the first would be the cherishing of an undying hope; and hope, it will not be contested, implies all the piety of effort and renunciation. It is the God-sent form of trust in the magic force and inspiration belonging to the life of this earth. We are inclined to forget that the way of excellence is in intellectual, as distinguished from emotional, humility. What one feels so hopelessly barren in declared pessimism is just its arrogance. It seems as if the discovery made by many men at various times that there is much evil in the world were a source of proud and unholy joy unto some of the modern writers. That frame of mind is not the proper one in which to approach seriously the art of fiction. It gives an author—goodness only knows why—an elated sense of his own superiority. And there is nothing more dangerous than such an elation to that absolute loyalty towards his feelings and sensations an author should keep hold of in his most exalted moments of creation.

To be hopeful in an artistic sense it is not necessary to think that the world is good. It is enough to believe that there is no impossibility of its being made so.

'Books' (1905); reprinted in *Notes on Life and Letters* (1921)

3. Rescue Work

Action in its essence, the creative art of a writer of fiction may be compared to rescue work carried out in darkness against cross gusts of wind swaying the action of a great multitude. It is rescue work, this snatching of vanishing phrases of turbulence, disguised in fair words, out of the native obscurity into a light where the struggling forms may be seen, seized upon, endowed with the only possible form of permanence in this world of relative values—the permanence of memory. And the multitude feels it obscurely too; since the demand of the individual to the artist is, in effect, the cry 'Take me out of myself!' meaning really, out of my perishable activity into the light of imperishable consciousness.

'Henry James, An Appreciation' (1905); reprinted in *Notes on Life and Letters* (1921)

4. Art and Temperament

... My own impression is that what he really meant was that my manner of telling, perfectly devoid of familiarity as between author and reader, aimed essentially at the intimacy of a personal communication, without any thought for other effects. As a matter of fact, the thought for effects is there all the same (often at the cost of mere directness of narrative), and can be directed in my unconventional grouping and perspective, which are purely temperamental and wherein all my 'art' consists.

Letter to Richard Curle (14 July 1913), *Life and Letters* (1927) ed. G. Jean-Aubry

5. To Make You See

... it is only through an unremitting never-discouraged care for the shape and ring of sentences that an approach can be made to plasticity, to colour, and that the light of magic suggestiveness may be brought to play for an evanescent instant over the commonplace surface of words: of the old, old words, worn thin, defaced by ages of careless usage.

The sincere endeavour to accomplish that creative task, to go as far on that road as his strength will carry him, to go undeterred by faltering, weariness, or reproach, is the only valid justification for the worker in prose. And if his conscience is clear, his answer to those who, in the fullness of a wisdom which looks for immediate profit, demand specifically to be edified, consoled, amused; who demand to be promptly improved, or encouraged, or frightened, or shocked, or charmed, must run thus: My task which I am trying to achieve is, by the power of the written word to make you hear, to make you feel—it is, before all, to make you *see*. That—and no more, and it is everything. If I succeed, you shall find there according to your deserts: encouragement, consolation, fear, charm—all you demand—and, perhaps, also that glimpse of truth for which you have forgotten to ask.

Preface to *The Nigger of the "Narcissus"* (1897)

Mavis Gallant

What Is Style?

I do not reread my own work unless I have to; I fancy no writer does. The reason why, probably, is that during the making of the story every line has been read and rewritten and read again to the point of glut. I am unable to "see" the style of the two stories presented here, and would not recognize its characteristics if they were pointed out to me. Once too close, the stories are already too distant. If I read a passage aloud, I am conscious of a prose rhythm easy for me to follow, that must be near to the way I think and speak. It seems to be my only link with a finished work.

The manner of writing, the thread spun out of the story itself, may with time have grown instinctive. I know that the thread must hold from beginning to end, and that I would like it to be invisible. Rereading "Baum, Gabriel" and "His Mother," all I can relate is that they are about loss and bewilderment, that I cannot imagine the people described living with any degree of willingness anywhere but in a city—in spite of Gabriel's imaginings about country life—and that a café as a home more congenial than home appears in both. The atmosphere, particularized, is of a fading world, though such a thing was far from my mind when the stories were written. It may be that the Europe of the nineteen-seventies already secreted the first dangerous sign of nostalgia, like a pervasive mist: I cannot say. And it is not what I have been asked to discuss.

Leaving aside the one analysis closed to me, of my own writing, let me say what style is *not*: it is not a last-minute addition to prose, a charming and universal slipcover, a coat of paint used to mask the failings of a structure. Style is inseparable from structure, part of the conformation of whatever the author has to say. What he says—this is what fiction is about—is that something is taking place and that nothing lasts. Against the sustained tick of a watch, fiction takes the measure of a life, a season, a look exchanged, the turning point, desire as brief as a dream, the grief and terror that after childhood we cease to express. The life, the look, the grief are without permanence. The watch continues to tick where the story stops.

A loose, a wavering, a slipshod, an affected, a false way of transmitting even a fragment of this leaves the reader suspicious: What is this too elaborate or too simple language hiding? What is the author trying to disguise? Probably he doesn't know. He has shown the works of the watch instead of its message. He may be untalented, just as he may be a gifted author who for some deeply private reason (doubt, panic, the pressures of a life unsuited to writing) has taken to rearranging the works in increasingly meaningless patterns. All this is to say that content, meaning, intention and form must make up a whole, and must above all have a reason to be.

There are rules of style. By applying them doggedly any literate, ambitious and determined person should he able to write like Somerset Maugham. Maugham was conscious of his limitations and deserves appreciation on that account: "I knew that I had no lyrical quality, I had a small vocabulary ... I had little gift for metaphors; the original striking simile seldom occurred to me. Poetic flights and the great imaginative sweep were beyond my powers." He decided, sensibly, to write "as well as my natural defects allowed" and to aim at "lucidity, simplicity and euphony." The chance that some other indispensable quality had been overlooked must have been blanketed by a lifetime of celebrity. Now, of course, first principles are there to be heeded or, at the least, considered with care; but no guided tour of literature, no commitment to the right formula or to good taste (which is changeable anyway) can provide, let alone supplant, the inborn vitality and tension of living prose.

Like every other form of art, literature is no more and nothing less than a matter of life and death. The only question worth asking about a story—or a poem, or a piece of sculpture, or a new concert hall—is, "Is it dead or alive?" If a work of the imagination needs to be coaxed into life, it is better scrapped and forgotten.

Working to rule, trying to make a barely breathing work of fiction simpler and more lucid and more euphonious merely injects into the desperate author's voice a tone of suppressed hysteria, the result of what E. M. Forster called "confusing order with orders." And then, how reliable are the rules? Listen to Pablo Picasso's rejection of a fellow-artist: "He looks up at the sky and says, 'Ah, the sky is blue,' and he paints a blue sky. Then he takes another look and says, 'The sky is mauve, too,' and he adds some mauve. The next time he looks he notices a trace of pink, and he adds a little pink." It sounds a proper mess, but Picasso was talking about Pierre Bonnard. As soon as we learn the name, the blues, mauves and pinks acquire a meaning, a reason to be. Picasso was right, but only in theory. In the end, everything depends on the artist himself.

Style in writing, as in painting is the author's thumbprint, his mark. I do not mean that it establishes him as finer or greater than other writers, though that can happen too. I am thinking now of prose style as a writer's armorial bearings, his name and address. In a privately printed and libellous pamphlet, Colette's first husband, Willy, who had fraudulently signed her early novels, tried to prove she had gone on to plagiarize and plunder different things he had written. As evidence he offered random sentences from work he was supposed to have influenced or inspired. Nothing, from his point of view, could have been more self-defeating. Colette's manner, robust and personal, seems to leap from the page. Willy believed he had taught Colette "everything," and it may have been true—"everything," that is, except her instinct for language, her talent for perceiving the movement of life and a faculty for describing it. He was bound to have influenced her writing; it couldn't be helped. But by the time he chose to print a broadside on the subject, his influence had been absorbed, transmuted and—most humbling for the teacher—had left no visible trace.

There is no such thing as a writer who has escaped being influenced. I have never heard a professional writer of any quality or standing talk about "pure" style, or say he would not read this or that for fear of corrupting or affecting his own; but I have heard it from would-be writers and amateurs. Corruption—if that is the word—sets in from the moment a child learns to speak and to hear language used and misused. A young person who does not read, and read widely, will never write anything—at least, nothing of interest. From time to time, in France, a novel is published purporting to come from a shepherd whose only influence has been the baaing of lambs on some God-forsaken slope of the Pyrenees. His artless and untampered-with mode of expression arouses the hope that there will be many more like him, but as a rule he is never heard from again. For "influences" I would be inclined to substitute "acquisitions." What they consist of, and amount to, are affected by taste and environment, preferences and upbringing (even, and sometimes particularly, when the latter has been rejected), instinctive selection. The beginning writer has to choose, tear to pieces, spit out, chew up and assimilate as naturally as a young animal—as naturally and as ruthlessly. Style cannot be copied, except by the untalented. It is, finally, the distillation of a lifetime of reading and listening, of selection and rejection. But if it is not a true voice, it is nothing.

NADINE GORDIMER

The Flash of Fireflies

Why is it that while the death of the novel is good for post-mortem at least once a year, the short story lives on unmolested? It cannot be because—to borrow their own jargon—literary critics regard it as merely a minor art form. Most of them, if pressed, would express the view that it is a highly specialized and skilful form, closer to poetry, etc. But they would have to be pressed; otherwise they wouldn't bother to discuss it at all. When Chekhov crops up, it is as a playwright, and Katherine Mansfield is a period personality from the Lady Chatterley set. Yet no one suggests that we are practicing a dead art form. And, like a child suffering from healthy neglect, the short story survives.

"To say that no one now much likes novels is to exaggerate very little. The large public which used to find pleasure in prose fictions prefer movies, television, journalism, and books of 'fact,'" Gore Vidal wrote recently (*Encounter*, December, 1967). If the cinema and television have taken over so much of the novel's territory, just as photography forced painting into wastelands which may or may not be made to bloom, hasn't the short story been overrun, too? This symposium is shoptalk and it would seem unnecessary for us to go over the old definitions of where and how the short story differs from the novel, but the answer to the question must lie somewhere here. Both novel and story use the same material: human experience. Both have the same aim: to communicate it. Both use the same medium: the written word. There is a general and recurrent dissatisfaction with the novel as a means of netting ultimate reality—another term for the quality of human life—and inevitably there is even a tendency to blame the tools; words have become hopelessly blunted by overuse, dinned to death by admen, and, above all, debased by political creeds that have twisted and changed their meaning. Various ways out have been sought. In England, a return to classicism in technique and a turning to the exoticism of sexual aberration and physical and mental abnormality as an extension of human experience and therefore of subject matter; in Germany and America, a splendid abandon in making a virtue of the vice of the novel's inherent clumsiness by stuffing it not with nineteenth-century horsehair narrative but twentieth-century anecdotal-analytical plastic foam; in France, the "laboratory novel" struggling to get away from the anthropocentric curse of the form and the illusion of depth of the psychological novel, and landing up very much where Virginia Woolf was, years ago, staring at the mark on the wall. Burroughs has invented the reader-participation novel. For the diseased word, George Steiner has even suggested silence.

If the short story is alive while the novel is dead, the reason must lie in approach and method. The short story, as a form and as a *kind of creative vision*, must be better equipped to attempt the capture of ultimate reality at a time when (whichever way you choose to see it) we are drawing nearer to the mystery of life or are losing ourselves in a bellowing wilderness of mirrors, as the nature of that reality becomes more fully understood or more bewilderingly concealed by the discoveries of science and the proliferation of communication media outside the printed word.

Certainly the short story always has been more flexible and open to experiment than the novel. Short-story writers always have been the subject at the same time to both a stricter technical discipline and a wider freedom than the novelist. Short-story writers have known—and solved by nature of their choice of form—what novelists seem to have discovered in despair only now: the strongest convention of the novel, prolonged coherence of tone, to which even the most experimental of novels must confirm unless it is to fall apart, is false to the nature of whatever can be grasped of human reality. How shall I put it? Each of us has a thousand lives and a novel gives a character only one. *For the sake of the form.* The novelist may juggle about with chronology and throw narrative overboard; all the time his characters have the reader by the hand, there is a consistency of relationship throughout the experience that cannot and does not convey the quality of human life, where contact is more like the flash of fireflies, in and out, now here, now there, in darkness. Short-story writers see by the light of the flash; theirs is the art of the only thing one can be sure of—the present moment. Ideally, they have learned to do without explanation of what went before, and what happens beyond this point. How the characters will appear, think, behave, comprehend, tomorrow or at any other time in their lives, is irrelevant. A discrete moment of truth is aimed at—not *the* moment of truth, because the short story doesn't deal in cumulatives.

The problem of how best to take hold of ultimate reality, from the technical and stylistic point of view, is one that the short-story writer is accustomed to solving specifically in relation to an area—event, mental state, mood, appearance—which is heightenedly manifest in a single situation. Take fantasy for an example. Writers are becoming more and more aware of the waviness of the line that separates fantasy from the so-called rational in human perception. It is recognized that fantasy is no more than a shift in angle; to put it another way, the rational is simply another, the most obvious, kind of fantasy. Writers turn to the less obvious fantasy as a wider lens on ultimate reality. But this fantasy is something that changes, merges, emerges, disappears as a pattern does viewed through the bottom of a glass. It is true for the moment when one looks down through the glass; but the same vision does not transform everything one sees, consistently throughout one's whole consciousness. Fantasy in the hands of short-story writers is so much more successful than when in the hands of novelists because it is necessary for it to hold good only for the brief illumination of the situation it dominates. In the series of developing situations of the novel the sustainment of the tone of fantasy becomes a high-pitched ringing in the reader's ears. How many fantasy novels achieve what they set out to do: convey the shift and change, to and fro, beneath, above, and around the world of appearances? The short story recognizes that full comprehension of a particular kind in the reader, like full apprehension of a particular kind in the writer, is something of limited duration. The short story is a fragmented and restless form, a matter of hit or miss, and it is perhaps for this reason that it suits modern consciousness—which seems best expressed as flashes of fearful insight alternating with near-hypnotic states of indifference.

These are technical and stylistic considerations. Marxist criticism sees the survival of an art form in relation to social change. What about the socio-political implications of the short story's survival? George Lukács has said that the novel is a bourgeois art form whose enjoyment presupposes leisure and privacy. It implies the living room, the armchair, the table lamp, just as epic implies the illiterates round the tribal story-teller, and Shakespeare implies the two audiences—that of the people and that of the court—of a feudal age. From this point of view the novel marks the apogee of an exclusive, individualist culture; the nearest it ever got to a popular art form (in the sense of bringing people together in direct participation in an intellectually stimulating experience) was the nineteenth-century custom of reading novels aloud to the family. Here again it would seem that the short story shares the same disadvantages as the novel. It is an art form solitary in communication; yet another sign of the increasing loneliness and isolation of the individual in a competitive society. You cannot enjoy the experience of a short story unless you have certain minimum conditions of privacy in which to read it; and these conditions are those of middle-class life. But of course, a short story, by reason of its length and its *completeness*, totally contained in the brief time you give to it, depends less than the novel upon the classic conditions of middle-class life, and perhaps corresponds to the breakup of that life which is taking place. In that case, although the story may outlive the novel, it may become obsolete when the period of disintegration is replaced by new social forms and the art forms that express them. One doesn't have to embrace the dreariness of conventional "social realism" in literature to grant this. That our age is threshing about desperately for a way out of individual human isolation, and that our present art forms are not adequate to it, it is obvious to see in all the tatty dressing-up games, from McLuhan's theories to pop art, in which we seek a substitute for them.

ALISTAIR MACLEOD

'At the Moment': Notes on Fiction

I am interested 'at the moment' in getting words down on the page that convey what it is like to be living a certain kind of life in a certain place and at a certain time in history. I believe that the writer should tell the truth about what he (or of course she) knows in a creative manner that is not necessarily 'holding a mirror up to life.' I do feel that fictional characters can often be as 'true' (or more 'true') than actual characters if their author creates them well enough. I like to think that writing is an act of communication and, as such, the writer should strive to be clear rather than coy. Being clear, to my mind, is not the same as being simplistic. I also believe that 'art' begins in the emotional part of the author which means that the writer should care or 'feel' deeply about his subject. If a writer has no sympathy for his characters or the human condition he will have difficulty arousing an emotional response in the reader. 'No tears in the writer—no tears in the reader,' is a quotation I remember from somewhere. This is, of course, not the same as going on emotional binges, crying on the page, etc. and I realize that 'strong feeling' is not art. However I believe that it often leads to the best art. There is a danger in over-intellectualizing emotion and/or intuition as Keats pointed out.

I think that if an author believes in the value of what he has to say through his work, he must be very persistent and strong in that belief and he must be 'willing to stand the rain.' There is a danger/temptation to be too much influenced by critical trends or the statements of those who worship at the altars of different religions—especially if they are considered the high priests of their time. It is good to remember that Henry James once dismissed the Dorset writer as 'poor little Thomas Hardy' and that Virginia Woolf said that the writings of Joyce reminded her of a young undergraduate scratching his pimples.

Some months before his death I was talking to George Ryga. 'Nearly all of the good literature,' he said, 'comes from all of the bad places.' I think of this statement more often now than I thought I would at the time. I think of it when reading *Wuthering Heights* or *The Mayor of Casterbridge* or *The Sound and the Fury* (rising out of that most maligned state of Mississippi) and I think of it when reading the work and criticism associated with the brilliantly determined David Adams Richards. I do not necessarily think of 'bad places,' but I do think of a kind of literature that rises out of the people and goes back to them. This is why undergraduates far removed from such books by space and time still sit on the edges of their chairs when they read them. This is the power and wonder of 'story.' It may well be that human nature does not change and that such books were written not for trends but 'for the record.' It is good to remember this as a reader and even more so as a writer. Good writing which is done with love and care and which 'is about something' will last a long, long time. And though sometimes in danger of being temporarily 'swamped' will, in the words of the late Stan Rogers, 'rise again.' I do believe.

ALICE MUNRO

What Is Real?

Whenever people get an opportunity to ask me questions about my writing, I can be sure that some of the questions asked will be these:

"Do you write about real people?"

"Did those things really happen?"

"When you write about a small town are you really writing about Wingham?" (Wingham is the small town in Ontario where I was born and grew up, and it has often been assumed, by people who should know better, that I have simply "fictionalized" this place in my work. Indeed, the local newspaper has taken me to task for making it the "butt of a soured and cruel introspection.")

The usual thing, for writers, is to regard these either as very naive questions, asked by people who really don't understand the difference between autobiography and fiction, who can't recognize the device of the first-person narrator, or else as catch-you-out questions posed by journalists who hope to stir up exactly the sort of dreary (and to outsiders, slightly comic) indignation voiced by my hometown paper. Writers answer such questions patiently or crossly according to temperament and the mood they're in. They say, no, you must understand my characters are composites; no, those things didn't happen the way I wrote about them; no, of course not, that isn't Wingham (or whatever other place it may be that has had the queer unsought-after distinction of hatching a writer). Or the writer may, riskily, ask the questioners what is real, anyway? None of this seems to be very satisfactory. People go on asking these same questions because the subject really does interest and bewilder them. It would seem to be quite true that they don't know what fiction is.

And how could they know, when what it is, is changing all the time, and we differ among ourselves, and we don't really try to explain because it is too difficult?

What I would like to do here is what I can't do in two or three sentences at the end of a reading. I won't try to explain what fiction is, and what short stories are (assuming, which we can't, that there is any fixed thing that it is and they are), but what short stories are to me, and how I write them, and how I use things that are "real." I will start by explaining how I read stories written by other people. For one thing, I can start reading them anywhere; from beginning to end, from end to beginning, from any point in between in either direction. So obviously I don't take up a story and follow it as if it were a road, taking me somewhere, with views and neat diversions along the way. I go into it, and move back and forth and settle here and there, stay in it for a while. It's more like a house. Everybody knows what a house does, how it encloses space and makes connections between one enclosed space and another and presents what is outside in a new way. This is the nearest I can come to explaining what a story does for me, and what I want my stories to do for other people.

So when I write a story I want to make a certain kind of structure, and I know the feeling I want to get from being inside that structure. This is the hard part of the explanation, where I have to use a word like "feeling," which is not very precise, because if I attempt to be more intellectually respectable I will have to be dishonest. "Feeling" will have to do.

There is no blueprint for the structure. It's not a question of, "I'll make this kind of house because if I do it right it will have this effect." I've got to make, I've got to build up, a house, a story, to fit around the indescribable "feeling" that is like the soul of the story, and which I must insist upon in a dogged, embarrassed way, as being no more definable than that. And I don't know where it comes from. It seems to be already there, and some unlikely clue, such as a shop window or a bit of conversation, makes me aware of it. Then I start accumulating the material and putting it together. Some of the material I may have lying around already, in memories and observations, and some I invent, and some I have to go diligently looking for (factual details), while some is dumped in my lap (anecdotes, bits of speech). I see how this material might go together to make the shape I need, and I try it. I keep trying and seeing where I went wrong and trying again.

I suppose this is the place where I should talk about technical problems and how I solve them. The main reason I can't is that I'm never sure I do solve anything. Even when I say that I see where I went wrong, I'm being misleading. I never figure out how I'm going to change things, I never say to myself, "That page is heavy going, that paragraph's clumsy, I need some dialogue and shorter sentences." I feel a part that's wrong, like a soggy weight; then I pay attention to the story, as if it were really happening somewhere, not just in my head, and in its own way, not mine. As a result, the sentences may indeed get shorter, there may be more dialogue, and so on. But though I've tried to pay attention to the story, I may not have got it right; those shorter sentences may be an evasion, a mistake. Every final draft, every published story, is still only an attempt, an approach, to the story.

I did promise to talk about using reality. "Why, if Jubilee isn't Wingham, has it got Shuter Street in it?" people want to know. Why have I described somebody's real ceramic elephant sitting on the mantelpiece? I could say I get momentum from doing things like this. The fictional room, town, world, needs a bit of starter dough from the real world. It's a device to help the writer—at least it helps me—but it arouses a certain baulked fury in the people who really do live on Shuter Street and the lady who owns the ceramic elephant. "Why do you put in something true and then go on and tell lies?" they say, and anybody who has been on the receiving end of this kind of thing knows how they feel.

"I do it for the sake of my art and to make this structure which encloses the soul of my story, that I've been telling you about," says the writer. "That is more important than anything."

Not to everybody, it isn't.

So I can see there might be a case, once you've written the story and got the momentum, for going back and changing the elephant to a camel (though there's always a chance the lady might complain that you made a nasty camel out of a beautiful elephant), and changing Shuter Street to Blank Street. But what about the big chunks of reality, without which your story can't exist? In the story *Royal Beatings*, I use a big chunk of reality: the story of the butcher, and of the young men who may have been egged on to "get" him. This is a story out of an old newspaper; it really did happen in a town I know. There is no legal difficulty about using it because it has been printed in a newspaper, and besides, the people who figure in it are all long dead. But there is a difficulty about offending people in that town who would feel that use of this story is a deliberate exposure, taunt and insult. Other people who have no connection with the real happening would say, "Why write about anything so hideous?" And lest you think that such an objection could only be raised by simple folk who read nothing but Harlequin

Romances, let me tell you that one of the questions most frequently asked at universities is, "Why do you write about things that are so depressing?" People can accept almost any amount of ugliness if it is contained in a familiar formula, as it is on television, but when they come closer to their own place, their own lives, they are much offended by a lack of editing.

There are ways I can defend myself against such objections. I can say, "I do it in the interests of historical reality. That is what the old days were really like." Or, "I do it to show the dark side of human nature, the beast let loose, the evil we can run up against in communities and families." In certain countries I could say, "I do it to show how bad things were under the old system when there were prosperous butchers and young fellows hanging around livery stables and nobody thought about building a new society." But the fact is, the minute I say *to show* I am telling a lie. I don't do it to show anything. I put this story at the heart of my story because I need it there and it belongs there. It is the black room at the centre of the house with all other rooms leading to and away from it. That is all. A strange defence. Who told me to write this story? Who feels any need of it before it is written? I do. I do, so that I might grab off this piece of horrid reality and install it where I see fit, even if Hat Nettleton and his friends were still around to make me sorry.

The answer seems to be as confusing as ever. Lots of true answers are. Yes and no. Yes, I use bits of what is real, in the sense of being really there and really happening, in the world, as most people see it, and I transform it into something that is really there and really happening, in my story. No, I am not concerned with using what is real to make any sort of record or prove any sort of point, and I am not concerned with any methods of selection but my own, which I can't fully explain. This is quite presumptuous, and if writers are not allowed to be so—and quite often, in many places, they are not—I see no point in the writing of fiction.

FLANNERY O'CONNOR

Writing Short Stories

I have heard people say that the short story was one of the most difficult literary forms, and I've always tried to decide why people feel this way about what seems to me to be one of the most natural and fundamental ways of human expression. After all, you begin to hear and tell stories when you're a child, and there doesn't seem to be anything very complicated about it. I suspect that most of you have been telling stories all your lives, and yet here you sit—come to find out how to do it.

Then last week, after I had written down some of these serene thoughts to use here today, my calm was shattered when I was sent seven of your manuscripts to read.

After this experience, I found myself ready to admit, if not that the short story is one of the most difficult literary forms, at least that it is more difficult for some than for others.

I still suspect that most people start out with some kind of ability to tell a story but that it gets lost along the way. Of course, the ability to create life with words is essentially a gift. If you have it in the first place, you can develop it; if you don't have it, you might as well forget it.

But I have found that the people who don't have it are frequently the ones hellbent on writing stories. I'm sure anyway that they are the ones who write the books and the magazine articles on how-to-write-short-stories. I have a friend who is taking a correspondence course in this subject, and she has passed a few of the chapter headings on to me—such as, "The Story Formula for Writers," "How to Create Characters," "Let's Plot!" This form of corruption is costing her twenty-seven dollars.

I feel that discussing story-writing in terms of plot, character, and theme is like trying to describe the expression on a face by saying where the eyes, nose, and mouth are. I've heard students say, "I'm very good with plot, but I can't do a thing with character," or, "I have this theme but I don't have a plot for it," and once I heard one say, "I've got the story but I don't have any technique."

Technique is a word they all trot out. I talked to a writers' club once, and during the question time, one good soul said, "Will you give me the technique for the frame-within-a-frame short story?" I had to admit I was so ignorant I didn't even know what that was, but she assured me there was such a thing because she had entered a contest to write one and the prize was fifty dollars.

But setting aside the people who have no talent for it, there are others who do have the talent but who flounder around because they don't really know what a story is.

I suppose that obvious things are the hardest to define. Everybody thinks he knows what a story is. But if you ask a beginning student to write a story, you're liable to get almost anything—a reminiscence, an episode, an opinion, an anecdote, anything under the sun but a story. A story is a complete dramatic action—and in good stories, the characters are shown through the action and the action is controlled through the characters, and the result of this is meaning that derives from the whole presented experience. I myself prefer to say that a story is a dramatic event that involves a person because he is a person, and a particular person—that is, because he shares in the general human condition and in some specific human situation. A story always involves, in a dramatic way, the mystery of personality. I lent some stories to a country lady who lives down the road from me, and when she returned them, she said, "Well, them stories just gone and shown you how some folks *would* do," and I thought to myself that that was right; when you write stories, you have to be content to start exactly there—showing how some specific folks *will* do, *will* do in spite of everything.

Now this is a very humble level to have to begin on, and most people who think they want to write stories are not willing to start there. They want to write about problems, not people; or about abstract issues, not concrete situations. They have an idea, or a feeling, or an overflowing ego, or they want to Be A Writer, or they want to give their wisdom to the world in a simple-enough way for the world to be able to absorb it. In any case, they don't have a story and they wouldn't be willing to write it if they did; and in the absence of a story, they set out to find a theory or a formula or a technique.

Now none of this is to say that when you write a story, you are supposed to forget or give up any moral position that you hold. Your beliefs will be the light by which you see, but they will not be what you see and they will not be a substitute for seeing. For the writer of fiction, everything has its testing point in the eye, and the eye is an organ that eventually involves the whole personality, and as much of the world as can be got into it. It involves judgment. Judgment is something that begins in the act of vision, and when it does not, or when it becomes separated from vision, then a confusion exists in the mind which transfers itself to the story.

Fiction operates through the senses, and I think one reason that people find it so difficult to write stories is that they forget how much time and patience is required to convince through the senses. No reader who doesn't actually experience, who isn't made to feel, the story is going to believe anything the fiction writer merely tells him. The first and most obvious characteristic of fiction is that it deals with reality through what can be seen, heard, smelt, tasted, and touched.

Now this is something that can't be learned only in the head; it has to be learned in the habits. It has to become a way that you habitually look at things. The fiction writer has to realize that he can't create compassion with compassion, or emotion with emotion, or thought with thought. He has to provide all these things with a body; he has to create a world with weight and extension.

I have found that the stories of beginning writers usually bristle with emotion, but *whose* emotion is often very hard to determine. Dialogue frequently proceeds without the assistance of any characters that you can actually see, and uncontained thought leaks out of every corner of the story. The reason is usually that the student is wholly interested in his thoughts and his emotions and not in his dramatic action, and that he is too lazy or highfalutin to descend to the concrete where fiction operates. He thinks that judgment exists in one place and sense-impression in another. But for the fiction writer, judgment begins in the details he sees and how he sees them.

Fiction writers who are not concerned with these concrete details are guilty of what Henry James called "weak specification." The eye will glide over their words while the attention goes to sleep. Ford Madox Ford taught that you couldn't have a man appear long enough to sell a newspaper in a story unless you put him there with enough detail to make the reader see him.

I have a friend who is taking acting classes in New York from a Russian lady who is supposed to be very good at teaching actors. My friend wrote me that the first month they didn't speak a line, they only learned to see. Now learning to see is the basis for learning all the arts except music. I know a good many fiction writers who paint, not because they're any good at painting, but because it helps their writing. It forces them to took at things. Fiction writing is very seldom a matter of saying things; it is a matter of showing things.

However, to say that fiction proceeds by the use of detail does not mean the simple, mechanical piling-up of detail. Detail has to be controlled by some overall purpose, and every detail has to be put to work for you. Art is selective. What is there is essential and creates movement.

Now all this requires time. A good short story should not have less meaning than a novel, nor should its action be less complete. Nothing essential to the main experience can be left out of a short story. All the action has to be satisfactorily accounted for in terms of motivation, and there has to be a beginning, a middle, and an end, though not necessarily in that order. I think many people decide that they want to write short stories because they're short, and by short, they mean short in every way. They think that a short story is an incomplete action in which a very little is shown and a great deal suggested, and they think you suggest something by leaving it out. It's very hard to disabuse a student of this notion, because he thinks that when he leaves something out, he's being subtle; and when you tell him that he has to put something in before anything can be there, he thinks you're an insensitive idiot.

Perhaps the central question to be considered in any discussion of the short story is what do we mean by short. Being short does not mean being slight. A short story should be long in depth and should give us an experience of meaning. I have an aunt who thinks that nothing happens in a story unless somebody gets married or shot at the end of it. I wrote a story about a tramp who marries an old woman's idiot daughter in order to acquire the old woman's automobile. After the marriage, he takes the daughter off on a wedding trip in the automobile and abandons her in an eating place and drives on by himself. Now that is a complete story. There is nothing more relating to the mystery of that man's personality that could be shown through that particular dramatization. But I've never been able to convince my aunt that it's a complete story. She wants to know what happened to the idiot daughter after that.

Not long ago that story was adapted for a television play, and the adapter, knowing his business, had the tramp have a change of heart and go back and pick up the idiot daughter and the two of them ride away, grinning madly. My aunt believes that the story is complete at last, but I have other sentiments about it—which are not suitable for public utterance. When you write a story, you only have to write one story, but there will always be people who will refuse to read the story you have written.

And this naturally brings up the awful question of what kind of a reader you are writing for when you write fiction. Perhaps we each think we have a personal solution for this problem. For my own part, I have a very high opinion of the art of fiction and a very low opinion of what is called the "average" reader. I tell myself that I can't escape him, that this is the personality I am supposed to keep awake, but that at the same time, I am also supposed to provide the intelligent reader with the deeper experience that he looks for in fiction. Now actually, both of these readers are just aspects of the writer's own personality, and in the last analysis, the only reader he can know anything about is himself. We all write at our own level of understanding, but it is the peculiar characteristic of fiction that its literal surface can be made to yield entertainment on an obvious physical plane to one sort of reader while the selfsame surface can be made to yield meaning to the person equipped to experience it there.

Meaning is what keeps the short story from being short. I prefer to talk about the meaning in a story rather than the theme of a story. People talk about the theme of a story as if the theme were like the string that a sack of chicken feed is tied with. They think that if you can pick out the theme, the way you pick the right thread in the chicken-feed sack, you can rip the story open and feed the chickens. But this is not the way meaning works in fiction.

When you can state the theme of a story, when you can separate it from the story itself, then you can be sure the story is not a very good one. The meaning of a story has to be embodied in it, has to be made concrete in it. A story is a way to say something that can't be said any other way, and it takes every word in the story to say what the meaning is. You tell a story because a statement would be inadequate. When anybody asks what a story is about, the only proper thing is to tell him to read the story. The meaning of fiction is not abstract meaning but experienced meaning, and the purpose of making statements about the meaning of a story is only to help you to experience that meaning more fully.

Fiction is an art that calls for the strictest attention to the real—whether the writer is writing a naturalistic story or a fantasy. I mean that we always begin with what is or with what has an eminent possibility of truth about it. Even when one writes a fantasy, reality is the proper basis of it. A thing is fantastic because it is so real, so real that it is fantastic. Graham Greene has said that he can't write, "I stood over a bottomless pit," because that couldn't be true, or "Running down the stairs I jumped into a taxi," because that couldn't be true either. But Elizabeth Bowen can write about one of her characters that "she snatched at her hair as if she heard something in it," because that is eminently possible.

I would even go so far as to say that the person writing a fantasy has to be even more strictly attentive to the concrete detail than someone writing in a naturalistic vein—because the greater the story's strain on the credulity, the more convincing the properties in it have to be.

A good example of this is a story called "The Metamorphosis" by Franz Kafka. This is a story about a man who wakes up one morning to find that he has turned into a cockroach overnight, while not discarding his human nature. The rest of the story concerns his life and feelings and eventual death as an insect with human nature, and this situation is accepted by the reader because the concrete detail of the story is absolutely convincing. The fact is that this story describes the dual nature of man in such a realistic fashion that it is almost unbearable. The truth is not distorted here, but rather, a certain distortion is used to get at the truth. If we admit, as we must, that appearance is not the same thing as reality, then we must give the artist the liberty to make certain rearrangements of nature if these will lead to greater depths of vision. The artist himself always has to remember that what he is rearranging is nature, and that he has to know it and be able to describe it accurately in order to have the authority to rearrange it at all.

The peculiar problem of the short-story writer is how to make the action he describes reveal as much of the mystery of existence as possible. He has only a short space to do it in and he can't do it by statement. He has to do it by showing, not by saying, and by showing the concrete—so that his problem is really how to make the concrete work double time for him.

In good fiction, certain of the details will tend to accumulate meaning from the action of the story itself, and when this happens they become symbolic in the way they work. I once wrote a story called "Good Country People," in which a lady Ph.D. has her wooden leg stolen by a Bible salesman whom she has tried to seduce. Now I'll admit that, paraphrased in this way, the situation is simply a low joke. The average reader is pleased to observe anybody's wooden leg being stolen. But without ceasing to appeal to him and without making any statements of high intention, this story does manage to operate at another level of experience, by letting the wooden leg accumulate meaning. Early in the story, we're presented with the fact that the Ph.D. is spiritually as well as physically crippled. She believes in nothing but her own belief in nothing, and we perceive that there is a wooden part of her soul that corresponds to her wooden leg. Now of course this is never stated. The fiction writer states as little as possible. The reader makes this connection from things he is shown. He may not even know that he makes the connection, but the connection is there nevertheless and it has its effect on him. As the story goes on, the wooden leg continues to accumulate meaning. The reader learns how the girl feels about her leg, how her mother feels about it, and how the country woman on the place feels about it; and finally, by the time the Bible salesman comes along, the leg has accumulated so much meaning that it is, as the saying goes, loaded. And when the Bible salesman steals it, the reader realizes that he has taken away part of the girl's personality and has revealed her deeper affliction to her for the first time.

If you want to say that the wooden leg is a symbol, you can say that. But it is a wooden leg first, and as a wooden leg it is absolutely necessary to the story. It has its place on the literal level of the story, but it operates in depth as well as on the surface. It increases the story in every direction, and this is essentially the way a story escapes being short.

Now a little might be said about the way in which this happens. I wouldn't want you to think that in that story I sat down and said, "I am now going to write a story about a Ph.D. with a wooden leg, using the wooden leg as a symbol for another kind of affliction." I doubt myself if many writers know what they are going to do when they start out. When I started writing that story, I didn't know there was going to be a Ph.D. with a wooden leg in it. I merely found myself one morning writing a description of two women that I knew something about, and before I realized it, I had equipped one of them with a daughter with a wooden leg. As the story progressed, I brought in the Bible salesman, but I had no idea what I was going to do with him. I didn't know he was going to steal that wooden leg until ten or twelve lines before he did it, but when I found out that this was what was going to happen, I realized that it was inevitable. This is a story that produces a shock for the reader, and I think one reason for this is that it produced a shock for the writer.

Now despite the fact that this story came about in this seemingly mindless fashion, it is a story that almost no rewriting was done on. It is a story that was under control throughout the writing of it, and it might be asked how this kind of control comes about, since it is not entirely conscious.

I think the answer to this is what Maritain calls "the habit of art." It is a fact that fiction writing is something in which the whole personality takes part—the conscious as well as the unconscious mind. Art is the habit of the artist; and habits have to be rooted deep in the whole personality. They have to be cultivated like any other habit, over a long period of time, by experience; and teaching any kind of writing is largely a matter of helping the student develop the habit of art. I think this is more than just a discipline, although it is that; I think it is a way of looking at the created world and of using the senses so as to make them find as much meaning as possible in things.

Now I am not so naïve as to suppose that most people come to writers' conferences in order to hear what kind of vision is necessary to write stories that will become a permanent part of our literature. Even if you do wish to hear this, your greatest concerns are immediately practical. You want to know how you can actually write a good story, and further, how you can tell when you've done it; and so you want to know what the form of a short story is, as if the form were something that existed outside of each story and could be applied or imposed on the material. Of course, the more you write, the more you will realize that the form is organic, that it is something that grows out of the material, that the form of each story is unique. A story that is any good can't be reduced, it can only be expanded. A story is good when you continue to see more and more in it, and when it continues to escape you. In fiction two and two is always more than four.

The only way, I think, to learn to write short stories is to write them, and then to try to discover what you have done. The time to think of technique is when you've actually got the story in front of you. The teacher can help the student by looking at his individual work and trying to help him decide if he has written a complete story, one in which the action fully illuminates the meaning.

Perhaps the most profitable thing I can do is to tell you about some of the general observations I made about these seven stories I read of yours. All of these observations will not fit any one of the stories exactly, but they are points nevertheless that it won't hurt anyone interested in writing to think about.

The first thing that any professional writer is conscious of in reading anything is, naturally, the use of language. Now the use of language in these stories was such that, with one exception, it would be difficult to distinguish one story from another. While I can recall running into several clichés, I can't remember one image or one metaphor from the seven stories. I don't mean there weren't images in them; I just mean that there weren't any that were effective enough to take away with you.

In connection with this, I made another observation that startled me considerably. With the exception of one story, there was practically no use made of the local idiom. Now this is a Southern Writers' Conference. All the addresses on these stories were from Georgia or Tennessee, yet there was no distinctive sense of Southern life in them. A few place-names were dropped, Savannah or Atlanta or

Jacksonville, but these could just as easily have been changed to Pittsburgh or Passaic without calling for any other alteration in the story. The characters spoke as if they had never heard any kind of language except what came out of a television set. This indicates that something is way out of focus.

There are two qualities that make fiction. One is the sense of mystery and the other is the sense of manners. You get the manners from the texture of existence that surrounds you. The great advantage of being a Southern writer is that we don't have to go anywhere to look for manners; bad or good, we've got them in abundance. We in the South live in a society that is rich in contradiction, rich in irony, rich in contrast, and particularly rich in its speech. And yet here are six stories by Southerners in which almost no use is made of the gifts of the region.

Of course the reason for this may be that you have seen these gifts abused so often that you have become self-conscious about using them. There is nothing worse than the writer who doesn't use the gifts of the region, but wallows in them. Everything becomes so Southern that it's sickening, so local that it is unintelligible, so literally reproduced that it conveys nothing. The general gets lost in the particular instead of being shown through it.

However, when the life that actually surrounds us is totally ignored, when our patterns of speech are absolutely overlooked, then something is out of kilter. The writer should then ask himself if he is not reaching out for a kind of life that is artificial to him.

An idiom characterizes a society, and when you ignore the idiom, you are very likely ignoring the whole social fabric that could make a meaningful character. You can't cut characters off from their society and say much about them as individuals. You can't say anything meaningful about the mystery of a personality unless you put that personality in a believable and significant social context. And the best way to do this is through the character's own language. When the old lady in one of Andrew Lytle's stories says contemptuously that she has a mule that is older than Birmingham, we get in that one sentence a sense of a society and its history. A great deal of the Southern writer's work is done for him before he begins, because our history lives in our talk. In one of Eudora Welty's stories a character says, "Where I come from, we use fox for yard dogs and owls for chickens, but we sing true." Now there is a whole book in that one sentence; and when the people of your section can talk like that, and you ignore it, you're just not taking advantage of what's yours. The sound of our talk is too definite to be discarded with impunity, and if the writer tries to get rid of it, he is liable to destroy the better part of his creative power.

Another thing I observed about these stories is that most of them don't go very far inside a character, don't reveal very much of the character. I don't mean that they don't enter the character's mind, but they simply don't show that he has a personality. Again this goes back partly to speech. These characters have no distinctive speech to reveal themselves with; and sometimes they have no really distinctive features. You feel in the end that no personality is revealed because no personality is there. In most good stories it is the character's personality that creates the action of the story. In most of these stories, I feel that the writer has thought of some action and then scrounged up a character to perform it. You will usually be more successful if you start the other way around. If you start with a real personality, a real character, then something is bound to happen; and you don't have to know what before you begin. In fact it may be better if you don't know what before you begin. You ought to be able to discover something from your stories. If you don't, probably nobody else will.

TILLIE OLSEN

From *Silences*

And, if in addition to the infinite capacity, to the daily responsibilities, there are children?

Balzac, you remember, described creation in terms of motherhood. Yes, in intelligent passionate motherhood there are similarities, and in more than the toil and patience. The calling upon total capacities; the reliving and new using of the past; the comprehensions; the fascination, absorption, intensity. All almost certain death to creation—(so far).

Not because the capacities to create no longer exist, or the need (though for a while, as in any fullness of life, the need may be obscured), but because the circumstances for sustained creation have been almost impossible. The need cannot be first. It can have at best, only part self, part time. (Unless someone else does the nurturing. Read Dorothy Fisher's "Babushka Farnham" in *Fables for Parents.*) More than in any other human relationship, overwhelmingly more, motherhood means being instantly interruptible, responsive, responsible. Children need one *now* (and remember, in our society, the family must often try to be the center for love and health the outside world is not). The very fact that these are real needs, that one feels them as one's own (love, not duty); *that there is no one else responsible for these needs*, gives them primacy. It is distraction, not meditation, that becomes habitual; interruption, not continuity; spasmodic, not constant toil. The rest has been said here. Work interrupted, deferred, relinquished, makes blockage—at best, lesser accomplishment. Unused capacities atrophy, cease to be.

When H. H. Richardson, who wrote the Australian classic *Ultima Thule*, was asked why she—whose children, like all her people, were so profoundly written—did not herself have children, she answered: "There are enough women to do the childbearing and childrearing. I know of none who can write my books." I remember thinking rebelliously, yes, and I know of none who can bear and rear my children either. But literary history is on her side. Almost no mothers—as almost no part-time, part-self persons—have created enduring literature ... so far.

If I talk now quickly of my own silences—almost presumptuous after what has been told here—it is that the individual experience may add.

In the twenty years I bore and reared my children, usually had to work on a paid job as well, the simplest circumstances for creation did not exist. Nevertheless writing, the hope of it, was "the air I breathed, so long as I shall breathe at all." In that hope, there was conscious storing, snatched reading, beginnings of writing, and always "the secret rootlets of reconnaissance."

When the youngest of our four was in school, the beginnings struggled toward endings. This was a time, in Kafka's words, "like a squirrel in a cage: bliss of movement, desperation about constriction, craziness of endurance."

Bliss of movement. A full extended family life; the world of my job (transcriber in a dairy-equipment company); and the writing, which I was somehow able to carry around within me through work, through home. Time on the bus, even when I had to stand, was enough; the stolen moments at work, enough; the deep night hours for as long as I could stay awake, after the kids were in bed, after the household tasks were done, sometimes during. It is no accident that the first work I considered publishable began: "I stand here ironing, and what you asked me moves tormented back and forth with the iron."

In such snatches of time I wrote what I did in those years, but there came a time when this triple life was no longer possible. The fifteen hours of daily realities became too much distraction for the writing. I lost craziness of endurance. What might have been, I don't know; but I applied for, and was given, eight months' writing time. There was still full family life, all the household responsibilities, but I did not have to hold an eight-hour job. I had continuity, three full days, sometimes more—and it was in those months I made the mysterious turn and became a writing writer.

Then had to return to the world of work, someone else's work, nine hours, five days a week.

This was the time of festering and congestion. For a few months I was able to shield the writing with which I was so full, against the demands of jobs on which I had to be competent, through the joys and responsibilities and trials of family. For a few months. Always roused by the writing, always denied. "I could not go to write it down. It convulsed and died in me. I will pay."

My work died. What demanded to be written, did not. It seethed, bubbled, clamored, peopled me. At last moved into the hours meant for sleeping. I worked now full time on temporary jobs, a Kelly, a Western Agency girl (girl!), wandering from office to office, always hoping to manage two, three writing months ahead. Eventually there was time.

I had said: always roused by the writing, always denied. Now, like a woman made frigid, I had to learn response, to trust this possibility for fruition that had not been before. Any interruption dazed and silenced me. It took a long while of surrendering to what I was trying to write, of invoking Henry James's "passion, piety, patience," before I was able to re-establish work.

When again I had to leave the writing, I lost consciousness. A time of anesthesia. There was still an automatic noting that did not stop, but it was as if writing had never been. No fever, no congestion, no festering. I ceased being peopled, slept well and dreamlessly, took a "permanent" job. The few pieces that had been published seemed to have vanished like the not-yet-written. I wrote someone, unsent: "So long they fed each other—my life, the writing—;—the writing or hope of it, my life—; but now they begin to destroy." I knew, but did not feel the destruction.

As for myself, who did not publish a book until I was fifty, I who raised children without household help or the help of the "technological sublime" (the atom bomb was in manufacture before the first automatic washing machine); who worked outside the house on everyday jobs as well (as nearly half of all women do now, though a woman with a paid job, except as a maid or prostitute, is still rarest of any in literature); who could not kill the essential angel (there was no one else to do her work); would not—if I could—have killed the caring part of the Woolf angel, as distant from the world of literature most of my life as literature is distant (in content too) from my world:

The years when I should have been writing, my hands and being were at other (inescapable) tasks. Now, lightened as they are, when I must do those tasks into which most of my life went, like the old mother, grandmother in my *Tell Me a Riddle* who could not make herself touch a baby, I pay a psychic cost: "the sweat beads, the long shudder begins." The habits of a lifetime when everything else had to come before writing are not easily broken, even when circumstances now often make it possible for writing to be first; habits of years—response to others, distractibility, responsibility for daily matters—stay with you, mark you, become you. The cost of "discontinuity" (that pattern still imposed on women) is such a weight of things unsaid, an accumulation of material so great, that everything starts up something else in me; what should take weeks, takes me sometimes months to write; what should take months, takes years.

I speak of myself to bring here the sense of those others to whom this is in the process of happening (unnecessarily happening, for it need not, must not continue to be) and to remind us of those (I so nearly was one) who never come to writing at all.

We must not speak of women writers in our century (as we cannot speak of women in any area of recognized human achievement) without speaking also of the invisible, the as-innately-capable: the born to the wrong circumstances—diminished, excluded, foundered, silenced.

We who write are survivors, "*only's*."[1] *One-out-of-twelve.*

1. For myself, "survivor" contains its other meaning: one who must bear witness for those who foundered, try to tell how and why it was that they, also worthy of life, did not survive. And pass on ways of surviving; and tell our chancy luck, our special circumstances.

"*Only's*" is an expression out of the 1950s Civil Rights time: the young Ralph Abernathy reporting to his Birmingham Church congregation on his trip up north for support:

I go to Seattle and they tell me, "Brother, you got to meet so and so, why he's the only Negro Federal Circuit Judge in the Northwest"; I go to Chicago and they tell me, "Brother, you've got to meet so and so, why he's the only full black professor of Sociology there is"; I go to Albany and they tell me, "Brother, you *got* to meet so and so, why he's the only black senator in the state legislature ..." [long dramatic pause] ... WE DON'T WANT NO ONLY'S.

Only's are used to rebuke ("to be models"); to imply the unrealistic, "see, it can be done, all you need is capacity and will." Accepting a situation of "only's" means: "let inequality of circumstance continue to prevail."

EDGAR ALLAN POE

On the Aim and Technique of the Short Story

The tale proper, in our opinion, affords unquestionably the fairest field for the exercise of the loftiest talent, which can be afforded by the wide domains of mere prose. Were we bidden to say how the highest genius could be most advantageously employed for the best display of its own powers, we should answer, without hesitation—in the composition of a rhymed poem, not to exceed in length what might be perused in an hour. Within this limit alone can the highest order of true poetry exist. We need only here say, upon this topic, that, in almost all classes of composition, the unity of effect or impression is a point of the greatest importance. It is clear, moreover, that this unity cannot be thoroughly preserved in productions whose perusal cannot be completed at one sitting. We may continue the reading of a prose composition, from the very nature of prose itself, much longer than we can persevere, to any good purpose, in the perusal of a poem. This latter, if truly fulfilling the demands of the poetic sentiment, induces an exaltation of the soul which cannot be long sustained. All high excitements are necessarily transient. Thus a long poem is a paradox. And, without unity of impression, the deepest effects cannot be brought about. Epics were the offspring of an imperfect sense of Art, and their reign is no more. A poem *too* brief may produce a vivid, but never an intense or enduring impression. Without a certain continuity of effort—without a certain duration or repetition of purpose—the soul is never deeply moved. There must be the dropping of the water upon the rock. De Béranger has wrought brilliant things—pungent and spirit-stirring—but, like all immassive bodies, they lack *momentum*, and thus fail to satisfy the Poetic Sentiment. They sparkle and excite, but, from want of continuity, fail deeply to impress. Extreme brevity will degenerate into epigrammatism; but the sin of extreme length is even more unpardonable. *In medio tutissimus ibis.*

Were we called upon, however, to designate that class of composition which, next to such a poem as we have suggested, should best fulfil the demands of high genius—should offer it the most advantageous field of exertion—we should unhesitatingly speak of the prose tale, as Mr. Hawthorne has here exemplified it. We allude to the short prose narrative, requiring from a half-hour to one or two hours in its perusal. The ordinary novel is objectionable, from its length, for reasons already stated in substance. As it cannot be read at one sitting, it deprives itself, of course, of the immense force derivable from *totality*. Worldly interests intervening during the pauses of perusal, modify, annul, or counteract, in a greater or less degree, the impressions of the book. But simple cessation in reading, would, of itself, be sufficient to destroy the true unity. In the brief tale, however, the author is enabled to carry out the fulness of his intention, be it what it may. During the hour of perusal the soul of the reader is at the writer's control. There are no external or extrinsic influences—resulting from weariness or interruption.

A skilful literary artist has constructed a tale. If wise, he has not fashioned his thoughts to accommodate his incidents; but having conceived, with deliberate care, a certain unique or single *effect* to be wrought out, he then invents such incidents—he then combines such events as may best aid him in establishing this preconceived effect. If his very initial sentence tend not to the outbringing of this effect, then he has failed in his first step. In the whole composition there should be no word written, of which the tendency, direct or indirect, is not to the one pre-established design. And by such means, with such care and skill, a picture is at length painted which leaves in the mind of him who contemplates it with a kindred art, a sense of the fullest satisfaction. The idea of the tale has been presented unblemished, because undisturbed; and this is an end unattainable by the novel. Undue brevity is just as exceptionable here as in the poem; but undue length is yet more to be avoided.

... Nothing is more clear than that every plot, worth the name, must be elaborated to its *dénouement* before anything be attempted with the pen. It is only with the *dénouement* constantly in view that we can give a plot its indispensable air of consequence, or causation, by making the incidents, and especially the tone at all points, tend to the development of the intention.

There is a radical error, I think, in the usual mode of constructing a story. Either history affords a thesis—or one is suggested by an incident of the day—or, at best, the author sets himself to work, in the combination of striking events to form merely the basis of his narrative—designing, generally, to fill in with description, dialogue, or authorial comment, whatever crevices of fact, or action, may, from page to page, render themselves apparent.

I prefer commencing with the consideration of an *effect*. Keeping originality *always* in view—or he is false to himself who ventures to dispense with so obvious and so easily attainable a source of interest—I say to myself, in the first place, "Of the innumerable effects, or impressions, of which the heart, the intellect, or (more generally) the soul is susceptible, what one shall I, on the present occasion, select?" Having chosen a novel, first, and secondly a vivid effect, I consider whether it can be best wrought by incident or tone—whether by ordinary incidents and peculiar tone, or the converse, or by peculiarity both of incident and tone—afterward looking about me (or rather within) for such combinations of event, or tone, as shall best aid me in the construction of the effect. …

> From "The Philosophy of Composition," originally published in *Graham's Magazine*, April 1846. Reprinted here from *Works*, XIV, 193–194.

With the vague opinion that to be original is to be unpopular, I could, indeed, agree, were I to adopt an understanding of originality which, to my surprise, I have known adopted by many who have a right to be called critical. They have limited, in a love for mere words, the literary to the metaphysical originality. They regard as original in letters, only such combinations of thought, of incident, and so forth, as are, in fact, absolutely novel. It is clear, however, not only that it is the novelty of *effect* alone which is worth consideration, but that this effect is *best* wrought, for the end of all fictitious composition, pleasure, by shunning rather than by seeking the absolute novelty of combination. Originality, thus understood, tasks and startles the intellect, and so brings into undue action the faculties to which, in the lighter literature, we least appeal. And thus understood, it cannot fail to prove unpopular with the masses, who, seeking in this literature amusement, are positively offended by instruction. But the true originality—true in respect of its purposes—is that which, in bringing out the half-formed, the reluctant, or the unexpressed fancies of mankind, or in exciting the more delicate pulses of the heart's passion, or in giving birth to some universal sentiment or instinct in embryo, thus combines with the pleasurable effect of *apparent* novelty, a real egoistic delight. The reader, in the case first supposed, (that of the absolute novelty,) is excited, but embarrassed, disturbed, in some degree even pained at his own want of perception, at his own folly in not having himself hit upon the idea. In the second case, his pleasure is doubled. He is filled with an intrinsic and extrinsic delight. He feels and intensely enjoys the seeming novelty of the thought, enjoys it as really novel, as absolutely original with the writer—*and himself*. They two, he fancies, have, alone of all men, thought thus. They two have, together, created this thing. Henceforward there is a bond of sympathy between them, a sympathy which irradiates every subsequent page of the book.

VIRGINIA WOOLF

Women and Fiction

The title of this article can be read in two ways: it may allude to women and the fiction that they write, or to women and the fiction that is written about them. The ambiguity is intentional, for in dealing with women as writers, as much elasticity as possible is desirable; it is necessary to leave oneself room to deal with other things besides their work, so much has that work been influenced by conditions that have nothing whatever to do with art.

The most superficial inquiry into women's writing instantly raises a host of questions. Why, we ask at once, was there no continuous writing done by women before the eighteenth century? Why did they then write almost as habitually as men, and in the course of that writing produce, one after another, some of the classics of English fiction? And why did their art then, and why to some extent does their art still, take the form of fiction?

A little thought will show us that we are asking questions to which we shall get, as answer, only further fiction. The answer lies at present locked in old diaries, stuffed away in old drawers, half-obliterated in the memories of the aged. It is to be found in the lives of the obscure—in those almost unlit corridors of history where the figures of generations of women are so dimly, so fitfully perceived. For very little is known about women. The history of England is the history of the male line, not of the female. Of our fathers we know always some fact, some distinction. They were soldiers or they were sailors; they filled that office or they made that law. But of our mothers, our grandmothers, our great-grandmothers, what remains? Nothing but a tradition. One was beautiful; one was red-haired; one was kissed by a Queen. We know nothing of them except their names and the dates of their marriages and the number of children they bore.

Thus, if we wish to know why at any particular time women did this or that, why they wrote nothing, why on the other hand they wrote masterpieces, it is extremely difficult to tell. Anyone who should seek among those old papers, who should turn history wrong side out and so construct a faithful picture of the daily life of the ordinary women in Shakespeare's time, in Milton's time, in Johnson's time, would not only write a book of astonishing interest, but would furnish the critic with a weapon which he now lacks. The extraordinary woman depends on the ordinary woman. It is only when we know what were the conditions of the average woman's life—the number of her children, whether she had money of her own, if she had a room to herself, whether she had help in bringing up her family, if she had servants, whether part of the housework was her task—it is only when we can measure the way of life and the experience of life made possible to the ordinary woman that we can account for the success or failure of the extraordinary woman as a writer.

Strange spaces of silence seem to separate one period of activity from another. There was Sappho and a little group of women all writing poetry on a Greek island six hundred years before the birth of Christ. They fall silent. Then about the year 1000 we find a certain court lady, the Lady Murasaki, writing a very long and beautiful novel in Japan. But in England in the sixteenth century, when the dramatists and poets were most active, the women were dumb. Elizabethan literature is exclusively masculine. Then, at the end of the eighteenth century and in the beginning of the nineteenth, we find women again writing—this time in England—with extraordinary frequency and success.

Law and custom were of course largely responsible for these strange intermissions of silence and speech. When a woman was liable, as she was in the fifteenth century, to be beaten and flung about the room if she did not marry the man of her parents' choice, the spiritual atmosphere was not favourable to the production of works of art. When she was married without her own consent to a man who thereupon became her lord and master, 'so far at least as law and custom could make him,' as she was in the time of the Stuarts, it is likely she had little time for writing, and less encouragement. The immense effect of environment and suggestion upon the mind, we in our psychoanalytical age are beginning to realize. Again, with memoirs and letters to help us, we are beginning to understand how abnormal is the effort needed to produce a work of art, and what shelter and what support the mind of the artist requires. Of those facts the lives and letters of men like Keats and Carlyle and Flaubert assure us.

Thus it is clear that the extraordinary outburst of fiction in the beginning of the nineteenth century in England was heralded by innumerable slight changes in law and customs and manners. And women of the nineteenth century had some leisure; they had some education. It was no longer the exception for women of the middle and upper classes to choose their own husbands. And it is significant that of the four great women novelists—Jane Austen, Emily Brontë, Charlotte Brontë, and George Eliot—not one had a child, and two were unmarried.

Yet, though it is clear that the ban upon writing had been removed, there was still, it would seem, considerable pressure upon women to write novels. No four women can have been more unlike in genius and character than these four. Jane Austen can have had nothing in common with Gorge Eliot; George Eliot was the direct opposite of Emily Brontë. Yet all were trained for the same profession; all, when they wrote, wrote novels.

Fiction was, as fiction still is, the easiest thing for a woman to write. Nor is it difficult to find the reason. A novel is the least concentrated form of art. A novel can be taken up or put down more easily than a play or a poem. George Eliot left her work to nurse her father. Charlotte Brontë put down her pen to pick the eyes out of the potatoes. And living as she did in the common sitting-room, surrounded by people, a woman was trained to use her mind in observation and upon the analysis of character. She was trained to be a novelist and not to be a poet.

Even in the nineteenth century, a woman lived almost solely in her home and her emotions. And those nineteenth-century novels, remarkable as they were, were profoundly influenced by the fact that the women who wrote them were excluded by their sex from certain kinds of experience. That experience has a great influence upon fiction is indisputable. The best part of Conrad's novels, for instance, would be destroyed if it had been impossible for him to be a sailor. Take away all that Tolstoi knew of war as a soldier, of life and society as a rich young man whose education admitted him to all sorts of experience, and *War and Peace* would be incredibly impoverished.

Yet *Pride and Prejudice*, *Wuthering Heights*, *Villette*, and *Middlemarch* were written by women from whom was forcibly withheld all experience save that which could be met with in a middle-class drawing-room. No first-hand experience of war or seafaring or politics or business was possible for them. Even their emotional life was strictly regulated by law and custom. When George Eliot ventured to live with Mr Lewes without being his wife, public opinion was scandalized. Under its pressure she withdrew into a suburban seclusion which, inevitably, had the worst possible effects upon her work. She wrote that unless people asked of their own accord to come and see her, she never invited them. At the same time, on the other side of Europe, Tolstoi was living a free life as a soldier, with men and women of all classes, for which nobody censured him and from which his novels drew much of their astonishing breadth and vigour.

But the novels of women were not affected only by the necessarily narrow range of the writer's experience. They showed, at least in the nineteenth century, another characteristic which may be traced to the writer's sex. In *Middlemarch* and in *Jane Eyre* we are conscious not merely of the writer's character, as we are conscious of the character of Charles Dickens, but we are conscious of a woman's presence—of someone resenting the treatment of her sex and pleading for its rights. This brings into women's writing an element which is entirely absent from a man's, unless indeed, he happens to be a working-man, a Negro, or one who for some other reason is conscious of disability. It introduces a distortion and is frequently the cause of weakness. The desire to plead some personal cause or to make a character the mouthpiece of some personal discontent or grievance always has a distressing effect, as if the spot at which the reader's attention is directed were suddenly two-fold instead of single.

The genius of Jane Austen and Emily Brontë is never more convincing than in their power to ignore such claims and solicitations and to hold on their way unperturbed by scorn or censure. But it needed a very serene or a very powerful mind to resist the temptation to anger. The ridicule, the censure, the assurance of inferiority in one form or another which were lavished upon women who practised an art, provoked such reactions naturally enough. One sees the effect in Charlotte Brontë's indignation, in George Eliot's resignation. Again and again one finds it in the work of the lesser women writers—in their choice of a subject, in their unnatural self-assertiveness, in their unnatural docility. Moreover, insincerity leaks in almost unconsciously. They adopt a view in deference to authority. The vision becomes too masculine or it becomes too feminine; it loses its perfect integrity and, with that, its most essential quality as a work of art.

The great change that has crept into women's writing is, it would seem, a change of attitude. The woman writer is no longer bitter. She is no longer angry. She is no longer pleading and protesting as she writes. We are approaching, if we have not yet reached, the time when her writing will have little or no foreign influence to disturb it. She will be able to concentrate upon her vision without distraction from outside. The aloofness that was once within the reach of genius and originality is only now coming within reach of ordinary women. Therefore the average novel by a woman is far more genuine and far more interesting today than it was a hundred or even fifty years ago.

But it is still true that before a woman can write exactly as she wishes to write, she has many difficulties to face. To begin with, there is the technical difficulty—so simple, apparently; in reality, so baffling—that the very form of the sentence does not fit her. It is a sentence made by men; it is too loose, too heavy, too pompous for a woman's use. Yet in a novel, which covers so wide a stretch of ground, an ordinary and usual type of sentence has to be found to carry the reader on easily and naturally from one end of the book to the other. And this a woman must make for herself, altering and adapting the current sentence until she writes one that takes the natural shape of her thought without crushing or distorting it.

But that, after all, is only a means to an end, and the end is still to be reached only when a woman has the courage to surmount opposition and the determination to be true to herself. For a novel, after all, is a statement about a thousand different objects—human, natural, divine; it is an attempt to relate them to each other. In every novel of merit these different elements are held in place by the force of the writer's vision. But they have another order also, which is the order imposed upon them by convention. And as men are the arbiters of that convention, as they have established an order of values in life, so too, since fiction is largely based on life, these values prevail there also to a very great extent.

It is probable, however, that both in life and in art the values of a woman are not the values of a man. Thus, when a woman comes to write a novel, she will find that she is perpetually wishing to alter the established values—to make serious what appears insignificant to a man, and trivial what is to him important. And for that, of course, she will be criticized; for the critic of the opposite sex will be genuinely puzzled and surprised by an attempt to alter the current scale of values, and will see in it not merely a difference of view, but a view that is weak, or trivial, or sentimental, because it differs from his own.

But here, too, women are coming to be more independent of opinion. They are beginning to respect their own sense of values. And for this reason the subject matter of their novels begins to show certain changes. They are less interested, it would seem, in themselves; on the other hand, they are more interested in other women. In the early nineteenth century, women's novels were largely autobiographical. One of the motives that led them to write was the desire to expose their own suffering, to plead their own cause. Now that this desire is no longer so urgent, women are beginning to explore their own sex, to write of women as women have never been written of before; for of course, until very lately, women in literature were the creation of men.

Here again there are difficulties to overcome, for, if one may generalize, not only do women submit less readily to observation than men, but their lives are far less tested and examined by the ordinary processes of life. Often nothing tangible remains of a woman's day. The food that has been cooked is eaten; the children that have been nursed have gone out into the world. Where does the accent fall? It is difficult to say. Her life has an anonymous character which is baffling and puzzling in the extreme. For the first time, this dark country is beginning to be explored in fiction; and at the same moment a woman has also to record the changes in women's minds and habits which the opening of the professions has introduced. She has to observe how their lives are ceasing to run underground; she has to discover what new colours and shadows are showing in them now that they are exposed to the outer world.

If, then, one should try to sum up the character of women's fiction at the present moment, one would say that it is courageous; it is sincere; it keeps closely to what women feel. It is not bitter. It does not insist upon its femininity. But at the same time, a woman's book is not written as a man would write it. These qualities are much commoner than they were, and they give even to second- and third-rate work the value of truth and the interest of sincerity.

But in addition to these good qualities, there are two that call for a word more of discussion. The change which has turned the English woman from a nondescript influence, fluctuating and vague, to a voter, a wage-earner, a responsible citizen, has given her both in her life and in her art a turn towards the impersonal. Her relations now are not only emotional; they are intellectual, they are political. The old system which condemned her to squint askance at things through the eyes or through the interests of husband or brother, has given place to the direct and practical interests of one who must act for herself, and not merely influence the acts of others. Hence her attention is being directed away from the personal centre which engaged it exclusively in the past to the impersonal, and her novels naturally become more critical of society, and less analytical of individual lives.

We may expect that the office of gadfly to the state, which has been so far a male prerogative, will now be discharged by women also. Their novels will deal with social evils and remedies. Their men and women will not be observed wholly in relation to each other emotionally, but as they cohere and clash in groups and classes and races. That is one change of some importance. But there is another more interesting to those who prefer the butterfly to the gadfly—that is to say, the artist to the reformer. The greater impersonality of women's lives will encourage the poetic spirit, and it is in poetry that women's fiction is still weakest. It will lead them to be less absorbed in facts and no longer content to record with astonishing acuteness the minute details which fall under their own observation. They will look beyond the personal and political relationships to the wider questions which the poet tries to solve—of our destiny and the meaning of life.

The basis of the poetic attitude is of course largely founded upon material things. It depends upon leisure, and a little money, and the chance which money and leisure give to observe impersonally and dispassionately. With money and leisure at their service, women will naturally occupy themselves more than has hitherto been possible with the craft of letters. They will make a fuller and a more subtle use of the instrument of writing. Their technique will become bolder and richer.

In the past, the virtue of women's writing often lay in its divine spontaneity, like that of the blackbird's song or the thrush's. It was untaught; it was from the heart. But it was also, and much more often, chattering and garrulous—mere talk spilt over paper and left to dry in pools and blots. In future, granted time and books and a little space in the house for herself, literature will become for women, as for men, an art to be studied. Women's gift will be trained and strengthened. The novel will cease to be the dumping-ground for the personal emotions. It will become, more than at present, a work of art like any other, and its resources and its limitations will be explored.

From this it is a short step to the practice of the sophisticated arts, hitherto so little practised by women—to the writing of essays and criticism, of history and biography. And that, too, if we are considering the novel, will be of advantage; for besides improving the quality of the novel itself, it will draw off the aliens who have been attracted to fiction by its accessibility while their hearts lay elsewhere. Thus will the novel be rid of those excrescences of history and fact which, in our time, have made it so shapeless.

So, if we may prophesy, women in time to come will write fewer novels, but better novels; and not novels only, but poetry and criticism and history. But in this, to be sure, one is looking ahead to that golden, that perhaps fabulous, age when women will have what has so long been denied them—leisure, and money, and a room to themselves.

Glossary

This glossary is not a bible or rule of law. It's a very subjective attempt to provide working definitions for words that come up over and over again in the discussion of short fiction. Every good teacher or student of literature will have his or her own definitions of plot, character, setting, and a host of other useful, and at times frustratingly vague, terms. The authors themselves often don't agree on the meaning and usefulness of critical terms. Flannery O'Connor said that describing a story in terms of plot, character, and setting is "like trying to describe the expression on a face by saying where the eyes, nose, and mouth are"; and John Hawkes goes even further by suggesting that plot, character, setting, and theme are the enemies of fiction.

A glossary is a point of departure. Consider these definitions as tentative probes, as starting-places for developing your own critical vocabulary, and remember Ralph Waldo Emerson's remark about consistency being "the hobgoblin of little minds." Much of the excitement of studying literature lies in the perpetual struggle with terminology and the gradual development of very personal insights and analytical skills.

If you want an even broader understanding of literary terminology than these brief capsule comments can provide, check out M. H. Abrams's *A Glossary of Literary Terms* and consider skimming all the notes on the authors in *The Art of Short Fiction*. In the notes you'll find a lively debate under way; actually, *crossfire* and *counterattack* might better describe the exchange, since authors can become quite heated and opinionated when it comes to discussing the craft. A similar excursion through the statements on the art of fiction and the act of critical reading is contained in the Afterwords, where Alice Munro talks about what is "real" in fiction and Mavis Gallant tackles the notion of "style," will prove equally useful and entertaining.

Action is what happens in a story, what the characters do or have done to them. Action may be distinguished from **plot** by not invoking causality or chronology and by not necessarily suggesting a unified sequence of events. Action may refer to external, physical events or internal, psychological events in the narrative. Action usually involves **conflict** and leads to some sort of **closure** or resolution, a change of behaviour or a change of heart, perhaps in the nature of that moment of illumination that Joyce called an **epiphany**. See also **plot** and pp. 59, 368.

Allegory is often taken to refer primarily to stories such as *Pilgrim's Progress*, in which the characters represent abstractions such as Faith, Truth, and Hope and the journey itself represents life. To some extent, literature is constantly edging towards the allegorical, since language is a symbolic medium and any verbal figure may be construed to represent both object and idea. So, too, all stories may be said to be representative, in an obvious way, of life as we know it.

However, although all literature leans in the direction of the symbolic and the allegorical, allegory, properly speaking, requires all, or most, of the key elements in a story to bear a one-to-one relationship with a parallel structure outside the narrative.

To say, for example, that a story about an unfortunate butcher in Toronto is an allegory of the Life and Crucifixion of Christ would, normally, entail identifying a close adherence to the biblical parallels; similarly, to call a story about the moral collapse of a professor of English in Edmonton an allegory of the Fall of Man would be rather meaningless unless we could identify in the text clear parallels to God, Eve, the serpent, and the Garden of Eden.

Antagonist, the character in a story who acts as a foil for, or stands in opposition to, the **protagonist**, or **hero**. The **conflict** between these characters constitutes the **action**, or **plot**. In modern stories, the antagonist is often simply a projection of some facet of the hero's character.

Atmosphere. Like **mood**, atmosphere may refer to the feeling that envelops all or part of a story, making it seem entirely, or by degrees, brooding, sinister, giddy, sad, or hilarious. However, atmosphere seems to be less a product of the laying on of descriptive detail (for example, Poe's dark, gloomy manors, cellars, and dungeons, with their sense of confinement and claustrophobia; or Alistair MacLeod's lonely, isolated, and elemental backdrops against which a small human drama is acted out) than the product of something less easily described. Eudora Welty's observations on this score are fascinating: "The first thing we notice about our story is that we can't really see the solid outlines of it—it seems wrapped in an atmosphere. This is what makes it shine, perhaps, as well as what initially obscures its plain, real shape."

Character. A character is a figure, consisting possibly of a name or title and a set of qualities, who plays a part in a fictional narrative. The part may be major or minor, depending on how much time is devoted to each character by the author. All fictional characters are fabrications, however close they might appear to be to figures in real life; thus they are all one- or, at best, two-dimensional. A flat character is one of limited complexity, who has been given only a few of what we think of as human qualities. A rounded character, given enough qualities to appear more complex, gives us a greater illusion of reality. The limits of the short story often necessitate giving all but the central character limited complexity.

Many writers suggest that plot is inextricably rooted in character. Henry James considered character to be the manifestation of plot; and plot, the expression of character.

Characters are created by way of a linguistic short-hand, which allows the observant and verbally gifted writer to find just the right word, the telling gesture, the significant detail, and the appropriate action to convince us to suspend our disbelief. A realist writer may concentrate most of his or her energy on physical details, including speech, gesture, clothing, and external action; a psychological realist will pay more attention to rendering the inner life of the mind and emotions, letting ideas and plot—even sentences—fragment and roll on in what has come to be called the **stream of consciousness**.

There is no shortage of kinds of characterization. Archetypal criticism tends to focus on fictional characters as types, such as the typical figures of romance literature: hero, heroine, villain, monster, sage, guide, and so on. The characters in allegorical fiction may be little more than ciphers, representing such ideas or philosophical positions as good and evil. A contemporary writer of fiction may exploit several kinds of characterization in a single work.

Character relations may be a useful term for discussing the patterning in a story, the way in which each character is associated with a different idea or value. By closely attending to the character relations in a story, along with the image-clusters, you may be able to make certain assumptions about the meaning that emerges as you read.

See notes and Afterwords on Munro, O'Connor, and others and pp. 32, 42, 141, 158–59, 196, 225, 232–33, 247, 324–25, 362, 366, 372.

Climax is the dramatic high point in a story, or the turning point in the action. The climax is usually followed by the **dénouement**, or untying (unravelling) of the **plot**, where debts are paid, conflicts are resolved, or knowledge is achieved. Many writers of short stories reject the notion of climax, conflict, and resolution, arguing that the short story, like the poem, requires more subtle organization and less mechanical expectations. Virginia Woolf, for example, insisted that "inconclusive stories are legitimate" and that stories should be open-ended. See also **closure** and **dénouement**.

Closure is a term used to refer to the wrapping up or resolution of conflicts and complications in a story. Stories that are too neatly tied up, with a clichéd or surprise ending, quickly fall out of favour with a sophisticated reading public, who are prepared to accept that art might well reflect the complexities of life, where death is not always a "neat" ending; in fact, it can be very messy for those left to pick up the pieces and, more so, for those who don't recognize it as an ending at all.

The convention of the open-ended story seems firmly entrenched in, if not actually the bone marrow of, the short story. See also **climax** and **dénouement**, as well as Woolf and Gordimer in the notes and Afterwords; also, Ian Reid's essay "Problems of Definition."

Concreteness and specificity in fiction are illusions achieved through a piling up of sensory detail, words and phrases that call up in the mind images and sounds and tastes and smells and textures from the empirical world. Since words are **symbols**, not trees, carburetors, or lipstick containers, the way they are used is crucial to creating the illusion of reality. For many years, the realist writer has insisted that his task is to *show*, not tell—not to speak of a character's suffering, but to set the character in motion and let the reader intuit the pain from what is said and done by the character. This kind of fiction favours narratives driven by descriptive detail directed at the senses and frowns upon so-called authorial intrusion.

More recently, however, Wayne Booth has argued in *The Rhetoric of Fiction* that telling is also *showing*. He suggests that we must not forget the fictional nature of fiction, that art is, first of all, not reality but artifice, *a thing made*, with its own rules and its own claim to existence in a world of things. Booth reminds us that authors can do, and have always done, exactly what they want in the game that is fiction, pretending to be all-knowing God, enjoying the role of puppeteer and commentator, stopping the narrative to make pronouncements about life and art, or accepting the limits of an ill-informed and self-deluded narrator who may be as unpleasant as she is unreliable.

However, it remains true that varying degrees of concreteness contribute to both authenticity of voice and the sense of playfulness that make us either suspend our disbelief or simply exult in pleasures of artistic sleight-of-hand. See pp. 351–53.

Conflict is basic to both drama and fiction and refers to the internal tension or external opposition faced by the central character. The conflict may be set off by a memory, event, or situation in the life of the central character. While most stories contain some element of conflict or complication, contemporary short fiction may not resolve its conflict at all, or at least not in the manner of the plot-driven story.

Dénouement refers, in French, to the untying of a knot. In drama and fiction, the term usually refers to that moment of truth in a story when the action has reached its peak, or climax, and the conflict is about to be resolved.

Dialogue is the term commonly used to describe what characters in fiction say to each other. Dialogue in fiction can be straightforward or, like the dialogue in drama (in say, Pinter or Chekhov), quite subtle and ironic, with as much left unsaid or implied. Beginning readers and writers of fiction often feel that a text doesn't look right unless it's peppered with bits of dialogue, but a serious writer will use dialogue sparingly or not at all. Hemingway's "Hills Like White Elephants" is notable for being an exception to this rule, though the story, which uses dialogue exclusively, is masterfully spare and transparent.

Convincing dialogue is not easy to create. A writer may benefit from a good ear, but imitating ordinary speech is not enough to produce convincing and efficient dialogue. As Guy Vanderhaeghe suggests, "Dialogue is really a literary convention; the writer does not attempt to reproduce speech but to reproduce the *effect* of the spoken word" (italics added).

Diction refers, simply, to word choice. A fiction writer may choose a limited range of diction, restricting himself or herself to words used in ordinary conversation, or take advantage of a wider choice of words. Often word choice is dictated by the impression a writer wants to give of his or her characters, particularly the narrator. An educated narrator may be characterized by an abundance of ornate words and sophisticated phrases, which simpler, more humble characters would regard as pretentious (they'd probably say *highfalutin*). Obviously, different levels of diction will be quite common in stories where there are several narrators and where dialogue is extensive.

Conrad insisted that fiction was composed of "words, nothing but words" and claimed that the right word was a lever with which an author could move the world. You might want to consult Owen Barfield's *Poetic Diction* or Winnifred Nowottny's *The Language Poets Use*. See also **character, imagery** and **style**, and Conrad in notes and Afterwords and pp. 355–56.

Dramatic irony occurs when the reader is aware of a discrepancy between a character's understanding of his or her situation and the real nature of that situation in the story.

Epiphany is a term that was first brought into critical usage by James Joyce. It refers to the sudden moment of illumination in a story, during which the central character sees herself or her situation in a new light. Of course, not all stories move towards an epiphany; in stories or novels with a naive narrator, the reader may come to an understanding of the nature of event and motivation that is beyond the ken of the narrator.

Episodic narration is the term applied to stories whose forward movement has less to do with character development than with the pleasure of inventing new and surprising episodes or incidents. These episodes may be entertaining, may even illustrate a **theme**, but they seldom advance our understanding of character.

Exposition is a term used to describe those passages in a story that present information considered essential to an understanding of the narrative, such as background information about a character or about preceding events. If this background information is presented in a dramatic form, rather than simply narrated, it's usually called a **flashback**. While the term *expository prose* is usually applied to non-fiction writing whose purpose is largely the transmission of information, exposition is often the place where a writer's greatest skill is evident and where, because the task of filling in details may seem more pedestrian, the greatest potential for failure resides. In such passages, the inexperienced author may be easily distracted by his or her own cleverness and abundant vocabulary.

Fantastical writing is as old as literature itself, encompassing the perception that there is more to life and human experience than is revealed by the world of the senses, or what is called empirical reality. Along with **science fiction**, fantastical writing has experienced a rebirth in this century, perhaps in recognition of the fact that reason and objective science have narrowed our range of experience without being able to spare us the horrors of war, hunger, social unrest, and spiritual malaise.

Writers such as Kafka, Cortázar, García Márquez, and Borges have been in the forefront of fantasy writing, stripping away such limiting conventions as credibility, coincidence, and consistency, allowing ghosts and mortals to intermingle and the most unlikely transformations and events to occur. See pp. 154–55, 359–61, 369.

Figurative language is the term used to describe language when it moves, for meaning or effect, beyond standard, or literal, usage. Some common figures of speech, (also known as *tropes*, or turns, which give the word new or extended meaning) are simile (describing one thing in terms of another: "He has an appetite like a blast furnace"), metaphor (a direct linking of different items without the use of *like* or *as*: "He is a pig"), personification, pun, hyperbole, paradox, and oxymoron. The figurative element in fiction may include syntax, with cuts and inversions that distort or alter meaning, or extend even to the overall structure of the story, where hyperbole (or exaggeration) may produce the tall tale or where the metaphorical impulse is so pervasive that the story slides into allegory.

First-person narratives are told by a character who refers to himself or herself as I and may be the central character or a mere observer in the story. It's a very intimate and engaging **point of view** from which to tell a story, but has definite limitations, since the first-person narrator can only speculate, unless told, on what is going on in heads other than his own or in situations where he is not present.

Flashback is the fictional technique of breaking the narrative flow of a story in order to inject, or insert, material from the past that is relevant to our understanding of character or situation. As a technique it's very telling, in both senses of the word, since flashback has to be employed subtly to avoid seeming clichéd and since it must be introduced at just the right moment, when something new is needed to advance the narrative and to sustain the interest of the reader.

Form is not an easy word to define, as it is often used in such a way as to make it indistinguishable from shape, **structure**, design, and all other words that have to do with the organization and patterning of elements in a story.

When Sherwood Anderson distinguished form from **plot** (in *A Story Teller's Story*), he was speaking of a subtler way of writing that would make the story less dependent on physical action or clever story ideas and more on other seeming intangibles: "For such men as myself you must understand there is always a great difficulty about telling the tale after the scent has been picked up. The tales that continually came to me in the way indicated above could not of course become tales until I had clothed them. Having, from a conversation overhead or in some other way, got the tone of a tale, I was like a woman who has just become impregnated. Something was growing inside me. At night when I lay in my bed I could feel the heels of the tale kicking against the walls of my body." Anderson, like the Romantic poets before him, is advocating organic form, the notion that every idea or situation (like the seed of a flower or tree) has its own inherent form, if the writer will take the time to discover it. He wanted his *words*—the clothing of the tale—to have the same subtlety and conjuring power as the brush-strokes of a master painter.

While not all short-story writers think of form in quite this way, most would agree that it is opposed to easy writing, or writing to a formula (as in the Harlequin romance, which often employs stock characters and interchangeable plots and settings). Eudora Welty calls form "the residue, the thrown-off shape, of the very act of writing." See also **structure** and the notes and Afterwords for O'Connor. See pp. 32–33, 58–59, 158–59, 195–96, 316–17, 359–60.

Frame story refers to a story that contains a story, or a story told within another fictional setting. A famous example is Conrad's *Heart of Darkness*, where Marlow's story of his fateful trip into the African jungle is told in the context of an "innocent" outing with his cronies on the Thames River near London.

Gothic elements in fiction are not unrelated to **myth**, but tend to focus on the working out of extreme, nightmare situations. Gothic fiction may concern itself with primal fears, such as rape and castration, or primal taboos such as incest. Whereas classic gothic tales in the nineteenth century may have required remote settings replete with darkness and decay, neo-gothic stories tend to locate the powers of darkness in the quotidian world of the motel, bus station, dentist's office, or bathroom.

Hero and **heroine** are antiquated terms derived mainly from the criticism of Classical drama and epic poetry, for the **protagonist** or central character of a work of literature. These terms seem particularly inappropriate for describing the protagonists or anti-heroes of short fiction, whose situations are so often humble and domestic.

Idiom usually refers to patterns of speech that are coloured by situation and locale, as in the phrase "local idiom." Flannery O'Connor is a strong advocate of using regional idiom, not to excess, where everyone in the story is wallowing in dialect, but as a means of placing and individualizing characters. She insists that "our history lives in our talk" and that "the sound of our talk is too definite to be discarded with impunity, and if the writer tries to get rid of it, he is liable to destroy the better part of his creative power."

Idiom cannot be entirely distinguished from—and is no substitute for—those other idiosyncrasies of speech and thought that go to make a character unique. See O'Connor in Afterwords (pp. 371–73).

Imagery. When Conrad used the word *image*, he was referring to things, events, and people called up before the senses, usually the reader's inner eye. In the sentence "The fat man drove to town in a blue station wagon" several images (or mental pictures) are immediately obvious. First, you have the overall image containing everything that is in the sentence. However, you also have an image of a man, an image of an action (driving), and an image of an object (the station wagon). Less obvious, but still significant, you have images imbedded in the adjectives: an image of rotundity in the word *fat* and an image of colour in the word *blue*.

An image is a word or group of words that calls up before the senses enough detail to make a reader feel that something concrete has been represented. Abstract words, such as *love*, *beauty*, and *truth*, are somewhat unreliable in fiction, as they call up nothing specific to the senses. The word *famine*, for example, is abstract and would not normally (except with the advent of television, when gaunt faces and bloated bellies are so common a sight) call up a concrete representation. However, in this line by Samuel Johnson—"Stern famine guards the solitary coast"—you can see how the idea assumes a quality (sternness), a place or habitation (the coast), and an activity (guarding), thereby assuming an impression of concreteness.

Patterns of imagery are repositories of meaning in a story. Sometimes, a group of images (those associated, say, with animals or machines) will cluster around a certain character. Along with character relations, image clusters help give a story shape and resonance. When an image recurs frequently, it may take on sufficient weight to become symbolic.

Interior monologue describes the convention of having a character reveal his thoughts directly to the reader, giving us the impression that we are engaged in psychic eavesdropping. Of course, the thoughts revealed to us are much more coherent on the page than we know them to be when we examine our own mental processes. Still, in the best interior monologues, the author will try to convey some sense of the internal chaos—fragmentation, illogic, discontinuity, et cetera—that are characteristic of the so-called **stream of consciousness**. See note on Virginia Woolf.

Limited omniscience is the most common, and perhaps the most flexible, narrative **point of view** from which to tell a story, because it usually involves complete knowledge about one character and the ability to speak directly about everything else that is happening in a story. In other words, it has some of the intimacy and immediacy of **first-person narration** and much of the flexibility of **omniscient narration**.

Magic realism is a term that has crossed over from painting (think of René Magritte,

Max Ernst, André Rousseau, and Alex Colville) to literature, and refers to a tendency to ransack the unconscious for images and to highlight certain aspects of the so-called real world in order to render them, once again, unusual. Like the **fantastical writer**, the magic realist may suspend the laws of nature, juxtapose objects unrelated in "reality," and draw them with such concreteness and specificity that they seem "more real than the real."

Gabriel García Márquez is often described as a magic realist, although he claims that nothing happens in his books that does not have its base in reality. His stories are imbued with a strange light, the half light between sleep and waking, where unexpected things happen and unexplainable states of mind prevail. *La vida es sueño*, the Spanish say—life is a dream. The magic realist's fictional world is certainly a world of dreams, in which a ghost, an out-of-body experience, or a sentient tree will be described with excruciating attention to detail.

See also **fantastical writing, metafiction**, and the notes on Borges and García Márquez.

Metafiction is a term that describes a type of fiction in which the techniques or conventions of writing have themselves become the subject of fiction. Wallace Stevens once insisted that all poems are about poetry; the same might be said in connection with short stories. And yet, as John Barth has suggested, "All fiction about fiction is, in fact, fiction about life." This paradox underlies literature of all ages. And some of the famous early practitioners of the novel—Cervantes in *Don Quixote*, Henry Fielding in *Tom Jones* and *Joseph Andrews*, and Thomas Sterne in *Tristram Shandy*, to take three familiar examples—enjoyed and exploited their own awareness of artifice and the act of writing. Self-reflexive fiction has become more common in this century, perhaps as an extreme reaction against the dominance of the realistic mode.

As Joe David Bellamy explains in the Introduction to *Superfiction*, "These fictions all dramatize the sweeping perception that art and language help *create* reality rather than serving as inert vehicles through which a self-evidently recognizable external reality is made manifest—a major ideological split between the new fiction and the old. Language, these writers are saying, *helps to constitute our reality*. Imagination (making things up) is a major form of perception, not a mere literary luxury but an absolutely necessary means of getting from one moment to the next." See Amy Hempel's "The Harvest" as an example of the metafictional impulse.

Mood is the prevailing or overriding feeling of a story (melancholy, anger, humour, terror, ecstasy, delight). Mood is determined not only by the nature of the **conflict** and the manner of its resolution, but also by the rendering of **setting** or locale, and the **tone** of the narration. Mood is often established in the first few lines of a story, by the way the narrator selects his or her words. Starting a story with a clichéd description of place or weather ("it was a dark and stormy night") may no longer be sophisticated enough to establish mood; however, a few key words or phrases that indicate all is not as it seems to be on the raincoast will quickly establish expectations of disaster, or a comic reversal of fortune. See also **atmosphere** and **tone**.

Myth is a means of organizing or making sense of the world, which draws on unconscious **symbols** known as archetypes that reveal to us the nature of reality. In its earliest forms, myth employed the figures of gods and heroes, working out their psychodramas on a grand scale. While these dramas have been largely domesticated in the realistic novel or story, substituting so-called ordinary humans in the most humble of circumstances, fiction continues, at one level, to be mythic, or mythopeic, since it endeavours to reveal through the use of symbols and symbolic action what is unknown, or only partially known, to the conscious mind.

Naturalism was a nineteenth-century movement that had its roots in the philosophical writings of Thomas Malthus, Charles Darwin, and Thomas Huxley. The naturalistic writer tried to present an objective, dispassionate but largely "realistic" portrait of ordinary life with a good deal of emphasis placed on detailing the relationship between character, destiny, and natural environment. Naturalist writers, such as Emile Zola, Stephen Crane, and Theodore Dreiser, were quite varied in their approaches, but most rendered a world where human behaviour was determined by nature and heredity.

Since naturalism was allied to science, it's not surprising that its methods of rendering "reality" might reasonably be expected to resemble those of the laboratory, particularly dissection, cataloguing, documentation, and analysis. Heavy emphasis was placed on the physiological and sociological, as opposed to the spiritual or imaginative, dimensions of human behaviour. Characters in thrall to their glands or to social forces beyond their control can be found in twentieth-century works by Thomas Hardy, James Joyce, William Faulkner, Frederick Phillip Grove, Eugene O'Neill, and Arthur Miller.

Novella, like the short story, is almost impossible to define. The novella has been called a story of a certain length, usually around 50,000 words, but sometimes ranging from 30 to 100 pages. Obviously, size alone won't serve as a reliable means of distinguishing the novella from either the long story or the short novel. The novella shares with the short story certain economies of style and characterization, often focussing upon the fate of a single individual. It seems driven, however, more by a desire to play out some lesson or truth about human society (the stifling of human love and spontaneity or the unredeemable ugliness of colonial greed and exploitation) than by any deep interest in human psychology. Indeed, character often seems to be subservient to a carefully articulated social situation and to a chain of events that neither dawdles nor sprawls, but which steps out smartly in the direction of the symbolic, even the allegorical. In this sense, the novella may be said to be the preferred form for a fictional drama that has a strong moral or philosophical thrust.

For further discussion of the novella, read the brief miscellany of quotations on pp. 348–49.

Omniscient narration, also known as third-person narration, assumes the god-like stance of knowing everything and having access to the minds and histories of all characters in a story.

Parable is the term used to describe a simple story that points up a moral or a religious lesson, such as those contained in the biblical accounts of the Prodigal Son and the Good Samaritan. Two of the earliest literary critics, Horace and Aristotle, concurred in the view that the chief aims of literature were to teach and delight; much subsequent critical debate has turned around the relative weight to be given each of these functions. A story that is blatantly "preachy" will quickly alienate a sophisticated reader; however, stories that are all dance, that seem to lack a moral centre, may prove to be equally limited and ephemeral.

Persona refers to the mask a poet or fiction writer puts on to tell a story. Akutagawa, in his story "In a Grove," employs a series of masks or personae, each of which adds to, and qualifies, our sense of what has transpired.

Plot is the series of actions, or events, that make up a story. These events are likely to be causally linked: A causes B; B leads to C; C produces D, and so on.

Plot is most often linked to **character**, some element inside or in the external circumstances of the character that drives him or her to act in a certain way. E. M. Forster suggests that curiosity and logic are central to plot. In *Aspects of the Novel*, he describes *story* as the "chopped-off length of the tapeworm of time" and distinguishes it from plot. Story, he says, is "the narrative of events in their time-sequence," whereas plot is "the narrative of events, with emphasis falling on causality. 'The king died and then the queen died' is a story. 'The king died and then the queen died of grief' is a plot."

Most writers and critics of short fiction are aware of the advantages and pitfalls of plot-driven writing. John Hawkes called plot one of the enemies of fiction. Sherwood Anderson rejected it in favour of **form**: "There was a notion that ran through all story-telling in America, that stories must be built about a plot and that absurd Anglo-Saxon notion that they must point a moral, uplift the people, make better citizens, etc. The magazines were filled with these plot stories and most of the plays on our stage were plot plays. 'The Poison Plot,' I called it in conversation with my friends as the plot notion did seem to me to poison all story-telling. What was wanted I thought was form, not plot, an altogether more elusive and difficult thing to come at."

See notes and Afterwords for Woolf (I can make up situations, but I cannot make up plots), Blaise (plot is the revelation of inevitability), Faulkner (the story makes its own plot), O'Connor, and others. See pp. 13, 32–33, 41–42, 141–42, 278, 297–98, 316, 325, 337, 377.

Point of view is the vantage point, or angle of vision, from which events in a story are told. The most common way of narrating a story is from the **omniscient**, or third-person, point of view, where the narrator knows everything and can dip in and out of the lives and minds of all the characters. Sometimes, the author will favour, or restrict himself or herself to complete knowledge of a single character, exercising what is called limited omniscience. While the omniscient, or third-person, narrator has greater freedom of movement in a story by virtue of knowing everything, many authors prefer the immediacy of **first-person narration**, telling the story from the point of view of a single character, who may be the **protagonist** or a mere observer of events. First-person narration is often more intense, because of the sense of total possession of one character's mind and the potential for piling on huge amounts of psychological detail; but this point of view imposes limits on what can be known by the narrator and, consequently, told to the reader about other characters. First-person narrative is, therefore, an ideal vehicle for irony, since the blind spots or limited vision of the narrator can be used for comic or ironic purposes. Such first-person narrators are often referred to as naive, or unreliable, narrators.

Although not as often as in the novel, the short story may also employ more than one narrator or more than a single point of view. Akutagawa's "In a Grove," cast in the manner of a detective story, is a polyphonic narrative, here containing numerous accounts of a murder, including that of the victim.

Protagonist refers to the **hero** or central character, whose problem or **conflict** constitutes the **action** or **plot** of the story.

Realism is a literary tendency that emerged in the eighteenth century with the journalistic fictions of Daniel Defoe, who claimed to be giving his reader the true-to-life stories of a one-time prostitute named Moll Flanders and a shipwrecked Robinson Crusoe. The history of fiction may be seen as a struggle between the realistic-reportorial impulse and the romantic-idealistic impulse, with the former gaining ascendance far into the twentieth century as fiction became the voice or sounding-board for a growing middle class. Technically, realism aims for accuracy of representation, rejecting coincidence and focussing instead on the probable and the believable. The realist writer, who purports to offer a slice of life, or to hold a mirror up to nature, usually focusses his attention on the unexceptional character engaged in his or her unadventurous, even humdrum, existence, living amidst failure, unfulfilled dreams, and rare moments of transcendence in food, sex, or television.

Joseph Conrad, Henry James, and Virginia Woolf were part of the reaction against literary realism, which they felt was too exterior and ignored the "hidden stream" of life. In its place, they offered what has come to be known as psychological realism, an attempt to offer a verbal approximation of the workings of the human mind, with its non-linear unfolding of events, its juxtaposition and counterpoint of images, and its more intensely poetic use of language. Joyce's *Dubliners* is often considered a triumph of the realistic mode, precisely because it manages to fuse external reality and the internal world of dreams. See pp. 24, 32, 78, 154–55, 246–47, 362–65.

Rhythm seems, at first, to be a term more relevant to poetry or music. However, prose also has rhythms that, though closer to the undulations of ordinary speech or conversation than to the measurable progressions of metrical verse, are nonetheless there to be enjoyed by the trained ear. The gap between poetry and prose seems less significant in the short story, where brevity and economy of expression are so important and where lyrical intensity is more often the rule than the exception.

Rhythm, or pacing, in fiction may refer not only to the shape and flow of individual sentences, but also to the patterning of ideas and events in the story, the way in which information is introduced, characters are developed, and events unfolded. You might want to consult E. K. Brown's *The Rhythm of the Novel*. See also **style** and **structure** as well as comments by Nadine Gordimer in the Afterwords.

Science fiction encompasses that area of **fantastical writing** committed to exploring and exploiting the fiction possibilities of science and technology. An early practitioner such as Jonathan Swift found much to parody in scientific institutions of his time and in the uses of technology to manipulate and oppress rather than liberate mankind. In addition to his biting satires of the abuse of science (attempts to breed hairless sheep, for example), Swift imagined in *Gulliver's Travels* a flying island that is not too far removed from the blimps, helicopters, and space stations so familiar to the *Star Wars* art and actuality of our time.

Jules Verne, H. G. Wells, and a host of more recent writers such as Bob Shaw and Ursula K. Le Guin have found scientific and technological speculation a fertile ground for critiquing our world and imagining different social and political models. Not surprisingly, the environmental crisis facing us has quickly challenged both the nuclear threat and Cold War power struggles for the attention of the writer of science fiction. See **metafiction** and **fantastical writing.**

Setting usually refers to the element of place in narrative fiction, the physical background or geographical location of the **action** in a story. If you think of an author setting the stage for his character, you will have a better idea of how the illusion of place is created, not by huge backdrops with intricately painted details, but rather by focussing attention on a few concrete particulars that are representative of the larger picture.

Weather, landscapes, and urban interiors (such as homes, apartments, factories, and stores) are all typical materials for the creation of setting. However, the props, or furnishings, of these rooms are even more useful than generic references to sea or mountain or clouds, and reveal a good deal about taste, social class, beliefs, and shared cultural values. See pp. 140–41, 218–19, 232–33, 246, 297–98, 362–65, 371–72.

Short story (see Ian Reid's attempt to define on page 334) encompasses plot-driven narratives, character studies, prose monologues, and a variety of hybrid shorter forms such as postcard fictions (Urbina's "Our Father Who Art in Heaven"), poetic meditations on history and place (Woolf's "The Fascination of the Pool"), and self-reflexive anti-stories such as Hempel's "The Harvest," in which the narrator admits and takes pleasure in her own unreliability, undercutting and revising the details of her own narrative. What all of these forms have in common, though, are an explicit or submerged narrative and a high degree of economy in the telling.

Stream of consciousness is a narrative technique that tries to create a verbal equivalent for human thought processes, emphasizing the fragmented, discontinuous (non-linear and non-logical) nature of consciousness. In the hands of Joyce, Virginia Woolf, and a host of other authors, stream of consciousness shifted the focus of fiction from the world of action and manners to the inner life and became an important technique in the repertory of psychological realism. See also **realism** and the note on Virginia Woolf.

Structure in a short story refers to the building blocks, the way in which the elements are arranged, or put together to make a more meaningful whole. French critics employ a useful term, *progression d'effets*, which translates literally as the progression of effects. Instead of being presented chronologically in the order of its happening, plot may be fragmented and discontinuous in the interests of heightening theme or more obviously reflecting the way the mind perceives and processes experience, moving backwards and forwards in time.

The term *structure* may be applied equally to the larger building blocks of fiction (such as **characters**, linear or non-linear **plot**, descriptive passages, pacing, **point of view**) and to the smaller linguistic elements (**diction**, **imagery**, metaphor, and **symbol**). However, sooner or later you end up saying that structure consists of everything in a story, which renders the term less than useful.

Many critics use the terms *structure* and *form* interchangeably, but it may be more useful to reserve the word *form* for the less mechanical elements shaping a work of fiction. Structure is a term borrowed from other arts, such as sculpture and architecture, which might lead you to think of it as the skeleton, or framework, of a story, form being the story's final fleshed-out shape or body—an interesting metaphor, but one that tends to link structure too exclusively with action or plot. See also **form**. See pp. 159, 173, 316–17.

Style is one of the most interesting and difficult terms used in literary discussions. M. H. Abrams describes style as a "characteristic manner of expression ... *how* a speaker or writer says whatever he says." He draws attention to **diction**, figurative language, **rhythm**, sentence structure, and rhetorical devices. I like this definition, as it suggests that the foundations of prose—indeed, all writing—are grounded in the way in which sentences are put together, in the very choice and deployment of words.

According to Annie Dillard in *Living by Fiction*, when you start to look closely at sentences, you begin to notice that some writers, such as Hemingway, are especially fond of a plain, journalistic style, with short, punchy declarative sentences or possibly loose, disjointed sentences that run on to inordinate lengths. Another writer, such as Faulkner, may employ a high style, using ornate or poetic prose with lots of figurative language, possibly formal **syntax**, and elevated **diction**. See pp. 32–33, 41–42, 150, 168–69, 178–79, 279, 324–25, 356–58, 385.

Consider Mavis Gallant's definition: style "is not a last-minute addition to prose, a charming and universal slip-cover, a coat of paint used to mask the failings of a structure. Style is inseparable from structure, part of the conformation of whatever the author has to say. ... Style in writing, as in painting, is the author's thumbprint, his mark. I do not mean that it establishes him as finer or greater than other writers, though that can happen too. I am thinking now of prose style as a writer's armorial bearings, his name and address. ... Style cannot be copied, except by the untalented. It is, finally, the distillation of a lifetime of reading and listening, of selection and rejection. But if the voice is not true, it is nothing." See Gallant in notes and Afterwords.

Symbol is created in a story when an image (a person, event, or object) begins to assume, by repetition or increased function, a more than local, or literal, significance, and comes to stand for more than itself. For example, a figure in a black coat might acquire symbolic value in a story by virtue of the nature and frequency of his or her appearances. It may not be accurate to say (except in the case of allegory) that the black coat equals death, but only that the image has acquired symbolic value to the point that its occurrence in the story brings to mind thoughts of death or mortal danger.

Authors quite often resent symbolic interpretations of their work, because they feel that such interpretations are usually oversimplified, reducing what may be a complex and multi-faceted work to a mechanical formula. The best stories, so it seems, are those in which the symbolism emerges naturally from the materials, from character and situation, rather than appearing stuck on like cake decorations.

It should be remembered, however, that language itself is a symbol system, using words or groups of words to represent objects, persons, feelings, and ideas. Thus, all literature is, by nature, symbolic. See pp. 297, 369.

Theme is often used to refer to the overriding subject or idea of a story. However, most fiction writers object to the term because it suggests that a complicated verbal structure, full of nuance and suggestion, can be reduced to a single sentence or a mere word. If a writer wanted to make a simple statement about love or death or computer maintenance, he or she would not write a story. The writer wants a reader to become immersed in the *how*—the technique, the words, the shaping principles—of the story, from which will emerge respect, understanding, and a deeper sense of what the author intends. See pp. 246, 368–69.

Tone is a musical term, often used to describe the author's attitude towards the characters and events in a story, sometimes eliciting such qualifiers as *whimsical*, *ironic*, *sarcastic*, or *satirical*. If you strip the music away from a song, you are left only with words and how they are spoken, the tone of voice, the little asides and descriptive details that give away important information. We can usually detect something, by listening closely to the narrator's voice, in his or her tone, that might betray the real motive for telling the story.

Tone may be revealed in a variety of ways, in the choice of **diction** (using, say, the word *contemplative* rather than the word *thoughtful* to describe a character), **imagery** (referring to a character in animal terms, as feline or simian), and in character relations (the particular groupings of characters, such as in a story). See also **mood** and **atmosphere**.